My Frozen Turbulence in KASHMIR

JAGMOHAN

ALLIED PUBLISHERS PVT. LTD.
NOIDA • MUMBAI • KOLKATA
CHENNAI • BANGALORE

ALLIED PUBLISHERS PRIVATE LIMITED

D-5, Sector-2, **Noida**–201 301
Ph.: 0120-4320295/2542557/4352866 • E-mail: delhi.books@alliedpublishers.com

17 Chittaranjan Avenue, **Kolkata**–700072
Ph.: 033-22129618 • E-mail: cal.books@alliedpublishers.com

15 J.N. Heredia Marg, Ballard Estate, **Mumbai**–400001
Ph.: 022-42126969 • E-mail: mumbai.books@alliedpublishers.com

No. 25/10 Commander-in-Chief Road, Ethiraj Lane (Next to Post Office)
Egmore, **Chennai**–600008
Ph.: 044-28223938 • E-mail: chennai.books@alliedpublishers.com

P.B No. 9932, No. 15, 3rd Floor (Next to Vijaya Bank), 5 th Cross, Gandhinagar, Karnataka, **Bangalore**–560009 Ph.: 080-41530285 / 22386239
• E-mail: bngl.journals@alliedpublishers.com/apsabng@airtelmail.in

Website: www.alliedpublishers.com

First Published September 1991
Second Edition, April 1992
Third Edition, June 1993
Fourth Edition, February 1994
Fifth Edition, July 1996
Sixth Edition, March 2002
Seventh Edition, January 2006
Eighth Edition, June 2007
Ninth Edition, January 2011
Tenth and updated Edition, July 2012
Eleventh and updated Edition, July 2014
Twelfth and updated Edition, February 2017

Reprint 2019-2024, 2025

ISBN: 978-93-85926-56-3

Published by Sunil Sachdev and printed by Ravi Sachdev at Allied Publishers Private Limited, D-5, Sector-2, Noida 201 301

My
Frozen Turbulence in
KASHMIR

About the Author

Shri Jagmohan, a recipient of Padma Shri (1971), Padma Bhushan (1977) and Padma Vibhushan (2016), has been an outstanding civil servant, Parliamentarian, Union Minister and original thinker and writer. Throughout his long and illustrious years in public service, he has worked, with an unmatched passion, for creating a model of fair, just and effective governance by fair, just and effective means.

Shri Jagmohan is known for making a significant contribution to the formulation and implementation of the Delhi Master Plan and for playing a Pioneering role in Planning and Implementation of Projects. He took over as Lieutenant Governor, Delhi in January 1980. He was the youngest Lieutenant-Governor of Delhi who held this prestigious office twice. His two-terms in the office are generally reckoned as the finest hour of Delhi's development. It saw successful organization of three major international events–Asian Games, Commonwealth Heads of Governments Meeting and Non-Alignment Movement Conference. During all these challenging years, he built for himself the reputation of being a public servant who gets things done in the face of heavy odds.

Shri Jagmohan was appointed as Governor of Jammu and Kashmir on April 26, 1984, when there were a series of subversion and terrorism-related incidents, aided and abetted by Pakistan. He successfully handled an explosive situation and overcame a series of crises. For a short time, the State was placed under the Governor's Rule, during which unprecedented development was witnessed through revamped and field-oriented administrative machinery. He was appointed for his second term, on January 19, 1990 at a time when pro-Pakistan and secessionist elements had virtually established their sway on Kashmir. However he is credited for pulling it back from their claws by way of a well-planned strategy which was swiftly and determinedly executed from January 19 to 26, preventing, *inter-alia,* tragedy like that of a Blue-Star or Tinanmen Square.

After his nomination by the President, Shri Jagmohan remained as an independent Member of the Rajya Sabha for about six years. After 1996, he won a hat-trick of Lok Sabha elections from New Delhi Constituency. He served as Union Minister in the Cabinet of Prime Minister Atal Bihari Vajpayee, for about five and a half years, and held charge of a variety of portfolios, including Communication, Urban Development, Tourism and Culture. His vision, his extra-ordinary hard and honest-work and even-handed approach to all the political parties, won him all round appreciation.

Shri Jagmohan has also established himself as a profound writer and thinker. His published works include over 700 articles in leading newspapers and journals and Nine books: Rebuilding Shahjahanabad; The Walled City of Delhi: Island of Truth; The Challenge of Our Cities; My Frozen Turbulence in Kashmir; The Soul and Structure of Governance in India; Shaping India's New Destiny; Crisis of Environment and Climate Change; Reforming Vaishno Devi and a case for Reformed, Reawakened and Enlightened Hinduism; and Triumphs and Tragedies of Ninth Delhi.

Shri Jagmohan's intellectual and literary standing can be seen from the fact that his book My Frozen Turbulence in Kashmir was described by Mr. Michael Foot, who was once the Shadow Prime Minister of Britain, as "a great book indeed and it tells me much more about Kashmir than I ever-learnt from any other place". About the same work, Dr. Mulk Raj Anand, the noted literary critic, wrote: "It is a brilliant work, written with verve which derives its power from the author's addiction to truth".

Apart from a number of managerial reforms, leading to the creation of scores of cultural hubs, such as those pertaining to **Quila Rai-Pathora, Kumbhalgarh and Ajanta-Ellora**, Shri Jagmohan formulated and implemented the historic reforms of the Mata Vaishno Devi Shrine during Governor's Rule in 1986. Consequent to the Shrine reforms, all round improvements have come about.

Apart from the three national awards mentioned above, he was honoured with cultural award by Australian Government and the Paul H. Appleby Award by the Indian Institute of Public Administration. He was conferred the degree of Doctor of Philosophy (Honoris Causa) by Kurukshetra University as well as by Guru Nanak University, Amritsar.

To
Radhicka, Sonali, Devika, Amayaah, Araddya, Srijan and Ajay
Seven Budding Aspirants
Who, I hope,
Would find a more Positive Work-Environment
To Realise Fully
Their Creative and Constructive Potential,
In Service of the Indian State and Civilization.

As in the case of earlier Eleven Editions of My Frozen Turbulence in Kashmir and its Hindi and regional languages translations, the author has donated the entire royalty of this book to a Charitable Trust set up in memory of his parents. The Trust, namely, **Amir Chand Dropti Devi Memorial Charitable Trust**, provides financial assistance to the poor and needy, especially the young students preparing for the competitive examinations.

Acknowledgements

Sincere thanks are due to the India International Centre, and its President, Shri Soli J. Sorabjee and Director, Air Marshal (Retd) Naresh Verma and also to Dr. S. Majumdar, Chief Librarian, and his helpful and humble staff–Ms. Shafali Bhatt, Sarvshri Rajeev Mishra, Ms. Hemlata, Ms. Kanchan Nagpal, Sarvshri Rakesh Chand, Sunil Sharma, Jagdish Prasad Dabral, Praveen Rawat and Kuldeep. The facilities provided have been excellent. Thanks are also due to former IIC Librarian Ms. Sushma Zutshi and Dr. H.K. Kaul and Ms. Sangeeta, Director and Network Manager, DELNET respectively for all the help and cooperation they have extended.

I owe a deep debt to my family members–my wife Uma, my daughter Deepika, my son Manmohan, my son-in-law Rajiv Kapoor and my daughter-in-law Nutan Manmohan. But for their reverential and encouraging attitude, I would not have found a congenial environment at home for undertaking an onerous task of writing a book in difficult times, covering a wide range of complex issues.

New Delhi JAGMOHAN

Extracts from Reviews

"Outpourings of a troubled, sensitive and dynamic mind... His observations about men and events are bound to ruffle many feathers... should be treated as a reference book on Kashmir."

–**S. Sahay** in *The Hindustan Times*

"In any other country, the publication of a book along the lines of Mr. Jagmohan's recent offering would have triggered off a fierce controversy and political furore... "

–**Swapan Dasgupta** in *The Times of India*

"It is really the sounding of a siren that Shri Jagmohan has done. Let people listen and understand that the question is of the survival or disintegration of the country."

–**Veena Saraf** *in Excelsior*

"On the controversy over Article 370 of the Constitution, Jagmohan opens a new viewpoint. No ex-Governor has written so bitterly before, nobody has examined the malady of Kashmir more minutely, arraigned so many high-ups, packed so much of political dynamite in one book."

–**Punyapriya Dasgupta** in *Deccan Herald*

"...the abiding value of the book lies... in raising larger and fundamental issues of Indian polity and society which the country would have to face squarely... "

–**Nancy Jetly** in *Sunday Times*

"...the one man who saved the Valley for the country last year, Jagmohan... His book (is) one of the most important to have been published in India... "

–**Arun Shourie** in *Economic Times*

"Frozen Turbulence is an evocative expression; the book chills the readers as it takes him through the heavy past, the dismal present and the bleak future. It is a work of monumental proportion and of great archival and historical importance... Jagmohan has a mass of background information and documentary evidence to support his thesis... "

–**V.N. Narayanan**, Editor-in-Chief, *The Tribune*

"It is a great book indeed and it tells me much more about Kashmir than I ever learnt from any other place."

–**Michael Foot** (British M.P. in a letter to Dr. Mulk Raj Anand)

"The book's strength is in its facts. For this reason alone, it should be compulsory reading for anyone professing an interest in Indian affairs."

—**N.S. Jagannathan** in *Indian Review of Books*

"Strong meat for Kashmiris. All his readers will lament the sordid ambitions and folly of those at the helm of affairs in Delhi and Srinagar who willfully left the country with a legacy of blood and tear in Kashmir... "

—**B.G. Verghese** in *Sunday Mail*

"As a history of both modern and ancient Kashmir, his account is invaluable. In many respects this is the first detailed honest and forthright narration of the series of lapses and blunders which have led to the present situation... The disclosures about corruption at the highest levels of the State administration and the vivid accounts of the politics of systematic deception leaves one breathless."

—**K.R. Sunder Rajan** in *The Pioneer*

"...a well-written book... presents a dismal picture of the state of mind of our political leaders... "

—**T.N. Kaul** in *Patriot*

"...it is a brilliant work, written with verve which derives its power from [the author's] addiction to truth... "

—**Mulk Raj Anand** in *Business & Political Observer*

"One has only to read Jagmohan's awesomely documented book to realise... He has minced no words about the indifference and incompetence and worse of Indian political leaders of all hues... The situation in 'Azad' Kashmir is no different... There is no Jagmohan there to tell the truth,... "

—**Bhabani Sen Gupta** in an article in *The Hindustan Times*

Preface to the Twelfth Edition

In the Preface to the First Edition, I had explained how truths of history had motivated me to write this book, and how important it was to underscore the fatal flaws of the Indian polity and the general proclivity of its leadership to nurse illusions and live in a world of its own make-believe. In the eleven Editions that have so far been published and updated, the 'tyranny of shallowness' that pervades the overall Indian system, with regard to the issue of Kashmir, has been manifesting itself, in one tragic form or the other, over the last several years. All this has been briefly brought out in the note containing the outlines of the Prefaces of the ten Editions. (2nd to 11th).

In the Eleventh Edition, which appeared in July 2014, soon after Narendra Modi Government assumed office on May 26, 2014, and which has been out of print for the last three months, I had, *inter-alia,* reflected upon the 'much needed expectations for inward and outward changes'. In this–Twelfth Edition–I have, added a new Chapter– XXV–titled: *Onward To A New Resolve,* and examined in what direction these expectations have moved, and how the harsh and cruel realities on the ground have been encountered during the eventful period of 33 months of the new regime, from May 26, 2014 to February 28, 2017.

I have also pondered over the connected issues of crucial significance: Are better days in store for the nation in which it could repair and renovate its leaky and rickety 'boat of destiny', retrofit it with new 'timber' and place its sail in the charge of a determined leader with expansive vision and penetrating mind?

In the background of India's 70 years of nightmarish Kashmir experience, I have also assessed whether the developments of the aforementioned period of 33 months hold out a promise of finding a new helmsman who could steer the 'boat' through stormy sea and turbulent winds and bring it safely to a calm and clean shore, from where a new journey, with a new mind and motivation, could begin.

The period in question is full of truly momentous events. The contents of Chapter XXIV provide an idea about their dimensions as well as their dense and diverse fall-outs. The ball is set rolling with the State Assembly Elections of November-December, 2014. It moves to the formation of the PDP-BJP coalition government, to the Agenda of Alliance, to encountering the unsavoury legacies of the past, to the passing away of Chief Minister Mufti Mohammad Sayeed, to the taking over of Mehbooba Mufti with her 'baggage of our boys in the jungle', and then to her disposition to rise to the occasion and face the combined onslaught of subversives, separatists, and pro-Pakistan elements, especially in the wake of Burhan Wani's death and the no holds-barred violence and agitation that followed it.

After analyzing the different facets of disturbances, Chapter XXIV unfolds the sagacious and subtle way in which Home Minister Raj Nath Singh diffused the crisis and ensured that the union government and the state government remained on the same page. It has also been indicated how the Home Minister and the Prime Minister saw to it that, notwithstanding the not too positive and helpful attitude of a section of All-Party Parliamentary Delegation, the fundamentals of their stand remained unaltered.

In the section dealing with India-Pakistan relations, it has also been spelt out how, despite the long history of disguised betrayal by Pakistan, another initiative was taken by Prime Minister Narendra Modi to build a shared vision of harmony and goodwill, and how this initiative, too, was frustrated by the treacherous terror attacks on the Pathankot Air-Base and Uri Brigade Headquarter.

The outrageous perfidies of the genre of Uri terror attack, coupled with the fanatical obduracy of the subversive outfits functioning in the valley, on the dictates of Inter Services Intelligence of Pakistan, under the umbrella organisation of All-Party Hurriyat Conference, pushed Prime Minister Narendra Modi towards what I have termed as New Resolve. This Resolve was ingrained in the traits of his leadership, and it found effective expression when he was faced with serious challenges simultaneously from internal and external forces inimical to India. He was virtually pushed to assume the role of a new helmsman.

The background of all this and the manner in which a number of action-plans were formulated by the new helmsman have been given in the section, titled New Resolve, in the Chapter XXIV. I have grouped the core components of the Resolve under the following heads/sub-heads:-

(i) To expose, thoroughly and persistently, at the United Nations General Assembly and other international fora, Pakistan as a state sponsor of terrorism and using it as an instrument of its policies.

(ii) To declare the incompatibility of Pakistan's credentials to hold the 19th SAARC Summit scheduled for November 2016 at Islamabad on account of its unwillingness to curb terrorists' groups from attacking fellow members.

(iii) To indicate firmly that hostility would be countered with hostility and the comparatively liberal treatment that Pakistan is presently enjoying with regard to river-water distribution and trade-regimes could be withdrawn and the Indus Water Treaty and Most-Favoured Nation Status revisited.

(iv) To demonstrate India's right to pre-empt terrorists from entering its territory by attacking their preparatory bases across the Line of Control/border.

(v) To continue earnest efforts to persuade the multi-lateral groups, such as BRICS, to denounce Pakistan as a malevolent force of terrorism which, apart from dehumanizing a large section of mankind, is undermining the basic objectives for the attainment of which such groups have been set up, namely, quick, coordinated and cohesive development.

(vi) To show how Pakistan is providing sanctuaries of safe haven to a number of dangerous terror-organisations who are bleeding the Heart of Asian Region.

(vii) To take up vigorously the issues pertaining to the large scale violations of Human Rights by the Pakistan Army in Baluchistan, Baltistan, Gilgit and Pakistan occupied Kashmir, and simultaneously counter Pakistan's diabolical disinformation campaign against India for 'committing atrocities and violations of human rights in Kashmir valley'.

The courage, consistency and 'resolute practicality' displayed by Prime Minister Narendra Modi, the promising new helmsman, in translating the above seven items of action on the ground have been delineated in the last portion of the Chapter. It concludes with the hope of emergence of a new pattern of life which is appeasement-free, terror-free, and in which the noblest strands and sinews of India's cultural heritage of treating service to man as service to God are regenerated, from Kashmir to Kanyakumari, providing an illuminating avenue for reaching the goal of a mighty, enlightened and forward-looking India.

Jagmohan

A Brief Note About the Outlines of the Prefaces of the Ten Editions (2nd to 11th) which have appeared between the First and the Twelfth Editions

The First Edition of this book was published in September, 1991. Public response to it had been very encouraging. It had also been warmly reviewed. The book underwent four reprints within first six months. It was soon translated/published in Hindi, Marathi, Urdu, Kannada, Gujarati, Telugu, Tamil, Malayalam and Bengali.

While responding to the need for the fifth reprint in March, 1992, I thought it more appropriate to update the book and add another chapter dealing with the events that had occurred since the publication of the First Edition. These events had affirmed what I had anticipated. A large section of the public felt unhappy over the superficiality and selfishness of those who wielded power at the Centre at that time.

As the ground-level condition worsened and the subversives and separatists expanded their sway, having been emboldened, a question was persistently asked by the concerned public men: why were national interests sacrificed at the altar of petty politics and why warning signals, so strongly hoisted, and recorded, by me were ignored? It was, therefore, no surprise that the Second Edition, which appeared in April, 1992, and the Third Edition which came up soon thereafter in May, 1993, were received with no less warmth than the first. The additional chapter was titled: *Tyranny of Shallowness and the Future of Kashmir.* It covered events, such as Jammu and Kashmir Liberation Fronts' marches, 'third' and 'fourth' options, Hazratbal, New Fault Lines.

In the Fourth Edition, the above chapter was expanded to cover developments upto February 5, 1994. These included United States' New Posture, Human Rights and International Power Politics, World Kashmiri Pandits' Conference, India-Pakistan Talks, Increasing Depth of Terrorism and level of ISI Activities.

Thereafter, it became a practice that whenever the current Edition went out of print, the next Edition was not only reprinted but also enlarged and updated with addition of a new Chapter.

The events from February 5, 1994 to July 1996 and events from July 1996 to February 18, 2002 were covered in the Fifth and Sixth

Editions. The Seventh and Eighth Editions took the book to June 2007. These included events such as Lahore Bus Yatra; Kargil War; Agra Summit; Attacks on the World Trade Centre and Indian Parliament, Continuance of Tension, Madrasas, Ideological Virus, War on Terror, Musharraff's Out of Box Suggestion, Self-Rule.

The Ninth Edition dealt with the developments upto January 1, 2011, including the terrorist attack on Mumbai, militant agitations in Kashmir, President Obama's visit and its signals for India-Pakistan-Afghanistan region. China's increasing presence in the Pakistan-Occupied-Kashmir was also touched.

The Tenth Edition extended the fold of my analysis to July 2012, with the assertion of 'my Kashmir truth' which spoke through the silent voices of about 50,000 dead Indians and also through the dilemma and discomfiture which American authorities faced in Afghanistan after discovering that Pakistan had all along been serving as a breeding ground for frenzied terrorists and acting as a deceitful ally.

With the Tenth Edition out of print for about two months, and with heightened interest of the public in the Kashmir affairs, especially in the aftermath of the 16th Lok Sabha Elections, the need for bringing out the updated Eleventh Edition, was obvious. A New Chapter–XXIV–titled: *A Season for inward and Outward Change: Undoing the Negative Politics of Articles 370*, was added to this Edition.

I have little doubt that the narration and analysis of the events brought out in all these Editions would impel a discerning reader to ask: why has 'my Turbulence in Kashmir remained frozen' for so long? He would also find my answer: India, in relation to Kashmir, had acquired a social, cultural and political ethos which were conducive to the growth of separatism, subversion and terrorism. Disruption and demagogy had penetrated deep into the texture of its democracy. And narrow ends of personal and political power had attained total ascendancy. In this environment, the chronic infections in the roots of the body-politic had remained, and erupted into high fever from time to time. Unless this environment undergoes an upward surge and propels the ethos of the social and political leadership into a healthier orbit, there would be no basic improvement and the 'frozen turbulence' would not melt and blow away.

Jagmohan

Preface to the First Edition

Why have I written this book? And why have I titled it 'My Frozen Turbulence in Kashmir'?

As a Governor of the State for two terms–April 1984 to July 1989 and January to May 1990–I was associated with some of the most crucial events of the contemporary period. I owe it to the nation and history to narrate and analyse these events in perspective and also indicate what I personally felt about them.

During the course of my governorship, the inner layers of the Indian soul, sickened and lacerated as these were by the disruptive forces of Indian politics and its superficiality and shallowness, came under sharp focus. The scenario deeply dismayed me. The surge of anguished feelings went on accumulating and soon assumed the intensity of a turbulence. On account of the position I held, this turbulence remained frozen inside. Now, I feel, is the time to provide an outlet to it.

Public interest in general and national interest in particular also demand publication of this book. A false picture has been painted either intentionally or out of ignorance. From the very first day of my second term, I had to wage not only the most grim and critical battle against terrorism but also an equally extensive and dangerous battle against disinformation. I could hold my own and even win the first battle, but not the second, such were the dimensions, frequency and fury of the avalanche of insinuations.

I have not made any assertion which I have not supported by solid evidence. This is in sharp contrast to the mode of 'disinformers' who weaved their versions on hearsay, or slanted, and sometimes wholly concocted, statements. Regrettably, some persons, who were in authority, also thought that they could resort to distortion of facts and accuse me of impropriety if I cited concrete evidence, such as letters, to expose them. Neither propriety nor any other norm of public behaviour permits one party to speak on a subject and expect the person adversely affected not to invite attention to irrefutable evidence to defend his position or reputation or safeguard public interest by disclosing the whole truth. For instance, it was stated by quite a few high-ups in authority that I had kept them in the dark about the dissolution of the State Assembly. But the written evidence on the subject knocks the bottom out of this assertion. Am I not entitled to invite attention of the public to this fact? In the same manner, when I am being wrongly criticised, am I not justified in showing the recorded "warning signals" of the time and point out where the responsibility actually rests? No one has the right to dish out self-serving disinformation and ask the other side to keep quiet.

Personally, I might have suffered in silence the 'slings and arrows' of this outrageous disinformation. But dictates of justice and truth and also the need to avoid future lapses, require that the facts should be made known immediately. Here, it may be relevant to indicate that Dr. Karan Singh in his *books–Heir Apparent* and *Sadar-i-Riyasat* and B.N. Mullick in his book, *My Days with Nehru,* reproduced a large number of letters.

The book has been divided into 17 chapters.

Chapter I deals with ten most critical days from January 19 to 28, 1990. It recalls the background of events and also describes the first of a series of stabs in my back.

The next chapter compresses the history of the State from pre-historic times to May 26, 1990.

Chapter III draws attention to the "Warning Signals" about the gathering storm and emphasises that to ignore these signals was to commit sins of historical proportions.

The next three chapters (IV to VI) lay bare the roots of the problem that lie embedded in the soft and permissive attitude of Central leadership, in the politics of deception, in the spurious democracy, in the habit of nursing illusions, in the unwholesome legacies of the past, in the fundamentalisation of religion, in the infirmities of administration, in public corruption, in environmental disruption, in regional differences, in disintegrative constitutional relationship, and in the overall dynamics of negative forces.

Chapter VII describes the facts and circumstances leading to the dismissal of Dr. Farooq Abdullah on July 2, 1984. It also indicates how my constitutional recommendations were put under the carpet. The role of the Governor and other constitutional authorities are also discussed.

The conditions before my arrival on January 19, 1990, have been portrayed in Chapter VIII, and Chapter IX deals with my approach to tackle the situation which had virtually reached a point of no return. It also shows how, ironically, efforts from three directions–of Rajiv Gandhi, Farooq Abdullah and Benazir Bhutto–converged against the same target.

The nature and pattern of subversion in Kashmir is brought out in Chapter X. It demonstrates that when the foundation is made of spurious material which is infested with white ants from within, a gale of low intensity is sufficient to bring the edifice down. It analyses, from original sources in Urdu, the motivational literature of the subversives, and points out how the militant strands of Islamic history have been selectively used and doctored to arouse religious frenzy and images of martyrdom, how the concepts evolved by Mao Tse-tung and Che Guevera have been adapted, and how cues for extensive use of mosques and clergy have been picked up from the Iranian Revolution. The chapter also discusses General Zia's Operation TOPAC and describes the precise manner in which terrorism was engineered and fanned from across the border.

Chapter XI details the reasons for my decision to dissolve the Assembly. It also explains the legal and constitutional position in this regard.

Chapter XII sketches the whirlpools of confusion and contradictions and exposes the hypocrisy of the declared aim of national consensus. It indicates the grave damage done by the visit of an all-party team to Srinagar on March 7, 1990 and shows how it nullified the advantages secured by me. It also reveals how my little candle of realism was subjected to nasty winds and how the appointment of George Fernandes led to the knocking out of the very base of the candle itself. This chapter also incorporates a letter which I wrote to the Prime Minister about George Fernandes, but which I never posted.

Chapter XIII exposes 'the hall of crooked mirrors' which the Committee called 'Initiative on Kashmir' fabricated on the foundations of deception, insinuations and prejudices. It shows how in the name of human rights, the Committee itself violated the most basic human right–the right to be heard before being condemned. The chapter also deals with the plight of Kashmiri Pandits and the quirks of their history.

Chapter XIV narrates how a series of innovative measures were introduced, how dynamic coordination was brought about, how administration was put back on the rails and motivated, how almost all the heinous crimes, including the kidnapping of Dr. Rubaiya Sayeed, the murders of Lassa Kaul, Mushir-ul-Huq, H.L. Khera, Abdul Gani, Saidulla, Dr. K.L. Ganju, and others were worked out, how a number of top terrorists were arrested, how, with the shifting of the capital, the task of re-asserting the authority of the State was successfully completed, and how the flags of JKLF no longer fluttered.

The scale and intensity of the deluge of disinformation are described in Chapter XV. It contains the full text of my open letter to late Rajiv Gandhi. It also deals with the question as to who is anti-Muslim, and indicates how the forum of Parliament was used to create a climate of prejudice, and how accusations were levelled in total disregard of the earlier stand of the accusers themselves. The chapter also analyses George Fernandes's style and its negative and unsettling effect on the situation.

Chapter XVI shows how in regard to Kashmir, India has repeatedly displayed a strange, almost suicidal, knack of converting successes into the festering stalemates. This chapter also includes an open letter to the Kashmiris.

The last chapter makes it clear that what the future holds for Kashmir and the rest of the country depends upon who would be at the steering wheel of history. It also dwells upon the need for fundamental reform and provides a glimpse of my ideas on the subject.

The real solution to the Kashmir problem lies in removal of the infirmities and the unhealthy forces that I have analysed in this book. The task can be performed only by a reformed, rejuvenated and motivated India, with a new vision, and not by an India that has become a hunting ground for small politics and whose shallow and superficial approach has exceeded all limits in Kashmir and whose leaders have exhibited almost infinite capacity to live under the shadow of illusions rather than face burning realities.

I may have been a bit critical of a few individuals. I did not want to be. But the truth of history gave me no choice. 'This criticism, moreover, is not personal. It is really a criticism of the negative forces that have rendered the country incapable of solving any of its basic problems with manageable costs and in a reasonable span of time.

Contents

Appendices

I. Sources of History of Kashmir.
II. Extracts from the Treaty of Lahore (March 9, 1846) and Treaty of Amritsar (March 16, 1846).
III. Naya Kashmir,
IV. Text of Sheikh Abdullah's letter of September 26, 1947.
V. The Resolution of the United Nations Security Council of August 13, 1948.
VI. Summary of Assurances given to India.
VII. Tashkent Declaration.
VIII. Shimla Agreement.
IX. Kashmir Accord.
X. Article 370.
XI. Particulars of the extensions of provisions of Indian Constitution to J&K.
XII. Particulars of Bomb Explosions (August 15, 1983 to July 2, 1984).
XIII. An Interview regarding Governor's Rule.
XIV. Farooq Abdullah's written statement to the Press (February 15, 1990).
XV. List of the Terrorist Organisations.
XVI. Excerpts from my interview with 'India Today'.
XVII. Brief particulars of cases registered during the period January 19 to May 26, 1990.
XVIII. Extracts from the Author's Suit.
XIX. Number and nature of crimes committed.
XIX B. Particulars of a few Typical Cases of Ignorant and Superficial Reporting.
XX. Accession and its validity.
XXI. Status of Different Areas of Jammu & Kashmir.
XXII. China's Stand.
XXIII. Inter Services Intelligences.
XXIV. Press notices requiring Kashmiri Pandits to leave the Valley within forty-eight hours.
XXV. Memorandum of National Conference.
XXVI. Resolution of Kashmir Bar Association (September 27-28, 1983).
XXVII. Pt. Jattu's letter: Pt II. Other Documents.
XXVIII. Delhi Declaration.
XXIX. Latest Data-Scale and Intensity of Militancy.
XXX. 'Back channel diplomacy'.

Appendices

CHAPTER I

My Frozen Turbulence

It has happened,
and it goes on happening,
and will happen again.

The plane suddenly dipped low. It was an air pocket. The small BSF plane could not take it easily. I was a bit shaken. So were my wandering thoughts. I was, perhaps, reminded that I was proceeding to a State full of terror and turbulence. It was early afternoon of January 19, 1990. I was once again airborne to J&K.

Six years earlier, on April 26, 1984, I had flown to the same State. It was experiencing rough weather even at that time. But, through the beautiful windows of the Boeing plane of Indian Airlines, the sun outside looked bright and sure. A large crowd of well-wishers had come to the airport to give me a warm send-off. This time, it was different. I had been woken up at midnight by a telephone call from I.K. Gujral, Foreign Minister. He asked me to attend an emergency meeting at Home Minister Mufti Mohammad Sayeed's house. There I was apprised of the grave crisis, and told to take, at the earliest, the special plane which was being kept ready for me. The break-neck speed of the departure and the near loneliness of the journey oppressed me somewhat. From the narrow window of the BSF plane, my tired eyes could hardly see anything except the grim haze that stretched from one end of the sky to the other.

I recalled that in early 1984, too, the State was experiencing frequent tremors. On February 3, that year, Ravindera Mhatre, an Indian diplomat posted at Birmingham, had been kidnapped by the activists of the Kashmir Liberation Army, an adjunct of the J&K Liberation Front, and murdered in cold blood on February 5. Six days later, Maqbool Butt, founder President of the J&K Liberation Front who had been sentenced to death for murder committed seventeen years earlier, was executed in Tihar Jail, Delhi. Both these events were casting their ominous shadows on New Delhi and Srinagar.

A few days later, three Central Ministers had met the President and complained that the secessionist forces were enjoying official patronage under the Chief Ministership of Dr. Farooq Abdullah, and these anti-national elements were dominating the Valley. On the other hand, Dr. Farooq Abdullah was threatening that if the Congressmen did not behave, there would be blood bath.

Earlier, during the State Assembly elections of June 5, 1983, the atmosphere in the State had been vitiated to such an extent that even naked men were sent into the crowd that had gathered at Srinagar Iqbal Park to hear Mrs. Indira Gandhi. In the agitation that followed the elections, public order remained continuously disturbed. On January 15, 1984, four supporters of the Congress Party were killed in police firing at Anantnag. Bomb blasts occurred with alarming frequency in the Valley. There were explosions at the time of the Independence Day Parade, in the Srinagar Indian Coffee House, in the house of Dr. A.S. Anand, Judge of the High Court, in Paladium Cinema at Lal Chowk, in the University Library Block and in the house of Sessions Judge (Retired), N.K. Ganju. Earlier, during the cricket test match between India and the West Indies, played at Srinagar on 19 October 1983, the country's image was badly tarnished. In full view of millions of television viewers, and in the presence of Chief Minister Dr. Farooq Abdullah, anti-India and pro-Pakistan slogans were raised. The National Flag was dishonoured. The Indian players were jeered at and pelted with pebbles and refuse.

In those days, processions were also being taken out, with telling frequency. People shouted such slogans as 'Pakistan Zindabad', 'Khalistan Zindabad', 'Noor-e-Chashm, Noor-e-Haq, Zia-ul-Huq, Zia-ul-Huq'. A new slogan, 'Muslim-Sikh Bhai Bhai, Hindu Quam Kahan Se Ayee' (Muslims and Sikhs are brothers; from where have these Hindus come?), had particularly sinister implications. Punjab had already been engulfed by the fire of fanaticism and fundamentalism. Flames of terrorism were leaping and threatening to reach J&K. The Valley was littered with dry, combustible faggots which could catch fire even by a stray spark. The entire border from Siachen downwards was in danger of getting destabilised.

A cup of tea was placed upon the small protruding table. "It would enliven you, Sir", said the smart attendant with a reverential smile. And it did.

From my briefcase I took out a file which an official of the J&K Resident Commissioner's office had handed over to me at the airport. It contained press clippings from July 12, 1989, onwards, that is, the date on which I demitted office of my first governorship of the State. I started glancing through it. "Pakistan Independence Day, August 14, celebrated with gaiety, and blackout and hartal observed on the Indian Independence Day, August 15; the National Flag burnt with crowd standing around and applauding", said one news story. "Kashmir nearly lost to nation", indicated the November 6, 1989 report of *The Statesman.* "Srinagar daily rocked by explosions', bemoaned *Patriot.* "There seems to be a strange conspiracy of silence about the reign of terror in the hapless Valley of Kashmir" was the comment of *The Times of India* of November 23. "Tikka Lal Taploo, Vice President of BJP, gunned down in front of his house in Srinagar"; "Justice Ganjoo brutally murdered in Hari Singh Street"; "P.N. Bhat, a well-known journalist, killed in Anantnag"; "Station House Officer of Maisuma Bazaar Police Station shot dead in the main bazaar"; "Total collapse of the administration"; "Terrorists rule the State"; and "Union Home Minister's daughter kidnapped", were the other horrible headlines. In sheer disgust, I stopped reading. I had read these reports in the daily press earlier. But on that day, seeing them in one heap, was truly depressing. I closed my eyes. My wandering thoughts once again seized me.

Why was the State subjected to periodic convulsions? Why do crises occur again and again? And why were the root causes of the current turmoil similar to those of the previous conflicts? A poem which, like the 'memory of music fled', had become a part of my intellectual sub-consciousness, came to my silent lips:

> It has happened
> and it goes on happening
> and will happen again
> if nothing happens to stop it.
> The innocent know nothing
> because they are too innocent.

The poor do not notice
because they are too poor.
And the rich do not notice
because they are too rich.
The stupid shrug their shoulders
because they are too stupid.
And the clever shrug their shoulders
because they are too clever.
The young do not care
because they are too young.
And the old do not care
because they are too old.
That is why nothing happens
to stop it.
And that is why it has happened
and goes on happening and will
happen again.*

Painful things, I thought, went on happening in our country with sickening frequency, because no one was really concerned about the fundamental issues of national reconstruction, of social and cultural rejuvenation, on the solid foundation of which alone a new moral and ethical order and a new pattern of politics and administration, suited to our requirements, could be built. Years ago, in the Epilogue to my book *Rebuilding Shahjahanabad*, I had penned a small poem, which read:

There cannot be
There will not be
Destruction or construction
Rebuilding or resurrection
Unless a new vision do we find
And create a revolution of the mind.

I had pleaded that, without a new vision, without a new mind, India could not rediscover its lost soul; it could not be re-born.

But such voices were never heard. The new edifice was built on rickety and moth-eaten foundations. At the most crucial turn of our history, our leadership failed to spot the correct path. Ideas were borrowed, not adapted or assimilated. We opened the window to let

*This is an English translation of a poem written by German poet Erich Fried.

in what we thought was fresh air. But we forgot to clean the stinking and slushy garbage that had accumulated inside our home. We did not know the art of digging out golden thoughts that lay buried underneath the debris and brushing and chiselling them and making them effective instruments of national regeneration. We walked on borrowed crutches and thought our muscles were strong. We ate the half-cooked food and believed that we had acquired sufficient strength to jump over the treacherous trenches which history had dug in our way.

Soon we fell by the wayside. Soon we found ourselves in the lap of quacks–on a dark and dingy road. At the dawn of our Independence, we aspired to build a mighty nation–"mighty in thought, mighty in action, mighty in culture and mighty in peaceful service to humanity". But we were caught in the quagmire of our own shallowness. We proceeded along with half an answer.

> Superficially–worse than being blind–
> We proceed along with half an answer
> Bearing our shallowness like a treasure.
> Then comes the snuffing out.
> Our inability to flee or fight
> And feathers of our tamed wings
> Becomes the nasty pillow for the night.

In regard to Kashmir, we inwardly recognised the infirmities of an immature democracy. We feared that in a plebiscite, ignorance, parochialism, and communal prejudice would be exploited. Yet we did nothing to eliminate those forces which fed this ignorance, this parochialism, and this communal prejudice. On the other hand, the politics of Kashmir was run in such a manner that these infirmities were multiplied. Over the years, the leadership betrayed its monumental superficiality, its monumental confusion, and an inexcusable lack of vision and sense of history.

How could one now expect the Kashmiris to act in a rational way? What had we done to merit a happy Kashmir? Had we not created a soft and permissive State? Had we not connived at the politics of deception and duplicity? Had we not allowed new Sheikhs, new Sultans, to emerge? Had we not underplayed the common identity of the deprived–his illiteracy, his hunger, his disease–and overplayed religious and regional identities? Had we not forgotten that India's destiny lay in unity amidst diversity, not in bowing before the bullies but in standing erect with a sense of purpose, not in creating vote banks for exploiting democracy, but in providing real democracy, real justice, and real freedom? Had we not permitted the forces of mediaevalism and monkism to prevail? And what precautionary steps did we take to minimise the damage that the storm of Islamic fundamentalism was bound to cause?

We relied upon fake coins and false 'gods'. We placed all our offerings in their bottomless baskets. We ignored the roots and the tendrils that were germinating beneath the surface. We did not look into cracks and crevices in our structure. We let the ants pierce into them and create still deeper cracks and crevices. Even when the structure was about to be reduced to rubble, New Delhi did not act. In my mind's eye I saw my letter of April 8, 1989, to Prime Minister Rajiv Gandhi in which I had said: "Today may be timely, tomorrow may be too late." But tomorrow had been allowed to turn into day after and the day after into yet another day after. Now that the structure had totally collapsed, here I was airborne, once again, to a troubled and tormented State, nestled in my little seat and bent with the heavy weight of dead albatrosses of the past around my neck, with a shaking cup and saucer before me and nothing but a grey, depressing haze outside. As if this was not enough, lethal political missiles began to be hurled at my little plane, as soon as it commenced its hazardous journey.

As the plane sailed over Pathankot and tilted to turn towards Jammu, bright rays of sunshine pierced through its windows, dispelling the gloom inside. A new resolve dawned upon me. Maybe, I thought, I would have to plough a lonely furrow. But the storm must be weathered. And with all the millstones around my neck, I should stand erect. I quietly worked out my approach and jotted down a few points for my policy statement.

The small plane had its own grace and charm. It came to a soft and steady halt, without the roar of a Boeing. I stretched my legs, straightened myself, and walked into the bright sunshine of Jammu airport. The cool breeze was so refreshing. I ran my fingers through my broken hairs and calmed the nerves underneath. After the usual formalities of reception, I drove towards Raj Bhavan through roads and avenues which seemed to speak to me in a friendly gesture and thank me for the little service that I had rendered them earlier.

A large number of people had gathered on the route, greeting me with smiling faces. They waved and clapped. I learnt from the local newspapers that the news of my appointment was received with a great deal of joy. There were celebrations. Crackers were burst, illumination was done and 'bhangra' performed. The newspapers carried photographs of the people dancing on the streets.

Why, I reflected, were the Jammuites so happy, so buoyant? Why did they stretch their necks from windows, from roof tops and the shop corners to have a glimpse of me? What had they gained? What advantages did they perceive? Why was the atmosphere permeated with an air of expectancy?

The people of India, by and large, I thought, had an innate desire for justice, truth and fair play. The Jammuites had seen these attributes in action in my earlier tenure. Their happiness today was, perhaps, a manifestation of this hidden desire. Could it not be inferred that it was only under the impact of exploitative democracy and a soulless political system that the Indian people sometimes exhibited propensities that were deplorable?

I left all such thoughts for consideration in calmer times. For the moment, I had to get on with the job of taking oath, assuming office, assessing the extent of chaos and collapse, and planning the strategy for restoration and reconstruction. The task was daunting. It would require all the skill in the world to swim across the political and administrative channel that had already been badly infested with merciless sharks.

I took oath of office in the evening. The ceremony had to be a rushed affair. Many people turned up, more than the seating arrangements could accommodate. The National Conference and Congress(I) boycotted the function. I could not understand their motive. Was that the time to save the Valley or to put a spoke in my wheel and obtain some assumed political advantage?

After taking the oath, I made a brief speech, a written one, an unusual thing for me to do. I did so because I wanted to make my approach absolutely clear. I said:

> It was way back in 1986 that I had the occasion to serve you last directly. You know my approach, and I know your manifold problems. I have always treated power as an instrument of service. I would deem it a privilege to serve you again with still greater dedication and determination.
>
> The current phase should be called not a period of Governor's Rule but a period of Governor's service. Constitutionally, I would

be a Governor. But, for all practical purposes, I would function like an orderly–a nursing orderly–to help the patient with love, compassion and service, to regain his health, become vigorous and vibrant, and lead a life of peace and productivity.

Every single penny would be saved to solve the problems of the poor, the sick and the needy. In view of the current conditions, I will draw only ₹ 1,000 as salary for food for myself and my family, out of ₹ 11,000 sanctioned under the J&K Constitution. There will be no State Party. Expenditure on government transport, telephones and other establishments will be curtailed. Top-heavy administration will be pruned. The pattern of development will be reoriented to meet the requirements of the common man.

All right-thinking people in the State are in deep anguish and agony. Whether A loses life or B, it is the blood of all of us that spills–the blood of our brothers and sisters, of our sons and daughters. We must stop all this. I assure full justice to all. Anyone with any grievance can come to see me.

Friends, we seem to have lost our moorings but I remind you of a couplet which says:

جہاں کارواں بھول جاتے ہیں رستہ
وہیں سے نکلتی ہیں منزل کی راہیں

(New routes are usually found only from places where the caravans lose their way.)

Let us gather ourselves and carve out a new path to a fair and just society by fair and just means. Let us devote all our energy, all our resources, to one supreme purpose–eradication of poverty and unemployment. Let us remember that one basic principle of all religions is to see the service to God in the service to the poor. I seek cooperation of all. I assure you, once again, of just, dedicated and determined service.

After the night's ordeal and the day's journey, I was tired. While speaking, my voice often choked. I wondered whether what happened was right. In the affairs of the State, emotions had hardly any place. But this was not the way in which my mind worked. It is the intensity of the feeling that puts life in thoughts and converts words into deeds.

After a few minutes, I moved away from the 'no tea party' ceremony. The Northern Command Army Commander, Lieutenant-

General Gobinder Singh, wanted to have discussions with me before returning to his headquarters at Udhampur. He apprised me of the extremely serious situation in the Valley. He told me that every time he spoke to the previous authorities about the rapidly deteriorating situation, he was assured that appropriate action would be taken. But nothing was done. I assured him that this would no longer be so.

Greetings and good wishes were galore. Many persons wanted to see me and speak to me. But my mind was elsewhere. Why had Farooq Abdullah resigned? Who had egged him on to do so? I recalled his public and recorded speech after I had sworn him as Chief Minister on November 7, 1986:

> Governor Sahib, we would need you very badly. It is, indeed, amazing that such remarkable work could be done by you in a short time through an imbecile and faction-ridden bureaucracy. If today three ballot boxes are kept, one for the National Conference, one for the Congress and one for you, your ballot box would be full while the other two ballot boxes would be empty. Please do not hesitate to pull my ears if I go wrong.

I thought to myself, "My administrative qualities have remained the same; my development disposition has remained unaltered; and my earnestness has not even been tested. What, then, was the justification for this somersault? Why, after creating the mess, intentional and unprincipled hurdles were being created for me? Could not small considerations be kept aside for resolving a national crisis?"

The following day, I wanted to proceed to Srinagar, but the helicopter could not cross Banihal which was under very thick clouds. Luck, chance, destiny–whatever one may like to call it–has always some part to play in human affairs. Had I reached Srinagar on that day, some damage could, perhaps, have been averted.

I went to the Jammu Secretariat and met a very large number of people and deputations. Most of them had a bunch of complaints against the previous regime. While I was listening to these grievances, I started getting frantic telephone calls from some persons in Srinagar, complaining that there had been large-scale searches by the police early in the morning in the Chota Bazaar and Guru Bazaar areas and about 250 youth had been picked up. Since I did not know what the matter was, I got in touch with Director-General of Police J.N. Saxena. He told me that alarming reports were being intentionally circulated, and that, after preliminary screening, about 200 youths had been released and only those suspected of serious crimes would be held up for further questioning. Saxena also informed me that a few days earlier, in the Guru Bazaar area, three Central Reserve Police personnel had been shot dead and searches had been conducted to apprehend the culprits.

Earlier, in the forenoon, I had spoken to Peer Ghulam Hassan Shah, retired Director-General of Police, and appointed him as one of my advisers. Shah accepted the appointment. On his suggestion, I even agreed to give him the rank of a Cabinet Minister. A press note was issued. Shah's appointment was flashed on the local radio. By noon, however, Shah had second thoughts. He told me that he could not accept the assignment as this would expose him and his family members to grave risks. It was at that moment that I realised how strong had become the hold of the terrorists. Even an officer with Peer Ghulam Hassan Shah's background, experience and reputation had to refuse a highly coveted assignment.

I went on working in the Secretariat and returned to Raj Bhavan late in the evening. The night that followed was the strangest night that I have ever lived. Hardly had I gone to bed when the two telephones at my bedside started ringing, almost continuously. At the other end, there were voices of alarm, of concern, of fright, sometimes muted voices of men too terror-stricken to speak. "Tonight is our last night", moaned one voice. "By morning, we–all Kashmiri Pandits–would be butchered", said another voice. "Send us aeroplanes; take us out of the Valley; evacuate us at night if you do not want to see our corpses in the morning", pleaded another. "Our womenfolk, our sisters, our mothers, would be abducted, and we menfolk slaughtered", shrieked yet another voice. Some callers told me that they would just hold on to their telephones so that I could hear the terrible slogans and exhortations that were emanating from hundreds of loudspeakers fitted on the mosques. The noises, they said, were deafening and it appeared that a number of recorded tapes were being simultaneously played at a very loud pitch, causing horrible effects in resonance and permeating the atmosphere with terror and fear of imminent death.

What was it all about? How was it that such a large number of loudspeakers had been installed and the same calls were being made from them? How was this technique of arousing mass frenzy acquired? Who had masterminded this well-knit organisation? And how was it that such a build-up remained unnoticed? Was it a case of default or connivance or both?

It was with some difficulty that I was able to contact, on phone, Srinagar Divisional Commissioner, Jalil Ahmed Khan, and Deputy Inspector-General of Police, S.S. Ali. I goaded them to take prompt action. I advised them to depute responsible officers to the troubled spots, and themselves remain at the police control room, and also keep the Army standby. I personally spoke to SSP Allah Bux, and motivated him to stretch all his resources. I knew he was the key man in the situation. I also got in touch with senior Army officers.

In between, there were telephone calls from the Ministry of Home Affairs. "Additional Home Secretary this side, Sir", was the worried voice. "We are getting frantic calls from Hindus from Srinagar. Hell seems to have broken loose. The Kashmiri Pandits are in utter panic. We cannot get any officer on phone in Srinagar." There were a number of other panic telephone calls from New Delhi. I assured everybody that I was taking action.

What incensed me most was that, at more or less the same time, 'ethnic revolt' in Azerbaijan and the 'Rumanian Liberation' were being telecast as a special programme. Large crowds were shown shouting: "We want freedom; we do not mind spilling our blood; death to the oppressors who have kept us in chains." If any proof of Government unimaginativeness or its disoriented functioning was needed, there it was. There could be no comparison between the case of Kashmir and that of Azerbaijan or Rumania. But it should have been understood that in the circumstances prevailing at that time, the Kashmiri youth would misread the message. Virtual incitement was provided by our own television. The timing of the telecast confirmed my impression that the political and bureaucratic mandarins of New Delhi had very little knowledge of the currents and undercurrents of the situation in Kashmir and its ground-level realities.

Throughout the night, I continued to ring up Srinagar officers to ascertain the situation and also to ensure that timely and coordinated action was taken. I was not sure either about the promptitude of the State Administration or its effectiveness. I was conscious of the fact that the same Administration had miserably failed on the eve of Guru Gobind Singh's birthday, January 13, 1989, when 15 persons were killed in Jammu, within an hour or so, at a short distance from Dr. Farooq Abdullah's office, even when the trouble could have been easily anticipated and elementary preventive action taken. It was only at about 4 a.m. that the crisis abated and I tried to get a wink of sleep before catching the morning flight to Srinagar.

I landed at the Srinagar Airport which was so familiar to me. But it looked somewhat different. The crispness in the air was absent. A dreary coldness seemed to have descended on it. The ebullience of officers, to which I was accustomed, was nowhere to be seen. Confronted with unusual events, they were not sure of themselves. Even their gestures appeared paralysed. Terrorism and the wayward administration of the past had taken its toll. Everything around looked so sullen, so grim. The tragedy that had overtaken Kashmir could be experienced in the eerie silence of its leafless trees–motionless, frozen, almost dead with terror.

After a moment, the convoy of cars moved towards Raj Bhavan through the city. There were small gatherings of people along the road and also around the few shops that were open on the airport road. Some officers at the airport had told me that I might stop at one or two points on the way, where people would like to submit memoranda about their demands. This was the practice in 1986, when villagers and persons living in poor localities had acquired a new reflex of listing genuine demands, as distinct from concessions, and presenting the same to me with the confidence that these would be accepted and action taken to get the decisions implemented immediately.

I, too, had the inclination to walk from one end of the busy street to the other. Knowing my disposition in this regard, a few enthusiastic officers of the local police, who had taken a special liking to my style of working in the field, had even made standby arrangements for my walks near the SMHS Hospital area. They thought that, as in the past, that would be my way of commencing my second tenure–walking through the heart of the city and thus walking through the heart of the people. But my instinct told me that things had changed and that such a step would be extremely rash, almost suicidal. Ruthless terrorism that had gripped Kashmir would not permit me to take the initiative. Its protagonists knew that the citadels of subversion and militancy, which they had built, could be breached through such walks. They would see to it that my first walk would be the last one too. Later on, I came to know that had I got down from the vehicle, where I saw crowds of people waiting for me, I would have been showered with bullets from the other side of the road, from a half-open shop.

From the very first day, the terrorists, the pro-Pakistan elements, the fanatics, the fundamentalists, and the vested political and bureaucratic interests, who feared exposure of their acts of omission and commission, had in their own ways decided to cripple and incapacitate me.

They knew that if I got a few days to entrench myself, the saner elements would rally around me, and I would be able to secure sufficient response for setting up a fair and just system of administration through fair and just means, and launch a drive against corruption and also initiate a new pattern of development which would knock out the social and economic base of subversion.

Uncommitted people in the Valley, I believe, were inwardly happy over my appointment. They thought that the good old days of 1986 might return. Those were the days when justice, fair play and common man-oriented development were seen, and the fair face of India was visible. When the people noticed spectacular developments–smooth and silken roads, crystal-clear water in the lakes, lush green city forests, liberal civic amenities, increasing number of schools in the rural and far-flung areas, and neat cities–they saw what the central assistance, properly utilised, could do. People, in fact, had started questioning what Sheikh Abdullah had done for them. They came to realise that it was corruption and maladministration, and not lack of assistance from the Central Government, that was the root cause of their economic and social problems.

But pro-Pakistan forces and forces of militancy had a separate game plan. They were not interested in justice, development, or a healthy face of India. On the contrary, these forces wanted that the person who symbolised these concepts, or who could revive the trend of 1986, should not be allowed to dig in. All means had to be used to annihilate his standing. These elements, in fact, worked overtime to ensure that Governor or President's Rule did not come. They wanted the State to drift, and indecision and indifference to continue. In fact, the TOPAC* plan had itself spelt out the strategy in this regard. It said: "Infiltrate the administration, demoralise it, and subvert all other instruments of power, but do not go to the extent that would invite Central intervention." Unfortunately, the Central Government aided and abetted the TOPAC plan, albeit unwittingly. It did not intervene, and allowed subversion to penetrate all components of the power structure.

What was still more unfortunate was that, notwithstanding the criticality of the Kashmir situation, every political party seemed anxious to exploit it to its advantage rather than make an earnest

*See Chapter X: 'Nature and Pattern of Subversion'.

contribution to help resolve it. My appointment itself was made a subject of controversy. The Left parties opposed it, the Congress(I) and the National Conference(F) opposed it, and some elements within the Janata Dal opposed it. All gave different reasons. But the commonality was the political exploitation rather than merit. I marvelled at their sense of responsibility, their commitment to the country's welfare, and their so-called intention to evolve a national consensus on Kashmir! When I was fighting with my back to the wall, they were sniping at me from the other side.

Another important development confounded the situation even before my arrival. Dr. Farooq Abdullah came to Srinagar on January 16. He held a meeting at the Police Headquarters. In this meeting he said that the National Front Government was taking serious note of non-action and that he was under pressure to show positive results. When some officers pointed out that they were not being allowed to do certain things, Dr. Farooq Abdullah lost his temper. He called the local police thoroughly corrupt, and asked the new Director-General of Police, J.N. Saxena, and Inspector-General CRP, Joginder Singh, to take the initiative. They said that they wanted to conduct searches in the area from where the terrorists often fired at paramilitary forces. In his usual flamboyance, Dr. Farooq Abdullah replied in anger: 'Do what you like.' Apparently he said so without applying his mind in depth and without ascertaining details and assessing the repercussions.

It was on the basis of these tempestuous discussions that Director-General Police, Inspector-General CRP, and SSP Srinagar city deployed the CRP in the night intervening January 19-20 in Chota Bazaar and Guru Bazaar area. I took oath of office at Jammu on January 19. I was given no information about the aforesaid matter.

When the searches were conducted, there was reaction. Dr. Farooq Abdullah, who had himself taken the aforesaid decision, secretly asked his partymen to incite the people against the searches. The sole objective was to create problems for the new administration which had taken over the previous evening. A number of his low-level proteges were seen in the mosques, acting as friends of subversives and playing a provocative role.

It was absolutely clear that the very nature of the Operation Search (January 19-20) was such that the Governor could not have ordered or organised this in a few hours' time. When Dr. Farooq Abdullah was confronted with this fact by a newsman, he took shelter behind technicality. He asked the newsman to show him his written orders.

He, thus, let down the poor Director-General Police and Inspector-General CRP and the SSP.

In my heart of hearts, I wished the Director-General of Police, Saxena, had publicly declared the truth and owned responsibility for the searches which were conducted under his orders and directions, without informing me. This would not only have been in accordance with the highest tradition of public service but would also have denied my denigrators any opportunity to mount false propaganda against me. I was their main target. They knew that if they could get me out of the way, their designs would materialise. By owning up what was his decision or product of Farooq's confused observation, Saxena would not have lost anything. We would not have let him down, as his action was bona fide. Regrettably, he could not pick up enough moral courage. My own principles of administration prevented me from saying in public that the decision had been taken by him or was implicit in Dr. Farooq's freakish behaviour.

On January 19 itself, Dr. Farooq Abdullah's party, the National Conference, issued a virulent statement. His game plan, which had been worked out in consultation with Congress(I), was to create as many hurdles as possible for the new administration.

In regard to these searches, I later on asked my Adviser, Ved Marwah, to conduct an inquiry. This is what Marwah observed in his report:

> Director-General of Police verbally told me that the searches had been planned earlier under the orders of the then Chief Minister, Dr. Farooq Abdullah. Apparently, the searches had been made to apprehend militants who, according to the information of the DGP, had been hiding in these areas.
>
> From all accounts it appears that the militants were prepared for such an agitation to take the State Government by surprise and declare independence from the Indian Union. The fact that the leaders of the agitation did not pursue their demand for an enquiry into these searches, only confirms this.

With my mind full of righteous indignation over the sad and sordid conditions of the country's politics, I entered Raj Bhavan. It looked so lonely, so silent. Nevertheless, it seemed to be taking a gloomy pride in standing as a lonely sentinel over the sad stillness of the vast Dal Lake whose flat and aging bosom reflected the frozen turbulence of my mind.

The office room wore a deserted look. It appeared to be frozen with inaction. From its corner, a small, worn-out sofa stared at me as if to say that history has its own logic, it offers its own opportunity, and the nations which do not understand its logic, or seize the opportunity offered by it, must bear the consequences and suffer. I had learnt at school that history is no blind goddess, and does not excuse blindness in others. Today, standing in this forlorn complex called Raj Bhavan, I realised how true this observation was. The pity was that for the blindness of others, I had to grope in the darkness, stumble around, and find a way to redemption and resurrection.

The office table was terribly dull. Its disproportionately long surface made me uncomfortable. My small notebook on it would make no impact, I thought. Involuntarily, I moved towards the chair which I had used before. It always appeared firm and straight. But, on this day, it was so cold, so cheerless. The low voltage in the bulbs added to the depression and seemed to symbolise the power vacuum in the State.

Outside, the events were moving with the same feverish speed as in the previous night. The voices of horror, fearful harangue and exhortations, soaked in Islamic fundamentalists' terminology, filled the air. Crowds were being goaded to gather in mosques. People were being mobilised from villages, from outlying areas and from the heart of the city. No civil authority seemed to exist. The passivity was unbelievable. The Director-General of Police later on told me that it had taken him more than six hours to get the Deputy Inspector-General out from his house for duty.

I found myself virtually shipwrecked on a lonely but known land. The airport, the trees, the hills, the lakes, the streets, the offices, the officers and Raj Bhavan–all were the same. And yet they were very different. Something had gone out of them–something that gives life and colour and meaning. The mood had changed, the expressions had changed, and the responses had changed. Everyone seemed to be in a state of shock, speaking in frightened whispers, in gestures. . . . Nothing, I thought, would be the same again. But life flows on. And fresh leaves do appear on the autumn trees.

Suddenly, the poetic mood gave way to the pragmatism of the practical administrator in me. The chillness of the room could no longer keep my mood down. It was time to warm up. I sprang up from my seat. Pacing up and down in my small room, I said to myself, "I must act. Kashmir would not be lost without a fight." The bunkers had to be repaired. Rearguard action had to be taken. Fight had to be resorted to with backs to the cold wall. The authority of the State had to be reasserted. Srinagar could not be allowed to be swamped by terrorists, the fundamentalists and their cohorts. The minorities could not be abandoned to be slaughtered. Panic reaction, I thought, should be left to Delhi, where people in power seldom find time to understand in depth what was really going on at the ground-level. Their source of information was always hearsay and distorted versions of the vested interests. Here, in this hour of deep crisis, decisions had to be taken and implemented in split seconds.

I spoke to my adviser, Ved Marwah, and called in Lt.-Gen. M.A. Zaki, Corps Commander, Northern Command. The three of us sat in my office. "We have hardly any time for discussion", I said. "Within a few minutes, we must act or suffer being overwhelmed." They agreed. Action was soon on. The curfew, which existed only in name, began to be enforced. The crowds which had gone berserk, burning public buildings–SIDC office complex at Natipora, Women's Polytechnic, Saida Kadal, Mehjoor Bridge, etc.–had to be dispersed. Firing had to be resorted to by the security forces at Hawal, Tulsi Bag, Gowa Kadal, Lal Bazaar, Safa Kadal, etc. Twelve trouble-makers lost their lives and many were injured. The militants and their propaganda outfits, and the rumour mill, which always worked overtime in Kashmir, were soon busy churning out stories of excesses, of atrocities, of hundreds of persons being killed. Well, loss of any human life is abominable, distasteful to me. I had made it clear in my very first speech: "Whether A loses life or B, it is the blood of all of us that spills."

Unfortunately, in public affairs, you have to put up with the lesser evil to eliminate the greater evil, and events do not always take the direction that you intend. Sitting in your office, you cannot really say with precision whether the force used was excessive. In such matters, poetic justice is not attainable. You would always have two versions before you. And in a situation like the one that obtained in Kashmir, no one from the public could say anything except what the terrorists wanted him to say. Even a whisper of deviation from their lips would invite certain death.

Even the most humane and enlightened administration has sometimes to administer a bitter pill. In what manner a particular situation would be dealt with has to be decided by the officer on the spot. As long as he acts in a bona fide manner, his judgment should not be ordinarily questioned.

By the evening, the city had become quiet. Order had been restored. The curfew restrictions began to be respected. Arson could not be indulged in with impunity. The first effective action to pull back Kashmir from the jaws of pro-Pakistan and pro-independence militants had been taken. An important part of the drama, whose final act had to be staged on January 26, had been thwarted.

At night I lay on my bed, reflecting upon the events of the day and their background. Injury to human lives has always made me uncomfortable. Human pain, human suffering, makes me uneasy.

I pity the people who have an insensitive mind. I distinctly remember how one day I was sitting at a rest-house near Pahalgam and watching the beautiful drama of the Lidder's waves–leaping, foaming, leaping still higher, and then hopping over to the next phase of their roaring journey. At that time a small group of retired Army officers approached me for a routine help to fish for trout in the stream. I asked my office to help. The officers went away happily over the prospects of getting some prize catches. Though I continued to watch the waves, the old thrill had gone. My mind was distracted. I brooded over the fate of the fish. What pleasure, I thought, would they get out of fishing as sport? Did they not think of the pain which the poor little trout experienced when the angler's hook pierced its soft flesh? Did they not think of the warm dark blood that oozed out of its body and then dissolved into the pure stream, leaving not a trace? Did they not share the agony which the trout underwent when pushed out of water before it breathed its last? Were they not touched by the last curl of its life?

But at the moment the mood was different. The stream, the trout, its soft flesh, its warm dark blood, flowing imperceptibly in the white stream, its frozen pain, its last curl, its gasping for breath and then becoming motionless, did not seem to matter. What mattered today was order, assertion of authority, integrity of the country. Whatever doubts I had, soon disappeared. Someone had to prevent greater losses; someone had to save the Lidder itself. And those equipped with Kalashnikovs and bombs were obviously not trouts who were being hooked by anglers. They were the bloody hyena thirsting for human blood. And the really guilty men were those who had allowed the tragic situation to develop, despite clear and timely warnings.

It was getting very late. "I must get some sleep", I argued with myself. "It is no use adding to my burdens with tormented thoughts. Such things never help."

I thought fresh wind would induce sleep. I got up from my bed and opened the window which had been closed by my ADC on considerations of security. It was a windless night. Yet I felt a calm waft of air hissing past my face. It had a message of its own.

The night was silent, dreadfully silent. But it was a silence that roared in my ears. At a distance across the lake stood the Shankaracharya Hill, symbolising our inner vitality–the volcanic* vitality that has now cooled inside the rock that bears the name of the great recreator of Indian cultural unity and who, like a Colossus, strode in the tenth century from Kanyakumari, "the lotus feet of the Divine Mother", to Kashmir, "the crown of India",** and ascended this hill to pray at the little Shiva temple that came into existence† between 2629 B.C. and 2564 B.C. and then proceeded to consecrate the Holy cave of Amarnath. Did this symbol of our innate strength have any meaning for our leadership of the day? Did it realise that India today required a new welding force–another cultural renaissance, another social and moral vision, which should stand like a Shankara's rock against the forces of decline and disintegration?

I looked in vain for the glimmer of light on my left, which used to come to Raj Bhavan from the flood-lit ruins of 'Pari Mahal'. Pari Mahal was built as a library and abode of learning by Dara Shukoh, the most learned, the most enlightened, and also the most tragic figure in the Mughal history. Here, he held spiritual discourses with saints and sufis of Kashmir*** under the guidance of his teacher, Mulla Shah, and evolved his thought which later found expression in his two treatises, "Majma-ul-Bahrain" (Unity of the Two Seas) and "Sarr-i-Asran" (Secret of Secrets), propounding the view that all religions taught the same fundamental truth and the 'Hidden Book' referred in the Quran was the Upanisads, as these "contained the essence of unity". But now even the ruins of catholic and integrative thinking were not allowed to be lighted by those to whom the Valley had virtually been handed over on a platter.

The hills around, shorn of trees, seemed to be staring at me with their tragic, stony looks. Corruption had fleeced them of their

---

* According to the geologists, this hill is a dormant volcano which cooled about 4 million years ago.

** These are the expressions used by the famous Tamil poet, Subramanya Bharati.

† This temple was repaired in 1360 B.C. by Gopaditya and again by Sultan Zain-ul-Abidin between A.D. 1421 and 1472.

*** Prince Dara Shukoh stayed in Kashmir in 1640, 1645 and then in 1654.

refreshing buoyancy, and the new breed of ravishers, with their lusty ventures, had plucked their long and thick hairs. In the other corner stood the hefty columns of yet another hotel building that was coming up on the bank of the Dal Lake, emptying its refuse on its fast rising bed. These were the shafts in my soul. All that was upward and divine in our heritage was, being brutalised.

The window, I thought, had deceived me. Instead of calming my nerves, it had stirred my inner being. I was again agitated with my frozen turbulence. Closing the window, I had a fleeting glance of the lake. It was silent, dead silent.

What was the way out of this seemingly intractable position? Obviously, I could not walk barefoot in the Valley full of scorpions–the Valley wherein inner and outer forces of terrorism had conspired to subvert the Union and to seize power. I must equip myself to face all eventualities. I could leave nothing to chance. A slight slip or error would mean a Tienanmen Square or a Blue Star or a formal declaration of a new theocratic state with all its international embarrassment.

The previous evening I had invited a deputation from the Chota Bazaar area. About twenty persons came to see me. Half of them were women. They were all wearing 'Choddar', and the general style of dress was in accordance with the newly prescribed 'code'.* Most of the talking was done by a middle-aged woman who was probably a teacher. She was highly articulate. She spoke in a measured tone, using both English and Urdu words. She reminded me that I had been to the deputationists' congested and stinking locality during 1986 Governor's Rule, and that the residents still had confidence in me. She complained that the police had been unfair and unjust.

The deputationists believed me when I told them that I was not at all aware of what had happened and that the decision to conduct searches had been made earlier. Before meeting them, I had ascertained the facts of the case from Director-General Police and Inspector-General CRP and ordered release of all except six young men against whom police was claiming substantial evidence. I apprised the deputationists of the position and assured them that the cases of the remaining six would also be settled within the next couple of hours. The deputationists went away, largely satisfied, though they continued to use strong words against the local SSP and

*See Chapter X: 'Nature and Pattern of Subversion'.

CRP staff. A responsive chord amongst the people, I thought, could still be struck.

I met the six young men personally. I was as sympathetic as a brother would be. I advised them to give up the wrong path. Two of them wept bitterly. They said they were being harassed by both the police and the terrorists. They were poor and their income had been badly affected. I ordered their immediate release. For all the six youth, I got some warm clothing.

I thought that compassion and sympathy that I had extended to the young men at a personal level would send my message of love and friendliness and hoist the right signal in the Chota Bazaar and the neighbouring areas. Things happened as I expected. But it was so only for a short while. What I had not reckoned with was the vicious disinformation campaign which the terrorists and their collaborators had adopted as a part of their overall strategy. They threatened all those who spoke of my help or made any mention of my work in the past about development and cleanliness of the city. The beneficiaries of Dr. Farooq's regime, in their own subtle and crafty manner, spread false rumours. I realised I was up against a massive stone wall with deep foundations in terrorism and disinformation.

Sensing what was to take place on and around January 26, I accelerated the pace of work. I met as many people as I could. I held as many discussions as possible with local officers. I opened my heart to the sincere and kept the 'quislings' at bay.

I was left in no doubt that a diabolical plan of subversion had been worked out. The final blow had to be struck on January 26, which also happened to be a Friday. Collection of about a million people was planned at the Idgah. In the city, they would be exhorted, through the mosques' loudspeakers, to proceed to the Idgah in small batches. Simultaneously, hordes of people would move from the outlying areas. From the neighbouring villages and small towns, the movement would be through buses and private vehicles. The 'namaz' would be performed with all the religious fervour. Slogans of independence would be raised. Shots would be fired in the air by the terrorists. Then, suddenly, the National Flag of the Union would be symbolically burnt and the flag of Islamic Republic hoisted. Foreign correspondents and photographers would be there in any number to report the event and take photographs.

The plotters had calculated that, being a Republic Day, the Government would have to allow free movement. And, judging by the past inaction, the organisers had convinced themselves that the Government would not interfere. The leaders and civil servants would be busy in Jammu, taking salute, and the local officers would not act. They could be made even to raise their hands as soon as the new flag went up. A few police officers would be there to lend a helping hand, if necessary.

The schemers had made all the preparations. They had kept the plan a closely guarded secret and wanted to spring a surprise at the eleventh hour. The only calculations they had not made was that the Farooq Government was no longer there. As early as on August 14, 1989, the previous Government had virtually permitted the terrorists to take salute in a parade at the Islamia College. The new factor had come in. And this was my appointment. The organisers took this into account but somewhat late and, as it turned out later, somewhat imperfectly. They thought that, in the first instance, I would not know what the game was, and even if I got scent of the matter, I would not have time to work out counter-strategy and implement it successfully. In any case, what could I do? Call in the Army and paramilitary forces, after hoisting of the new flag, to disperse one million people, make a Tienanmen Square or a Blue Star, and thus subserve the very purpose of the terrorists and their supporters across the border? And what could the Army do if one million people just decided to sit at the Idgah and refuse to move?

In the meanwhile, I went ahead speedily to weld as many broken tools as possible and forge new ones to meet the challenge. A broad strategy had been thought of by me. And this was to attain maximum results with minimum casualties and in the shortest possible time.

To create an extremely critical situation one or two days before January 26, an absolutely false rumour was spread, in accordance with a pre-planned design, that four jawans' of the Kashmir Armed Police had been shot dead by the paramilitary forces. The agents provocateurs were simultaneously at work within the Armed Police and the local police stations. Some of the policemen started deserting their posts, and a sizeable section of the Kashmir Armed Police surrounded the office of the Director-General, shouting derogatory slogans and calling for 'blood for blood'. It was a near mutiny. The conspiracy was to bring about total mutiny on the eve of January 26 or on January 26 itself. The foreign journalists also reached the spot and attempted to record the slogans on their tapes. But we did not lose nerve. I quickly deputed Adviser Jamil Qureshi to the office of the

Director-General to take 'holding action' by initiating some sort of a dialogue with the policemen and suggesting that those who had grievances could even meet the Governor. In the meanwhile, a contingent of the Army was brought near the place of trouble to convey the impression to the trouble-makers that the Administration would act quickly to disarm the J&K Armed Police. Simultaneously, the Central Reserve Police personnel were despatched to the police station. This had a lightning effect, and the designs of the conspirators and subversives were frustrated.

On the evening of January 24, I was informed by Divisional Commissioner Jalil Khan that Akali leader Simranjit Singh Mann had come to the State Guest House and that he wanted accommodation for him as well as a retinue of his armed bodyguards. Accommodation, of course, had to be given. It was a matter of courtesy. Jalil also informed me that Mann wanted to meet me. Mann had not given prior information to anyone, nor was any intelligence agency able to inform me about his intended arrival. Such was the state of the intelligence machinery. I was totally surprised by Mann's arrival.

Why should Mann arrive at Srinagar unannounced? What was the purpose of his mission? While I was weighing all these misgivings in my mind and discussing them with the officers concerned, Inspector-General of Police (CID), Amar Kapoor, rang me up to say that Mann had met a number of foreign journalists at Broadway Hotel and told them that he wanted the State Government not to enact a second 'Blue Star'. This statement added to the mystery of Mann's visit.

About the same time, information was received that Dr. Farooq Abdullah was coming to Srinagar from Jammu, and that he wanted certain facilities at the airport as well as at his house. These facilities had to be given. But there were no apparent compulsions for him to come at that time and in the circumstances then prevailing. Did he not realise that his presence would merely cause further strain on the security apparatus? Or was his purpose different? Why did he choose this Moment? Why did he not come earlier? In fact, the accusation against him was that, when in office, he had securely cushioned himself at Jammu.

Simranjit Singh Mann came to see me the following morning. His talk with me was somewhat patchy and disoriented. As Mann was talking to me, an urgent wireless message came. Four IAF officers, including, Squadron Leader Ravi Khanna, had been shot dead by the terrorists, while they were waiting at Rawalpura bus stand for their vehicle to pick them up. This ghastly crime shocked me. I picked up the phone and issued instructions for a vigorous search of the area. Mann's instant advice was that I should not order searches. "It would serve no useful purpose", he said.

After another five minutes, Mann left. He told me that he was going back to Punjab via the rest-house where he was staying. Before leaving, he made a statement to the press that he had advised the Governor to ensure that no 'Blue Star' was enacted in Srinagar. He did not refer to the expression 'Blue Star' in his talk with me. Why did he mention this in his press statement? Was it a slip or something else? Was he aware of the huge crowd being collected at the Idgah on January 26? If his purpose was to make a statement to the press after speaking to me, why could he not do so after contacting me on the phone from Chandigarh or Amritsar?

By that time, however, I had more or less decided about the strategy for January 26. But I kept my thinking close to my chest. If I gave any premature indication, I thought, it might be divulged to the militants and they might change the plan and create more serious problems.

Late in the evening of January 25, I made it known to a few of my close aides that I would not be going to the winter capital, Jammu, to take the Republic Day salute. The risk of leaving the city of Srinagar was too great. Anything could happen. I had to be there to take quick decisions, to meet an unforeseen situation, or modify our strategy if the militants changed their operational plan at the eleventh hour.

With the brutal killings of four IAF officers and sudden visits of Mann and Dr. Farooq, new tensions, new suspicions had arisen. The Air Force was shocked and angry. The airmen had questions in their eyes: "Was it to see our brave officers being killed like pigeons in treacherous attacks that we undertook 704 hazardous sorties from October 27 to November 17, 1947, to save Kashmir Valley from the ravages of the raiders? Would this be the end-result of Major-General Thimayya's historic action of taking tanks to snow-covered Zojila Pass at the height of 11,578 feet or that of the amazing feat of Air Commodore Mehar Singh who flew his plane at 23,000 feet above the sea level without oxygen on the hitherto uncharted course and landing at a hastily laid rough airstrip at the height of 11,500 feet?"

I went to the Air Force colony along with Lt.-General Zaki, met senior officers, and personally consoled the bereaved families. Mrs. Khanna, the young widow of Squadron Leader Khanna, struck me as unusually courageous and gentle. Her tragedy was immense, and it was writ large on her pale face. But she did not utter a single word against either Muslims or Kashmiris. Her only appeal to me was to ensure that other families were not struck with such tragedies. Lt. General Zaki and I also went to the military hospital to see the injured airmen.

The tragic incident of brutal murder of the four IAF officials also confirmed the impression that a sizable section of the police had been infiltrated or had come to the conclusion that the terrorists at that time had acquired so much ascendancy that it would be expedient to help them–indirectly, if not directly–by inaction, if not by active collaboration. The Adviser, Qureshi, whom I requested to make an on-the-spot inquiry immediately after the killing took place, reported:

> The Rawalpura shooting incident of January 25, 1990, wherein Squadron Leader R.K. Khanna and three others were killed and ten injured by the extremists, at about 0730 hours in the morning, is a result of absolute lack of pluck and failure, at the operational level, manifest from the lack of action of the J&K Armed Police outpost located within a stone's throw of the three places where the actual shooting took place. Altogether about 40 rounds were fired by the extremists, apparently from 2 to 3 automatic weapons and one SA pistol. The assailants drove up to the victims in a two-wheeler Honda and a Maruti Gypsy and, after accomplishing their task, took a clockwise circuit of the roundabout and vanished towards the bypass. The J&K Armed Police post, located near the place of occurrence in a pucca building, had one head constable and 7 constables with 8 × 303 rifles with 50 rounds of ammunition per rifle and had, at the precise time of the occurrence, 5 men including the head constable present. They did not react.

To frustrate the overall strategy of the militants and to hit their operational plan at its roots, I had already decided to impose curfew from January 25 afternoon and to enforce it strictly, even in lanes and by-lanes. The underlying objective was to prevent the crowd from gathering. I was certain that, once the crowd gathered at the Idgah, then situations like those of Blue Star and Tienanmen Square could not be prevented. Frenzied speeches would be made to incite the crowd and the cry of 'Jihad' and independence would be raised in the name of Islam. The armed terrorists would assure the crowd that they would hit back if the police or the army moved in. The mass of people could just sit down and challenge the army and paramilitary forces to do what they liked.

One thing for which the militants were not fully prepared was the imposition of strict curfew. They believed that it would be unthinkable to impose curfew on the Republic Day, and even if curfew was imposed, it would be impossible to enforce it. But the strategy of posting the police and paramilitary forces at street corners, that is, at the very point from where rivulets were to flow and join other rivulets to form a torrent, upset the calculation of the subversives and their supporters.

The Administration meant business. People got the message. Loudspeakers did blare out, exhorting the people to come out. But this had little impact. Psychologically, the position had changed. Terrorists could be told by their passive supporters that they could do nothing. Terrorism could no longer be taken as sport. For any subversive venture the price had to be paid.

This was our first major victory on the physical as well as psychological front. The torrent had not been allowed to be formed. The rivulets had been dyked near their point of origin.

For the night, I had taken special measures to illuminate Government buildings and also to have street lights burning. The terrorists had 'issued instructions to the people' to observe blackout and not to permit illumination of any buildings or burning of street lights. They had threatened to blow up the power houses and electric substations. But they could not succeed in any of these designs.

In the evening, I came out of my office to have a look at the city. Most of the lights were on. The street lights were burning brightly. The government buildings were illuminated. Srinagar, in fact, was never so well lighted as it was on that night. For the sake of records, I got some of the important localities photographed. I felt as if a new candle of light, of hope, had started burning within me. My instructions to the Power Department, the Srinagar Municipality, the Police, the P.W.D. and various other public bodies had been obeyed. Respect for authority, call it fear if you like, had started having its impact.

I contrasted this phenomenon with the blackouts of the earlier Republic Days and Independence Days, when the so-called popular Governments were in power. What used to upset me most in this regard was that the miscreants indulged in the blackouts for fun, for sport, for securing some sort of mischievous thrill and the

Governments of the time took everything light-heartedly. Even some of the functionaries of the administration derived secret pleasure out of these events. Consequently, over the years, it became second nature with most of the youth to indulge in the business of embarrassing pro-India forces and secure wide publicity in the process. Tolerance was mistaken for cowardice, non-action for acquiescence, and the administration's blind eye for a wink of encouragement. This is how habits are formed. The attitude of taking the authorities lightly struck deep roots.

At night I had sound sleep for first time since January 17, 1990. I felt a certain warmth in the otherwise cold bed. But the incipient hope proved to be short-lived. On the morning of January 28, when I was feeling relaxed and strong after more than a week of tension and apprehension, I received the first of a series of stabs in the back. I learnt from the local newspapers that Dr. Farooq Abdullah had been taken to Delhi for talks. Apparently under the instructions of higher authorities, the Director of Intelligence Bureau, Joshi, came to Srinagar in a special plane, had discussions with me about the situation in the Valley and then flew to Jammu the next morning. He did not tell me anything about his mission in Srinagar or Jammu–of contacting Farooq and Mohammad Shafi and taking them both to Delhi for what the newspapers said 'talks with the Central Government'.

Why could not I be told about it? Why could not I be consulted? Did the top political functionaries have no trust in me, or were they afraid of facing me or my logic, or were they suffering from schizophrenia? Did they trust and mistrust the same man at the same time? I felt greatly perturbed. What was the intention? Did they only want to use me to overcome the administrative crisis and then discard me to suit their narrow political ends? For a moment I thought I was being cynical. This could not be the case. But subsequent events showed how inconsiderate certain persons in authority could be. Here was I, willing to lend a helping hand in resolving a national crisis of immense magnitude and complexity, without taking any salary, and with all the risks to my life and the lives of my near and dear ones. And here they were, ever so ready to play their game of deception on the political chessboard. In sheer exasperation I shouted to myself, "These are small men, product of a shallow and superficial age. So used are they to narrow thinking that they could not see even the apparent tragedy in what they were doing."

The main problem with which I was confronted was to secure loyalty, support and enthusiastic cooperation from the officers. Who would extend the necessary support and cooperation if the impression went round that I was merely a bird of passage, fluttering my wings for just a few days? The initiator of the move hardly realised the practical implications of what they were doing. More than anything else, it convinced me that confusion and crudity were the hallmarks of the decision-makers at the top. They were wholly ignorant of the ground-level reality. Nor were they aware of the roots of the problems and the forces which shaped the psychological disposition of the contemporary Kashmiri. In these circumstances, I thought, to be brave was to be foolish, to be patriotic was to be a masterless dog whom a few might pity but most would forget after it is consigned to municipal mortuary. Some of the tragic chapters in our history bear ample testimony to this. Our contemporary ethos, I felt, was adding one more tragic chapter to this history.

On January 30, after returning from New Delhi, Dr. Farooq Abdullah made a press statement. He accused the Governor's administration of committing genocide and imposing undeclared martial law. He attacked me personally for unleashing a 'reign of terror'. He also alleged that restrictions had been placed on the press to keep the people in the dark about the real happenings.

Here was a leader who levelled irresponsible accusations against the Administration which was trying to tackle a grave national crisis. Here was a leader who virtually incited the people to hate the authorities. Here was a leader who propagated, knowing fully well that it was not true, that Kashmiri Muslims were being exterminated as a race. Yet he was the person whom the Union Government invited for discussions, over my head, and to whom it intended to hand over power. What could be a more crude, more confused, way of dealing with the crisis, and also more unjust and unfair? What better proof was needed of the closing of the Indian mind? It could not think beyond a few decadent ideas or personalities. It could explore no new avenue. It had reached the end of its tether.

I was depressed by this attack of confusion and crudity. I thought of sending in my resignation. But seeing the grave situation as I did–a virtual Pakistan or theocratic Islamic state staring me in the face–I changed my mind. To do so, I convinced myself, would be a disservice to the nation. No administrator, I argued with myself, burnt with inner rage as much as I was burning, and no one could develop that intensity of motivation which I had acquired for saving Kashmir. The nation, I was sure, did not know the extent to which the cancer of subversion had spread in the Valley. I, therefore, calmed myself and decided to write a letter to the President, with a copy each to the Prime Minister, the Home Minister and the Vice President. This letter dated January 30 read, inter alia, as under:

> Respected Rashtrapatiji,
>
> It is exactly 10 days ago that I took over. I could not snatch even a single minute to write even a brief report. The situation was so grim and critical.
>
> Due to total inaction, unbelievable incompetence, widespread corruption and passive connivance, the administrative machinery and all other levers of power structure had been taken over by the subversionists and their collaborators. Majority of the officials are active or passive supporters of these elements. The remaining are mortally afraid.
>
> Unfortunately, in our country, the people go over to the winning side. Since subversionists have been scoring one victory after another in the last six months or so, the public has gone over to their side. Listed terrorists are openly harboured, given money, food and vehicles. Quite a number of officers even salute them. Senior officers turn their face the other way. Jailors and doctors help detenus in escaping. Some of the pistols issued to the political workers are being used for the commission of the crimes. When I took over, Kashmir stood almost on the point of no return.
>
> It was, indeed, a miracle–maybe providential–that Kashmir was saved on January 26, and the nation spared of acute national and international embarrassment. The story of this day is a long one and need to be told in depth at a later stage.
>
> Using my past contacts with the officers and the people, I am re-asserting the authority of the State. Some of the branches of power structure have started leaning towards me. But my mission in this respect has been seriously undermined by the impression that is being created by Dr. Farooq Abdullah that he is returning to power. Neither bureaucracy nor other organs of the State polity would cooperate with me if such an impression persists.
>
> I think the gravity of the situation in Kashmir has not dawned upon the nation. The fundamental issue today is whether the nation

wants to keep Kashmir or hand it over to Pakistan or accept an independent theocratic State. I would beg of you to send our critics to Kashmir. Reality may dawn upon them. They may find that they were unwittingly playing an unpatriotic role. It would be a grave tragedy to hand over power at this stage to those very elements who have brought the State to the brink of disaster.

I have invited eminent journalists of the country to see things for themselves. They include Nikhil Chakravartty, Arun Shourie, Inder Malhotra, R.K. Mishra, Kuldip Nayar, Pran Chopra, H.K. Dua, etc.

I have accepted the assignment solely with the motivation of lending a helping hand in overcoming a national crisis. I have exposed myself and my family to grave personal risk. I am not even drawing my pay. My approach has been spelt out in my policy statement which I made immediately after I took over.

I have done my bit in regard to the events of January 26 and I am proud of it. But it may be difficult for me to continue if the current impression persists and I am not fully supported in public. I have already a broken and shattered Administration at my disposal. If the Commander, too, is everyday sniped at, the chances of success could well be imagined.

In my view, the way to solving the Kashmir crisis is:

i. Assert vigorously the authority of the State and create an impression in the public that, no matter what the cost be, the subversionists and their collaborators would be firmly dealt with and eliminated;

ii. Create solid, sound and healthy institutional framework;

iii. Adopt an absolutely just and fair approach to people in regard to day-to-day administration and speedily redress the backlog of grievances;

iv. Reorient the development pattern in the State to stop big wastage;

v. Implement vigorously stimulus economic packages such as recruitment of 7,000 BSF personnel and 3,000 teachers, etc.;

vi. Dissolve the State Assembly immediately and hold elections after six months or so. By that time some of the subversive elements would be eliminated and some would prefer to participate in the elections. And various groups would balance each other out. A new leadership may emerge which, besides looking to the Union, would enjoy real support of the people, particularly the youth, and would not be so corrupt and callous as the previous State Government.

It would be wrong, if not suicidal, to resort to short cuts or temporary solutions. Infection has gone deep into the vital organs. Unless this infection is first exterminated, we would stumble from one critical situation to another.

Yours sincerely,
(Jagmohan)

Could I have spelt my stand in a more straight and forthright manner? But the decision-makers in Delhi were far from being clear. They could not evolve a basic policy framework and then stick to it resolutely. They remained prisoners of their old reflexes, their limited moorings. They were only used to patchwork solutions. They did not realise that eradication of terrorism in Kashmir depended not on appeasement of ugly forces of subversion, not on short cuts of holding talks with the terrorists, not on bringing back a defunct and discredited leadership and nursing new illusions, not on working through crippled, emaciated and soulless institutions, but on charting out a new course, creating a new motivation, acquiring new commitments to translate words into deeds, reforming institutions, and evolving a new ethos which would bring new vision, new insight and new earnestness to the task.

Terrorism does not happen by accident or by mere outside stimulus. It has a long gestation period. It makes its inroads slowly. If unchecked at the initial stage, it soon attains the take-off stage, accelerates, gathers momentum, spreads in different directions, rolls over its victims, and destroys them ruthlessly. Like a blood-fed hound, it becomes more and more ferocious and gobbles up more and more innocent people. This is exactly what has happened in Kashmir. The current malady is deep-rooted. Its infection had been spreading unchecked. It has now seized the vital organs of the body and become almost irreversible.

To see the tragic spectacle of such a serious malady being subjected to a patchy and irresolute treatment was a very sad experience of my first ten days in office.

The terrorists were training their guns at me. Benazir Bhutto, Amanullah Khan and their workers were hurling their propaganda missiles from the other side. Dr. Farooq Abdullah was coining his worst invectives to incite Kashmiri Muslims against me. New Delhi was emitting incompatible signals. Most of the political parties were resorting to intentional falsehood to project me as anti-Muslim and to sabotage my earnest efforts to establish a friendly rapport with the Muslim bureaucracy and the youth as I had done in 1986.

It became increasingly clear to me that, in the current political ethos, with shallowness and superficiality gripping the levers of power, our country could not fully overcome any crisis, much less the crisis of the dimensions of Kashmir. Nevertheless, I persuaded myself to believe that I had a national obligation to discharge. With all the frozen turbulence in my mind, with all the millstones round my neck, and with my back badly wounded by the stabs from the rear, I proceeded ahead.

CHAPTER II

Survey of History

There is a secret agreement between the past generations and the present ones.

—Walter Benjamin

Why History?

Kashmir has been in the news for quite some time, yet the ignorance about its past and present is amazing. Even when knowledgeable people talk about J&K, they give the impression as if only the Valley and a few personalities matter. Other regions of the State and their interaction with one another, and many more issues of fundamental importance, rooted in its history, culture and ethos are either ignored or side-tracked. Therefore, before proceeding further, it would be pertinent to provide a brief survey of its history.

Events, attitudes, traits and beliefs do not spring from nowhere. They have deep roots. And the seeds of these roots are planted in the past. Some plants bend with age and wither away in course of time; some shed their leaves temporarily but sprout them again under congenial conditions; and some are uprooted totally by the storms and tornadoes of history. But there are others that remain, influencing silently and imperceptibly the social, political and cultural environment. We all live in the social and cultural cage that has been fabricated in the past, though new light and fresh breeze of the present continue to reach us through the gaps in its bars.

To say that the contemporary scene alone is ours and we have nothing to do with the past is to take a very narrow view of reality. For, to be aware of the present without being aware of the past, is to have a deceptive view of things. Cicero rightly observed, "Not to know what took place before you were born is to remain for ever a child."

When I landed in the Kashmir Valley during my first tenure in April 1984, I was fascinated, despite the obvious wounds that had been inflicted on its landscape, by the beauty of its streams and springs, its meadows and mountains. But looking at it in the background of its unfortunate history, I wondered how much of heartlessness was hidden in the hard strata of those mountains, how many betrayals had been scattered over those meadows, and how much of hardship and misery had flown with those streams.

Viewed in the context of the deeds of its kings and their courtiers, the history of Kashmir, with a few illuminating exceptions, is a long and lamentable tale of conspiracies and collusions; of incessant upheavals, intrigues and counter-intrigues; of repulsive pettiness and nauseating profligacy; and of monstrous vices and abominable crimes. It has often been said that history repeats itself. But in the case of Kashmir, history appears to have repeated itself many times over, both as tragedy and as farce. Vincent A. Smith correctly remarked, "Few regions in the world could have had worse luck than Kashmir in the matter of Government."

But history does not tread the path trodden by Kings and Sultans alone. It treads many other little paths, through the lanes and by-lanes, peeping into the closed doors of the matter and the mind. History is the biography not only of the ruler but also of the ruled, and whichever area it traverses, its direction is influenced by the wind blowing from the ideas that emanate from the spiritual workshop of the community–its religion, culture and traditions.

Seen from the plane of ideas, the history of Kashmir would reveal what a beautiful cradle it has been of ancient culture. "The ancient India has nothing more worthy of its early civilisation than the grand ruins of Kashmir." The remnants of hundreds of temples, stupas and viharas and numerous schools of thought would show how in ancient times it has been a nursery of two great religions of India–Hinduism and Buddhism–and how these religions met and mingled in the mindscape of the people. Kashmir's own creative contribution to the Hindu thought, particularly to the evolution of the monistic philosophy of Saivism, known as 'Trika Sastra', has been truly historic. And when Islam made its appearance in the middle of the fourteenth century, it acquired its own distinct hue in the Valley.

A clear and well-focussed spectacle of history, covering the ruler and the ruled and their social and spiritual dispositions is, therefore, essential for viewing contemporary problems in their proper perspective and examining their roots, both old and new.

Antiquity

There are good geological and mythological reasons to believe that the Kashmir Valley was once a vast span of water, similar to a huge dam, walled by high mountains. There was some habitation on the higher ranges which were not under water. Over the years, as a result of violent geological upheavals such as earthquakes, the mountain walls were breached at a few points and the water gushed out, forming the Valley in its present shape.

According to legend, as narrated in *Nilamata Purana*, the name of the Valley at one time was Satidesa. Over the years, a person by the name of Jalodbhava, 'water-born', came to live here. When Jalodbhava was a child, Brahma had blessed him with "indestructibility under water". As he grew up, he became arrogant and cruel. He caused widespread death and destruction. Nila, who had brought up Jalodbhava, was exasperated. He sought the help of his father, Kashyap, who was a great sage. Kashyap, in turn, approached Brahma, Vishnu and Siva for help. Vishnu took the initiative. He proceeded to kill Jalodbhava. But the latter knew that he could not be destroyed if he remained under water. He, therefore, took refuge in Satisara, the lake. Vishnu and the other gods accompanying him decided to cut the mountains. Thereafter, "the water flowed out with force, terrifying all beings with its violent rush and sound and overflowing the tops of the mountains with curved waves like Himalaya touching the sky". With water having been drained out thus, Jalodbhava could no longer stay under water. To save himself, Jalodbhava resorted to magic. He created darkness all around. But Siva soon came to the scene to remove the darkness, holding the sun and the moon in his hands. Jalodbhava was then spotted and beheaded by Vishnu with his discus.

The land that emerged thus began to be inhabited by people other than the few original inhabitants. Brahma, Vishnu, Siva, and Kashyap carved out a few hermitages of their own. This, perhaps, is the reason why a number of places in Kashmir, like the holy cave of Amarnath, are considered sacred by the Hindus.

Legends are, after all, legends, and do not provide hard evidence. But this legend is not irreconcilable with the principles of geology. The description in *Nilamata Purana* about the draining of water from the Valley is reconcilable with the geological scenario of violent earthquakes, accompanied by darkness and cloudburst. Even otherwise, life evolves with gradual as well as calamitous changes. Few of us realise that the earth in its present shape came into being about 5,000 million years ago. "Sometimes", says Frederic Drew, the famous geographer, "traditions are valuable as showing how in early times some races of mankind had learnt to interpret aright the geological records of the history of their dwelling places."

Incidentally, it is not improbable that after the bursting of the 'dam' which the Kashmir Valley once was, the plains of north-west India, where pre-Aryan Mohenjodaro-Harappan civilisation existed, were completely submerged in flood waters and all human beings perished. This could be the reason for the sudden dis-appearance of the Harappan civilisation.

Recent excavations at Burzahom, near Srinagar, show that there was habitation in the Valley around 2000 B.C. But the identity of the earliest inhabitants, who lived in pits and buried their dead along with the pet animals in their compounds, has not so far been established.

The Nagas were the earliest known inhabitants. A few other tribes appeared on the scene a little later. These are Khasas, Dars, Bhuttas, Damars, Nishadas, Tantrings, etc. The Aryans moved in considerable numbers after water flowed out and large areas of land became available for settlement. The legend revolving around Jalodbhava may really be a description of the struggle between the natives and the Aryans who came in about 800 B.C. from the areas now known as Uttar Pradesh, and who by that time had acquired iron instruments and also the skill to cause small cuts in the rocks and remove obstruction to the flow of water. By draining out water, the Aryans made it difficult for their enemies, the native tribes, to hide.

In course of time, the Aryans acquired dominance throughout the Valley and set up their institutions of governance. Monarchy was firmly established. The King was treated as a divine being. This would be evident from what Lord Krishna told the people while making Yasovati sit on the throne: "Kashmir-land is Parvati; know that its king is a portion of Siva."

Sources

The main source of ancient Kashmir's history is Kalhana's epic historical poem, *Rajatarangini* (River of Kings). The Hindus of ancient India were not known for writing history. Kalhana's book makes a welcome departure from that tradition. The observations made in the poem on various aspects of life show the depth of Kalhana's mind and also the range of his perception. The book is of such great merit that it has itself become an invaluable part of Kashmir's history and also of ancient Indian literature. It could be favourably compared with the celebrated epic poem *The Lusiads* of the Portuguese poet, Camoes. The book was written in A.D. 1148-50. While it provides insight into the entire period of ancient Kashmir, it gives a fairly accurate and exhaustive account of the events and social and economic conditions from the eighth century onwards. Kalhana was followed by Jonaraja, Srivara, Prajybhatta, Suka, Ksemendra and other chroniclers. But they were prone to exaggeration and embellishments. For the later period, there are a number of other sources which have been summarised in Appendix I.

In his poem *Gerontion*, T.S. Eliot wrote:

> History has many cunning passages, contrived corridors
> And issues, deceives with whispering ambitions,
> Guides us by vanities.

The narratives of ancient Kashmiri historians bear the truth of Eliot's observations. But we have little other material to fall back upon. All that we can do is to carefully sift facts from fantasies. Internal evidence and sustainable probability can also serve as our guide.

Period of Hindu and Buddhist Kings

Gonanda, the first known King of Kashmir, was a relation and friend of Jarasandha, King of Magadha. The latter was father-in-law of Krishna, King of Mathura. Gonanda went to the help of Jarasandha, but he was defeated and killed by Krishna. Jarasandha's son, Damodara, then became the King of Kashmir. To avenge his father's death, he proceeded to fight Krishna. But he, too, was killed. Yasovati, Damodara's widow, who was pregnant at the time of her husband's death, ascended the throne with the support of Krishna. When a son was born to her, he was formally crowned as the King under the name of Gonanda II. Being an infant and of little consequence, he was not asked for help either by the Pandavas or by the Kauravas during the *Mahabharata* war.

These events not only show that the kings of Kashmir and those of the various other parts of North India had strong links with one another but also indicate that hereditary monarchy had come to stay in Kashmir and the days of tribalism were over.

After Gonanda II, Kashmir was ruled by at least 43 kings. They were all weak and insignificant. Thereafter, Asoka (273-232 B.C.) extended his control over Kashmir. He encouraged Buddhism in the Valley. During his time, viharas and stupas were built at Vita Staktra and Sus Kaletra. Asoka was, however, not intolerant of Hinduism. He got the old Siva temple of Vijayesvara repaired. Two new Siva temples, known as Asokesvara, were also constructed. Asoka also founded the ancient capital, Srinagari, about five kilometres away from the present city. According to Kalhana, it was "resplendent with wealth".

After Asoka's death, the Mauryan Empire began to disintegrate. Jalauka, Asoka's son, became an independent monarch of Kashmir. Meanwhile, there was revivalism of Hinduism in North India, and the wave of this revivalism also reached Kashmir. Under its influence, Jalauka destroyed a few Buddhist viharas and built two new Siva temples at Srinagari and Nandi-Kshetra.

Three centuries later, Kashmir passed under the control of the Kushans. Amongst the known Kushan rulers were Kaniska, Huska and Juska. Kaniska was the most powerful monarch whose rule extended to north-western India and Central Asia. Kashmir was the fulcrum of his activities for the spread of Buddhism which he earlier adopted. Buddhism became the state religion and Kashmiri missionaries carried its message to China and far-off places in South-Central Asia. The fourth Buddhist Council was held by Kaniska in Kashmir at a place called Kundalvara.

The Kushans were followed by a number of local rulers including Abhimanyu, Vibhisana I, Indrajit, Ravana and Vibhisana II. Their names, which are familiar to the readers of the *Ramayana*, suggest close cultural affinity between Kashmir and North India. During the reign of these kings Saivism made headway. Buddhism suffered. One of the kings, Nana, burnt thousands of viharas and granted Buddhist villages to the Brahmins.

In the first half of the sixth century A.D., Mihira-Kula, a Hun general, came to occupy Kashmir's throne. He rose to power in North

India after the decline of the Gupta Empire. But he lost the war against a confederacy of Indian chiefs. He escaped to the Valley and seized power. He ruled from A.D. 515 to 550. He was a cruel king. Kalhana mentions that the people could forecast his arrival by seeing the vultures that flew ahead of him. His sadistic disposition became a part of the Kashmiris' sayings. While crossing the pass near Hastivanj, an elephant fell down the hill. Mihira-Kula so enjoyed the terrified cry of the dying elephant that he caused the fall of another 100 elephants to feel the repeated thrill of the scene.

After Mihira-Kula, the Huns ruled Kashmir for some time. But the local rulers soon regained power, and the second Gonanda dynasty came into being. King Meghavabana of this dynasty is worthy of special mention. He stopped slaughtering of animals. During the rule of this dynasty, King Vikramaditya of Ujjain exercised a loose suzerainty over Kashmir.

Hiuen Tsang, the celebrated Chinese traveller, came to Kashmir in A.D. 631. At that time, the Karkota dynasty was ruling over Kashmir, and its founder, Durlabhavandhana, was the King. Hiuen Tsang was well received. He stayed in the Valley for two years, and visited almost all the important places associated with Buddhism.

According to Hiuen Tsang, the King of Kashmir held sway over as distant places as Taxila, Hazara, Poonch and Rajourie. He was a powerful monarch, and had a vast kingdom to rule. He controlled the route from Kabul to Kashmir. But he was not totally independent. Emperor Harshavardhana, whose capital was Kanauj, exercised a weak form of suzerainty over Kashmir. The economy of Kashmir was in good shape. The Valley was full of fruits and flowers. Buddhism was fairly widespread. There were about 5,000 Buddhist monks and over one hundred Buddhist monasteries. There were also four Asokan 'Chaityas', each containing a very small relic of Buddha's body. The sacred 'tooth-relic' of Buddha was also with the King of Kashmir. But Harshavardhana took it away.

Hiuen Tsang thought poorly of the Kashmiris of the time. He recorded: "They are volatile and timid; they are good-looking but deceitful. They are fond of learning and follow both Buddhism and Hinduism."

The most outstanding king of the Karkota dynasty was Lalitaditya who ruled for 37 years from A.D. 724 to 761. He was motivated by an ambition similar to that of Alexander the Great. This would be evident from what he is believed to have stated to his ministers: "For rivers, the ocean is the limit but nowhere is there a limit for those aspiring to be conquerors." The unsettled conditions in northern India after the collapse of the Gupta Empire, the exhaustion of the Deccan kingdoms by mutual conflicts, and the power vacuum in the area west of Kashmir afforded ample opportunities to Lalitaditya to realise his dreams of conquering more and more areas. He is believed to have gone as far as the banks of Cauvery in South India and also to Konkan and Kathiawar in the west. In the east, he extended his hold up to Bengal. In the north-west of the Valley, he established his sway over Ladakh and a portion of western Tibet. He had in his employment a brilliant Chinese general, Cankunya. Lalitaditya also had some contacts with the Chinese Emperor. Most probably he and the Chinese ruler cooperated with each other to check the power of Tibet.

While some of the claims, particularly in regard to southern expeditions, made on behalf of Lalitaditya, appear to be incorrect, the fact remains that he was the greatest conqueror and warrior that Kashmir has ever produced.

Lalitaditya was also a great administrator and a great builder. He reorganised the administrative machinery and added new functionaries, including chief minister, senior chamberlain, master of horses, and keeper of treasury. He built a number of new towns with beautiful temples, stupas and viharas and decorated them with gold and silver images. He also assigned a number of villages to the newly built shrines.

Lalitaditya's most memorable act was the construction of the glorious temple of Martanda, in honour of the sun-god, at a site now called Matan. About this famous construction, Stein said, "The ruins of this splendid temple are still the most striking objects of ancient Hindu architecture in the Valley." In the same strain, Younghusband observed, "The temple is built on the most sublime site occupied by any building in the world–finer far than the site of Parthenon, or of the Taj, or of St. Peters. It is second only to the Egyptians in massiveness and strength and to the Greeks in elegance and grace. No one without an eye for natural beauty would have chosen that special site for the construction of a temple and no one with an inclination to the ephemeral and transient would have built it on so massive and enduring a scale."

Similar imposing dimensions and conceptual grandeur are visible in the ruins of Purihaspura which have been recently excavated.

During Governor's rule of 1986, I had tried to resurrect its lost glory and make it an attractive tourist spot. But time and opportunity were not with me.

Lalitaditya was a staunch follower of Hinduism. He worshipped Lord Vishnu intensely. But he was equally liberal towards Buddhism. In fact, his rule is considered as "the golden period of Kashmir Buddhism". On a single vihara–Raja Vihara–he is believed to have spent about 84,000 tolas of gold. He patronised learned men without any distinction of creed and territorial loyalty. He brought to his court two great poets from Kanauj–Bhavabhuti and Vakpatiraja.

Due to the misrule of Lalitaditya's successors, the dynasty collapsed by the middle of the ninth century.

For the next century and a half, the course of Kashmir's history was influenced by the looks and dispositions of two women. One, Jayadevi, gave a new dynasty, Uptala, which produced one of the finest kings of Kashmir–Avantivarman; and the other, Didda, dominated the scene for about 50 years and set in motion forces which ultimately led to the decay and decline of Hindu rule in Kashmir. Both were women of captivating beauty and charming features.

Jayadevi was born in a poor family, eking out a livelihood as distillers of liquor. She became widow at a very young age. King Jayapida happened to see her. He was fascinated by her beauty and brought her to the palace. The King died soon thereafter. But the King's son and successor, Lalitapida, was equally charmed by Jayadevi. Because of her influence over the king, her brothers became all powerful. Ultimately, one of her brothers' grandsons, Avantivarman, became the King and founded the new dynasty of Uptala.

Never before were the Kashmiris so happy and prosperous as during the 28 years' rule of Avantivarman (A.D. 855-883). Under his benign rule, Kashmir became a land of piety, peace and plenty. Avantivarman did not wage any war, and concentrated his energy and resources on development and welfare activities. With the help of a local genius, Suyya, he was able to execute many drainage, irrigation and agricultural improvement schemes. Food production increased and prices fell. For instance, the price of one 'Kharwan' of rice came down from 200 to 36 dinars. Suyya was hundreds of years ahead of his times. His scheme of diverting the course of Jhelum was a forerunner of the present-day multipurpose river valley projects.

Avantivarman showed concern for conservation and anticipated the modern movement in this regard. He prohibited killing of any living creature. To use the words of Kalhana, “At that time, the shad fish left the cold water without fear, and coming to the river banks sunned their backs in the autumn sun.” The King’s irrigation adviser. Suyya, imposed a permanent ban on killing of animals and birds in the Wular Lake.

Avantivarman’s time witnessed building activity on a large scale. The stability and prosperity of the kingdom enabled Avantivarman, his ministers and relations to found new towns and construct new temples and ‘maths’. The King himself founded the town of Avantipur and built two magnificent temples therein, namely, Avantisvamin and Avantisvara. Even the ruins of these temples are a great tourist attraction. Practically everyone stops at Avantipur on his way to Pahalgam to see these temples. Percy Brown remarked, “Whereas Martand was an expression of the sudden glory when Kashmir re-established the consciousness of its own might, Avantisvamin temple is a sophisticated and more elegant structure produced by a maturity of experience acquired during the passage of time.”

Sura, a minister of the King, founded the town of Sunapora, the present-day Hurpor, and the King’s irrigation adviser, Suyya, built the town of Suyyapur, modern Sopore. In honour of Siva and Sura ‘maths’ and to provide accommodation to the rishis and pious men, Sura also built the Suresvara temple in village Ishabara on the bank of the Dal Lake.

All these constructions show that Hinduism had gained predominance in Kashmir and Buddhism had been relegated to the background. Most of the buildings were adorned with multi-armed and multi-headed images, indicating the ascendency of the caturryuha form of Vishnu worship. The King was also very humble and liberal. The needs of the Brahmins and the poor were attended to.

Avantivarman also patronised scholars and men of letters. They were nominated, to the King’s Sabha. Many other privileges were conferred on them. Prominent amongst the scholars were Ramata, who was known for his grammatical sciences, and Bhatu Kallata, a great philosopher who was a disciple of Vasugupta, founder of Advaita Saivism, and did much to propagate the views of his master.

From all points of view, Avantivarman’s time was a glorious period in Kashmir’s history. There was peace; there was development; there was justice; there was understanding between the King and his ministers; there was piety and even awareness of conservation; and there was attachment to higher ideals of religion, art and culture. The King's pious disposition can be seen from the fact that he used to listen to the recital of *Bhagvadgita* from his sickbed, and he passed away while listening to the 'slokas' from this holy book.

Avantivarman's successor, Samkaravarman, disturbed the peace and prosperity of the kingdom by resorting to unnecessary military expeditions. He imposed heavy taxes and levies and resorted to forced labour, 'begar'. It used to be said that the King had 'spared nothing from his exactions except breathing'.

The successors of Samkaravarman were kings of poor calibre. The Uptala dynasty ended in A.D. 939, when Yasaskaradeva, a Brahmin, was crowned king. But the rule of the Brahmin dynasty lasted only ten years. In A.D. 949, Parva Gupta, chief minister of the Brahmin king, enacted a coup, killed the King, and ascended the throne.

It was during the reign of the Gupta dynasty that Didda, the daughter of the King of Lohrin, came to the forefront. Lohrin is presently located in Poonch district. Didda was married to the second Gupta King, Ksema Gupta (A.D. 950-958). She dominated the Kashmir scene for about 50 years, first as queen, then as regent for her son and grandsons, and finally a direct ruler.

Didda's sway over her husband was such that King Ksema Gupta was called Didda Ksema. At the time of Ksema Gupta's death, Didda was willing to perform *sati*. But she retracted her steps on the advice of a section of the courtiers who were jealous of the chief minister. She became a regent for the minor king Abhimanyu II, and vanquished her adversaries one by one. As Kalhana observes, "The lame queen whom no one thought capable of stepping over a cow's footprint got over the ocean-like host of her enemies, just as god Hanuman got over the ocean."

Didda was extremely beautiful, highly intelligent, and uncommonly wayward. She had a Byronic streak in her personality. Like Byron, she too had a limp in her leg. But she turned it to her advantage, a stance that captivated her numerous lovers. She literally walked in beauty like the limping light of a dancing lamp in her court. On some occasions she could be voluptuous beyond imagination, while on other occasions she would exhibit no emotions and stand firm like a rock and overcome all challenges to her authority. She conferred favours, including physical, to the courtiers and senior functionaries of the kingdom, and then got rid of them, sometimes through secret killings. She is even believed to have caused the death of her three grandsons. In between, she performed many acts of piety and built temples and 'maths'. Her last paramour, Tunga, a young Khasa herdsman, who was later made chief minister and Commander-in-Chief, outlived her. She died in A.D. 1003.

Didda was one of those enigmatic characters of history whom one condemns as well as admires. She survived the politics of intrigue, murder and debauchery for about 50 years and held the troubled kingdom together through sheer competency and courage. But she also caused incalculable harm by being sinister and sinful and by spreading moral pollution all around.

Before her death, Queen Didda was able to manipulate the crown for Samgramaraja, a member of her family from Lohara–the principality to which she herself belonged before her marriage. Thus, a new dynasty, the first Lohara dynasty (A.D. 1003-1101), came into being. With this, the Kshatriyas came to rule Kashmir.

During the time of Samgramaraja (A.D. 1003-28), Sultan Mahmud of Ghazni skirted Kashmir after defeating Trilochanapala of the Sahi kingdom. Samgramaraja's successor, Ananta (A.D. 1028-63), a weak king, came under the influence of the Sahi princes of Punjab, who took refuge in Kashmir after Mahmud Ghazni. They also brought about the marriage of the King with Suryamati, the daughter of the ruler of Jalandhar. The increasing influence of the Sahi princes and Queen Suryamati caused widespread resentment, and the kingdom witnessed frequent turmoils. Ananta, though a well-meaning ruler, could not assert himself and committed suicide in desperation, unable to bear the taunts of his wife, Suryamati. This chastened the Queen. Struck by remorse, she performed *sati* and burnt herself on the funeral pyre of her husband.

Ananta was followed by Kalsa (A.D. 1063-89) and Harsa (A.D. 1089-1101). The latter made himself infamous by plundering the wealth of temples and dishonouring divine images. In this regard, Kalhana observes, "To defile the statues of gods, Harsa had excrement and urine poured over their faces by naked mendicants."

There seems to be no plausible explanation for the obnoxious behaviour of the King. Some scholars attribute it to the influence of Islam which prohibited image worship. Some other scholars suggest that he was under the hypnotic spell of an evil mendicant. Whatever be the reason, Harsa's conduct show to what low depth the kingdom of Kashmir had descended. To use the expression of Kalhana: "In the form of Harsa, some demon had descended to the earth to destroy this land hallowed by gods, tirthas and risis." As if to prove that misfortunes do not come alone, the Valley was visited by epidemics, floods and famines.

Among the kings of the second Lohara dynasty, there were only two who deserve notice. They were Uccale (A.D. 1101-11) and Jaya Simha (A.D. 1128-55). The former tried to repair the damage done during the rule of Harsa. He reformed the administration, removed corrupt officials, and amended the criminal code to punish the delinquents, not by sending them to jail, but by directing them to do social work. In this regard, he was a precursor of the modern movement of reforming and rehabilitating the criminals. He had a strong sense of justice. To ensure that his subjects were not harassed by petty functionaries, and were otherwise happy, he used to move incognito in towns and villages. Uccale also rebuilt some of the temples and 'maths' destroyed by Harsa and re-installed the images in them. But he was highly conceited, vain, and given to fits of anger. Quite often, he behaved like 'a mad dog'. This marred his otherwise benevolent regime.

Jaya Simha, who ruled for about 28 years, was truly a great king, in the traditions of Lalitaditya and Avantivarman. His period is considered as the "age of Aryan renaissance in Kashmir". Though much of his time and energy was spent in curbing factions, revolts and intrigues of ambitious men and pretenders to the throne, he undertook various measures to improve the moral tone of society. He himself set high standards of conduct. The poor were helped at the time of marriages and religious functions. Liberal grants were given to scholars and needy Brahmins. Prostitution was curbed, particularly in the capital, which was placed under the charge of an upright prefect, Dharya. Jaya Simha built a number of new temples and 'maths', including the famous `Simhapura Maths'. To ensure proper maintenance of the new buildings, he made permanent endowments in their favour.

After the death of Jaya Simha in 1155, the process of decline and decay which had started during the time of Didda and Harsa, and which was temporarily halted by Uccale and Jaya Simha, hastened. The next two hundred years saw only weak and selfish kings who showed no will to set the house in order. An effete and insignificant dynasty of Bopadeva (A.D. 1171-1286) was followed by an equally indolent and impotent dynasty of Damra (A.D. 1286-1320).

It was in this atmosphere of moral decay, economic decline, and social and political disruption that foreign adventurers started arriving in the Valley. Two such foreigners were Shah Mir and Rinchana. The former settled in a village near Baramulla and the latter in the Lar. Both were helped by the Damra King, Suhadeva, by grant of 'jagirs', and both were destined to play crucial roles in shaping the course of the future history of Kashmir.

A fatal blow was struck to the Hindu kingdom of Kashmir by the invasion, in 1320, of Dulacha, a Mongol warrior and adventurer who hailed from Turkistan. As no vigil was kept at the passes, Dulacha swept everything before him. King Suhadeva exhibited woeful cowardice. He tried to buy off the invaders but failed. Dulacha entered the Valley as "a lion enters the cave of a deer". The people of Kashmir died as "insects in a fire". Men were put to sword and women and children taken away as slaves. The invaders looted and burnt the villages and the cities that came in their way. In the words of Jonaraja, "Kashmir became almost like a region before creation."

Rinchana who hailed from Ladakh and had migrated to Kashmir after his father, a local chief, had been killed in the power-struggle with the Baltis, took advantage of the disorderly conditions and, unmindful of the good deed done to him by King Suhadeva, plundered the area around the Lar Valley.

Jonaraja colourfully describes the situation thus: "Dulacha was like a billow in the water; and on the hill, Rinchana was like a tempest, while the chief men in the town (Srinagar), the prosperous and the rich, were struck with fear. As the kite swoops on the young ones of the birds thrown out of their nests, so the swift army of Rinchana seized the people of Kashmir." The only obstacle in the way of Rinchana was chief minister Rama Chandra who had proclaimed himself as king after the flight of Suhadeva in the wake of Dulacha's invasion. Rinchana got Rama Chandra murdered by deceitful means and seized the throne. Thus, the kingdom of Kashmir came to be ruled by a Ladakhi Buddhist.

Muslim Sultans

To conciliate the people, Rinchana married the daughter of Rama Chandra, Kota Rani. He restored order and set up an efficient and just administration under the charge of Shah Mir. To ingratiate himself further with the people, he wanted to become a Hindu. But his proposal was turned down by Kashmiri Brahmins. He then embraced Islam, a religion which a section of his subjects had already adopted. He assumed the title of Sultan Sadr-ud-Din. Kashmir, thus, got its first Muslim ruler.

The first Muslim Rule was, however, short-lived. Rinchana died in 1323, leaving behind a minor son, Haider. The courtiers invited Udyanadeva, brother of the late king Suhadeva, to accept the throne. He did so. To strengthen his position, Udyanadeva married Kota Rani, widow of Rinchana.

King Udyanadeva was a weak and lazy ruler. The real control over the kingdom was exercised by Kota Rani. At that time, another invader, Achala, a Turko-Mongol adventurer, appeared in the Valley. Udyanadeva fled to Ladakh, but Kota Rani and Shah Mir joined hands and defended the Valley. Achala retreated. People were overjoyed. Shah Mir became their hero. He became a *de facto* ruler, though King Udyanadeva had returned.

Udyanadeva died in A.D. 1338. To forestall Shah Mir, Kota Rani kept the death of her husband secret for four days, and, after moving to the safe fort of Indrakot, proclaimed herself as the next ruler. In the struggle that followed, Shah Mir came out victorious and assumed kingship under the title of Sultan Shams-ud-Din. According to a Persian chronicler, Shah Mir asked Kota Rani to marry him. She made a pretence of acceptance. But in the bridal chamber, she stabbed herself and pointing to her intestinces said: "Here is my acceptance." She soon bled to death.

Muslim rule in Kashmir commenced on a favourable note. Shah Mir's regime (A.D. 1339-42), though brief, acted like a soothing balm on an aching body. The Sultan adopted a humane, enlightened and just approach. He reduced the taxes and treated Hindus and Muslims alike.

The next important Sultan was Shihab-ud-Din (A.D. 1354-73) grandson of Shah Mir. In fact, his rule has been called, "from the political and military point of view, as the most glorious epoch in the history of Muslim Sultanate in Kashmir". He not only curbed the growing power of feudal chiefs and consolidated his position but also undertook extensive military expeditions to the north, north-west and south of Kashmir. As Jonaraja puts it, "Deer-eyed women attracted not his mind, nor the pleasure of drinking, nor the light of the moon; only the march with his army was dear to him."

During Shihab-ud-Din's regime, the Valley, particularly the city of Srinagar, suffered badly under the impact of a devastating flood.

"There was not a tree, not a boundary mark, not a bridge, not a house that stood in the way of "the flood which it did not destroy." To overcome this calamity, the Sultan rose to the occasion admirably. He provided prompt relief to the affected people. He also built a new town on higher ground near Hari Parbat and named it Laxminagar after his queen Laxmi. He was a just ruler and generally tolerant of Hindus.

Hindal, the younger brother of Sultan Shihab-ud-Din, succeeded him. He assumed the title of Qutub-ud-Din (A.D. 1373-89). It was during his time that Sayyid Ali Hamdani came to Kashmir and Islamic practices began to be adopted rather strictly.

The Islamic zeal attained fanatical proportions under the next ruler–Sultan Sikandar (A.D. 1389-1413) who came to be known as 'But-Shikan', destroyer of idols. "There was no city, no town, no village, no wood, where the temples of gods remained unbroken." The Sultan even tried to pull down the famous temple of Martand but later gave up the effort. Under the influence of the Baihaqi Sayyids, the Sultan banned un-Islamic practices such as drinking, gambling, dancing and playing of musical instruments. The Hindus were subjected to 'jizia', and forbidden to apply 'tilak' on their forehead. Sikandar also introduced an institution of Sheikh-ul-Islam to ensure that the injunctions of Islam were fully observed.

A relentless campaign for conversion to Islam was launched, under the charge of the Sultan's chief minister, Malik Saif-ud-Din. The chief minister's original name was Suha Bhatta. He renounced his Hindu faith to accept Islam. The zeal of this newly converted minister knew no bounds. He unleashed a reign of terror against those who resisted conversion. It is believed that the Sultan and his chief minister threw into the Dal Lake all the sacred books of the Hindus that they could lay their hands on, and seven maunds of sacred threads of murdered Brahmins were burnt. It is from this period that the predominance of Muslims in the population of the Valley begins.

During Sultan Sikandar's regime, a large number of sufi saints and Islamic scholars came to Kashmir from Persia and Central Asia. About 700 Sayyids accompanied Mohammad Hamdani, son of Ali Hamdani. Through them, the influence of Islam spread further in Kashmir. A large number of mosques were also built at that time, including the famous Bijbehara Mosque and the Jama Masjid in Srinagar.

Sikandar's policy was continued by his son, Sultan Ali Shah. He too remained under the influence of the chief minister Saif-ud-Din.

The next Sultan, Zain-ul-Abidin (A.D. 1420-70), turned out to be the most tolerant and benevolent ruler that Kashmir has known. It has been correctly remarked that "history can give few examples where the policy of the father was so completely reversed by the son. Where Sikandar destroyed, Zain-ul-Abidin restored; where the former banished, the latter recalled." Zain-ul-Abidin's reign, following that of Sikandar and Ali Shah, was, in the words of historian Srivara, "like the cooling sandal paste after the heat of summer in a desert had departed".

All restrictions against the Hindus were removed. Cow slaughter was banned. Killing of fishes in the springs considered sacred by Hindus was prohibited. He also allowed rebuilding of demolished temples. He himself got a few of them reconstructed. He recalled Pandits who had fled the Valley due to persecution, and assigned them responsible positions on merit. He got Hindu *Sastras* as well as the *Mahabharata* translated into Persian.

Sultan Zain-ul-Abidin was a many-splendoured genius. In the sphere of religion, he was a precursor of Akbar; in the field of construction, he proved to be the Shah Jahan of Kashmir. He distinguished himself equally in the realm of learning, art and culture. He had an innovative mind and introduced a number of new items of commerce and industry. His orientation towards welfare and development led to the laying out of a large number of canals which not only helped in draining out water from marshy and low-lying areas, thereby making them fit for cultivation, but also in providing irrigation facilities to parched areas.

All this resulted in manifold increase in agricultural production. As pointed out by Moorcroft, while the annual rice production in 1822-23 was 20 lakh 'kharwans', it was 77 lakh kharwans during the time of Zain-ul-Abidin.

The Sultan also reconstructed the administrative machinery. He came down with a heavy hand on corrupt officials and judges. He held the village headman responsible for crimes committed in his jurisdiction. He set up an efficient system of collecting information. It is said that the Sultan came to know "all about his subjects except their dreams". Prices were subjected to strict control, hoarding was eliminated and arbitrary levies were abolished. To check the widespread evil of forgery and cheating, registration of documents was made compulsory.

Zain-ul-Abidin not only revived old arts and crafts but also introduced a number of new ones. "Kashmir became a smiling garden of industry" and made significant progress in wood carving, papier-mache, silk, shawl and carpet weaving. This is what Mirza Haider wrote in *Tarikh-i-Rashidi* in 1543: "In Kashmir one meets with all those arts and crafts which are, in most cities, uncommon, such as stone polishing, stone-cutting, bottle-making, gold-beating. This is all due to Sultan Zain-ul-Abidin."

As a builder, Zain-ul-Abidin made his mark by constructing a number of new towns–Naushahr, Zainapura, Zaina Kot and Zainagiri. He developed a beautiful island in the Wular Lake. His royal palace was the finest building of the time in the whole of the East. It was a twelve-storeyed building, with each storey having 50 rooms, halls, and corridors decorated with carvings and frescoes.

The Sultan was no less adept in the art of war and conquest. He reorganised the army. He introduced the use of gun powder and also fabricated a few cannons. He established control over Ladakh and Baltistan, and also subjugated the hill principalities of Naushara, Rajouri and Lohara.

Zain-ul-Abidin has justly earned the reputation of being the greatest Sultan of Kashmir who reigned for half a century. Srivara was right in saying that "the King's virtuous mode of government in the 'Kali Yuga' became glorious like the very middle of 'Satya Yuga'. At the time of his death, it was felt that the "crown became lustreless, the earth and the sky became gloomy, justice and generosity, learning and power, glory and pomp, peace and tolerance departed."

Sultan Zain-ul-Abidin's sons proved unworthy of their illustrious father. In the intrigues and the counter-intrigues that followed his death, the caucus of the Sayyids gained ascendency at the court, making the Sultan a mere puppet in its hands. In the early stages of their arrival in the Valley, the Sayyids were respected. But they soon acquired power and position which caused much heart-burning amongst other courtiers. Their arrogance also alienated the people whom, to use the expression of Srivara, they "treated as grass". The administration became callous. "Accepting bribes was considered by the officers as virtue, oppressing the subjects was regarded as wisdom and the addiction to wine and women was reckoned as happiness."

The Sultan lost all interest in governance. He preferred to spend his time amongst beautiful women whom he collected around himself and who, taking full advantage of his infatuation, elicited undue favours from him and collected bribes from the people.

The fortunes of the Sultanate in Kashmir began to decline rapidly. The next 120 years saw only intrigues and conspiracies. One weak Sultan followed another, while factions of the courtiers–the Sayyids, the Magreys, the Chaks and the Dars–indulged, their power games in the most unscrupulous manner. Religious differences added to the fury of the conflicts. The Chaks were fanatically attached to the Shia faith, and the Sayyids and the Magreys were equally strong in their adherence to the Sunni faith, and, as a result, the people suffered. Their miseries were compounded by the epidemic that swept the Valley in 1515-16. As the chronicler Shuka puts it: "The number of the dead could not be counted either in the villages or in the capital. Men could hardly get a piece of cloth at their last moment. Friends did not weep for friends, what to speak of sorrowing for others."

It was in these unsettled conditions that Mirza Haider Dughlat, a Mughal general, entered the Valley. He was in the service of Humayun. When the latter was defeated by Sher Shah at Kanauj in 1540 and his army was in retreat, Mirza Haider moved into the Valley in November 1540 with only 400 soldiers. He met with practically no resistance. He was aided and abetted by the Magreys and the Sayyids. He soon established his full control and ruled the Valley for the next eleven years (1541-51) in the name of Humayun.

Mirza Haider's administration provided welcome respite to the Kashmiris. The Mirza revived the industry which was languishing after the death of Zain-ul-Abidin. The trade also picked up. The general economy improved. But Mirza Haider unduly favoured the Mughal generals, gave them all high posts and distributed jagirs to them after depriving the local nobility of the same. This resulted in revolt against him. In the ensuing struggle, he was killed.

After Mirza Haider's death, the local factions returned to the scene. In the ensuing scramble for power, the Chaks emerged victorious. Things came to such a pass that in 1561, in the open court, Ali Chak snatched the crown from the Sultan and put it on the head of his brother Ghazi Chak. Thus was founded the Chak dynasty. But it did not change the conditions materially. Conflicts and conspiracies continued. A section of the Kashmiri nobility approached Akbar with the request that he should annex Kashmir.

From the near anarchic conditions, Kashmir was rescued by the Mughals who established their full control over it in 1589, when Emperor Akbar himself came there. The last Sultan, Yaqub Shah, after putting up plucky resistance, wrote a letter of apology in which he said, "His (Yaqub Shah's) prayer now was that His Majesty would send him his special slipper so that he might place it on the crown of his head and prostrate himself at the Emperor's threshold."

The last two Chak rulers, Yusaf Shah and Yaqub Shah, are worthy of special mention. The romance of the former with Habba Khatun, known also as Zooni, the moon, is an unforgettable saga of Kashmir's literary and cultural history. She came from a humble stock. Her husband maltreated her. Yusaf Shah was struck by her beauty and her melodious songs. He manipulated her divorce and married her.

Habba Khatun was a gifted poetess. Her mournful songs, composed to express the pangs of her separation from Yusaf Shah who had been detained by the Mughal Emperor Akbar, are tender expressions of deeply felt emotions that are highly personal and yet universal. In one of her lyrics, she says:

> The distant meadows are in bloom
> With flowers in various colours spread far and wide.
> Come, let us to the mountain meads.
> Sweet is the ritual of love.
> I would deck you, my love, with ornaments
> And in henna dye your hands.
> I would anoint the body with fragrant kisses.
> Offer you wine in golden goblets
> And give the lotus of love which blooms in the lake of my
> heart.
> I shall strew the meadows with flowers for thee!
> Come, come, my Lover of Flowers.

Habba's language is of ordinary folk, 'a well of Kashmiri undefiled', and her style sincere, artless, and autobiographical. She gives expression to her inner emotions with rare candour and spontaneity, as in her songs, "Come and enjoy my blossoming" or in the following lyric:

> Within the house I stayed hidden from view,
> Once outside, my name was on every tongue,
> Hermits, in their urge to see me, gave up
> their penance in the woods.
> My shop was brimful with its stock,
> And the whole world was keen to see it,
> My precious wares exposed, the prices crashed,
> As the day sank in the west!

Her voice is that of a humanist, of a mortal of flesh and blood, who feels the pangs of separation intensely and longs for fulfilment of her love:

> The radiance of your form illumines darkness,
> Love, would you come but once!
> On pretext of fetching water I slip out of home
> in the dark,
> Leaving the water-pot in the stream I call at your
> casement;
> Tarry not, come to me, Love, lest the fierce northerly
> gale breaks the earthen pail to pieces.

Habba's love-lyrics symbolise Shelley's immortal lines: "Our sweetest songs are those that tell of saddest thought."

Yusaf Shah showed no inclination to resist the might of the Mughals. But his son, Yaqub Shah, was a man of mettle. He wanted to stand up against Akbar. But the Sultanate of Kashmir had been crippled by internal factions and intrigues. Yaqub's persecution of Sunnis had turned a large section of Kashmiris against him. And the Mughal army had little difficulty in entering Srinagar on October 14, 1586.

The Mughals

In *Ain-i-Akbari*, Abul Fazl recorded: "On all the sides, mountains, which raise their heads to heaven, act as sentinels. Though there are six or seven roads, yet in all of them there are places where if some old women rolled down stones, the bravest of the men could not pass. On this account, former princes did not think of conquering it and prudence turned them away from such a wish." But this natural fortress fell to Akbar easily not only because of the superior might of the Mughal Empire but also because the people of Kashmir had become sick of the mismanagement of their Sultans. The defence of the passes had been badly neglected. More often than not, the defenders themselves joined the invaders.

Even before Akbar, the Mughals had been treating Kashmir as a part of their empire. First, Kamran held it for a few months in 1531, and then Mirza Haider Dughlat ruled Kashmir on behalf of Humayun from 1541 to 1551. Though Mirza was overthrown, the Mughals never relinquished their claim over Kashmir. Moreover, one powerful faction or the other of Kashmir's court was always in touch with the Mughals.

In 1589, Kashmir became a province of the Mughal Empire. It was ruled through a Governor, known as Subedar. Though the Mughals could not rid Kashmir of the recurring menace of floods and famines, they gave it a just administration. Peace prevailed. Kashmir became a hub of Central Asian trade. Akbar himself visited the Valley thrice–first in 1589, then in 1598, and again in 1601. The Mughal institutions and pattern of administration were introduced. The isolation of Kashmir came to an end. Earlier, when famines and floods visited the Valley, the people died in very large numbers. But with links now effectively established with the mainland, foodgrains could be quickly imported through the two roads which the Mughals built over the Pir Panjal and Jhelum Valley passes. For example, in 1638, in the wake of unprecedented floods, huge quantities of foodgrains were brought from Punjab under the orders of Emperor Shah Jahan. In sharp contrast to this, in the famine of 1576-78, during the regime of Ali Shah Chak, about half the population of the Valley died or migrated. Similar was the misfortune of the Kashmiris in earlier famines and floods.

Some notable social reforms were also carried out by the Mughals. For example, Jehangir put an end to the evil practice of *sati* and infanticide. In some areas of the kingdom, even Muslims came under the influence of the prevailing Hindu customs and buried their women alive along with their dead husbands. Unwanted female children were also killed.

Akbar's successor, Jehangir, fell in love with Kashmir. He visited the Valley six times. In his memoirs, he has paid glowing tributes to its beauty. He wrote, "Kashmir is a garden of eternal spring, a delightful flowerbed, and heart-expanding heritage for 'dervishes'. Its pleasant meads and enchanting cascades are beyond all description. There are running streams and fountains beyond count." About a site near the present-day Gulmarg, the Emperor observed, "It is a page that the painter of destiny has drawn with the pencil of creation."

Jehangir's son, Shah Jahan (1627-58), was equally fascinated by Kashmir. He, too, made several trips to the Valley. It was during the times of Jehangir and Shah Jahan that the world famous Mughal gardens were developed in Kashmir, including Shalimar, Nishat, Achabal, Chasme Shahi and Pari-Mahal. All these added to the natural beauty and tranquility of Kashmir.

Apart from order and stability, Jehangir and Shah Jahan brought elements of leisure and festivity in the depressing atmosphere of the last days of the local Sultanate. Thomas Moore's words in *Lalla Rukh*:

All love and light
Visions by day and feast by night

relate to Nur Jahan, Jehangir, the Mughal nobility, and the 'festival of roses' and point to the general enlivening of the social environment of the Valley.

Aurangzeb (1658-1707) administered Kashmir efficiently. But his puritanical disposition did not go well with Kashmir. He visited the Valley only once, in 1665. Francois Bernier, a French physician, who was included in Aurangzeb's entourage, has described the Kashmir scene of the time thus: "The Kashmiris are celebrated for wits and considered more intelligent than the Indians. In poetry and science they are not inferior to the Persians. They are also very active and industrious. But what may be considered special and which promotes the trade and fills it with wealth is the prodigious quantity of shawls which they manufacture."

During Aurangzeb's long reign of 49 years, Kashmir saw 14 Governors. They generally ruled well. But one of them, Iftikar Khan (1671-75), persecuted the Brahmins, and they approached the ninth Sikh Guru, Tegh Bahadur. They complained: "We suffer great atrocities, sacred threads (*janeus*) are forcibly taken off our persons. Cows are killed. *Janeus*, a maund and a quarter in weight, are snapped in a single day." The Guru consoled them and said, "Go and tell the Mughal rulers that if they converted Tegh Bahadur they would all voluntarily accept Islam." This infuriated the Imperial Court and led to the Guru's martyrdom. And the Sikh faith and history took a new turn.

After Aurangzeb's death, the Mughal Empire began to crumble. The central authority over Kashmir was lost. The Valley once again became a hotbed of intrigues, violence and bloodshed. The Governors appointed by the Imperial Court seldom came to Kashmir. On account of the continued power struggle at Delhi, they thought it expedient to stay in the capital. They administered Kashmir through their Deputy Governors who were really not accountable to anyone.

The devastating flood followed by the horrible famine of 1746-47 completely shattered the regime. About three-fourths of Kashmir's population perished. A large number of people were seen crawling their way to India. Most of them died on the way due to exhaustion. Gone were the great days of the stable Mughal Empire when massive movement of foodgrains to the Valley could be effected. The Mughal

Empire had lost everything except its sonorous title and ceremonial privileges. About Shah Alam's power and position, for example, there was a popular distich of the time:

Badshah Shah Alam
Az Delhi ta Palam.
(King Shah Alam
From Delhi to Palam.)

It was in the midst of such chaotic conditions that two influential local leaders invited Ahmad Shah Abdali to invade Kashmir and establish his rule. He seized the opportunity and sent a strong force in 1753 under Abdul Khan Isk Aquasi. The last Mughal Governor, Alaquli Khan, had in the meantime been displaced by a local upstart, Abdul Qasim Khan. The Afghan general defeated Qasim and established Afghan rule in Kashmir.

The Afghans

The nobles who approached Akbar to annex Kashmir made a good judgement. Kashmir got peace and justice for about 120 years. It was only after the disintegration of the Mughal Empire that mismanagement and misrule returned to Kashmir. But those who invited Ahmad Shah Abdali did not realise that they were really calling a barbarous horde to their garden of nature. The unfortunate people virtually jumped from the frying pan into the fire. And 67 years of brutal Afghan rule caused them untold miseries. The local feelings in this regard were reflected in a couplet which, when translated, would read: "I enquired of the gardener the cause of the destruction of the garden; drawing a deep sigh he replied that it was the Afghans who did it."

The very first Afghan chief, Abdullah Khan Isk Aquasi, appointed by Abdali, extracted rupees one crore from the local merchants. He lined up all the Kashmiris whom he considered rich and ordered them to part with all their wealth or face death. Such was the rigour of his torture that some traders committed suicide by jumping into the Dal Lake. The Afghan army ransacked the houses of the common people and looted whatever they could lay their hands on. The Kashmiris never had it so bad.

After five months of plunder and torture, Aquasi returned to Kabul, leaving Kashmir under the charge of Abdullah Khan Kabuli. Aquasi also appointed Sukh Jiwan Mal, a Hindu Khatri adventurer, as chief adviser to Kabuli. A local noble, Abdul Hassan Bandey, wanted to rid Kashmir of the Afghans' cruel rule. He persuaded Sukh Jiwan Mal to do away with Kabuli and declare himself independent. In pursuance of the common plan of Bandey and Sukh Jiwan Mal, Kabuli was assassinated. Sukh Jiwan Mal became virtually independent. He appointed Bandey as his chief minister. The team worked smoothly. For a while, the Kashmiris got a just and sympathetic administration. Abdali sent first Khwaja Kijak and then Aquasi to chastise Sukh Jiwan Mal. Both of them were defeated. On the second occasion, a number of Afghans were taken prisoner and paraded in the streets of Srinagar with Kashmiri crowds jeering and spitting at them.

Sukh Jiwan Mal established unquestioned sway over Kashmir. He declared his allegiance to the Mughal Emperor who granted him the title of Raja. The people were happy, though their happiness was marred by natural calamities. A devastating famine occurred in 1755 and two years later swarms of locusts descended on the Valley. People were reduced to such famished conditions that they ate the dead locusts after boiling them in water.

When force did not yield results, Abdali resorted to stratagem. Through his agent he wrecked the cordial relations between Raja Sukh Jiwan Mal and his chief minister, Abdul Hassan Bandey. Taking advantage of the situation, Abdali sent his third expeditionary force in 1762 under the leadership of Nur-ud-Din Khan Bamzai. A major portion of Raja Sukh Jiwan Mal's army deserted him. He was captured, blinded and sent to Ahmad Shah Abdali at Lahore, where he was mercilessly killed by throwing him under the feet of an elephant.

With the re-establishment of Afghan rule, the miseries of the people redoubled. The Kashmiris had the misfortune of being ruled by two upstarts–Lal Khan Khattak and Faqir Ullah. Both were tyrannical to the extreme. The former was given to fits of insane rage and sometimes got an entire family killed on mere suspicion. He was particularly hard on Hindus. Faqir Ullah was equally inhuman. He got hundreds of Kashmiri Pandits killed because he suspected that his father had been killed at the instance of a Kashmiri Pandit, Kailash Dhar, who was a nobleman at the time.

The next Afghan Governor of note was Amir Khan Jawnsher. He left the affairs of the province to his chief minister and himself indulged in merry-making. He fell in love with a beautiful Hanji girl and married her. He spent most of his time in her company in a luxury house which he built on an artificial island in the middle of the Dal Lake. The relations of the girl exploited her influence over the Governor. They indulged in inexcusable vandalism and destroyed about 700 Mughal gardens to secure material for building their houses. To Amir Khan, however, goes the credit of building the first bridge in Srinagar–Amira Kadal. He also built Sher Ghari, presently the Old Secretariat. A canal linking the Dal Lake with the Anchar Lake was also built during his time.

Taking advantage of the preoccupations of Timur Shah, the Afghan ruler at Kabul, Amir Khan declared himself independent. Being a fanatic Shia, he started persecuting the Sunnis. Many Sunni nobles were arrested and executed on flimsy grounds. When complaints in this regard reached Timur Shah, he despatched a strong force under Haji Karim Dad Khan who defeated Amir Khan's forces in a second attempt, mainly through the desertion of his army.

During the regime of the next two Governors–Haji Karim Dad Khan and Asad Khan–the Afghan misrule in Kashmir touched its lowest depth. In 1783, George Forster*, an officer of-the East India Company, visited Kashmir. While recounting the cruelties perpetrated by Karim Dad Khan, Forster described how for minor offences the alleged culprits were tied together in pairs and thrown into the river, and how women were sexually abused. About Asad Khan, Forster recounted the story that was current at that time. "A film on one of his eyes had baffled the attempts of many operators, and being impatient at the want of success, he told the last surgeon, who had been called in, that if the disorder was not remedied within a limited time, allowing but a few days, his belly should be cut open; the man failed in the cure and Asad Khan verified his threat."

Forster, incidentally, did not have a good opinion of the Kashmiris. Initially, he sympathised with their miserable lot. Subsequently, however, he wrote, "Experience has driven me to the conclusion that I had never known a body of men more impregnated with the principles of vice than the natives of Kashmir." Earlier, Abul Fazl had talked about the Kashmiris in the same strain: "The bane of this country is its people."

Asad Khan, intoxicated by power, soon declared himself independent in 1784 and assumed the title of Nadir Shah II. Timur

*Forster's impressions are recorded in his letters.

Shah had to send two military expeditions to re-establish his authority in Kashmir. When the new Governor, Madad Khan, assumed control, he found Kashmir a deserted and forlorn place. "A few famished and miserable looking people were all that was left of its once opulent villages and towns." A year earlier, due to shortage of food and the cholera epidemic, people had died like flies. In the beginning of his rule, Madad Khan was sympathetic and adopted a helpful attitude towards the people. But the machinations of Kashmiri nobles and officials succeeded in turning him against them. He adopted ruthless methods. The familiar pattern of Afghan oppression and cruelty returned. And the people suffered.

Another Afghan Governor, Ata Muhammad Khan, had earned notoriety for his insatiable lust for beautiful Kashmiri women. The Hindu parents became so apprehensive that they had the good looks of their girls sullied to evade the attention of the Governor's agents.

Jabbar Khan, the last Afghan Governor, persecuted the Hindus relentlessly. A Pandit nobleman, Birbal Dhar, unable to see any longer the Kashmiris being tormented and tortured, approached Maharaja Ranjit Singh for help and 'provided him with valuable information about the strength and deployment of Jabbar Khan's forces. Ranjit Singh had earlier made two unsuccessful attempts to capture Kashmir, once in 1812 and again in 1814. This time, success greeted Ranjit Singh. The Sikh forces, under the able command of Misser Dewan Chand, defeated Jabbar Khan at Shopiyan on July 15, 1819, and triumphantly marched into the capital the next day.

Thus ended 67 years of Kashmir's nightmare. The tragedy of the Afghan rule in Kashmir lay in its predatory nature. The Valley was treated not as a province to be justly administered as a part of a larger empire, but as an area from which maximum amounts could be extracted to finance military expeditions elsewhere. Ruthless exactions and violent suppression were inherent in the attitude of the Afghans. And they went all out to break the will of the people to resist. The Kashmiris were so much subdued that in the later part of their rule, the Afghans could hold the entire Valley with just 3,000 soldiers. In the beginning, they required at least 20,000 soldiers. But by over-extracting Kashmir's wealth, they ruined its economy. They had killed the hen that laid the golden egg.

The Sikhs

Maharaja Ranjit Singh was so happy over the annexation of Kashmir that he ordered special illumination of Lahore and Amritsar for three nights. He nursed 'a deep desire to visit Kashmir. In a letter he wrote, "Would that only once in my life I could enjoy the delight of wandering through the gardens of Kashmir fragrant with almond blossoms, and sitting on the fresh green turf!" But he was not destined to have his wish fulfilled. Although he ruled for 17 years after his forces conquered Kashmir, Ranjit Singh could not visit it even once.

Sikh rule in Kashmir lasted only 27 years (1819-46). But it saw ten Governors. Misser Diwan Chand was the first Governor. He remained for a short time. Moti Ram was the second. He held the office twice. He was gentle and sympathetic. He restored, to some extent, the confidence of the people. He is known for having banned killing of cows and punishing the offenders with death. But he was easy going. The extent of corruption and unfair exactions prevalent in his time can be seen from the fact that one of his subordinates collected ₹ 30 lakhs and misappropriated it.

The third Governor, Kirpa Ram, was popular. He carried out many improvement works, including development of the Rambagh Gardens. He was a colourful personality in the mould of Emperor Jehangir. A lover of dance, music and nature, he was in harmony with the Kashmiri ethos. He spent much time in a pleasure-boat in the Dal Lake. Even his boat was rowed by women musicians and dancers. He earned the nickname of "Kirpa Shroin"–Kirpa, "the sound of the boat paddle". But he was not remiss in his duties. He was able to collect a revenue of ₹ 42 lakhs annually for the treasury of Lahore. Due to intrigues at the Sikh Darbar, Raja Dhyari Singh, chief minister, manoeuvred to have Kirpa Ram recalled in disgrace under the orders of Ranjit Singh.

Prince Sher Singh was the next Governor. He spent his time in drinking and neglected his work even during the severe famine of 1832. When Col. Mihan Singh, popularly known as Colonel Sahib, arrived in 1833 as the next Governor, he found the people living in great distress. He promptly imported foodgrains from Punjab and provided relief in taxes. He administered the province justly and efficiently. The Sikh troops, used to illegal extortions, resented the Governor's actions. With the death of Maharaja Ranjit Singh in 1839, indiscipline and instability had spread all over his kingdom. On April

17, 1841, the Sikh troops mutinied and murdered the Governor. He was followed by inconsequential Governors. The last Governor, Imam-ud-Din, was made to surrender possession of Kashmir to Raja Gulab Singh in 1846 in pursuance of the Treaty of Amritsar.

Except for the brief period of Kirpa Ram's governorship, the Sikh rule in Kashmir was far from being benign or just. While the Hindus were treated slightly better, the Muslims were maltreated and subjected to a number of disabilities. Their mosques were locked. Even Jama Masjid was closed to public prayers. At the time of the commencement of Sikh rule, a local commander, Phula Singh, had even fixed a gun to blast the famous Shah Hamadan mosque on the grounds that it had been built over a Hindu temple. But Birbal Dhar interceded and the mosque was saved. The Mullahs were forbidden to give call for prayers. But the Kashmiris as a class were despised. If a Sikh killed a Hindu, the compensation allowed was four rupees, and if a Muslim was killed, the corresponding amount was two rupees.

"The Sikhs", as correctly observed by Younghusband*, "were not so barbarically cruel as the Afghans; but they were hard and rough masters." Their main objective was to collect the maximum amount of money, no matter what the long-term consequences would be. When the Sikh rule commenced in Kashmir, the annual revenue extracted was ₹ 62 lakh. In the last year of the rule, the amount came down to only ₹ 10 lakh. Such was the extent of impoverish-ment caused by the short-sighted approach of the Sikh rulers.

A crisp and fairly accurate idea about the Sikh rule can be formed from the observations made by Moorcroft** and Vigne†. The former wrote, "The Kashmiris were exorbitantly taxed by the Sikh Government and subjected to every kind of extortion and oppression by its officers." Describing the conditions of the 'unpaid porters' who were seized by the Sikh soldiers, Moorcroft, noted, "They were tied together by a cord fastening their arms and driven along the road, and at night, to prevent their escape, their legs were bound with ropes." In

* Younghusband was a British Political Resident in Kashmir. He travelled extensively in Kashmir and other areas around the Himalayas and also Central Asia and China.

** Moorcroft was a veterinary doctor in the military stud branch of the East India Company. He travelled extensively in the areas of Mansarovar, Kulu, Ladakh, Kashmir, and Bokhara.

† Vigne, who was interested in geology, and botany, came to study Kashmir in 1835.

the eastern part of the Valley, Vigne saw "numerous but ruined villages; many of the houses were tenantless and deserted, the fruit was dropping unheeded from the trees; the orchards were overgrown with a profusion of wild hemp and wild indigo".

History of Jammu: Rise of the Dogras

Gulab Singh, founder of the Dogra dynasty, was an unusually gifted person. He was born in 1792 in a family which traced its ancestry to Raja Ranjit Deo, the famous ruler of the Jammu region from 1742 to 1780.

According to tradition, Jammu was founded about 3,000 years ago by Raja Jambhu Lochan brother of Bahu Lochan, who built the fort of Bahu on the bank of Tawi. Recent excavations near Akhnoor show that Jammu formed part of the area covered by the Harappan civilisation. Remains of the Mauryan, Kushan and Gupta times have also been found. Its antiquity and long tradition are slowly coming to light. In precise terms, however, we hear of Jammu around A.D. 900. The memoir of Timur refers to the sack of Jammu in A.D. 1398-99. After the collapse of the Mughal Empire, Ranjit Deo quickly brought twenty-two small Dogra chieftains under his control. During his regime, the Duggar area prospered and Jammu attained the zenith of its glory. The town became a thriving centre of trade and commerce. Hugel, who travelled in the area at that time, described Jammu "as one of the richest towns in India".

During the last phase of the Dogra dynasty, the Duggar region was drawn into the orbit of the rising Sikh power. Jammu was attacked by the Sikh forces, and it was in the defence of Jammu–the battle of Gumat–that Gulab Singh, at the young age of 16 years, distinguished himself. When Gulab Singh's feat of valour came to the notice of Maharaja Ranjit Singh, he took Gulab Singh in his service. The two brothers of Gulab Singh, namely Dhyan Singh and Suchet Singh, were also employed by the Maharaja.

In the various military campaigns undertaken by Ranjit Singh, Gulab Singh exhibited his unmatched skill, courage, loyalty, and organisational ability, particularly in regard to the sieges of Multan and Jalandhar and subjugation of the tribes of Yusafzai in 1819 which enabled the Maharaja to capture Peshawar. In recognition of Gulab Singh's services and as a part of his overall strategy to create a subordinate military power between the Sikh and the Afghan domains, Ranjit Singh granted a number of estates, including Jammu, to Gulab Singh. The title of Raja was conferred upon him, and he was given permission to raise his own force.

Ranjit Singh followed the mediaeval system of farming out provinces for revenue. This system and the title of Raja gave opportunities to Gulab Singh to organise military operations to bring Reasi, Kishtwar, Rajouri, Chenani and other small principalities under his effective control. Jacquemont, who travelled through Gulab Singh's territory in 1831, observed, "Gulab Singh is more the master of his own house than is Ranjit Singh in distant possession."

At the Lahore Darbar, the other two brothers, Dhyan Singh and Suchet Singh, attained positions of eminence. The former became the chief minister. Thus, the Dogras acquired a dominant position in the Jammu region and also at the court of Maharaja Ranjit Singh. About the power of the three Dogra brothers, C.M. Wade, the British Political Agent at Ludhiana, wrote, "They held an immense tract of territory in the plains, besides the monopoly of the salt mines, and by means of farming the transit duties, from Sutlej to Peshawar, have their officers stationed in all principal towns and exercise more or less influence or interference in every department of the government."

Ladakh's History and its Inclusion in the Dogra Domain

The most significant military achievement of Raja Gulab Singh was the inclusion of Ladakh in his province. In 1834, with the implied consent of Ranjit Singh and the East India Company, Gulab Singh deputed his most brilliant general, Zorawar Singh, to conquer Ladakh, the most strategic area having borders with China and Tibet, and also a nerve centre of wool trade with Central Asia. At that time, Ladakh was an independent kingdom under the suzerainty of the Grand Lamas of Tibet.

Ladakh, "the little Tibet of India" and the "roof of the world", is a cold desert.* It lies to the east of the Kashmir Valley. Its elevation varies from 2,440 to 4,570 metres above the sea level. It is sparsely populated. Its density of population is only 2 per square kilometre. But its strategic importance is immense.

Cunningham, in his book published in 1854, described Ladakh thus: "The general aspect of Ladakh is extreme barrenness. No trace of man or of human habitations would meet the eye, and even the

*See also Chapter IV: 'Roots' (Section: Regional Roots).

large spots of cultivated land would be but small specks on the mighty waste of a deserted world. But a close view would show many fertile tracts covered with luxuriant crops and picturesque monasteries, from which the chant of human voices ascends high in daily prayer and praise".

In earlier stages of its history, Ladakh formed part of the larger area covering Western Tibet and Baltistan and Gilgit. It was loosely divided amongst petty chieftains, some of whom came under the sway of Kanishka. Buddhism travelled to Ladakh from India via Kashmir. The description given by Hui Chao, a Chinese pilgrim, who travelled in the territory in A.D. 727, argues that Buddhism which came from India had established its hold on the people of Ladakh at a time when even Tibet had not become Buddhist. Later on, however, when the Lama form of Buddhism came to be accepted in Tibet and in India Buddhism was virtually wiped out with the rising tide of Hindu revivalism, Ladakh became a part of "the spiritual and cultural empire of Tibet".

Territorially, the south-western portion of Ladakh came under the control of the great ruler of Kashmir, Lalitaditya (A.D. 724-61); and in the preceding century, Stron-tsan-gam-po, the most powerful ruler of Tibet, had extended his sway over its eastern portion. But the rulers of Kashmir and Tibet soon lost their control, which in any case was loose, and the local Lahchen dynasty came into being in A.D. 842. It was one of the members of this dynasty, Rinchana, who, as we have noted earlier, fled to the Valley to escape local troubles, became its, ruler embraced Islam and founded the Muslim Sultanate.

During the time of Zain-ul-Abidin (A.D. 1420-70), Mirza Haider Duglat (A.D. 1541-51) and the Mughal rule in Kashmir, Ladakhi Rajas accepted a loose form of suzerainty over them. But more often than not, it was a mere posture. For example, Bernier, while referring to the Ladakhi King's undertaking to Aurangzeb to pay an annual tribute, recorded, "No person doubts that this treaty would be totally disregarded as soon as Aurangzeb has quitted Kashmir and the King of Ladakh will no more fulfil his stipulations than he did those of the treaty concluded between him and Shah Jehan." Moreover, these periods of submission were brief and Ladakh was mostly ruled by independent or semi-independent rulers.

Sengge (Lion) Namgyal (1616-42) was its most outstanding ruler. He brought a large number of kingdoms, including Zanskar, under his control. He helped in establishing a number of monasteries, including the world famous Hemis Monastery. He also built an equally famous nine-storeyed palace at Leh.

In a series of spectacular marches which have few parallels in the annals of Indian history, Zorawar Singh subjugated Ladakh, including Zanskar, and also Baltistan. In another bold but extremely hazardous venture in 1841, General Zorawar Singh tried to establish control over Tibet. As K.M. Panikkar pointed out, "Before Zorawar Singh, no army from Hindustan had attacked Tibet. No Indian ruler had thought of conquering it and no Indian general accustomed to the heat of the plains had ever dared to face the hostility of the Tibetan climate." Zorawar Singh took Rudok, Garo and Taklala Kote. There, unfortunately, he was encircled by Tibet and caught in a snow storm. He fought bravely at the height of 15,000 ft. But he was destined to meet his Waterloo there and was killed.

In the words of K.M. Panikkar, "Thus died Zorawar Singh, a soldier of whose achievements India could justly be proud. To have marched an army not once or twice, but six times over the snow-clad ranges of Ladakh and Baltistan, 15,000 feet above the sea-level, where the air is so rarefied that people from the plains can hardly live with comfort, is a wonderful achievement. To have conquered that country after successive campaigns and reduced it to a peaceful province is an exploit for which there is no parallel in Indian history. His greatness will shine through the pages of Indian history as that of a great and noble warrior".*

In the wake of Zorawar Singh's death, another force under Wazir Ratnu was sent. A formal agreement between the three parties – the Dogras, the Ladakhis and the Tibetans – was arrived at. The boundary between Ladakh and Tibet was fixed, and Ladakh was ceded to Gulab Singh. Thus, as a result of Zorawar Singh's unique military ventures in Ladakh, it became a part of the Dogra domain and subsequently of the Indian Republic. Had this not happened, the Chinese claims of suzerainty over Tibet might have been extended to Ladakh.

General Zorawar Singh was a born military genius–"the finest soldier that India produced in the nineteenth century." During my visits in 1984-1985 to Kishtwar, Leh, Kargil, Daras, Pyuangong Lake, Chushul and various other far-flung inhospitable areas of Ladakh, I wondered how General Zorawar Singh and his troops could have

*K.M. Panikkar: *The Founding of the Kashmir State*, p. 82.

braved such difficult climatic and topographical conditions and how they could have moved with such speed and precision. It is unfortunate that his remarkable campaign has not been fully recognised. I could hardly find any befitting memorial in his honour. This prompted me to take the initiative through the Mata Vaishno Devi Shrine Board, of which I happened to be the Chairman. From the funds of this Board, I started renovating the ruined Reasi Fort with which Zorawar Singh was associated, and developing a large park around it. This memorial complex was named after Zorawar Singh. I did so because the General was also a devotee of Vaishno Devi, and I had separately decided to honour all the great devotees of the Mata.

With the death of Ranjit Singh in 1839 and the Anglo-Sikh wars, in the last of which the Sikhs were decisively beaten at Sobraon in 1845, the Sikh kingdom virtually disappeared. Earlier, on September 15, 1843, due to court intrigues and a scramble for power amongst various factions, Dhyan Singh, the powerful Dogra Wazir, was brutally murdered. The Dogra influence at the Lahore Durbar suffered a steep decline. Efforts were also made to deprive Gulab Singh of his territory. But even in this grave crisis, Gulab Singh remained the cool tactician that he was. He, in fact, turned adversity into opportunity.

When the Anglo-Sikh conflict came to a boiling point, Gulab Singh cleverly turned the situation to his advantage. While the Sikhs wanted his help because he was their most important feudatory chieftain, the British interests lay in not permitting the combination of the Sikh and the Dogra powers. Gulab Singh deftly interposed himself between the two warring parties. On the one hand, he professed loyalty and friendliness to the Lahore Durbar, and, on the other, he remained in secret touch with the British. He wanted to use his trump card only when the power of the Sikh army had been broken.

Following the death of Ranjit Singh in 1839, there were three principal actors–the British, the Dogras and the Sikhs–on the stage of north-western India, where a tense drama of power struggle was played for the next seven years. The British were modern, scientifically organised, farsighted and clear in their imperial objectives. The Dogras were hardy, ambitious, feudal, not well-equipped militarily, but had the good fortune of being led at the moment by a sound, sagacious and experienced leader. The Sikhs were martial, brave, with a strong army, but reckless, ill-disciplined, riven with factions and jealousies and virtually leaderless. In the circumstances, complete success of the British in attaining their objectives was not surprising. Gulab Singh realistically accepted the position of 'subordinate alliance' to the British and in the process secured a vast princely State free from the vagaries of the Lahore Durbar. The Sikhs lost all their power and position which they had built over the last fifty years.

Princely State of Jammu and Kashmir

After the defeat of the Sikhs, two separate treaties were executed. The Treaty of Lahore, which incorporated the terms of settlement between the Sikhs and the British Government, was signed on March 9, 1846. A week later, on March 16, 1846, a separate Treaty, known as the Treaty, of Amritsar, was signed between Raja Gulab Singh and the British Government. Relevant extracts of the two Treaties have been given in Appendix II. It would be noted that by virtue of the first Treaty the Sikhs ceded certain areas to the British Indian Government on account of their inability to pay the indemnity of rupees one and a half crore that was demanded by the British; and by virtue of the second Treaty, the British Government transferred 'forever in independent possession' some of the ceded areas, including Kashmir, because of Gulab Singh's willingness to pay ₹ 75 lakh out of the total amount of indemnity demanded by the British. Thus, Kashmir passed on to the Dogras in consequence of the terms of the Treaties, and not in consequence of a 'sale deed'.

At the first glance, it may appear rather strange that the British Indian Government did not annex the Valley. Younghusband wrote, "Surprise has often been expressed that when this lovely land had actually been ceded to us, after a hard and strenuous campaign, we should ever have parted with it for the paltry sum of three-quarters of a million sterling." But the British had a subtle and long-term purpose. This becomes evident from the despatch dated March 19, 1846, from the Governor-General, Lord Hardinge, to the Secret Committee of the East India Company. It said:

> I request Your Honourable Committee's attention to the treaty made with the Maharaja Gulab Singh, by which a Rajput principality of the hill districts has been constructed, extending from the Ravi to the Indus, and including the province of Kashmir. The Maharaja is declared by the treaty independent of the Lahore State and under the protection of the British Government. As it was

of the utmost importance to weaken the Sikh nation before its Government could be re-established, I considered the appropriation of this part of the ceded territory to be the most expedient measure I could devise for that purpose, by which a Rajput dynasty will act as a counterpoise against the power of a Sikh prince, the son of the late Ranjit Singh, and both will have a common interest in resisting attempts on the part of any Mohammaden power to establish an independent state on this side of the Indus, or even to occupy Peshawar.

The Dogra dynasty lasted for a little over hundred years. This period saw four Maharajas–Gulab Singh (1846-57); Ranbir Singh (1857-85); Pratap Singh (1885-1925); and Hari Singh (1925-52).* But the dynasty was always at the mercy of the British Government. Maharaja Gulab Singh himself had no illusion about it. He wrote to the Governor-General: "I am ready to sacrifice my life and property as a proof of my obedience to Your Honour. Anyone who is faithful to the Honourable Company has to remain faithful with his heart and soul."

At the time of the commencement of the Dogra rule, the conditions in Kashmir were deplorable. Baron Schonberg, who travelled in the Valley at that time, observed, "I have been in many lands but nowhere the conditions of human beings present a more saddening spectacle than in Kashmir. It vividly recalled the history of Israelites under the Egyptian rule, when they were flogged at their daily labour by their pitiless task-masters." Lt. R.G. Taylor, who visited Srinagar in 1846, portrayed an equally dismal picture. He recorded, "Srinagar town presents a very miserable appearance. The houses were tumbling. The streets were filthy for want of drainage. None of the bazaars looked well-filled. Forced labour was prevalent and the wages of the artisan were very low." Most of the people lived on a small quantity of rice. The Bomba and Khaka tribesmen often made inroads and the Galawan dacoits harassed the people. Gulab Singh employed stern, often inhuman, measures to restore order. Corruption had become a way of life. For paltry considerations, large tracts of State lands had been gifted away. On the assumption of rulership of the Valley, Gulab Singh found that more than 3,100 land grants had been made. He ruefully remarked that he had parted with 75 lakh

*The State acceded to India on October 26, 1947, but the hereditary rule of the Dogras was abolished in 1952.

rupees for an area three-fourths of which comprised mountains and water and the remaining one-fourth given away as 'Jagir' grants.

High principles of governance were unknown to the Dogra rule which largely remained personal and feudal in character. But the conditions substantially improved. Peace and stability itself was a boon. A few welfare measures also were taken. 'In this regard, the British Indian Government exercised a healthy influence on the Maharaja.

At that time, the British Indian Government had two main policy objectives in J&K: first, to establish a tight control over the Maharaja, particularly in regard to the strengthening of its hold on areas of strategic importance such as Ladakh and Gilgit, and, secondly, to bring about a stable and reasonably just administration which could maintain law and order, prevent disaffection, and undertake rudimentary development work, such as construction of roads which would also serve its military and commercial interests.

In the uprising of 1857, the Dogras sided with the British. Though the latter were pleased with the Maharaja and readily agreed to Gulab Singh's suggestion in regard to the succession of his son, Ranbir Singh, the Government of India did not relax its somewhat aggressive attitude. Already, in 1852, an 'officer on special duty' had been forced on the Maharaja. In 1867, the British Trade Agency was established at Leh, and the control of the trade route to Central Asia passed on to the British-Indian Government. In 1884, a permanent Resident Political Agent was stationed in the capital.

With the appointment of the Resident, British control over the state affairs increased. Even in regard to insignificant administrative issues, such as land grants, the Resident's will prevailed. Commenting on the powers of the Resident and the so-called reform of the Kashmir administration by transferring some of the functions of the Maharaja to the Kashmir Council, William Digby* said:

> The Government of the country is vested to all practical purposes in the Resident alone. Indeed it is not possible for anybody to set foot in that country without a written permission from him. His will is law; he is king, and has surrounded himself

*William Digby was a Liberal Member of the British Parliament. In his note, "Condemned Unheard", he severely criticised the British Indian Government for accusing Maharaja Partap Singh of mismanagement to give justification for intervention in the affairs of the State.

with his own friends and proteges, and turned out many an old and faithful servant of the State. Nobody dares to open his mouth in that country, and if anyone is so bold as to raise the most feeble protest, he is threatened with the 'most serious consequences'.

The British Government justified its intervention on the grounds of misgovernance by the Maharaja. But the real purpose was to secure complete control over the frontier region in the north. As William Digby put it, "It was Gilgit that the Government of India wanted."

More often than not, intervention was made to such an extent that the Maharaja looked like a poor and helpless petitioner. For instance, when Maharaja Pratap Singh was divested practically of all control over the Government and the administration was handed over to the Kashmir Council, the members of which were hand-picked by the British-Indian Government, the Maharaja wrote a letter on May 14, 1889, to the Governor-General, which speaks for itself. He said:

> If, after a fair trial being given to me, I do not set everything right, and am found not to rule to the satisfaction of the Supreme Government and my people within the prescribed time, Your Excellency's Government is at liberty to do anything that may be considered advisable. In case this liberty is not allowed to me by the Supreme Government, and I have to remain in my present most miserable condition, I would most humbly ask Your Excellency to summon me before you–and I will be most happy to obey such summons–and shoot me through the heart with Your Excellency's hands, and thus at once relieve an unfortunate prince from unbearable misery, contempt, and disgrace for ever.

In view of the British Government's pervasive and decisive intervention in the affairs of J&K, it would be more appropriate to call the period 1846 to 1947 as the period of Dogra-British rule rather than of Dogra rule alone.

While intervening in the affairs of the State, the British Indian Government was primarily motivated by its concern for the protection of its imperial interests. But intervention was justified on other grounds as well. For instance, during the famine of 1878-79, the Maharaja's administration proved unequal to the task of providing effective relief.

Nor was the British intervention without its healthy fall-outs. By compelling the Maharaja to use the services of a sizeable number of British civil servants, the local administration, to some extent, was imparted a modern outlook. Some of the British officers served the State admirably. Walter Lawrence, Settlement Officer, was the most outstanding amongst them. From 1889 to 1893, he carried out work of truly historic dimensions. He evolved a fair and rational system of land settlement in place of the corrupt and chaotic one. Forced labour, 'begar', was abolished. The revenue demand was fixed for fourteen years. Payment of revenue in cash was prescribed, and occupancy rights were conferred upon the tenants working on undisputed lands.

On account of the pressure of the British Government and also on his own initiative, the Maharaja undertook constitutional reforms on a moderate scale. This was done through the Constitution Acts of 1924 and 1927. On July 13, 1931, there were serious riots outside the Srinagar Jail in which 21 persons were killed. The riots were attributed to the general dis-content amongst the Muslims. On the insistence of the British Resident, an Inquiry Committee under the chairmanship of a British officer, Bertrand J. Glancy,* was appointed. The recommendations of the Glancy Committee report generated further pressures on the Maharaja for reforms. In 1934, he promulgated another Constitution Act which introduced a dyarchical form of Government. The subjects were divided into two groups. Group I comprised 'reserve subjects' which remained under the exclusive charge of the Maharaja, and Group II comprised 'transferred subjects', the administration of which was entrusted to the Ministers. This Act also provided for a 75-member Legislative Assembly (Praja Sabha), including 37 elected members.

Political Awakening

While the Maharaja was proceeding with limited constitutional reforms, the freedom movement in India was gathering momentum under the leadership of the Indian National Congress. The Muslim League was also emerging on the scene. These developments were bound to influence events in the State of J&K. A number of young men received higher education at Lahore and Aligarh and returned to the State with new political and social awakening. Sheikh Mohammad Abdullah was one of them.

---

*See also Chapter IV: 'Roots' (Section: Regional Roots).

In 1932, a political organisation, by the name of Jammu and Kashmir Muslim Conference, was founded, and Abdullah was elected its first president. The Muslim Conference began with modest demands. Its main objectives were to work for social, economic and cultural betterment of Muslims and to secure for them a larger share in civil services and army jobs.

By 1934, differences had arisen in the Working Committee of the Muslim Conference in regard to the attitude to be adopted towards the Franchise Committee which the Maharaja had appointed as a part of his scheme for limited constitutional reforms. This was the beginning of the division of the political movement in the State. As a consequence of these differences, the Working Committee was dissolved, and Chowdhry Ghulam Abbas was appointed sole dictator of the Muslim Conference. Abbas's talks with the Prime Minister of the State failed. He gave a call for civil disobedience movement which evoked very little response. Abbas was arrested and sentenced to imprisonment for six months.

In other princely States of India, too, the freedom movement was having its impact. The Indian National Congress was the motivating force behind it. It also took deep interest in what was happening in J&K. The local leadership soon saw the advantage of eliciting support of the national leaders and also broadening the base of its movement against the Maharaja's Government. In 1938-39, the Muslim Conference was renamed as 'All Jammu and Kashmir National Conference' and its membership was opened to all classes, irrespective of their religion. The initiative in this regard was taken by Maulana Sayeed Masoodi and Sheikh Mohammad Abdullah. The latter, in his presidential address, pleaded: "In order to secure responsible government, it is essential that we invite Hindus, Sikhs, Buddhists and Harijans to join us. They too are steeped in ignorance. They too pay taxes. They too face hunger. The institution of the responsible government is as necessary for them as for us."

In 1944, the National Conference adopted, as its manifesto, a programme called 'Naya Kashmir'. It envisaged a pattern of parliamentary democracy in the State, with independent judiciary, and also a programme of social, economic and educational reforms. A summary of this document has been added as Appendix III.

In the summer of 1944, in an attempt to establish his hold in J&K, M.A. Jinnah visited the State. He came on the plea of rest but accepted receptions in his honour. In the reception given by the

National Conference, both Sheikh Abdullah and Jinnah indulged in what may be called exercises in ambivalence. At the reception held by the Muslim Conference, however, Jinnah came out openly in its favour. He said, "The Muslims have one platform, one 'Kalma' and one God. I would request the Muslims to come under the banner of the Muslim Conference and fight for their rights."

Jinnah also presided over the annual session of the Muslim Conference. In his address, he described the National Conference as a 'band of gangsters'. Later, when the National Conference launched its 'Quit Kashmir' movement, Jinnah labelled it as "an agitation carried on by a few malcontents who were out to create disorderly conditions in the State". Clearly, Jinnah and the Muslim League did not give much quarter to Sheikh Abdullah, and Chowdhry Ghulam Abbas and the Muslim Conference were preferred. This must have convinced Sheikh Abdullah that his political future would be bleak if the State joined Pakistan. In his autobiography, *Atish-e-Chinar*, Sheikh Abdullah himself acknowledges the hostility which Jinnah displayed towards him. He writes, "At that time, Jinnah was intoxicated by power. He thought it beneath his dignity to talk to a poor and resourceless nation. When this equation of power went against him, he woke up in panic from his dream. But by this time, the snake had passed; only its line remained."

During Jinnah's visit, Moulvi Yusaf Shah also came in for some sharp tongue-lashing from Jinnah. He described the Moulvi as a "rotten egg". He also told the Moulvi, "I advise you to remain aloof from politics. In Kashmir, we want a leader, and not a Mullah."

By this time, the National Conference had become disillusioned with the system of dyarchy. It discovered that the system was nothing but an 'organised puppetry'. The close rapport which Sheikh Abdullah had developed with Jawaharlal Nehru, Maulana Azad, Khan Abdul Ghaffar Khan and other national leaders had given him and his colleagues in the National Conference great confidence. The arrival of the Cripps Mission in India at that time also raised new hopes. In a telegram to the Mission, the National Conference said:

> As Mission is at the moment reviewing relationship of Princes with the Paramount Power with reference to treaty rights, we wish to submit that for us in Kashmir re-examination of this relationship is vital matter because hundred years ago in 1846 land and people of Kashmir were sold away to servitude of Dogra House by British

for seventy-five lakhs of Sikh rupees equivalent to fifty lakhs of British Indian rupees. As such, case of Kashmir stands on unique footing and people of Kashmir press on Mission their unchallengeable claims to freedom on withdrawal of British power from India.

On May 10, the National Conference, under the leadership of Sheikh Mohammad Abdullah, launched the 'Quit Kashmir' movement. In his speech on May 17, 1946, Sheikh Abdullah said, "The tyranny of the Dogras has lacerated our souls. It is time for action. You must fight slavery and enter the field of 'Jihad' as soldiers. Every man, woman and child will shout 'Quit Kashmir'. The Kashmiri nation has expressed its will. I ask for plebiscite on this question." On May 20, he was arrested. The other prominent leaders of the National Conference were also detained. Nehru demanded immediate release of Sheikh Abdullah and himself proceeded to Kashmir to make arrangements for the Sheikh's defence. The Maharaja, presumably under the advice of his Prime Minister, Ram Chandra Kak, prohibited Nehru's entry into the State. Nehru defied the prohibition order and was arrested. This event, besides causing a great public stir, permanently impaired the relations between Maharaja Hari Singh and Nehru. As subsequent events showed, Nehru was never able to get over his hostility towards the Maharaja, and Sheikh Abdullah exploited it to the hilt. Nehru was, however, persuaded by the Congress Working Committee to return to Delhi. Later on, Sheikh Abdullah was released on what has been described in certain quarters as his qualified apology to the Maharaja. In his letter of September 26, 1947, Sheikh Abdullah wrote: "I assure Your Highness that myself and my party have never harboured any sentiment of disloyalty towards Your Highness' person, throne or dynasty. I assure Your Highness the fullest and loyal support of myself and my organisation. Not only this, but I assure Your Highness that any party within or without the State, which may attempt to create any impediments in our efforts to gain our goal, will be treated as our enemy and will be treated as such." The full text of his letter has been given in Appendix IV.

Some prominent leaders of the National Conference, including Chowdhry Ghulam Abbas, joined the Muslim Conference. In October 1946, the Muslim Conference launched Direct Action campaign under the leadership of Mirwaiz Moulvi Yusaf Shah. Chowdhry Ghulam Abbas and a few other leaders of the Muslim

Conference were arrested. This showed the increasing influence of the Muslim League on the Muslims of J&K.

Mirwaiz Moulvi Yusaf Shah displayed extreme hostility to the Indian National Congress and the National Conference. Deploring what he called interference of the Congress, he said in a statement on September 25, 1946:

> The Hindu capitalists want to get the State into their grip, but I warn that if the Government of J&K gets terrified at the might of the Congress and strikes an unholy alliance with the National Conference fascists, it will have to face the terrific opposition of the Muslims. And this sinister alliance will be smashed to pieces. The Muslims of Kashmir have warded off Pt. Nehru's invasion in 1940, 1945 and 1946. Now he is again out to make a fresh attempt and it is the duty of the Kashmiri Muslims particularly and all the well-wishers of the country to smash up this onslaught.

In another revealing and interesting statement, issued on May 10, 1947, Chowdhry Hamidullah Khan, President, Muslim Conference, urged the Maharaja to declare himself independent. He said:

> If Kashmir has to keep itself aloof from carnage and bloodshed, it should lose no time in adopting a strong and bold policy. His Highness the Maharaja Bahadur should declare Kashmir independent immediately. A separate Constituent Assembly to frame the Constitution for the State, according to the wishes of the people, should be established at once. His Highness the Maharaja Bahadur will receive the cooperation of Muslims in carrying out this policy. The Muslims form 80% of the population. They are represented by the Muslim Conference. The Muslims will welcome the Maharaja Bahadur as the first constitutional ruler of independent and democratic Kashmir.

Forces and Actors on the eve of Indian Independence

Thus, on the eve of the country's Independence, a number of forces were operating on the political firmament of the State. There was the National Conference headed by Sheikh Mohammad Abdullah. It dominated the Valley but had only limited influence in Jammu and Ladakh. It had developed close rapport with the leaders of the Indian National Congress, particularly Jawaharlal Nehru, but its equation with the Muslim League was marked by hostility. Mirwaiz Moulvi

Yusaf Shah, who had wild and fanatical following in the downtown area of Srinagar city, was antagonistic both to the National Conference and to the Congress. Then, there was the Muslim Conference which had little following in the Valley but had acquired rapid strength amongst the Muslims of the Jammu region during the last two years on account of its ideological affinity with the Muslim League, which had the potential of spreading its influence in the Valley also. Voices for independent Kashmir were also being raised here and there. The Maharaja was yet another force. The Dogra Rajputs of Jammu considered him their own kith and kin. The relations between him on the one hand and Sheikh Abdullah and Pandit Nehru on the other were marked by mutual distrust and dislike. None of the three leaders was able to rise above his pride and prejudices while taking vital decisions in regard to the future of the State.

All these forces and actors were soon to play their part in the first act of the tragic Kashmir drama. The Maharaja was indecisive. Jinnah was impatient. Pandit Nehru was caught in between his idealism and the stark realities of the situation. Sheikh Abdullah, with streaks of megalomania and duplicity embedded deep in the layers of his mind and with Jinnah's doors closed to him, was nursing secret ambitions to carve out a Sheikhdom for himself and his coterie. It appeared that all these actors were pushed on the stage with illusions of their own. Each one of them imagined different outlines of the plot and believed that the drama would end the way he desired. Consequently, there was confusion and inconsistency on the stage. Mistakes after mistakes were made. One jarring note was followed by another. One miscalculation gave rise to another. And Kashmir soon found itself in the whirlpool of national and international controversy and conflict.

First Mistake: Flirtation with the Idea of Independence

The first grave mistake was made when Maharaja Hari Singh flirted with the idea of independence. With the passage of the Indian Independence Act (1947) and consequent lapse of paramountcy, the princely States were technically free.* But, in practice, the only option open to them was to accede either to India or Pakistan. In June 1947,

*The Indian National Conference, in its resolution of June 1947, contested the view of paramountcy. It said: "The relationship between the Government of India and the States would not be exhausted by lapse of paramountcy. The lapse does not lead to the independence of the States."

Lord Mountbatten paid a four-day visit to Kashmir. He advised the Maharaja to make up his mind. But the Maharaja dodged him. In the meeting to be held on the day of Mountbatten's departure, the issue was to be finally discussed. The Maharaja pretended an attack of colic, and the meeting was cancelled. In this connection, Mountbatten later recalled: "On every one of those four days, I persisted with the same advice: ascertain the will of your people by any means and join whichever Dominion your people wish to join by August 14 this year, He did not do that, and what happened can be seen. Had he acceded to Pakistan before August 14, the future government of India had allowed me to give His Highness an assurance that no objection whatever would be raised by them. Had His Highness acceded to India by August 14, Pakistan did not then exist, and therefore could not have interfered. The only trouble that could have been raised was by non-accession to either side, and this was unfortunately the very course followed by the Maharaja."*

Mahatma Gandhi also came to Srinagar in July-August 1947. He called upon the Maharaja on August 1. Except that Mahatma Gandhi advised the Maharaja not to remain in conflict with his people, nothing is clearly known about the conversation between the two. But if Gandhi's mission was to persuade the Maharaja to make up his mind one way or the other, he failed to achieve his objective. The only visible fall-out of the visit was the replacement of Prime Minister R.C. Kak by Major-General Janak Singh on August 10.

Gandhi's visit to Kashmir in July-August 1947, his meeting with the Maharaja on August 1, dismissal of R.C. Kak from the office of Prime Minister on August 10, release of Sheikh Abdullah on September 29, after tendering an 'unqualified apology' in his letter of September 26, strengthening of the road link between Pathankot and Jammu, and the scheme to construct a boat bridge over the river Ravi, all would seem to suggest that ground was being prepared for accession of the State to India; at least, the possibility was not being ruled out. There is, however, no hard evidence to support the Pakistani charge that a 'sinister design' had been worked out by India to secure the accession of the State. This charge, in fact, stands refuted not only by the assertion of Lord Mountbatten but also by the unambiguo us statement of three services Chiefs of India who were all British, namely, General R.M. Lockhart, Chief of the Indian Army;

***Time Only To Look Forward: Mountbatten's Speeches.*

Air Marshal T.W. Elmhirst, Commander of the Royal Indian Air Force; and Rear Admiral J.T.S. Hall, Chief of the Royal Indian Navy. In a joint statement,* they said:

> On 24 October the Commander-in-Chief, Indian Army, received information that tribesmen had seized Muzaffarabad. This was the first indication of the raid.
>
> Prior to this date, no plans of any sort for sending Indian tosses into Kashmir had been formulated or even considered.

In any case, if option of Kashmir's accession to India was being kept open, there was nothing wrong in it. India never accepted the two-nation theory. It was justified in believing that if both the Maharaja and Sheikh Abdullah, who at that time had the support of the Valley people, had expressed desire to join the Union, it would have demonstrated the hollowness of the two-nation theory. The issue was largely one of ideology and the Indian perspective, and not of territorial extension. The tragedy of India lay not in the conceptual framework, but in being wayward and impractical in execution.

India's 'tryst with destiny' arrived on August 14-15. To reword Jawaharlal Nehru's historic words, at the stroke of midnight when the world slept, India woke to light and freedom. But in Kashmir, the Maharaja was having his dreams of independence–dreams that had been planted in his mind by ambitious advisers and flatterers. The only thing of note that happened on that day was special illumination of Srinagar, Jammu and Leh to celebrate the birth of the two dominions of India and Pakistan and retrocession of paramountcy.

Clearly, Maharaja Hari Singh was badly advised. Prime Minister Ram Chandra Kak and 'Raj Guru' Swami Sant Dev had planted the idea of independence in his mind. The Swami was the prototype of the present-day 'godmen' who, notwithstanding their apparent fraudulent claims, exercised, to the misfortune of the country, considerable influence over the minds of some of the top politicians of the country. I learnt quite a few things about this Swami. He lived in the house which is presently Srinagar Raj Bhavan. Earlier, it was a palace which the Maharaja had specially built for his fourth wife, mother of Dr. Karan Singh. Subsequently, many celebrities, including Tej Bahadur Sapru and Gopalaswamy Ayyangar, occupied this house. Afterwards it became a Government guest house. It was a favourite

*Josef Korbel: *Dangers in Kashmir*.

haunt of Jawaharlal Nehru during his visits to Kashmir, as it provided a fascinating sunset-scene over the Dal Lake with the last few rays of the sun shimmering through Hari Parbat and Shankaracharya Hill. That such a palace, with a car and many other facilities, was made available to Swami Sant Dev, was an index of his influence over the Maharaja. It was the Swami who had predicted to the Maharaja that a still brighter future awaited him, implying thereby that he would, with the lapse of paramountcy, become independent. Like the 'weird sisters' in *Macbeth*, the Swami appeared to have won the Maharaja with his "honest trifles only to betray him in greater consequences". The poor Maharaja lost even what he had before August 1947. Interestingly, when the Maharaja left Srinagar for Jammu at 2 a.m. on October 27 in a great hurry he found that the Swami, who had been advising him to stay at Srinagar, was going ahead of the caravan.

In response to the telegram of August 12 from the Prime Minister of J&K, Pakistan agreed to enter into a 'Standstill Agreement' with it with effect from August 15, 1947. An offer of a similar agreement was made to India, but the latter sought some clarifications and asked for more time. But the plan to grab J&K by force was already taking shape in Pakistan. The 'Standstill Agreement' was violated. The State was subjected to an effective economic blockade, causing acute scarcity of essential commodities.

Lapses

A grave crisis was in the offing. It was an inevitable consequence of a series of lapses on the part of the state and central authorities. In entertaining the idea of 'independent state', Maharaja Hari Singh showed little understanding of the international power politics that had emerged in the post-Second World War and rapidly decolonizing world. For a strategically located state, such as J&K, it was virtually impossible to escape being a zone of conflicts between the two power-blocks, the Anglo-American and the Soviet Russia, or even to survive subterfuge of Pakistan.

The Maharaja also failed to keep in mind that the game of partition of India had been played by Britain to safeguard its geo-strategic interests in Afghanistan and Central Asia. Nor did he realize that Jinnah could be quite ruthless in his approach and deploy the 'direct-action' strategy which had paid rich dividend to him in attaining his goal of Pakistan. Unfortunately, the Maharaja, at a crucial turning point in the history of J&K, chose to grope in the world of his own make-belief. A deeper understanding of the emerging conditions, and not lending his ears to the flatterers and manipulators, would have enabled him to see that the best course for him, his subjects and the country as a whole, was to straightway accede to the dominion of India. But he continued to dither.

Apart from Prime Minister R.C. Kak who, in quite a few quarters, was believed to have been working surreptitiously for the State's accession to Pakistan, the background of highly acrimonious relations between the Maharaja and Nehru was another inhibiting factor. Neither of the two was able to rise above his bias. For Nehru, the Maharaja was a figure of 'blind hate' and Sheikh Mohammad Abdullah an attractive 'buddy' who had to be pleased at all costs. On the Maharaja's side, Nehru's 'supercilious disregard' of Hindu-Dogra's feelings was beyond tolerance.

By the time the stark realities at the ground-level dawned upon both Nehru and Maharaja, and corrective measures were taken up with the urgency that was warranted, substantial damage had been done. Pakistan's plan to destabilise the State's civil administration and scatter its armed forces along the border had come into operation. The range of this plan was enlarged and deepened, when Jinnah's overtures* to tempt Maharaja Hari Singh to accede to Pakistan did not cut any ice. Communal passions were worked up and incitement to subversion intensified. With the stronger dozes of lethal frenzy being injected daily in the atmosphere, the conditions in Jammu region, which were by and large peaceful till September 1947, turned bloody and brutal. The next few weeks were replete with grim tragedies – attacks and counter-attacks by communities.

A contemporaneous and candid account of tragic happenings of this genre would be found in the letter** written by the State Prime Minister Mehar Chand Mahajan in respect of Mahatma Gandhi's remarks made on December 27, 1947, in his post-prayer speech,

* These overtures were made to Prime Minister M.C. Mahajan through Major Shah, an emissary and confidant of Jinnah, who was ostensibly in Kashmir as a tourist. p. 142: M.C. Mahajan: *Looking Back*.

**This letter, from the point of view of historical perspective, is significant. It reveals not only the background in which the story of the so called Poonch Revolt was weaved, but also the vacillation, on the part of key leaders, both at the state and central level , which caused many a sided confusion in the process of decision making. It also shows a fatal proclivity of Sheikh Abdullah to resort to intentional disinformation to secure his personal ambitions and serve his ends of power. M.C. Mahajan: *Looking Back*. p. 159.

about the killings and abductions of Muslims in Jammu province. The following extracts from this letter speak for themselves:

> It seems to me that the speech has been made on a false representation of facts. I am sure you will revise your opinion on knowing the true state of affairs. ...A very large number of Hindus and Sikhs were killed and their women abducted. It is also true that a considerable number of Muslims were killed and a number of their women were abducted. The wave of insanity that prevailed in the East and West Punjab took hold of the State territory. ...Muslims suffered the most in parts of Udhampur and Riasi Districts and in parts of Kathua and Jammu Districts. ...The Muslim population in a part of the Riasi District on the side of the Chenab, in Bhadarwa and Kishtwar and in the Rajouri area became very aggressive. In these parts the Hindu and Sikh population has been practically wiped out and a very large number of their women have been abducted and are in the possession of the local Muslim population. In the Mirpur District, the Hindu and Sikh population has been exterminated. ...It was not humanly possible to stop all that took place when men had become insane and started behaving like jungle animals...

Clearly, the post-prayer-speech remarks of Mahatma Gandhi were the outcome of false complaints of Sheikh Abdullah and his coterie against Maharaja Hari Singh and his Prime Minister Mehar Chand Mahajan. The motivation was to ease out Mahajan from the State and reduce the power of the Maharaja to that of a titular head. Such engineered complaints were, later on, used by Pakistan to prop up a handy narrative with regard to the so called revolt in the Poonch and Jammu regions of the State'.

'Poonch Revolt'

There was, in fact, no such revolt. Stray processions and protests, dovetailed to violent incidents, arising out of communal disturbances, spelt out above in M.C. Mahajan's letter to Mahatma Gandhi, were counted as ingredients of the 'revolt'.* The narrative was designed to

*In any case the observations made by the protagonists of the 'Poonch Revolt' - have been too vague to carry conviction. For example, Alastair Lamb, in his book, *Crisis in Kashmir, 1947 to 1966*, satisfies himself by saying: "The Poonch rebels *appears* to have soon established contact with tribal country, where they sought aid in arms. ...At the outset the Poonch rising *appears* to have been less a communal than an attempt to overthrow the oppressive rule of the Maharaja".

provide an excuse for letting loose on Kashmir a large army of religiously aroused wild tribals called Lashkars.* These Lashkars were under the spell of mystic and fanatic tribal leaders, such as Pir of Manki Sharief. They were fed with false stories of atrocities 'committed' by the Hindus and Maharaja's troops on the Muslims of Poonch and Jammu regions. In dissemination of this falsehood and in engineering commotion and violence here and there, prominent role was played by two pro-Pakistan leaders of the region–Sardar Mohammad Ibrahim, a lawyer, and Abdul Qayyum Khan, a member of the landed gentry . It is they and their ring-masters in Pakistan who talked incessantly of the revolt against the oppressive rule of the Maharaja, without caring to explain how the pain of oppression was suddenly felt in August-September, 1947, and that, too, near the border. The real purpose of the narrative was to give a cover to the wholly unprovoked and unjustified attack on the valley for which clandestine preparations were already on. As rightly pointed out by Vincent Sheean, "By September 1947, the Pathan tribals had been converging on the borders of J&K".**

Deceitful Belligerency

An incisive reading, in between the lines, of what Maj. General Akbar Khan had recorded in his book, *Raiders in Kashmir*,*** should leave no one in doubt that, by way of an informal and 'secret militarialy structured support', a plan for tribal invasion and forcible occupation of the State had been worked out. At the instance of a top Muslim League leader of Pakistan, Mian Iftikharuddin, the plan was drawn up by Akbar Khan. It was approved at the high-level meeting, chaired by Prime Minister Liaquat Ali Khan at Lahore, in the first few days of October 1947. The immediate operational requirements were attended to. About 4000 rifles and huge quantity of ammunition were made available from the Army/Police stores. 'The Prime Minister also promised to obtain some light machine guns from a war dump in Italy'. 'Help from Pakistan Air Force also started coming in, in the shape of winter clothing, ammunition and some weapons'. 'Commi-ssioner of Rawalpindi was another enthusiast who was busy collecting

* Lashkar is a unit of traditional fighting force of tribesmen. Each unit has generally a strength of 1000.

** Vicent Sheean : *Nehru – 10 years of Power.*

*** Maj. General Akbar Khan: *Raiders in Kashmir*. Army Publishers, Delhi.

funds, rations, weapons'.* Khan Abdul Qayyam Khan, the Chief Minister of North-West Frontier Province, was no less active in providing arms, ammunition, motor transport and fuel to the tribesmen and other invaders.

By October 20, 1947 Lashkars comprising about 5000 tribesmen had been mobilised. The number was mentioned in the telegram which the Commander-in-Chief of India received from his Pakistani counterpart about the attack and occupation of Muzzaffarabad and Domel by tribesmen. Obviously, the plan prepared by Akbar Khan, the decisions taken at the Prime Minister Liaquat Ali Khan's Lahore meeting and the follow-up action in the military and civil arenas had been kept as a closely guarded secret. The Commander-in-Chief of Pakistan, a British officer, remained unaware of all that was being worked out to grab the State of J&K. However, in the ultimate analysis, Pakistan's sinister hand in invading the valley was too pervasive, too glaring, to be covered by the fig-leaf of 'Poonch revolt', the incidents attributed to which, as brought out in earlier section of this Chapter, were largely a spill over of Punjab disturbances and both-way movement of refugees through Jammu region.

As J&K State's accession to India came to be known on the morning of October 27, 1947, another high level meeting presided over by Pakistan Prime Minister Liaquat Ali Khan was held the same evening. Like the earlier one, this meeting was termed as unofficial and top secret. Amongst various considerations of strategy, the proposal of Akbar Khan to snap the only road-link from India to Kathua-Jammu was discussed: "I suggested only that tribesmen may be allowed to make the attempt. I thought that three Lashkaras of a thousand each should be used. The tribesmen were available and I offered to go with them".** An important decision taken in this meeting was to set up a Liberation Committee of which Akbar Khan was a key member. He was also designated as Military Adviser to the Prime Minister.

Aggressive and Domineering.

From day one, Nehru was convinced that invasion by the tribesmen had full assistance of Pakistani authorities. It had been planned and

* The statements put within single inverted comas here would be found on pages 15, 16, 19 and 20 of Akbar Khan's book, titled *Raiders in Kashmir*.

**All this, too, has been mentioned in Akbar Khan's book on pages 27 and 28. On page 27, it has also been stated: "The same evening the first Provisional Government of Azad Kashmir came into existence, with Sardar Ibrahim as President."

finalised, at least a fortnight earlier than it began with all its pitiless fury. Again, in the month of December 1947 when, amidst comparatively calmer battle fronts, Pakistan tried to occupy Uri again, Nehru burst out in anger against its deceitful belligerency: "The only inference to draw from this is that the invasion of Kashmir is not an accidental affair resulting from the fanaticism or exuberance of the tribesmen but a well-organised business with the backing of the state. The present objective is Kashmir. The next declared objective is Patiala, East Punjab and Delhi. On to Delhi is the cry all over West Punjab". Nehru could not have been more expressive of his inner feelings about Pakistan's aggressive and domineering outlook.

With regard to the internal conditions emerging in the state at that time, an idea can be formed from the report published in Tribune of October 23, 1947 which stated:

> "Pakistan had been developing Hitlerian appetite and Hitlerian strength. Not a day passes when reports do not come indicating that Pakistan's intentions are acquisitive and its plans are aggressive. West Punjab and Frontier Pakistani crusaders, masquerading as pleasure seekers, had poured into the Valley and besides carrying on subtle poisonous propaganda were organizing 'stabbers and fire-raisers' squads. Menacingly, Jinnah caps were visible everywhere."

Simultaneously, military skirmishes all along the border from Gilgit to Mirpur were manipulated to disperse the State forces, the total strength of which was only nine infantry battalions and two mountain batteries. On October 22, as briefly indicated earlier, a full-scale tribal invasion, backed by Pakistan regulars, was launched. The tribesmen*, comprising Afridis and Mahsuds and the Pakistani regulars, the 'volunteers' and the 'freedom fighters' were all operating under the overall command of Akbar Khan, a Major General in Pakistani army, who was given the code name of 'General Tariq'.** The State Administration was so unprepared that it could not destroy the vital Krishan-Ganga bridge at Muzzaffarabad for want of dynamite. Muzzaffarabad fell on October 23. The Maharaja realized the gravity of the situation. On October 24, he

* These tribesmen were known as the hardest and the cruelest fighters in the world.

**Tariq was a Moorish warrior who fought heroically in Spain for the cause of Islam.

approached the Government of India for assistance. On the same day, the Mohara power station was captured by the raiders and Srinagar city was plunged into darkness. The following day, V.P. Menon, Secretary of the Ministry of States, flew to Srinagar to assess the situation. Menon noted the "stillness of the graveyard all round". At the Maharaja's Palace, Lieutenant Colonel Sam Manekshah, who accompanied Menon as a sort of Military Attache, remarked: "I had never seen such disorganisation in my life".

Accession

Consequent upon the discussions with V.P. Menon, immediate help was sought from the Government of India by the Maharaja and accession to it offered. In his letter of October 26 to Lord Mountbatten, Maharaja Hari Singh said:

> With the conditions obtaining at present in my State and the great emergency of the situation as it exists, I have no option but to ask for help from the Indian Dominion. Naturally they cannot send the help asked for by me without my State acceding to the Dominion of India. I have accordingly decided to do so and I attach the Instrument of Accession for acceptance by your Government.

Accepting the* accession, Lord Mountbatten wrote to the Maharaja on October 27:

> 'In the special circumstances mentioned by Your Highness, my Government have decided to accept the accession of Kashmir State to the Dominion of India. It is my Government's wish that, as soon as law and order have been restored in Kashmir and her soil cleared of the invaders, the question of the State's accession should be settled by a reference to the people. Meanwhile, in response to Your Highness's appeal for military aid, action has been taken today to send troops of the Indian Army to Kashmir to help your own forces to defend your territory and to protect the lives, property and honour of your people.'

Saving the State

In the developments from October 22 onwards, time was the most crucial factor. Every minute mattered. The State forces under the

*See also Appendix XX.

command of Brigadier Rajinder Singh, though hampered by large-scale desertions of Muslim troops, fought to the "last man and last bullet" at Uri delaying the advance of the main horde of raiders for two crucial days. The Uri bridge was also destroyed by the retreating force, thereby gaining another one day. Brigadier Rajinder Singh died like a hero and made an invaluable contribution in saving the State. The Maharaja got the time to seek and obtain India's help.

Baramulla fell into the hands of the raiders on October 24-26. Overtaken by their wild habits, they indulged in large-scale looting, burning, raping and killing. As noted by Father Shanks, "The tribesmen–great, wild, black beasts they were–came shooting their way down from the hills on both sides of the town. A 20-year old Indian nurse, Philomena, tried to protect a Muslim patient whose baby had just been born. She was shot dead first. The patient was next".* Even the St. Joseph Convent was destroyed, and the Assistant Mother Superior and three nuns were brutally murdered. After visiting Baramulla, the correspondent of the *New York Times* wrote, "Surviving residents estimate that 3,000 of their fellow townsmen, including four Europeans and a retired British officer and his pregnant wife, were slain." The raiders hardly realised that the time spent by them in committing their abominable crimes would turn out to be their punishment, as it enabled the Indian forces to land at Srinagar airport on October 27 and ultimately push back the raiders inflicting heavy casualties on them.

On October 27, a few planes of the Indian Air Force hovered over Srinagar airport carrying the first batch of Indian troops under the command of Lt.-Colonel Ranjit Rai. It was not certain whether the airport was still held by the State Forces. After landing, Lt.-Colonel Rai led the small contingent of the troops towards Baramulla. He dug his defences at Pattan and engaged the raiders near Baramulla. He lost his life in this bold venture. But this unnerved the raiders. They thought that the Indian Army had arrived in strength.

In another bold move, Major Somnath Sharma engaged the raiders at Badgam as they had reached very near the airport (November 3). He was outnumbered 7 to 1. But he showed unbounded courage and inflicted heavy casualties on the enemy. He was killed. He was awarded Param Vir Chakra posthumously, the first Indian to have received the highest gallantry award of the land. In the meantime,

*Korbel: *Dangers in Kashmir,* p. 76.

reinforcements arrived, and the airport was secured. The sacrifice of three brave soldiers–Lt.-Colonel Ranjit Rai, Major Somnath Sharma and Brigadier Rajinder Singh–made an unforgettable contribution in saving Kashmir.

No less heroic was the organizational initiative and drive shown by Sardar Patel. When the raiders were on the outskirts of Srinagar and Lt. Col. Ranjit Rai and Major Somnath Sharma of the Indian Army had been killed, being heavily outnumbered, Patel, accompanied by Defence Minister Baldev Singh, flew to the State capital, assessed the situation on the ground, and on return to New Delhi ordered stoppage of all airline services and diversion of all planes for flying troops to Srinagar. The timely arrival of reinforcements enabled Brigadier Sen to lure the raiders in the net of Indian forces, near Shaltang, and attack them on November 5 from three sides, with Indian Air Force lending support. The raiders were routed. They retreated in panic. Three hundred of them were killed. The battle of Shaltang (November 7) proved decisive. It removed all threats to Srinagar. Three days afterwards, advancing Indian troops recaptured Baramullah. But for the shortage of petrol which halted their advance at the crucial moment, they would have also got back Mirpur and Muzzaffarabad. The process of retreat by the enemy on almost all fronts had begun.

In the north of the Valley, Gilgit, a strategic area cradled by the mighty Himalayas and Karakoram, was grabbed by Pakistan. The British-Indian Government had virtually forced the Maharaja in March 1935 to give this strategic area to it on lease for sixty years. With the impending lapse of paramountcy and the British declaration to give back the possession to the Maharaja, he sent Brigadier Ghanshara Singh as Governor of Gilgit. At the instigation of Pakistan, the Muslim army officers mutinied on October 31 and took the Governor prisoner. The Garrison Commander, Major Brown, a British officer, hoisted the Pakistani flag formally on November 4.

Many Dogra officers did not comprehend the new reality. They did not realise that the propaganda of the Muslim League had overtaken the professional loyalty and discipline of their Muslim troops. Col. Hari Singh, for example, was ordered to disarm his Muslim troops. He frowned upon the very idea. He could not imagine that his comrades-in-arms who had fought side by side with him in World War II would betray him. But they did. Col. Hari Singh paid with his life for his lack of a correct appreciation of the situation. He was murdered while asleep.

The Pakistani raiders also made a determined bid to occupy Ladakh. But it was saved by the superior strategy and grit of the Indian military and air force. In this regard, two daring actions deserve special mention. One was the amazing feat of Air Commodore Mehar Singh to fly his plane on May 24, 1948, at 23,000 feet above the sea level without oxygen on a hitherto uncharted course and landing at the rough strip of Leh airport located at the height of 11,555 feet. This enabled the Indian forces to be airlifted to Leh and build up defence for Ladakh which was at the mercy of the enemy. The second unique feat was of Major-General Thimayya who took his tanks to snow-covered Zojila Pass at the height of 11,578 feet on November 1, 1948. His officers surprised the raiders and destroyed 25 of their bunkers. Demoralised, they ran away in a hurry. General Thimayya's feat has been compared to Hannibal crossing the Alps with his elephants. Till that time no one in history had taken tanks to such a height in such hazardous conditions.

To United Nations: Another Mistake

On January 1, 1948, India took the case to the United Nations. On January 12, to provide a smoke-screen to Pakistani aggression, Sardar Ibrahim Khan, President of Azad Kashmir, declared that 99,000 volunteers were being trained to liberate Kashmir.

Taking the case to the United Nations was yet another mistake. The case got enmeshed in the international power politics. At every stage, India faced rough weather. And Kashmir became almost a permanent item on the agenda of the United Nations. As a backdrop, it needs to be underlined that, in this respect, too, Sardar Patel had tried to put the trajectory of events in the right orbit. He bemoaned disposition of Mountbatten and Nehru to seek intervention of the United Nations. He was perturbed to see the text of the radio broadcast of October 28, 1947 which carried India's declaration to hold plebiscite under the U.N. auspices. In the words of V. Shankar*, "Sardar Patel noticed the embarrassing commitment. He commissioned me to go to the Broadcasting House and ask Pandit Nehru to delete the offending phrase 'under U.N. auspices' but to retain the commitment made at the time of accession, namely that the wishes of the people would be ascertained. I made haste to go to the Broadcasting House but by the

*V. Shankar : My Reminiscences of Sardar Patel. p. 133.

time I reached there, Pandit Nehru had already begun his broadcast* and in a few minutes the deed was done. That commitment has ever since been a millstone round our necks." Patel was also against Gopalaswamy Ayyangar being sent as leader of the Indian delegation to the UN and Sheikh Abdullah as member. He preferred Sir Girja Shankar Bajpai to the former; about the latter, he feared that the "Sheikh's flamboyant personality might easily swamp the boat."

India's complaint was made under Chapter VI of The Charter of the United Nations, which pertains to 'Pacific Settlement of Disputes', and not under Chapter VII, which relates to 'Action with Respect to Threats to Peace, Breaches of the Peace, and Acts of Aggression'. Initially Indian approach was rather mild. Later on, however, she became more assertive, and insisted upon vacation of aggressive Pakistan. She underlined:

> Since the aid which the invaders are receiving from Pakistan is an act of aggression against India, the Government of India are entitled, in international law, to send their armed forces across Pakistan territory for dealing effectively with the invaders.

But, in the absence of reference under Chapter VII, the Security Council could find grounds to take its own time. Even otherwise, its handling of the situation savoured of timidity and procrastination.

Pakistan refuted the Indian allegations. Its Foreign Minister, Sir Zafrullah Khan, stated before the Security Council, "The Pakistan Government emphatically deny that they are giving aid and assistance to the so-called invaders or have committed any act of aggression against India." But when the United Nations Commission on India and Pakistan, which was set up in pursuance of the UN Security Council resolution of April 17, 1948, arrived at Karachi, Pakistan admitted the presence of its troops 'since May' and 'in self-defence'. Sir Owen Dixon, who later became representative of the United Nations in place of the Commission on India and Pakistan, observed: "When the frontier of the State of J&K was crossed by the hostile elements, it was contrary to international law and when, in May 1948,

*In another broadcast on November 2, 1947, Nehru reiterated: "We are prepared when peace and law and order have been established to have a referendum held under the international auspices like the United Nations. We want it to be a fair and just referendum to the people, and we shall accept their verdict. I can imagine no fairer and juster offer."

Kashmir White Paper. op. cit. pp. 52-55.

units of the regular Pakistan forces moved into the territory of the State, that too was inconsistent with international law."

The United Nations Security Council passed four resolutions on Kashmir. The first, of January 1948, merely urged the two Governments to take measures to improve the situation. The second resolution, of April 17, 1948, recommended setting up of a 5-member Commission "to proceed to the subcontinent and there place their good offices and mediation at the disposal of the Governments of India and Pakistan". The third resolution, of August 13, 1948, was the most significant. It has been reproduced in Appendix V. This resolution has three parts. Part I related to the 'cease-fire'. Part II made it incumbent upon Pakistan to withdraw all its forces, regular and irregular, while India was required to reduce the strength of its forces. And Part III said, "The Government of India and the Government of Pakistan reaffirm their wish that the future status of J&K shall be determined in accordance with the will of the people and to that end, upon acceptance of the Truce Agreement, both Governments agree to enter into consultation with the Commission to determine fair and equitable conditions whereby such free expression of the will be assured." The fourth resolution was merely a supplement to the third resolution.

The subsequent stand of the Government of India was that the question of taking up of Part III would arise after the provisions of Part I and Part II were carried out. In this regard, it also needs to be noted that before India agreed to 'cease fire' with effect from January 1, 1949, some assurances were given to it during the course of discussions and correspondence with the UN Commission for India and Pakistan. These assurances have been listed in Appendix VI. It will be seen that one of the assurances was that "the plebiscite proposal shall not be binding upon India if Pakistan does not implement Part I and Part II of the resolution of August 13, 1948".

On March 21, 1949, Admiral Nimitz was designated Plebiscite Administrator. The United Nations Military Observers were also deputed to assist in settling the cease-fire line and supervising it. On July 27, 1949, the karachi Agreement was drawn up on the basis of which the cease-fire line was delineated and ancillary points settled.

Separately, the President of the Security Council, General McNaughten, proposed large-scale demilitarisation of the entire area. As this proposal equated India with Pakistan, that is, the aggressor and the victim of aggression, and virtually ignored the fact that the accession of J&K to India was legal and complete–the fact which the Legal Adviser of the UN Commission fully conceded–India rejected it. The McNaughten proposal was also not compatible with the Security Council resolution of August 13, 1948.

On March 14, 1950, the Security Council decided to appoint a representative of the Commission to carry out its work. Sir Owen Dixon was the first holder of this assignment. He formulated, after discussions with the parties involved, what is known as the 'Dixon Plan'. This plan envisaged virtual partition of the State. Dixon held that the entire area could be divided into three regions: (i) the region about which there was no doubt that it wished to accede to India; (ii) the region which undoubtedly wished union with Pakistan; and (iii) the region in respect of which there could be doubt about its wishes. He recommended that plebiscite should be held only in regard to the region falling in the third category.

The Dixon Plan was rejected by both India and Pakistan. In April 1951, the Security Council appointed another representative, Dr. Graham. He laboured for two. But his recommendations, too, were rejected by both the countries. And the stalemate* continued.

From 1954 onward, India persistently invited the attention of the world community to the material change that had taken place in the situation consequent upon Pakistan's acceptance of military aid from the USA and also her becoming a member of the western bloc. At the initial stage of the discussions at the United Nations, the USSR adopted a lukewarm attitude. This was the time when Jawaharlal Nehru was being described as the "running dog of the western imperialism". Later on, however, when the cold war between the two major power blocs intensified and Pakistan moved into the western bloc, India received strong support from the USSR. In January 1952, the Soviet delegate to the Security Council accused the USA and the UK of interfering in the internal affairs of Kashmir and declared that the Constituent Assembly of the State would solve the problem. The Soviet support became absolutely firm and clear during the course of the Bulganin and Khrushchev visit to Kashmir, in December 1955. The latter declared: "The question of Kashmir as one of the States of India has already been decided by the people of Kashmir."

*This stalemate, viewed in conjunction with Shimla Agreement (see page 104), implies divisions, on ground, of thc erstwhile princely State into four areas. The legal status and other details of these are given in Appendix XXI.

The endeavors of Dr. Frank P. Graham, who had been appointed to succeed Sir Own Dixon as Representative of the United Nations in 1951, to evolve a satisfactory formula for demilitarization of the State did not produce any tangible results. India remained firm in repulsing any proposition which equated the 'aggressor, Pakistan, with the victim of aggression'. The intractable realities of the two opposing view points virtually ended in a deadlock.

It was only after four years that the Security Council deliberated upon the issue again, when Pakistan objected to the resolution of the Constituent Assembly of Jammu and Kashmir, which declared that 'the State of Jammu and Kashmir is and shall be an integral part of the Union of India'. Attempts were made in 1957 and then again in 1962 to make both Pakistan and India to agree to mediation. But these proved as barren as the earlier ones. Eventually, in June 1962, an Irish resolution, brought before the Security Council with the backing of Western power block, was vetoed by Soviet Russia.

During the 1957 and 1962 debates in the Security Council, India encountered criticism. But the head of Indian delegation, Krishna Menon* used the opportunity to do some plain speaking. He beamed the searchlight on Pakistan's aggression and fearlessly exposed the "imperialists' game". He regretted: "Here, the politics of power alignments, religious fanaticism, personal antagonism, take precedence over the fundamental principles of UN Charter." With equal emphasis, he brought home the double-standards of Pakistan and its supporters: "Why is it that we have never heard voices in connection with the freedom of the people under the suppression and tyranny of Pakistani authorities on the other side of the cease-fire line? Why is it that we have not heard here that in ten years, these people have not seen a ballot paper? With what voice can either the Security Council or any one coming before it demand a plebiscite for a people on our side who exercise franchise?"

Menon countered the argument about India's commitment to hold a plebiscite: "The commitment about a plebiscite is usually spoken of as though it were the law of the Medes and Persians, but what does it amount to? It amounts to an expression of a wish on the part of the

*The quotes, put within the inverted comas, are based on Krishna Menon Speeches on Kashmir at the United Nations in 1957 and 1962, published by Sanchar Publishing House, in association with Krishna Menon National Memorial Committee, and edited by E.S. Reddy and A.K. Damodaran.

two Governments. The expression of a wish is far less than what may be called an international obligation."

Krishna Menon did not evade the issue of plebiscite. Instead, he laid bare its limitations. He elaborated that self-determination in the case of J&K would be nothing but a religious self-determination which would be wholly incompatible with the secular polity of India. He underlined: "We refuse to recognise what is called the two-nation theory. We are not a theocracy. Whether it be in Pakistan or India, whether they be Hindus, Muslims, Christians, their ancestries are pretty much the same."

In respect of each and every material point concerning the Kashmir issue, Menon took the battle to the opponents' court and showed that, in dealing with Pakistan and its mentors, offence was the best part of defence. He did not succeed–nobody could–in moulding the attitude of the super-powers at the Security Council. But, at home, he 'set millions of pulses racing' and filled them with a sense of pride. Even his "caustic tongue and imperial disdain" were taken as an expression of national self-assertion.

Political Developments

While the matter was dragging on at the international level, the events moved swiftly in J&K and a momentous change took place. With the accession of the State to India, Sheikh Abdullah was first appointed by the Maharaja to head what was called the Emergency Administration. On March 4, 1948, he was appointed the Prime Minister with a Council of Ministers. He came to acquire practically all the executive powers of the government. As a political analyst put it, "Where the Maharaja was required to be consulted, he was bullied; and where he was needed to be informed, he was ignored." In whatever he did, reasonable or unreasonable, he was supported by Jawaharlal Nehru, much to the chagrin of Sardar Patel. The Maharaja was exasperated not only by the proceedings at the United Nations but also by the agressive* attitude of Sheikh Abdullah. On January 31, 1948, he sent a letter to the Home Minister in which he expressed his frustration in these words:

> There is an alternative possible for me and that is to withdraw the Accession and that may kill the reference to the UNO because

*After M.A. Jinnah's death in September 1948, Sheikh Abdullah's attitude became more aggressive. He thought that his bargaining power vis-a-vis India had improved.

> Indian Union will have no right to continue the proceedings before the Council if the Accession is withdrawn. The result may be a return to the position the State held before the Accession.

Complaining to the Home Minister about the insulting attitude of the Sheikh, the Maharaja in his letter of April 20, 1948, said:

> I refer to the wild and baseless allegations that are being made against me that I left the Capital at the dead of night and removed truckloads of furniture and other belongings. I would ordinarily have dismissed these allegations but, to my great regret and profound shock, they have found expression in some of the utterances of my present Prime Minister.

In another letter of May 6, 1949, to Sardar Patel, the Maharaja said:

> Nor would it be fair on my part to conceal from you my own feeling that while Sheikh Abdullah has been allowed to depart from time to time as suited his inclinations from the pledged and written word, to act consistently in breach of the loyalty which he professed to me prior to his release from jail and the oath of allegiance which he took when he assumed office, and to indulge openly along with his colleagues in a campaign of vilification and foul calumny against me, both inside the State and outside, I should have had to be driven from position to position–each of which I thought I held on the advice of the State's Ministry.

The Maharaja was eventually humbled and made to leave the State. Shorn of its veil, it was a case of forced abdication. On June 20th, 1949, the Maharaja issued a proclamation vesting all his powers in Yuvraj Karan Singh. Sheikh Abdullah took Karan Singh for granted and went on taking all sorts of decisions even when there was no elected legislature to whom he could be responsible.

Constitutional Relationship

A special status was accorded to the State by way of Article 370*–the Article which has been a matter of controversy ever since. The State was also to have its own Constitution. Though this Constitution was finally adopted on January 26, 1957, its motivation and objectives were spelt out in the National Conference resolution of October 27, 1950. This resolution said:

---

*See Chapter VI: 'Roots: Article 370'.

We view with great concern the repeated failure of the United Nations to redress the wrongs of aggression of which the people of the State continue to be victims. The failure, in its opinion, is due to the continued concessions given to Pakistan by placing a premium on her intransigence. The time has come when the initiative must be regained by the people to put an end to this indeterminate state of drift and indecision.

On May 1, 1951, the Yuvraj issued a proclamation instituting the Constituent Assembly which would be elected from electoral districts to be carved out on the basis of one district for every segment of 40,000 population. Elections were held in the middle of October 1951. All the 75 seats were won by the National Conference–73 unopposed and two after contest. The Jammu Praja Parishad boycotted these elections. On October 31, the Constituent Assembly met under the chairmanship of Maulana Masoodi and commenced its deliberations.

Three Developments

After the execution of the Instrument of Accession on October 27, 1947, and adoption of the Indian Constitution on January 26, 1950, the Jammu and Kashmir State was irrevocably brought under the territorial and constitutional jurisdiction of India. The jurisdiction exercised by the Maharaja stood dissolved.

At this point of time three developments were simultaneously taking place. One pertained to the resolution of the political and constitutional issues; the second to the Praja Parishad agitation; and the third to the outward eruption of the inner propensity of Sheikh Abdullah to have an independent Kashmir.

Delhi Agreement

In regard to political and constitutional issues, the fundamental question was: what would be the constitutional structure of the State and how it would fit into the overall framework–political, legal and financial–laid down by the Constitution of India. With Sheikh Abdullah's hidden ambition to carve out a virtual Sheikhdom for himself and his coterie and with his uncanny technique of exploiting India's difficulty with regard to holding of plebiscite, differences arose between him and the Central leaders, particularly in regard to the issues of fundamental rights, citizenship, jurisdiction of the Supreme Court, Election Commission, Comptroller and Auditor General, emergency provisions, etc. After considerable irritation, felt but not openly expressed, a broad agreement, known as the Delhi Agreement, was arrived at. It was announced in the Union Parliament on July 24, 1952, by Nehru. On August 19, the Constituent Assembly of the State also approved it.

The provisions of the Delhi Agreement included abolition of the hereditary rulership; vesting of the residuary powers in the State; continuance of special citizenship rights for the 'State subjects'; flying of a separate flag for the State with the national flag also finding a supremely distinct place; and, subject to certain restrictions and limitations, extension of provisions of the Indian Constitution in respect of fundamental rights, emergency powers of the President and jurisdiction of the Supreme Court.*

Immediately after the announcement of the Delhi Agreement, the State Constituent Assembly proceeded to abolish the institution of the hereditary monarchy. The formal resolution was passed on August 21, 1952. The Head of the State was designated as the Sadar-i-Riyasat. He was to be elected by the State Legislative Assembly, for a period of five years, from amongst the persons who were "State Subjects of Class I". He was to be recognised by the President of India and hold office at his pleasure.

Praja Parishad Agitation

There was a substantial section of Indian opinion which thought that Sheikh Abdullah was being unduly appeased and national interests were being sacrificed. The Jammuites were particularly unhappy. They were incensed at the derogatory remarks which the Sheikh frequently made against the Dogra dynasty. For instance, on June 10, 1952, while speaking in the Constituent Assembly on the report of the Basic Principles Committee, Sheikh Abdullah said, "The people, under the guidance of National Conference, have sacrificed their lives, have gone to jails, and have lived in narrow cells inhabited by serpents and scorpions. Hundreds of womenfolk have been dishonoured, hundreds made to crawl on their bellies and thousands rendered martyrs by shedding their blood." Such observations showed little regard for facts or truth. These were also, in the changed circumstances, not called for. They merely added to tensions in Jammu.

*See Chapter VI: 'Roots: Article 370', for details.

The agitation in Jammu was led by the Praja Parishad. The main plank of the agitation was, 'Ek desh mein do vidhan; ek desh mein do nishan; ek desh mein do pradhan nahin chalenge'–"in one country, two constitutions; in one country, two flags; in one country, two prime ministers", would not be tolerated.

At the national level, it was strongly supported by Jana Sangh which was highly critical of the Delhi Agreement and reacted to it in these words: "Sheikh Abdullah has secured the most unreasonable of his demands without conceding anything substantial. Every concession that Nehru has secured is limited by a proviso which almost nullifies it. This is not likely to gain Kashmir for India but will certainly endanger the security and development of J&K." Syama Prasad Mookerjee, President of the Bharatia Jana Sangh, himself proceeded to Jammu. But he was arrested on May 11, 1953. He died in custody on June 23. There was a wave of national anger against Sheikh Abdullah. Nehru's own standing in the public suffered. Mookerjee's body was taken to Calcutta where he was given the biggest funeral in the history of the city.

Even with regard to the Delhi Agreement, for which Nehru was severely criticised by the Praja Parishad, the stance of Sheikh Abdullah turned out to be insincere. In fact, to let him abolish the hereditary rulership and allow him to deal with the remaining items of the Delhi Agreement later was another mistake. If it had been insisted that all parts of this Agreement should be implemented at one go, most of the subsequent troubles could have been avoided. After securing implementation of what suited him, Sheikh Abdullah referred the remaining clauses of the Agreement to the sub-committees of the Constituent Assembly, causing intentional delay. Even Nehru was dismayed by his crafty approach. He felt that he had been caught on the wrong foot. In his letters of August 6 and 7, 1952, to Abdullah, he lamented that his position in Parliament would become untenable if changes were made by the Kashmiri leaders in the Delhi Agreement. Again, on June 28, 1953, Nehru wrote to Abdullah: "To me it has been a major surprise that settlement arrived at between us should be by-passed or repudiated. That strikes at the root of all confidence. My honour is bound up with my word." But Abdullah was unmoved. He even avoided visiting Delhi for discussion, though he was invited by Nehru himself. Arrogance of power and visions of an independent Sheikhdom had wholly seized him.

Independent Sheikhdom

Around this time, Sheikh Abdullah started showing colours which almost every Central leader who came in contact with him, with the exception of Nehru, suspected him to possess beneath his pro-India, and even pro-Nehru, veneer. On April 10, 1952, he made an aggressive speech at Ranbirsingh Pura in which he denunciated the Indian press and the Indian Government and even accused them of communalism. On June 22, he commented that Indo-Kashmir relations were at a crucial stage. Again, on July 13, 1952, during the course of his 'Martyr Day' speech, he declared that the interference of the Central Government in the affairs of the State would not be tolerated. On May 3. 1953, Adlai Stevenson came to Srinagar and had a long meeting with Sheikh Abdullah, causing grave misgivings about the intentions of the latter. The *New York Times,* in its issue of July 5, published a map hinting at the independent status for the Valley. On July 10, speaking at Mujahid Manzil, Abdullah said, "A time will, therefore, come when I will bid them goodbye." While speaking on the 'Martyrs Day', on July 13, 1953, he again commented, "It is not necessary that our State should become an appendage of either India or Pakistan."

All these events and pronouncements, taken together, should leave nobody in doubt that Sheikh Abdullah was dreaming of becoming an independent ruler of Kashmir and the Anglo-US bloc was, at that point of time, encouraging him to entertain such dreams. This impression stood reinforced by the statement of Clement Attlee made on November 11, 1953, in London that "Kashmir should belong neither to India nor to Pakistan but be independent."

The attitude of Sheikh Abdullah caused grave concern to the Central leaders. It also caused a sharp rift in the State Cabinet. On August 7, 1953, majority of the Cabinet Ministers, including the Deputy Prime Minister Bakshi Ghulam Mohammad, accused him of creating a sense of uncertainty and suspense in the minds of the people. The Sadar-i-Riyasat suggested an immediate meeting of the State Cabinet but the Sheikh ignored it. He proceeded to Gulmarg. Sensing that Abdullah's designs were sinister, the Sadar-i-Riyasat immediately dismissed him and the Sheikh was arrested at Gulmarg.

In the early hours of August 9, Bakshi Ghulam Mohammad was sworn in as the Prime Minister.

In a radio broadcast, after assumption of office, Bakshi justified the proceedings against Sheikh Abdullah by saying: "Betrayal of the country's interests was in the offing. The slogan of independence was highly misleading. An independent Kashmir, under the influence of an imperialist power, will be a grave threat to freedom and independence of the Indian and Pakistani people. Another Korea may be staged here."

Bakshi-Ghulam Mohammad was an effective administrator. He firmly dealt with the disturbances following Sheikh Abdullah's detention. In these disturbances, 70 persons lost their lives.* In his autobiography, *Atish-e-Chinar,*† Sheikh Abdullah puts the number of casualties between 2,000 and 3,000. He says, "On hearing the news of my arrest, volcanic demonstrations erupted against Bakshi Ghulam Mohammad. Between 2,000 and 3,000 Kashmiris were killed by police bullets." But this assertion is incorrect and based on hearsay.

Bakshi Ghulam Mohammad understood that to build a workable relationship between the Union and the State, closer constitutional links had to be forged between the two. He put an end to the obstructive attitude of the State Government in regard to the implementation of the Delhi Agreement. On May 14, 1954, the first Constitution (Application to J&K) Order was issued by the President, extending certain provisions of the Constitution of India to the State. Other measures, as detailed in Chapter VI, on Article 370 followed. On April 1, 1959, the permit system for entry into the State was also done away with.

Bakshi's approach to political as well as law and order problems was pragmatic. When the Plebiscite Front** was founded by Mirza Afzal Beg on August 9, 1955, with the blessings of Sheikh Abdullah, he allowed the organisers to hold meetings and let off their steam.

On January 8, 1958, Sheikh Abdullah was released. When, however, the Sheikh's supporters caused riots after his speech at

---

* Official records.

† This autobiography has been written by Yusaf Teng, Secretary, J&K Academy of Art, Culture and Language, which is really an official body and of which the Chief Minister is the President. It is claimed that what has been recorded therein was dictated or told to the author by Sheikh Abdullah. Some doubts have, however, been expressed about it by a section of the press. In any case, *Atish-e-Chinar* is apparently inaccurate in many respects and does not indicate the source or the data on the basis of which various assertions have been made.

** For details, see Chapter VI: 'Roots: Article 370'.

Hazratbal on February 21, in which one person died and 21 were injured, Bakshi adopted a tough line, arresting the rioters and putting them on trial. On October 20, 1958, 68 out of the 80 accused in the Hazratbal murder and rioting case, including three ex-Members of Parliament and two former Deputy Ministers, were committed to the Sessions Court.

Earlier, on April 29, 1958, Sheikh Abdullah was re-arrested. He, Mirza Afzal Beg and 22 others were charged with conspiracy under the Kashmir Conspiracy Case to cause forcible annexation of the State by Pakistan.

Bakshi Ghulam Mohammad's outlook was constructive and development-oriented. Under his Prime-Ministership, substantial development work was carried out in all the three regions of the State.

Bakshi Ghulam Mohammad, however, suffered from three disabilities. First, he was painted as a betrayer of the Kashmir cause; the Plebiscite Front carried out a virulent propaganda against him. Secondly, his political rivals within the National Conference continuously sniped at him and carried tales to New Delhi. Thirdly, the coterie around Bakshi Ghulam Mohammad built a system of personal and political patronage and indulged in gross nepotism and corruption.*

The cumulative effect of all these disabilities was that an atmosphere of extreme hostility and suspicion was built against Bakshi Ghulam Mohammad. In a fit of bravado, Bakshi Ghulam Mohammad offered to resign under the 'Kamaraj Plan', though this Plan had no relevance to Bakshi who was not a member of the Congress organisation. His offer was accepted by Jawaharlal Nehru. He resigned on October 4, 1963. But Bakshi had a strong hold over the party. In defiance of the wishes of the Central leaders, he got his protege, Shamsuddin, elected as leader of the legislative party. Shamsuddin became the Prime Minister and Bakshi did the back-seat driving.

Bakshi's opponents and also the public at large had, however, seen the signal that the top Central leadership was no longer enamoured of him. The tempo of hostility against him and his supporters increased. And this found expression in what is known as the Moe-e-Muqaddas case: theft of the hair of Prophet Mohammed—the Holy Relic.

On December 27, 1963, the 'Holy Relic' was found missing from the Hazratbal Shrine. The window had been broken open and the Relic taken away. The news spread like wild fire. The crowd gathered.

---

*See Chapter V: 'Roots: Hidden Veins' (Section: Public Corruption).

It appeared as if hell had broken loose. Shops were closed. A hotel and a cinema belonging to the brother of Bakshi Ghulam Mohammad, and the Kothi Bagh police station were set on fire. The administrative machinery collapsed. A large number of senior officers of the Government of India, including the Director, Intelligence Bureau, B.N. Mullick, moved to Srinagar and tried to restore order.

B.N. Mullick declared that the investigations showed that the theft was an insider's job. He announced that the shrine would be kept free from watch for some time, so that the man who had taken away the Holy Relic could keep it back safely. This is exactly what happened on January 4, 1964. The Holy Relic was placed back surreptitiously. But this did not satisfy the public. The agitation continued. On February 3, 1964, however, 15 Muslim divines, headed by Sayeed Mirak Shah, identified the Holy Relic and declared it as genuine. The agitation died down.

Almost all the basic questions in regard to this incident still remain unanswered. Who committed the theft? Was it the work of a Pakistani agent or some elements in the Plebiscite Front? Or was the Holy Relic taken out at the instance of Bakshi Ghulam Mohammad to show it to his ailing mother who was lying on her death-bed at Jammu?

In any case, the incident exposed the near fatal flaws of the Kashmir political and administrative set-up. Unfortunately, no real lesson was learnt and no fundamental reform of the institutional framework was undertaken. Only patchwork was done. Shamsuddin was made to resign.

Ghulam Mohammad Sadiq became Prime Minister on February 29, 1964. The denominations 'Prime Minister' and 'Sadar-i-Riyasat' were changed to 'Chief Minister' and 'Governor', respectively, through an amendment of the Jammu and Kashmir Constitution with effect from May 30, 1965. After this date, G.M. Sadiq remained Chief Minister till his death on December 12, 1971.

Sadiq adopted a soft attitude towards Sheikh Mohammad Abdullah. Jawaharlal Nehru had all along been feeling uneasy about the Sheikh's trial in the Kashmir Conspiracy Case which had been going on since May 21, 1958. Though the long time taken by the proceedings was largely due to the delaying tactics of the accused and though the Magistrate found prima facie case of conspiracy against all the accused and committed them to the Sessions Court on January 25, 1962, Nehru and Sadiq together decided to withdraw the case. The formal order of withdrawal was issued on April 8, 1964, and Sheikh Abdullah was released.

After his release, Sheikh Abdullah received tumultuous receptions wherever he went in the State. In Delhi he had an emotional meeting with Jawaharlal Nehru and stayed as his guest.

In May 1964, Sheikh Abdullah went to Pakistan. On May 25, he had a meeting with Ayub Khan. The following day, he went to Muzaffarabad, the capital of 'Azad Kashmir'. There, on May 27, he received the news of Jawaharlal Nehru's death and immediately returned to New Delhi. In his talk with Ayub Khan, Sheikh Abdullah broached the proposal of confederation between India and Pakistan. In his book, *Friends and Not Masters*, Ayub Khan recounted: "When Sheikh Abdullah and Mirza Afzal Beg came to Pakistan in 1964, they (too) had brought the absurd proposal of a confederation between India, Pakistan and Kashmir. I told them plainly we should have nothing to do with it. It was curious that whereas we were seeking the salvation of Kashmiris, they had been forced to mention an idea which, if pursued, would lead to our enslavement".

The Sheikh, then, came to the Valley. He again changed his stance and started making highly anti-Indian speeches.

In February 1965, Sheikh Abdullah went abroad with his wife, ostensibly for the purpose of Haj. But during this visit he indulged in political* propaganda which was highly embarrassing to India. On March 28, 1965, he met even Chou En-lai,** Prime Minister of China. His passport was, therefore, cancelled. On return he was arrested at Delhi Airport on May 9, 1965.

In the meantime, Pakistan had formulated yet another plan to seize Kashmir through internal sabotage and a swift and surprise attack in August 1965. A force† of 30,000 men, comprising both regulars and 'Mujahids' and 'Razakars', was organised under the command of General Malik to launch a subversive campaign on a large scale. As soon as the snow melted, hundreds of infiltrators, disguised as local Kashmiris, entered the Valley (August 5, 1965). The Indian authorities came to know about it only when the infiltrators had reached the outskirts of Srinagar. At about the same time, Pakistan

---

* See Chaptrr IV: 'Roots' (Section: Regional Roors).

** This meeting was widely seen as Sheikh Abdullah's willingness to become a "Tool of Pindi-Peking Conspiracy" against India in respect of Kashmir.

† Michael Carver: *War Since 1945*. p. 223.

started its skirmishes on the border. On September 1, 1965, the Pakistan Army launched a massive attack with 90 tanks in the Chamb Jaurian sector. The objective was to take over Kashmir through a blitzkrieg. The military aid given by the USA had made the army rulers of Pakistan overconfident. Ayub Khan even boasted that he could launch an attack in the morning and have his breakfast next morning in New Delhi. But the overconfident generals soon realised their limitations.

The infiltrators could not make much headway. Their dialect, idiom and faulty training betrayed them. They were hounded and apprehended one by one. The local population did not rise in revolt as was expected by the Pakistani authorities. India, on the other hand, mounted a counter-offensive on the Lahore border on September 5, 1965. It also moved its troops towards Sialkot. Consequently, pressure on the Chamb Jaurian sector eased. Pakistan's plan of taking over the State by force failed once again. After an initial failure, the Security Council succeeded in making both the parties agree to a cease-fire on September 22, 1965.

The USSR assumed the role of an honest broker. It had special interest in bringing about peace between India and Pakistan, as it was apprehensive of China's increasing influence in the region. While the hostilities were going on, China assumed aggressive postures* against India. On September 16, China gave a three-day ultimatum to India "to dismantle all its military works for aggression on China-Sikkim boundary". Again, on September 19, China declared all-out support to the people of Kashmir in their "struggle for right of self-determination". At about the same time, the Chinese declared that they would not sit idle.

After the 1962 war, China had changed its stand with regard to Kashmir. Earlier, it had taken either a pro-India or a neutral stand. For instance, on March 16, 1956, Chou En-lai had told the Indian envoy, "People of Kashmir have already expressed their will regarding accession with Indian Union." Again, on May 31, 1962, China had told India that its attitude of "never getting involved in dispute over Kashmir is well-known throughout the world".

The efforts of the USSR succeeded. On January 10, 1966, the Tashkent Declaration was signed, in the presence of Kosygin and

---

*For subtle shifts in China's stand on Kashmir, during different phases of its relationship with India, see Appendix XXII.

Bulganin, by the Indian Prime Minister, Lal Bahadur Shastri, on behalf of India, and the President of Pakistan, Ayub Khan, on behalf of Pakistan. Both the parties agreed to withdraw their troops to the position held by them on August 5, 1965. The text of the Tashkent Declaration is at Appendix VII.

The Indo-Pak conflict of 1965 has been described by a number of observers as the most useless and fruitless war which cost both the countries heavily in terms of men, material and finances. But this observation is not wholly true. India definitely stood to gain. After the Tashkent Declaration, the interest of the international community in the Kashmir problem abated. Pakistan also learnt to its cost that any future intervention in Kashmir would not remain restricted to the area around Kashmir but would amount to a full-scale war between India and Pakistan.

After the Tashkent Declaration, the political atmosphere in the Valley cooled down. On December 8, 1967, Sheikh Abdullah was released. With the passage of time, less attention was paid to him by the public, though the activities of the Plebiscite Front continued with unabated vigour. On January 8, 1971, Sheikh Abdullah, Mirza Afzal Beg and G.M. Shah were expelled from the State. On January 12, the Plebiscite Front was banned.

At the end of 1971, the liberation movement in Bangladesh gained momentum. The Indian Army moved into Bangladesh. In December 1971, a regular war started. On December 3, in the north, Pakistan attacked J&K. Fierce land and air battles followed for a fortnight. On December 16, Pakistani forces surrendered in Bangladesh. India declared unilateral cease-fire. Pakistan also accepted cease-fire on December 17. The war thus ended with spectacular victory for India and coming into being of the independent state of Bangladesh.

After the conflict, the Prime Minister of India, Mrs. Indira Gandhi, and the President of Pakistan, Z.A. Bhutto, held bilateral discussions, as a result of which the Shimla Agreement was formulated and signed by the two countries on July 3, 1972. The text of this Agreement has been given in Appendix VIII. It would be noted that this Agreement, *inter alia*, contained the following:

> That the two countries are resolved to settle their differences by peaceful means through bilateral negotiations or by any other peaceful means mutually agreed upon between them.

In order to initiate the process of the establishment of durable peace, both the Governments agree that:

(i) Indian and Pakistani forces shall be withdrawn to their side of the international border.

(ii) In J&K, the line of control resulting from the cease-fire of December 17, 1971, shall be respected by both sides without prejudice to the recognised position of either side.

From July 1972 onwards, the Shimla Agreement became the cornerstone of Indo-Pakistan relations. It has stood the ground, though the parties have sometimes tended to give it different interpretations.

After the Bangladesh War and Pakistan's humiliating defeat with its about 90,000 troops surrendering to the Indian Army, and the execution of the Shimla Agreement which made the Kashmir issue really a bilateral one, the attitude of the recalcitrant leaders of Kashmir like Sheikh Abdullah and Mirza Afzal Beg underwent a change. Their ardour for Pakistan or independent Kashmir diminished. They started making conciliatory speeches. Mrs. Indira Gandhi also thought it expedient to arrive at some settlement with Sheikh Abdullah. Negotiations started between the two parties in 1972. After 3 years of protracted talks between G. Parthasarathi and Mirza Afzal Beg, an agreement, known as the Kashmir Accord,* was signed on February 24, 1975. The text of this Agreement has been reproduced at Appendix IX.

In the spirit of the Kashmir Accord, Chief Minister Syed Mir Qasim, who had taken over after the death of G.M. Sadiq on December 13, 1971, and had played a significant role in bringing about the Accord, resigned. The Congress Legislative Party elected Sheikh Abdullah as its leader. He was sworn in as Chief Minister on February 25, 1975. Three other non-Congress ministers† joined his Cabinet.

The understanding between the Congress and Sheikh Abdullah did not last long. It turned out to be a love-hate relationship. While on the one hand Sheikh Abdullah lauded "Jawaharlal's vision and statesmanship, combined with Indiraji's courage and decisiveness",**

---

* See Chapter IV: 'Roots' (Section: Kashmir Accord).

† These were Mirza Afzal Beg, D.D. Thakur and Sonam Narboo.

** 'Sheikh Abdullah's speech in the Legislative Assembly on February 24, 1975.

on the other, he turned down the suggestion that he should join the Congress Party. Instead, he revived the National Conference and became its president on April 13, 1975, thereby creating a piquant situation in which he held the office of the Chief Minister on the sole legislative support of one political party and at the same time functioned as president of another political party.

On July 5, 1975, Sheikh Abdullah dissolved the Plebiscite Front and merged it with the National Conference. On August 15, he openly welcomed ten Congress members, including Abdul Ghani Lone, who defected to the National Conference. This created a rumpus in the Congress Party. The differences were, however, resolved, and a coordination committee comprising two representatives of each party was set up on October 13. On October 21, Sheikh Abdullah announced expansion of his Cabinet in which he included four Congressmen who were picked by him without consulting Mrs. Indira Gandhi. She retaliated by instructing the four Congressmen not to join the ministry. The swearing-in ceremony had to be cancelled.

Thus, within a period of less than eight months, wide cracks appeared in the edifice built on the foundation of the Indira-Abdullah Accord of February 1975. There were other incompatible planks in this edifice which made it unstable.

The National Conference leaders frequently described the period of 23 years from August 9, 1953, to February 25, 1975, as a "dark patch in the history of Kashmir". About the development of the State during this period, the perceptions and pronouncements of the two parties also differed widely. Sheikh Abdullah himself commented: "An artificial and exhibitionist show of false progress was put up. The people of the State refused to yield before the temptation and the terror that followed August 1953."[†] Such comments naturally caused a great deal of resentment amongst the Congressmen.

Eventually, the precarious structure collapsed under the impact of Parliamentary elections of March 1977, when the Congress party was routed in northern India. Anticipating that Sheikh Abdullah would break relations with the Congress and arrive at a settlement with the Janata Party, the Congress Party, which had a strength of 45 members in the Legislative Assembly of 73,* withdrew support to

† Sheikh Abdullah's presidential address at a Session of the National Conference held at Jammu on April 24, 1975.

* Two seats were vacant at that time.

him on March 25, 1977, and staked its claim to form the Ministry. But Sheikh Abdullah secured dissolution of the Assembly from Governor L.K. Jha. The Congressmen were incensed. They described Sheikh Abdullah's action as a "sordid act of political betrayal", an "effrontery by a Chief Minister who had the support of only three members". The Governor's decision, too, was dubbed as "undemocratic, morally indefensible and constitutionally questionable". But the die had been cast. Sheikh Abdullah had successfully outwitted the Congressmen.

It was the time of the 'Janata' wave. In the State, the Janata Party unit was set up with Maulana Masoodi as its convener. A number of disparate parties and groups, including the Awami Action Committee of Moulvi Farooq, gathered under its umbrella, causing considerable worry to the National Conference. But Sheikh Abdullah resorted to his familiar technique of arousing parochial feelings and planting apprehensions in the minds of Kashmiris about the abrogation of Article 370. He went to the extent of saying, "We shall not hesitate to secede from India if we are not assured a place of honour and dignity in terms of the safeguards provided for the people of the State under Article 370 of the Constitution. We shall remain part of India only with dignity and honour. There had been much watering down of Article 370 since 1953. We have to strengthen it with all our might." During the period of electioneering, Sheikh Abdullah fell sick. According to his detractors, he feigned sickness to win sympathy of the masses.

Sheikh Abdullah's semi-fascist propaganda yielded results. In the elections held on June 30, 1977, the National Conference won 39 seats in the Valley, out of 42, and seven seats, mostly from the Muslim majority districts in the Jammu region, out of 32, and both the seats from Ladakh. The Janata Party got only two seats in the Valley and 11 in Jammu. The Congress was practically wiped out in the Valley; in the Jammu region, it got 10 seats primarily due to the infighting between the Janata Party and its rebel candidates.

The Janata Party fared badly because it had no clear policy or programme. Its leaders spoke with discordant voices. For instance, Subramaniam Swamy declared in Jammu that he would have Article 370 abrogated. A.G. Lone took a diametrically opposite view and said that Article 370 would be strengthened. Asoka Mehta talked vaguely about the Janata Party's intentions of changing the Kashmir policy of Jawaharlal Nehru.

Sheikh Abdullah was sworn in as Chief Minister on July 9, 1977. His spectacular victory had the effect of strengthening the authoritarian streaks in his personality. The circle of power around him became narrower. Small caucuses, both in the administrative and political arena, attained ascendency. Absolute power brought in its wake corrupting and corroding influences. His administration showed little sensitivity to complaints of corruption and regional discrimination.

To keep the emotional fervour of the Kashmiri masses at a high pitch and in his favour, Sheikh Abdullah resorted to such controversial measures as the Resettlement Bill and withdrawal of cases against 30 hardcore activists of Al Fatah. In a subtle and crafty way, he also prepared the ground for Dr. Farooq Abdullah's succession to chief ministership. The probable contenders were either eliminated from the National Conference or their wings clipped. For instance, Mirza Afzal Beg was asked to resign on September 25, 1978, and four days later was expelled from the party. The local anti-defection law was also so designed as to strengthen the hold of Sheikh Abdullah's coterie on the power structure of the State.

After a stormy and eventful life, Sheikh Abdullah passed away on September 8, 1982, securing one of the most crowded funerals in the history of the country. Dr. Farooq Abdullah, as expected, succeeded him as Chief Minister. Because of the behind-the-scene support of Mrs. Indira Gandhi and Governor B.K. Nehru, the transition was smooth. But the relations between Mrs. Indira Gandhi and Dr. Farooq Abdullah soon soured. During the course of the State Assembly elections of June 1983, serious conflicts developed between the Congress(I) and the National Conference. Simultaneously there was a spurt in anti-national activities. The relations between the Centre and The State Government became tense. The Punjab events also started casting their long shadows on J&K. The frequency of violent disturbances increased.

The State, as indicated in Chapter VII entitled 'July 2, 1984', was in turmoil, when I assumed the office of Governor on April 26, 1984. In the circumstances, as narrated by me in the said chapter, Dr. Farooq Abdullah's Ministry was dismissed by me on July 2, 1984, and G.M. Shah became the Chief Minister. His Ministry, too, was dismissed by me on March 7, 1986. Governor's Rule was imposed by me under Section 92 of the Jammu and Kashmir Constitution. It continued for six months. Thereafter, the State was brought under President's Rule under. Article 356 of the Constitution of India, and I continued to administer it on behalf of the President for a further period of two months.

Following the Rajiv-Farooq Accord, the coalition Ministry of the National Conference and Congress(I), with Dr. Farooq Abdullah as Chief Minister, came into being on November 7, 1986. Fresh elections to the State Legislative Assembly were called for in March 1987. The coalition parties swept the poll. But the fairness of these elections was doubted by a sizeable section of the people. Because of this and many other fundamental reasons, as analysed in the three chapters entitled 'The Roots', the storm started gathering in the Valley and engulfed it with full force in the second half of 1989.*

I relinquished charge of my office on July 12, 1989. In the circumstances stated by me in Chapter I entitled 'My Frozen Turbulence', I was appointed Governor for the second term on January 19, 1990. I resigned on May 26, 1990.

The activities of organisations like the Plebiscite Front, the Al Fatah, the Jammu and Kashmir Liberation Front and other subversive organisations; major events like the Kashmir Accord (February 1975), State Assembly elections of June 1977, June 1983 and March 1987, and Parliamentary elections of December 1984 and November 1989; controversial measures like the Resettlement Act; the decisions which involved important constitutional and political issues such as dismissal of Dr. Farooq Abdullah's Ministry by me on July 2, 1984, and G.M. Shah's Ministry on March 7, 1986, and Dr. Farooq Abdullah's resignation on January 18, 1990, and other significant issues, have been dealt with by me, in a larger perspective, in the subsequent chapters. I have, therefore, not thought it necessary to go into all these issues in this chapter. Likewise, the trends, currents and undercurrents have not been delineated here, as these have been elaborated in proper context, in the next chapter–'The Warning Signals'.

All the events and developments which I have traced, all the catalogues of omissions and commissions which I have shown, all the debris of betrayals and conspiracies which I have scanned, and all the dramas of many grim tragedies and triumphs which I have unfolded, during the long journey of over two thousand years have made Kashmir what it is today. Quite a few wounds which history has inflicted upon it are still unhealed and others have left their deep scars.

---

*See Chapter VIII: 'Conditions Before My Arrival'.

At the most crucial turn of its history in the middle of 1947, a great healer, a great mind, was needed to stitch old wounds and smoothen old scars. Unfortunately, that did not happen. Reliance was placed only upon cosmetics. The new actors had only polished exterior, it soon wore off. As would be noted in the Chapters IV, V and VI, the significance of roots was not grasped. New seeds of reform were not planted and new crucibles of integration not fashioned.

CHAPTER III

Warning Signals

History is no blind goddess,
and it does not excuse blindness in others.

From the beginning of 1988, I had started sending warning signals to the Union Government about the gathering storm. But the men at the helm of affairs had neither the time nor the inclination, nor the vision, to see these signals. For the sake of letting the nation know the truth, for the sake of correcting distortions, for the sake of shooting down lies, half truths, concoctions, and for the sake of learning from the history of omission and commission, let me acquaint you with some of the signals which I persistently gave. These signals were so clear, so pointed, that to ignore them was to commit sins of true historical dimensions.

I reproduce below notes from my diary. These notes had been incorporated in my monthly reports to the President, with a copy each to the Prime Minister and the Home Minister.

My diary notes for the month of August 1988 contained the following:

> Large-scale violence and public disorder involving loss of 9 lives and police firing on at least a dozen occasions; spill-over of the happenings from across the border; and visits of Kashmiri youth, owing allegiance to subversive groups, to Pakistan for getting training in arms to create Punjab-like terrorist movement in the State, are some of the events which provide clue to the undercurrents and trends of the month.

The fragility of the social and political structure of the State and the infirmities of the administrative set-up stand exposed once again. Manifest in the events is also the sway of forces of fanaticism and fundamentalism.

The Reasi agitation for securing District status for the Reasi Sub-Division focuses attention on another unhealthy feature of the State's landscape, *viz.*, regional jealousies.

In my notes for the month of July, I had indicated that the bomb blasts, the petrol pump robbery, the Poonch disturbances, the aggressive posture of Moulvi Farooq and his collaborators, the mounting tempo of pro-Pakistan activities, the tactics of Jama'at-i-Islami, the latent sympathies and parochial loyalties of a section of Administration, the increasing indifference of the so-called secular forces, and failure of the ruling partners to inject enthusiasm in their party workers, are all points of the compass which foretold an emerging storm. This storm did emerge. And it lashed the Valley with varying degrees of intensity throughout the month. Unforeseen events like the sudden death of General Zia-ul-Haq added to its fury.

Parallel to all these developments was the movement of Kashmiri youth to Pakistan for securing arms and getting training in their use for terrorist activity.

To recount the main events: On the night intervening July 31 and August 1, there were two bomb blasts and one dacoity. On August 4, one electronic watch time-bomb was found at Lakhanpur, which was defused before it could do any damage. On August 12, there was an explosion in an auto-rickshaw in the main bazaar of Jammu. On August 14, Pakistan Independence Day, a number of green flags were hoisted in the interior of Srinagar city and other towns of the Valley. On August 15, India's Independence Day, black flags were put up at a number of places. On August 16, clashes took place between the police and the pro-Pakistan processionists on Nallah-mar road. The processionists were shouting anti-India slogans and asking for the opening of Rawalpindi road–a demand that had been put up a few days earlier by Moulvi Farooq. In the ensuing clash, one person was killed in police firing and about 50 persons were injured. A police jeep was also burnt down and a few shops were damaged. On the 16th night, an attempt was made to set on fire Rishi Peer Temple in Srinagar.

On August 17, late in the evening, when the news of General Zia's death came, large crowds gathered in the down-town area of Srinagar and shouted anti-India and anti-Russia slogans. Though curfew was imposed, rioting took place at a number of places in Srinagar, Baramulla, Pulwama and Bhaderwah. Violence continued for four days and police had to open fire in which four persons were killed on August 18, and one on August 21.

On August 23, violent clashes took place in the Shia-dominated localities and curfew was clamped. On August 24, about 50 Shias going to Abiguzar for Moharrum procession were attacked and stones were thrown at them. Srinagar city was again placed under curfew. Due to extreme tension between the Shias and the Sunnis, the Moharrum procession was abandoned. Though the abandonment of the procession prevented the anticipated clashes, it brought down the prestige of the Administration. On August 26, after Friday prayers at Jamia Masjid, wherein 'fateh' was offered for the late General Zia-ul-Haq, the crowd, while dispersing from the mosque, turned violent. The police resorted to firing in which three persons died and five others received gun shots.

On August 31, there was a bomb explosion in an unoccupied, stationary bus at Anantnag. One person standing near the bus died.

The responsibility for the bomb explosions on the night of July 31 and August 1 has been claimed by the J&K Liberation Front. Some posters and press notes in this regard were circulated.

While the surface cause of the disturbances has connection with one event or the other, the fundamental cause has to be found in the character of Kashmir's polity and administration and the economic and social fabric of its society and its current cultural ethos.

In regard to the disturbances, a number of basic questions arise. How is it that on Pakistan Day green flags were hoisted and on India's Independence Day black flags were brought out? Why did General Zia's death become an occasion for large-scale rioting in Srinagar, Baramulla, and other towns, when there was no such rioting anywhere in Pakistan? How can one explain the current behaviour of the rioters, when it is remembered that, in April 1979, large-scale anti-Zia demonstrations took place following the execution of Zulfikar Ali Bhutto, and the properties of Jama'at-i-Islami workers were looted and burnt on the suspicion that General Zia was receiving support from this organisation?

The answer, in broad terms, to all these questions lies in the deep-rooted disposition of local Kashmiri leadership to exploit religion and whip up pro-Pakistan sentiments. Whosoever has been out of power has found it expedient to talk of 'opening the Rawalpindi road'; of 'all Kashmir rivers flowing towards Pakistan' and of 'resettlement of brethren who have gone to the other side'. For regaining power, or for cornering public attention, or for capturing newspaper headlines, these are considered to be the best slogans. No one has, unfortunately, effectively discouraged this disposition, much less penalise it.

The youth, the element which actually takes part in violence, is either illiterate and easily exploitable by the communal and fundamentalist leaders, or educated but frustrated on account of the unjust system which affords him limited opportunities for employment or ignores his merit due to unfair methods of recruitment and selection. Frustrations and fanaticism, mediaevalism and 'monkism', exist side by side. And this keeps the pot boiling. It spills over the edges whenever any outside stimulus is provided or extra heat is generated locally. Neither the traditional norms of mediaeval authority nor the modern norms of fairness and justice are available. The Kashmiri youth is getting the worst of both the worlds.

All the local groups and regional parties rely, not on hard and honest work to win over the Kashmiri masses, but on emotive and mediaeval issues to prop up their political standing. In this attitude lies the fundamental malady of Kashmir's polity and administration. Instead of grappling with the reality and tackling the problem from its roots, shortcuts are resorted to and personality-oriented politics is encouraged. This, in turn, breeds individual ambitions, and makes power an end in itself. In the ensuing intrigues, public disorders are caused. A good part of the administrative energy and resources is consumed by these disorders, and a major portion of the resources that remain is misapplied to suit the social and economic elite upon whose shoulders alone the current set-up rests.

In the context of these realities, the current imbalanced and inequitous development is not surprising. About 90% of the urban and urbanisable lands are owned by the new elite. Large-scale speculation, racketeering and profiteering go on, filling the coffers of those who are already rich and influential. The re-distributive content of the much adumbrated rural land reforms has also been subverted by the amendment of 1978 by which orchards were exempted from the purview of land ceiling and flood-gates for establishing 'neo-landlordism' in the State were opened. Now 10% of the population control about 50% of the rural assets, and the top 30% account for 82% of these assets. Obviously, in a State where about 80% of the total assets are controlled by less than 15-20% of the people, there could be neither social nor economic justice. Further, priorities and patterns of development leave very little resources for genuine development. Consequently, education suffers, civic services are neglected, public health gets little attention, and environment and ecology come under severe pressure.

In the circumstances, injustices remain; frustrations remain; ignorance and illiteracy remain; and so do the opportunities for manipulation and exploitation. Today it may be X; tomorrow it will be Y; the day after tomorrow it will be Z and the like–all talking in the same strain, all singing the Pakistani songs and songs of Article 370 and Kashmiris' identity, without meaning even an iota of good for the poor and the downtrodden masses.

Already a section of the National Conference, apprehending that it is losing the battle on emotive and exploitative fronts, has started raking up the dead issue of 'resettlement'. . . . The Youth Wing of the National Conference has, on August 2, 1988, submitted a memorandum in which it has asked me to request the President to accord assent to the 'Resettlement Bill' which has been passed by the State Legislature, 'representative of six million people of the State'. The memorandum says: "We the people of J&K feel that the roots of the accession are gradually eroding by not implementing the 'Resettlement Act'. We hope that the people of J&K State will not be forced to think "otherwise" which will not be liked by the Government of India, if the 'Resettlement Act' is not given assent in the near future." Implicit in these words is the threat. Implicit in these words is also the desire and inclination to resort to techniques of 'exploitative democracy' and use the issue which had served the electoral ends of the National Conference so well in the past. The long-term damage that is done to the Kashmiri psyche and the State's emotional integration with the Union is not its concern.

The reaction of various parties to the disturbances and the handling of the situation by the State Government varied. The Bharatiya Janata Party demanded imposition of Governor's Rule on account of the alleged failure of the coalition Government to deal with the situation effectively. The Awami National Conference of G.M. Shah, too, asked for the imposition of Governor's Rule. In a strongly worded statement G.M. Shah deplored the 'casual and callous manner in which the State Government was dealing with an explosive situation' and asked the Central Government and the Governor to intervene and dismiss the incompetent alliance Government. He even advised policemen not to obey orders of firing by the authorities. The People's Conference of A.G. Lone exhorted the people to launch a campaign for the ouster of the Chief Minister who was perpetrating 'atrocities in collusion with the Centre'. The Muslim United Front (Jama'at-i-Islami group) also condemned the State Government, for the frequent imposition of curfew and for resorting to firing. The Muslim United Front (Abbas Ansari group) demanded the resignation of the State Government for its inability to protect the 'Moharrum' procession. The Awami Action Committee condemned the 'callous and indiscriminate killing of the innocent people'. The party president, Moulvi Farooq, published a list of 16 youth who wert killed in police firing during the last three months. He demanded the Chief Minister's resignation. Mufti Mohammad Sayeed of Jan Morcha also strongly criticised the Chief Minister and the Police and paramilitary forces and their so-called 'patrons in Delhi' for creating a dangerous situation in the State.

At the party level, both Congress(I) and National Conference(F), by and large, played a supine role. The frequently-talked-about common political fight of National Conference and Congress(I) against the anti-national and communal forces was nowhere in sight. The workers and leaders of these parties were conspicuous by their absence when fundamentalist and pro-Pakistan elements were all over Srinagar city and other towns of the Valley. The administrative machinery was left high and dry, and its effectiveness in the political vacuum could not but be limited. All this shows a disconcerting trend.

It is now known that about 50 Kashmiri youth had gone to Pakistan and obtained training in terrorist activity. Some of them have returned with lethal weapons like the Chinese assault rifle.

It appears that Amanullah Khan, the Chief of 'Jammu and Kashmir Liberation Front', is masterminding subversive activity with the help of the Pakistan authorities. Amanullah is eliciting support of Kashmiri youth who mostly belong to pro-Pakistan splinter groups like the People's League, the Islamic Students' League, the Mahaz-e-Azadi and the J&K Liberation Front. Amanullah's objective is to train these youth and make them operate on the same pattern as the Punjab terrorists.

Two bomb explosions on the night intervening July 31 and August 1, and the bomb explosion at the Anantnag bus stand on August 31, appear to be the handiwork of the newly trained group in subversion.

Unfortunately, the intelligence agencies failed to detect in time the movement of the Kashmiri youth to Pakistan. These agencies came to know of the movement only when some of the youth returned from Pakistan after training with weapons.

There have also been reports that some Kashmiri youth had gone to Punjab to establish contact with the Punjab terrorists and make common cause with them. They are, however, understood to have received only a lukewarm response.

On a different level, events from across the border are likely to cast their shadows on the State. Maybe, General Zia's death has the effect of pouring cold water on subversive activity. Maybe, on the other hand, electoral compulsions of the coming elections in Pakistan impel its leaders to talk increasingly of the 'Kashmir issue' and cause ripples here. Already the issue has been raised in the meeting of the Non-Aligned group. Junejo's party has also been referring to it time and again.

While vigilance needs to be mounted to prevent fall-out of subversion from across the border, the real defence against terrorist activity in the State lies in reforming and reorganising the State administration and securing sound and balanced development and at the same time dispensing even-handed justice in regard to selections and appointments.

The deficiencies of the J&K administrative set-up, particularly those of police, were brought home once again during the disturbances of the month. Poor intelligence prevented advance planning. Even when trouble was anticipated sound strategy was not forthcoming.

The general administrative ethos of the State administration also leaves much to be desired. Too many holidays are enjoyed. Too little productive work is done. Time and energy are wasted in peripheral issues. Overheads are high. The Secretariat is overstaffed. Daily wagers continue to be appointed, causing unnecessary strain on the State Exchequer. Both in regard to providing a cost-effective administrative machinery and meeting the challenge of subversive elements, the State is nowhere near the mark. There is a crying need for reform. A new look and motivation need to be imparted. Arrangements for obtaining timely intelligence need to be made forthwith. Panic reactions cause confusion and leave too many lacerated wounds and bitter memories.

Confidence in purity of public life remains low. A number of cases, which, to say the least, reek with moral garbage, are coming to light, and the undercurrent of corruption continues to flow.

To sum up, the trends and undercurrents reveal that the polity and the administration of the State are not in good health. The Congress(I) is in disarray. The National Conference shows no spark, no vigour. The drumbeaters of parochialism and fundamentalism are working overtime, and the secularists have surrendered initiative. Subversion is on the increase. The shadows of events from across the border are lengthening. Lethal weapons have come in. More may be on the way. The intelligence agencies have not proved equal to the task. The chinks in their armour stand exposed by the undetected movement across the border. As if these problems were not sufficient to fill the cup of trouble, regional agitations have cropped up. The face of democracy is being increasingly pimpled by exploitation. The overall fabric of the State shows too many loose threads, too many weak stitches.

Though similar notes had been recorded by me in the months of April and June 1988, I have considered it necessary to make the above extensive reproduction from the notes for the month of August 1988. This reproduction not only shows that I have not become wise after the events but also reveals the extent of irresponsibility displayed by those whose duty it was to take action at the Central level.

My notes for the month of September read, inter alia, as under:

The subversive activity showed no sign of abatement in the month of September. If anything, the activity intensified.

On September 10, late in the evening, some unidentified persons opened indiscriminate firing at Ranibagh Mandir, Srinagar. On the night intervening September 17 and 18, an attempt was made on the life of DIG Kashmir Range, Ali Mohammad Watali, and his family members, by four young men armed with sophisticated weapons. One of the terrorists died in the armed scuffle, and his Russian made gun was seized. It is believed that the attackers were members of the Jammu and Kashmir Liberation Front and had been given arms training in Pakistan. On September 22, the house of N.K. Ganjoo, a retired Sessions Judge, who sentenced Maqbool Butt to death, was fired upon. On September 23, at about 8 p.m., the lane between the offices of DIG Kashmir and IG, CID, was subjected to indiscriminate firing. On the night intervening September 24 and 25, motor-cycle borne terrorists fired at the sentry on duty at the Srinagar Museum.

Interrogations of some of the detainees reveal that quite a number of young men crossed the border for securing arms training, and have returned for carrying out subversive and terrorist activities. The most unfortunate aspect of the whole affair is that not a single person could be apprehended while going to and returning from Pakistan, not a single weapon could be detected, and not a single motivator could be spotted. The matter came to light when bullets started flying and bombs exploding.

From religious platforms, the Moulvis invariably give political advice. They concern themselves less with religion than with politics. Some of the 'religious czars' in their respective areas have built their entire political following by addressing Friday congregations. Even political stalwarts have been making important speeches from the Hazratbal and other shrines.

Organisations like Jama'at-i-Islami, Ummat-e-Islam, Islamic Students' League and Ahl-e-Hadis have been mounting their attack on the local practices and drawing inspiration from Islamisation of Pakistan and Bangladesh. The educational institutions, spreading narrow ideas in the impressionable minds, were supposed to be closed. But words were not translated into deeds. The citadel of the old and cherished values continues to be eroded from its foundations.

In the Governors' Conference, held on October 10 and 11, 1988, under the chairmanship of the President of India, and which was attended by the Vice-President, the Prime Minister, the Home Minister and other senior ministers of the Union Cabinet, I expressed my opinion on the basis of the above-mentioned notes in my diary. Everyone seemed to agree with my analysis. And yet no action followed.

In the notes recorded for the month of January 1989, I again brought out how subversives were getting more emboldened, how their pronouncements were becoming more aggressive and bellicose, and how the Chief Minister, Dr. Farooq Abdullah, was showing a shocking lack of concern and seriousness.

In my notes pertaining to the month of February 1989, I once again dwelt at length upon the points of the compass which foretold the storm. I recorded:

> Subversive and terrorist activities continue unabated. During the month, 11 hartals were organised, dozens of bombs were exploded, hundreds of persons were injured, and two died.
>
> Observance of 'Martyr Maqbool Butt Day' and publication of *Satanic Verses* provided cover to the subversionists to whip up emotions and give call for 'bandhs' and agitations.
>
> 'Maqbool Butt Day', on February 11, saw extensive trouble in the Valley. As a dress rehearsal, explosions started even two days before the so-called martyrs day. On the 'Day' itself, practically all shops in Srinagar and other major towns were closed. Violence occurred on a fairly large scale.
>
> The disturbances of February 11 showed the Government in poor light–politically as well as administratively.
>
> At the political level, no activity on the part of the workers of National Conference(F) and Congress(I) was visible. Surprisingly, though the city of Srinagar is represented by the National Conference(F) MLAs in the State Assembly, not even a few shops could be got opened. The passivity of the political leaders of the ruling alliance can be interpreted either as a case of studied indifference or of extreme irresponsibility. These leaders appear to be taking a self-destructive course–a course which is leaving the field wide open for the subversive elements like Jammu and Kashmir Liberation Front, People's League, Jama'at-e-Tulba, Muslim Students' Federation, Al Jung and Zia Tigers, etc. The Chief Minister, unfortunately, chose to be away to Australia and Singapore. This, besides leaving the political workers leaderless, caused much resentment amongst the general public.
>
> Hardly had the trouble on Maqbool Butt Day subsided when disturbances broke out following police firing in Islamabad on a crowd which was protesting near the American Cultural Centre against the publication of *Satanic Verses* in the USA. In the snap

'bandh' on February 12, and the accompanying disturbances, one person was killed in police firing. These bandhs and disturbances were followed by similar happenings on February 13, 14, 16 and 26. The usual pattern was to start stoning the public vehicles and attacking the police after Friday prayers and speeches at the mosque. The refrain of these speeches was condemnation of 'conspiracies against Islam'.

The subversionists are proving successful in their designs to inject heat in the political environment. The poster campaign is going on. New terrorist outfits like 'Al Jung' and 'Zia Tigers' are emerging. Militancy is mounting. Hit-and-run tactics are being increasingly employed. Some of the ring leaders like Shabir Shah continue to hoodwink the police and evade arrest.

The continued failure of the State Government to redress the grievances of the people and to show results in the realm of development add to the tension and enable the fundamentalists and secessionists to exploit religious frenzies and seize such opportunities as are afforded by events like the publication of *Satanic Verses.* In fact, to a considerable extent, the present troubled state of affairs is the result of the accumulated anger of the people against the malfunctioning of the Government.

Apart from the outfits which directly resort to terrorism, there are groups which fan the forces of subversion and create a climate conducive to its growth. The activities of these groups are indirect, but they are equally lethal, as they sustain the psychological base on which subversion is built.

The call given by subversive elements for observing January 26, 1984, as Black Day was fully responded and the hartal was total. The communal, parochial and subversive elements are becoming more active and the administration is getting more isolated. Neither the National Conference(F) nor the Congress(I) is showing any inclination to face the challenge at the political level. A large amount of arms and ammunition brought from across the border has also yet to be recovered. The local intelligence network is not proving equal to the occasion. Moreover, the subversive elements enjoy overt as well as covert support of a sizeable section of the politicians, particularly those belonging to Jama'at-i-Islami, People's Conference, People's League and Mahaz-e-Azadi. The distribution of cassettes by Jama'at-i-Islami workers, containing speeches of Syed Ali Shah Geelani and the late Maqbool Butt of the Kashmir

Liberation Front, inciting the youth to take up arms against India, also indicate the same pattern. Mohammad Altaf Khan alias Azam Inquilabi, who crossed over to the Pakistan side of the Line of Actual Control, is still actively operating from that side. He and his supporters are even now getting all help from Amanullah Khan of the Kashmir Liberation Front which is now operating under the name of 'Hamhaz'.

The political needle of Kashmir invariably responds to the developments in Pakistan. The recent statement of Ms. Benazir Bhutto, calling for solution of Kashmir issue and removal of 'Siachen irritant', are taken here as an indication of her adopting a stand similar to that of the late President Zia. On February 7, Ms. Benazir Bhutto demanded that India should withdraw its forces from the Siachen Glacier. In regard to the Kashmir issue, she said: 'Our position is based on the UN Resolution, according to which the question of the accession of the State of J&K to Pakistan or India is to be decided through the democratic method of a free and impartial plebiscite. In the Shimla Agreement, when we say that we have agreed to have bilateral negotiations with India, it is on the basis of UN Resolutions.' Though the fundament-alist and die-hard elements in Kashmir still do not look upon Ms. Bhutto as their supporter, they are no longer as downcast as they were when she scored over Islamic Jamohri Ittehad and was elected the Prime Minister. They believe that, due to the compulsion of internal politics of' Pakistan, Ms. Bhutto, sooner rather than later, will be forced to take a tough stand against India with regard to the Kashmir issue. That is one of the basic reasons for their continued efforts to escalate subversion and to keep the Kashmir issue in the limelight. The 'Rushdie affair' has come as a godsend to these elements. Even other political forces, which are not so inimical to the Union, joined in condemning Rushdie. No one seems to bother that most of the people who are agitating, both in Pakistan and India, against the *Satanic Verses*, are not even literate. They are merely becoming an instrument of exploitation in the hands of Mullahs and leaders who are adept in whipping up religious frenzy.

In Kashmir, as is well known, religion has always been a handmaid of politics. From Sheikh Abdullah to the present political leaders, practically all except the leaders of the National

Congress have exploited it for political purposes. This is particularly true in the Valley where every Friday political speeches and religious sermons are mixed. It is, therefore, not surprising that most of the disturbances that have taken place in the month, have occurred after the Friday prayers when the crowds were dispersing from the mosque.

In the month of May 1989, I recorded:

The youth is sullen and angry. It is taking refuge under religion whose appeal helps it to gain sympathy and support of the common folk. The main secessionist outfit–J&K Liberation Front–has already announced setting up of ten hit Squads. It has also claimed support of the Islami Jamhoori Ittehad of Pakistan. It has announced in the handout that the 'Al Jehad' hit Squad will be headed by Javed Ahmed Mir, the 'Hamza' Squad by Abdul Gaffar, the 'Victory Commandos' by Muzaffar Shah, the 'Azad Janwaz Commando Force' by Ghulam Hassan Lone, the 'Shaheed Zia Tigers' by Mohammad Asraf, the 'Al Fatah' Squad by Javed Ahmed, the 'Sadai Janwaz' Commando Force by Abdul Hamid, the 'Al Maqbool' by Mushtaq Ahmed, the 'Muslimeen Commando' force by Safed Rasool Aqadhan, and the 'Pak Commando' force by Roofi Islam.

In April and May 1989, I wrote two personal letters to Rajiv Gandhi inviting his attention to the critical conditions. My letter of April 8 was as follows:

Dear Prime Minister,

The situation is fast deteriorating. It has almost reached a point of no return. For the last five days, there have been large-scale violence, arson, firing, hartals, casualties and what not. Things have truly fallen apart. Talking of the Irish crisis, British Prime Minister Disraeli had said: 'It is potatoes one day and the Pope next.' Similar is the present position in Kashmir. Yesterday it was 'Maqbool Butt'; today it is '*Satanic Verses*'; tomorrow it will be 'repression day' and the day after it will be something else. The Chief Minister stands isolated. He has already fallen–politically as well as administratively; perhaps, only constitutional rites remain to be performed. His clutches are too soiled and rickety to support him. Personal aberrations have also eroded his public standing. The situation calls for effective intervention. Today may be timely, tomorrow may be too late.

Yours sincerely,
(Sd.) Jagmohan

My letter of May 14 read as under:

Dear Prime Minister,

From May 8 to 13, there have been 14 bomb blasts and six cases of firing and cross-firing. Four persons died and about 20 were injured. A tourist bus proceeding from Gulmarg to Srinagar was fired upon, and four tourists were injured. The current administrative and political structure has once again proved unequal to the task. During the 'hartal' period, no worthwhile activity has been visible at the political front to counter the move of the subversionists. What is still more worrying is that every 'victory' of the subversionists is swelling their ranks, and the animosity is being diverted against the Central authorities. I have indicated my anxiety to the Chief Minister.

Yours sincerely,
(Sd.) Jagmohan

All these clear and pointed warnings were, unfortunately, ignored. For everything, there is a time. An infection in the body has to be eliminated before the disease becomes irreversible. If neglected, the consequences have to be faced. And the nation today is paying a heavy price for the neglect of the past.

CHAPTER IV

The Roots

What are the roots that clutch,
What branches grow
Out of this stony rubbish!

—T.S. Eliot

In the preceding chapter, I have given a broad picture of the warning signals—the signals which had been hoisted by no less an authority than the Governor of the State. But no attention was paid to these warnings. What to speak of the distant thunder, even the shrieking voices of the storm around the house were not heard. So intoxicated were the guardians with the heady wine of conceit and caprice that even creaking and crumbling doors did not stir them.

In this and the next two chapters, I intend to lay bare the roots and tendrils which gave rise to the current crop of separatism and subversion. Poisonous seeds were persistently planted in the Kashmiri psyche. And these were liberally fertilised. Those, whose obligation it was to stop these plantations and fertilisation, were not aware of even the elementary lesson of history: to compromise with evil was only to rear greater evil; to ignore the inconvenient reality was only to compound it; to bow before the bully was only to invite the butcher next day.

Fall-out of a Soft and Permissive Attitude

On October 2, 1988, the birthday of Mahatma Gandhi, his statue was to be installed in the new High Court complex at Srinagar. The function had been announced. The Chief Justice of India, R.S. Pathak, was to do the formal installation. But a few Muslim lawyers objected. They threatened to cause disturbance at the time of the function. The Chief Minister gave in to the bullying tactics. The function was cancelled.

What were the implications of what happened? A secular Kashmir, part of a secular India, could not have, even in its highest seat of justice, the statue of the Father of the Nation, of a sage who laid down his life for communal harmony and about whom Einstein had said that "generations to come would scarcely believe that such a man ever trod on the earth". Who was the person spearheading the move against the installation? It was none other than Mohammad Shafi Bhat, an advocate of the J&K High Court and an active member of the National Conference, who was later given party ticket for the Srinagar Lok Sabha seat in the elections held in November 1989.

At that time, there was a National Conference(F)-Congress(I) Ministry in office. Such was its lack of adherence to principles, such was its disposition to cling to power, such was the character of Congressmen who formed part of the Ministry that not even a little finger was raised when the function was cancelled.

The bully's appetite could not have been whetted better. Intimidation could not have secured better results. The trouble-makers could not have perceived a more casual and non-committed adversary. Was it not natural for them to nurture higher ambitions and think that more spectacular results could be achieved by deploying a more aggressive and threatening strategy? Only those who are extremely naive would believe that, in the context of the Kashmir situation, softness and surrender on basic principles would not act as invitation to terrorism and militancy.

What is the mental make-up of those who held key positions in the State, drew high salaries, and are still enjoying pensionary and other benefits from the Indian Exchequer? Here is Mufti Baha-ud-Din Farooqi, former Chief Justice of the J&K High Court, speaking through the writ petition* filed by him:

> That, nearly forty-two years back, India annexed the J&K State by manipulation, fraud and force against the declared wishes of the people of the State.

*Writ petition of June 1990.

Is it not treachery? Is it not sedition? Is it not deplorable? I leave it to you to decide. But one thing is clear. It is a sad reflection on the permissive Indian State.

In the same writ petition, Mufti Baha-ud-Din goes on to affirm:

> The people of the State scented mischief and continued the freedom struggle with added determination. . . . That soon after the Indian Army landed in Kashmir, it mounted a powerful offensive on freedom fighters and imposed a reign of terror in the State.

The ex-judge and ex-member of the National Conference considers that the raiders from Pakistan were freedom fighters and that the Indian Army did not go there to defend Kashmir but to establish a reign of terror. Note, further, his averment:

> The Indian Government worked on the plan to weaken and dismember Pakistan and to maintain hegemony on Kashmir through sheer might.

Can anyone believe that it is not a rabid India-baiter or a Pakistani agent or the chief of some subversive organisation, but a former Chief Justice, who is making such statements on oath? But who is to be blamed for such situations? Is it some crafty people or those who allowed themselves to be fooled by such people? Is it not the soft underbelly of the Indian State that has given birth to deceptions and disloyalties?

A few members of the All-India Services (IAS, IPS, IFS, etc.) floated a cooperative society with the objective of meeting their bona fide requirements of housing. The society was registered in June 1985 under the name of Rajtarangini.

A fierce controversy was raised about this case primarily on the grounds that non-State subjects could not acquire residential plots even as members of a housing society. Some prominent members of the National Conference such as Abdul Rashid and Sharif-ud-Din Shariq raised the issue in the State Assembly in March 1988 and severely criticised the registration of the society. This was done despite the fact that the officers had to render lifelong service in the State and their number was only 32. The members of the IAS and IPS were described as agents of the colonial power. They were compared with the officers of the East India Company. Erosion of Article 370 was seen. A conspiracy to upset the balance of population, was alleged. Prosecution of the 'conspirators' was demanded. The officers, in sheer disgust, dissolved the society. No one got any land.

What was disconcerting in this case was not that fault was found with the registration of the society, but the attitude displayed, the contemptuous words used against the Union and its representatives, and the notions that were instilled in the minds of the Kashmiris. There has always been a strong tendency on the part of Kashmiri politicians to project themselves as heroes fighting the imperialists who were out to spread their tentacles at the expense of the poor natives. Could not anyone see that small heroes of the day, taking malicious pleasure in running down the symbols of the Union, and creating their political base on the bashing of the imperialists, would be displaced by the bigger heroes of tomorrow, who would wield a bigger and more brutal stick, the Kalashnikov, and derive more sordid pleasure out of the game, and also receive louder applause from the 'victims'? A psychological atmosphere of hatred could not but lead to violence and bloodshed.

So much dust was kicked up by the local National Conference leaders that the case was gleefully lapped up by the Pakistani media. One leading pressman commented:

> Rajtarangini cooperative housing society had been formed by Indian officers in Kashmir to purchase land for construction of their own houses and thus be able to attain Kashmiri citizenship. This smacked of the action of the Jews who settled in Palestine as 'uprooted refugees' and ultimately drove out the Arabs from their own lands. Under a plot, the Indian officers in Kashmir formed a society, got it registered, obtained government monetary aid, purchased land and was dead set to construct houses for its members. The thing got leaked. There was hue and cry in the press, on the pulpits, in the mosques, and even in the legislative assembly of Kashmir. Members of the Kashmir National Conference also raised a storm. The atmosphere in Kashmir became dangerous.
>
> The result was that the Hindus from India, on their own, voluntarily dissolved the housing society and said it had failed or had been condemned by the people of Kashmir.

> This is what has happened to the Indian officers' cooperative housing society. And this is what will ultimately happen to the Indian imperialist designs on Kashmir. Let the Indian rulers learn a lesson from the incident. All Muslim members, opposition as well as ruling, have lined up against this colonising society. And this is the opinion of every Muslim of Kashmir about the forced marriage of Kashmir with India. Let India ponder over the whole thing.

Just imagine a housing society of 32 officers raising a spectre of colonisation of Kashmir which had a population of seven million at that time. Just see the comparison of this wholly innocuous desire of a few officers to secure land in their own country with the case of settlement of Jews in Palestine. But who were responsible for this venomous propaganda? None but the leaders of the National Conference, the senior coalition partner at the State level, and an ally of the ruling party at the Centre. What did one expect out of this diseased womb? Would not such politics of paradoxes extract its price? Would not the psychological atmosphere of hatred lead to violence one day?

The Union Government enacted the Religious Institutions (Prevention of Misuse) Act, 1988. It was made applicable to all the States of the Union except J&K. Because of Article 370, the concurrence of the State Government was needed for extension of this law to the State. But the same was not given. Why? Because J&K is different; its personality, its identity, is different. What an argument for not having a law which aimed at prevention of misuse of religious premises for political purposes!

Nowhere was this law more needed than in the State of J&K. Nowhere were religious places misused more than here. Nowhere were the seeds of fanaticism and fundamentalism sown more assiduously than from the pulpits of mosques here, every Friday. Nowhere has it been preached more regularly than here that Indian democracy was un-Islamic, Indian secularism was un-Islamic, and Indian socialism was un-Islamic. And yet, neither the State Government which was ruled by two supposedly secular parties, nor the Union Government took the matter seriously. The Union Government did not discharge its obligations to pressurise or persuade the State to fall in line with the rest of the country. What intrigued me most was that the law, which was considered good for about 100 million Muslims in other parts of India, was not considered good for 4 million Muslims of Kashmir.

What was the use of the nationalist forces ruling the country when they would not act in the national interest; when they remained mental slaves of the politics of communalism; when they were inclined to place reliance on words rather than on deeds; when they did not lead, but succumbed; when they encouraged, and not vanquished, the separatist elements; when, instead of building a new society, strong in human and spiritual values, they did everything, wittingly or unwittingly, to repair, renovate and strengthen the old, decaying and smelly citadel of obscurantism; and when they invariably gave precedence to expediency over the basic goals and principles of our Constitution? What could be the result of all this? Did it require any unusual insight to understand where such spurious forces would take us?

On April 8, 1988, at a Friday prayer meeting at Anantnag, the Imam of Delhi Jama Masjid made a virulent speech. He fomented pro-Pak sentiments and stoked the fire of fundamentalism and parochialism. His inner motivation was evident from his reference to UN resolutions on Kashmir and the emphasis which he placed on their implementation both in letter and spirit. Two days after this speech, there were a series of explosions in a Pakistani ammunition depot, near Rawalpindi, causing loss of life and property. On the following day, there were widespread disturbances in Srinagar, Anantnag, and other towns of the State.

The Imam's activities during his visit had surcharged the atmosphere. The explosions in the ammunition depot provided the ignition point, and large-scale disturbances broke out. In these disturbances, one person died, and about 100 were injured. Three vehicles, including one army jeep, were set ablaze, and seven shops were ransacked. These violent disturbances coincided with the visit of Sri Lanka's Prime Minister, Mr. Premadasa, to the Srinagar city. The agitators shouted slogans against India and also against the killing of Sinhalese Muslims in Sri Lanka.

Why did the Imam act in the manner he did? Why did he indulge in what to a discerning mind was plain incitement and plain communalism? Why was sympathy shown to the sufferers of the Pakistani ammunition depot tragedy by organising hartals, while no such sympathy was shown to the victims of Bhopal gas tragedy who also happened to be Muslims? Why did disturbances coincide with the visit of Shri Premadasa? Why were the agitators not even slightly afraid of exhibiting extra-territorial loyalties?

The answer to these and allied questions lies in the general tendency to blink over the evil, to adopt a short-term approach, to do a little patchwork here and a little patchwork there, and hope that the poisonous stream that flows in the body politic of the State will somehow or the other disappear if the eyes are shut. This is not the law of life. This is not what nature permits. Poisonous streams do not die so easily. They usually move on and on, cutting deeper channels and occasionally overflowing the banks and depositing their poisonous silt in areas beyond their beds.

A soft and permissive attitude was not characteristic only of the period from which I have taken the above instances. It was there from the very beginning. An example or two may be given.

To strengthen his leadership amongst the Kashmiri masses of the Valley and do something dramatic on Martyrs Day, July 13, 1949, Sheikh Abdullah sent to Yuvraj Karan Singh draft of a law which provided for expropriation, without payment of compensation, of 10,000 holdings/jagirs in excess of 182 canals. Since the proposed law affected a very large number of people, the Yuvraj gave the draft to Vishnu Sahay, Secretary of Kashmir Affairs, and sought the advice of the Government in the matter. Sheikh Abdullah came to know about it. He was furious. He told the Yuvraj that he had no business to ask for Union Government's advice even informally and that he was merely required to sign the law as a constitutional head of the State. The Yuvraj informed Vishnu Sahay what Sheikh Abdullah had told him. Nevertheless, the Government of India advised him to return the proposal with the note that since the law had far-reaching consequences and there was not even a Legislative Assembly at that moment, it should be examined in consultation with the Union Government.

Despite the Government of India's clear stand, Sheikh Abdullah went ahead with a dramatic announcement of the law at the Martyrs Day public meeting at Lal Chowk, Srinagar. Gopalaswamy Ayyangar wanted that the Government of India should react by declaring the so-called 'law' of Sheikh Abdullah null and void. But Jawaharlal Nehru did not permit this, and the Sheikh had his way.

What is pertinent here is not whether the law was progressive or not, whether it had a communal tinge or not, or whether it was legal or fair, but whether the Government of India should have shown a paralysis of will and thus encourage the Sheikh to get into a habit of defiance and to act virtually as a Sultan. The Government of India failed to realise at the time that its continued appeasement of the Sheikh would ultimately lead to a situation when he would have to be pulled down from his high pedestal by resorting to the extreme measure of dismissing and arresting him, with unhappy consequences for all concerned.

The spirit of Munich has, for most of the period of the last 43 years, determined the attitude of the Indian decision-makers towards Kashmir. A vague hope has been entertained: tomorrow it will be all right. But it will never be all right. The logic of history is against it. The logic of justice is against it. The morality of non-submissiveness to evil is against it.

Catholicity and compassion are one thing, timidity and permissiveness quite another. Hollow and hypocritical values and soft and superficial attitudes never help. They do not placate, but encourage aggressive dispositions. Buying peace for a moment at the cost of basic values only means planting the seeds of trouble and turmoil for the future. It also hastens the process of degeneration on the other side. It creates over-confidence. A timely signal of firmness dampens the propensity to bully. It acts as a brake. It helps the party in regaining its balance. Permissiveness, in the ultimate analysis, spells disaster on both the sides–in fact, for all concerned, even for those who simply choose to stand and watch from the sidelines. Is it not self-evident from what is now happening in Kashmir?

Politics of Deception and Duplicity

To the flaws that were inbuilt in the soft and permissive attitude were added the flaws inherent in the politics of duplicity and deception which became a characteristic feature of the J&K scene. Around every basic principle, insincerity and inconsistency were woven. Whether it is the issue of secularism, autonomy or democracy, different postures could be adopted at different times or at different places by the same leader. Of Sheikh Abdullah, for instance, it was said that he could be "a communalist in Kashmir, a communist in Jammu, and a nationalist in New Delhi".

Most of the Kashmiri politicians were adept in speaking with two voices. They could be secular as well as communal, democratic as well as dictatorial, accessionist as well as pro–Pakistan. The underlying motivation was not principles but power–power for the person and for the coterie around. If the Central leaders allowed the Kashmiri leaders to rule the State in whatever manner they liked, whether or not it was in the interest of the country as a whole or even in the interest of the State, they swore by principles of democracy, socialism and secularism, and accession to India was declared as final. If, on the other hand, any question was raised in regard to the exercise of authority, or any personal ambition was checked, accession became temporary and issues of autonomy, or identity and of the personality of Kashmir were raised, and communal feelings aroused.

Before Sheikh Abdullah lost power in August 1953, he generally sang the song of secularism. But when the Congress Party was established as a separate political entity in J&K, Sheikh Abdullah issued a 'fatwa', religious decree, labelling the Congress Party as an organisation of infidels, 'kafirs'. He declared in the true style of a religious dictator that it would be a sin to offer the funeral prayer, 'namaz-e-janaza', for Muslims who were members of this party.

Would a true secularist issue a 'fatwa'? Would he use the language which Sheikh Abdullah used? Was it any different from the language of an obscurantist or a fundamentalist? Would not religious excommunication of political opponents lead to mediaevalisation of politics and make people narrow-minded and intolerant? Would not Islam, and not secularism, become the base of their political loyalties? And would this not act as an inbuilt attraction for Pakistan? Z.A. Bhutto understood this clearly. That is why he boasted to Dr. Farooq Abdullah in 1974: "Let India double the aid which it is giving to Kashmir, say, for three years. For the same period, Pakistan will stop all aids to 'Azad Kashmir'. Thereafter, plebiscite may be held. The result will still be in favour of Pakistan."

Sheikh Abdullah politicised religion; he paved the way for fundamentalism and built an emotional bedrock against India. His secularism was phoney, a mere stance to suit his power game. He, like his son subsequently, and other National Conference leaders, was neither communal nor secular. He was a mere power seeker. His stance was determined by the strategy of his power game. Nowhere has the faith of the unlettered populace been so unashamedly exploited, and nowhere has it been so cynically blinked at, as in Kashmir.

After regaining power, consequent upon the signing of the Kashmir Accord (1975), Sheikh Abdullah once again became the high priest of secularism. But what Sheikh Abdullah did during the State Assembly elections in 1977, once again showed that he exploited Islam to the hilt. At first, after Mrs. Gandhi lost Lok Sabha elections in 1977 and Janata Government came to power, he wooed the Janata Party and asked two Members of Parliament belonging to his party–Begum Akhtar Jahan and Abdul Ahad Vakil–to support it in the Lok Sabha. But as soon as the Janata Party decided to fight State Assembly elections on its own, he berated it on communal grounds. In April 1977 he observed, "Kashmir Congress is a dirty gutter. Democracy will undoubtedly thrive under Janata Party. We yearn to be its ally. Jan Sanghis are our brothers." But barely after a month, in June 1977, he said, "Janata Party is anti-Muslim, Jan Sanghi in new garb. The hands of Jan Sangh leaders are still soiled with Muslim blood." He sent his workers, with *Quran* in hand, exhorting the Kashmiri Muslims not to vote for a party of the infidels.

Since leaders like Sheikh Abdullah benefited by exploiting religion for political purposes, is it not understandable that the present-day youth should be deploying essentially the same strategy? The hundreds of loudspeakers installed on the mosques, and speeches delivered from the pulpits, are nothing but continuation and intensification of practices started by Sheikh Abdullah and his National Conference. When Dr. Qazi Nissar, chief of Ummat-i-Islami, was assailed by the National Conference leaders for exploiting religion for elections in March 1987, he shot back:* "Who taught us to do so? What had Sheikh Abdullah been doing in his life time? Did he not make his speeches from Hazratbal Shrine? Have the National Conference workers forgotten the 1977 and 1983 elections when they moved with the Holy Quran in their hands to seek votes?"

The same phenomenon of duplicity and deception was noted with regard to accession. Basically, Sheikh Abdullah was neither for India nor for Pakistan. It was his power game that got precedence over everything else. What suited him at a particular moment was all that mattered. From 1947 to 1952, he went on proclaiming that accession of Kashmir to India was based on fundamental principles and was irrevocable. In 1948, he told Jawaharlal Nehru, "We have made our choice and linked our destiny with India, and nothing can separate us now." On March 7, 1949 he announced, "We have decided to work with and die for India."

---

*Dr. Qazi Nissar's interview with *The Hindustan Times,* July 7, 1987.

While he was making such solemn declarations, he was sounding various quarters for support to the idea of having an independent Kashmir. As early as January 28, 1948, Sheikh Abdullah discussed the subject of independence with the American officials. This is evident from the note sent by Warren Austin† to the State Department after an interview with Sheikh Abdullah on January 28, 1948. Again, on April 14, 1948, Sheikh Abdullah gave an interview to Michael Davidson of *Scotsman* in which he said, "Independent Kashmir, guaranteed by United Nations, may be the only solution." Sheikh Abdullah suggested to Sir Owen Dixon in 1950 that one possible solution of the Kashmir issue would be independent Kashmir. At that time, Sheikh Abdullah also wanted to enter into bilateral talks with the leaders of 'Azad Kashmir'.

This was the working of the mind of a person whom Nehru, in a letter to the Maharaja on November 13, 1947, described as "the only person who could deliver the goods in Kashmir".

The same phenomenon of duplicity and deception was witnessed with regard to the implementation of the Delhi Agreement. As indicated in Chapter II, after getting the part of the Agreement which was favourable to Abdullah implemented Sheikh Abdullah changed his colours.

At that point of time Nehru's position looked almost pathetic. Having placed all his eggs only in one basket, Nehru did not know how to save the eggs when the basket itself started tilting. In almost all his letters on Kashmir during the period 1952 to 1953, he made repeated use of the expression "I do not know". For instance, in his letter dated April 25, 1952,* to Sheikh Abdullah, Nehru said, "For the moment, it is not clear to me what I should do." Likewise, in his letter dated April 27, 1953,†† to Bakshi Ghulam Mohammad, Deputy Prime Minister, Nehru remarked: "I do not mind dealing with any matter but I quite feel helpless about this Kashmir issue because I do not

---

† See "Warren Austin to State Department on interview with Abdullah, 28 January, 1948", *Foreign Relations of United States* 1948. Vol. 5 , Part I, p. 292. The report (Sept. 1950) of Loy Henderson, the US Ambassador to India, is another piece of confirmation. Henderson noted: "in discussing future Kashmir, Abdullah was vigorous that it should be independent."

* For full text see *Letters to Chief Ministers 1947-1964* (G. Parthasarathi, ed.), Govt. of India, 1985.

†† For full text see letters as referred in Chapter VI of Dr. S. Gopal's *Jawaharlal Nehru: A Biography*. Vol. II, 1979, Oxford University Press, New Delhi.

know where I stand." In yet another letter to Sheikh Abdullah on August 25, 1952, he laments, "Meeting with the United Nations officials, or developments in Pakistan do not worry me in the least. What has sometimes worried me is what happens in Kashmir, because I have found doubt and hesitation there, and not clarity of vision or firmness of outlook.* In his letter to Maulana Azad of March 1, 1953,† Nehru wrote, "My fear is that the Sheikh, in his present state of mind, is likely to do something or take some step which might make things worse."

Earlier, too, Nehru had been stumped by Abdullah's duplicity. On July 4, 1950,* in his letter to Sheikh Abdullah, he said, "I have not thought of Kashmir or of you in that way and so I am rather at a loss how to act when the very foundation of my thought and action has been shaken up."

Having ignored the streaks of duplicity and deception in Sheikh Abdullah's outlook and having earlier showered disproportionate praise on him, Nehru was very badly caught on the wrong foot in August 1953 when he found that there was no alternative but to dismiss Sheikh Abdullah. Because of his imbalanced approach, which led him to self-contradictory decisions, he damaged his own international standing and tarnished the country's image. India had to hear such adverse comments as these from Bertrand Russell: "When one observes that the high idealism of Indian government in international matters breaks down completely when confronted with the question of Kashmir, it is difficult to avoid a feeling of despair."* Nehru's critics also got the opportunity of branding him as 'a Brutus', 'a fraud'.

It has been made out in certain quarters that Nehru did not know about Sheikh Abdullah's dismissal and arrest. Gundevia, for instance, makes such a claim. But nothing could be more unconvincing than this. Nehru was so possessive about Kashmir policy that not even its minor components could move without his specific approval. How could such a major event as Sheikh Abdullah's arrest take place without Nehru nodding his head in its favour?

---

* For full text see *Letters to Chief Ministers 1947-1964* (G. Parthasarathi, ed.), Govt. of India, 1985.

† For full text see letters as referred in Chapter VI of Dr. S. Gopal's *Jawaharlal Nehru: A Biography,* Vol. II, 1979, Oxford University Press, New Delhi.

Even Sheikh Abdullah, whom Nehru always went out of the way to prop up, had harsh words about him. This is what Abdullah said about Nehru in *Atish-e-Chinar*:†

> Nehru used to call himself an agnostic. But he was also a great admirer of the past heritage and the Hindu spirit of India. His interpretation of the Indian history, though not always based upon accurate knowledge, approximates to the interpretation of revivalists like K.M. Munshi and Dayanand Saraswati. He considered himself as an instrument of rebuilding India with its ancient spirit.
>
> In Nehru's outlook, therefore, imprints of Machiavelli's political philosophy and jugglery are found. That is why the disciple of the principled philosopher and saint, Mahatma Gandhi, was at the same time very much fond of Chanakya. Jawaharlal Nehru employed Machiavellian approach towards us in Kashmir. He dealt with Pakistan in the same fashion. At international level also he exhibited the same Machiavellian outlook with regard to Hungary and other issues.
>
> Nehru could go to any extent to fulfil obligations towards his friends. But this he would do only if his personal power and position were not adversely affected. He would change his stance and colour when his own standing was in jeopardy. When I ceased to be useful to him, he had me sent to jail. At his instance, Bakshi Ghulam Mohammad betrayed his mentor and his nation. But when he, too, was not needed by Nehru, he was thrown out of the window like a rotten fruit. Likewise, when his own position was threatened, Krishna Menon, who was only carrying out Nehru's policy, and whom I also never liked, was made a sacrificial goat, disgraced and removed from the Cabinet.
>
> In the end, the Chanakya in Nehru ruined him. In respect of his China policy he was not only wounded politically but also suffered mentally. As an inheritor of Gandhi's legacy, he tried to become a champion of high moral principles. But his standing began to be viewed with suspicion and his claims lost all validity on account of the manner in which he dealt with Kashmir.

†Pages 351-355, translated from Urdu by the author. About *Afish-e-Chinar,* see earlier footnote. When this book was given Sahitya Akademi Award posthumously, the Hindustani Writers Guild protested on the ground that the book contained quite a few observations which were evidently inaccurate (UNI report, February 19,1989).

Poor Nehru got it both ways–from his political foes as well as his friends. The real culprit was the politics of deception and duplicity initiated by Sheikh Abdullah. Had he shown even a modicum of sincerity with regard to the issue of accession, most of the subsequent troubles and turmoils could have been avoided.

What Sheikh Abdullah did after August 1953 was equally inconsistent. Most of his speeches and actions were wholly irreconcilable with his earlier stand. He virtually toed the Pakistani line. He remained in touch with Pakistani authorities through the workers of 'War Council' and 'Plebiscite Front'.* With the help of Pakistani agents, he managed to have his letter sent to the Security Council. He even entered into a criminal conspiracy to overthrow the government with the help of men, material and money from Pakistan. When he was released on January 8, 1958, he entered the Valley with a great deal of fanfare and made anti-India speeches at various places. Though he miserably failed to re-establish his control over Mujahid Manzil, the National Conference Party headquarters, on January 17, 1958,** and his call to boycott the Republic Day celebrations on January 26, 1958, did not evoke any worthwhile response, he continued to whip up mass hysteria by exploiting the religious faith of the poor, non-discerning populace and exhorting them to act as martyrs of Islam had acted against the oppressor. When he was re-arrested on April 29, 1958, a draft resolution of the Plebiscite Front, virtually endorsing the Pakistani stand, was recovered from his house. During the course of the Kashmir Conspiracy Case, Sheikh Abdullah used the forum of the court to carry out extensive anti-India propaganda. In fact, for most of the time up to 1972, he tilted heavily in favour of Pakistan. It was Sheikh Abdullah's pro-Pakistan attitude that, in part, encouraged Pakistan to make another attempt to grab Kashmir by force in 1965. But when it suited his ends, he signed the Kashmir Accord (1975) and changed his stance.

There was validity in the criticism of his detractors who said that the 'place of honour' about which Sheikh Abdullah talked for 22 years

---

* See Chapter II: 'Survey of History'; and subsequent sections of this chapter on the Kashmir Accord and the Plebiscite Front.

**On this day, Sheikh Abdullah had given a public call for massive gathering at Pather Masjid, ostensibly for Friday prayer, but actually for setting the crowd after the prayer on the Mujahid Manzil, which is located just opposite the mosque. Huge crowds gathered. But the Sheikh himself did not appear, his courage having failed him at the eleventh hour.

meant "Chief Ministership for himself and subsequently for his son, Dr. Farooq Abdullah; membership of Parliament for his wife, Akbar Jahan; ministership for his son-in-law, G.M. Shah; and lucrative posts for his other friends and relations."

What is true of Sheikh Abdullah is also true, to some extent, of G.M. Shah and Dr. Farooq Abdullah. When G.M. Shah was the Chief Minister, he was all out for India; for him, accession was irrevocable and final. When he went out of power, he started saying, "Every Kashmiri Muslim is a Pakistani. I am also a Pakistani; a great mistake was made by acceding to India." Till 1975, when the National Conference was out of power, Dr. Farooq Abdullah kept company with Amanullah Khan. In 1974, he even went to the extent of saying, "For independence of Kashmir every child would give his blood." His recorded speech was believed to have been broadcast from Azad Kashmir Radio from January 22 to 26, 1990, to incite Kashmiris to rise in revolt against India.

A.G. Lone, at one stage, was a Congress Minister. At that time, India was seen by him as the haven of secularism and democracy, and accession was considered as a sound and valid decision. But the moment he lost office, he put on different spectacles. India became communal and colonial, and accession was described as a tragic blunder. When he found that incitement to violence would pay him richer political dividend, he went to the extent of praising the Sikh assassins of General A.S. Vaidya and virtually goaded the Muslim youth to emulate them.

In 1986, a Pakistani journalist, who originally hailed from Baramulla, came to see me. During the course of our talk, I asked him as to what impression he had gathered during his visit. He said, "I can say something definitely only about the politicians as I have met a large number of them. Those who are in power at the moment are with India and those who are not, are for Pakistan."

Illusions

The politics of deception and duplicity created different illusions for different actors of the drama. The Central Government, particularly Jawaharlal Nehru, nursed one type of illusion, while Sheikh Abdullah and his National Conference entertained another type of illusion. Therein lay the tragedy of Kashmir. The Union leaders expected that, in course of time, Kashmir would get fully integrated in the Union, disproving the two-nation theory, while Sheikh had an inner compulsion to act like a semi-independent monarch and establish a virtual 'Sheikhdom' with no one to question him.

Even Sardar Patel was taken in by the Indian illusion. When V. Shankar expressed doubt about the wisdom of Sardar Patel agreeing, albeit against his better judgement, to the draft of Gopalaswamy Ayyangar in regard to the special status of Kashmir, he remarked: "After all, neither Sheikh Abdullah nor Gopalaswamy is permanent. The future would depend upon the strength and guts of the Indian Government and if we cannot have confidence in our own strength we do not deserve to exist as a nation."

Different expectations which these illusions created amongst different actors of the drama did not materialise. They simply could not. Illusions were, after all, illusions. They could not even stay as illusions for long. The political, social and religious realities shattered them.

Since false hopes had been raised and emotions worked up, subsequent disappointments turned into bitterness, and bitterness into frustrations, and frustrations into conflicts. And, then, with the passage of time, new illusions were entertained, new hopes raised and new bitterness, frustrations and conflicts followed. The cycle went on. And it goes on even now. Perhaps, it will go on in future also.

The Indian leadership did not realise, and has not done even now, that it was the illusions that needed to be eliminated. The castles in the air had to be replaced by concrete citadels raised on firm foundations. Actual realities had to be respected. The closed circuit of old thinking had to be replaced by a new model. Unhealthy consequences of permissiveness had to be recognised. The inbuilt deception and insincerity, and the disposition to keep alive the two-nation theory, had to be done away with.

Kashmir Accord

The Kashmir Accord* of February 1975 was another manifestation of the old habit of entertaining illusions. After the Bangladesh War and in the light of the changed circumstances, negotiations took place between the representatives of Sheikh Abdullah and Mrs. Indira Gandhi. After long, almost tortuous, negotiations, the Kashmir Accord was signed in February 1975.

*See also Chapter II: 'Survey of History'.

The main provisions of the Kashmir Accord were that Article 370 would remain and the residuary powers would continue to vest in the State Government. It also stipulated that "where any provision of the Constitution of India had been applied to the State of J&K with adaptations and modifications, such adaptations and modifications can be altered or repealed by an Order of the President under Article 370, each individual proposal in this behalf being considered on its merits; but provisions of the Constitution of India already applied to the State of J&K without adaptation or modification are unalterable." The full text of this Accord is given in Appendix IX.

In essence, the Kashmir Accord did not change the constitutional relationship between the Union and the State. It was primarily a device to bring Sheikh Abdullah back to power and also give an impression that certain aspects relating to autonomy could be reviewed. Mrs. Indira Gandhi brought out the essence of the Accord when she said in her statement to Parliament on February 24, 1975, "Nobody had denied Sheikh Abdullah the previous role. In between, he seemed to have changed his mind and there was disagreement and estrangement. Now that he is again expressing his willingness to work for unity, for secularism, we welcome him."

The Kashmir Accord was, undoubtedly, beneficial in some respects. As stated by Swaran Singh in Parliament in justification of the Accord, "The need for change was that there was an influential section of public opinion in J&K which still was not in the mainstream of Indian nationalism." In the international arena also, India's case could perhaps be better understood. This was evident from the unhappiness of Pakistan over the signing of the Accord. Z.A. Bhutto gave a call for hartal to protest against the Accord.

But the Accord did not tackle the fundamental problems. The emotional ingredients of Article 370 remained intact. The forces which had, in the first instance, created a situation that led to the events of August 1953, were not really vanquished. Nothing was done to ensure that the communal card and the card of Kashmir's identity were not played to strengthen the personal power and position of Sheikh Abdullah and his family. Nor was any remedial measure taken to stop the unhealthy fall-outs from the politics of deception and duplicity. Avenues that could set the clock back were not effectively plugged. And Sheikh Abdullah did put a number of items* in the

*See Chapter V: 'Roots: Hidden Veins'(Sections: Administrative Roots, and Regional Roots).

reverse gear. He soon became a 'mini Sultan' again. There was nothing wrong in burying the unsavoury past. But putting the unpleasant dirt underneath the carpet did not help. It began to ooze out and soon a suffocating atmosphere was created.

Swaran Singh hailed the Kashmir Accord as "an accession of heart and mind and an act of faith". Sheikh Abdullah described it as re-establishment of trust and confidence. He said, "We have established a solid foundation for mutual cooperation." But it was soon discovered that the solid foundation was made of spurious and substandard material. Cracks started appearing. By 1977, the super-structure collapsed. Another illusion stood shattered.

Mir Qasim in his book, *Dastan-e-Hayat,* primarily blamed Mrs. Gandhi for the failure of the Kashmir Accord. He thought that Mrs. Gandhi was always suspicious of Sheikh Abdullah and Mir Qasim, and the decision of the Congress(I) Legislature Party on March 26, 1977, to elect a new leader and withdraw support to Sheikh Abdullah was the last nail in the coffin of the Kashmir Accord. But Mir Qasim is only partly right. He does not adequately explain as to why it was necessary for Sheikh Abdullah to convert the Plebiscite Front into National Conference, why Mrs. Gandhi was not consulted in clear terms about the nominee of her party in the State Cabinet, why Sheikh Abdullah was keen to induct A.G. Lone in his ministry, the person who had earlier deserted the Congress Party, and why the Sheikh acted in an arbitrary manner and rewarded the Plebiscite Front workers and leaders with bonanzas, such as pensions for freedom fighters. The Accord was a failure not only because a section of the Congress(I) Party of J&K was hostile to it from the very beginning but also because the basic contradictions and incompatibilities were not resolved and the concept of autonomy was allowed, as in the past, to degenerate into licence under the umbrella of the 'democratic dictatorship' of Sheikh Abdullah.

Reverse Gear

The Resettlement Act. After the Kashmir Accord of 1975, and particularly after the State Assembly elections of 1977, the process of integration of the State with the Union was put in the reverse gear. Further extensions of the provisions of the Indian Constitution and Central laws to the State virtually stopped, even when these were in public interest and highly beneficial to the common folk. The bogey of autonomy was raised from time to time. The pattern of All-India Services was subverted. And the protective wall of Article 370 was raised higher. But the most glaring manifestation of the reverse gear was the J&K Grant of Permit for Resettlement Act, 1982.

The manner in which the Resettlement Act was brought in, provides yet another example of how the 'local Sultans' invariably tried to strengthen their position, whenever they thought that they needed to do so, by stoking parochial and communal sentiments. The emotional integration of Kashmir with the rest of the country was of least concern to them.

The ostensible objective of the Resettlement Act, 1982, was to provide for the resettlement of Kashmiris who had migrated to Pakistan-Occupied Kashmir or Pakistan itself, and to unite the Kashmiri families who had been separated from their kith and kin. In a pamphlet titled *Why Resettlement Bill,* it was, *inter alia*, claimed that the legislation fulfilled a constitutional requirement and facilitated return and resettlement of the State subjects. But such claims were mere rationalisations, and sounded hollow.

The real objective of the Resettlement Act was to present Sheikh Abdullah and the National Conference as champions of Kashmiri unity and Kashmiri identity, lionise the Sheikh further, blow up his image, create an atmosphere which would facilitate 'coronation' of Farooq Abdullah as the Sheikh's successor, make a show of autonomy and independence, display a bit of insolence towards the Central Government, undermine the Kashmir Accord, give some shape to what has been called the 'Greater Kashmir' plan by ensuring effective Muslim majority for the districts of Poonch and Rajouri, and bring about a general situation in which the basic issues of progress and welfare were forgotten by the masses and no one questioned the honesty* of the leaders.

As was expected, the Resettlement Bill raised a fierce controversy. Hundreds of representations were received by Governor B.K. Nehru and the Central Government. The Governor took some time for considering these representations and making up his mind. Even this was objected to by G.M. Shah, then minister in Sheikh Abdullah's cabinet, and he demanded that the Governor should sign the Bill or resign.

---

*See Chapter V: 'Roots: Hidden Veins' (Section: Public Corruption).

B.K. Nehru decided to send a message to the legislature pointing out the infirmities of the Bill, including the legal and constitutional ones. But Dr. Farooq Abdullah, who became Chief Minister after the death of Sheikh Abdullah on September 8, 1982, persisted and got the Bill passed on October 4, 1982, from the State Assembly for the second time. The Governor had no option but to give his assent. After discussions with the new Chief Minister, Dr. Farooq Abdullah, the Central Government sought the advice of the Supreme Court, where the case is still pending.

In regard to the entire controversy about Resettlement Bill the way it was started, and the way it was given a temporary burial, a number of questions arise. Where was the justification? Could the fact of three wars–1947, 1965 and 1971–be ignored? Would not the return of the so-called Kashmiri families cause social and economic disruption and also pose a serious threat to the security of the country? Who would guarantee that spies and saboteurs do not move in? How could a Bill, which basically related to the grant of citizenship rights, be enacted by the State Legislature? And how could the children of the migrants, born and brought up in Pakistan, be given Indian nationality?

These questions were important in themselves, and reflected on the insular, parochial and separatist thinking of Sheikh Abdullah and the National Conference. But there were other questions, too. And these were of far greater significance for the future. Was not the Resettlement Act a move to create an environment which would give birth to the movement for an independent Kashmir? Were not conditions being created, seeds being planted, minds being re-fashioned, dormant emotions being stocked and pro-independence feelings being strengthened to ask for what the Jammu and Kashmir Liberation Front is asking now? Is it difficult to see that the Jammu and Kashmir Liberation Front has similar motivation? The thinking of the protagonists of the Resettlement Act and the thinking of the supporters of the current liberation movement spring from the same root, that is, the separatist psyche.

Spurious Democracy

In regard to another basic issue–democracy–the same ambivalence, the same deception and the same disposition to build personal nests, were present. The brand of democracy which Sheikh Abdullah and his coterie cultivated in Kashmir was largely based upon negative factors and forces. It was built around mediaeval instincts and sectarian emotions. It stoked the personality cult, and did not hesitate to employ intimidatory tactics. It was essentially manipulative and fascist in character. It created imprisoned and prejudiced minds and then hijacked them to the ballot boxes. Clearly, such a spurious coin could not hold ground for long.

What I have stated above would be evident from the way Sheikh Abdullah prepared the ground for dynastic succession, and also from the manner in which the National Conference fought the elections during the period beginning from the Kashmir Accord (February 1975) to the Rajiv-Farooq Accord (November 1986).

On August 21, 1981, Sheikh Abdullah made a speech at Iqbal Park, Srinagar. The English translation of a part of the speech* is as follows:

> In 1930, Pt. Motilal Nehru had entrusted the presidentship of the Indian National Congress to the new generation led by Pandit Jawaharlal Nehru, and we have seen how that had served well. Today, I find myself standing on the same delicate crossroads. I am handing over the presidentship of the National Conference to the new generation represented by Dr. Farooq Abdullah. This is a great honour and a big test. The crown that I am putting on his head is full of thorns; I hope that Dr. Farooq Abdullah will be worthy of it. I pray to God that he may come out successful in the test.
>
> I have nursed this nation, the Kashmiri people, with a lot of care, and have bathed this nation with tears. I have dedicated the best part of my years in the service of the nation. I would like that the younger generation should be worthy of the trust.
>
> Colleagues, my heart is full, keeping the greatness of the occasion in view. I am grateful to God that he had selected me for discharging a great trust. I am grateful that he gave me strength since 1931.
>
> I thank all those friends and colleagues who were my fellow-travellers and who supported me on all difficult occasions. If I did not have their trust and confidence, I could not have discharged the trust given to me. I bow my head to these colleagues who had risked their lives in the freedom struggle. I also pay my respects to the martyrs who sacrificed their lives in the service of the nation, those sisters who sacrificed their own 'suhag' for the country.

*This was penned in Urdu by the person on duty at the public meeting.

The occasion of the speech was annual convention of the National Conference, but the real purpose was the 'coronation' of Farooq Abdullah.

The speech is significant. It brings out some of the dominant traits of Sheikh Abdullah's personality. He wants responsibility to be entrusted to the younger generation. But whom does he choose? His son, Dr. Farooq Abdullah. See how he projects himself, how he speaks of his sacrifices, his 'having bathed the nation with his tears'. See how he covers up his real intention and reminds the audience that Motilal, too, had handed over Congress presidentship to Jawaharlal. It does not matter if the circumstances were different or the decision-making process was different. Note also how he again and again describes Kashmiris as a nation and whips up the issue of identity. See how he talks of his life long friends who made innumerable sacrifices for him, and then proceeds to ignore the stoutest of them, Mirza Afzal Beg, and also other senior leaders of his party like G.M. Shah* and places the 'crown' on the head of his son, thereby bottling up many legitimate aspirations. When asked by Sheikh Abdullah to sign the 'personal loyalty pledge', Mirza Afzal Beg had resisted and demanded the matter to be discussed in the party forum. Sheikh Abdullah agreed. But, within a few hours, he asked for Beg's resignation. Beg remarked "If a person cannot trust 47 years of loyalty and friendship, how could he trust declaration of two sentences?" Afzal Beg was the principal architect of land reforms, the live wire of the Plebiscite Front, and the sole negotiator of the Kashmir Accord. No one could have served Sheikh Abdullah better through thick and thin, and no one else could have been made a worse sacrificial goat at the altar of the personality and dynastic cult.

In the same speech, Sheikh Abdullah talked of economic and social disparities of the Maharaja's time. He did not mention the disparities that he had himself created. He also brought in the communal factor: "In India, even after 34 years, Muslims live with a fear psychosis." At the same time he knew that, at that moment, when he was manoeuvring to have his son installed in his place, it was not expedient to rub the Central leaders, such as Indira Gandhi beyond a point. He, therefore, also quoted what Abul Kalam Azad had said at the Ramgarh Congress Session: "I am a Muslim and I am proud to be so. The culture of Islam is my health and it is my duty to protect it.

*See Chapter VII: 'July 2, 1984: Dismissal of Dr. Farooq Abdullah'.

But, with all this, I feel proud that I am an Indian and it is our duty to forge ahead with the Indian national cause."

Election Techniques

The elections in Kashmir during the above period (February 1975 to November 1986) were fought by the National Conference with fascist techniques. The electorate was never allowed to think on rational grounds. It was assiduously propagated that if the Kashmiris wanted to get rid of 'slavery', they must vote for the National Conference. The cult of personality, built around Sheikh Abdullah, was exploited. The Sheikh was portrayed as a champion of Kashmiri freedom, as a destroyer of Central leaders.

The weakness of the Central Government, its vacillation, its frequent changes in stand, its lack of commitment to clear goals, the ostrich-like attitude of the Governors, the disproportionate praise of Sheikh Abdullah and his family, all emboldened the National Conference to follow the above course. Quite a sizeable section of the Central leadership, the press and the opposition were taken in by the double talk or were influenced by extremely narrow political considerations. None showed the courage to call a spade a spade or work hard to understand the deeper currents.

The combined effect of all these factors was that elections during the period in question ceased to have any real meaning for democracy or the national cause. They turned out to be mere exercises for keeping the unpatriotic elements alive. They gave an opportunity to the unscrupulous leaders to whip up communal and local prejudices and exploit the innocent and the ignorant, and maintain their complete sway by resorting to almost treasonable activities.

There is a preponderance of evidence to support my contention. But here I would restrict myself to the campaign of the National Conference(F) during the Lok Sabha elections of December 1984 and invite attention to a few posters, reproduced hereunder, that were widely circulated at that time. All these posters were printed and distributed by the National Conference.

Poster (I) suggests in a telling manner that all Kashmiris are in chains. Who has put these chains? Obviously, India. The entire 'Kashmiri nation' is identified with the National Conference(F). The last line of the poster pointedly says that the 'plough *(Hul)* is the symbol of 'your struggle, your freedom', etc. Struggle against whom?

توڑ اس دستِ جفاکیش کو یارب جس نے
روحِ آزادیٔ کشمیر کو پامال کیا
اس جفاکیش ہاتھ کو کاٹ ڈالیے جو مظلوموں کے خون سے رنگا ہوا ہے
اس ہاتھ کو ہمیشہ کیلئے توڑ دیجئے جو ریاستی عوام کی آزادی کا بدترین دشمن ہے
ہل پر مہر لگایئے
آپ کی جدوجہد آزادی اور آپ کے جمہوری حقوق کے تحفظ کی علامت ہے

(I)

(II)

(III)

Freedom from what? Are the Kashmiris not already free? Do they consider themselves slaves?

At the top of the poster is a verse which means "O! God, break this hand of the cruel–the hand that has destroyed the soul of Kashmir's freedom."

The poster further says that "this hand which is stained with the blood of the innocent victims should be cut for all times to come". Does it not mean the 'Indian' hand?

What does this poster, in its context, mean? What is its effect in totality? What does it convey to the Kashmiris? And what is the intention of the National Conference(F)? Does the message of this poster fit in with the speeches, announcements and declarations made by Dr. Farooq Abdullah in other places in India?

Poster (II) shows the map of Kashmir and a young Kashmiri boy, with his horror-stricken face, perched inside the boundary line. He lies prostrate with a spear being pushed in his chest by a strong and brutal hand. The hand is shown emerging from outside Kashmir, that is India. The sinister meaning is obvious. The cruel and blood-thirsty Indians are butchering innocent Kashmiris. The bloody hand, the strong fist, and the blood around the boy's chest, convey their own meanings, especially to the Kashmiris.

Poster (III) shows bayonets and rifles being pointed against Kashmir. Whose bayonets and rifles are these? The Kashmiris will certainly take them as India's. The wording: 'think, think for a while' exhorts the people to think that they are surrounded by the enemy.

There was another poster with the pamphlet titled: *Operation New Star*. The poster described the girl as a daughter of the 'nation'—Kashmiri nation. It exhorted the Kashmiris to avenge her blood by voting for the National Conference(F). The pamphlet said that the innocent girl was the victim of bullets of Indian security forces, implying that these forces were aliens and were killing innocent girls. The damaging nature of the propaganda was compounded by the fact that the girl had died in an accidental firing by an official of the Kashmir police when a procession was taken out by the Shia Muslim community.

The democracy which Sheikh Abdullah, Farooq Abdullah and National Conference built in Kashmir was exploitative in nature. It drew sustenance from techniques which could provide only temporary gains to the wielders of power. The hate propaganda created revulsion against India on the one hand, and, on the other, hid the poor and corrupt* performance of the State Government.

If the Kashmiri youth today has started hating India, is it the fault of the youth or of those who indulged in or permitted propaganda of this nature? The tragic irony becomes all the more pronounced when it is remembered that this was being done by a party about whose supreme leader, Sheikh Abdullah, President Sanjiva Reddy said in October 1977 at Srinagar, "For his achievements, Sheikh Abdullah deserves to be called Sher-i-Kashmir (lion of Kashmir) as also Sher-i-Bharat (lion of India)."

Another dark side of Kashmir's democracy was its oligarchic, possessive and intolerant character. Interestingly, Mohammad Amin Chughtai, an Urdu poet of Jammu, had sensed its nature** as early as in the forties. About Sheikh Abdullah's idea of 'New Kashmir', he versified thus:

تمنا شیخ جی کی ہے نیا کشمیر بن جائے
نیا کشمیر بن کر آپ کی جاگیر بن جائے
اگر کوئی مخالف بات ان کے سامنے کرے
تو بخشی کی چھری اک آن میں شمشیر بن جائے

* See Chapter V: 'Roots: Hidden Veins' (Sections: Administrative Roots, and Roots in Public Corruption).

**In his letter of December 11, 1947, to Sardar Patel, Mehar Chand Mahajan also complained about the Nazi's type of administration which Sheikh Abdullah was setting up.

The gist of the above verse is: It is the desire of the Sheikh that a new Kashmir should come into being, and thereafter it should become his personal fiefdom. If anyone says anything to oppose him, the Bakshi's stick should at once turn into a sword and take care of the opponent.

Spread of Infection

As it was bound to happen, the environmental insincerity soon seeped into the power structure itself, howsoever tight the inner crust was. A tendency developed to deceive old colleagues and close associates. Bakshi deceived Sheikh Abdullah who behaved no better and badly let down Mirza Afzal Beg, his lifelong senior party colleague. Moulvi Farooq who was helped by Bakshi Ghulam Mohammad in becoming the Mirwaiz turned against his benefactor and caused Bakshi the maximum damage in public esteem during the 'Moe-e-Muqaddas'* agitation. Mutual doubts and suspicions spread to such an extent that all the Ministers of Dr. Farooq's Cabinet were taken to the grave of Sheikh Abdullah on September 14, 1982, immediately after the swearing-in ceremony at Raj Bhavan, and made to take a pledge of loyalty to the new Chief Minister by holding in hand a small quantity of the earth from the grave. But such tactics could not withstand the environmental reality. It was none other than Dr. Farooq's own sister, Mrs. Khalida Shah, who brought him down from the office of the Chief Minister. The mother, Begum Sheikh Abdullah, sided with the son, and Kashmir witnessed the tragi-comic spectacle of Begum Sheikh Abdullah doing the 'namaz-e-janaza', funeral prayer, for her daughter, thereby proclaiming that so far as she was concerned, her daughter was dead. The ease with which friendships, loyalties and postures were changed was truly amazing. This greatly undermined the moral tone and tenor of the society, and frequently exposed the State to convulsions of violence and instability. In this connection, I will give only one recent example–the phenomenon called 'Double Farooq'.

During the first half of the year 1988, the two Farooqs–Dr. Farooq Abdullah and Moulvi Farooq–were political allies. But, almost continuously, one was trying to run down the other. Their stand brought out the intriguing nature of Kashmir politics and the

*See Chapter II: 'Survey of History'

proclivity of the Kashmir politicians to blow hot and cold at the same time. In this regard, a local commentator humorously but significantly observed in April 1988: "There is every possibility that the future history of Kashmir will revolve round the activities of the two Farooqs-one blowing hot and cold from Jamia Masjid and the other blowing cold and hot from Hazratbal Shrine. They have nothing in common except deception and ambivalence."

On June 9, 1988, disturbances broke out in Srinagar city. These disturbances continued, with intermittent pauses, till June 15. Five persons were killed and about 100 injured. The ostensible cause of these disturbances was the protest of 'the people' against the decision of the State Government to enhance the electricity rates. But the real cause was the highly irritating relationship between the two 'Farooqs', and the ambition of Moulvi Farooq to carve out a larger political niche for himself in the State politics.

The hike in the electricity rates did not affect 93% of the consumers. Whatever impact it had on the industry was largely in the Jammu region. Yet the agitation was organised in the Valley, particularly in Srinagar, in the central portion of which Moulvi Farooq had sizeable following. The trouble was mainly engineered by him. Using mostly the Jamia Masjid as his political platform, he lambasted the Chief Minister in every conceivable way. For instance, on June 17, he described Dr. Farooq Abdullah as "wholly undependable", and accused him of following 'anti-people' policies. Simultaneously, in an attempt to boost his own image, he referred to the sacrifices made by the 'Mirwaiz dynasty' and drew the attention of the public to the role played by the Awami Action Committee in the Moe-e-Muqaddas agitation of 1964. On another occasion, he described Dr. Farooq Abdullah as "immature and unstable" and a "friend when out of power" and a "foe when in power" Dr. Farooq Abdullah, too, became more pungent in his remarks. On June 18, he described Moulvi Farooq as a "mere hen" and said that today's moulvis had no character–they talked religion in the day-time and saw blue films in the night.

Earlier, Begum Sheikh Abdullah, 'Madre-e-Meharban', as she was called at that time, had been saying that Moulvi Farooq and Dr. Farooq were her two sons, two eyes. These remarks, in the context of what they were doing to each other in mid-1988, looked highly ironical, and spoke volumes about the quicksand of Kashmiri politics. The poor people were the sufferers. In the June 1988 agitation, five precious lives were consumed by the rivalries and conflicts of the two leaders–Dr. Farooq and Moulvi Farooq–who were supposed to be political allies. And the State was subjected to agony for days.

What was still worse, no hesitation was generally shown in adopting blatantly unfair means to secure personal and political ends. For instance, in the Lok Sabha elections of December 1984, G.M. Shah and his cabinet colleagues had drawn out a diabolical 'scheme'* to secure victory for the candidates of the Khalida faction of the National Conference for the three Lok Sabha seats from the Valley. But for the timely information received by me and my subtle but effective intervention, the 'scheme' would have been carried out and the State thrown into a whirlpool of violence and bloodshed.

The wholly contradictory stand taken by the leaders, without even batting their eyelids, also tended to create an atmosphere of cynicism and revulsion which struck at the very root of healthy polity and administration. For quite a length of time, Sheikh Abdullah had been issuing 'fatwas' against Congressmen, describing them as "dirty insects of the gutter" who were unworthy even of burial in Kashmir; and yet in February 1975, he had no hesitation in becoming the leader of the Congress legislative party and functioning as Chief Minister with its support. From May 1983 to February 1986, the Congress(I) had been telling the nation that Dr. Farooq was a 'security risk', and Rajiv Gandhi himself called him anti-national and accused him of having links with subversive and pro-Pakistan elements. Still, without caring to give any explanation to the public for the sudden change in its stance, the Congress(I) entered into an 'Accord' with him, fought State Assembly elections of March 1987 together, with means the fairness of which was strongly doubted, and joined his Ministry as the only coalition partner. And, so far as Dr. Farooq Abdullah was concerned, it was even difficult to keep count of his inconsistent postures and statements.

Unwholesome Legacies

The roots of the current crop of violence and terrorism in the State also lie in some of the legacies of the past. Two such legacies, one of the Plebiscite Front and the other of 'Al Fatah', are particularly relevant.

---

*See Chapter V: 'Roots: Hidden Veins' (Section: Roots in Public Corruption).

Plebiscite Front. The Plebiscite Front was founded by Mirza Afzal Beg on August 9, 1955. Earlier, immediately after Sheikh Abdullah's arrest, a 'War Council' had been set up to muster support for his cause. It was this Council that was converted into the Plebiscite Front by Afzal Beg who had been released on health grounds in November 1954.

The main inspiration behind the Plebiscite Front was Sheikh Abdullah. He remained its mentor and guide. But, for tactical reasons, he did not formally join it. He wanted to keep certain options open.

The basic objective of the Plebiscite Front was to press for the demand for holding a plebiscite under the auspices of the United Nations to decide about the future of the State. This demand was voiced at every public meeting that the Front organised. The Front also described the Indian Army as an army of occupation. During the Indo-Pak conflict of 1965, it even justified infiltration of Pakistanis into the Valley. The Front kept secret links with Pakistan wherefrom it received substantial financial and propaganda support. According to a report* published in Pakistan in 1976, the Front received about ₹ 7.5 crore from Pakistan during the period between 1954 and 1974.

During the hey-day of the Plebiscite Front, Sheikh Abdullah, who had earlier been dubbed as an Indian stooge, was hailed as a hero in Pakistan. He was even offered a Pakistani passport.

The activities of the Plebiscite Front increased following the withdrawal, in April 1964, of the Kashmir Conspiracy case. After a brief spell of moderation, virulent propaganda against India was set in motion. The Kashmiris were exhorted again and again to 'throw away the Indian yoke'. The anti-India propaganda was carried on by Sheikh Abdullah even in foreign press and outside India when he, accompanied by Afzal Beg, went for Haj pilgrimage in early 1965. In an article published in the *Foreign Affairs Quarterly* in April 1965, he lambasted the attitude of the Government of India and justified his demand for a plebiscite. He intentionally embarrassed India by suggesting, in a press interview at Cairo, that President Nasser of Egypt should intervene to bring about unification of the two parts of Kashmir. He also demanded that the Algiers Afro-Asian Conference

*See in *Indian Express* report, June 26, 1987.

Amanullah Khan, in his autobiography, 'Jeh-ed Musalsal' confirms (p. 325) that Sheikh Abdullah got finances from Pakistan. In 1980, Mirza Afzal Beg, too, accused Abdullah of having collected crores of rupees.

(1965) should discuss Kashmir as a problem of divided people. Abdullah even met Chou En-lai to elicit support for his views on Kashmir. Chou invited him to Peking.

The Government of India took strong exception to the hostile activities of Sheikh Abdullah and Mirza Afzal Beg. Both of them were detained when they returned from Haj on May 8, 1965.

The Tashkent Declaration (1966) had the effect of throwing cold water on the Kashmir issue. The international community practically lost interest in it.

In January 1968, Sheikh was released. The propaganda of the Plebiscite Front again started making deeper inroads. The total control of Sheikh over the Auqaf fund, and the liberal use of religious platform for anti-India propaganda enabled the Plebiscite Front to enrol as many as five lakh members at one stage.

The Plebiscite Front did not participate in the first two State Assembly elections on the grounds that these were held under the Constitution of the State which it did not recognise. However, the Front participated in the elections of the local bodies and made its presence felt in a big way.

After the Bangladesh War, the Plebiscite Front got a big psychological setback. Its rank and file also showed signs of exhaustion. At that time, Sheikh Abdullah started making statements that he would be holding negotiations with the Central Government. These negotiations, conducted by Mirza Afzal Beg, ultimately led to the signing of the Kashmir Accord and the disbandment of the Plebiscite Front–rather its virtual conversion into National Conference.

The Plebiscite Front was, no doubt, disbanded but its bitter legacy remained. All its members could not be accommodated in the new power structure, although quite a few of them received lots of unmerited benefits. Some of its members, ideologically against Sheikh Abdullah's stand, wanted the struggle for plebiscite to continue. The dissatisfied elements, aided by the permissive environment, ultimately joined organisations which, in times to come, were to indulge in subversive activities. What was, however, more damaging was that when the Plebiscite Front had weakened as a force after the Bangladesh War, and also under the impact of the time, it was virtually revived by arriving at a settlement with Sheikh Abdullah by way of the Kashmir Accord (February 1975). The attitude once again was to keep legs on two stools with the inevitable result of falling in between.

Al Fatah. The legacy of Al Fatah and other terrorist organisations was no less serious. Past cases of espionage, bomb blasts and even hijacking of planes had left their mark on the mental make-up of the Kashmiri youth. In the Kashmir Valley, during the five-year period from January 1965 to January 1971, no less than 80 underground cells and espionage rings operated including Al Fatah, Al Baro and Al Kashmir. During this period, 281 (.303) rifles, 309 guns, 8 sten-guns, 4 light machine-guns, 44 revolvers, 431 hand-grenades, 66 (2") mortar shells, 5 automatic rifles, 65 bayonets, 117 detonators, 30 bombs, 2 rocket launchers, 3 wireless sets and 1,600 lbs. of explosives were recovered by the police. This list would show the extent to which subversive activity continued even after the Indo-Pak War of 1965 and the Tashkent Declaration of 1966.

The period following the Tashkent Declaration was dominated by the organisation called Al Fatah. This organisation commenced its activity in 1966. Gradually, its ranks swelled. By 1969, it had become a full-fledged organisation with a political wing and with a well-planned strategy of economic and militant subversion. Its activities were at its peak in 1971, when, after arrests in a bank dacoity case, the recruits were detected and the organisation was practically smashed.

Al Fatah derived its name from an Arab guerilla organisation committed to the liberation of Palestine. It alludes to a Quranic verse which implies "assistance from God and imminent success". The organisers also drew inspiration from such diverse elements and movements as the Hungarian struggle for Independence, the Cuban revolution and the Che Guevara tactics.

The main organiser and leader of Al Fatah was Gulam Rasool Zehangir. In course of time, he secured support of some young men whom he was able to motivate with a great deal of success. Notable amongst them were Syed Sarwar who, on his own, had earlier set up an organisation called Students' Revolutionary Council, Fazal-ul-Haq Qureshi, and Nazir Ahmed Wani. Before its liquidation by police in 1971, the organisation had about 200 recruits on its list, 40 of whom were extremely active and highly motivated.

The primary objective of this organisation was to indulge in espionage, bomb explosions, dacoities and other acts of subversion. Its strategy included destruction of holy places such as 'Maqdoom-Saheb-Ke Ziarat', and arouse communal passion. It also brought out posters under the caption 'Red Kashmir', and gave a call for independent Kashmir.

The top leaders of Al Fatah were guided, trained and motivated by officers of Pakistan Intelligence–Major Habibullah, Major Qaisar Qureshi, Major Tufail, Major Asgar, and Zafar Iqbal Rather. They crossed the border several times. They remained in touch with the Pakistan Embassy to secure guidance and help. They also infiltrated into government offices. For instance, Mohammad Ishaq Manhas, Head Assistant in the State Secretariat, was an active member of the organisation. Separately, Pakistan officials arranged for a sizeable quantity of arms to be smuggled, through one Saleem Jehangir, the idea being to make these arms available to the activists of Al Fatah as and when they needed them.

Al Fatah drew substantial support from the Plebiscite Front leaders, particularly Mirza Afzal Beg. The youth wing of the Front worked in close liaison with the Al Fatah's special organisation–Youngmen League add Student Federation. Mirza Afzal Beg remained in clandestine touch with Gulam Rasool Zehangir.

Al Fatah was responsible for three major incidents of terrorism in Kashmir, namely, (i) attacking and killing of Constable Charan Dass of BSF at Nawkadal bridge on February 3, 1967; (ii) dacoity on April 1, 1970, at Tehsil Education Office, Pulwama, from which about ₹ 72,000 was looted; and (iii) Hazratbal bank dacoity on January 2, 1971, during the course of which ₹ 97,000 was looted.

It was during the Hazratbal bank dacoity case that police was able to find a clue which led to the detection and ultimate arrest of most of the members of the organisation. The investigation also revealed that a large quantity of arms had been kept by Saleem Jehangir at Char-e-Sharief. When the residence of Jehangir was raided, 12 sten-guns, 13 (.38 bore) revolvers and a number of bags containing ammunition were recovered.

The investigation also revealed that there was a diabolical plan of kidnapping and assassinating VIPs, including Chief Minister and Ministers, who would become easy targets during the elections of 1971.

It should be evident that the current wave of terrorism is not without precedence. Maybe, Al Fatah and other terrorist organisations operated on a comparatively small scale. But the underlying motivation, the technique of operation, the strategy of subverting the loyalty of government servants and securing outside help for internal subversion, are not different. For example, Fazal-ul-Haq Qureshi, a leading figure of Al Fatah, who was given a government job under the scheme of rehabilitating 'misguided youth', later became a top activist of Hizbul Mujahideen. After the arrest and interrogation of a terrorist who was keeping 12 bombs in his house at Soura, the conspiratorial links of Qureshi became known and he was arrested. At that time, he was working as an Accounts Officer in the State Secretariat.

Dynamics of Negative Forces

All the negative forces spelt out above–the attitude of softness and permissiveness; the politics of deception and duplicity; the spurious democracy; the disposition to nurse illusions and sweep the unwholesome legacies under the carpet–had their own internal dynamics. They continued to operate in one form or the other. The politics of deception and duplicity was not confined only to the National Conference and other local groups. The Congress Party, too, was not free from this malaise. In 1983-84, it described Dr. Farooq Abdullah as anti-national, a "security risk".

Speaking in the course of a debate in the Lok Sabha on change of government* in J&K, the Congress(I) MPs virtually portrayed Dr. Farooq Abdullah as a traitor. Rajendra Kumari Bajpai, for instance, said, "Dr. Farooq Abdullah has always contacts with people who thought in terms of separating Kashmir from India. He has personal relations with leaders of the Kashmir Liberation Front. After coming to power also, he continued his contacts with these people and that was why he had started giving encouragement to Jama'at-i-Islami and Jama'at-i-Tulba which were their militant wings. These people started raising slogans which had never been heard earlier."* Zain-ul-Bashir commented that "there was a constant link between the extremists of' Punjab and the Chief Minister of J&K".* B.R. Bhagat charged: "Facts had borne out clearly that Dr. Farooq Abdullah was indulging in anti-national activities.* Dr. Abdullah endeared himself to the Pakistan-Occupied Kashmir based militants and they tried to exploit this to the full and, therefore, invited Dr. Farooq Abdullah to attend the annual session of the Plebiscite Front in Mirpur (Pak-Occupied Kashmir) in 1974. And it was during this visit that Dr. Farooq Abdullah came in contact with

*This refers to discussions under Rule 193 on the recent developments in J&K. Lok Sabha Debates, July 30, 1984 (23 July-27 August 1984).

Amanullah Khan and Maqbool Butt. Dr. Abdullah in his public utterances appealed to the people of Kashmir to rally round the Plebiscite Front functioning on both sides of the ceasefire line and categorically stated that he stood firmly for the inalienable right of the Kashmir people to determine their future."* Kamal-ud-Din Ahmed* also expressed grave misgivings about the patriotism and sincerity of Dr. Farooq Abdullah. He said: "The events in Punjab and Kashmir had confirmed that there was a very serious conspiracy for the balkanisation and disintegration of our country. Dr. Abdullah had been in the company of organisations like Akali Dal, Plebiscite Front, Jama'at-i-Islami, Jama'at-i-Tulba and JKLF. It was a serious matter which the entire country had to take note of. Dr. Abdullah also aligned himself with Moulvi Farooq who did not believe in the accession of Kashmir to India. The way Dr. Farooq Abdullah conducted the Kashmir Government had compelled the MLAs to part company with him."

And yet it was the same Farooq Abdullah with whom Congress(I) entered into a hearty alliance and in whose defence its leaders, including Rajiv Gandhi, strained every nerve to denounce me when I made a determined effort in January-February 1990 to get back the levers of the power-structure from the hold of the subversionists. Neither the Congress(I) as a party nor any of its leaders ever cared to make it clear whether intentional lies were resorted to earlier or later. They treated the Indian public with cynical contempt and thought they could get away with anything.

The Rajiv-Farooq Accord (November 1986) was another reflex of spurious democracy and the habit of nursing illusions. It was an unwritten Accord, a mere declaration to work together and form a coalition government of the National Conference and the Congress(I). There was an informal understanding that power would be shared in the ratio of 60:40.

The Accord might have yielded positive results if it had been inspired by reformative zeal and constructive approach. But both parties joined hands merely to serve their selfish ends. In practice, the Accord only resulted in enlarging the circle of predatory and insensitive oligarchy. No new healthy seedling was planted. On the

*This refers to discussions under Rule 193 on the recent developments in J&K. Lok Sabha Debates, July 30, 1984 (23 July-27 August 1984).

contrary, whatever solid work was done during Governor's Rule to build an honest and sound institutional framework was undone. The manner in which the State Assembly election of March 23, 1987 were conducted caused grave misgivings about their fairness. In some constituencies, counting was suspended and the margin of victory for the National Conference candidates turned out to be smaller than the votes rejected. The margin of victory in Beejbehara was 100, in Wachi 122, and in Shopian 336, while in these constituencies the number of votes declared invalid was 1,172, 1,703 and 1,122 respectively. These elections, unfortunately, were followed by the arrest of a number of top-ranking leaders, of the Muslim United Front.

The unpalatable reality soon emerged on the surface. It found expression in the angry outburst of the individuals and leaders. Abdul Rashid Kabuli, National Conference MP, said: "Our image is shattered. Farooq's image is already one of suppression, suffocation and rigging."* Likewise, Mir Mustafa, an Independent MLA, lamented: "During Governor's rule, the State didn't take an extra paisa from the Centre and yet schools, roads, hospitals, drinking water were made available, and justice was on the roadside. Within a few months, the Governor had shown results. What became apparent during the Jagmohan period was that, given an atmosphere of an efficient and people-oriented administration, the Valley's fundamentalism is only skin-deep. The people's demand then was not for Nizam-e-Mustafa or for Pakistan, but for jobs, more representation in Central Government departments and fair recruitment policies. Even Qazi Nissar, who had been jailed by the Governor for disturbing the peace, admitted: 'Yes, there is sadness now that the reforms made for the State's benefit have been reversed.' The de-weeding of the Dal Lake has ground to a halt. Playgrounds under construction in rural areas are gathering dust. Government doctors–despite a high court ruling that the Governor's ban on private practice was in the public interest–are back in business as usual. There is also a move to abolish the subordinate selection boards–set up under Jagmohan–to wipe out the Statewise favouritism and bribery involved in the recruitment of non-gazetted officers."

The Accord was also used to create new illusions. Pompous declarations were made by Dr. Farooq Abdullah about the closure of the schools run by Jama'at-i-Islami. A misleading impression was created by no less a person than the Prime Minister, Rajiv Gandhi,

*Interview with *India Today,* September 15, 1987.

about a special assistance of ₹ 1,000 crore to Kashmir. Actually, it was nothing but manipulation of figures. Apart from the undesirability of such deceptions, the false promises proved counter-productive. They merely added to the atmosphere of irritation and frustration.

The Rajiv-Farooq Accord, accompanied as it was by the characteristic superficiality of the two leaders and non-performance of the State Government, resulted in strengthening the dynamics of negative forces and providing an environment in which unhealthy crops from unhealthy roots could grow faster. It was both an offshoot of environmental determinism and a contributor to that determinism. The inevitability to the damage and disaster was inbuilt in the polluted climate, the degraded soil, the infected seeds, and the defective vision of the men behind the ploughs.

CHAPTER V

Roots: Hidden Veins

Having cut the hide, you have
Pegged down yourself.
What kind of seed had you sown
To expect an abundant harvest?
—Lal Ded

There are some fundamental forces that govern the life of a nation. These forces constitute the hidden veins of its social and political order. Religion is one of these veins—the most vital and significant.

Religious Roots

Throughout human history, religion has remained a potent force, despite all the pounding it has received from thinkers like Marx who called it opiate for the people and Freud who termed it as a collective neurosis of the masses. In this regard, I am reminded of a talk between Cardinal Gonsalvic and Napoleon. The Cardinal was pleading the case for the Catholic Church. Napoleon got annoyed on some point and shouted at the Cardinal: "Your Eminence, are you not aware that I have the power to destroy the Catholic Church?" The Cardinal smiled and replied: "Your Majesty, we, the Catholic clergy, for the last 1,800 years have done our level best to destroy the Catholic Church. We did not succeed. You will not succeed either." This conversation brings out in a telling manner the staying power of religion, notwithstanding its internal and external destroyers.

Failure at the Turning Point

In the religious orders of the Sufis and Rishis of Kashmir, there were ingrained noble traditions of love and harmony, peace and piety, compassion and catholicity. These traditions were not made use of. They were not refashioned, rejuvenated and reinterpreted to suit the new social and political realities that were bound to arise after the attainment of independence. It was a case of failure of the leadership at the turning point of history.

At this most crucial moment, Kashmir failed to look beneath the surface and grasp the significance of the underlying religious and cultural forces–the reconstruction and rechannelisation of which would have provided a solid and sound foundation to Kashmir's new polity and its relationship with India. This relationship could have been of mind and soul and not based merely on a trite constitutional provision–Article 370.* The inner beauty and lustre of the Kashmiri's Islam could have provided the spiritual underpinning to its positive link with India. But, unfortunately, the reverse gear was clutched. Not only were the healthy traditions in Kashmir's culture damaged and destroyed but unhealthy ones were propped up and fertilised.

I have already indicated how Sheikh Abdullah did not hesitate to use Islam to attain his political ends, whenever he found it expedient to do so. After his death, his son, Dr. Farooq Abdullah, and the National Conference as a party, adopted a similar line. This would be evident from the manner in which the National Conference conducted its election campaigns† for the State Assembly in 1983 and for Lok Sabha in December 1984. In fact, all along, there have been elements in the National Conference who exhibited a marked Islamic orientation. Sometimes these elements acted as fanatically as any fundamentalist group would act. For instance, Attaullah Suhrawardy, a senior leader of the National Conference, and a former Minister and Deputy Speaker, made the following remarks in a speech in the State Legislative Council:

> I am first a Muslim and then an Indian. Islam does not need the support of anyone for its spread. It is spreading on its own. At the time of partition there were only four and a half crore Muslims in the country. However, in spite of the bloody communal riots in Bhiwandi, Moradabad, Aligarh and other areas, killing thousands of Muslims, the population of Muslims has increased to 14 crores. . . . As for the question of conversion of all to Islam, it is

* See Chapter VI: 'Roots: Article 370'.

† See Chapter IV: 'Roots' (Section: Spurious Democracy).

the fundamental duty of a Muslim to strive for conversion and any Muslim who does not remember this duty, does not deserve to be called a Muslim.

What is Islam?

It is difficult to provide any precise definition of Islam. Undoubtedly there is a core, but there is a vast area around it which is full of uncertainty and admits of different interpretations. Every Muslim would agree that there is only one God and Prophet Mohammed is His messenger. But there is little agreement beyond it. Islam's principles and ideas have been subjected to different interpretations at different times and in different conditions.

During the course of his inquiry into the anti-Ahmedia riots of 1953 in Pakistan, Justice Munir asked 'Ulmas' as to what was their definition of a Muslim. A wide variety of answers were given. Justice Munir remarked: "If 'Ulmas' could not agree on such a simple question, how could the common man understand?" This example brings out the dilemma of indicating, in precise and definite terms, what principles and practices conform to Islam and what do not.

"If", as Goethe said, "Islam means submitting to God, we all live and die in Islam." The problem is not with regard to the centre but the periphery–the periphery that touches economic, social, cultural and political issues of day-to-day life."

Distinct Colour

Islam in Kashmir acquired its own distinct colour and hue. As Sir Aurel Stein noted, "Islam made its way in Kashmir not by forcible conquest but by gradual conversion." Coercive methods were occasionally employed, as it happened during the regime of Sultan Sikander. But its spread was largely the result of the work undertaken by the missionaries like Saiyid Ali Hamdani and Saiyid Muhammad Hamdani. Though it was adopted rapidly, it did not displace most of the local customs, beliefs and practices. Even otherwise, in their basic ingredients, the Sufi and Rishi orders, which constituted the core of Islam in Kashmir, were not irreconcilable with the general milieu and spiritual disposition of the people. These orders were essentially eclectic and catholic in outlook.

Till the very recent times–till, in fact, the intrusion of Jama'at-i-Islami and some other fundamentalist organisations–the Kashmiri ethos had been largely shaped by the two religious orders–the Sufis and the Rishis–which appeared on the Kashmir scene in the fourteenth–fifteenth century. The Sufi order in Kashmir was mainly served by the saints and preachers from Persia and Central Asia, while the Rishi order, which also drew inspiration from the general Sufi thought, had a deeper imprint of local mystical traditions and was propagated by the sons of the soil.

Attributes of Sufism

Within Islam, Sufism has been one of the most significant spiritual movements. It arose out of the 'inner rebellion of conscience' against social injustices of the time, and also as a reaction to over-intellectualism of hair-splitting of the theologians.

There are a few pronouncements in Quran, which seem to suggest that the Prophet was not appreciative of asceticism or escapism. According to the Sufi saints, however, Sufism represents the essence of Islam. These saints believe in the oneness of God, the day of judgment, the system of punishment and reward, etc., but they lay much greater stress on the inner purification and personal and direct approach to God. They advocate piety and purity of life. Simplicity, austerity and continuous efforts at self-improvement are their guiding stars. They believe that the true meaning of 'Jihad' is to wage a war against the evils that reside inside man, and true victory can be attained by curbing worldly desires and carnal pleasures. They hold that God should be loved for the sake of love for Him and not for seeking any selfish gain As one Sufi saint, Rabia, puts it: "I have served Him only for the love of Him and out of desire for Him. My love for him has so possessed me that no place remains for loving any other thing."

Kashmiri Sufi Order

The beacon light of the Sufi order in Kashmir was Saiyid Ali Hamdani. He is popularly known as Shah-i-Hamdani, Lord of Hamadan. He was born in 1314 at Hamadan. He was a great scholar and preacher. He wrote 170 books and monographs. He was both an *alim* (scholar-thinker) and a Sufi saint. He came to Kashmir in 1372 with 700 disciples. He came for the second time in 1379 and stayed for two and a half years. He made his third visit in 1383. He travelled throughout the Valley, spreading the message of Islamic mysticism, and securing conversions to his faith. He left disciples at a number of places, particularly at important centres of Hindu religion and culture, such as Avantipura and Muttan. He played a major role in the Islamisation of Kashmir. The process of Islamisation undoubtedly started before the arrival of Saiyid Ali Hamdani, but he and his followers greatly accelerated it. They established 'khankas' and 'madrasas' from where the message of Islam was propagated throughout the Valley. He is rightly called 'Bani-i-Islam' in Kashmir.

Saiyid Ali Hamdani's Sufi beliefs can be considered at two levels. At one level, he holds the view that the creator and the creature are two distinct realities; the creator has no form–nothing is like Him, "whatsoever one conceived of Him He is beyond that". At another level, he believes that the creature, by leading a pure and pious life, and through pure and pious contemplation, can attain mystical union with the creator. Hamdani wants man to be perfect. He emphasises that those who adopt the right path fulfil the purpose of God, because God created man only to manifest Himself.

Saiyid Ali Hamdani was followed by his missionary son, Saiyid Muhammed Hamdani, who was more aggressive in his approach. Accompanied by 300 Saiyids, he came to Kashmir in 1394. He stayed in the Valley for 22 years. It was because of his influence that the Sultan displayed proselytising zeal.

Kashmiri Rishi Order

Compared to the Sufi order, as propagated by Saiyid Ali Hamdani, the Rishi order was more liberal, non-missionary and rooted in the local traditions. The two stalwarts of this order were Lal Ded and Sheikh Nuru'd-Din.

Lal Ded was born sometime between 1317 and 1320 in a well-to-do family of Pompore. She was brought up in an atmosphere of piety. She was married at an early age. Her husband and in-laws maltreated her. She left her home and became a wandering ascetic. She used to move in forests with hardly any clothes on. Her sayings and verses along with those of Sheikh Nuru'd-Din constitute the essence of the Rishi order. Lal Ded's great influence finds expression in her own saying:

> Whatever I uttered with my tongue
> Became a 'mantra'.

Lal Ded's poetry has the stamp of a born genius. Her imagery, phrases and metaphors are so spontaneous and familiar in the environment of Kashmir that one is left wondering at her power of expression and grasp of inner and outer reality of life around. Sheikh Nuru'd-Din was right when he said, "Lal Ded is an 'Avatar' and 'Yogini'." Another telling, observation about her is: "Passion for God set fire to all she had."* But the best description is her own:

> A tapasvin into the world came I,
> And bodha illumined my path to the Self.

Sheikh Nuru'd-Din was about 30 years younger to Lal Ded. He was born in 1378 or thereabout in the family of a watchman. After the death of his father, his brothers made him join in their ventures of theft. But he was a pious man and given to contemplation. He became a great Owaisi mystic. He was the real founder of the Kashmiri Rishi order. He set up cadres of dedicated Rishis and established centres of his movement in every 'paragana'. He attained great fame and popularity. Sultan Zain-ul-Abidin attended his funeral (1439) and the Afghan Governor Ata Muhammad Khan struck coins in his honour in the early nineteenth century.

Impact

The Rishis had a tremendous impact on the social and cultural life of Kashmir. Of them it has been remarked that "they converted the Valley into a paradise". A seventeenth century poet wrote: "The candle of religion is lit by the Rishis; they are the pioneers of the path of belief. The heart-warming quality of humble souls emanates from the inner purity of hearts of the Rishis. This vale of Kashmir that you call a paradise owes a lot of its charm to the traditions set in vogue by the Rishis."

Abul Fazal too was impressed by the role of the Rishis. He reckoned that there were about 2,000 such Rishis during his time. He observed: "The most respectable class of people in Kashmir are the Rishis. Although they have not abandoned the traditional and customary forms of worship, they are the true worshippers. They do not denounce men belonging to other faiths. They do not seek worldly objects. For the benefit of the people, they plant fruit-bearing trees. They abstain from meat-eating and do not marry." Emperor Jahangir spoke in the same strain: "Although the Rishis have not

*This observation about Lal Ded is of Sheikh Nasir-ud-Din; it was quoted by Baba Dawud Mishkati in his *Asrar-ul-Abrar* (The Secrets of the Pious) written in A.D. 1654.

acquired learning, they live a frank and unostentatious life. They criticise nobody and do not demand anything."

Beliefs

The Rishis deprecated sham and hypocrisy. One of the famous verses of Sheikh Nuru'd-Din is:

> O mulla, your rosary is
> like a snake,
> You begin to count the
> beads when
> Your disciples come near;
> You eat six meals one after
> the other.
> If you are a 'mulla', then
> who are the thieves?

The Rishis denounced theoretical knowledge. In this regard Sheikh Nuru'd-Din remarked:

> A spiritual guide seems like a pot full of nectar,
> Which may be trickling down in drops.
> Having a heap of books beside him,
> He may have become confused by reading them.
> On examining him we found him empty in mind.

The Rishis also laid great stress on conquering worldly desires. According to the story associated with the life of Sheikh Nuru'd-Din, he once saw fish being cooked at a shop. He was tempted to have it. He went near the cooking place. But, after a moment's reflection, instead of picking up fish, he picked up a burning stick from the hearth and put it in his mouth. His tongue was burnt. He cried out: "O my 'nafs', the fish for you is this burning stick." The Sheikh held that the wants, the greed, were the root causes of trouble in this world. He says:

> The nafs has disturbed me greatly,
> The nafs has ruined me entirely.
> It is the nafs which makes us destroy others.
> The nafs is the slave of the devil.
> To serve the nafs is to thrust ashes
> into one's own eyes.

How then can one expect to see?
The nafs is just like a rebellious calf,
which should be tied up.
It should be threatened with the stick of fasting.

Lal Ded echoes similar sentiments:

I will weep and weep for you, my Soul.
The world has caught you in its spell.
Though you cling to them with the anchor of steel,
Not even the shadow of the things you love
Will go with you when you are dead.

The Rishis grasped the profound truths of life and expressed them in simple idioms. They believed that God was everywhere and one can realise Him by merging the individual self in the all-pervasive, all-powerful Self (God). Sheikh Nuru'd-Din once observed: "When I was able to recognise my own self, I was able to recognise God; both loss and gain became identical to me and distinction of life and death disappeared."

The same belief was expressed by Lal Ded:

The pilgrim sannyasi goes from shrine to shrine,
Expecting to meet Him who abides within his own self.

Before the current turmoil, the Kashmiris' well-known disposition not to kill, emanates from the preachings and practices of the Rishis. They abhorred killing and meat-eating. Like Jains, they were careful not to cause harm even to insects and grass. Sheikh Nuru'd-Din, for instance, stopped walking on grass. He even gave up eating fresh vegetables.

Kashmir's Islam, as propagated by the Rishis, was akin to Kabir's religion. For instance, this is what Lal Ded observed:

Shiv abides in all that is, everywhere;
Do not discriminate between a Hindu and a
Musalman;
If thou art wise, know thyself;
That is true knowledge of the Lord.

At another place Lal Ded said:

I renounced fraud, untruth, deceipt;
I taught my mind to see the One in all my fellow-men.

How can then I discriminate between man and man
And not accept the food offered to me by brother man?

Sheikh Nuru'd-Din also expressed identical thoughts:

There is one God,
But with a hundred names.
There is not a single blade of grass,
Which does not worship Him.

The virtues of Kashmiri Islam—contemplation, asceticism, renunciation, abstinence, simplicity, co-existence, etc.—are common to the virtues admired in the best of Hinduism, Buddhism and Jainism. It is more in tune with the Indian pluralist society. It was also because of these virtues ingrained in the Kashmiri psyche that no bloodshed, no intolerance, no communal frenzy was exhibited in 1947 when the rest of the subcontinent was severely jolted by the storm of narrow communalism and fanaticism.

We are the progeny of the same parents,
Then why should we differ?
Let Hindus and Muslims together adore God alone.
We came to this world like partners,
We ought to share our joys and sorrows together.

It is, indeed, a pity that such edifying thoughts and beliefs, stamped upon the spiritual landscape of Kashmir, were not perceived and their significance was not grasped. Every leader at the Central and State level developed an obsession with his game of power and totally ignored the religious and cultural roots that could make politics scrupulous, institutions fruitful and the social order of the Union and Kashmir harmonius and integrated. The exploiters, in pursuit of their petty aims, showed no hesitation in uglifying the landscape and planting the seeds of narrowness and narcissism, and thus causing poisonous trees of disharmony and disruption to appear on the scene.

Jama'at-i-Islami

Over the years arose new political forces who calculated that by enlarging the National Conference's strategy of using Islam in times of need and by fundamentalising Kashmiri Islam, they could acquire a stronger foothold on the political landscape of the State. In this arena, the most potent and pervasive force was Jama'at-i-Islami. It tilted

Kashmiri social and political ethos towards fundamentalism and fanaticism. It reshaped the undercurrent of Kashmir's polity and administration. It spread pro-Pakistan sentiments even among groups which were otherwise not in favour of merger of Kashmir with Pakistan. It is, therefore, necessary to go into its background at some length.

The Jama'at-i-Islami-Hind was founded in India in 1938 by Sayyid Abdul A'Ls Maudoodi, when he circulated its draft constitution amongst a few prominent Muslims of his way of thinking. This draft was adopted with a slight modification in 1941. Maudoodi developed the concept of Nizam-e-Mustafa, that is, the system as enunciated by the Prophet Mohammad. He wanted total supremacy to be given to Quran and 'Sunna'. He held that political sovereignty vested in God; that the ruler, who could rule only on behalf of God, should be the most virtuous Muslim and the Umah (Muslim community) must elect only such a person as the ruler.

Maudoodi gave a pre-eminent place to the Islamic way of life. He believed in the supranational character of Islam. He denounced nationalism. He once remarked that Muslim nationalism was as contradictory a term as a 'chaste prostitute'. He wanted to mould the entire social, moral, political and economic system of the world in accordance with the tenets of Islam.

The set-up envisaged by Maudoodi was totalitarian. By its very nature, it could not be democratic in the conventional sense. Maudoodi himself called it a 'theo-democracy', a vague sort of democracy functioning in accordance with the divine laws.

Before the partition of India on August 15, 1947, Maudoodi was opposed to the creation of a separate state of Pakistan. He thought that, unless the Islamic way of life could be brought about, Pakistan would be another un-Islamic godless state. After the establishment of Pakistan, however, Maudoodi changed his stance. He started working for making it an Islamic state. He became extremely rigid about his beliefs. He played an extremely active part in causing anti-Ahmadia riots in West Punjab in 1953. He was sentenced to death, but later on freed. His fanaticism came out vividly in his testimony before the Munir Commission which was set up by the Government of Pakistan to enquire into the anti-Ahmadia riots. Over the years, the Jama'at-i-Islami became a potent force in Pakistan and played a prominent role in supporting Gen. Zia-ul-Haq, in first throwing out Zulfikar Ali Bhutto and then executing him.

Maudoodi's entire thinking is fundamentalist to the core. His concepts are obviously muddled. Who would enforce God's supremacy on His behalf? If there are differences of opinion in regard to the interpretation of the Quranic injunctions, whose interpretation would prevail? Will the ruler, exercising God's sovereignty, submit himself to the authority of those who give interpretations different from his? Who would assess the qualification on the basis of which a person could be declared as the most virtuous and selected to be the head of state? And where is the guarantee that, once selected, the ruler would remain most virtuous?

Absence of clear answers to such questions explains the contradictions, uncertainties, and impracticabilities of the Islamic state as envisaged by Maudoodi. That is why, in actual practice, wherever any Islamic state was sought to be established, it turned out to be dictatorial, leaving religious tenets to be exploited for personal and political purposes. It has been correctly pointed out that "Of all forms of oppression, the most dangerous are the laws and restrictions forcibly imposed on people in the name of religion. This is what the Monks, through collaboration with the ruling classes, did. What was not from God was thrust, in His name, upon the people to enslave and suppress them."

In India, after August 1947, a separate organisation, under the name of Jama'at-i-Islami-Hind was again set up. The Indian Jama'at-i-Islami does not concern itself with the idea of setting up an Islamic State. It links the Indian Muslims with Umah Islamiya, and aims at improving the lot of the Indian Muslims as a part of the world Muslim community. It is primarily engaged in the task of safeguarding the religious and cultural identity of Indian Muslims–their personal laws, their language, their religious endowments, etc.

To propagate its views, the Jama'at-i-Islami-Hind is running 548 libraries, 386 reading rooms, 240 study circles, 266 nursery schools, 344 part-time 'maktabs' or elementary schools, 36 junior high schools and 23 colleges. It is also running a central institute at Rampur. It controls over 700 mosques, and from these mosques its leaders address congregations every Friday. The Jama'at has also published 491 books in Urdu, 77 in Hindi and 78 in English on the Quran and various facets of its ideology.* It is also bringing out a number of

*These data, collected in 1986, were based upon the Jama'at's reports. These give a broad idea of what its activities are.

newspapers and journals from Delhi, Rampur, Calcutta, Guwahati, Ahmedabad, Hyderabad, Mangalore, Calicut and Madras.

Significantly, the Jama'at-i-Islami-Hind supports secularism and considers it a blessing for the Indian Muslims. On the other hand, Jama'at-i-Islami, Pakistan, labels secularism as an unmitigated evil and the worst enemy of Islam. These opposing stands taken in India and Pakistan expose the hypocrisy expediency and cynicism of the Jama'at-i-Islami's ideology which makes a mockery of its concern for purity and piety.

The Jama'at-i-Islami of J&K is not a part of the Jama'at-i-Islami-Hind. It is a separate and independent organisation. It was established in 1942 at Shopian by Maulvi Ghulam Ahmed Ahar in collaboration with Syed Shahab-ud-Din and other like-minded persons.

Both in theory and practice, the Jama'at-i-Islami of J&K is on the same wave-length as of Jama'at-i-Islami of Pakistan. It rejects secularism and socialism. It denounces what it calls 'Indian colonialism' and 'Brahminical imperialism'. It contemptuously labels the Union Government as Delhi Darbar. It considers Kashmir's accession to India as disputed. For all practical purposes, it works for Kashmir's merger with Pakistan. It believes in Islam-inspired political mobilisation. It has set up strong cadres of dedicated, disciplined and religiously motivated workers to carry out its social and political programmes. It advocates the establishment of Nizam-e-Mustafa in accordance with Maudoodi's ideas. It hails Gen. Zia-ul-Haq's endeavours to Islamise the state and society in Pakistan. It criticises modern norms of social and moral behaviour. It wants the Kashmiri society to be reformed and re-fashioned in accordance with the principles and ideas of 'Shariat'.

A clear idea about the aims, objectives and motivation of the Jama'at-i-Islami emerges from the writings and speeches of its present prominent leader, Syed Ali Shah Geelani. In his book *Ye Bhee Ek Rukh Tha Tasveer-e-Kashmir Ka* in Urdu, he articulates his views in a poetic and colourful style which has great fascination for the Kashmiri youth who, as a class, are given to sentimentality and emotionalism.

In regard to the argument that the issue of plebiscite and accession has now become dead, Geelani says: " 'Much water has flown down the Jhelum'–this sentence is often written by our journalists. To these friends, I ask whether human rights have also flown with the waters of Jhelum. The moral principle of mankind has not flown with this water. Nor have the urges and passion for freedom, nor the parameters of culture and civilisation." In respect of his political beliefs, he makes it clear: "The politics of socialism and secularism is totally unsound. I do not like any Muslim to adopt socialism and secularism as his political ideal."

In another booklet titled *Mukadama-e-Ilhaq*† (Trial of Accession), the Jama'at-i-Islami speaks to the people in these words: "You, the nation of Kashmiri Muslims, how long will you continue to remain easy-going slaves! These high cinema buildings, public houses where nude women perform dances, these liquor shops in every street, these centres of a permissive society where men and women get together unashamedly, these schools and colleges, all these indicate that your culture and heritage is being snatched from you. Who has reduced to dust the Taj Mahal of your civilisation? Who has atrophied the souls of your young men? Who has undermined your religion and faith? How long will you be put to sleep with lullabies? How long will you allow yourself to be manipulated for the selfish power game of others? How long will you remain victims of atheism and godless philosophies? Are you waiting for the time when, as it happened in Afghanistan, your mosques will be converted into places where faithless people would gather and the pages of your Koran would be used for cleaning dust and rubbish?"

The booklet goes on to say: "Your enemies are bent upon destroying your identity and faith. They are pressing in full strength with their army and weapons. If you ignore this warning, be sure that the history of Muradabad will be repeated here. Like the lands of Bhiwandi, Chaibasa, Aligarh, Hyderabad, Jabbalpur and Assam, your lands would also be dyed with blood. You are facing a ruthless imperialist power whose Brahminical psyche is bringing new troubles for you every day. If you do not understand even now, you will not find any place in the pages of history."*

This booklet also contains doctored views, taken out of context, of Lord Mountbatten, Jawaharlal Nehru, Prem Nath Bazaz, G.M. Kaul, Sisir Gupta and Dr. Karan Singh. It also carries a brief summary of Maudoodi's ideology.

Such views, expressed in a highly emotional and religious tone, continued to be propagated with impunity for a number of years till January 1990. No counter-strategy was formulated and implemented.

† This publication has been brought out by Jama'at-i-Islami and is addressed to the people of Kashmir in direct form. Translation from Urdu to English is by the author.

* The translation from Urdu is by the author.

Nothing effective or concrete was done to educate the people about the inaccuracy of the Jama'at-i-Islami propaganda and the pitfalls of fanaticism and fundamentalism and the fatal injury which the hegemony of Pakistan would cause to Kashmir's identity and culture.

Consequently, the Jama'at-i-Islami, with one or two brief intervals of low fortune, continued to gain strength. On the political plane, it went on advocating, with increasing belligerency, that accession of Kashmir to India was not final, that 'jihad' was a legitimate weapon for the Muslims, that the Iranian revolution was worthy of emulation, and that Gen. Zia-ul-Haq's programme of Islamising Pakistani society and state was inspiring and admirable. On the social plane, the Jama'at-i-Islami carried out a virulent campaign against family planning saying that the programme was un-Islamic and a clever device of the Central Government to convert the Muslim majority into a minority in the State. On the educational plane, it went on planting seeds of fundamentalism and parochialism through its 150 schools and madrasas. A typical example of what was being taught to the children was the following portion of a poem prescribed for Class III:

> Little children, be very calm
> I will tell you what is Islam.
> You may be few and without army
> But you must fight for Islam.

Another passage from a book for primary classes reads: "We are Kashmiris and our country is Kashmir. It is surrounded by India, China and Iran."

The visit of Madine University's delegation in June 1980 to which Jama'at-i-Islami played host and which was also entertained officially by Sheikh Abdullah, acted as a pat on its back. A leading member of the delegation, Professor Addul Samad, made it clear that for bringing about Islamic revolution, both individual and society have to be prepared. In pursuance of this objective and its overall objective to prepare the minds of the youth towards such a revolution, a large number of schools were set up and the scale of activity increased. The basic objective was to indoctrinate the young children in fundamentalist ideology through the schools run by it and its front organisation Ahl-e-Hadis. For these institutions substantial funds flowed from Saudi Arabia. The oil in the middle-east also placed a lot of wealth in the hands of Saudi Sheikh and this enabled them to provide substantial funds for such activities. Practically nothing was done to close the schools or to control them in any other way. Both Sheikh Abdullah and later on Dr. Farooq Abdullah fulminated against these schools but did practically nothing and the crop of youth, trained and indoctrinated, continued to grow and increase.

Because of the Jama'at-i-Islami's operation at social, educational and cultural levels and the growing number of its workers, it had always more strength beneath the surface than above it. And its electoral performances of the past are no indication of its real hold on the people. It contested three elections, first in 1972, then in 1977, and then again in 1983. Subsequently, in 1987, it fought elections as a constituent of the Muslim United Front. In 1972, it secured five seats and 7.18% of the votes polled. In 1977, it secured only one seat and 3.59% of the votes polled. In 1983, it did not get any seat but the percentage of its votes increased to 3.88.

The above voting pattern does not present the real picture. In the 1977 and 1983 elections, the National Conference, by its very communal, parochial and pro-Pak stance, virtually displaced the appeal of the Jama'at-i-Islami. It did exactly what the Jama'at-i-Islami was intending to do. The youth organisations, now aligning with Jama'at-i-Islami, are, in essence, no different from the youth organisations which aligned with the National Conference at the time of the elections in 1977 and 1983. The programmes of the Jama'at-i-Islami and the National Conference looked similar when the National Conference adopted a pro-Pakistan and anti-India attitude. Their public appeals merged. They looked like twin sisters. During the 1983 Assembly elections, for instance, Dr. Farooq Abdullah fulminated against 'Indian domination'. He even threatened to hold elections under the supervision of the United Nations and not of the Election Commission of India.

When the Kashmir Accord was signed by Sheikh Abdullah in 1975, the Jama'at-i-Islami strongly opposed it. A number of active workers of the Plebiscite Front, who were not in favour of the Accord and who were on the same wave-length as of the Jama'at-i-Islami, left the Front. The organizations, however, suffered a set-back in 1977, when Zulfikar Ali Bhutto was executed in Pakistan. The local Muslims believed that this execution was due to the influence of the Jama'at-i-Islami of Pakistan on President Zia-ul-Haq. They went on a rampage and burnt a number of houses belonging to the local Jama'at-i-Islami workers.

The set-back of the Jama'at-i-Islami was short-lived. It quickly regained its position and, in fact, strengthened it. This was due partly to the maladministration and consequent frustration amongst the youth, upon which the Jama'at-i-Islami encashed, and partly to the proclivity of the National Conference leaders to whip up and make use of those very emotions which constituted the base of the Jama'at-i-Islami. This was the electoral strategy which Sheikh Abdullah adopted in June 1977, Dr. Farooq Abdullah in June 1983 and G.M. Shah in December 1984. The dangers inherent in this phenomenon were forcefully pointed out by me to the Union Government. In my letter of February 12, 1985, to Prime Minister Rajiv Gandhi, I wrote:

> This is about firing and other incidents that took place in Srinagar yesterday in connection with observance of first death anniversary of Maqbool Butt.
>
> On surface, the trouble is connected with the Maqbool Butt day. But the underlying cause is the increasing strength of the anti-national forces which received a tremendous boost by the sudden decision of the Chief Minister to release Syed Ali Shah Geelani, leader of the Jama'at-i-Islami, and his followers. This decision was announced by the Chief Minister on December 6, 1984, in a dramatic fashion. Even when the issue involved the security of the State,* he did not care to consult me or the Central Government. In fact, I came to know about the decision only from the newspaper reports.
>
> Ever since the aforesaid release, Geelani has been making highly objectionable speeches, preaching Islamic fundamentalism and accusing India of forcible occupation of Kashmir. Of late, he has been organising training camps in which ring leaders of Jama'at-i-Islami have been exhorting the party cadres to propagate that by joining Pakistan, the Kashmiris would have not only served the cause of Islam but also secured, like Pakistanis, a large number of jobs in the Muslim world.
>
> What is most disconcerting is that, notwithstanding the secessionist and treasonable activities which have been mentioned even in the otherwise sketchy reports of the State intelligence, no action has been taken against Geelani. This has naturally emboldened other

*According to the 'Rules of Business', cases involving Security of the State have to be shown to the Governor before issuing any order.

anti-national groups like Mahaz-e-Azadi, People's League, Kashmir National Liberation Front, etc.

I may take this opportunity to indicate that, in violation of Article 44 of the J&K Constitution and the Rules of Business, the Chief Minister is keeping me in the dark with impunity by withholding information even with regard to vital matters involving the security of the State and creation of parallel police cadres etc.

For the consumption of the public and the Central Government, the Chief Minister has been making a few pro-national statements. In actual practice, however, he has been doing everything to encourage communal, proautonomy and secessionist forces. These forces are more pernicious than others, because they preach Islamic fundamentalism mixed with pro-Pak sentiments. Once these forces become part of the Kashmiri ethos, permanent damage will be done. No amount of subsequent political engineering would be able to solve the basic problems that would be created. Whatever solution may be thought of, the present situation needs to be remedied.

Rajiv Gandhi, unfortunately, remained insensitive to all such pleadings and warnings.

The other parties and groups also found it expedient to make use of Islamic fundamentalism to secure quick political gains. These included the People's League, the Islamic Jama'at-i-Tulba, the Islamic Students' League, the Ummat-e-Islam, the Tahfazul-ul-Islami, the Islamic Study Circle, the Mahaz-e-Azadi, and the Anjumane Itehade Musalmeen. The People's League which was founded on September 30, 1974, by Nazir-Ahmed Wani, one of the accused in Al Fatah case, and the leadership of which was subsequently taken over by Farooq Rehmani and Shabir Shah, propagated that the duty of the followers of Islam was to throw out the Indians from Kashmir. The Islamic Jama'at-i-Tulba, the students' wing of the Jama'at-i-Islami, launched a special drive, under the leadership of Tajamul Islam, to indoctrinate the Muslim youth. The Islamic Students' League's constitution itself declared that 'soldier's life was a basic part of Islam'. Umat-e-Islam, which was founded by Dr. Qazi Nissar on March 4, 1986, did everything to fan the fire of fanaticism and in the process to build leadership for himself amongst the ignorant Muslim masses on narrow religious emotions.

In pursuit of political power, the normal course of which was blocked by an over-possessive and manipulative oligarchy, every political party or group tried to outdo the other in plucking whatever healthy roots were there in the soil and sowing the new seeds of fanaticism and fundamentalism. The tragic harvest* is there for everybody to see.

Administrative Roots

A stable and sound administrative set-up is a *sine qua non* for a stable and sound political set-up. In J&K, unfortunately, stability and soundness are absent from both the set-ups. Here, one compounds the weaknesses of the other.

History provides ample evidence of the fact that a strong and motivated bureaucracy can play a major role in welding disparate groups into a unified entity and in bringing about rapid social and economic advancement. Japan after the Meiji Restoration and Germany in the nineteenth century are striking examples in this regard. On the other hand, as is evident from conflicts in most of the Third World countries, weak, venal and faction-ridden bureaucracies can spell disaster. They can sharpen ethnic, regional, and communal cleavages and retard social and economic progress.

In view of the manifold problems of J&K, its administration should have been strong, smooth, honest, objective, apolitical, dynamic, innovative and creative. But, by and large, it acquired the opposite attributes. It became casual, parochial, flabby and wooden. Politics seeped into its structure.

Politics and administration cannot be kept in watertight compartments; in fact, they are integrated items of the same framework. They breathe the same air, practise the same values, and grow in the same national ethos. In any case, no administration functions in a spiritual or ideological vacuum. It is deeply influenced by political culture. If this culture is unhealthy, the administrative system is bound to be deformed. An infected administrative set-up, in turn, renders the political culture still more unhealthy. One adds to the infirmities of the other.

This is exactly what has been happening in J&K, particularly after the Kashmir Accord. After 1975, the new political power structure that came into being tended to make the administration more insular, and

---

*The swelling wave of fanaticism and fundamentalism and the manner in which it sheared the politics of the state into narrower, nastier and terror-ridden groups have been brought out in the subsequent chapters of the book.

more subservient to its narrow ends. The elements in the administration, whom this trend suited, egged on the political bosses to move further in the same direction. Soon, at the higher echelons, a group of senior Kashmiri officers came to acquire disproportionately large influence upon the Chief Minister, Sheikh Mohammed Abdullah. On the one hand, this group, along with a few auxiliary groups at the middle and lower levels, began to serve personal and party interests of the top politicians of the regime; on the other, it started feathering its own nests and securing a hold on the power structure. The personality cult built around Sheikh Mohammed Abdullah was cleverly exploited. Thus, a politico administrative power elite emerged on the scene. And self-aggrandising cliques in politics and in the administration began to subserve each other's interests.

Most of the officers who were given key assignments were aligned with those forces which wanted to keep the State as much away from the national mainstream as possible. For example, the Chief Secretary, in the early eighties, was almost a fanatic in his pro-autonomy stance. He systematically set at naught all that was needed for healthy Centre-State relationship. He stifled pro-Union forces and made it difficult for the Central agencies to function effectively in the State. For instance, he was instrumental in issuing an order, on March 19, 1982, which made it virtually impossible for the Army to acquire any land.

The result of all this was that the role of the All-India Services was rendered inconsequential. A number of posts were made ex-cadre. For instance, I noticed in November 1984, that in the Police department alone, one post of Director-General, three posts of Inspectors-General, six posts of Additional Inspectors-General and forty-seven posts of Superintendents of Police were kept out of the all-India police cadre, Parallel State cadres emerged. Intake of IAS and IPS officers virtually stopped. The State as well as the all-India cadres developed acute distortions. Manipulation acquired sway. Favouritism increased. Justice became a frequent casualty. Regional loyalties deepened. Accusations of communal and ethnic bias were freely made. Even when a decision was taken on merit, its fairness was hardly accepted. The State machinery lost its credibility. Corruption made deeper inroads. The productivity of the administration declined. Fruitless controversies were raised. Avoidable tensions were created between the State and the Centre.

There were a few exceptions. Some of the officers were highly competent. But they were either caught in the vortex of politics, or they preferred to remain on the fringe, sulking over their inconsequential role, and hoping that some day the political fortune of the State would change and they would play an influential role in the power structure. A couple of officers, who were undoubtedly brilliant, preferred to use their talent in the service of manipulative politics between the Centre and the State on the one hand and the Congress and some Opposition parties on the other.

Under the weak and wayward leadership of Dr. Farooq Abdullah, the rot in public services deepened. Sheikh Abdullah knew how to utilise competent officers from amongst those who constituted the coterie around him. Moreover, he had his hold on cliques and groups. Dr. Farooq Abdullah lost even that. Gaps between words and deeds widened. Dr. Farooq was also obliging in distributing administrative patronage. Bureaucracy proliferated. By the mid-eighties, the administration acquired so much of extra weight that its expenditure became the highest in the country and its productivity the lowest. The wage bill of the State consumed about 43 per cent of its non-plan expenditure. During the seven-year period, 1982 to 1989, the annual growth in the number of its employees was 4.38 per cent as against the national average growth of 2.7 per cent. An index of the poor productivity of the State administration was the quarterly ranking done by the Central Ministry of Programme Implementation in regard to the implementation of the 20-point programme; it was invariably at the bottom rung of the ladder.

'Groups', 'grooves' and 'godfathers' were the three main characteristics of the J&K administration when I assumed charge of the office of Governor, for my first term, on April 26, 1984. Higher services were largely divided into factions. They were jealous and suspicious of one another. They were given to undercutting and intrigues which were mediaeval in spirit and concept but modern in technique and application. A strong, just and inspired leadership, and an enlightened, progressive and straight-forward policy could still have salvaged the position. But neither Dr. Farooq Abdullah nor G.M. Shah could rise above the old and entrenched reflexes. The Central leadership, which came on the scene after Mrs. Indira Gandhi, showed little understanding of the ground-level realities and tended to place its eggs in the bottomless baskets of a few individuals.

The descent, though halted in 1986, could not be arrested. The whimsical elimination of some competent field officers made the matters worse. And the State Administration during Dr. Farooq Abdullah's tenure from November 7, 1986, to January 18, 1990, became a by-word for inefficiency and ineffectiveness.

The truth of the above assertion can best be demonstrated by narrating and analysing an incident that happened on January 13, 1989, in Jammu, in an area which was hardly a few hundred yards away from the State Secretariat, where the Chief Minister, Dr. Farooq Abdullah, and his cabinet colleagues and Chief Secretary were present.

January 13, 1989, happened to be the eve of the birthday of Guru Gobind Singh. A procession was organised on the occasion. Some of the young participants carried banners which described Mrs. Gandhi's assassins–Satwant Singh and Kehar Singh–as martyrs. According to the District Magistrate and the Police, the processionists, at the point of the commencement of the procession, were asked not to display these banners. And they agreed. But when the procession approached Purani Mandi, a thickly populated area in the heart of the city, the aforesaid banners were again taken out and anti-national and provocative slogans were raised. This annoyed some of the Hindu shopkeepers and residents of the area who allegedly showered brickbats on the procession. According to another version, it was the processionists who started looting shops, and set about 50 'khokhas' on fire. The procession broke up in confusion and rioting started. Some of the young participants of the procession, while running in different directions, burnt parked vehicles and indulged in various acts of hooliganism. In the ensuing clashes, 12 persons lost their lives, 120 were injured, 125 vehicles were damaged, and property worth several lakhs was destroyed.

An unpardonable lack of foresight was exhibited by the Administration. Even rudimentary precautions were not taken. And when violence began, the inner paralysis hijacked the will to act. Practically, at a stone's throw from the Chief Minister's Secretariat, for five hours there was free-for-all. No administration seemed to exist. No policeman was willing to lift a finger, even when cars and shops were being burnt in his presence. Brutal attacks, and even killings, evoked no response from the Police. Not a single Police lathi was wielded, not a single tear gas shell was exploded, and not a single shot was fired.

There was a clear alert after the execution of the two assassins of Mrs. Indira Gandhi. There was also acute tension after the hanging of four persons by the terrorists in Gurdaspur District. The Akal Takht Chief, Darshan Singh Ragi, had given a call for the observance of a protest week from January 6 to 13.

Unfortunately, no eventuality was foreseen, and the procession was allowed without collecting hard intelligence. An inadequate and ill-equipped contingent of police was deployed with the procession. Provocative banners were not seized. Inflammatory speeches made by a section of the processionists were not checked. Even when it became clear that shops were being closed and the atmosphere was becoming explosive, no real vigil was mounted.

It was an abject failure on the part of the special branch of the State Police. It had neither assessed the mood of the people, nor gauged the intensity of their emotions. Senior officers did not apply their mind in depth. Deployment was poor. No reserves were kept at strategic points. Even the Police control room remained in a poor state of organisation. On the day of the procession, both the Commissioner and the Adviser (Home) chose to be away from the headquarters. Such was their lack of comprehension of the underlying currents. Such was the state of intelligence that had been fed to them. Mental alertness, it was obvious, was something that could not be provided by any outside stimulus. Casualness and callousness had seeped into the administrative ethos of the State and that was bound to cause many avoidable tragedies.

How did this sorry and sordid state of affairs come about? How did the law and order machinery become so indolent and incompetent? And why was there all-round deterioration? Some of the reasons I have indicated above. Another basic reason was the unjust and unfair system of recruitment to subordinate services, such as teachers and inspectors, and unashamed corruption and naked politicisation that was exhibited in this regard. An example would make it clear. This example pertains to the recruitment of police inspectors and sub-inspectors in January-February 1986.

Apparently, before the process of selection commenced, the Director-General of Police got some lists from the Chief Minister and other influential politicians. The candidates whose names were given on these lists had to be formally selected by the Director-General in the selection board set up by him. The partners in the distribution of patronage, however, quarrelled among themselves. The Agriculture

Minister picked up a row over the issue. Here is an eyewitness account of what happened at the cabinet meeting where this matter cropped up for discussion which had not been anticipated earlier.

> The trouble started when the Director-General of Police explained the selection procedure that he had adopted. He said that, in accordance with the Chief Minister's instructions, he had decided to select 70 per cent of the candidates by 'open merit' and 30 per cent on the recommendations of the leaders of the ruling party. The Police Chief also disclosed that, with regard to selection from Baramulla District, he had consulted two leaders of the ruling party, who were close confidants of the Chief Minister. This provoked the Agriculture Minister who also came from Baramulla area. He taunted that the two 'close confidants' were not the only leaders from Baramulla. He, too, represented the same District. An infuriated Chief Minister interjected to say that the two leaders in question had fought for him, and he could not forget their sacrifices. The Agriculture Minister remarked that he, too, had sacrificed a lot. This further annoyed the Chief Minister. 'What sacrifices have you made? You are a thief. You have swallowed ₹ 6 lakhs. Give me account of that money.' The Agriculture Minister shot back, 'You are a bigger thief. You have swallowed ₹ 28 lakhs. You should first render account of this amount. Government is not your fiefdom. You have recruited all your relations against important posts.' The Chief Minister lost control and shouted, 'You get out from my house.' The Agriculture Minister shouted back, 'This is neither your personal property nor your family jagir. Who are you to ask me to get out?' The Chief Minister started rolling his sleeves and menacingly advanced towards the Agriculture Minister.

I have cited this case to show how the future custodians of law and order were being recruited and what unhealthy nexus existed between the politicians and the institutional framework; also the extent to which the Administration had become venal and corrupt. The Justice Ayyangar Commission, which was set up in January 1965, to inquire into the allegations of corruption against Bakshi Ghulam Mohammad, had in his report, *inter alia*, observed: "The most saddening and depressing of the materials placed before me were the affidavits of the officials who confessed to have knowingly done improper acts extending even to tampering with official records to the prejudice of the State and the State property and monies in carrying out the desire or orders of Bakshi Ghulam Mohammad to benefit him or his relations". Unfortunately, in this arena, the position remained the same; rather it worsened. More often than not, the politicians and the administrators in J&K were willing to enter into unholy alliances to butcher justice, fair play and all that goes to make efficient, effective and healthy institutions.

Another incident, of a slightly different character, is also worth citing. It pertains to the recruitment of bus drivers to the State Road Transport Corporation in the year 1984-85. In this case, the Transport Minister gave a list of 150 persons to the Managing Director of the Corporation and told him to appoint these persons as drivers. When the Managing Director indicated that certain procedures for selection had to be gone through, he was instructed not to bother about these procedures. And when, after 2 or 3 days, the Managing Director pointed out that a number of persons in the Minister's list did not possess even a driving licence, he was told to get them licences. "What is your use as Managing Director if you cannot arrange even a few driving licences?" was the comment of the Minister. To what depths had fallen the process of selection and appointment! Even the requirements of public safety were given a go-by. No wonder, the J&K State had the highest accident rate in the country.

Such callous disregard of public safety and elementary principles of justice was, to some extent, due to the fact that the elections in J&K were won by the National Conference, not on the record of road safety or honesty in administration, but on emotive slogans whipping up parochial, regional and communal feelings.

The low-level politicisation of the recruitment procedure brought in many other undesirable features. Sometimes only one type of persons got recruited. These persons constituted a homogeneous block. They had more or less the same political dispositions and loyalties. One typical example of this phenomenon was the recruitment of hundreds of Class IV employees in the Sher-e-Kashmir Medical Institute of Sciences which had been financed to the extent of ₹ 62 crore by the Planning Commission through the Central Government. A single telephone call from 'Mujahid Manzil', the headquarters of the National Conference, could assemble all these employees for demonstration anywhere. They could use the buses of the Institute. When Mrs. Indira Gandhi went to Srinagar in 1983, almost all these employees were despatched to the airport to show black flags to her.

Thus, ironically, the Central Government helped, with its own funds, in the creation in Kashmir of instruments which were used against it with impunity. If a little imagination had been displayed and, along with the financial aid, proper procedures of selection had been insisted upon, such a situation could have been avoided. Recruitment through employment exchanges, for instance, would have prevented growth of such a solid block of officials having the same political attachment.

I tried to set the matter right. During the short period of Governor's Rule for six months, from March 7 to September 6, 1986, I carried out a major reform in this area. Using my legislative powers, I promulgated the J&K State Subordinate Services Recruitment Act, 1986. But the tradition of manipulation and nepotism was so strongly ingrained in Kashmir's political system that as soon as Dr. Farooq Abdullah came back to power in November 1986, his government proceeded to repeal this Act. When the repealing bill was submitted to me for assent, I sent a note to the State Cabinet on August 7, 1987. The note, which speaks for itself, read as under:

> Let me at the outset make it clear that I have no intention of substituting the judgement of the State Cabinet or that of the Legislature with my own judgement. Nevertheless, it appears necessary to indicate the motivation underlying the J&K State Subordinate Services Recruitment Act and the circumstances under which the said Act was promulgated by me under Governor's Rule.
>
> A number of cases had come to my notice in which favouritism had been exercised on a large scale through unstatutory or ad-hoc selection board. This, besides undermining faith in justice and fair play, had caused considerable social tensions and given rise to frustration and anger amongst the youth. In this regard, the following instances are cited:
>
> (a) In early 1985, the opportunity to fill hundreds of vacancies of school teachers was fully exploited. Candidates with B.A. and M.A. qualifications were ignored and Matriculates with 3rd division were appointed as teachers. In one case, three female members of an influential political element were appointed, ignoring many other highly meritorious candidates. It was not realised that, apart from the intrinsic unfairness of the selection, appointments of poorly equipped teachers had deleterious

effect upon the education of the students and made them incapable of competing on merit in any examination for competitive selection.

(b) Consequent upon the frustration caused by selections, in May 1985, one candidate set himself on fire or, as the alternative version goes, tried to set the office of the District Education Officer on fire. The incident demonstrated the anger and frustration of the meritorious candidates against the selection procedure adopted.

(c) Recruitment of bus drivers, village level workers and subordinate police personnel in 1985-86 revealed a truly tragic state of affairs.

(d) In the statutory public undertakings, the influential elements found special opportunities to resort to nepotism and malpractices. In one case alone, that of selection pertaining to Loan Officers in the State Financial Corporation, four sons of influential political elements were appointed.

It was to prevent such miscarriage of justice and resultant irritation and frustration that a regular institutional framework, based on Statute and manned by wholly independent persons, whose terms and conditions of service were guaranteed by law, was provided. This framework was so fashioned and the Act so designed that the process of selection was insulated from day-to-day pressures of political and other extraneous elements and confidence of the public was gained in regard to fairness of selection. In such matters, justice has not only to be done but should also appear to have been done.

There was a larger and long-term purpose, too. By creating public faith in pre-eminence of merit, an urge had to be created in the youth to activate their talent which otherwise remained latent or dormant. In the process, not only the individual was to gain by acquiring better standards of performance but also the society which would be better served. There was also subsidiary objectives such as reducing the load of administrative work which arose out of complaints and counter-complaints and the court cases.

But this note elicited only a polite reply. The matter was brought to the notice of the Government of India. It, too, did not do anything.

The values which the political rulers of the State practised and the casualness with which the Central Government treated issues of crucial importance of the public administration come out vividly in a case that happened in connection with the Lok Sabha elections in 1984-85.

In December 1984, I got timely information of the plan of Chief Minister G.M. Shah's coterie to manipulate victory for his son, Muzaffar Shah, in the Lok Sabha elections from the Srinagar constituency. I immediately flew to Srinagar from Jammu and called a meeting of senior officers of the Division and the Director-General of Police. In the meeting I reminded the officers that the elections were being held under the supervision, of the Election Commission of India and it was the Commission's instructions, and no one else's, that were required to be followed. I also made a few general observations about their legal, administrative and moral obligations. The officers got the hint and distanced themselves from the 'plan' which, to say the least, was diabolical both in its dimensions and likely consequences.

The 'plan' failed. Muzaffar Shah lost badly. But the political rulers who were used to having their ways unchecked, retaliated. Punitive transfers were ordered on a large scale. I tried to check this vendetta but found myself powerless. The indifference of the Central Government was appalling. Even my personal discussions with the Prime Minister and my demi-official letter to him on the subject had no effect. In my letter of January 9, 1985, I, *inter alia*, wrote:

> Large-scale punitive transfers have been ordered, and enforced within a few hours. All those officers who have acted on our informal advice to ensure fair elections and thus prevent large-scale violence in the Valley, have been victimised and humiliated. The haste is deliberate and part of the design to make me and the Central authority powerless to influence the course of events. A dangerous and explosive situation is being created which will have extremely deleterious effects, short-term as well as long-term, on the political and administrative landscape of this most sensitive State.

The local bureaucracy, faction-ridden as it was, also did not show any awakened sense of responsibility. Some of them gleefully seized the new opportunities.

Soon after the elections, G.M. Shah, Chief Minister, specially called for the personal file of Hamid Ullah Khan who was Divisional Commissioner, Srinagar, at the time of the elections. He recorded the following remarks:

I have found him outstanding in sycophancy and untrust-worthiness.

This unprincipled and arrogant display of power showed to what low level the administrative and political life in the State had descended.

The following points which Hamid Ullah Khan made in his representation to me during Governor's Rule need to be particularly noted:

Throughout 1985-86, save 23 days of March 1986, I had been kept absolutely idle, without any assignment whatsoever. I proceeded on leave soon after the Lok Sabha elections of 1984 and reported for duty in the Secretariat on 1.4.85 and thereafter kept waiting for a posting till March 8, 1986, when I was posted as Divisional Commissioner, Kashmir, by His Excellency the Governor (after the imposition of Governor's Rule on March 7, 1986). As I did not perform any function during the period under report the question of assessing my performance and making observations should not arise.

When the elections to the Lok Sabha were announced in November '84, Mr. G.M. Shah decided to field his son from the Srinagar Lok Sabha constituency. For ensuring his success he did not consider any means foul. It all began with the induction of G.N. Kochak as the Revenue Minister.

Soon after his being sworn in as a Minister, Kochak called me to inform of the decision to put up Muzaffar Shah as the NC(K) candidate from Srinagar constituency and asked me in embarrassingly clear terms to ensure the success of the ruling party candidate.

The Chief Minister, G.M. Shah, arrived in Srinagar on 4.12.84 to launch the election campaign of his son. He did so in his own style. Instead of holding a public meeting, he first summoned me along with the Director-General Police, Peer Ghulam Hassen Shah, and the DIG Kashmir (Range), Watali. He had no compunctions in asking us in his peculiar perverse way to use our positions for getting his son elected.

Before his return to the winter capital on 22.12.84 the Chief Minister called a meeting of the Deputy Commissioners where he asked them to go by the orders of Kochak who he said was functioning as Home Minister. Kochak summoned me and the

DIG Kashmir to the Chief Minister's residence where, in the presence of Begum Khalida Shah, he made the most gory proposition of exploding bombs in the Valley to create scare and keep people away from electoral involvement. This, in his wisdom could make massive rigging possible. He said he would 'not mind if 10/15 persons got killed in the process'.

The polling over, another war of nerves was started by the Chief Minister, the Revenue Minister and their supporters. Kochak called the Director-General Police, the DIG Kashmir and me on 25.12.84 to his residence where he came out with his plans to tamper with ballot boxes and sought our help in carrying out the unholy design. He even made the shameful suggestion of forcing the Returning Officer of Srinagar constituency, G.Q. Pardesi, to declare Muzaffar Shah elected even while the counting of votes was on.

On 27.12.84 instructions of Chief Minister were conveyed to me by Director-General Police that the DIG Kashmir and I should meet Begum Khalida Shah. That we did. Muzaffar Shah was also present. The macabre demand from the mother-son duo followed a cup of coffee. Their perversity of thought came out in full when Mrs. Khalida Shah suggested that in any case the result of the elections would be followed by bloodshed and killings. 'Why not make the best out of it and get Muzaffar elected?'

Meanwhile, reports were received that in their desperation the ruling party planned to blow up the treasury, the repository of the ballot boxes. The administration responded by making heavy police bandobust around the treasury and cordoning off the area from all sides.

While the counting was on, at a tardy speed rather, as a result of the hurdles created by the ruling party musclemen, reports came that they had planned to set the counting hall on fire as a last-ditch battle to swing the outcome of the elections in their favour. The Returning Officer ordered the Police to be deployed inside the counting hall. The CRPF men were posted on duty accordingly. This frustrated the designs of the ruling party as after the failure of their arson bid their band of toughs, called election agents, led by a notorious anti-national and anti-social character Bashir Ahmed Tota tried to destroy the ballot papers. They tried to assault the officials on duty in the counting hall. The Provincial President of NC(K) A.R. Shah abused me and the DIG Kashmir Watali. He contacted Begum Khalida Shah on phone from the counting centre and wanted the DIG Kashmir to talk to her. He did not oblige. On the following day the Chief Minister ordered the Director-General Police to withdraw the police force from the counting hall. The Director-General expressed his inability.

On 7.1.1985 the Secretary to Government, General Deptt., informed me on telephone that I should hand over charge of office of the Divisional Commissioner, Kashmir, and proceed on leave which had been sanctioned.

While I was on leave the Government issued large-scale transfer orders. All the officers connected with the election process in Kashmir Division were transferred in the very first Cabinet meeting held after the elections.

When I reported to the Chief Secretary for duty on 1st April 1985, I was not adjusted anywhere. I was not even allotted a room and I had to fight for a place for myself to sit in the Secretariat. The seniormost Commissioner of the State had to rest content without even the elementary facility of an orderly for over a year.

In a manner characteristic of Nazi Germany, secret police was made to keep me and other victimised officers under surveillance.

This unseemly persecution of senior officers for the 'sin' of upholding law and Constitution continued till the last day of the G.M. Shah regime. But, unfortunately, it seemed to be nobody's business anywhere in the country except for one man whose affectionate concern sustained us through this most difficult period. We kept His Excellency the Governor informed of all that we had to suffer and but for his sympathies some of us might have broken down in the face of the atrocities of the Government. Even while the election process was on, His Excellency the Governor was pleased to issue clear instructions to us to ensure free and fair elections.

I have considered it necessary to quote at some length from Hamid Ullah Khan's representation because it gives an accurate idea of the values practised in Kashmir's politics. What G.M. Shah's coterie did, or attempted to do, was by no means peculiar to them. Some other political regimes, both preceding and succeeding, had been equally guilty. It was immaterial whether they resorted to one type of tactics or another. The common feature was the blatant unscrupulousness.

What could be the long-term consequences of this moral chaos? Where could such political and administrative perversion lead to?

During Governor's Rule, the All-India Services–the Indian Administrative Service, the Indian Police Service, and the Indian Forest Service–were restructured, their cadres rationalised and their general morale given a boost. To make the process of recruitment fair and just, an independent statutory Subordinate Services Selection Board was established. For dealing with the quasi-judicial matters, independent tribunals were set up. A vigorous drive was launched against corruption and a lot of dead-wood chopped off to infuse new life in the services. Twenty-two senior officers were compulsorily retired. A system of public interviews was introduced to enable even the poorest and the most resourceless to have direct access to me. This system not only helped in prompt disposal of public grievances but also acted as a 'cat-scan', for the entire administrative machinery. It enabled me to see clearly as to what was happening at different levels of administration. Under this system, I met about 22,000 persons from different walks of life. This made the entire machinery active, alert and responsive to the public needs and humanised it.

When Governor's Rule was about to end, I had advised the Union Government to ensure that the institutional framework, which I had created and which they themselves had applauded, was not dismantled by the State Government, particularly when this government was coming into being as a result of the Rajiv-Farooq Accord. Verbal assurances were given in plenty. In practice, however, nothing was done.

The political masters were soon back at their old game of petty manipulation and jockeying for personal and party patronage. To take just one example, in mid-1989, 1,100 posts were created in Agriculture Department. In regard to filling of these posts, a dispute arose between the coalition partners–whether the posts would be divided between the National Conference(F) and the Congress(I) in the ratio of 80 : 20 or 70 : 30 or 60 : 40. The dispute not only delayed appointments but also caused considerable strain between the two political parties. This happened when subversion and terrorism were knocking violently at the door of the State Government.

The practice of not giving district posting to IAS and IPS officers also returned. In 1988, for instance, against 14 cadre posts of Deputy

Commissioners, only six IAS officers were working. Likewise, against 14 cadre posts of Superintendents of Police, only five IPS officers were working. The tendency of giving preference to non-IAS and non-IPS officers not only reduced the role of the All-India Services but also resulted in the re-emergence of an unhealthy nexus between the politicians and the public services at the field level, giving rise to a new wave of corruption and malpractices. In February 1988, I found that in the preceding nine months over rupees three crore had been spent on employing daily wagers at the instance of the Ministers. And the graph of nepotism went on rising. Small but troublesome principal-ities were being daily created.

There were many other infirmities from which the State Administration under Dr. Farooq Abdullah suffered. In March 1988, I assessed the situation in this regard and noted that the administration was top-heavy. In a State with a population of about seven million, there were as many as 10 Additional Chief Secretaries, three Directors-General of Police and a dozen officers in the rank of Inspector-General of Police and Additional Inspector-General of Police, causing diffusion of duties and responsibilities. The political leadership seemed unable or unwilling to end groupism in higher services. And this further lowered the already low productivity of the administration. Eleven Government Undertakings were in the red. They suffered losses to the tune ₹ 71 crore. This sorry state of affairs was largely due to over-staffing, non-modernisation, and absence of a proper work-culture. The extent of over-staffing could be seen from the fact that for every bus, there were 6 drivers and 8 conductors and cleaners.

"Few regions in the world could have had worse luck than Kashmir in the matter of Government", wrote Vincent A. Smith about the mediaeval period. This observation is not applicable to contemporary Kashmir. But this period, too, has not been lucky in having a healthy administration. Except for brief intervals, Kashmir's administration, even after October 1947, showed dispositions which were more feudal and parasitic in nature than modern and altruistic. It was nowhere near a steel frame; it was not even a structure built with graceful bamboos. Its rickety edifice was too often shaken by the whims and caprices of housekeepers like G.M. Shah and Dr. Farooq Abdullah. No wonder, it collapsed like a house of cards by the push of its own contradictions.

Roots in Public Corruption

On May 2, 1988, a three-storeyed building of a Children's Hospital at Jammu collapsed. It came down like a house of cards. At the initial stage, it was feared that about 100 children and their guardians and hospital staff were the victims of the tragedy. Luckily, the final toll turned out to be not as high as was earlier apprehended. Ten persons lost their lives and 27 were seriously injured.

The gruesome tragedy, wholly man-made, symbolised the deep-rooted corruption in the administration of the State. The building was only five years old. Apparently, substandard material had been used, and all norms of safety were sacrificed at the altar of the new 'god of money'–the god who had found many devotees amongst administrators, engineers and politicians. The tragedy also brought out other deep-rooted maladies–wrong methods of selection, appointments and transfers of engineers, influence exercised by political elements when contracts are settled, general casualness of the bureaucracy, and the absence of any worthwhile civil rescue machinery. But for the Army's timely assistance, loss of life would have been much higher.

In March 1988, G.M. Shah disclosed, in a public statement, that he had paid ₹ 1 lakh to the Awami Action Committee chief, Mirwaiz Moulvi Farooq, for securing his help in getting Muzaffar Shah elected from Srinagar City parliamentary constituency in the December 1984 Lok Sabha elections. While it was generally believed that G.M. Shah was speaking the truth, no one asked him where from he got this amount and whether he accounted for it in his income-tax returns and other documents. Neither any State agency nor any Central agency made enquiries, despite the fact that the allegations were made by no less a person than the former Chief Minister.

In another public statement on July 16, 1988, G.M. Shah alleged, "Dr. Farooq Abdullah has a fleet of motor vehicles of latest models, valued at ₹ 32 lakh, of which only one motor-bike is worth ₹ 73,000. I demand that the Chief Minister should indicate the source of income from which he purchased these vehicles." There was no response.

I have cited these examples to show that corruption in Kashmir was so endemic that its occurrence was viewed with cynical forbearance. It had benumbed the body and the soul. Construction of spacious and costly bungalows and farmhouses by the politicians, businessmen and bureaucrats, their life-style and conspicuous consumption, the proliferation of Marutis like ants on the roads, and the low yield of taxes, were all indications of large-scale corruption prevailing in the State. But practically nothing was done to eliminate it. Consequently, while the beautiful streams and rivulets, which murmur their way all over the Kashmir Valley, are losing their purity and silken colour due to environmental degradation, the messy river of corruption continues to flow with uninterrupted ugliness.

During the first few months of my posting in April 1984, I wondered why there was such extraordinary rush for government jobs; why posts were created even when there was absolutely no need for them; why people were willing to pay huge amounts as bribes for small jobs; and why Ministers and other political elites considered that they had earned a lifelong gratitude of their kith and kin by securing minor jobs for them.

The answers to these questions, I soon found, lay in one simple fact–the jobs in J&K had more than normal importance. They brought in a lot of extra income. Once appointed, the official did not have to exert much. There were too many holidays, too little official work, too many avenues for making quick money. If one was a doctor, one could earn huge amounts by seeing the patients in private clinics and by not attending to the normal hospital work; if one was a teacher, one could start a tuition class in the house and fleece the students, being harsh on those who did not ask the teacher for tuition and favourable to those who engaged him. Since jobs were secured by unfair means, the appointees had easy conscience, and experienced no inner pricks in doing blatantly wrong things.

Corruption had debilitated and dehumanised the entire system. In June 1986, during Governor's Rule, I went to Kishtwar on tour. It was a practice with me to visit, during my tours, hospitals, schools, offices of civic bodies, streets and other places where the public came in direct contact with the administration. At the Kishtwar hospital, I saw a young boy of about 15 years who was in great agony. He had a nasty fall and both of his arms were badly fractured. On inquiry, the father of the boy told me that the doctor in charge of the hospital had asked him to take the boy in a taxi to Jammu, as he required extensive surgery to set his broken limbs in position, and this would involve an expenditure of ₹ 2,700, besides an extremely painful journey over a long and difficult hilly terrain. The poor father did not have even ₹ 20 with him. I arranged for the money and had the boy sent to Jammu. But that was beside the point.

The event pointed to a corrupt and soulless system which, in theory, had the plan targets fulfilled, but in practice did not provide any service even to the most needy. The event also laid bare the cruel fangs of the 'power elites' network and doctor-politician nexus in the State. I found that the Kishtwar hospital had an operation theatre. It had also a qualified surgeon. But there was no anaesthetist, though there was a sanctioned post for the same. I learnt that, as private practice was allowed to the Government doctors, the anaesthetists, with the help of their political godfathers, managed to stay in Srinagar or Jammu, where they could make a lot of extra money by attending private clinics.

Many other instances of gross inhumanity and virtual robbing of the poor patients came to my notice. I banned private practice of government doctors and simultaneously sanctioned non-practising allowance to them. The step was warmly applauded by the press and the public. Hospital service improved dramatically. Malpractices were reduced. Availability of free medicines became easy. Teaching in medical colleges became regular. When some doctors challenged my order in the High Court, it was held to be valid and in public interest. But as soon as the so-called popular ministry returned, it reversed the most popular reform, causing much annoyance and frustration to the common people. In Kashmir, corruption and closely-knit power circle of a few caucuses have made democracy a meaningless charade.

Just as honesty and compassion move hand in hand, corruption and callousness travel together. It is the culture of public corruption that makes the administration inhuman as well as costly. Fundamentalist and moralist trends, witnessed in Kashmir during the last decade, are, to some extent, reactions to the culture of corruption, callousness and consumerism. The discontentment of the public on account of corruption undermines the image of the government and swells the ranks of the fundamentalists. For instance, Farooq Rehmani, former chairman of the People's League and a leader of the subversives had been propagating for years: "What to speak of the outsiders, even our own people are treating us like sheep and plucking our wool mercilessly."

The Union Government, by and large, turned a blind eye to the existence of widespread corruption in Kashmir. When Bakshi Ghulam Mohammad became Prime Minister in 1953, he used to appease and placate the Kashmiris. He brought substantial funds from the Central Exchequer and used them liberally for distributing patronage and for carrying out development work.

Bakshi Ghulam Mohammad was, in his own right, a great leader, a great organiser, and a great propagator of Hindu-Muslim unity. He rose from the ranks and understood the pains and problems of the common Kashmiri. But his tragedy was that, instead of restructuring the society, reforming its base, and modernising the administration, he relied upon feudal norms and also made fortunes for himself, for his family members and for his friends. His political opponents, both at the State and Central levels, kicked up a lot of dust. Ultimately, he was eased out of office under the Kamaraj Plan. On January 30, 1965, a Commission of Inquiry was set up, under the J&K Commission of Inquiry Act, 1962, to inquire into the allegations of corruption against Bakshi Ghulam Mohammad. Justice Ayyanger constituted the one-man Commission.

The findings of the Ayyanger Commission broadly confirmed what was already known to the public. So far as the objective of the Bakshi's political opponents was concerned, it was achieved; he was practically finished as a political force. But the Commission singularly failed to eliminate or reduce corruption in the State. The streams of corruption continued to flow. In fact, what happened subsequently showed that Bakshi Ghulam Mohammad was 'more sinned against than sinning'.

A booklet, titled *Lal Kitab,* catalogued acts of corruption committed by Sheikh Mohammed Abdullah and his family members. In the early eighties, it was being circulated clandestinely. Maybe the booklet was politically motivated. But the specificity of the allegations was such that only the Sheikh's 'historic greatness' prevented the people from believing the charges. In any case, it cannot be denied that corruption thrived under the very nose of the Sheikh, though it was a sick nose and could not smell the stench of corruption around. In the forest leases, in the allotment of lands for hotels, in making concessions to industrialists, in giving contracts, in disposing of government property, and in the misuse of the lease agreements, corruption was more than evident.

After 1977, Sheikh Abdullah acquired almost unlimited powers. And corruption acquired new fangs and depth in Kashmir. The power-circle grew closer; the roles of politicians and civil servants virtually merged; the curtain of Article 370 acquired a thicker and more malevolent texture; and increasing reliance came to be placed upon money-power and exploitation* of parochial emotions rather than on solid, sound and honest work. And one could easily see the operation of the well-known dictum of Lord Acton: "Power corrupts, and absolute power corrupts absolutely".

By way of illustration, I would give only one example. And this pertains to the construction of a number of hotels on the bank–rather the bed–of the Dal Lake, along what is now called the boulevard. Here, scores of plots were allotted, at cheap rates, to influential businessmen for construction of hotels and commercial complexes. A permanent wound was inflicted on the silvery bosom of the lake. The damage was compounded by allowing the sewer from these constructions to flow into the lake and by not leaving any space for public parking. A modern slum has now come into being, right on the bank of the lake, ravaging its landscape, silting its bed, and multiplying its slushy weeds. Everybody in the power-circle, perhaps, gained–the politician, the businessman and the bureaucrat. But the shrinking mass of the lake and its stinking portion will remain as a tragic legacy of the culture of corruption and of power.

This is what Abida Hussain has recorded in the book *Life of Sheikh Abdullah:*

> Sheikh Abdullah and his family were persons of modest means before he came to power as Chief Minister. Today, his known immovable assets are estimated to be worth more than twenty crores of rupees. This phenomenal accumulation has taken place mainly within a short span of time, from 1975 to 1981. His assets are mainly in the shape of illegally-occupied government lands of the highest commercial value in the State and a series of palatial buildings that have come up over these lands. Needless to add that these buildings have been constructed with the money and materials obtained from all sorts of dubious sources from contractors working with governmental departments.**

About the income tax raids,[†] this is what Mohammed Farooq Rehmani, Chairman of the Peoples' League wrote: "While the general

---

* See also sections on 'Administrative Roots' and 'Roots in Environmental Disruption' in this Chapter and also Chapter V: 'Roots: Article 370'.

** Reproduced from Farooq Rehmani's book in Urdu, *Sheikh Abdullah ke Naqoosh* (translation by author).

† Income Tax authorities carried out in 1981 simultaneous raids on some top ranking carpet dealers in the country. At Srinagar, the raiding party was attacked. The State leaders, including Dr. Farooq Abdullah, M.P., incited the mob. At a few places the seized document were snatched and thrown in the Dal Lake. 47 of the 69 officials were injured.

public in Kashmir had become very happy about the income tax raids to detect hidden income, Sheikh Abdullah felt extremely annoyed and expressed his resentment. There was no doubt that Sheikh Abdullah had become a protector of capitalists and racketeers who made unmerited gains through dishonest means and the honest practices and laws were meant only for the un-influential poor people: Sheikh Abdullah and his family considered themselves above law."

During the regime of G.M. Shah, from July 2, 1984, to March 6, 1986, further damage was sought to be done by making available the vacant tract near the new hotel complex to a retired Major-General of Pakistan Army who was persuaded to claim it as evacuee property. I came to know about it, and was able to stall the proposal.

What Dr. Farooq Abdullah did was truly amazing, and showed how cynical and nasty had become the power structure and how hypocrisy and expediency held complete sway.

During the course of a seminar in early 1984, which I inaugurated, Dr. Farooq Abdullah lambasted the Sheikh's decision to allow hotels on the boulevard. He said, "A great crime was committed by permitting construction of these hotels. They should all be burnt. They have raped and pillaged the bank of the lake." I was happy to hear these words. I thought, Dr. Farooq was an enlightened leader, conscious of the need to prevent environmental degradation. But it did not take long to discover that he could be a perfect wolf in sheep's clothing. A few months after the above declaration, Dr. Farooq Abdullah himself permitted, and even laid the foundation-stone of a big hotel complex at a most unsuitable spot*–the spot which is causing maximum pollution to the lake, maximum uglification of the landscape, and the longest and the deepest cut in the green hills by knifing a road through them and providing for the movement of hundreds of light and heavy vehicles every day. Nothing could be a sadder example of saying one thing and doing exactly the opposite. In fact, over the years, it became a special feature of Kashmir's political scene to denounce, on the one hand, corrupt practices with loud statements and, on the other, indulge in, directly or indirectly, such practices.

The existence of corruption on a large scale during Sheikh Abdullah's rule was indirectly recognised by Dr. Farooq Abdullah, when he became Chief Minister after the Sheikh's death in September 1982.

---

*See: Chapter VI: 'Roots: Article 370'.

He excluded from his ministry quite a few prominent leaders of the National Conference–D.D. Thakur, G.N. Kochak and G.M. Bhaderwahi–who were ministers in the Sheikh's cabinet. Dr. Farooq wanted to kill two birds with one stone. He wanted the ambitious men in his father's cabinet to be kept away and at the same time, give the impression to the public that he was out to eliminate corruption from public life. That Dr. Farooq Abdullah's ministry was no paragon of virtue or in any way different from the previous regime, soon became evident.

Dr. Farooq Abdullah also appointed a commission of inquiry, under the Commission of Inquiries Act, to look into the allegations of corruption particularly in regard to the allotment of housing plots to certain erstwhile ministers in Sheikh Abdullah's ministry. Justice Kotwal, retired Judge of the J&K High Court, was appointed to hold such inquiry. But as soon as G.M. Shah's ministry came into existence and the erstwhile ministers in the Sheikh's cabinet also became ministers in G.M. Shah's cabinet, the Kotwal Commis-sion was promptly wound up. On the other hand, a cabinet sub-committee was appointed to go into the allegations of corruption and improprieties committed by Dr. Farooq Abdullah. This sub-committee, headed by the Deputy Chief Minister, D.D. Thakur, castigated Dr. Farooq Abdullah for his aberrations, malpractices and anti-national activities. But nothing came out of these inquiries and counter-inquiries.

The list of improper decisions taken during the time of G.M. Shah and of Farooq Abdullah are too long to be narrated or analysed here. One typical example would suffice.

From December 1987 onwards, a large number of complaints were received against the Asra Builders, a land-colonising private company floated in 1987 by Raman Mattoo, son-in-law of P.L. Handoo, Revenue and Urban Development Minister in Dr. Farooq Abdullah's ministry. The allegations were that, with the active connivance of Handoo, the Asra Builders had purchased large areas of land on the periphery of Jammu city, in violation of revenue and municipal laws, and sold the same in the shape of residential plots without getting the layout plan and the service plan sanctioned by the competent authority, and, in the process, secured huge unmerited monetary benefits. I brought this to the notice of the Chief Minister, Dr. Farooq Abdullah, and wrote three letters to him on the subject. In my third letter of December 28, 1987, I, *inter alia*, said: "I am sorry to point out that the activities of the Asra Builders are still going on. In this connection, I am enclosing a photostat copy of the advertisement which the Asra Builders have issued in the local newspapers. I cannot understand how residential plots can be sold without getting the layout plans sanctioned from the Municipal or Development Authority and following the municipal and town planning regulations, and also without first developing the colony and providing services in accordance with the said sanctioned plan. Even a glance at the advertised layout shows that only plots have been carved out on paper. What the Asra Builders are doing is a negation of all principles of town planning, regional development and environmental safeguards. It is obvious that racketeering and speculation in land is taking place with impunity. Apart from being illegal and irregular, this type of activity will burden the posterity with heavy financial and environmental costs."

Udhey Chand, General Secretary, Panthers Party, and Dr. Qazi Nissar, the Chief of Umat-e-Islam and 'Mirwaiz' of South Kashmir, approached me, separately, for permission to prosecute P.L. Handoo under the Prevention of Corruption Act. I sent their applications for comments to the Chief Minister. But no reply was received.

S.N. Kakkar, an eminent jurist and former Law Minister in the Union Cabinet, whose advice was obtained by the Vigilance Department, opined that the 'Asra Builders' had violated several provisions of law. But, instead of taking action on the report of S.N. Kakkar or sending to me comments on the applications of the Panthers Party and Umat-e-Islam, the Chief Minister, with the obvious intention of gaining time and circumventing the straightforward legal course, manoeuvred to have the case referred to a House Committee of the Legislature. Obviously, the House Committee was not a suitable body for dealing with the case. It soon came to a dead end.

No institution can remain unaffected by the political and social environment around it. The judiciary in the State was no exception. It too was infected by the prevailing virus of corruption. Vicious groupism in the High Court further fouled the atmosphere. Several recommendations made by me in regard to remedial measures were not attended to by the Central Government. Nor was any reply sent as to why it was not possible to accept my recommendations. Consequently, the decline in the judiciary became steeper, and quite often one witnessed the tragic spectacle of unjust situations being caused by the machinery of justice.

Notwithstanding the fact that the cancer of corruption was eating into the vitals of the State and the society, the gravity of the problem was never realised. The politicians were in no mood to adopt a sincere approach, the officials were in no mood to dissociate themselves from the unhealthy political elements, the elites were in no mood to change their habits of circumventing the laws, and the courts were in no mood to appreciate the damage that was being caused by their too frequent intervention in favour of the suspects. The nature of public corruption, thus, became highly disintegrative* and its scale became so large that the social arid political system was bound to crack under its impact. It caused conflict among those involved in it and also between the beneficiary and the non-beneficiary. The day of reckoning, obviously, could not be far way.

Roots in Environmental Disruption

The state of the environment of any place is an indication of its spiritual health. In the issues of environment are involved the deeper issues of culture, values, politics and the economic and social outlook of a community.

The validity of this proposition is borne out, in a striking manner, by the case of Kashmir. Here, nature has endowed the Valley with beautiful gifts, but the inner forces of matter and mind are stamping these gifts out of existence at a rapid pace. The brutalisation of the landscape, the silting of the great lakes and rivers, the pollution of air, water and soil are manifestations of the phenomenon. The priorities and patterns of development, coupled with the whimsicalities of decision-making, have greatly contributed to it. It is the greed, and not the green, that generally motivates. In view of the breathtaking beauty of the natural landscape, the attitude should have been: "Oh Mother Earth, we salute you; pardon us for touching you with our feet." But Kashmir's natural beauty is being ravaged by the beast, the new beast that has found a safe refuge in the minds of the new elites and is fed liberally by the forces of exploitative democracy. This is evident from the fate of the lakes, rivers, forests, soil, cities, etc.

The famous Dal Lake, which was described by Abul Fazal as the 'delight of the world', has shrunk from 24 sq. km to about 10 sq. km.

*In his essay on "The Political Consequences of Corruption" *(Comparative Politics,* July 1986), Michael Gohuston draws clear distinction between integrative and disintegrative corruption. The former links people and groups but later causes serious conflicts.

Even at present, about 15 tonnes of phosphorus and 320 tonnes of nitrogen are flowing into it every year. The floods of 1987 showed how badly the natural flow of water in the Lake had been disrupted by encroachments. About 1200 houses built around the lake were damaged and 12 lives lost. The total loss was estimated at ₹ 85 crores. The fate of the other lakes such as Wullar and Manasbal is not different. The Anchar and the Gilsar lakes are now extinct.

The River Jhelum, the lifeline of the Valley, is getting silted at an alarming speed. The Pohru catchment area alone sends 24 lakh cubic feet of slit into it every year. The liquid and the solid wastes of the entire Valley go into it. Now, even rains of moderate intensity send the river in spate, causing huge damage to property and crops. In the floods of 1986, 1987 and 1988, the losses were estimated to be ₹ 84 crore, ₹ 328 crore and ₹ 212 crore respectively.

Not long ago, the Shiwaliks of Jammu and the high mountains of Kashmir supported one of the densest and richest subtropical and temperate forests of the world, covering more than 60 per cent of the total land area. But, of late, particularly after the mid-seventies, there has been virtually licensed massacre of green trees. Till two years ago, about 4 crore cubic feet of timber were being extracted every year from the forests of the State. A recent study revealed that during the period 1952 to 1976, about 91 thousand hectares of forest land was lost to various 'development' projects. For meeting the annual firewood needs, even now 5 lakh quintals are being made available in the city of Srinagar alone. For the whole State, the current requirement of firewood is believed to be 100 lakh quintals.

The problems arising from pollution of air, water and soil, caused by cement factories, stone crushers, brick kilns, smelting industries and unchecked use of chemicals, have become very serious. Hardly one per cent of the applied chemicals reaches the target and the rest is absorbed by the environment. Against the national average of 500 grams/ha. of pesticides, the Kashmir region uses 6,000 to 12,000 grams/ha. of fungicides for the orchards.

It is astonishing that even after 43 years of freedom there is total absence of a sewerage system in the summer capital of the State. Hardly one or two per cent of the houses in the main city have flush latrines with soakage pits. Night-soil is carried on head or in poorly maintained vehicles, spreading foul smell all along. Various diseases such as the hookworm, are widespread. Boatmen living in 'dongas' and the inhabitants of the houseboats dispose of their refuse in the

River Jhelum or Dal Lake, making them virtual sewer pits and sewer drains. A study recently made by the Hydro-Biology Laboratory of the Government S.P. College revealed that the drinking water supplied in some parts of Srinagar city was worse than the polluted water of the River Jhelum. It was also revealed that supply of this type of polluted water posed a threat to wild life, particularly in the Dachigam National Park.

All this has happened, and is happening, not only because of rampant corruption and maladministration but also because of the perverse priorities of so-called development and the unashamed gap between what is said and what is done. Ecological consciousness is confined only to words. Let me give a few examples.

A vast area of about 907 hectares of land, littered with trees, shrubs and wild growth, was lying neglected near Pari Mahal, Shankaracharya hill and Zeethyar hills. It was being subjected to encroachments and vandalism. A few government departments were using it as a dumping ground for stores. Natural springs had been covered with debris. Artificial pits, full of stagnant water, were breeding mosquitoes.

While going to my first public function on May 9, 1984, I noticed this area. In my inaugural speech, I referred to it and said: "This area has great potential for development into a City Forest." I pleaded: "Let us create an environment which will enable the visitor to the Valley to come in contact with its physical and spiritual beauty, so that when he leaves, he is not only externally refreshed but internally beautified."

> As the sun dries the morning dew,
> Let the strains of our visitors
> Disappear,
> At the very site of this beautiful land.

In his speech, the Chief Minister, Dr. Farooq Abdullah, warmly applauded the idea. He said: "As a young, dynamic and imaginative person, the eyes of Jagmohan have caught the area which requires prompt attention. I, too, have young blood. The two 'young bloods' could join hands and create a revolution in the State." But it turned out to be an empty rhetoric. Nothing was done either by Dr. Farooq Abdullah or G.M. Shah who followed him. The area continued to be in a state of neglect.

During Governor's Rule, I ordered that this area be developed into a City Forest, a sort of natural woodland within the Srinagar metropolis. The entire land was fenced with chain-links, keeping intact the natural topography, and walkways were created for walkers. The stores were removed, the artificial pits were filled, and old springs were revived and repaired. Natural growth and shrubs and marshes were preserved. Nature was restored to its pristine simplicity and charm. Barren and desolate chunks were earmarked for fresh plantation, and thousands of school children were regularly brought from schools with the twin objective of securing mass plantation of trees and providing nature's education. A conservation centre was also set up in the old dilapidated building. It was adapted to the need for holding exhibitions, painting competitions and for showing films on nature and wild-life. In one corner, a wild-life sanctuary was also created. Hanguls and other animals were reared therein.

The entire complex became a heaven for nature's lovers. Thousands of morning and evening walkers began to experience a new life–a clean and crisp environment, free from any kind of fume and noise, with birds chirping, trees and shrubs swinging, streams and springs murmuring, and beautiful and harmless animals playing and dancing around. Nothing more attractive, nothing more inexpensive, nothing more delightful could be asked for by the common man. The tourists, too, found it an extremely pleasant place to loiter, away from the humdrum life of a city dweller.

The project became the talk of the Valley–nay, of the entire State. People in Jammu began to ask for a similar City Forest. The All-India Society of Nature Photography hailed it as a masterpiece of nature's preservation. Even the State Board of Wild-life, after the termination of Governor's rule, passed a special resolution, eulogising the project. Ironically, the general resolution eulogising my services to the upgradation of ecology and environment of the State was moved by the Chief Minister himself.

All this has been destroyed. Gone are the walkways, the springs, the wild-life created. Gone also are the hundreds of trees and shrubs. A huge sprawling and artificial golf course is being laid at a phenomenal cost of over ₹ 10 crore. A thing of beauty, which was 'a joy for ever', has been mutilated. Instead, an 'elite course' which could, if at all justified, have been constructed anywhere else, has been created.

For me, it is a matter of great personal pain and anguish. One cannot bear the sight of one's own creation being destroyed. But, for general public, it is an act of grave injustice. It is like snatching away even fresh air and visual delight from them. What is still more tragic is the pattern of development–a pattern for the elites and by the elites, a pattern which is highly expensive, lop-sided, and wholly out of tune with our requirement.

The golf course would not help in the growth of Srinagar tourism. On an average, only two or three foreign tourists play golf in Srinagar during summer and that too on non-rainy days. These tourists are not golf-minded and they hardly spend anything on the game. Srinagar climate being what it is, the foreign tourists generally move to cooler resorts like Gulmarg and Pahalgam. The disadvantages of the golf course project are far more than the advantages that may accrue.

Now, a huge tract, extending to several kilometres, would have to be maintained. Scores of golf boys and staff would have to be appointed. It will consume millions of gallons of water. In brief, the pattern of development, which is simple, inexpensive and capable of enhancing the quality of the common man's life, and is beneficial to the overwhelming majority of the people has been abandoned in favour of a highly expensive, elite-oriented, lop-sided pattern.

Thousands of morning walkers, groups of students and teachers coming for a picnic, visitors to the conservation centre, artists, animal and bird lovers, and other users of the City Forest felt deeply hurt by its virtual destruction. They found themselves helpless before the arrogance of power of a whimsical head of Government. Their frustration had to be experienced to be realised. Once a group of young students saw me and complained that the trees they had planted in my presence at a special function on Oct. 2, 1986, had all been bulldozed. I was upset but did not show my feelings. In fact, I had spoken several times to the Chief Minister about this case, but, as was usual with him in the post-November 1986 period, he held out promises only to falsify them later without batting an eyelid. The impression that the Centre would be indifferent to Governor's report had got into his head and made him more irresponsible and erratic. To the young complainants I tried to suggest that, after the termination of Governor's rule I had little say in the matter, and whatever I could do I had already done by advising the Chief Minister not to touch even a blade of grass in the City Forest, because by doing so he would not only destroy a very popular and lovable project but also remove from the scene a new pattern of development which could be studied in depth and which was inexpensive, simple, and more tuned to our heritage of living in harmony with nature. A young boy in the group, a bit irritated, shot back, “Sir tell us, who is higher in authority–the Governor or the Chief Minister? You must ask him to stop all this vandalism and replant our trees, otherwise we would be forced to do something else.” I was surprised at the intensity of his feelings. All such frustrations were bound to swell the wave of subversion once it got going. Those standing by the wayside were impelled by their inner revulsion to applaud and to shout hurrah to the marchers on the road. The stream of discontentment and disenchantment was joined by small rivulets of anger and revulsion and soon turned it into a formidable torrent, overflowing the banks and washing away whatever little protective barriers the saner forces had built.

Regional Roots

It was an accident of history that had brought different ethnic communities under the Dogra dynasty in the forties of the last century. Factors of geography, language, race, religion and culture separated them. Jammu, Kashmir and Ladakh constituted distinct regions. The ‘Pahari’ tribes had different characteristics. ‘Gujjars’ and ‘Bukerwals’ had their own nomadic ways of living. Apart from the overall cultural unity of India, the only common bond between them was the autocratic rule of the Maharaja.

At the dawn of Indian Independence, a wise and constructive leadership, with vision, would have blunted and smoothened the rough and rusted edges of ethnic differences and weaved for them a new economic, social, political and cultural fabric–the fabric that was very badly needed by the poor people to change their tattered and stinking clothes and come out of their dark and depressing houses, with a new sense of dignity and direction, into the bright and sunny days of freedom. Unfortunately, that was not to be. On the contrary, under the peculiar brand of democracy that was contrived, the State became a hotbed of religious and regional tensions.

Rivalries and suspicions between the two main regions–J&K–are deep-rooted, and these have been surfacing time and again. The communal factor has also been playing its part. As early as in October 1924, both the regional and communal factors were manifest in the six petitions submitted by the Muslim clergymen of Kashmir to Lord Rippon. Thest petitions alleged that the "religion of Islam" was being dishonoured and the Muslims were being deprived of education and jobs, though they "always willingly responded to the call for men and material of the Supreme Government".*

Unfortunately, contemporary politicians of different hues have found it expedient to exploit the regional and religious issues. Some Kashmiri politicians, particularly the National Conference leaders, whenever they found their influence in Kashmir waning, have been using the 'Jammu card' to bolster up their own leadership in the Valley. For instance, the occasional outbursts in public of Sheikh Abdullah against Maharaja Hari Singh, wholly unnecessary and unjustified in the post-independence period, was as much a product of his innate arrogance as of his political strategy to secure a stronger hold on the Kashmiri mind. Likewise, some politicians in the Jammu region have been using the 'Kashmiri card' to gain ascendency in their own area. For their self-interest, thus, the political elements have not allowed harmony and homogeneity to develop in the State.

During the Dogra regime, quite a few of the higher posts were held by officers of the British-Indian Government, whose services the Maharaja was persuaded to use. The other top posts were mainly held by the Dogra Rajputs whose families were close to the ruling dynasty. A few loyal members of the Muslim feudal class were also accommodated.

With the spread of English education and the emergence of a new political consciousness, the details of which have been given in Chapter II entitled "Survey of History", the Kashmiri Muslims began to demand adequate share in government jobs. Following the violence of July 13, 1931, and general unrest, the Maharaja, under the pressure of the British-Indian Government, appointed a Commission to look into the grievances and complaints of the different communities. The Commission was headed by Bertrand J. Glancy, a British officer. The communal and regional imbalances were looked into by the Commission. It recommended that all vacancies in the State services should be advertised and it should be ensured that all communities received a fair share of the government appointments. The Commission also recommended that in regard to local appointments, the residents of the district concerned should be recruited.

*By this, the petitioners meant the British Indian Government.

The recommendations of the Glancy Commission gave nominal relief to the Kashmiri Muslims. The basic problem was the economic backwardness of the State. Job opportunities were few. Expectations of the people were never fulfilled. Discontent continued and found expression in occasional agitations.

After October 1947, the State Government came to be dominated by the Kashmiri leadership. It was now the turn of the Jammu people to feel aggrieved. They felt that their legitimate rights and interests were being sacrificed to favour the Kashmir region.

Due to continuing regional tensions and frequent agitations in the Jammu region, the State Government appointed, on November 6, 1967, a Commission known as the Gajendragadkar Commission. This Commission examined the regional disparities in depth and made a number of recommendations, including the recommendation of setting up a Statutory State Development Board and Statutory Regional Development Boards for the three regions–Jammu, Kashmir and Ladakh. The Commission noted that Jammu and Ladakh had been victims of political neglect. It also observed, "Even if all the matters were equitably settled, there would still be a measure of discontent unless the political aspirations of different regions of the State are satisfied."

Most of these recommendations were either not accepted or were not implemented. And wherever the process of their implementation was initiated, it was half-hearted. Sheikh Abdullah himself assailed* the report of this Commission. Consequently, the Jammuites continued to nurse grievances. In December 1978, regional resentment resulted in serious students' riots in Poonch, Rajourie and Jammu. Curfews had to be imposed and firing resorted to. On December 26, 1978, an All-Party Jammu Action Committee was formed to launch an agitation for the redressal of the grievances of the Jammu region. Sheikh Abdullah was accused of letting loose a reign of terror. The public agitation on the issue continued for 94 days. To cool public tempers, the State Government appointed another Commission under the chairmanship of Mr. Justice S.M. Sikri, retired Chief Justice of India. Its terms of reference were similar to those of the Gajendragadkar Commission. This Commission submitted its report on August 25, 1980. But its recommendations, too, met with a fate similar to that of the earlier Commission.

*Statement of Sheikh Abdullah on October 12, 1977.

Separately, the issue in regard to the creation of additional districts became highly controversial. In October 1972, the State Government appointed two Committees under the chairmanship of A.S. Kadri, Financial Commissioner, for the two divisions of Srinagar and Jammu. These Committees recommended that no new district should be created either in Jammu or in Kashmir Division. However, on July 1, 1979, the State Government suddenly decided, on its own, to create three districts in the Srinagar Valley, namely Badgam, Palwama and Kupwara, and one in the Ladakh region, namely Kargil. This decision of the State Government was considered arbitrary and partial to the Valley. It was followed by a number of agitations in the Jammu region, including a prolonged agitation in Kistwar.

On November 12, 1981, the State Government appointed another Commission under the chairmanship of Justice J.N. Wazir, retired Chief Justice of the J&K High Court, to go into this question. The Commission recommended the creation of three more districts in the Jammu region–Kistwar, Samba and Reasi–and one more district, Bandipur, in the Srinagar Valley. The recommend-ations which mostly went in favour of the Jammu region, have remained unimplemented, though they were made as far back as on January 3, 1984.

In the light of this background, the Jammuites had been feeling hurt and aggrieved. Their catalogue of grievances had been expanding. The inner frustration of the region has often found expression in regional agitations. Two recent agitations, one pertaining to the 'Darbar move' (1987) and the other to the creation of Reasi district (1988), need to be mentioned in this regard.

In October 1987, Dr. Farooq Abdullah's Government made a sudden modification in the normal pattern of shifting of the State Government Secretariat and other offices from Srinagar to Jammu. This change in the practice–popularly known as the 'Darbar move'–resulted in a major agitation and gave rise to a number of other problems.

The practice of the 'Darbar move' has been in vogue since 1870. The people of Jammu looked upon the new decision as an act of grave discrimination against them. They apprehended that it was a first step towards making Srinagar the permanent capital of the State, and that it would damage the economy of the Jammu region.

Apparently, the decision was taken by the Chief Minister without really applying his mind to the matter, and without preparing any formal and proper agenda note for the Cabinet. The haste with which the decision was announced to the press and the way the press note was worded, emphasising some aspects of the decision and ignoring the others, further compounded the mistake and created an impression amongst the people in the Jammu region that their interests had been thrown to the winds in a somewhat cavalier fashion, and that Dr. Farooq Abdullah was out to favour the people of the Valley to serve his narrow political ends.

The agitation lasted for about five weeks, during which total 'bandh' was observed for a number of days in Jammu, Udhampur and various other towns of the Jammu region. The student community was also very much worked up. The State Government closed the educational institutions indefinitely. In view of the solidarity displayed by the Jammuites in their opposition to the move, as also their hardening attitude, the Union Home Minister, Buta Singh, came to Srinagar on November 12 to discuss the situation with the Chief Minister. Soon thereafter Dr. Farooq Abdullah announced cancellation of the order.

Although the *status quo ante*, ordered by the Government, did not harm the interests of the Kashmiris in any way, a section of the people there reacted with indignation and anger. The Srinagar Bar Association gave a call for Kashmir 'bandh' as a protest against what it called bowing down of the State Government before the agitators in Jammu. The 'bandh' call received wide support and the day also saw a few untoward incidents. Stray incidents of violence also occurred in Srinagar on the following four days.

Though the agitation ended after five weeks, it left a trail of bitterness, and caused a lot of tension between the two regions of the State. The national interests suffered. Parochialism gained potency. Regionalism touched deeper cords and revived old memories of the Praja Parishad agitation in Jammu. Even a demand for a separate State of Jammu began to be made seriously.

The incident also revealed the immaturity and superficiality of the decision-making process of Kashmir's Administration. If the decision had not been taken in haste and if all the pros and cons had been properly weighed beforehand–the implications of the move were obvious even to a man of common intelligence–the hosts of problems which arose later could have been avoided.

The decision in regard to the 'Darbar move' was unfortunate, and its timing wholly inappropriate. It was, indeed, tragic that when the

State Administration should have been tackling the problems arising out of drought and numerous other problems connected with development, its time, energy and resources were allowed to be wasted on agitations which were wholly avoidable. The observation that "nothing would darken the economic future of our country more effectively than the politics of pendulum" was extremely relevant to the situation that emerged in the State then.

The second agitation was launched in support of a demand for the creation of a separate Reasi district. As noted earlier, the Wazir Commission had recommended the creation of a separate district of Reasi. Since this recommendation remained unimplemented, an agitation was started in September-October 1988. During the first ten days, the State Government practically took no action and virtually abdicated its authority. The agitators declared Reasi as a district and appointed their own Deputy Commissioner. Subsequently, the leaders were arrested. The agitation continued for two months during which 'hartals', 'dharnas' and processions became a regular feature. On some assurances given by the State Government, the agitation was suspended.

After October 1947, a strong feeling has grown over the Jammu region that the political domination of the State by the Valley leadership has resulted in grave injustices to the Jammu region. It is believed that the Central leadership has been appeasing the Valley and a number of decisions have been taken which favour Kashmir at the expense of the Jammu region.

It will be noticed that these grievances are largely valid. In the next chapter I have analysed the misuse of Article 370 in this regard. There seems to be little justification for having one seat in the Legislative Assembly for 73,000 of population in the Kashmir Valley and for 90,000 in the Jammu region.* Nor is there adequate justification for locating a disproportionately large number of important institutions and projects–the Institute of Medical Sciences, Engineering College, Dental College, Agricultural University, Veterinary College, Convention Hall, the Cable Car project, etc.–in the Valley. The distribution of the plan funds is also unfair.

The need for development in the Valley cannot be minimised. But it should not be forgotten that regional discriminations cause acute

*For details, see Chapter VI: 'Roots: Article 370'.

tensions and give rise to law and order problems in the tackling of which valuable resources of the State are consumed, thereby undermining its general capacity to bring about speedy development and attain higher productivity.

Ladakh

"When the rest of India rejoiced in 1947 over its indepen-dence, the Ladakhis found themselves out of the frying pan into the fire. Instead of becoming free sons of free India, they were left at the mercy and step-motherly treatment of the Government of J&K." These sentiments are expressions of regional frustrations and tensions which have gripped contemporary Ladakh, and are frequently repeated in some form or other. In a memorandum submitted to me in March 1990, the Ladakhi Buddhist Association said, "Gandhiji and other Indian national leaders emancipated the Indian masses from the oppressive alien domination, exploitation, feudal and colonial rule. But we the people of Ladakh, with a distinct identity, have been pushed under the oppressive political domination of the Kashmiris, and denied the fruits of freedom and national independence. In the last forty-two years of Independence we not only have suffered rampant Kashmiri political domination but also the severe stresses and strains of separatism."

As noted in Chapter II entitled "Survey of History", Ladakh, though sparsely populated, has territory which is double the size of J&K combined. It has an area of 98,000 sq. kilometres with an altitude range of 4,000 metres. Its population, according to the 1981 census, is 1,20,000. It has a long border both with China and Pakistan. Its strategic importance is immense.

The scenic beauty of Ladakh is unique. It has the fascination of stillness. Its barren and rugged grandeur creates an impact of its own. The vast nothingness simply grips the mind. It symbolises the vast unknown reality of human existence.

The landscape of Ladakh is treeless except for the area where water is available from the river Jhelum and other rivulets. Here poplar and willows grow. Some of its regions experience heavy snowfall. One of its small towns, Daras, is the second coldest place in the world. Here the temperature goes down to below –40°C. It was here that some members of the Indian expedition group to Antarctica were acclimatised.

Ladakh has very little rain. More than 300 days in a year are totally sunny. In the shade, one experiences freezing cold. In the sun, the heat is intense and unbearable. If one sits on a chair with his head in the sun and feet in the shade, the head may get a heat stroke, while the feet will suffer frost bite.

Ladakh's landscape resembles the moonscape. After visiting Ladakh for the first time, I used to humorously remark to my friends that the Americans made a mistake in spending billions of dollars in sending Armstrong to the moon. They could have sent him to Ladakh. He could have seen the moon and also found it less inhospitable.

In the Leh region of Ladakh, which is predominantly Buddhist and has a population of 67,000, the Dalai Lama is more revered than in the present-day Tibet. It is often described as the spiritual outpost of Tibetan Buddhism. Some observers believe that it is more Tibetan than Tibet itself.

The Kargil area is inhabited predominantly by Shia Muslims (80%). They are highly conservative and puritanical in their outlook. They come from the Mongol, Tarachho, Maghmi, Brukpa and Mangrik stocks.

It is unfortunate that even this 'moonscape with vast nothingness' has not escaped the poisonous fall-out of the present-day manipulative politics. In July-October 1989, this remote region whose people were well known for being "cheerful, willing and good-tempered, ready for laugh and not quarrelsome",* saw prolonged and, on occasion, violent agitation, led by the Ladakhi Buddhist Association.

In justification of their agitation, the Ladakhi Buddhists said, "Today the people of Ladakh realise that the gentleness and tolerance inherent in their age-old culture are being mistaken for cowardice and helplessness". They have finally launched a movement, not against any religious community as a whole, but "against the root cause of all the feuds and problems in Leh, the Kashmir Government, the source of all the evils". The Association alleged, "Although Ladakh suffered discrimination all along in the last 42 years of independence, it did particularly so after Sheikh Abdullah's coming back to power in 1975. A political schism was surreptitiously set forth, which succeeded in separating Leh and Kargil into two separate districts. In separating

*This description was given by Fredric Drew in his book *Northern frontier* of *India*. See also Chapter II. 'Survey of History'.

Kargil from Leh district, the Sheikh's intention was to remind the Kargilis, who are predominantly Shia Muslims, that historical and cultural ties are insignificant factors in Islamic polity which he was trying to impose on the State. With Dr. Farooq Abdullah coming back to power, the Ladakh Affairs Department was virtually turned into a defunct Department."

The Association pointed out, "The Government of India never responded favourably to our sincere conviction; instead, they made us to be governed by Kashmiris during these decades to our utter ruin. In the post-independence period, we have been reduced to the status of slaves in our own homeland. The impact of the oppressive rule unleashed by the Kashmir Government over us has obliterated our cultural and social ethos."

The Buddhists felt that they were being accorded step-motherly treatment, and their economic, educational and administrative needs were being intentionally ignored by the State Government. They pointed out that the pass percentage in a number of schools in Ladakh was zero, because the State Government never cared to fill the posts of teachers. Urdu had been imposed as an official language and 'Bodhi' was neglected.

The Association also alleged that a number of rich and resourceful Kashmiri businessmen had set up antique shops in Leh. Besides indulging in clandestine sale of Ladakhi antiques, which drained the area of its cultural wealth, these businessmen cornered even the few good economic opportunities that existed in the region.

The Ladakhi Association vehemently complained that "Being assured of Article 370, the Kashmiris have trained their guns on the minuscule Buddhist population with the ultimate objective of assimilating them in the Islamic faith. The State Government, dominated by Kashmiri Muslims, have been openly encouraging conversion of Ladakhi Buddhists to Islam. The underlying idea has been to disturb the balance of population in favour of Muslims. Conversion has assumed a menacing proportion in the recent years. The Islamic fundamentalists and zealots have been encouraged by the State Government to carry out a relentless campaign of conversion. By using monetary power and fraudulent propaganda means they have converted hundreds of Buddhist girls to Islam. Underlying the conversion campaign is the design to Islamise Ladakh and to consolidate the Valley based on separatist and secessionist politics."

Another ground of strong resentment was the appointment of certain Kashmiri officers who allegedly established a nexus with 'Argoras'—a tiny community of Kashmiri Sunni Muslim elite traders who settled in Ladakh years ago—and misappropriated the plan funds and thus deprived Ladakh of whatever little development that could have taken place.

Yet another grievance of the Ladakhis was that in Dr. Farooq Abdullah's ministry of 1989, there were 30 ministers, but not a single one from their region. They raised a number of other questions: "How does the government justify the inclusion of departments such as tourism, power and horticulture in the district plan of Leh, when in other districts these departments receive funds from the State sector? How is it that the World Bank aided Social Forestry Scheme received ₹ 24 crore in the last 4 years and Leh district was not covered at all? At the senior level, the local officers are not appointed in Ladakh on the plea that they would not be objective, but why is this criterion not employed in Kashmir where exactly the opposite tune is played?"

As brought out in the next chapter, most of the current problems of the State have arisen due to misuse of Article 370 and disposition of the Kashmiri politicians to shape the power structure of the State to the advantage of the Valley.

The special needs of Ladakh have also been overlooked. When I visited the region in 1984 for the first time and toured its remote and almost inaccessible areas like Chushul, Pong-gong lake, Zanskar and Nubra, what struck me most was the usual administrative machinery in wholly unusual environment. The pattern of administration was practically the same as in any other district, notwithstanding the fact that the problems of environment and ecology and those rising out of the far-flung habitations were fundamentally different. But for the presence of the Army and its helpful attitude, the Ladakhis living in the remote areas would be, like primitive people, totally at the mercy of the weather conditions and deprived of any facility which the present-day civil government should provide.

No wonder, some of the development projects have been lingering for decades. The Stukna Hydel Project was started about 30 years ago, and when I visited it, quite a part of it still remained to be completed. The Army Commander of Northern Command, Lt. General M.L. Chibber, told me that when he was working as a Captain in the area, the Stukna Project had begun, and it was going on even after he had become the Army Commander.

During Governor's Rule of 1986 I took some steps to meet the special requirements of Ladakh. For Leh town, the Leh Development Authority was set up to undertake urban improvement works and modernise civic services. The objective was to give a clean and new look to the town and boost tourist traffic. A whole-time Chief Engineer was appointed for Ladakh. The officer selected, Dawa, was a Ladakhi. He was popular and known for his honesty, integrity and deep local knowledge. A housing project, specially suited to the climate of 'hot sun and freezing cold', was formulated. Work for the construction of 200 dwelling units with the trombe wall system which enabled retention of the day's heat for keeping them warm at night was begun.

To provide stimulus to local language and literature, both the Kashmir University and the Jammu University were asked to set up separate departments of Ladakhi studies.

To cater to the special needs of the environment and ecology of Ladakh, the Ladakhi Ecological Society, a non-Governmental voluntary organisation, was encouraged to expand its activities and cover more items. The Central Department of Environment was also brought in the picture in a big way.

I had also formulated a number of long-term schemes and envisaged institutional changes to meet the administrative requirements of far-flung areas. But, thanks to the political elements operating at Srinagar and New Delhi, Governor's Rule was abruptly brought to an end. Not only were the plans for institutional changes abandoned but some of the decisions were quietly reversed. For instance, Chief Engineer Dawa was transferred. This greatly irritated the Ladakhis. Subsequently, Dawa resigned.

The treatment meted out to Dawa became, beneath the surface, one of the focal points of the prolonged and violent agitation of the Ladakhi Buddhist Association of 1989.

It should be evident that quite a few serious problems of the State emanate from regional roots. As I have indicated in the last chapter of this book, for doing constructive and creative work and for bringing about much needed reforms and renovations, a particular kind of motivation, a particular kind of urge and impulse is needed. In its absence, harmony amongst different regions, different communities, cannot develop. On the contrary, the position would go on worsening. Already, the Ladakhi Buddhist Association is once again on the verge of launching an agitation for the Union Territory status, and Jammu might erupt any time under the impact of the fall-out of events in the Valley. Some regional antipathies are inherent in the situation. Many more, unfortunately, are being added by petty politics, absence of vision and constant refusal to look to the roots.

Blood Stream

I have shown the hidden veins through which the blood stream of Kashmir's political and social life flows. While doing so, I have kept in mind what Polybius, the Greek historian, said in the 2nd century B.C.: "If you take from history all explanations of cause, principle and motive, and of the adaptation of the means to the end, what is left is a mere panorama without being instructive, and though it may please for the moment, it has no abiding value."

CHAPTER VI

Roots: Article 370

For them, power is everything, fairness nothing. They have created a land without justice, a land full of crudities and contradictions.

–Author's diary
(August 15, 1986)

One of the strongest roots of Kashmiri separatism and alienation lies in Article 370 of the Constitution of India, which gives special status to the State of J&K. It is an issue which involves not only historical, constitutional, political, social and eco-nomic considerations of far-reaching consequences, but also psychological and emotional ones. A fierce nation-wide controversy has often been raised about it. Its deletion or retention has been advocated with equal vehemence. But one fundamental aspect has always been lost sight of. That pertains to its misuse by vested interests.

While pondering over the need for fundamental reforms during Governor's Rule, I wrote in my diary in August 1986: "Article 370 is nothing but a feeding ground for the parasites at the heart of paradise. It skins the poor. It deceives them with its mirage. It lines the pockets of the 'power elites'. It fans the ego of the new 'Sultans'. In essence, it creates a land without justice, a land full of crudities and contradictions. It props up politics of deception, duplicity and demagogy. It breeds the microbes of subversion. It keeps alive the unwholesome legacy of the two-nation theory. It suffocates the very idea of India and fogs the very vision of a great social and cultural crucible from Kashmir to Kanyakumari. It could be an epicentre of a violent earthquake in the Valley–an earthquake, the tremors of which would be felt all over the country with unforeseen consequences." Thereafter, I communicated my views to the Union Government and made a number of suggestions to create a new institutional framework in the State. But these were ignored. A great opportunity was missed.

Over the years, Article 370 has become an instrument of exploitation in the hands of the ruling political elites and other vested interests in bureaucracy, business, the judiciary and bar. It has set in a vicious circle. It breeds separatist forces which in turn sustain and strengthen Article 370. Apart from the politicians, the richer classes have found it convenient to amass wealth and not allow healthy financial legislation to come to the State. The provisions of the Wealth Tax, the Urban Land Ceiling Act, the Gift Tax, etc., and other beneficial laws of the Union have not been allowed to operate in the State under cover of Article 370. The common masses are prevented from realising that Article 370 is actually keeping them impoverished and denying them justice and also their due share in the economic advancement.

What were the circumstances under which Article 370 was incorporated in our Constitution? What are its contents? And how, over the years, has dilution of this Article taken place, if at all? It is necessary to deal with these questions before proceeding further.

Maharaja Hari Singh sought the help of the Government of India when Pakistan attacked the State on October 24, 1947, in the name of Azad Kashmir forces. On October 26, 1947, he executed an Instrument of Accession by way of which he surrendered the jurisdiction of three subjects–Defence, Foreign Affairs and Communication–to the Union Government. The format of this Instrument of Accession was exactly the same as was executed by other heads of the princely States. On the insistence of the Government of India, it was agreed that the final decision with regard to accession would be taken by the Constituent Assembly of J&K. For the intervening period, that is, from the time of the execution of the Instrument of Accession to its consideration by the Constituent Assembly of the State, temporary provisions had to be made in the Constitution of India. And this was done by incorporating Article 370.

The sum and substance of Article 370 is that with regard to J&K, in addition to Defence, Foreign Affairs and Communication, the Union Parliament can make laws with regard to the items in the Union and Concurrent Lists but only with the concurrence of the State Government. This puts the J&K State on a special footing. While the

Union Parliament has unfettered powers to make laws for all the States in respect of items included in the Union and Concurrent Lists of the Constitution, it can do so with regard to J&K only with the consent of the State Government.

It would be noticed from the contents of Article 370, which is reproduced in Appendix X, that it was transitional in nature. The Constituent Assembly of J&K ratified the State's accession to India in February 1956. With this ratification, the issue of accession was finally settled but the issues in regard to jurisdiction of Parliament to subjects other than Defence, Foreign Affairs and Communication were kept flexible. The President could, with the concurrence of the State Government, extend provisions of the Indian Constitution to the State of J&K.

The first order of the President of India, under Article 370, was issued in 1950. The order applied to the State of J&K those provisions of the Indian Constitution which were related to the three subjects stipulated in the Instrument of Accession. The proposals to extend more items of the Indian Constitution to J&K were further discussed by the representatives of the Union Government and the State Government. At that time Sheikh Mohammad Abdullah was the Prime Minister of J&K. Consequent upon the discussions, an understanding was arrived at between the two Governments. This understanding is known as the Delhi Agreement* (1952) in pursuance of which the President of India issued the Constitution (Application to J&K) Order 1954. Under this Order, a number of provisions of the Indian Constitution were extended to the State. This Order was amended from time to time extending more provisions of the Indian Constitution to the State. Particulars of these extensions are given in Appendix XI. Separately, the Constitution of J&K was amended in 1966 to change the denomination of Sadar-e-Riyasat to that of Governor and of Prime Minister to Chief Minister.

The position, in brief, today is that besides the subjects of Defence, Foreign Affairs and Communication, a number of provisions of the Indian Constitution stand extended to the State of J&K. Important amongst these extensions are Article 356 and the jurisdiction of the Supreme Court, the Election Commission, and the Comptroller and Auditor General.

*See Chapter II : 'Survey of History'.

There is, however, still a vast area which remains under the exclusive jurisdiction of the State Government. It includes a substantial portion of the Concurrent List and also Residuary Powers. Article 352, which enables the President to declare a proclamation of national emergency, is applicable only in a limited way. Article 360 which empowers the President to issue proclamation of financial emergency is also not applicable. Neither can the President suspend the Constitution of the State, nor can he give any direction under Article 365.

The State has a Constitution of its own which is an unfortunate by-product of Article 370. No other State of the Indian Union has a separate Constitution. All other States have a uniform structure; it is laid down in Part IV of the Constitution of India.

The provisions of the J&K Constitution create a number of problems, particularly in regard to the right to hold property, right to citizenship, and right to settlement. The citizens of India do not automatically become the citizens of J&K. They have no constitutional right of settlement in the State. The Constitution of India recognises only one citizenship. But the citizens of J&K enjoy double privileges– one as citizen of India and the other as citizen of the State. Those who are not citizens of the State of J&K are subjected to a number of disabilities. They cannot hold any property in the State. They have no right to vote in the election to the State Assembly or local bodies or panchayats and co-operative societies, etc. What is still more unjust is that if a woman*, belonging to J&K, gets married to a person who is not a citizen of J&K, she loses her property; she cannot even inherit property from her parents. These provisions of the Constitution are anachronistic, legally and constitu-tionally antiquated, create emotional barriers between the State and the Union, and are otherwise incompatible with the fundamental principles of justice and fair play. The unhealthy position is compounded by the fact that the State has its own flag and its own emblem. On the Government buildings, the National Flag and the State Flag are flown and the Ministers belonging to National Conference usually fly the National Flag as well as the flag of the National Conference.

As indicated in the three opening paragraphs of this Chapter, Article 370 is not in the interest of the common folk of the State. A few examples may be given.

*Women are issued State-subject certificates which are valid till marriage.

The case of renewal of lease to Nedous Hotel in March 1988 is a typical example of how a small caucus exploits Article 370. In this case, the original lease of Nedous Hotel expired in June 1980. In March 1988, the State Government renewed, retrospectively, the lease for a period of 95 years from June 1980, for an annual rent of ₹ 52,000 which would be doubled during the last 10 years of the lease period. Simultaneously, permission was given to the lessee to sub-lease the property to the Indian Tobacco Company which runs a chain of hotels under the name of Welcomgroup for an annual rent of ₹ 14 lakh which would be doubled in the years to come, making the annual rent in the last decade of the lease period to ₹ 30 lakh. In other words, the lessee would get over ₹ 19 crore as rent from the Welcomgroup during the period of the lease and pay to the Government, during the same period, a rent of ₹ 80 lakh, thereby obtaining a net unmerited gain, at the expense of the State, of ₹ 18.20 crore as an intermediary. If the property, comprising about 11 kanals of land, had been put to auction or allotted on the basis of competitive tenders, the State Government would have got several crore as lease money.

The case of the hotel at Karal Sangri, now known as Santuar Hotel, is another example of perfidy under the protective wall of Article 370. In this case, a five-star hotel has been constructed on the hill-top overlooking the Dal Lake.

The case came to my notice, when T.N. Kaul, Ambassador to the USSR, came to see me in Srinagar in mid-1985. He was on holiday, and staying at Chashmashahi Guest House. He told me that the hillock, Karal Sangri, which provided a beautiful view from Chashmashahi, was being ravaged to make a road. I had the matter looked into. I found out that during the Chief Ministership of Syed Mir Qasim, some exploratory work for constructing a few government huts at the site was undertaken. But nothing was actually done. When Sheikh Mohammad Abdullah came to power, a portion of the site was quietly purchased by an influential local businessman with the tacit understanding that permission for the construction of a hotel at the site would be given. During Dr. Farooq Abdullah's ministry, a vague sanction of sorts was also obtained from Srinagar Municipality. While the businessman was in search of a resourceful hotelier from outside the State, whom he could virtually sell the plot with the sanctioned building plan, Dr. Farooq Abdullah's ministry fell. After lying low for some time, the businessman, with the reported help of Muzaffar Shah, son of G.M. Shah, Chief Minister, got the building plan re-validated.

By that time, a suitable party–Santuar Hotel–had been located and proper understanding arrived at. It was at that stage that the cutting of the hillock started.

Dr. Farooq Abdullah's party, National Conference(F), who were aware of the modus operandi of the businessman, made several complaints to me about the alleged misdoings of Muzaffar Shah. On September 14, 1985, the two former ministers of Dr. Farooq Abdullah's ministry, P.L. Handoo and Mohammad Shafi, met me in this regard. So possessed were they of the issue that they virtually forced me to come out of the office and see how a site of natural beauty was being uglified and how the ecology of the Dal Lake was being damaged.

Governor's Rule was imposed in the State on March 7, 1986. On an examination of the files, I detected a number of irregularities, both in regard to the ownership of the land and the so-called sanction. The project was cancelled. I was happy that a grave ecological disaster had been averted. Besides stabbing the landscape, I thought, the hotel would have caused a huge quantity of silt and sewer to flow into the lake. But, soon after the termination of Governor's Rule, I noticed hectic construction activity at the site. On inquiry, I was told that none other than the Chief Minister, Dr. Farooq Abdullah, had himself laid the foundation stone of the hotel complex. Tragically, the person and the party who made the loudest noises, alleging corruption and environmental damage, got the project going, thereby enabling the local businessman and his hotelier-associate to secure huge financial gains at the expense of the State.

The case demonstrates in a classic manner how money-making and power-building cliques and coteries rape and ravage the State economy and ecology under cover of thick and thorny bushes of Article 370, and how the tragedy of Kashmir is inbuilt in the politics of deception and economics of exploitation.

If commercial sites are allotted on the basis of auction or competitive tenders open to everyone in the country, innumerable benefits would flow to the State. Land resources would not be cornered by the intermediaries. The State's environment would not be damaged. Black money would be reduced. The corrupt and the crafty would have a smaller base to operate from. Conspiratorial links between the ruling and business elites would be snapped. Since nothing would be required to be done in a surreptitious manner, damage to ecology and environment would be minimised. Capital would come from outside the State. Employment opportunities would increase for the local population. The society would become more open. And the process of development would be quickened.

During Governor's Rule in 1986, I put a complex, known as Hari Niwas, for the setting up of a hotel, to open auction, without any restriction regarding residence in the State. This complex belonged to the erstwhile Maharaja. In the early seventies, Dr. Karan Singh sold it to the State Government for ₹ 50 lakh. It remained practically unutilised. In the open auction, a bid of ₹ 6 crore was received. To prevent the power elites from raising the bogey of Article 370 and misleading the poor masses, I simultaneously announced that the auction proceeds would be utilised for laying sewers in the city. By linking the auction proceeds with the city development scheme, beneficial to the poor of the city, the harmful effect of Article 370 in restricting the resource-base of the State, was demonstrated.

The Urban Land (Ceiling and Regulation) Act, 1976 is applicable all over India. But it was not extended to J&K. What has this non-extension to do with the special status of J&K? It was primarily to protect the vested interests of the ruling elite that this Act was not extended.

In March 1988, I had the occasion to examine six serious cases of public corruption. In one case, there were allegations against the Revenue Minister and his son-in-law. In the second case, the previous Revenue Secretary and the previous Revenue Minister were involved. In the third case, a member of the erstwhile royal family had secured huge monetary benefits through underhand transactions. In the fourth case, manipulation in the records of evacuee property was noticed. In the fifth case, the son of the erstwhile Chief Minister allegedly secured expensive land in the heart of the city. In the sixth case, a top leader of a political party was believed to have secured compensation for the land much in excess of the normal rates. In all these cases two aspects were common: urban lands and political and bureaucratic elites. By cornering valuable lands and speculating upon them, huge unaccounted amounts were collected. This unhealthy activity would have been contained by the extension of Urban Land (Ceiling and Regulation) Act, 1976. But the vested interests saw to it that this did not happen.

Article 370 has also been misused to build a political oligarchy. For instance, the Central legislation to prevent defection in the legislatures was not extended to or adopted in toto in the J&K State. The local legislation is so designed that it virtually vests the Party Chief with dictatorial powers. In the State law, now in force, it is not the Speaker, but the Party Chief, who decides whether a particular member of the legislature has defected or not. In other words, he is the head of the government as well as the head of the party; he is the one who distributes party tickets; he is the one who nominates ministers; and he is the one who sits in judgement and takes the final decision, in the event of his leadership being questioned either by a minister or by a party member of the legislature. The law was enacted by way of the Constitution of J&K (Eighteenth Amendment) Act, 1987. It provides: "If any question arises as to whether a member of the House has become subject to disqualification under this schedule, the question shall be referred for the decision of the Leader of the Legislature Party to which such member belongs and his decision shall be final." It entrenches the personality cult and virtually sanctions constitutional dictatorship of the party leader.

I have already mentioned the case of a woman of J&K losing her rights if she gets married to an Indian who is not a citizen of the State. By way of illustration, let me cite a recent case. Dr. Rubeena Nasrullah who was a 'permanent resident/citizen of the State' got her MBBS degree and applied for the postgraduate course in the Government Medical College. She had a State subject certifi-cate and submitted it with her application. But she was asked to produce "permanent residence certificate after marriage" implying thereby that her status after marriage had changed. She applied to the authorities for the grant of the requisite certificate. She was refused. Why? Because she had married an Indian citizen who was not a citizen/subject of the J&K State. Dr. Rubeena Nasrullah had to file a writ petition* in the High Court under Article 226 "for quashing of the State authorities' communication dated February 6, 1985, directing her to produce 'permanent residence certificate after marriage' and declining to accept her eligibility to seek admission to the postgraduate course on her failure to produce the certificate demanded".

The basic question here is: what is the approach of those who govern the State of J&K and of the Indian policy-makers who permit such governance under the cloak of Article 370 and its corollary, the State Constitution? A person who is a citizen of India, and also a

*Writ petition, Dr. Rubeena Nasrullah versus the State of J&K, filed in the State High Court on February 11, 1985.

citizen/permanent resident of J&K cannot secure admission in the medical college established with the finances of the Union Government merely because she had married an Indian citizen. Can anything be more unjust, more primitive, than this?

The case of displaced persons from West Pakistan is a still worse example of gross injustice. In the wake of partition, a few thousand families from West Pakistan migrated to J&K and settled there. They are now in the State for decades. But these unfortunate persons, who were forced to migrate due to compulsions of circumstances beyond their control, have been denied elementary human rights. They, their children and grandchildren have no citizenship rights in J&K. They cannot participate in the elections to the State Assembly or municipality or panchayat. They cannot even secure loans from the State Government or its agencies. Young boys and girls cannot get admission to medical, engineering or agricultural colleges in the State.

Is it not tragic that this is happening in a part of our country–a country that has been taking pride, in season and out of season, in its sense of social, economic and political justice; a country that has been shedding tears about human rights of South Africans and Palestinians? The basic question here is not the number of persons involved, but the national propensity to play the politics of appeasement for narrow gains, and to sacrifice compassion and commitment at the altar of expediency.

In the present-day world, there are four classes of offenders who generally remain unidentified. There is a class which commits offences by invisible manipulation. An example of this class is the top elites who bend the economic system to their sole advantage and cause disease and death by keeping a large section of the people famished. There is another class of offenders who commit offences by planting what may be called environmental time bombs and by injecting poison, not in the body, but in the land, air and sea. There is yet another class of offenders who thrive on the art of disinformation and prevent reality from dawning. There is still another class of offenders who commit offences by omission, which, in essence, is no different from commission. We all know it and yet we are silent. In the case of displaced persons in question and other such cases, the entire country is guilty–guilty of omitting to look into inequities and inhumanity hidden in Article 370 and its by-products.

There are a few other basic questions that need to be raised regarding Article 370. What is its rationale, its raison d'etre? What is so special about Kashmir that this Article is not applicable to other States? If Article 370 is there to protect and preserve the cultural entity of Kashmir, then such a provision should have been made for all the States. The need for preserving the cultural entity is common to all the States. Could it be said that the cultural personality of Bengal or Kerala or Tamil Nadu need no protection? What then has Kashmir got which other States of India do not have? Is it that it is the only Muslim majority State? Does it not follow that in the continuation of Article 370, there is a tacit acceptance of the two-nation theory?

We denounced the two-nation theory, proclaimed to the world that in India religion did not constitute the basis of separation or distinction. Ironically, it is we who are applying the two-nation theory in Kashmir. And we are doing that in the most unfortunate, most suicidal manner. Pakistan, which owes its birth to the two-nation theory, exists, after all, with its own resources. But here in Kashmir, Article 370 and the issue of autonomy are designed to be manipulated in such a way that a virtual Sheikhdom or Sultanate, or mini-Pakistan, has been nurtured with Indian money. Unfortunately, we have neither the inclination nor the depth of perception to see through the game. The in-built attitude of the Kashmiri leadership towards India is: "When you are going, what would you leave; and when you are returning, what would you bring?" The relationship is sought only for securing Indian finances and not for building a lasting relationship on truly just, secular and progressive basis. Any Union law or administrative measure, howsoever beneficial to the masses, is spurned.

The protagonists of Article 370 often argue that its retention is necessary for giving substantial autonomy to the State. But what has desirable autonomy to do with this Article? When other States in the Union ask for greater autonomy, they do not mean separation of identities. They really want decentralisation and devolution of power, so that administrative and development work is done speedily and the quality of service to the people improves. In J&K the demand for retaining Article 370 with all its pristine purity, that is, without the alleged dilution that has taken place since 1953, stems from a different motivation. It emanates from a clever strategy to stay away from the mainstream, to set up a separate fiefdom, to fly a separate flag, to have a Prime Minister rather than a Chief Minister, and a Sadar-i-Riyasat instead of a Governor, and to secure greater power and patronage, not for the good of the masses, not for serving the cause of peace and progress or for attaining cultural unity amidst diversity, but for serving the interests of the 'new elites', the 'new Sheikhs'.

How recognition of the two-nation theory is implicit in Article 370, and how the legacy of this theory shapes the State's communal psyche, would be evident from the attitude of its leaders towards the family welfare programme. Almost all the local political parties and groups find it expedient to talk against this programme. For instance, G.M. Shah, Chief of the Awami National Conference and former Chief Minister, recently said: "The official birth control programme is aimed at reducing the State Muslim majority to a minority. The Muslims constituted 80 per cent population of the State in 1947; they have now been reduced to only 54 per cent. In another 10 years' time, the Muslims would be reduced to a minority–48 per cent of the total population." Such statements, besides being statistically false, seriously undermine the family welfare programme and reflect the inner thinking of the obscurantist and fundamentalist elements. They dub the family welfare programme as un-Islamic, and a conspiracy of 'Hindu India' to reduce the Muslims to an insignificant minority. It is because of this attitude that, during the decade 1971 to 1981, the growth of population in J&K has been the highest in the country. It is 29.6 as compared to the national average of 25. The achievements have invariably fallen far short of the targets.

And what are the practical aspects of Article 370 and the autonomy syndrome? Is autonomy really feasible in the context of the Kashmir situation? Has it any meaning in practice?

Both for plan and non-plan finances, J&K is heavily dependent upon the Union Government. Its five-year plans are wholly funded by the Centre. A substantial part of its non-plan expenditure is also met by the Union. For instance, in the budget for the year 1988-89, about 74 per cent of its revenue receipts were by way of transfers from the Central Government. While the State got about ₹ 1,003 crore from the Central Government as grants* and loans, its own total receipts were about ₹ 234 crore. The State's salary bill for the same year was about ₹ 277 crore, that is, more than its own receipts. Had the State been truly autonomous and left to its own resources, it could not find a

*Recently, in 1990, as a measure of further concession or appeasement, whatever one may like to call it, the pattern of assistance has been changed to 90% grant and 10% loan, though this principle of assistance has been followed only in the case of new States in the north-east which were once Union Territories.

single paisa for any plan or development work. It could not also pay salaries to a good number of its employees. In view of its extremely weak financial position and its narrow economic base, autonomy for J&K is neither feasible nor desirable.

In the absence of full financial integration with the Union, J&K would be nothing but a mediaeval autarchy like in the Maharaja's time, when the per capita income was only ₹ 11 and out of that, too, 21 per cent had to be paid as taxes; 93.4 per cent of the population was illiterate; there was only one boys' primary school for every 66 square miles and one girls' primary school for every 467 square miles; and the total annual expenditure on agriculture, public health, industries, roads, irrigation and education was only ₹ 36 lakh*. In 1947-48, the State Budget envisaged a total expendi-ture of ₹ 4.81 crore. The corresponding figure for the year 1988-89 was ₹ 1,237 crore. In 1947, the per capita State expenditure was ₹ 15. In 1988-89, the per capita State expenditure on plan alone was ₹ 645. These comparisons indicate the enormous benefits which financial integration with the Union has brought to Jammu and Kashmir. During the Seventh Five-Year Plan, the State got Union finances to the extent of ₹ 1,838 crore–₹ 1,400 crore for plan expenditure and ₹ 438 crore to meet non-plan resource gap. In the course of the last 43 years, the Union Government has pumped several thousand crores† in J&K. In the case of this State, the per capita financial assistance from the Centre has been far above the national average. It is getting 2.57% of the total grant disbursed by the Centre, while its population is 0.8% of the country's population. For instance, in the year 1989-90, the per capita central grant for J&K was ₹ 1122, while it was ₹ 552 for Himachal Pradesh, ₹ 425 for Assam, ₹ 109 for Bihar, ₹ 91 for U.P., and ₹ 67 for West Bengal.

Take another issue–the extension of Article 356 of the Constitution to J&K. This Article enables the President to bring the State under President's Rule. It is often said that the extension of this Article constitutes encroachment on the State's autonomy. But no one asks a connected question: if there is a breakdown of the constitutional machinery in the State or if the State refuses to comply with any direction concerning Defence, Foreign Affairs or Communication, what will happen in the absence of President's powers under

---

*The data are based upon the 1941 Census of the State.

†According to an estimate done in 1989-90 this figure works out to Rs. 70,000 crore.

Article 356? Suppose the Governor has the corresponding powers; then does it not mean that the President would have to submit to the decision of the Governor, his own appointee? Again, suppose the Governor is made Sadar-i-Riyasat who is not appointed by the President, but is elected by the State Assembly; then would not granting the final say to the Sadar-i-Riyasat amount to subordinating the Union to the State?

Take another practical problem. Defence is a Union subject, while land acquisition is the subject assigned to the State. If the Union Government wants to establish a cantonment at a particular place, the land for the same would have to be acquired by the State Government. Suppose the State Government refuses to acquire that land. The only remedy available would be to impose Presidential will by invoking provisions of Article 356. In other words, in day-to-day working of the administration, a number of cases would arise in which the needs of the Union would have to be met by the State. And in case of the State's refusal to comply with the requirements of the Union, the will of the Union has to be enforced.

The current wind blowing in East Europe in favour of autonomy is sometimes advanced as an argument for giving greater autonomy to certain regions. But this argument ignores the stage of our social and economic development. To think of greater autonomy before tackling the problems of poverty, backwardness, illiteracy, obscurantism and parochialism, would be like putting the cart before the horse. Let us not imitate and destroy ourselves. Our 'warlords' would not be guided by any higher principles of freedom and human development but by a petty and narrow outlook and cause bloodshed and misery all around. Such false notions of autonomy picked up from alien environments will lead the country to Balkanisation and society to fragmentation.

Those who talk of Kashmir's autonomy tend to ignore the vast and varied socio-cultural phenomena of the State of J&K. The Jammuites have different aspirations. They are wedded to 'ek vidhan, ek nishan, ek pradhan' (one Constitution, one flag, and one President). Their culture and personality are distinct. The Muslims of Poonch and Rajouri have different cultural traits. So is the position with the people living near the border with Himachal Pradesh. Gujjars and Bakarwals, too, constitute a distinct group. Ladakh is totally different.

If Article 370 is retained or the issue of autonomy is overplayed, then every regional and cultural unit would demand an equivalent of

Article 370 or 'autonomy' to counter the domination of the Kashmiris. The claims and counter-claims would be unending and the State's fabric would be further ruptured.

The people of the Jammu region nurse a long-standing grievance that, under cover of Article 370 and the State Constitution, the decisions over the years have been so manipulated by the Valley-leaders that the power structure in the State has permanently tilted in favour of the Kashmir region. In this connection, it is pointed out that for the Lok Sabha, Jammu returns one member for every 1.4 million people, while Kashmir sends one representative for every one million. Jammu's total area is 70 per cent larger than Kashmir's and has 45 per cent of the State's population. But Jammu has only 32 seats, out of 76, in the State Assembly, and Kashmir has 42. While Jammu returns one member for every 90,000, Kashmir returns one for every 73,000. While three new districts were suddenly created in the Valley in 1979, none of the three districts recommended by the Wazir Commission (1981-83) has been created in the Jammu region. The distribution of plan funds is also unfair. For instance, about half a million tourists, on an average, come to the Valley; while in Jammu, the Vaishno Devi Shrine alone attracts over two million cultural and religious tourists, thereby contributing a great deal to the economic development of the State. Practically nothing is spent by the State toward providing infrastructural facilities to these tourists. Even the road to Katra on which thousands of buses and other vehicles move every day is very narrow. On the other hand, huge funds–sometimes 90 per cent of the tourism budget–are allocated to the Valley. The two current projects, Gulmarg Cable Car and Srinagar Golf Course, would consume ₹ 50 crore. In Jammu, the Dogra Art Gallery, which has rare *objets d'art*, remains in an utter state of neglect. Again, the Jammu region has a total area of 26,293 sq. km and 3,500 km* of roads; the Kashmir region has 15,853 sq. km area and 4,900 km of roads. Thus, in the case of Jammu, 18% of the area is covered by roads, while in Kashmir the corresponding percentage is 40.

The Ladakhis, too, are highly resentful that the leverage of Article 370 has been placed in the hands of the Kashmiri leadership. They have been complaining that, instead of being made "free sons of free India", they have been thrown "at the mercy of the Kashmiris". They

*These data indicate the position in the year 1987.

are often heard saying, "If India is going to keep us under the Kashmiri domination, then it is as bad as being under the Chinese." As early as 1949, in an impassioned plea to Prime Minister Nehru for taking Ladakh directly under the care of the Union Government, the Ladakhi Buddhist Association said, "Tibet is the cultural daughter of India, and we of the 'lesser Tibet' seek the bosom of the gracious mother to receive more nourishment for growth to full stature. Will the great mother (India) refuse to take to her arms one of her weakest, forlorn and distressed children?" Unfortunately, such noble sentiments did not evoke any worthwhile response. And, on account of the provisions of Article 370, the Valley leadership acquired almost unlimited control over Ladakh, and even those institutional safe-guards which were available elsewhere in the country were denied to the Ladakhis. The violent agitation of Ladakhi Buddhists in July-September 1989 was an expression of their strong resentment against what they called the Kashmiri domination and exploitation.

The primary task in J&K is not the circulation of the fake coin of autonomy and fooling the people in the name of cultural entity, but to eliminate poverty, hunger and disease and carry out balanced development by stressing the commonality of the deprived and the underprivileged. Unless backwardness is eradi-cated, there would be no real freedom and democracy. Even Kashmir culture would stagnate. Abrogation of Article 370 would, in fact, help in removing poverty and backwardness which, in turn, would help in rejuvenating Kashmiri culture and enhancing the cultural personality of the State as a whole. No culture can advance in isolation. It requires cross fertilisation. It requires the 'stimulus of contact'.

Some leaders and analysts continue to say that Article 370 is a matter of faith. But they do not proceed further. They do not ask themselves: what does this faith mean? What is its rationale? Would not bringing the State within the full framework of the Indian Constitution give brighter lustre and sharper teeth to this faith and make it more just and meaningful?

In a similar strain, expressions like 'historical necessity' and 'autonomy' are talked about. What do these terms mean in practice? Does historical necessity mean that you include, on paper, Kashmir in the Indian Union on the one hand at a huge cost and give it back, in practice, on the other hand, on a golden platter? And what does autonomy or the so-called pre-1953 or pre-1947 position imply? Would it not amount to the Kashmiri leadership saying: "You will send and I will spend; you will have no say even if I build a corrupt and callous oligarchy and cause a situation in which Damocles' sword of secession could be kept hanging over your head?"

Can Article 370 be abrogated? If so, how? It has sometimes been argued that it is not constitutionally permissible to abrogate this Article without the approval of the Constituent Assembly of the State. It is said that a plain reading of the Constitution makes the position clear in this regard. The relevant portion of Article 370 reads:

> Notwithstanding anything in the foregoing provisions of the article, the President may, by public notification, declare that this article shall cease to be operative. . . .
>
> . . . Provided that the recommendation of the Constituent Assembly of the State referred to in clause (2) shall be necessary before the President issues a notification.

An essential prerequisite of the Presidential declaration is the recommendation of the Constituent Assembly. In other words, even if the Union Government decides to abrogate this Article, it cannot constitutionally do so by itself as this would involve positioning of the State's Constituent Assembly and getting its recommendations. The amending powers under Article 368 of the Constitution would also not help.

On the face of it, the aforesaid argument is impressive. But no provision of the Constitution can be read in isolation. Article 1 is of far more fundamental importance. It reads:

1. *Name and Territory of the Union.* India, that is Bharat, shall be a Union of States.
2. The States and territories thereof shall be as specified in the First Schedule.
3. The territory of India shall comprise: (a) the territories of the States; (b) the Union territories specified in the First Schedule; and (c) such other territories as may be acquired.

J&K is the 15th State in Schedule 1 of the Constitution, and Article 1 applies to it in its entirety. On the other hand, Article 370 is transitional. The very heading of part XXI of the Constitution reads: "Temporary, transitional and special provisions." Thus, at the time when Article 370 was framed, the understanding was that it would stay for a short time and cover the transitional period. Since the State's Constituent Assembly no longer exists, the question of its consent under Article 370 does not arise. Consent of a dead body or a non-existent body has no meaning. The Constitution can, therefore, be amended under Article 368 by the Union Parliament which represents the people of the State also. Thereafter, the aforesaid proviso requiring the recommendation of the Constituent Assembly could be deleted. After this deletion has been carried out, the President can make the necessary declaration and Article 370 would stand abrogated.

Whenever there is any incompatibility between one provision of the Constitution and another, the more fundamental provision would prevail. The Courts, while interpreting the Constitution, would have to give due regard to the changed circumstances, and the overall national objective for which the Constitution was framed. Article 1, as pointed out above, is of basic importance. It relates to the territorial integrity of the country. No State has any right to secede, unlike the States in the USSR. The territorial and political matters pertaining to the entire country are the concerns of the Union Parliament, and it has the overriding right to ensure that nothing happens which has the effect of undermining the territorial integrity of the country.

The current situation in Kashmir shows that Article 370 has created a separatist psyche and thus threatened the territorial integrity of the Union. The Union Parliament, therefore, must act. And the Courts, when called upon to interpret the Constitution and reconcile the provisions of Article 1, Article 368, and Article 370 must accept the argument in favour of the territorial integrity and not interfere with the Parliament decision to delete Article 370, particularly when this Article is being used as an instrument of injustice, and the fundamental objective of the Court itself is to ensure justice and end unjust situations. In other words, if the Court makes a creative and dynamic interpretation of the Constitution, then it would certainly uphold deletion of Article 370 after its sub-clause has been deleted by the constitutional amendment under Article 368.

Provisions of Article 355 of the Constitution of India are also of crucial significance. This Article casts on the Union of India the duty to protect the States against external aggression as well as internal disturbances. If Article 370 stands in the way of the Union of India in discharging this paramount constitutional duty, it must go. In the present context, when J&K has become vulnerable to both external aggression and internal rebellion, and Article 370 is playing no small part in enabling the hostile elements to cause internal disturbances and facilitating external aggression, it is incumbent upon the Union Government to take steps to delete this Article to effectuate the duty cast upon it by Article 355. Thus, if Article 370 is read along with Article 1 and Article 355, an amendment of the Constitution under Article 368 to delete the proviso to Article 370 would be perfectly valid, and after the said deletion of the proviso, the President's declaration deleting the entire Article 370 would make the position absolutely clear.

It may also be pointed out that it is possible to take away the teeth of Article 370 by deleting Article 35A. If this deletion takes place, Articles 19(1)(e) and (g) will come into full play. Articles 19(1)(e) and (g) declare:

> All citizens shall have the right
> (a) to reside and settle in any part of the territory of India; and
> (b) to practise any profession, or to carry on any occupation, trade or business.

Part III of the Indian Constitution is already applicable to the State of J&K. With unrestricted application of Articles 19(1)(e) and (g), any Indian can settle in J&K, and all irrational, unjust and anachronistic provisions of the J&K Constitution in regard to the rights of settlement and citizenship, which are incompatible with the Indian Constitution, would go.

The defenders of the restrictions regarding State subjects have sometimes pointed out that these restrictions were imposed not by the State Government or by Sheikh Abdullah after 1947, but by the Maharaja on the representation of the Dogra and Pandit Sabhas in 1893. This plea is totally misplaced. We are not being guided by the values, thinking and circumstances of 1893, but by the present-day aspirations and fundamental principles of the Indian Constitution. What is not in the interest of justice must go, whatever be its background. The unfairness of these restrictions were noted as far back as 1931-32, when Bertrand Glancy, Chairman of the Grievances Committee, observed in his report:* "The present definition of the State subjects appears to be unduly rigid; domicile in the State for a thousand years cannot, according to this definition, qualify a man. It would seem both unfair and inexpedient to deny the right to franchise

---

*See Chapter II: 'Survey of History', and also Chapter V: 'Roots: Hidden Veins' (Section: Regional Roots).

to a man who has so far identified himself with local interests as to make his domicile in the State over a consecutive period of five years."

These restrictions were continued, and given constitutional protection, with less than honest intentions. It was intentionally 'forgotten' that the restrictions were primarily imposed by the Maharaja to keep the British away from Kashmir.

In the case of displaced persons about whose plight I have made brief comments earlier in this chapter, the Supreme Court recognised the injustice that was being done to them but could not provide any relief on account of Article 370 and the provisions of the State Constitution and the laws made thereunder. I reproduce below the relevant portion of the Supreme Court's† observations:

> The persons who migrated from West Pakistan to the State of J&K in the wake of 1947 partition and have settled down in the State of J&K and who are citizens of India and who also have the right to participate in elections to Parliament, have very anomalous right within the State. They are not entitled to be included in the electoral rolls of the State Assembly, they are not entitled to be elected to a village Panchayat, they are not even entitled to purchase any land and they are also not entitled to be appointed to any service under the State govern-ment. All these denials and deprivations are the consequence of the definition of a permanent resident under Section 6 of the J&K Constitution. It is to be noticed here that these provisions are not open to challenge as inconsistent with the right guaranteed by Part III of the Constitution of India because of the Constitution Order, 1954, issued by the President of India under Article 370(I)(d) of the Constitution by which Article 35(A)* was added to the Constitution in relation to the State of J&K. The net result is that these persons, though citizens of India and entitled to various fundamental rights guaranteed by the

† Supreme Court's judgement of February 20, 1987.

* Article 35(A) was added to the Constitution of India in 1954, not by amending the Constitution by way of Article 368, but by issuing Presidential Order under Article 370. It defines permanent residents of J&K, and confers on them special rights and privileges. It also restricts rights and privileges of all other citizens of India in respect of their fundamental rights–rights of settlement and citizenship–guaranteed under Article 35 of the Constitution. It is of doubtful constitutional validity. Its

Contd.

Constitution, are not in a position to enjoy many of these rights within the State of J&K though they are domiciled in that State for over 40 years.

In the circumstances, in view of the peculiar constitutional position obtaining in the State of J&K, we do not see what possible relief we can give to them. All that we can say is that their position is anomalous and it is up to the legislature of the State of J&K to take action to amend legislations such as the Jammu and Kashmir Representation of the Peoples Act, the Land Alienation Act, the Village Panchayat Act, etc. so as to make the persons, who have migrated from West Pakistan in 1947 and who have settled in the State of J&K since then, eligible to be included in the electoral rolls, to acquire land, to be elected to the Panchayat, etc. This can be done by suitably amending the legislations without having to amend the J&K Constitution. In regard to providing employment opportunities under the State Government, it can be done by the government amending the J&K Civil Services rules. In regard to admission to higher technical educational institutions also, the government may make these persons eligible by issuing appropriate executive directions, without even having to introduce any legislation. The petitioners have a justifiable grievance. Surely they are entitled to expect to be protected by the State of J&K.

The suggestions of the Supreme Court that such unfair laws might be amended by the State legislature, have been ignored. Unfortunately, the underlying motivation of the State rulers is not justice but playing petty politics, creating little hegemonies and keeping the poor

---

ramifications, and those of Article 370, have been analysed, in the context of current of realities, in subsequent portion of the book. Its contents are:

"*Art. 35A. Notwithstanding anything contained in this Constitution, no existing law in force in the State of J&K, and no law hereafter enacted by the State, –*

(a) Defining the classes of persons who are, or shall be, permanent residents of the State of J&K; or

(b) conferring on such permanent residents any special rights and privileges, or imposing upon other persons any restrictions, as respects –

(i) employment under the State Government;

(ii) acquisition of immovable property in the State;

(iii) settlement in the State; or

(iv) right to scholarships and such other forms of aid as the State Government may provide.

and the resourceless of different regions in a state of perpetual confusion and conflict.

A parallel is sometimes drawn to restrictions imposed by the Himachal Pradesh Government on purchase of land in the State by outsiders. This parallel is also misconceived. The Himachal Pradesh law, which was enacted by the Central Government when Himachal Pradesh was a Union Territory, is primarily designed to protect the interests of the poor and ignorant cultivators. It is open to constitutional scrutiny under the Indian Constitution and is subject to fundamental rights. The Courts can strike down any provision which does not qualify under the clause of reasonable restrictions. Moreover, the restriction is not absolute. The purchase of agricultural land can be made with the permission of the State Government. In the case of J&K, the bar is absolute and even the Supreme Court cannot intervene, as has been pointed out in the above-quoted judgment.

On August 21, 1962, in reply to Pandit Prem Nath Bazaz's letter concerning Article 370, Jawaharlal Nehru wrote:

> As a matter of fact, much has been done in spite of the Article in the Constitution which is supposed to give a special status to Kashmir and gradually what little remains will also go. The question is more a sentimental one than anything else. Sentiment is sometimes important but we have to weigh both the sides and I think no change should be made in the matter for the present.

This letter shows that Nehru himself did not rule out future change with regard to Article 370. And so far as sentiments are concerned, it is quite clear by now that they have operated in the opposite direction and strengthened the separatist and subversive psyche which, in turn, have threatened the very unity and integrity of the country. It is time that the seed that has given birth to an unhealthy plant is pulled out from its roots.

Retention of Article 370 has sometimes been justified by saying that it is not a wall but a tunnel. On December 4, 1964, Gulzari Lal Nanda, Union Home Minister, said, "Through this tunnel, a good deal of traffic has already passed; more will pass now." A few days later, M.C. Chagla, Education Minister, observed, "Through Article 370, the whole of the Indian Constitution could be applied to J&K."*

*M.C. Chagla, however, wanted the separate Constitution of J&K to be scrapped.

It may be an ingenious position to take in theory, but it ignores the stark reality that the gates of this tunnel are manned by someone else. And what happens if this tunnel is blocked, as was done after 1975, with the sole exception of the period of Governor's Rule† from March 7 to September 6, 1986? Even otherwise, does it make any sense to go through a precariously built tunnel when a straight, firm and wide avenue is available?

An argument has also sometimes been advanced that if Article 370 is abrogated, Kashmir's link with India would stand terminated. This argument is too legalistic to have any meaning in practice. Would India become a colony again if the British Parliament were to amend the Indian Independence Act retrospectively, which it is legally competent to do?

The above argument also ignores Article 1 and other provisions of the Constitution of India. It assumes that, after deletion of Article 370, nothing else would be added by way of rectification or clarification or elaboration. It also assumes that India today is what the British Parliament wanted it to be, and Kashmir was not a part of India earlier. It gives precedence to the narrow technicality of law over the basic reality that is India–India from Kashmir to Kanyakumari that has existed for thousands of years in the minds and hearts of its people, the India that its intellect and emotions, its philosophy and poetry, its life and literature had given birth to. The Russian Nobel laureate, Solzhenitsyn, has rightly observed, "A society which is based upon the letter of the law and never reaches any higher is taking very scarce advantage of high level of human possibilities. The letter of the law is too cold to have any beneficial influences on the society. Whenever the issue of life is woven in legalist relations, there is an atmosphere of moral mediocrity, paralysing man's noblest impulses." In similar strain, Thomas Jefferson said, "Laws and institutions must go hand in hand with the progress of the human mind. . . . We might as well require a man to wear the coat that fitted him as a boy, as civilized society to remain ever under the regime of their ancestors."

History also tells us that civilisations decline when they begin to deceive themselves, when they begin to confuse technicality of law with intrinsic justice. The legal institutions of a dynamic and

†During this period, as many as 29 laws were enacted by me or beneficial Union laws extended by virtue of these executive and legislative powers vesting in me under Section 92 of the J&K Constitution.

progressive society have to adjust to the changing social and economic realities. They must respond to the new urges and aspirations.

It should be evident that Article 370 and its by-products, the separate Constitution of J&K; and Article 35A of the Indian Constitution, must go, not only because it is legally and constitutionally feasible to do so, but also because larger and more basic considerations of our past history and contemporary life require it. This Article and its accompanying paraphernalia need to be abrogated. It serves as an instrument of perpetrating injustices and inequities. It facilitates the growth and continuation of corrupt oligarchies. It fans and feeds the forces of parochialism and obscurantism. It implicitly recognises the two-nation theory. It acts as a breeding ground for separatist emotions. It puts false notions in the minds of the youth, and it creates narrow grooves and narrow loyalties. It gives rise to regional tensions and conflicts, and even the autonomy assumed to be available is not attainable in practice. The distinct personality and cultural identity of Kashmir can be safeguarded without this Article. It is socially regressive and causes situations in which women lose their rights if they marry non-State subjects an persons staying for decades in the State are denied elementary human and democratic rights. And, above all, it does not fit into the reality and requirements of India and its vast and varied span. What India needs today is not petty sovereignties that would sap its spirit and aspirations and turn it into small 'banana-republics' in the hands of 'tin-pot dictators', but a new social, political and cultural crucible in which the age-old traditions of pluralism and tolerance, of truth and rectitude, of fairness and justice, and of compassion and catholicity, are melted, purified and moulded into a vigorous and vibrant set-up which provides real freedom, real democracy, and real resurgence to all.

CHAPTER VII

July 2,1984: Dismissal of Dr. Farooq Abdullah

To everything there is a season;
A time to keep silent, and
A time to speak.

A common weakness of some of our political commentators is that they seldom try to ascertain the facts before making 'authoritative' observations. In the process, the reality gets submerged under layers and layers of superficial criticism. History has a way of correcting itself, but only with the passage of time. Such is the position with regard to my decision of July 2, 1984, to dismiss Dr. Farooq Abdullah from the office of the Chief Minister. This decision is still referred to in certain quarters with less than *bona fide* intentions. It is, therefore, necessary that I should deal with it in its full context and perspective.

Who is an Ideal Governor?

After I took oath as Governor of J&K on April 26, 1984, I was asked a number of questions by the pressmen who attended the oath-taking ceremony. I parried these questions by saying that an ideal Governor was one who talked as little as possible and heard, read and saw as much as possible. Next morning, these observations were carried prominently in the newspapers. Many suggested that I should spell out my concept of an ideal Governor. I got an opportunity to do so, while presiding over a public lecture delivered by Justice V.R. Krishna Iyer on April 4, 1989, at the Jammu University on Centre-State relations. What I said appeared in a section of the national press and needs to be recapitulated and elaborated here.

To me, the Governor of an Indian State appears to be a person having a crown on the head and fetters on the feet. The following Urdu couplet fits his position well:

مصور نے بنائیں کیا کیا تصویریں ہیں
سر پہ تاج ہے پاؤں میں زنجیریں ہیں

An ideal Governor is one who talks as little as possible, who does not make unnecessary comments in public and who does not say anything to denigrate the Head of Government or the Council of Ministers or any other component of the power structure. Our erstwhile President, Sanjeeva Reddy, once said: "Fortunately, Kamaraj had no son or sons-in-law." It was a dig at Indira Gandhi, Morarji Desai and Charan Singh. Dr. Radhakrishnan, too, used to make uncomplimentary remarks on Jawaharlal Nehru. He even told the American Ambassador, Chester Bowles, that it would be better to have President's Rule for a few months throughout the country after Nehru ceased to be the Prime Minister, implying thereby gross mismanagement of public affairs by Nehru. Such utterances by the constitutional head not only lower the image of important public functionaries but also reduce his own effectiveness in times of constitutional crises.

Sometimes the Governors find themselves in an unenviable situation. It is seldom appreciated that the constitutional crises which the Governors are called upon to deal with are not of their making. They are thrust upon them, and they are required to decide intricate issues, with manifold ramifications, not in months or days but within a few hours.

If 'milk-pure' action is expected from the Governor, other components of the power structure should also act in a milk-pure way. For instance, in regard to a floor test, the role of the Speaker has to be considered. We all know what happened in the Tamil Nadu Assembly, when the Speaker, directly or indirectly, manoeuvred to ensure that only 98 out of 223 persons participated in the vote.

What should the Governor do if some other components of the power structure destroy the very moral and ethical basis of constitutional provisions? Should, for instance, the Governor nominate an illiterate person under the clause of the Constitution which requires persons of intellectual and literary eminence to be nominated? Again, should he criticise the President in his customary Address to the legislature when he himself holds office at his pleasure?

The Constitution is not an end in itself. It is a means to an end–the end of leading an organised and orderly life in an environment which is conducive to peace, progress and productivity. Otherwise, the Constitution will degenerate to such an extent that democracy would be reduced to an elective dictatorship.

Then there is the question of constitutional responsibility. Every component of the power structure must act in a reasonable and responsible manner. In this connection, I am tempted to cite an example of the British Prime Minister, Baldwin, who in 1926 wanted to go on holiday for a week on health grounds. At that time a coal strike was on in Britain. The King expressed his surprise that Baldwin should be away from the capital at a time like that. Poor Baldwin had to submit a medical certificate to satisfy the King. Such are the constitutional norms practised by the British Prime Minister. How many of our elected heads of State Governments show such respect and consideration to the constitutional heads?

Sometimes the Governor is criticised by persons who, at the time of making comments, are not in possession of full and true facts. And for reasons of office, the Governors have to keep quiet. Moreover, constitutional words and expressions admit of different interpretations and have to be read in the totality of the circumstances. The political and administrative environment cannot be ignored by a responsible Governor.

Political analysts sometimes refer to traditions and conventions. But where are such conventions? If anyone analyses the decisions taken by the Governors since the enforcement of the Constitution, one would hardly find any consistent pattern. Different Governors have taken different decisions even in regard to circumstances which were similar in nature. The golden principle is to assess the discretionary position of the Governor in the light of national security and integrity and general welfare of the people. To make him act in a particular manner in all circumstances would amount to playing with fire.

Acting in the overall national interest, the ideal Governor must display courage and vision at the time of a crisis. He should not act as a cipher, or as a rubber stamp, or as a foggy old man standing in a corner with a wooden face and stony eyes. The Governor has a 'reserve area' of power which remains dormant in day-to-day affairs of the State but becomes crucial in moments of crisis. If he has to do in all circumstances what his advisers tell him to do, then it would be more rational and economical to have a robot or not to have him at all.

Ignorance

For a proper appreciation of the case in regard to the dismissal of Dr. Farooq Abdullah, it is necessary to keep in view what I have stated above and also the special circumstances in which I was called upon to take the decision in the light of the provisions of the Constitution of J&K.

Ignorance of the correct position in regard to the J&K Governor is so widespread that even a leading national newspaper wrote an editorial comment without knowing that J&K had a separate Constitution, that the Governor of J&K was appointed under that Constitution, that in the event of a breakdown of the constitutional machinery he could take over administration of the State under Section 92 of the J&K Constitution and issue a proclamation in this regard with the concurrence of the President of India, and that he need not make a report to the President, as is done by other State Governors under Article 356 of the Constitution. It was partly due to this type of ignorance that some adverse comments were made in regard to my action.

Practical Experience

There was also another fundamental reason. Much of what was written about the role of the Governor was written by those who had no practical experience of dealing with complex situations which could not be precisely imagined by the framers of our Constitution and which defy description within the parameters of its phraseology.

Did the constitution-makers envisage a situation in which the Chief Ministers would act like Sultans or establish a wholly partisan administration, or put their hand-picked CID officials at the Raj Bhavan in the garb of security men to spy on the Governors, or deny them even crucial information or provide them with only coloured versions, or generally belittle their position by rejecting even ordinary proposals emanating from the Governor's office in regard to establishment or maintenance matters? Did the founding fathers anticipate that there would be Chief Ministers who would frequently attempt to keep the Central authorities at bay by whipping up regional, religious and parochial emotions? Did they think that the Chief Ministers will be paying only lip service to the rule of law and take no action in actual practice against their supporters? Did they visualise that Government servants in a State would in open public speeches threaten to kill the President of the Union or the Prime Minister and the State Chief Minister would take no action against them even in the shape of transfer from a sensitive position, let alone any action in the shape of departmental proceedings or prosecution in the court of law for an obvious criminal offence? Or did our Parliament, while agreeing to a special status for J&K and incorporating Article 370 in our Constitution, understand that this provision would be used, not to safeguard the interests of the poor Kashmiris, but to build an oligarchy of the elites who would manipulate the system to keep the separatist forces alive and prevent the State from joining the mainstream? Or did they anticipate a situation in which the Governors would be asked to nominate social and political delinquents to the Upper House under the category of persons of eminence?

Justice Krishna Iyer has somewhere remarked that the framers of the Constitution never intended to have Chakravartis and Maharajas in the garb of Governors. This is, undoubtedly, true. But did the framers of the Constitution want the Chief Ministers to play that role and to bend the constitutional structure to suit their selfish ends of staying in power by strangulating the soul of the democratic system and also imprison the minds of the people by weaving a web of communal and parochial prejudices around them?

Viewing the happenings in the context of Kashmir, it is not to be regretted that the Governors have acted more often, but that they have acted too late and have been too negligent to check the malady at the incipient stage and have been too much inclined to follow the line of least resistance. They have been too deficient in their commitments to safeguard the system. In fact, one of the reasons why norms and principles dear to the constitution-makers have not taken roots is that most of the State Governors assumed the role of innocent idlers and silent spectators of the wrongdoings of the Chief Ministers and have shown a marked tendency to compromise with what contains infection for the spread of the disease. Otherwise, in J&K, during the period 1975 to 1984, how could, the basic structure of the All-India Service, so essential for integrity and unity of the country, be allowed to be undermined? How could, during the same period, the judiciary be allowed to become wholly subservient to the chief executive? How could patronage in the shape of appoint-ments, promotions, admissions to professional colleges and allotment of lands, etc., be allowed to operate in such a manner that only about 200 or so families have benefited? And how could a power structure, with deep vested interests in the separatist tendency, be allowed to be entrenched? Subsequent unpalatable and assailable decisions could have been avoided had the tendency to remain mute spectators not taken grip earlier.

Hard Realities

Critics are usually unaware, or are only superficially aware, of such hard realities. Nor do they take into account the attitude of other agencies. Can, for instance, the Governor at the time of the constitutional crisis of the type with which I was confronted, ignore the attitude of the Chief Minister, the attitude of the Speaker, the attitude of political parties and the attitudes of various functionaries whose vested interests are linked with the current power structure? Pure actions of the Governor depend upon the pure disposition of the Chief Minister, the Speaker, the political parties and other components of the power structure. One cannot expect wholly unassailable decisions from the Governor when the other parties involved are not prepared to follow the rules of the game. An overall atmosphere of responsibility, of respect for the spirit of the Constitution, is what is really needed.

Ill-informed Criticism

My critics did not know, and perhaps never cared to know, that on July 2, 1984, I had very strongly urged the President/Union Government to permit me to impose Governor's Rule under Section 92 of the J&K Constitution, and that it was only when this legitimate constitutional option was denied to me that I had to choose the lesser of the two evils—G.M. Shah's Ministry in preference to Dr. Farooq Abdullah's Ministry.

After the dismissal of Dr. Farooq Abdullah and coming into being of G.M. Shah's Ministry, there was a spate of ill-informed criticism. At first, I decided to keep quiet. Time, I thought, will reveal the truth. But when criticism exceeded certain limits, I decided to give to the public at least a glimpse of my stand. I did so, in a letter to *The Times of India* which was published on August 24, 1984. The letter was in reply to the criticism of my action by L.P. Singh, former Governor of Assam, in an article published three days earlier in the same newspaper. This letter of mine is reproduced below:

To August 22, 1984

The Editor,
The Times of India,
New Delhi.

Dear Sir,

In regard to Shri L.P. Singh's article–Governor's Role in Crisis–published in your esteemed daily of August 18, 1984, I wish to state the following:

On Shri L.P. Singh's own reckoning, he has been out of touch with the Kashmir affairs for about 14 years. Would it, therefore, not have been appropriate for him to refrain from expressing any opinion, particularly when such an opinion, coming from a person of his background and experience, is likely to be taken as authoritative?

So far, I have resisted the temptation of correcting superficial or misinformed criticism. The nature of some of the facts, moreover, is such that they cannot be disclosed to public at this stage. But, in view of what is being commented upon even in responsible quarters, it seems necessary to put at least some of the records straight, notwithstanding the limitations imposed upon me by my office and the confidentiality of certain facts.

Is the Governors' Committee's recommendation, to which Shri L.P. Singh has referred, an end in itself? Should the Governor ignore the political and administrative environment in which he is called upon to exercise his judgement? Should he not be guided by the solid evidence which is in his possession about the behavioural pattern of certain individuals, groups and communities? Should he sidetrack the national interests and requirements of public order and tranquility and adhere to the narrow confines of a Committee's observation which has neither any validity in law and Constitution nor bears the stamp of Government and Parliamentary acceptance? Should he seek transitory applause from a section of the press or public for his 'demonstrable impartiality' or have courage to take upright though unpopular decisions? I am convinced that if the situation had been viewed from a narrow angle, without considering the totality of the circumstances, a highly tragic situation, as in Punjab and Assam, would have developed, involving huge loss of life and property and grave damage to national integrity. I hardly need to point out that 'the only thing necessary for the triumph of evil is for good men to do nothing'.

Shri L.P. Singh has referred to the recommendations of the Governors' Committee only in part. Is it not a fact that the same Committee categorically stated that it would be unwise and unrealistic to provide any rigid guidelines to the Governors, and that the Governor should come to his own conclusion keeping in view the circumstances of the case? Did not the Committee say that no two cases could be identical? If Jammu and Kashmir's case does not fall in the special category, then I cannot conceive of any other case which would.

Shri L.P. Singh has omitted to state that the then Janata Government made it clear to the Lok Sabha on November 17, 1977, and the Rajya Sabha on November 18, 1977, that it did not consider it necessary to accept the aforesaid recommendations in regard to the summoning of the Assembly. If calling of the Assembly in every such case is so sacrosanct, as is now being made out, why did not the Government and Parliament say so clearly in November 1977? Why did it not even consider it necessary to issue a letter of advice to the Governors in this regard?

Has anyone tried to think what facts were disputed that needed to be resolved by the Assembly vote? In this case, the facts were not disputed. That Dr. Farooq Abdullah was in minority was beyond doubt. He himself did not, and could not, contest it. All evidence was provided to him in writing and in person and nothing was done behind his back. In fact, by referring to his opponents as defectors, he admitted that they had turned against him. Then, like an obscure 'mantra', the meaning of which nobody bothers to enquire, why is it being chanted again and again that the Assembly should have been convened?

No responsible Governor could have ignored the stark realities of the situation. Allowing the minority Government of Dr. Farooq Abdullah to continue, even for a short while, would have implied turning a blind eye to the well-grounded apprehensions that 'instant' rallies would have been organised, communal and extremist elements exploited, public hysteria whipped up, administrative machinery misused, the 'traitors' dealt with appropriately, and the police made to say later on that, in view of the 'spontaneous' upsurge and understandable anger of the people, it could do nothing. In this connection, it would not be out of place to recall what Shri B.K. Nehru wrote to Dr. Farooq Abdullah in January 1984: "Your opponents were afraid, firstly, that in the interval between their coming to me and the vote in the House their houses would be burnt and their families attacked by the Police under your orders. They were afraid, secondly, that the Rules of the House would be so bent as to preclude a fair and free debate and vote from taking place. I recognised the validity of these fears on both counts."

If mere clerical or post office role is to be assigned to the Governor, then he, particularly the Governor of J&K, would be nothing but a mute spectator, watching from the sideline the sordid game of the disruptionists.

'Even the angels are not all of one opinion.' But I have no doubt that as all the facts about the nursing of extremists, disruptionists and communal forces, to be exploited for such eventualities as arose on July 2, 1984, comes to public notice, it would be fully appreciated that, having regard to the general powers of the Governor, the particular facts of this case, and the political and administrative environment in which I was called upon to exercise my judgement, the decision taken by me to dismiss Dr. Farooq Abdullah's ministry was constitutionally valid, administratively justified and in the overall national interest and in the interest of public order and tranquility. At the moment, I only feel 'a certain gloomy pride in having dared to do the right'.

Yours faithfully,
(Sd.) Jagmohan

Time to Speak

The publication of this letter had an electrifying effect. Almost all other leading newspapers published its contents in the form of a news story. A number of people, including my erstwhile critics, recognised the force of my arguments, and started talking about the other side of the picture. They pressed me to come out with all the details. But I did not want to get into controversies while holding office. My reply was: 'For everything there is a time–a time to keep silent, and a time to speak.' Now, I think, is the time to speak, and speak clearly and comprehensively, dealing with all the insinuations, innuendoes and points of criticism, including those relating to the replacement of B.K. Nehru by me.

Appointment

On March 25, 1984, a Rashtrapati Bhavan communique announced my appointment as Governor of J&K. Different inter-ests reacted in different ways. I was myself caught in two minds–happy at being elevated to Governorship and unhappy at the prospect of leaving Delhi in the service of which I found a great deal of creative satisfaction and whose poetry, pain and pathos had occupied a special corner in my heart. The people of Delhi, too, had generally identified me with the life and development of the city and were somewhat dismayed. In its lead story of the day, *The Times of India* correctly described the mood. It said:

> Many in Delhi will miss Lt. Governor Jagmohan who will himself miss Delhi, his first love. He has served Delhi for long–for seven years as the Chairman of the DDA and two terms as the Lt. Governor of Delhi and of Goa, Daman and Diu. During all these challenging years he built for himself the reputation of being a man who gets things done in the face of heavy odds. He appeared to take his assignment in Srinagar in his characteristic spirit that a job worth doing is worth doing well. He is the only civil servant who, in recent times, has left an indelible mark in the life and landscape of the capital.

The Hindustan Times editorial of March 28, 1984, commented:

> Jagmohan is not a politician although he is conversant with nuances of politics. He has a mind of his own and that is precisely the reason why a few Congress-I leaders in the Union Territory are happy at his departure.

In its editorial of the same day, the *Patriot* said:

> The threat from across the border is no more a 'figment of imagination' of India, as General Zia-ul-Huq would like the world to believe. The morale of the people in J&K is the first line of defence and this must not be allowed to become weak due to indecisiveness or confusion. Under the given circumstances

Jagmohan with his well-known administrative efficiency shown in his handling of the affairs of Delhi, cutting through bureaucratic red tapism, eminently fits the requirements of that office in Srinagar.

The editorial comments of *The Times of India* of March 28 were:

It would appear that the Prime Minister feels that in the country's troubled security environment which inevitably impinges on J&K and the revival of pro-secessionist elements there, the State needs a Governor with a more activist temperament. In that she has made a good choice. Jagmohan is a doer. In the circumstances of J&K, his role cannot realistically be merely titular. Dr. Farooq Abdullah would himself recognise this to be the case.

The Statesman of March 28 observed:

While it remains to be seen whether the former Lt. Governor of Delhi will be ready to break with his predecessor's principled precedent and oblige the KPCC (I) at Dr. Farooq Abdullah's expense, Congressmen are entitled to entertain high hopes of his cooperation. After all, Mrs. Gandhi was sufficiently impressed to promote him immediately after being re-elected in 1980, and later to recall him to Delhi's Raj Niwas in time for Asiad.

One Urdu newspaper humorously remarked that people had been commenting that, after extraordinary hard work connected with CHOGM, ASIAD and NAM, Jagmohan was being sent to recoup his health in Kashmir and also make in the process Dr. Farooq Abdullah more healthy.

Insinuations

The insinuation of some politicians and political commentators that I was being sent to J&K as a part of Mrs. Indira Gandhi's "overall designs" in the State somewhat saddened me. I, therefore, told the Prime Minister's office that, if the idea was to assign higher responsibilities to me, as had been mentioned to me, I could be sent to Punjab–a posting which, in my opinion, involved higher responsibilities than those concerning Kashmir. I was politely told that, whereas the Prime Minister was appreciative of the gesture, she was not willing to accede to my request partly because I was a Punjabi and partly because she thought Kashmir was equally important. She believed that it was of crucial importance to ensure that J&K did not become another thorn in the soft flesh of India.

Briefing

When I called upon Mrs. Gandhi, she was at pains to emphasise that there were strong forces, both within and outside the country, which were bent upon 'encircling' India and creating permanent headache for her in Punjab, Kashmir, North-East and in Tamil Nadu-Sri Lanka area. She spoke about the recent happenings in Kashmir and commented briefly about the various parties and personalities involved. She thought that B.K. Nehru had become rather old, and certain forces of destabilisation were taking full advantage of the fact. About Dr. Farooq Abdullah, she was both bitter and light-hearted. She talked of his boyish, inconsistent and erratic ways. She thought that he was under the influence of some crafty men and, whenever it suited him, he would whip up communal and parochial emotions and promote 'hate-Centre' feelings. She was particularly worried about his extraordinary friendship with Sikh fundamentalists in Punjab.

Presumably it was at her instance that M.K. Rasgotra, the then Foreign Secretary, invited me for a cup of tea at his house and briefed me about the possible developments around the Indian border, particularly in regard to Kashmir's border with China and Pakistan. Our position in regard to the Siachen Glacier was explained in detail.

After four days of the announcement of the appointments and transfers, B.K. Nehru came to Delhi. He invited me to have breakfast with him at the Kashmir House in New Delhi. Earlier I had met him twice. Once, at his suggestion, I took him round to various areas where new development works were carried out by the Delhi Development Authority. After the visit he wrote to me a very warm and appreciative letter. I was struck by his truly Nehruvian catholicity of mind and his paternal attitude towards young officers like me. I had also met him in 1964-65 at his Washington Ambassadorial residence with a group of middle level officers under a training programme sponsored by the Indian Institute of Public Administration. I could hardly imagine that one day I would be taking over from him. I was somewhat sorry over his transfer. He said that he wanted to stay a little more in Kashmir and he would take about a month to pack up. I told him that he could take his own time and, so far as I was concerned, there was no hurry at all.

B.K. Nehru gave me a briefing typical of the old civil servants. He said that the situation was very bad and that the people invariably talked of Kashmir's identity, and that there was a great deal of misunderstanding and bad blood between the Centre and the State, and the Prime Minister and the Chief Minister were on different wavelengths. He did not criticise Dr. Farooq Abdullah but thought that he was immature and erratic.

There were many others who gave advice. I heard everybody and made no comments. Even when Mrs. Gandhi briefed me or Mr. B.K. Nehru indicated his viewpoint, I largely kept quiet. My approach was to first understand the situation fully. There were, of course, a number of genuine friends and well-wishers who thought that there were too many scorpions in the paradise of Kashmir, that I would be ditched even by my apparent friends, and that I was sure to meet my Waterloo there. I took all such advice and comments in my stride. I was subjected to conflicting emotions. Delhi had a strong pull for me. There were personal and family problems. My son had to be put into a hostel which would affect his studies as well as his career. Even in regard to emoluments, strange though it may seem, I did not gain anything.

Propaganda Technique

With all these briefings, and press comments, I took over after more than a month of the issue of Presidential warrant in regard to my appointment. But inference was still being drawn in certain political quarters that I had been sent by Mrs. Gandhi with a purpose. This upset me and made me all the more cautious. But at the same time I argued, within myself, whether this inference was not a propaganda technique to keep me away from the correct path, to make me hesitant to act even when the national interests and requirements of security warranted me to act. What I found within the first few days of my assuming office caused me a lot of concern. The anti-national forces dominated the scene. Come what may, I resolved, I would not fumble and compromise with anything wrong and fundamentally evil.

I seldom pray in regard to my personal career or administrative matters. But whenever I do, I always say: "Give me the courage to do the correct thing, even when I am in the minority of one." Such prayers, in moments of difficulties and crises, have invariably provided immense confidence and enabled me to take decisions which, I knew, would make me unpopular with a particular section of the people, but which, with the passage of time, would be seen as basically fair, just, and sound, and in the overall interest of the community and the State.

Tension-ridden Atmosphere

The atmosphere in the State was thick with tensions. It had been badly vitiated by the State Assembly elections held on June 5, 1983, and also by the underlying forces and elements which I have discussed in the three previous chapters entitled "Roots".

During the aforesaid elections, the party managers resorted to fascist techniques. Lies were intentionally spread. Religious and regional feelings were unscrupulously exploited. To strengthen his position in the Valley and to create a mental climate in which anti-Centre, pro-plebiscite, and Muslim votes would constitute one solid phalanx in his favour, Dr. Farooq Abdullah joined hands with Mirwaiz Moulvi Farooq, though the latter did not abandon even temporarily his pro-plebiscite and pro-Pakistan stance. The Maulvi's uncle, the previous 'Mirwaiz', Yusaf Shah, had migrated to Pakistan and become 'president' of 'Azad Kashmir'. Dr. Farooq Abdullah spoke different languages at different places. But in the Valley he subtly enlisted the support of the groups which once formed the core of the 'Plebiscite Front' and which formally parted company with Sheikh Abdullah when he entered into the Kashmir Accord (1975). Dr. Abdullah himself propagated in the Valley: "This election is a plebiscite to allow the people to say which political party, National Conference or Congress(I), they liked." Mrs. Indira Gandhi and the Congress(I) party, on the other hand, aroused the apprehensions of the Jammuites about Pakistan and the elements in the State who were favourably disposed towards it.

The result of all this was a sharp polarisation of the voters on communal and parochial lines. The Valley and the Muslims overwhelmingly voted for the National Conference and the non-Muslim-dominated area of the Jammu region and the Hindus for the Congress(I).

During the election campaign, there were a number of ugly incidents which left a trail of bitterness and hostility. For instance,

Mrs. Gandhi's meeting on June 3, at Iqbal Park, Srinagar, was violently disturbed and indescribably indecent tricks were employed. There were conflicts between the Central and the State agencies also. Some of the Returning Officers even defied the instructions of the Election Commission of India. About 10,000 personnel of the paramilitary forces were sent to the State for the election duty, particularly for providing mixed force at the polling booths, but the State authorities assigned them inconsequential work, leaving the polling booths under the exclusive charge of the local police. Dr. Farooq, on the other hand, objected to the presence of a large number of Central officers and observers of the Election Commission of India in the State.

Due to coalescence of the political and administration elements at the field level, allegations of rigging in favour of the candidates of the National Conference could not be dismissed lightly. There were specific complaints of booth capturing at 18 polling stations spread over ten constituencies. At many places a large number of unaccountable ballot papers were found. In Zadibal constituency, for example, the National Conference candidate 'secured' 90 per cent of the votes polled even when in the hey-day of Sheikh Abdullah in 1977 the party candidate got 51 per cent votes. The State Congress Chief, Mufti Mohammad Sayeed, bemoaned, "This is exactly like Bhutto's 1978 Election in Pakistan. It has no legitimacy. It is based upon fraud." The Congress(I) filed as many as 40 election petitions. Dr. Farooq, on the other hand, accused the Election Commission of India of playing a partisan role.

Security and Administrative Environment

From August 15, 1983, onwards there were a series of bomb explosions to which I have made a brief reference in Chapter I. In connection with one such incident at the time of the Independence Day function, the investigations were pursued at the instance of Mrs. Indira Gandhi. Four suspects–Iqbal Qureshi, Altaf Qureshi, Altaf Mahajan and Majid Lala–were arrested. Iqbal Qureshi was the brother of Hashim Qureshi who had hijacked an Indian Airlines Fokker Friendship plane in 1971. Altaf Qureshi was the brother of Ashraf Qureshi who was a co-hijacker. The presence of such dangerous persons showed the direction in which the wind was blowing.

On October 13, 1983, highly deplorable acts of subversion were witnessed during the one-day international cricket match between India and the West Indies. The Indian players were humiliated, hooted, heckled, abused and even assaulted with rotten fruits, pebbles and flag sticks. Pakistani flags were waved. Attempts were made to dig up the pitch. In September 1986, during Governor's Rule, there was another one-day international match between India and Australia which was conducted in an orderly manner. At that time, Kapil Dev, the Indian Captain, spoke to me of his horrible experience of October 13, 1983. He said that some of his team-mates thought that they would be killed. The ugly incidents which took place in full view of millions of television viewers sent a wave of anger throughout the country. The nation received another shock when the Indian diplomat, Ravindera Mhatre, posted at Birmingham, was kidnapped and then murdered in the first week of February 1984, by the terrorists of 'J&K Liberation Army' which was really a militant organ of the Plebiscite Front. This tragic incident was seen as a direct outcome of the disturbed conditions in the Valley and total inaction against anti-India, and pro-Pakistan elements. In fact, these elements and a sizeable section of the National Conference workers at the grassroots level were not at different emotional wavelengths. The execution of Maqbool Butt on February 11, 1984, added to the tension in the State.

Another factor of considerable significance that emerged at that time was the nexus that developed between the Muslim and Sikh youths who were hostile to the Union Government and frequently indulged in subversive activities. On May 29, 1984, for instance, a violent procession was taken out by these elements at Srinagar, ostensibly to protest against Bhiwandi riots that took place a fortnight earlier. Seven vehicles belonging to the Army and the BSF were attacked and five jawans injured. Highly provocative slogans, like "Pakistan Zindabad"; "Khalistan Zindabad"; "Noor-e-Chashm, Noor-e-Huq–Zia-ul-Haq, Zia-ul-Huq", were raised. On June 7, another combined procession was organised in which naked swords were freely brandished. The crowd went on a rampage and set a number of shops and houses on fire, including the Arya Samaj School and the Nirankari Bhavan. The Hanuman temple was also attacked, the 'pujari' beaten and the idol thrown into the Jhelum.

Many other incidents of a similar nature took place. In regard to the period August 15, 1983 to July 2, 1984, I have particularised all the incidents having a bearing upon the State security and public order in Appendix XII. This, when read with what I have stated above, will provide a clear of security and administrative conditions prevailing at the time of the constitutional crisis of July 2, 1984.

Politics of the Family

Politics was in the blood of Sheikh Abdullah's family. His eldest daughter, Mrs. Khalida Shah, was as politically ambitious as her brother, Dr. Farooq Abdullah. Like Lady Macbeth, she too wanted her husband to be 'king'. There was also a background of frictions between the sister and the brother. Many stories were current about their jealousy and the Sheikh's special liking for Khalida and his dislike for the non-serious Dr. Farooq Abdullah.

G.M. Shah always felt that he had a better claim to the Chief Ministership of the State and the leadership of the National Conference. He was not reconciled to Sheikh Mohammad Abdullah's decision to pass on the crown to his son. He would comment, albeit in a hushed tone, that he had stood by the Sheikh in difficult times, gone to jail, laboured hard as Secretary of the 'Plebiscite Front' and acquired a vast experience of the party machine, while Dr. Farooq Abdullah enjoyed himself all the time in England, and took years to obtain his medical degree, and then secured the father's *gaddi* through 'palace intrigues'!

G.M. Shah was later accused of betraying Dr. Farooq Abdullah. But he could with equal justification point out that it was he who was first betrayed by Sheikh Abdullah who, incidentally, also betrayed Mirza Afzal Beg, his lifelong associate and partner in all his trials and tribulations.

G.M. Shah lay low for some time. He made an outward show of loyalty to Dr. Farooq Abdullah. During the State Assembly elections of June 1983, he quietly managed, through his mother-in-law. Mrs. Sheikh Abdullah, to secure party tickets for at least eight of his supporters. Shah saw his opportunity when the relations between the Congress(I) and the National Conference soured, and the former sent encouraging signals to him. About half a dozen erstwhile ministers in the Sheikh Abdullah cabinet, who were unceremoniously dropped by Dr. Farooq. Abdullah when he became the Chief Minister in September 1982, after the Sheikh's death, clandestinely joined hands with G.M. Shah.

Separately, the Congress(I) started a public agitation against rigging in election and misrule of Dr. Farooq Abdullah. A number of demonstrations were held. During the course of one such demonstration on January 15, 1984, the police resorted to firing in which four Congress supporters were killed. This further embittered the relations between the Congress(I) and the National Conference. The mood of the Congress(I) at the moment was reflected by Mohammad Shafi Qureshi, Congress(I) leader and former Union Minister, when he said, "It is strange that if you raise the slogan of 'Azad Hindustan Zindabad' you get killed; but if you shout 'Pakistan Zindabad' or 'Indian dogs go back', you prosper and make hay." K.C. Pant also accused Dr. Farooq Abdullah of becoming a "willing prisoner in the hands of anti-national forces". On his part Dr. Farooq Abdullah criticised the Congress(I) with equal vehemence. He even threatened that if the Central Government did not give liberal financial assistance, he would turn to Saudi Arabia for help. He called the Congress(I) party in Kashmir as a "group of burglars and goondas" who could not remain without power.

The relations between the State and the Central Government were also strained, particularly in regard to the allegations about the existence of training camps in J&K for the Sikh activists. Dr. Farooq Abdullah had obtained the support of the Akalis in the State elections of June 1983. He had also developed a soft corner for the Sikh activists. P.C. Sethi, Union Home Minister, wrote a number of letters to Dr. Farooq Abdullah on both the counts. He expressed the Union Government's deep apprehensions over the training camps and the dangerous liaison that was developing between the subversive elements in Punjab and J&K. Sethi also deplored the increase in the activities of secessionists and pro-Pakistan elements in the Valley. Dr. Farooq Abdullah and the State Government vehemently denied these allegations. But the controversies caused much acrimony and friction between the two Governments.

By the end of January 1984, it was no longer a secret that G.M. Shah and his supporters had decided to topple Dr. Farooq Abdullah's Ministry with the help of the Congress(I). From the letter of B.K. Nehru of January 27, 1984, to which I have made a reference subsequently in this chapter, it was clear that the matter was taken up with him and he in turn had spoken to Dr. Farooq Abdullah and secured an assurance from him that he would seek a vote of confidence in accordance with the normal rules and after proper notice and debate.

Sheikh Abdul Jabbar, an MLA from Kangan, was the first to raise the banner of revolt. He submitted a memorandum to the President of India listing the misdeeds of Dr. Farooq Abdullah and demanding his dismissal. The reaction of Dr. Farooq Abdullah's supporters was true to the Kashmiri style of politics. They resorted to intimidation and hounded Sheikh Jabbar wherever he went. G.M. Shah and Mrs. Khalida Shah came out openly in support of Jabbar on April 24, 1984. Mrs. Khalida proceeded to Kangan to address a public meeting in support of Jabbar. She was assaulted on the way and injured.

Separate Conventions

The rupture between Dr. Farooq Abdullah and G.M. Shah was formalised when their groups decided to have separate conventions of the party. G.M. Shah decided to have his convention on May 23, 1984, and Dr. Farooq Abdullah a few days later.

The convention, organised on May 23 by the dissidents headed by G.M. Shah, removed Dr. Farooq Abdullah from the presidentship of the party and expelled him from the primary membership of the National Conference. In his place, the convention elected Mrs. Khalida Shah as the leader of the National Conference. They called their group the "real National Conference".

The prominent leaders who attended the convention organised by G.M. Shah were D.D. Thakur, G.N. Kochak, M.K. Tickoo, A.R. Shaheen and all former Ministers in Sheikh Abdullah's Cabinet. According to the claim of the organisers, 2,300 delegates of the National Conference attended this convention.

The resolution passed at this convention said that the election of Dr. Farooq Abdullah as party leader was a 'Himalayan blunder', that the period of his 18-month-old presidentship was a black spot in the history of the National Conference, that within three days of taking over as Chief Minister he removed all senior leaders who were Ministers in the Cabinet of Sheikh Abdullah, that he even indirectly accused them of corruption and thereby cast doubt on the wisdom and perception of Sheikh Abdullah himself, that he was constituting Commissions of Inquiry to discredit senior leaders and Ministers in the Sheikh Abdullah Cabinet, that he was entering into an alliance with known communal and pro-Pak elements like the Awami Action

Committee, and that during his stewardship of the State its economy had gone down. The discussions at the convention also ridiculed Dr. Farooq Abdullah's non-serious, unpredictable and enigmatic nature and his infinite capacity to contradict himself and create confusion all around.

The reaction of Dr. Farooq Abdullah and the National Conference was typical. Instead of allowing the conventionists to talk over their plans, Dr. Farooq Abdullah, his party workers and his administrative machinery decided to put all sorts of impediments to the holding of the convention. Trucks were not allowed to be hired under one pretext or another. Even hotel accommodation, for which advance money was deposited by the organisers of the convention, were got cancelled through pressure exerted by the local administration. All this gave an opportunity to G.M. Shah and his supporters to kick a lot of dust and secure wide publicity. G.M. Shah, D.D. Thakur, G.N. Kochak and others met me with petitions in which they bitterly complained about the fascist techniques of Dr. Farooq Abdullah.

While the organisers of the convention called it a great success, and their claims were adumbrated with banner headlines by their supporters in the press, Dr. Farooq Abdullah and his party colleagues termed it as a great 'tamasha' of a few manipulators. The significance of the convention, however, lay not in its success or failure in terms of the number of people or leaders it attracted but in the locus standi that it gave to Mrs. Khalida Shah's group as a component of the party that had split. What Farooq Abdullah failed to realise was that the very holding of the convention implied that G.M. Shah had been assured of clandestine support of certain MLAs who, for obvious reasons, could not come out in the open at this stage. He persuaded himself to believe that Shah had no support. Instead of becoming vigilant, he became more complacent.

Tensions All Around

There were thus acute tensions all around–tensions between the State and the Centre, between the National Conference and the Congress(I), between Dr. Farooq Abdullah and Mrs. Indira Gandhi, and also amongst the members of Sheikh Abdullah's family. Pro-Pakistan and pro-Khalistan elements were nursing their own designs. The atmosphere was badly surcharged. A slight mishandling or miscalculation on my part would have caused the entire ammunition dump to blow up with one big bang, spreading death, destruction and bitterness in its wake. In our country, unfortunately, no one notices when a tragedy is avoided and grave damage is prevented.

A Crucial Night

On July 1, 1984 at 10.30 p.m., I was informed by my security staff that a group of MLAs and MLCs, led by G.M. Shah and D.D. Thakur, wanted to come to Raj Bhavan and meet me with an important request. It was hinted that they had withdrawn their support to Dr. Farooq Abdullah's government which had been reduced to minority, because the Congress(I) Legislature Party had also decided to support the new group. I told the security staff to tell the group that they could come in the morning at 8.30 a.m. But the group persisted. Its reply, conveyed through the staff, was somewhat like this: "If the police had been independent, there would have been no problem and we would not have bothered you at this odd hour. Our real problem is the wholly captive administration. The moment you ask the police to give protection, the news of our gathering would be immediately communicated to Dr. Farooq Abdullah and, with the connivance of the police, hooligans and criminals would be set on us. We would be slaughtered, our houses would be burnt and our families harmed. If you would like to see us only in the morning, let us enter the Raj Bhavan premises so that we are not attacked if the news of our gathering leaks out."

I recognised that the apprehensions of the group were not without basis. Nevertheless, I stuck to my earlier view. The only concession I made was that they could see me at 7 a.m. instead of 8.30 a.m.

I was somewhat perplexed by this sudden development. Although it was in the air that G.M. Shah and his group were planning to bring down Dr. Farooq Abdullah's Government, with the help of Congress(I), yet the possibility looked rather remote. There were, in fact, indications that the misunderstanding between Dr. Farooq Abdullah and Mrs. Gandhi was about to be resolved. She herself told me at the end of June that if Dr. Farooq Abdullah took effective action against the disruptionists, she would, in the totality of the circumstances, ignore his many other aberrations. His crafty friends, she thought, were taking advantage of his immaturity and egging him on to adopt a dangerous course which, besides bringing Muslim and Sikh fundamentalists together, would enable Pakistan to play its own game.

In the light of my talk with Mrs. Indira Gandhi at the end of June, the decision of the local Congress(I) leadership to encourage G.M. Shah and to join hands with him, looked a little surprising.

I soon collected myself and realised that it was not the time for me to consider why a particular event was occurring but to do some quick thinking to ensure that in the morning when the conflict between the anti-Farooq group and the pro-Farooq group came to surface, the State did not go up in flames, and hostile forces within the Valley and across the border did not take advantage of the tense situation.

I came down to my office which was located on the ground floor of Raj Bhavan. As was my practice, to deal with the crisis and attain clarity, I noted down a few points. I visualised various possible situations that might arise in the morning. On one basic point, I soon became absolutely clear. To the extent it was feasible, I would not allow public order to be disturbed and human lives to be lost. Lost lives cannot be retrieved. But our political leaders, after exploiting the masses, themselves change sides and subvert all values on which real freedom and democracy rest. I was acutely conscious of the petty game which politicians had been playing in Kashmir. I knew how superficial was their commitment to any cause and how most of them had shown no qualms of conscience in basing their power on the forces of obscurantism, communalism and regionalism. It would be morally indefensible to let human lives be lost for the sake of such leaders. For them power was everything; people or principles or values did not count for anything.

Both groups, I thought, would feather their own nests. Both would serve the same elite class. Both would try to fool the poor. Both would resort to disinformation and fascist techniques. Both would mislead the people in regard to Article 370 of the Indian Constitution.

Safety of the people and their property and protection of national interests, without sacrificing the requirements of intrinsic justice and intrinsic fair play, as distinct from superficial justice and surface fair play, became, therefore, my primary objective. I decided to assume an activist's role while remaining within the parameters of the Constitution. It was quite clear to me that if any consideration of constitutional passivity was allowed to prevail, disastrous consequences would follow.

The first task I took upon myself was to telephone Cabinet Secretary, C.R. Krishnaswamy Rao Saheb, and Home Secretary, M.M.K. Wali, and inform them about the situation that might arise in the morning. I did not say anything on behalf of the State Government, but simply informed them. This I did because the past experience was that whenever any disturbance or conflict occurred, the Central Government installations and offices were the first targets of attack by the trouble-makers. Even military vehicles were not spared. There was also danger of places of great religious and historic importance being blown up or damaged, thereby arousing religious emotions of the entire populace as were aroused during the Prophet's hair theft incident in December 1963-January 1964. It was my duty to inform the Union Government, and to informally suggest to them, for their consideration, whether they should not arrange Central police force to remain in or near the Valley, so that no time was wasted in making effective arrangements for protecting vital installations in the event of large-scale disturbances breaking out in the morning.

Much was subsequently made out of this action of mine by a section of the press. It was stated that I had acted as if the State Government had been taken over by me. Nothing could be farther from the truth. I had not issued any order or made any request for and on behalf of the State Government. To promptly inform the Union Government of a situation which had the potential of causing serious public disorder and even undermining the security of the State was not merely an act of ordinary prudence or public responsibility but also a constitutional duty. Above all, it was a human obligation to protect human lives–an obligation above all other obligations.

On page 3 of his booklet, *My Dismissal,* Dr. Farooq Abdullah says: "Why did the Governor have to make special arrangements for meeting law and order situation which he envisaged would develop if I was not to be illegally dismissed?" The answer to this is that I thought I should inform all concerned and leave it to them to keep the forces nearby. My understanding was that the force would be needed whatever be the outcome of my decision in the morning. If Governor's Rule came, as I was contemplating, I needed the force; if Dr. Farooq continued and if there was breakdown of law and order, the force would be needed. So would be the position if the Shah Government took over and his opponents started causing disturbances on a vast scale. In all this, I did not pass any order. I informed; I suggested; I alerted. Initiative is nowhere prohibited, particularly when it is in public interest, and when the underlying motivation is not to allow innocent masses to become victims of the power-play of unscrupulous politicians.

I also got in touch with Lt.-Gen. M.L. Chibber, General Officer Commanding, Northern Command, on the phone. I apprised him of the developments. I advised him to alert his officers and instruct them not to get provoked by any act of misguided civilians, such as stoning of Army vehicles on routine duty. I also suggested to him to come over to Srinagar so that quick decisions could be taken if the situation became serious. The presence of about 10,000 fanatic and violence-prone followers of the Awami Action Committee leader, Moulvi Mohammad Farooq, was, I thought, too significant a factor to be ignored. Nor was I sure which way the six battalions of J&K Armed Police would look. The recruitment of this force, I was told, was made with a bias in favour of those elements who were fed on anti-Centre emotions.

Like an imaginative and sound strategist of an administrative organisation, I attempted to visualise all possible scenarios, including the worst one, and make provision for them. Some of the greatest mishaps in the administration have been caused by those who remained cocksure of events taking a particular course. Wooden-headedness of a sizeable section of the present-day administration and its inability to get to the core of the issues in question are its fatal flaws—flaws which have led to innumerable riots and consequent loss of life and property, besides undermining the forces of national cohesion and stability.

I also got in touch with the local Chief of the Intelligence Bureau, K.P. Singh. He told me that at the moment the public was not aware of what was happening, but the news was bound to spread in the morning and some leaders would attempt to bring crowds on the streets and incite them.

The exchange of information with K.P. Singh reinforced my view that no risk could be taken and no theoretical consideration should be allowed to stand in the way of arriving at a quick and final decision in the matter. I was aware of the main provisions of the J&K Constitution, yet I thought it prudent to go through the relevant provisions once again. Interpreting the Constitution is not a routine work. It depends upon the context and the circumstances in which its provisions are studied. It would be unwise, I thought, not to consider all the possibilities, but it would be equally unwise to deal with the problem with any preconceived idea. My approach to tackle the crisis should depend upon the stand which different parties involved took in the morning.

A Crucial Day

All this thinking, all this exchange of information, all this reading and scribbling took practically the whole night. So absorbed was I in the situation that I hardly realised that it was already 3 a.m. of July 2, 1984. After satisfying myself that I had done all that was practicable and possible, I went upstairs to sleep. I had a sound sleep for two hours, the type of sleep which one gets after feeling that a job has been conscientiously and diligently done and the consequences, good or bad, have to be accepted with stoic calmness.

When I returned to the office at 7 a.m. I was told that the group headed by G.M. Shah had already arrived and was waiting in a hall that was about 30 to 40 metres away from the main building. I was told that Iftikhar Hussain Ansari, leader of the Congress Legislature Party, was also with them. I pondered over the situation again for a few minutes and then allowed the deputation to see me at the appointed time.

G.M. Shah presented to me a letter dated June 28, 1984, which was signed by 12 MLAs, namely, Munshi Habibullah, Kargil; Mohammad Dilawar Mir, Rafiabad; Hissam Din Bandey, Hazratbal; Sheikh Abdul Jabbar, Kangan; Talib Hussain, Rajouri; Dr. Mehboob Beg, Anantnag; Hakim Mohd. Yasin, Khansahib; Mohammad Khalil Jawhar, Bandipur; Gurbachan Kumari Rana, nominated; Ghulam Hassan Mir, Gulmarg; Khem Lata Wakhlu, nominated; and Sonaullah Dar, Pulwama. This letter read:

> Your Excellency, we hope, is aware of the internal rift in the ruling National Conference. In September 1982, consequent upon the sad demise of our beloved Leader Sher-i-Kashmir, we had elected Dr. Farooq Abdullah as the Leader of National Conference Legislature Party by a unanimous decision in the hope that he will uphold and follow the path and the principles laid down by his father. Dr. Farooq Abdullah, during the last nineteen months or so, has miserably failed in following the principles and the programme of the party and its late Leader. He first dismissed the entire Cabinet of Sher-i-Kashmir on the pretext that it was a corrupt Cabinet. This resulted in maligning the name of our great leader who presided over that Cabinet for a long time.
>
> Throwing to winds the directions of Sher-i-Kashmir and the party, he entered into an unholy alliance with anti-social elements and fundamentalists who had been fought by Sher-i-Kashmir for as long

a period as 52 years. The party structure was changed beyond recognition and undesirable elements were pampered and the real workers ignored–so much so that G.M. Shah who had given his life and blood for the party and who suffered for decades along with Sher-i-Kashmir was expelled from the party along with D.D. Thakur, a close confidant of the late Leader, and a large number of other senior leaders. At this stage, we the undersigned expressed our solidarity with G.M. Shah as we felt that he alone could save the party from disintegration. We unmistakably indicated to Dr. Abdullah that he had lost our support and that we no longer could support his Government and its policies.

In the Assembly meeting on January 27, 1984, we apprehended that Dr. Abdullah, having known that he had lost the support of the majority of the House, out of sheer desperation would recommend dissolution of the Assembly or obtain a resolution of the Council of Ministers to that effect. That day Dr. Abdullah and his Ministers threatened us and under duress obtained a vote of confidence which is not our voluntary vote.

We submit that Dr. Abdullah and his Government having lost the support of the majority of the Lower House of the Legislature has no moral or constitutional right to recommend the dissolution of the House. We, therefore, pray that any such recommendations as and when made may kindly be ignored and rejected.

We would further submit that Shri G.M. Shah in whose leadership we have total faith and who has the confidence of the other sections of the House also be called upon to form a Government which shall be stable and which we are sure would carry out the policy and the programmes of our Leader, Sher-i-Kashmir.

This application was accompanied by a note dated July 2, 1984, of an independent MLA, Ali Mohammad Naik, and a letter dated July 2, 1984, of Moulvi Iftikhar Hussain Ansari, Leader of the Congress(I) Legislature Party.

G.M. Shah volunteered to present before me the 12 MLAs. He wrote another application in my presence, in continuation of the earlier application, and produced the 12 MLAs before me who signed again in my presence. The second application read as under:

In continuation of our letter dated 28.6.1984 we the following Members of the J&K Legislative Assembly belonging to the

> National Conference present ourselves personally before your goodself and submit that we have withdrawn our support from the Government headed by Dr. Farooq Abdullah. Consequent upon the withdrawal of our support, Dr. Farooq Abdullah has lost the confidence of the majority of the members of the Legislative Assembly.
>
> We have elected G.M. Shah, MLC, as our Leader. We, therefore, request your goodself to call upon G.M. Shah to form the Government of the State.
>
> We further submit that twenty-six (26) Members of the Congress(I) Legislature Party have pledged their support along with an independent Member Ali Mohd. Naik.

I asked the group led by G.M. Shah as to why they could not exhibit their strength in the Legislative Assembly. Their reply was simple: "The Speaker will play a partisan role. This has already been demonstrated in the last session when all rules were suddenly relaxed and vote of confidence obtained by Dr. Farooq Abdullah, despite the assurance earlier given by him to B.K. Nehru that such a vote would be sought in the normal way and no unfair pre-emption would be resorted to. Certain elements in the State Police as also hooligans would be set on us, and the fascist method of arousing crowd hysteria against us would be employed." I saw weight in the argument, but remained somewhat sceptical. What type of democracy were we having in Kashmir when hooliganism and fascist techniques could determine the course of events?

I took the documents from G.M. Shah and his colleagues and asked them to wait in the hall. I telephoned Dr. Farooq Abdullah and requested him to come to Raj Bhavan. He said he would have his bath and then come. It took him about 45 minutes to arrive. Meanwhile, I got photostat copies made of the letter of G.M. Shah and his colleagues. During this time Lt.-General M.L. Chibber also arrived. I offered him a cup of tea and apprised him of what was happening. When my ADC announced that Dr. Farooq Abdullah had come, I asked him to make him sit in the drawing-room, where I went, leaving Lt.-General Chibber to have his tea in my office.

After the usual courtesies and greetings, I spoke to Dr. Farooq Abdullah somewhat in these words: "There is a bit of a political crisis. We have to take everything calmly. We should ensure that, whatever be the decision, nothing would be done or said which would create a law and order problem. Here are the letters which have been given to me by G.M. Shah and others. Shah claims that you are now in minority and demands that you should be removed and he, being in majority, should be sworn in as Chief Minister. Shah also claims that due to the explosive situation created in the State and the sham vote which was obtained on January 27, 1984, he did not expect fair trial of strength to be carried out on the floor of the Assembly."

Dr. Farooq Abdullah's immediate reaction was one of bewilderment. He saw the names and muttered some incoherent words, including thieves, rogues and the like. He did not challenge the authenticity of the applications or the signatures appended thereon. It appeared that he was expecting "these thieves", "these rogues" to behave in the manner they were doing. So sure was he about what he thought was the treacherous behaviour of these MLAs that he did not verify whether what G.M. Shah was claiming was correct. In his booklet,* *My Dismissal,* he himself says: "I did not want to see the faces of all those who had deceived me." From the names he could quickly see that revolt against him was the outcome of his own game of dropping some erstwhile Ministers of Sheikh Abdullah's Cabinet and some others whose ambitions he had frustrated.

Dr. Farooq Abdullah struggled for expression. He did not really know what to say. Noticing the uncertain state of his mind, I said: "Look, Doctor, you must realise the dimensions of the crisis. You are in clear minority. Obviously, it will not be possible for me to keep a minority Government in office. You will have to resign. You must understand my limitations and also appreciate my overwhelming anxiety to maintain public order in this sensitive State. I cannot take any risk. I can rely on you but not on your supporters in the streets. The best that I can do–and this will also be fair to all concerned–is to impose Governor's Rule under Section 92 of the J&K Constitution and have the other issues sorted out subsequently."

The moment I mentioned Governor's Rule, Dr. Farooq Abdullah literally jumped from his seat. He seemed to have got new life in him. "Governor Sahib, I am grateful to you for this suggestion", he said. Regaining his full confidence, he added: "Not to these thieves, not to these scums; keep the reign with you as long as you like." The awkwardness in our talks certainly disappeared. Tension in the minds

*This booklet was written by S. Sahni, former Director of Information, J&K, as per the version given by Dr. Farooq Abdullah.

eased. We briefly spoke about the conditions which justified the imposition of Governor's Rule. I thought that the crisis had been got over. But in my optimism, I had not taken into account the twists and turns of Kashmir's politics and the machinations of certain individuals and forces.

I told Dr. Farooq Abdullah that it would be better if he confirmed in writing that he supported my idea of bringing the State temporarily under Governor's Rule. He, without any hesitation, agreed. He stated he would go home, draft the letter with the help of P.L. Handoo and send the same. Such a letter, I must make it clear, was not needed by me for any legal or constitutional purpose. I thought it would be of use to me in pressing the President/Union Government to concur in the issuance of the Governor's Proclamation under Section 92 of the J&K Constitution. I could tell the President/Union Government that, apart from my satisfaction as envisaged under Section 92* of the J&K Constitution, Dr. Farooq Abdullah also was supporting the measure and his cooperation would help me in maintaining law and order—a factor of fundamental importance in my calculations.

As Dr. Farooq Abdullah moved out of the drawing-room, the door of the office-room, which faced the drawing-room, was left ajar. Dr. Farooq Abdullah saw Lt.-General Chibber and greeted him. They knew each other well. After Dr. Farooq Abdullah left, I briefly talked to General Chibber about the internal security scheme. I also told him that the State was likely to come under Governor's Rule. He thought that this was the best thing to do at the moment. Soon thereafter General Chibber left and I told him that I would keep him informed of further developments.

I am mentioning this apparently inconsequential fact, as it was insinuated in a section of the press that General Chibber had been called by me to intimidate Dr. Farooq Abdullah. This is far from the truth. Dr. Farooq Abdullah entered the office-room only after meeting me in the drawing room and having happily agreed to my suggestion in regard to the imposition of Governor's Rule.

I was very anxious to prevent violence in the streets. Kashmir crowds are easily excitable. They soon get hysterical. It is immaterial whether they support or denounce a particular cause. Once they get into an emotional and tense mood, nothing can prevent them from acting simultaneously from different parts of the city, particularly in

*See Chapter XI: 'Dissolution of the Assembly'.

the city of Srinagar. Erection of road blocks and stoning of buses and cars are their speciality. There is a touch of light-hearted hooliganism in their behaviour. They are mostly unemployed or underemployed, and have little, by way of recreational activity, to keep them occupied. They are not even aware of the justness or otherwise of the causes they seemingly espouse. An overwhelming majority of them are the ones against whom firm action cannot be taken without feeling sorry for them.

Since Maulvi Farooq, Chairman of the Awami Action Committee, had a frenzied following of about 10,000 violence-prone persons and as he was the key figure in regard to the maintenance of public order in the heart of Srinagar city, I immediately invited him to Raj Bhavan on the plea that I wanted to seek his wise and mature advice in regard to the constitutional crisis. The Maulvi was happy that the Governor was seeking his invaluable advice. And I was happy to keep him engaged in Raj Bhavan till arrangements for maintaining law and order in the city had been made.

While I was trying to settle explosive issues quietly and quickly, the All India Radio flashed the news, in its 8 o'clock news bulletin, that 13 MLAs headed by G.M. Shah had gone to Raj Bhavan to indicate in person to the Governor their withdrawal of support from Dr. Farooq Abdullah's Government and press their claim for the installation of G.M. Shah as Chief Minister on the grounds that he enjoyed support of the majority of the MLAs. It was also stated that these MLAs and the leader of the Congress(I) Legislature Party, Moulvi Iftikhar Hussain Ansari, were demanding the dismissal of Farooq Abdullah's Government which had been reduced to a minority. When my staff told me about the news bulletin I was upset. I wondered whether it was a case of foolhardiness or someone was intentionally sabotaging my efforts to prevent disturbances. Nevertheless, I took prompt measures to counter the adverse repercussions of this broadcast. One such measure was to immediately invite Moulvi Farooq to my residence and the other was to speed up decisions in regard to consultations, letter-writing and sorting out of constitutional and administrative issues.

I dictated a top priority wireless signal to the President with a copy each to the Cabinet Secretary, the Home Secretary and the Secretary to the Prime Minister. This signal read as follows:

> Law and order and security of the State seriously threatened by activists/disruptionists and also by the political instability that has been caused by the withdrawal of support to the Chief Minister and his Ministry by 13 MLAs (12 of the ruling National Conference and 1 Independent). With the withdrawal of support by these MLAs, Dr. Farooq Abdullah has lost absolute majority in the Legislative Assembly. I am satisfied that a situation has arisen in which the Government of the State cannot be carried on in accordance with the provisions of the J&K Constitution. I want to issue proclamation immediately under Section 92 of the J& K Constitution assuming to myself all or any of the functions of the Government of the State vested in or exercisable by any body or authority in the State. Solicit your concurrence immediately under sub-section 5 of Section 92 of the Constitution. Position serious.

I also spoke on the phone to the Cabinet and Home Secretaries. I impressed upon them the necessity of communicating to me forthwith the requisite concurrence for issuing the proclamation under Section 92 of the J&K Constitution. I argued that under the said section, it was the satisfaction of the Governor about the breakdown of the constitutional machinery that formed the crux of the issue. More than that, I argued, the time was of essence, and if in the state of uncertainty some incidents took place the situation could abruptly go out of hand. The Home Secretary and the Cabinet Secretary agreed with my assessment and promised early action. The latter told me that Mrs. Gandhi was busy in discussions with Jayawardene, Sri Lanka's President, and he would be able to talk to her as soon as the discussions were over. I told him that Dr. Farooq Abdullah, too, had agreed with me and his agreement would help me in ensuring that law and order was not disturbed. Both the Cabinet Secretary and the Home Secretary recognised that it was a plus point in the situation and they would speed up the process of obtaining concurrence. I also spoke to the President personally.

At the same time, I asked my staff to call the Chief Secretary and the Director General of Police. The Chief Secretary had gone for his morning golf and was unaware of the situation. The Director General of Police heard of the developments while he was on his way to Raj Bhavan. When they arrived I informed them of what was happening. I reminded them of their legal and administrative obligations. For enforcement of law and order and for maintenance of public peace they did not require any orders from the political head or the Governor. I simply elucidated the position to instil confidence in them and advised them to remain alert.

A little earlier, I had sent, through a special messenger, the following letter to Dr. Farooq Abdullah:

> My dear Chief Minister,
>
> 13 MLAs of the Legislative Assembly of J&K (12 of the National Conference Party and one Independent) have approached me in person this morning. They told me, and have given in writing, that they have withdrawn their support to your Government and pledged their support to Ghulam Mohammad Shah, MLC. Simultaneously, Moulvi Iftikhar Hussain Ansari, MLA, and leader of the Congress(I) Legislature Party, J&K, has informed me in writing and in person that the Congress(I) Legislature Party, having a strength of 26 MLAs, has decided to support Ghulam Mohammad Shah. A copy each of the communications is enclosed.
>
> I am satisfied that you no longer enjoy the majority support of the Legislative Assembly and have, therefore, forfeited the right to continue as Chief Minister and to head the Government.
>
> In these circumstances, I advise you to submit your resignation as Chief Minister forthwith.
>
> With kind regards,
>
> Yours sincerely,
> (Sd.) Jagmohan
>
> P.S.: We have since met and discussed the matter. You advised me to impose Governor's Rule under section 92 of the J&K Constitution and keep the Legislative Assembly in suspended animation. I shall be grateful if you could kindly send me your confirmation in this regard in writing immediately.

The existence of this letter and two other crucial facts would show that Dr. Farooq Abdullah and his Council of Ministers had forfeited their right to give me any more advice. At 7 in the morning, at the time of demonstrating his majority, G.M. Shah and his supporters had demanded that I should not accept any advice that might be tendered by the Chief Minister in regard to the dissolution of the Assembly. In fact, the advice of the Chief Minister whose minority position stood proved not only on the basis of the physical presence of his opponents but also on the basis of the documents and who himself accepted the factual position in this regard, could not be considered *bona fide*. The question might have been different had Dr. Farooq Abdullah and his Council of Ministers approached me with a request in this respect a day earlier. Secondly, there was also the background of B.K. Nehru's letter of January 27, 1984, to which I will refer later in detail. In the concluding portion of this letter, B.K. Nehru had made it clear in these words: "I write to say that in these circumstances, if and when such a delegation were to come to me and I were convinced through the counting of heads–a procedure which I have hitherto stubbornly refused to follow–that you had lost your majority I would have no option but to dismiss your government as all proper constitutional process has now been unfairly pre-empted."

I once again got in touch with the Cabinet Secretary and the Home Secretary. Both of them informed me that my signal had been discussed with the Prime Minister and she had tentatively agreed to my request and called a special meeting of the Cabinet Sub-committee on Political Affairs and soon thereafter the President's approval would be obtained and sent to me. The Cabinet Secretary told me that this approval was likely to be made available to me by 1 p.m. Immediately thereafter I called G.M. Shah and D.D. Thakur who were sitting in the waiting hall in my office and told them that, in my opinion, the best available option was to impose Governor's Rule for the time being. Their faces fell. They said that it would not be fair, and went out for consultations.

The information conveyed to me by the Cabinet Secretary relieved me of my anxiety. With the help of the Chief Secretary, Mir Nasarullah, I set about drafting the press note to be issued after the imposition of Governor's Rule explaining the reasons for the same and appealing to the public to extend full cooperation to the new administration.

As there was delay on the part of the Chief Minister in sending to me the promised letter, I asked the Chief Secretary to go to his house and ascertain the position. After quite some time, the Chief Secretary returned with the letter which, to my surprise, was different from what had earlier been agreed to by the Chief Minister. I was sure that the Chief Minister had been guided, rather misguided, by some of his over-clever colleagues. The issue really was not one of constitutional nicety but of political judgement and clear thinking. It was G.M. Shah, and not Dr. Farooq Abdullah, who stood to lose most by the imposition of Governor's Rule. If his supporters had gathered merely for securing power, they would have fallen apart. I had no doubt that if

Dr. Farooq Abdullah had even a rudimentary knowledge of the J&K Constitution and applied his own mind, he would have come to the right decision and sent me the promised letter and thus spared me the unenviable task of dismissing him.

The letter which Dr. Farooq Abdullah sent through the Chief Secretary read:

Excellency,

I am in receipt of your letter D.O. No. GS-I (PAG) dated 2nd July 1984, as also its enclosures. I have considered the matter in depth in consultation with the colleagues of my Cabinet and wish to inform you that democratic traditions require that the question of loss of confidence should always be tested on the floor of the House. In fact, the letter addressed to Your Excellency by signatories makes reference to a letter shown to have been addressed to you on 28th June 1984, the contents whereof are not known to me. Anyway, I don't feel you are not in the know of the anti-defection law in the State which disqualifies a Member for violation of the Whip of the party. 12 signatories including 2 nominated members have lost their right of vote and as such all that they have written cannot be of any consequence. I would, on behalf of the Cabinet and myself, advise you to immediately summon the session of the Legislature so that confidence of the Legislature enjoyed by me is demonstrated.

In the latter part of the letter you have referred to discussion which you had with me early this morning that I advised you to impose Governor's Rule under section 92 of the Constitution. No doubt we discussed alternatives but all those options are available on my failure to show that I enjoy confidence of the Legislature which can be demonstrated on the floor of the House. I, therefore, reiterate that the Assembly be summoned forthwith so that on my failure to demonstrate confidence of the House we can next consider the options available to us under the Constitution of the State. If, however, you do not want to conform to this democratic method I, on behalf of my Cabinet, would request you to accept our advice of dissolving the Legislative Assembly so that we go back to our people.

With kind regards,

Yours sincerely,
(Sd.) Dr. Farooq Abdullah

Dr. Abdullah knew that I had made it clear to him in the morning that in the surcharged atmosphere I could not convene the Assembly, that the meeting of the Assembly could be held only after a few days of Governor's Rule when proper arrangements for the maintenance of law and order could be made and all possibilities of street fights and demonstrations eliminated.

A few important points in regard to this letter need to be noted. First, this letter came after I had asked for Dr. Farooq Abdullah's resignation and after he had enthusiastically concurred with my idea to impose Governor's Rule and leave other issues to be settled subsequently in a calmer atmosphere and in an administrative environment which would inspire confidence and entail no risk in regard to the breakdown of the administrative machinery.

Secondly, this letter admitted, by implication, that 12 MLAs of his party had gone against him and withdrawn their support to his Government. Therefore, the criticism that the head count in Raj Bhavan decided the issue is totally wrong. The documentary evidence coupled with his own statement that 12 MLAs had defected, left no question of the number to be decided by the Governor. It stood settled by the claim of one party–G.M. Shah–and by the admission of the other party–Dr. Farooq Abdullah. So far as the issue of disqualification of these 12 MLAs was concerned, the J&K High Court alone could declare them as disqualified in terms of the local law on the subject. Till the High Court had done so I had to treat them as qualified MLAs. Even otherwise it was quite clear from the provisions of the law that these MLAs had not incurred any disability. Incidentally, the J&K High Court later ruled that these MLAs were not defectors and the National Conference had split.

Thirdly, Dr. Farooq Abdullah evaded direct answer to his having agreed in the morning to the imposition of Governor's Rule. Instead, he made a vague reference to the matter and stated that this was one of the options discussed and asked for the summoning of the Assembly and that the other options available in the Constitution could be considered afterwards. In this connection, the question arises as to how he could demonstrate his majority when he was in minority at the moment. Did he want to win back the so-called defectors during the intervening period or would he use the office of the Speaker in not allowing the 12 MLAs to vote or adopt any such dubious means or in the meanwhile recommend certain MLAs to be made Ministers?

Fourthly, Dr. Farooq Abdullah should have also known that after he had been asked to resign, he had no valid right to demand dissolution of the Assembly. Nor would it have been appropriate for me to grant the same. Dissolution is always an exceptional remedy. A well-known constitutional expert, Sir John Marriot, rightly says, "Under no circumstances is the Cabinet entitled to demand dissolution of the Parliament from the Crown". Dr. Eugene A. Forsay, in his brilliant treatise, 'The Royal Power of Dissolution of Parliament' observes, "The enormous increase in the power of the Cabinet, and especially of the Prime Minister, raises the question whether the reserve power of the Crown to force or refuse dissolution may not be one of the few safeguards against dictatorship by 'the leader of the junta' wielding for the moment the power of the office. The British constitutional system was never intended to be a plebiscitary democracy, in which Parliament exists and debates only on sufferance, under threat of dissolution at any moment by the government in office. A system of that kind has certainly no right to the title of 'parliamentary government', and it may at least be questioned whether it has any right to be called democratic."

Letting down two Governors

Dr. Farooq Abdullah's inconsistency upset me. Here was a man to whom I was trying to extend justice in the most trying circumstances. And he was letting me down. On page 12 of his booklet, *My Dismissal,* Dr. Farooq Abdullah says: "On July 2, 1984, Delhi turned down the Governor's recommendations to impose Governor's Rule." Here is a clear acknowledgement of the fact that I was in favour of Governor's Rule. How can the Union Government and the Governor be in conspiracy if they were working at cross purposes and if the recommendations of the latter were turned down by the former? The real trouble lay in the fickle nature of Dr. Farooq Abdullah and the superficial hold he had on the administrative machinery and constitutional provisions. If Dr. Farooq Abdullah had stuck to his agreement with me I would have pressed the President/Union Government for the imposition of Governor's Rule and the Union Government would in all probability have agreed. I had to cut a sorry figure before the Union Government when the promised confirmation was not forthcoming from the Chief Minister and what was sent was contrary to what was earlier agreed. "Did we not tell you that he was thoroughly unreliable?" Dr. Farooq Abdullah's detractors at the

Union Government level asked. My basic objective in pressing for Governor's Rule was to first set the institutional framework right and then hand over the administration to the Chief Minister in majority.

I was not the only one who had been let down by Dr. Farooq Abdullah. He had done the same to B.K. Nehru also. After giving him solemn pledge to conduct the Assembly proceedings in a fair manner and by following the normal procedures, Dr. Farooq went back upon his promise. And this is what an angry B.K. Nehru wrote to him on January 27, 1984:

> As you are well aware, for several weeks past the possible defectors from among the National Conference MLAs have been suggesting to me that if and when 13 of them come to me in a body expressing their lack of confidence in you and your ministry, together with an assurance of support from the 26 members of the Congress Legislature Party in the Assembly I should forthwith dismiss your government and instal a new Chief Minister in whom the combination of the Congress Party and the defectors (who would then form the majority) have confidence.
>
> I have consistently told them that I would not do so because the proper place to display their want of confidence was on the floor of the Legislative Assembly. I said that I would, instead, ask you to advise me to summon the Assembly at short notice so that the motion of no confidence in you could be properly moved, properly debated and properly voted upon.
>
> They were hesitant to follow this course for two reasons. They were afraid, firstly, that in the interval between their coming to me and the vote in the House their houses would be burnt and their families attacked by the Police under your orders. They were afraid, secondly, that the Rules of the House would be so bent as to preclude a fair and free debate and vote from taking place. I recognised the validity of these fears on both counts but nevertheless felt that the maintenance of constitutional propriety was paramount and the risks should be taken.
>
> I learnt–not from you–that this morning as soon as the Assembly resumed its session after hearing the Governor's Address, when only certain routine business was slated to be transacted, you introduced a motion expressing the confidence of the House in yourself, that in breach of the normal rules the 7-day notice required for such a motion was waived and that an

immediate vote was insisted upon and taken without debate while the Congress Party was actually in process of leaving the House in protest. This motion of confidence was carried without dissent from among the members left in the House.

Under the rules a motion of no confidence is now barred from being moved in the Assembly while the present session lasts. I write to say that in these circumstances, if and when such a delegation were to come to me and I were convinced through counting of heads–a procedure which I have hitherto stubbornly refused to follow–that you had lost your majority I would have no option but to dismiss your government as all proper constitutional process has now been unfairly pre-empted.

This letter is very significant from another aspect also. It contains the Governor's clear indication that he had been left with no option but to decide the fate of Dr. Farooq Abdullah's Ministry through counting of heads. As I have discussed above, I mainly relied upon the documents of both the parties and exercised the option for the imposition of Governor's Rule. But had I proceeded solely on 'counting of heads in Raj Bhavan', I would have been fully justified on the basis of the above-quoted letter of my predecessor in office, B.K. Nehru.

To my surprise, I was informed by the Cabinet Secretary a little after 3 p.m. that the Cabinet Sub-Committee had decided not to convey the President's concurrence in terms of the provisions of Section 92 of the J&K Constitution. How this change from the morning thinking came about, I cannot definitely say. Maybe it was due to lack of proper appreciation of ground-level realities; maybe it was in consequence of pressure exerted by certain vested interests on the Union Government; maybe it was due to the annoyance of the Sub-Committee and the Prime Minister on the volte-face of Dr. Farooq Abdullah; maybe it was due to the combination of all these factors.

I was disappointed by the final outcome of my efforts. Constitutionally, I was left with no other option but to swear in G.M. Shah. I had already asked Dr. Farooq Abdullah to submit his resignation. Another factor that existed in the corner of my mind was that the Shah Government and the bureaucratic set-up of the time would not be hand-in-glove with each other and the stranglehold of the partisan administration would be loosened. In any case, so far as I was concerned, I was quite clear in my mind that if all the planks of decision-making were in my hands I would have imposed Governor's Rule on July 2, 1984.

As it was dangerous to have a power vacuum in the State, I called upon G.M. Shah to form the government. I obtained an assurance from him that he would convene the Assembly within one month. On the pale and tired faces of G.M. Shah and D.D. Thakur, I found a sudden glow of happiness. They were keen to get into the saddle immediately.

The swearing-in ceremony was scheduled to be held at 5.30 p.m. A crowd was soon collected by Shah and his supporters. They tried to demonstrate that they had popular backing and the people were happy over the departure of Dr. Farooq Abdullah. I immediately cautioned G.M. Shah and told him not to do anything which would provoke a counter-reaction. I also told him that he would have to deal with his political opponents with respect and courtesy and there should be absolutely no harassment to anyone, and every effort had to be made to bring about a congenial and peaceful atmosphere.

Proving Majority Twice

It would be incorrect to say that the Governor had given one month's time to G.M. Shah to prove his majority, as had been alleged by Dr. Farooq Abdullah. His majority already stood proved. All that I had asked him to do was to convene the Legislative Assembly within one month and seek a vote of confidence within that period; in other words, to prove his majority once again. I had made this absolutely clear in my letter of July 7, which was sent by me in reply to Dr. Farooq Abdullah's letter of the same date. Both these letters are reproduced below. Dr. Farooq Abdullah's letter read:

July 7, 1984

Dear Governor Sahib,

With greetings.

An announcement was made on 2nd July 1984 simultaneously with the swearing in of new leader of twelve defector-members of Legislative Assembly that Assembly session would be called to test the majority support of the leader of this defector group. It is 7th July 1984 today and no notice has been issued so far which apparently is bound to delay convening of the Legislative Assembly beyond one month. At this stage the defectors are engaged in further efforts to tamper with the basic loyalties of the captive group functioning as members of the

Council of Ministers and others who have refused to fall in line with their nefarious anti-people activities. You did not accept my advice to convene the Assembly immediately against all accepted norms of democratic behaviour and for reasons best known to you and instead placed newly called-in man under obligation to have confidence of the House verified within one month which solemn understanding he is not complying with.

The leaders of All-India Opposition too understandably have taken up this matter with you during their meeting in the interests of restoration of people's faith in organic law of our State and the country. I am told that you assured the All-India delegation that steps will be taken to have the Assembly convened within a reasonable time—outer limit having been fixed, *viz.*, 30 days from 2nd July 1984. I request you to have the commitment solemnly given fulfilled as soon as it can be.

With regards,

Yours sincerely,
(Sd.) Dr. Farooq Abdullah

My reply was:

My dear Dr. Abdullah

Thank you for your D.O. letter No. 11/NC/7/84/PP, dated the 7th July 1984, regarding summoning of the Legislative Assembly for confirming majority support to the Government led by Shri G.M. Shah on the floor of the House.

I would like to reassure you that Shri Shah was invited to form the Government subject to a written undertaking that he would again prove his majority on the floor of the House within one month from the date of assuming office.

I have passed on a copy of your letter to the Chief Minister for initiating action if he has not already done so.

With kind regards,

Yours sincerely,
(Sd.) Jagmohan

False Assumptions: Conspiracy of Silence

It should be clear that, apart from being politically motivated, the criticism of my decision was based upon inaccuracies and false assumptions. It is indeed amazing that during the extensive discussions in both the Houses of Parliament neither any Union Minister, including the Home Minister, nor any representative of the National Conference (Farooq) who knew that I had constitutionally moved for the imposition of Governor's Rule and requested the President, in accordance with the provisions of the J&K Constitution, to convey his concurrence, clearly mentioned this crucial fact. Is it morally and constitutionally defensible? Does it not raise a question of privilege? Is the Minister entitled to suppress material and vital fact?

I was hurt by this conspiracy of silence but could do nothing. My success in achieving the basic objective of preventing volcanic eruption in the State was my only solace at the moment. Fortunately, even amidst intentional slant and distortion, a section of the press was able to capture the essence of the situation. For example, the national daily *Patriot* of July 10, 1984, in its leading article titled "Why Kashmir did not go up in flames", said:

> At the very outset, it needs to be emphasised that Governor Jagmohan handled an extremely delicate situation on 2 July, with exceptional perspicacity, competence, sensitivity and farsightedness. From the moment the curtain went up, he was able to win the confidence of all sections and impress upon them that he was acting in fairness and impartiality. He refused to meet the thirteen supporters of G.M. Shah at midnight when they rang him up on 1 July. Next morning when they gave him a signed memorandum withdrawing their support to Dr. Abdullah, Jagmohan insisted that each one of them append his or her signature in his presence. Without losing a moment, he called Dr. Abdullah and gave him a photocopy of the letter submitted by these MLAs, informed the Chief Minister that he had lost the majority and told him that in the situation he had only two alternatives: either to invite G.M. Shah to form a ministry or impose Governor's Rule. Dr. Abdullah personally favoured the latter course, but, on second thoughts, wanted time to consult his colleagues. The Governor agreed, but at the same time, he sent a formal letter informing the Chief Minister that he had lost his majority and placed on record his proposal for Governor's Rule.
>
> Dr. Abdullah did not challenge that thirteen MLAs had withdrawn support, though he described them as defectors. Nor did he deny that Governor's Rule was suggested by him, but qualified that it was one of the options. It was clear that the advice given by a Chief Minister who has lost the support of the majority is not binding. Under the anti-defection law of J&K, only the High Court can declare a legislator as a defector.

While these consultations were in progress, Jagmohan took immediate administrative and political initiatives to prevent the situation from worsening. Additional forces were requisitioned and airlifted from Madhya Pradesh and Bihar. The local army commander flew to the airport in a helicopter to arrange for their deployment. There was an impressive show of strength in Srinagar, particularly in trouble-prone areas. Rounding up operations against pro-Khalistani and pro-Pakistani elements were set in motion. Anti-social elements were put behind bars and thus the sources of mischief were immobilised.

Simultaneously, the Governor called Maulvi Farooq to Raj Bhavan, informed him that Dr. Abdullah had lost his majority and expressed the hope that the Mirwaiz would cooperate in maintaining peace and communal harmony in the city. It is no secret that Maulvi Farooq's followers are present in considerable numbers in the trouble-prone areas and play a leading part in starting disturbances in Srinagar. This had its own effect.

The daily emphasised:

> The opposition leaders cannot afford to ignore the fact that the country will always give first priority to questions of national security, setting aside technicalities of constitutionalism.

The daily went on to say:

> Everyone who knows in detail the events since the beginning of this month is aware that but for Jagmohan's competent and perceptive handling of the situation during the critical phase, events could have taken a much more frightening turn. Even Dr. Farooq Abdullah has so far not said anything against the Governor because he knows fully the role that the Governor played. In private talks every section in J&K appreciates the manner in which the Governor has conducted himself. The opposition parties, however, can derive political mileage only if they make the Governor the focus of attack. But this is not a farsighted approach.

In a similar strain the magazine *Link*, in its issue dated July 15, 1984, pointed out:

> National security is the paramount issue in J&K. Governor Jagmohan, by all accounts, acted in a manner which prevented a serious breakdown of law and order in this sensitive border region.

> This is an achievement which deserves unreserved acclaim. The opposition parties, in their anger, understandable no doubt, should not overlook the value of Governor's role in J&K, a State in the Indian Union; but it is not just any other State.

The magazine noted:

> Of late, religious fundamentalism has been forged by imperialism as a major instrument of destabilisation of ancient societies. Forces of reaction and subversion have been conjuring up a scenario of convergence between Sikh and Muslim communalism with a view to cutting off Punjab and Kashmir from the rest of the country. The political task in J&K is to defeat this conspiracy and frustrate these plans.

Referring to my role, the *Link* observed:

> Governor Jagmohan combined mobilisation and display of force, as distinct from use of force, with fairness and reasonableness. He kept open lines of communication with all those who mattered. He brought into play the elements of statesmanship and deft psychological handling during the first 24 hours of the changeover, thereby creating conditions in which heat and passion of the moment were dissolved and a sober approach was taken by all sides. But a Governor, even if he is as dynamic, fair and farsighted as Jagmohan, cannot be a substitute for political process which will determine the future course of events.

Foul Intentions: The Role of the Speaker

That Dr. Farooq Abdullah and his supporters intended to play foul became still more clear from the role that the Speaker, Wali Mohammad Itoo, played. As required under the anti-defection law of the J&K State, the Speaker, on a complaint lodged by the National Conference Party, referred the case to the High Court to seek its decision on the status of the 12 MLAs in question. After hearing all the parties concerned, the Chief Justice, in his judgement of July 30, 1984, said: "I hold that the 12 MLAs have not incurred any disqualification within the meaning of Section 24-G of the Represen-tation of the Peoples Act. The reference is answered accordingly."

The court made it clear that whip, if any, has to be with regard to policy and not with regard to leadership. It ruled that a legislator could not be said to have "given up the membership" of the party by refusing to support the leadership of the party.

When the Chief Justice was pronouncing his judgement, the Speaker made a crude attempt, against the provisions of the law, to withdraw the reference. In this connection, the Chief Justice ruled that "the High Court was a court of record and no party could treat the matter pending before it as withdrawn at the party's sweet will".

The Speaker went further and crossed all limits of propriety. In utter disregard of the provisions of the J&K Constitution, the provisions of the anti-defection law and the verdict of the High Court, he himself passed an order disqualifying all the 12 MLAs and declaring their seats vacant.

Constitutionally and morally, what could be worse than this? The Speaker, knowingly and intentionally, and, in collusion with Dr. Farooq Abdullah, passed a wholly illegal order. He did not show even the slightest sensitivity to the fact that he had himself made the reference to the High Court. Such were the principles and norms practised by those who were shouting themselves hoarse about the democratic traditions and assailing my decision even when they knew it was as 'milk-pure' as it could be in the circumstances and nothing could be more appropriate–constitutionally, administratively and morally–than the imposition of Governor's Rule for a short period.

On July 31, at 10 a.m. the special session commenced as scheduled. I deputed my Secretary to watch the proceedings of the House. There were three items of business for the House: (i) motion of confidence in the Ministry headed by G.M. Shah; (ii) motion of no confidence against the Speaker, Wali Mohammad Itoo; and (iii) election of the Deputy Speaker. Since the business for the day included a no-confidence motion against the Speaker and his conduct on the previous day left nobody in any doubt about his intentions, the Leader of the House, Ali Mohammad Naik, Education Minister, requested the Speaker to take up the motion of no confidence against him in the first place or step down making way for a member of the panel of Chairmen to preside over the business. Since the Speaker refused to accede to the request, 43 members of the Assembly stood up in support of the Leader's motion and the Speaker was removed. Rangil Singh, a member of the panel of Chairmen, presided. Thirty-one members of the National Conference (Farooq), walked out of the House in protest against the removal of the Speaker.

The motion of no confidence against the Speaker was taken first and carried with forty-two members in favour and none against. The House then elected Mangat Ram Sharma as the new Speaker who presided over the remaining business of the House. The motion of confidence in the Ministry of G.M. Shah was carried unanimously. The House next elected Ghulam Din Malik, proposed by the Leader of the House, as Deputy Speaker. The new Speaker announced in the House that he had rescinded the order of his predecessor, issued on the previous day, disqualifying 12 MLAs of the House from being members of the J&K Legislative Assembly as, according to him, these orders were erroneous, violative of the Constitution and in defiance of the High Court decision on the reference made by the ex-Speaker himself.

Procedural technicalities and behavioural norms apart, the question as to who was in majority had once again been clearly answered. And the issue in regard to the disqualification or otherwise of the MLAs also stood settled by the verdict of the High Court. The very fact that the Speaker and Dr. Farooq's group was avoiding the trial of strength on the motion of no confidence against the Speaker showed that their group was in minority and was intending to misuse the office of the Speaker.

Sanctity of the Floor-Test

In regard to the sanctity of the floor-test, it may be relevant to invite attention to the Tamil Nadu case. On December 24, 1987, M.G. Ramachandran, Chief Minister, suddenly died. The Governor S.L. Khurana invited the next senior member of the Cabinet, V.R. Nedunchezhiyan, to assume the office of the Chief Minister. On January 2, supporters of Mrs. Janaki Ramachandran of the AIADMK approached the Governor and informed him that they had decided to support Janaki Ramachandran, instead of V.R. Nedunchezhiyan. The Governor invited Mrs. Janaki Ramachandran to hold the office of Chief Minister. He asked her to prove her majority in the House within three weeks. There was some confusion in regard to the Governor's requirement of majority. According to one version, he wanted Mrs. Janaki Ramachandran to prove absolute majority in the total membership of the House but later on changed the decision to imply majority of those present at the time of voting.

When it became clear on the day of voting that the Congress(I) Party would vote for the Jayalalitha faction of AIADMK, the supporters of Mrs. Janaki Ramachandran, in connivance with the Speaker, P.H. Pandian, evolved a strategy of declaring all their opponents as defectors.

The voting was fixed for January 28. The House met at 10 a.m. The Speaker, Pandian, straightway announced that he had received a telephonic call 10 minutes earlier intimating that five Congress(I) members were resigning from the Assembly. He adjourned the House till noon. When the House met at noon, the Speaker immediately declared that he had decided to disqualify six members, including the former Chief Minister, V.R. Nedunchezhiyan and his four Cabinet colleagues. He once again adjourned the House till 3 p.m.

In the intervening period the group favouring Mrs. Jayalalitha and the supporters of Congress(I), numbering 122 in total, met separately and elected their own Speaker, S. Sivaraman of Congress(I). In the 'Session' of the 'House' chaired by this Speaker, a 'no-confidence motion' against Mrs. Janaki Ramachandran's Government was passed.

When the House chaired by Pandian met, he cleared the House, with the help of the police, of all the opponents. However, a few MLAs managed to remain there. A vote was taken in these circumstances. Pandian declared that confidence had been expressed in favour of Mrs. Janaki Ramachandran. Before taking the vote, the Speaker disqualified the entire Jayalalitha faction under the anti-defection law. Earlier, in the first session, he had disqualified six members of this faction. Five Congress(I) members had resigned. Ten members of DMK had been disqualified in 1986 by Pandian for taking part in the anti-Hindi agitation. One seat was vacant on account of the death of a member. Thus, the Speaker made it possible for Mrs. Janaki Ramachandran to obtain a vote of confidence with 98 supporters in the House which had a total strength of 223.

It should be evident to what level 'floor test' can be taken. The basic structure of the Constitution and the dictates of justice require that the Governor should assess the real, and not manipulated, majority and he should not follow any rigid procedure but use his discretion, keeping in view the special circumstances prevailing at the time the constitutional crisis arises.

In the Andhra case, too, the Speaker played a wholly partisan role. On the last day of the 30-day limit set by the Governor for N. Bhaskara Rao to prove his majority in the Assembly, the Speaker adjourned the House abruptly on the childish plea that he was not feeling well. Soon thereafter, he sent his resignation. Evidently, his intention was to give more time to Bhaskara Rao.

Likewise, in the constitutional crisis of West Bengal in 1967, the role played by B.K. Banerjee, Speaker of West Bengal Assembly, was wholly untenable. He went to the extent of declaring that he did not recognise the new Government sworn in by the Governor. The Supreme Court had the occasion to comment upon the conduct of the Speaker. It said, "The Speaker had no right to declare a Ministry, appointed and duly sworn in by the Governor, as unconstitutional. By doing so, the Speaker had acted in a partisan manner and forfeited his right to be Speaker."

In view of these telling examples of grave improprieties and illegalities, could the Speaker be expected to act in a just and impartial manner when the fate of the party to which he himself belongs has to be decided? In fact, over the years, the Speaker's office has become highly politicised.

Where are Conventions?

In view of the correct position, as stated above, I hardly need to refute the criticism in regard to the alleged violation of traditions and conventions. But I wondered what traditions, what conventions, in the context of Indian decisions, were these critics talking about? Conventions of the Constitution, according to Dicey's classic definition, consist of "customs, practices, maxims, or precepts which are not enforced or recognised by the courts", but "make up a body not of laws but of constitutional or political ethics". Where are such conventions, so far as the decisions of the Governors are concerned?

If one analyses the decisions taken by the Governors since the enforcement of the Constitution, one would hardly find any pattern. Different Governors had taken different decisions, even with regard to the circumstances which were similar in nature. For instance, in 1952, the Rajpramukh of Travancore-Cochin dissolved the Assembly on the advice of the Chief Minister who had lost majority in the Assembly. But in similar circumstances dissolution was refused to Gurnam Singh in Punjab in 1967, to Charan Singh in Uttar Pradesh in 1968, to Raja Naresh Chandra Singh in Madhya Pradesh in 1969, to Sukh Dev in Orissa in 1971, and to Hitender Desai in Gujarat in 1971. Again, the Governors had not followed the same course in appointing Chief Ministers where there were different claimants for the post. While some had invited the leader of the largest party in the Assembly, the others had assessed the total following of the different claimants. For instance, in 1967, in West Bengal and Bihar, the Congress Party leader was not invited to form the Government even when the Congress Party was the largest single party in the Assembly. On the other hand, in Uttar Pradesh as well as in Rajasthan, the leader of the single largest party, which happened to be the Congress Party, was invited to form the Government. Further, in regard to the method of assessing the claims and counter-claims, different approaches were adopted by different Governors. Some had followed the list system, some had relied on the physical verification system, and some had combined the list and the physical verification systems. For instance, in Gujarat, in 1971, Shriman Narain followed the principle of list-cum-physical verification. In 1952, the Governor of Madras, Sri Prakasa, first nominated Rajagopalachari to the Upper House and then invited him to form the Government. In other words, he chose a person who was not a member of either of the two Houses and used his discretion in appointing him. Yet again, in regard to the prorogation of the Assembly, the Governor of J&K, Bhagwan Sahay prorogued in 1970 the Assembly on the advice of G.M. Sadiq, even when 35 out of 62 MLAs of the Congress Party in the J&K Assembly had withdrawn support from Sadiq in favour of Syed Mir Qasim. K.C. Reddy, Governor of Madhya Pradesh, did likewise. On the other hand, Dharam Vira, Governor of West Bengal, dismissed the Ajoy Mukhejee Ministry on the grounds that it did not follow the Governor's advice to summon the Assembly immediately. Thus, while the Governor of J&K and the Governor of Madhya Pradesh did not follow the principle of putting the Executive and the Legislature together, the Governor of West Bengal proceeded against the Ministry on the grounds that it did not agree to the Executive and the Legislature coming together.

I am not saying whether Governor 'A' or Governor 'B' followed the correct course. The point I am trying to drive home is that different Governors have taken different decisions, and no tradition or convention worth the name has been established.

In the case which I was called upon to decide, the Chief Minister, Dr. Farooq Abdullah, asked for dissolution only after I had called upon him to resign and the irrefutable documentary evidence, which he himself did not contest, showed him in clear minority. My decision not to dissolve the Assembly was, therefore, much more justified than in the case of the Governor who had refused to dissolve the House despite the fact that the Chief Minister concerned had recommended dissolution even before he was asked to resign. In this connection, it may be pointed out that when the Governor of Punjab dissolved the Assembly on the recommendation of Prakash Singh Badal, when his majority had become doubtful on account of the defections in the Akali Dal, his decision was strongly criticised and it was alleged that the Governor was in league with the Sant Akali Dal.

Discretion

The basic question is whether, in such contentious circumstances, the Governor has any discretion. It is crystal clear that he has. If he uses the discretion in a particular manner, he may open himself to criticism by the parties or groups who stand to suffer because of the decision, but the decision itself cannot be called illegal or unconstitutional. The correct approach to assess the worth of the Governor's decision is to evaluate it in the totality of the circumstances, including the political and administrative environment in which he is called upon to exercise his discretion. To make him act in a particular manner in all circumstances would be totally unrealistic and dangerous. The position would be much worse than the position obtaining now in which a slight aberration may creep in here and there. No Governor can really keep the Chief Minister going who has not the majority in the Assembly. In the case of Andhra Pradesh, the majority was with N.T. Rama Rao and no matter what the Governor, Ram Lal, did, the position became quite clear within a few days. On the other hand, the majority in J&K was not with Dr. Farooq Abdullah and he and his colleagues could make a lot of noise but could not prove majority on any of the occasions that came their way from July 1984 to November 1986 when the Shah Ministry was dismissed by me.

The Constitution makes it nowhere obligatory to have the trial of strength of the different claimants only on the floor of the House. In the well-known Nigerian case, the Privy Council stated the correct position with unmatched straightforwardness. In this case, the Governor of the western region of Nigeria, on the receipt of a letter signed by 66 members of the Assembly, which had a total strength of 124 members, saying that they did not support the Prime Minister, removed him from office and appointed another in his place. No vote was taken on the floor of the House.

The case came before the Privy Council which observed:

> It appears somewhat unreal to draw a firm dividing line between votes and other demonstrations where the issue of support is concerned. The difficulty in limiting the statutory power of the Governor in this way was that the limitation was not to be found in the words in which the makers of the Constitution decided to record their description of his powers. There would have been no difficulty at all in so limiting him if it had been intended to do so. The ultimate decision was that there was nothing which legally precluded the Governor from forming his opinion on the basis of anything but votes formally given on the floor of the House.

In a similar strain, the Calcutta High Court ruled:* "The exercise of the pleasure of the Governor is a matter entirely in the discretion of the Governor. This right of the Governor is absolute and unrestricted. It is not fettered by any condition or restriction."

If the Governors were to be made to act in a particular manner on all occasions, what difficulty was there in making a provision to this effect in the Constitution? At the time of framing of the Constitution, there was a proposal to issue an Instrument of Instructions to the Governor. This proposal was, however, given up, primarily because it was felt that it would be unwise to make a rigid provision and the Governor should be allowed to exercise his judgement and discretion on the merits of the case.

In the case of the privileges of the Members of Parliament, it was specifically provided in the Constitution that they would have the same privileges as were available by conventions to the Members of the House of Commons in Britain. Similar provisions could have been made in the Constitution to say that the Governor would act in the same manner and in accordance with the same conventions as are prevalent in Britain and he would function on lines similar to those of the Crown vis-a-vis the Ministers and the Chief Minister. But even this was not done. The truth of the matter is that the framers of the Constitution had misgivings about the nature of our democracy. Dr. Ambedkar had observed that our democracy was only a top-dressing on a soil which was essentially undemocratic. He was, therefore, not inclined to trust the Legislature wholly.

*AIR 1969: 198: M.P. Sharma versus P.C. Ghose and others.

About the discretion of the Governor, the Sarkaria Commission recorded the present position as under:

> Whatever might have been the views of the framers of the Constitution, it would appear from a plain reading of Article 163 that clauses (1) and (2) of the Article confer on the Governor the general power to exercise discretion in respect of any of the functions entrusted to him by the Constitution. The expression 'by or under the Constitution' in clause (1) can be taken as covering all situations in which the power to exercise discretion is either expressly mentioned or necessarily implied in the relevant Articles. Further, a decision of the Governor to act in his discretion in a particular situation is protected from being questioned by any court or other authority by clause (2).

The observations made by a well known Constitution expert, Seervi, are also relevant. He says, "After the Supreme Court's decision in Shamsher Singh's case (A.I.R. 1974 S.C. 2192)–the proposition that the Governor is required to act in his discretion only by express provisions is no longer good law, for, both the judgements (of A.N. Ray, C.J., and Krishna Iyer, J.). In that case held that in some cases the Governor had power to act in his discretion as a matter of necessary implication."

In an article,* Justice (Rtd.) A.K. Das of Calcutta High Court, commenting upon my decision, observed: "In this particular case, the Governor has applied the 'pleasure doctrine', not arbitrarily but most judiciously and after confronting Dr. Farooq Abdullah with the evidence against him–the evidence which he never controverted. Recommendations of the Chief Minister who has lost majority has no validity. The action of the Kashmir Governor is neither illegal nor unconstitutional and the row created over the dismissal is uncalled for."

The then Minister of Home Affairs, P.V. Narasimha Rao, defending my decision in the Lok Sabha, said:

> The two developments, namely, losing majority and ineffectiveness in checking anti-national forces were not mutually exclusive. As regards the legal and constitutional side of propriety, it might be recalled that even during the debates in the Constituent Assembly,

*The *Amrita Bazar Patrika,* July 12, 1984.

it had been very clearly laid down that the term 'during pleasure' was always understood to mean that the pleasure would not continue notwithstanding the fact that the Ministry had lost the confidence of the majority, and the moment the Ministry had lost the confidence of the majority, it was presumed that the Governor would exercise his pleasure in dismissing the Ministry. We had any number of cases where Governors had exercised their discretion. There was not a single case in this country where the majority of a Chief Minister had been actually, in point of fact, tested on the floor of the House. If the present Governor of J&K, like many other Governors in India, had explored the possibility of another democratic alternative and found it viable, it was not wrong.

Regrettably, Narasimha Rao did not add that I had constitutionally moved for the imposition of Governor's Rule.

Here, it may be relevant to invite attention to what President Sanjiva Reddy did in July 1979. He called for the lists of supporters of Charan Singh and Moraji Desai. He acted on these lists and not on any floor test. He did not even ask for individual declarations in writing from members whose names were found in both the lists. He refused to give extension of little time to Morarji Desai and invited Charan Singh to form the Government on the basis of the lists of doubtful validity, drawn by bosses of various caucuses. He knew full well that Charan Singh's supporters comprised ten heterogeneous groups and a few individuals who had no common programme or policy. He ignored the fact that Morarji Desai had a backing of 219 members which constituted a single solid block with a common programme and policy.

As was expected, Charan Singh could not face the Parliament. Reddy accepted the advice of the Prime Minister who had really no majority support at any point of time. Against his own precedent of inviting the leader of the Opposition, Y.B. Chavan, he did not give an opportunity to Jagjivan Ram to form a government. He arbitrarily rejected his plea that "the views of leaders of some of the parties do not reflect those of a significant number of their followers".*

Notwithstanding what President Sanjiva Reddy did, he, in his retirement, chose to criticise my procedure which took into account solid evidence which was not contested by any of the parties involved. In my case, moreover, the compulsions of security environment also

*Jagjivan Ram's letter of August 21, 1979.

existed; the continuance of Dr. Farooq Abdullah and his 'hijacked services and police' would not have allowed a free and fair test. No such compulsion had to be taken into account by Sanjiva Reddy. It is unfortunate that even the top leaders of our country show little hesitation in taking self-contradictory stands. Nor did Sanjiva Reddy care to ascertain the correct facts before making comments. He did not know that, so far as I was concerned, I had moved for the imposition of Governor's Rule and not for the installation of the G.M. Shah Ministry.

"In the provinces you are going to have democracy from toe to neck and autocracy at the head. I would have cited how the Governor who was an agent of British Imperialism has all along been attempting to smash my party. What was being done by the Governor under British Imperialism may also be repeated...." Thus spoke Bishwanath Das in the Constituent Assembly, when the provisions in regard to the role and functions of the Governor, were being discussed.

The apprehensions voiced by Bishwanath Das did not take into account the fact that the Governor during the British regime was inclined to safeguard the imperial interests of the empire, whereas after Independence, the Governor had to safeguard the integrity of the Union. Without Governors and their disposition to safeguard the interests of the Union, the country would run the risk of being torn apart. The Founding Fathers of the Constitution were conscious of the need to provide safeguards against fissiparous tendencies to which India has always been prone.

The Governor is the "linchpin of the constitutional apparatus of the state".* His position needs to be strengthened and his office and image improved. A conscientious and active Governor can play an extremely useful role in correcting the aberrations of egocentric democracy, in improving the norms of public behaviour and raising the general moral temper and tone of the society. I would illustrate my point by giving two examples.

On January 21, 1985, G.M. Shah's Cabinet decided to confer proprietary rights to the lessees of the State land at half the market value and also to regularise all unauthorised occupation of 'nazool lands'. The two issues were really separate but were intentionally mixed to diffuse the issues. A sketchy and ambiguous agenda note was prepared. The attempt was to camouflage the real intention of

*Sarkaria Commission Report.

benefiting the rich and influential lessees, including a number of ministers and senior civil servants.

The case came to my notice in the second week of February 1985. I wrote to the Chief Minister on February 13. In my letter, I, *inter alia*, said:

> I am writing to invite attention to the Cabinet decision No. 67 of January 21, 1985. The subject of the item has been listed as under:
>
> 'Transfer of leases on proprietary basis–Conferment of proprietary rights on unauthorised occupants of 'nazool land.'
>
> This item really relates to two separate issues, one regarding conferment of proprietary rights and the other relating to regularisation of unauthorised occupation of 'nazool' land.
>
> So far as the first issue is concerned, it is not clear why principles of town planning and rationale of lease system are being ignored, and why proprietary rights are being conferred by charging only 50% of the market value of the land. There seems to be no justification for doing so, particularly when the lessee, after acquiring the assets at half the market value, would be able to sell the same at full market value and thus earn huge profits. The larger the property, the greater the benefit. In other words, the richer the man, the more rich he would become.
>
> In the absence* of Urban Land Ceiling Act, Capital Gains Tax, Wealth Tax, Gift Tax and such other taxes, which are leviable in other parts of India but not in Kashmir, the decision in question would mean a big, and wholly unmerited, bonanza to the richer classes, and would lead to speculative transactions in lands.
>
> It is also not clear as to what will be the principle or criteria for determining land values. Usually such matters are decided in quasi-judicial manner on clearly stipulated regulations. But in this case, the final decision has been left to the Revenue Minister.
>
> The second issue relates to the unauthorised occupation of 'nazool lands', the decision would be disastrous from the point of view of future planning and preservation of environment. Is it true that large parts of land along the Dal Lake are in unauthorised occupation and some large tracts of agricultural land are in possession of a few other influential persons?

*See also Chapter VI: 'Roots: Article 370'.

> It is obvious that the case has large financial implications. It involves huge land assets of the State, and would benefit at State expense a large number of rich and influential persons.
>
> In view of the aforesaid considerations, I would suggest that the entire matter should be reconsidered and examined in greater depth and, till then, implementation of the decision should be held over.
>
> If, even after reconsideration or otherwise, the State Government wishes to adhere to the decision already taken, necessary note along with the relevant file/files may be sent to me for perusal.

This letter shook the Chief Minister and the Ministers. It also jolted the senior civil servants who had prepared an inadequate agenda note. They realised that someone was looking into the matter in depth and had seen through the game. They procrastinated for some time. But I continued to insist. The clique soon thought discretion was the better part of valour. The case was shelved and finally dropped.

In the period following the Lok Sabha elections in 1984, G.M. Shah's Cabinet virtually went on a 'looting spree'. It became reckless in transferring* senior officers and appointing undeserving persons in key positions. One such case pertained to the appointment of the Chairman of the Jammu and Kashmir Bank. A person of doubtful integrity against whom three vigilance cases were pending, and who was known for advancing business interests of the ruling caucus was proposed to be appointed. I wrote to the Finance Minister and the Governor, Reserve Bank. I indicated:

> The State Government have decided to appoint a person as Chairman of the Jammu and Kashmir Bank against whom three vigilance cases stand registered.
>
> The move is actuated by considerations other than merit. When I asked the State Government for a report, a sketchy and somewhat misleading information was sent to me. Simultaneously, the officers of the Vigilance Department were pressurised to clear the case immediately.
>
> The charges against the proposed appointee are serious. My own inquiries not only confirm these allegations against him but also reveal much greater depth of corruption.

*See Chapter V: 'Roots: Hidden Veins' (Section: Administrative Roots).

There are such strong vested interests that my advice at local level is not going to be heeded. I am, therefore, bringing these facts to your notice for taking such action as you may consider necessary. I might suggest that the Central Government should advise the Reserve Bank of India to ensure that an entirely independent and honest person, preferably from outside, is appointed as Chairman of the J&K Bank—at least till such time as thorough inspection is carried out by the Reserve Bank.

By taking a subtle initiative in the matter, I was able to prevent the appointment and consequent damage.

There were a number of other cases in which I sent notes and letters to the Chief Minister. Since the Cabinet had no real answer to the questions raised by me in these cases, it became jittery. The Chief Minister and the Deputy Chief Minister complained to Rajiv Gandhi whom I sent the following letter:

> I am merely asserting my right to know, right to obtain reports, which has been given to the Governor under Article 44 of the J&K Constitution and the Rules of Business (extracts enclosed).
>
> I have no doubt that if this right had been previously asserted, the late Sheikh Abdullah and his family would not have been in possession of huge assets. Nor would have 'pro-autonomy' forces built such strong levers of power in business and bureaucracy.
>
> I have taken pains to study every aspect of Kashmir situation since 1947. One of our major problems has been our inability to stand firm, at the right moment, against the browbeating and bullying tactics.

What I am trying to drive at is that the Governor should not be a mere sage in contemplation, occasionally fluttering his old and ineffectual wings in the void, but a sage in action, whenever the occasion demands, whenever the evil crosses certain limits. I am not arguing for interference in day-to-day matters of administration or in cases where two views on honest and *bona fide* considerations could be taken. But the Governor must intervene, and intervene effectively, when the cliques and coteries combine or where the minister and the legislatures act in a self-serving manner as in the case of allotment of plots, the particulars of which have been given in Chapter XII. The interests of the common man and the State must be safeguarded.

Real Culprit

The problems arise not because the Governor has a sizeable area of discretionary powers but because the political elements that have come to power at the Centre from time to time have not been able to rise above petty considerations. If the intentions of the political elements are *bona fide*, there should be no difficulty in following the principle which T.T. Krishnamachari indicated while speaking in the Constituent Assembly. He said, "I would at once disclaim all ideas that we in this House want the future Governor who is to be nominated by the President to be in any sense an agent of the Central Government. I would like that point to be made very clear, because such an idea finds no place in the scheme of Governor we envisage for the future." Again, if political parties are really sincere in setting at rest all controversies with regard to appointment, tenure, removal and role and functions of the Governor, why do not they get together and accept in toto what the Sarkaria Commission has recommended on the subject? What, after all, is the use of setting up such Commissions and then to allow their recommendations to remain on the shelf? Today no constitutional office is so insecure as that of a Governor. It is only he who can be transferred or fired at the whims of the Union Government. His tenure has been reduced to that of a work charged employee, if not a daily wager.

What the Chandra Shekhar Government did in dismissing the Tamil Nadu Government, without even bothering about the Governor's report, shows the extent of constitutional improprieties to which the Union Government could resort and get away with it.

The real culprit is the unprincipled politics. In the recent times, no political party in power at the Centre has shown any sensitivity to constitutional morality.

The leaders, who later joined hands in 1977 under the banner of Janata Party, used to criticise Mrs. Indira Gandhi for misusing the office of the Governor. But when the Janata Party came to power, it appointed Governors on partisan considerations. Some of them got the office merely as rewards. They were clearly unsuitable for the assignment. I remember that, when I became Lt.-Governor of Delhi on February 17, 1980, and got the opportunity to attend my first Governors' Conference, I found that quite a few Governors were hard of hearing and unable to get up from their seats without the assistance of their ADCs. So old and decrepit had they become.

The National Front Government of V.P. Singh, which came to power at the end of 1989, outdid all previous Governments. It changed the Governor *en masse*. It made a mockery of the term 'five years' mentioned in the Constitution itself. The very fact that 'pleasure of the President' was withdrawn in almost all the cases simultaneously showed that it was done on political considerations and not on considerations of individual merit. The decision virtually changed the position of the Governor from an independent constitutional entity to that of an employee of the Central Government who could be removed even without a show cause notice–a right which even the pettiest of the officials enjoy. When the Chandra Shekhar Government came to the scene it showed equal insensitivity to the spirit of the Constitution. It sent signals to the Governors in no uncertain terms: "Either toe our line or quit."

Unfortunately, no President has shown constitutional courage to protect the office of the Governor and the independence, dignity and honour of the incumbent. No one has threatened to resign if the ruling party persisted with its course of making the Governor as its political agent rather than an agent of the Constitution. In my case, even this much suggestion or advice was not given by the President to the Prime Minister or the Home Minister that the Government should at least tell Parliament that the Governor wanted Governor's rule to be imposed, and it was the Union Government which had not accorded its concurrence to the issue of declaration for which the Governor had constitutionally moved the President in terms of Section 92 of the J&K Constitution.

The President of India has forgotten that he is not only the head of the State which has a system of responsible parliamentary government but also the apex of the federal structure; that he is elected by an electoral college comprising MPs and MLAs; and that there is a constitutional provision for the impeachment which has no relevance if he has always to act as a cipher. If the President refuses to sign on the dotted lines in cases where he thinks that the Governor is sought to be transferred or removed or asked to resign before his term of five years, by the Union Government in a State ruled by a different party, and if he threatens to resign or otherwise takes the nation into confidence, no Prime Minister would trifle with the office of the Governor, and the dignity and stature of both the institutions–the Governor and the President–would go up.

The truth is that there is a national “malady that afflicts us all”. As Dr. Ambedkar observed at the time of the adoption of the Constitution: “However good a Constitution may be, it is sure to turn out bad because those who are called to work it happen to be a bad lot.”

CHAPTER VIII

Conditions Before My Arrival

Things fall apart, the centre cannot hold
Mere anarchy is loosed upon the world
The blood dimmed tide is loosed, and everywhere
The ceremony of innocence is drowned;
The best lack all convictions, while the worst
Are full of passionate intensity.

–W.B. Yeats

Some political elements have been trying to propagate the view that conditions during National Conference-Congress(I) coalition Government were not so bad as they became subsequently. This view is misleading as well as superficial. It ignores facts. It forgets the origin, the roots. It places symptoms above the fundamental malady. Before the imposition of Governor's Rule on January 19, 1990, there was a total mental surrender, and dense clouds of chaos and collapse had completely covered the Valley.

A force, an administration, that surrenders neither causes nor takes casualties. It betrays the country by an attitude of surrender. The nation would have woken up to the grim and tragic consequences of this attitude if the Kashmir administration had remained in the hands of Dr. Farooq Abdullah till January 26* instead of January 19, 1990.

For the conditions prevailing up to July 12, 1989, when I relinquished charge of my first term, I have given my assessment in Chapter III

*See Chapter I: 'My Frozen Turbulence'.

on 'Warning Signals'. In this chapter, I would confine myself mainly to the events between the period July 1989 to January 19, 1990.

Terrorism Comes with a Bang

On October 27, 1988 a Maruti van was parked at Lal Chowk. There was an explosion in it. A bomb had apparently been planted in the van shortly after it was parked. The van was destroyed. Eleven passers-by including a young Muslim woman advocate, were seriously injured. The poor lady lost her foot.

Terrorism had struck. It was going to be a ruthless venture. It did not matter if an innocent Muslim woman was badly injured in the process. An acute scare had to be caused. I had, as indicated in the earlier chapter, warned that 'today might be timely; tomorrow would be too late'. And that tomorrow had, unfortunately, arrived with a bang. More explosions, more acts of terrorist violence, were to follow with increasing rapidity and ferocity.

At about 7 a.m., on July 13, 1989 a bus of CRP came, as usual, to pick up the jawans who had finished the duty for the day. As they were boarding the bus, a volley of bullets was showered on it. The firing was calculated and determined. It came from the neighbouring houses as well as the roadside. The bus hurriedly drove away, returning the fire at the same time. In the ensuing panic and confusion, some attackers melted in the crowd and some disappeared in the adjoining narrow lanes and by-lanes. Two CRP jawans died. Ten were seriously injured. Four innocent passers-by also lost their lives.

Almost all the characteristics of contemporary terrorism could be seen in the attack. Elements of surprise, swiftness, careful planning, and mingling with and melting in the crowd were all there. Attempts to frighten and overawe the public and secure extensive publicity in the national and international media were also obvious. The basic pattern had been set. And it was to be repeated in varying forms and shapes.

On July 17, the Jammu and Kashmir Liberation Front made a formal announcement, claiming responsibility for the attack on CRP. It declared: "Such attacks would go on till the Indian tyranny and imperialism are ended." After a few days, another terrorist organisation–Hizbullah Islamia Jamhoria–made a similar announcement. It also gave a stern warning to the 'traitors' and said that they would be given exemplary punishment.

On July 20, there was a bomb explosion in the ladies toilet of Khayam Cinema. The incident showed that some women, too, had been roped in the terrorists' organisations. On July 29, acid was thrown on two young Muslim ladies who were moving about without 'burqa'. It was intended to serve as a warning to those who did not pay heed to the 'instructions' issued by some of the fundamentalists' groups to the women to observe strict 'purdah'.

In the month of August, incidents of violence, intimidation, subversion and terrorism continued with alarming frequency. Pakistan's Independence Day, August 14, was celebrated with gusto and gaiety. On August 15, 'hartal' was observed on the call of various subversive and terrorist groups. Even the shops owned by Ministers and their relations were closed. Tricolours were burnt. Black flags were hoisted over private houses and even on some public buildings. Traffic was not allowed to ply. Bomb blasts left almost 60 persons injured on this day. Earlier, letters had been sent to the parents of the school-going children, warning them of dire consequences if they allowed their children to participate in the Independence Day parade or any other function connected with the Independence Day celebrations. At night, the street lights were switched off. Even the Secretariat building was engulfed in darkness.

On August 17, a State Government bus was hijacked near Tangmarg at the point of a pistol and blown up after ordering the passengers to alight. More than 50 persons were injured in the violent incidents on August 18, and on August 21, Mohammad Yusaf Halwai, a leader of the National Conference, was shot dead in the heart of Srinagar downtown near Safakadal. Earlier, the terrorists exploded bombs in the house of Shafi Qureshi, President of the Provincial Congress(I) Committee. This was the comment which Shafi Qureshi himself made to the press on August 18. "It was for the first time that the secessionists had become so bold as to organise Pakistan independence day celebrations under the very nose of the Government. A march past was held at the Government stadium and even 21 rounds were fired, symbolising the 21-gun salute. The police did nothing to stop this anti-national act. My own house was badly damaged when a bomb exploded in the garage. My Maruti van was damaged beyond repair." Ironically, it were persons like Qureshi who started criticising me when I initiated firm action against those who were taking 21-gun salute, exploding bombs, burning tricolours, and killing innocent people in broad daylight.

The National Conference-Congress(I) Government of Dr. Farooq Abdullah seemed to have been struck with paralysis. Its unconcern and incompetence were appalling. And so was the indifference and ineffectiveness of the two main political parties. There was no one to allay the fears of the people, no one to mobilise public opinion, no one to throw a counter-challenge. Verbal harangue was the only weapon that the leaders of these parties possessed. And that, too, had lost its effect due to over-use.

Sheikh Abdullah's death anniversary fell on September 8, 1989. The National Conference leadership contented itself by holding a meeting at the heavily guarded mausoleum of the Sheikh. The subversives had given a call for observing this day as a deliverance day, 'yome-e-nijat'. This call was responded to. A near total 'hartal' was observed in Srinagar, Anantnag, Baramulla and other towns of the Valley. There was not much traffic on the roads. Effigies of the Sheikh were burnt. At night, about 90 per cent of the houses did not put on the lights. A virtual blackout was observed.

Could anyone believe that it was the same Sheikh Abdullah on whose death seven years ago, a veritable sea of humanity, with 'sanye shero'—our lion—on its lips, had come out in the streets of Srinagar, and at the time of whose funeral two days later every window, every roof-top and every lodge was occupied? Was it not clear that either, his greatness was made of artificial material and had a mere coating of gold, or those who stepped into his shoes were made of such impure and slushy clay that their acts of commission sucked his greatness even out of the grave?

In none of the other cities, any activity on the part of the National Conference workers or leaders was seen. So ineffective had the organisation become. It could not, rather would not, assert itself even for a person whom it was never tired of calling 'Sher-e-Kashmir' and 'Baba-e-Quam' (father of the nation). It left the avenues of Kashmir free for the subversives to march on.

On September 14, Tikka Lal Taploo, 58-year-old Kashmiri Pandit and an advocate of High Court and also the Vice President of the J&K unit of the Bharatiya Janata Party, was coming out of his house in Chinkara Mohalla, Srinagar. Two young men, wearing helmets, appeared before him. One of them greeted him, presumably to confirm his identity. The other suddenly pulled out a Kalashnikov and pumped in five bullets from close range into the abdomen of Taploo. He lay motionless in a pool of blood. Half a dozen other bullets, which sailed past his body and got embedded in the nearby wall, spoke of the ruthlessness of the attack and the cool confidence with which it was carried out. Fear of authority did not exist at all. The assailants walked away in broad daylight.

A signal had been hoisted for the Kashmiri Pandit community. It was at the mercy of the subversives. They could kill any member of the community any time. If a Pandit was not safe in the heart of Srinagar city and that, too, in a locality inhabited by a large number of Pandits, how could anyone of them be safe in the isolated pockets of the far-flung and scattered villages. Fear began to haunt them.

To other nationalists also the message was loud and clear. As the JKLF put it in its press statement after the assassination, "We will kill all those who say that Jammu and Kashmir's accession to India is irrevocable; we shall continue our armed struggle." Tikka Lal Taploo was a dedicated social worker and a patriot to the marrow of his bones.

Ajaz Dar's* 'martyrdom' day was observed on September 18, his first death anniversary. Dar was a young man who was killed in a scuffle with security men outside the house of Srinagar DIG, Ali Mohammad Watali, on the night of September 18, 1988. Dar and three of his companions had gone to the DIG's house with weapons to assassinate Watali who was considered as an active symbol of the State authority. Ironically, about two years later, four top leaders of JKLF were arrested from the house of Watali's brother.

Posters, eulogising Dar's supreme sacrifice, were circulated and pasted on a large scale. Poems were composed in his honour. Prayers were said in mosques. Markets, schools and colleges remained closed. The propaganda machinery of the subversives worked furiously. But the State apparatus hardly stirred. Posters were not removed, and no counter-move worth the name was made. Consequently, public emotions were aroused. And a halo of martyrdom was successfully woven around Ajaz Dar.

The day witnessed a number of violent incidents. At Nawa Kadal, two Chinese-made hand-grenades were hurled at a police party, injuring 16 persons, including 10 policemen. The Deputy Inspector General, CRP, N.K. Tiwari, was attacked by a two-hundred-strong mob at Basant Bagh, when he was proceeding to the site of the incident at Nawa Kadal. He had to fire in the air to scare the mob away. Near the Idgah, a police patrol car was also fired upon.

---

*See Chapter III: 'Warning Signals'.

At Safa-Kadal, the J&K Bank was attacked and damaged. Indiscriminate firing was resorted to by twelve subversives as Ali-Kadal locality. Kalashnikov rifles were also flaunted.

Over 50 persons were injured in the violence. With the State machinery not planning any strategy in advance, the subversives did what they wanted to do. They secured a big psychological advantage. And militancy made deeper inroads in Kashmir.

The President of the People's League, Shabir Ahmed Shah, was arrested on the night of September 27-28 near Ramban, on the Srinagar-Jammu highway. The trap for the arrest was laid by the Intelligence Bureau. It was a neat operation. But, for some unaccountable reasons, Shabir Shah was not taken to Jammu for detention but brought back to Srinagar, under the instructions of Director General of Police, Ghulam Jilani Pandit. This was a signal for trouble in the Valley. Large-scale disturbances occurred in the Valley, exposing again wide chinks in the armoury of the State machinery. For four days, there was complete 'hartal' in Srinagar and other major towns. Five persons died in firing. A number of public buildings were set on fire. These included the Sopore Handicraft Centre, the Baramulla Sheep Husbandry Office, a boys' school at Tahab in Pulwama District, a girl's school at Ratnipora, and a wooden bridge near Pahalgam. A Chinese-made hand-grenade was also hurled at Lal Chowk, causing all-round panic.

The ruling alliance did not make even a symbolic move to mobilise their followers and break the strike. Its irrelevance became all the more pronounced.

Administratively, the position turned out to be still more disconcerting. The Deputy Commissioner of Srinagar, Pardesi, flatly refused to sign the warrant of detention of Shabir Ahmed Shah. The Deputy Commissioner of Anantnag also adopted the same attitude. The Advocate-General did not appear before the Court to represent the State. He tried to pass on the responsibility to the Additional Advocate-General and the Government counsel. They, too, did not appear. All this gave further fillip to the subversive movement. A large number of paid advertisements started appearing in the local newspapers, announcing dissociation with the National Conference and the Congress(I). If important functionaries of the State were terror-stricken or otherwise unwilling to discharge their elementary duties, and with the higher State and Central authorities all the time looking the other way, the fear amongst the rank and file of the political workers at the grassroots level was natural.

The month of October 1989 was equally troublesome. Violent incidents continued. There were about 50 bomb explosions, causing injuries to 39 persons, and scores of cases of arson. There were fifteen incidents of firing by the terrorists in which three persons were killed and a dozen injured.

Shabir Ahmed, Sub-Inspector of Police, did some useful work in containing terrorism in his area in District Kupwara. He was rewarded by way of out-of-turn promotion. On the night of October 2, three terrorists came to village Wagoora, where Shabir Ahmed's brother, Bashir Ahmed Hakim, lived. Through the ventilator of Hakim's house, they fired indiscriminately with Kalashnikov, killing Ahmed's wife and 10-year-old daughter. It was a murder most brutal, most foul. Even the child was not spared. Neither the mother nor the daughter had anything to do with the duties and obligations of the Sub-Inspector. But the terrorists would not entertain any such consideration. Their objective was to terrorise. And in this they succeeded.

On October 5, a powerful hand-grenade was thrown in the main bazaar, injuring 17 persons, including five policemen. An attempt was also made to assassinate Assistant Sub-Inspector of Chattabal Police Station.

As brought out in Chapter II on 'The Survey of History', October 27 has great significance in the history of Kashmir. It was on this day in 1947 that the first batch of Indian troops, under the command of Lieutenant Colonel D.R. Rai, landed at Srinagar.* At that time, the raiders were within a few hours' march to the Capital. Colonel Rai decided to engage them at Baramulla. Heavily outnumbered, he died fighting valiantly on its outskirts. In another heroic deed, Major Somnath Sharma laid down his life in his attempt to save the Srinagar airport. But in October 1989, the Valley was once again in the grip of 'raiders'—not outside but inside raiders. It appeared that all the sacrifices made by the brave soldiers of India since October 1947 had been brought to naught. The extent of political and administrative mismanagement was, indeed, unpardonable. For two days—October 26 and 27—the Valley was paralysed by 'hartal' the call for which was given by seccessionists and terrorists.

---

*See Chapter I: 'My Frozen Turbulence', and Chapter II: 'Survey of History'.

On November 4, N.K. Ganjoo, retired District and Sessions Judge, who, as the presiding officer of the special court set up under the Enemy Agents Act, had sentenced Maqbool Butt to death on a murder charge, was gunned down by three young terrorists in broad daylight at the busy Hari Singh High Street. The objective was not only to dramatise the ascendancy of the subversives but also to instill fear in the minds of the judiciary. The signal did not go unnoticed, as the subsequent behaviour of the local judiciary showed.

With the Lok Sabha elections approaching, the subversive activities were accelerated. More than 50 bombs and grenades were exploded during the month of November. The frequency of 'hartals' and processions also increased. Nehru's birthday, November 14, was observed as a 'black day'. Women staged a violent demonstration as a protest against the arrest of Hameed Sheikh, a top terrorist. Hameed had been injured in an encounter with the police, and was under treatment in the Soura Medical Institute. The doctors of the Institute put every conceivable hurdle in the way of the police to interrogate Hameed. The entire State apparatus, as detailed in Chapter X on 'Nature and Pattern of Subversion', had come under the control of subversionists and their collaborators.

By October 1989, the subversives had also made inroads in the Doda, Bhadharwa and Kishtwar areas of Jammu division. Processions were taken out by the Muslims in these areas to protest against the arrest of Shabir Shah. On October 14, Islamic flag was hoisted in Doda and provocative speeches were made in the mosques. On October 27 and 28, a 'hartal' was observed by the Muslims in these towns. Extension of terrorist activity to Doda and adjoining areas was a part of programme to realise the 'Greater Kashmir' plan.*

Inter-Party and Intra-Party Quarrels

While the State was on the verge of an explosion, neither the National Conference nor the Congress(I) was doing anything to counter the subversive forces. On the contrary, they were quarrelling amongst themselves. Not only that, between the two parties also there was deep-rooted distrust. They were constantly plotting against each other. After all, not long ago, the Congress(I) leaders were painting

*This plan envisaged merger of the Muslim majority areas of Jammu division with the Kashmir Valley.

Dr. Farooq Abdullah as an agent of the Liberation Front. No less a person than Janak Raj Gupta, a senior leader of the Congress(I), who later became a Lok Sabha member, had virtually charged Dr. Farooq Abdullah of being a pro-Pakistani subversionist. Speaking in the State Legislative Assembly on March 15, 1984, Jank Raj Gupta quoted extensively from *Insaf*, an Urdu weekly published simultaneously from Muzaffarabad and Rawalpindi and said that Dr. Farooq Abdullah visited Pakistan and Pakistan-Occupied Kashmir in 1974 on the invitation of the Ansari group of the Plebiscite Front which was an active wing of the Liberation Front. At that time Dr. Farooq had openly declared support for independence of Kashmir. He had gone to the extent of saying that if Sheikh Abdullah did not accept his views he would revolt against his father. Old hostility and misgivings could not disappear easily.

In the circumstances prevailing in the State, the inter-party and intra-party squabbles were nothing but an undiagnosed death wish. While the house was on fire, the managers inside were busy quarrelling over the distribution of the spoils of office. So overtaken were they by their chronic malady of securing power that they would not see the danger to all of them from the rising flames on the outer wall.

Equally damaging was their habit of washing dirty linen in public. This further tarnished the image of the two parties and made them objects of contempt and derision. Could such parties fight the national battle against organised and determined subversion, both from within and without?

A few telling examples of the phenomenon may be cited. In June 1989, Mohammad Shafi Qureshi, President of PCC(I), made highly critical remarks about the outlook and performance of the National Conference. He did not even spare Sheikh Abdullah. He said, "The Sheikh exploited the people of the State for personal gains. A few families have, through corrupt practices, cornered all the wealth of the State". Separately, in an apparent attempt to wrest the initiative from the National Conference, Qureshi suggested that the Union Government should invite the 'militants' for talks.

The National Conference was no less virulent in its hostility to and criticism of the Congress(I). On October 20, Dr. Farooq Abdullah's inner feelings betrayed him. He said that the Central Government was following "the British policy of divide and rule." He even went to the extent of telling the Kashmir Chamber of Commerce that "the Kashmir Muslims were not being trusted by New Delhi". He reverted to the familiar tactics of blowing hot and cold at the same time, and saying one thing in the Valley, another in Jammu, and still another in Delhi.

Open bickerings, and even hostility, were not confined to the coalition partners alone; these extended, with equal vehemence, to the factions within the parties also. The Congress(I) house was particularly divided. In July, relations between the two main factions, one led by the PCC(I) Chief, Mohammad Shafi Qureshi, and the other by the Power Minister, Ghulam Rasool Kar, deteriorated.

The squabbles in the National Conference were not so pronounced as in the Congress(I). But there was a strong undercurrent of resentment against Dr. Farooq Abdullah and his coterie. On September 16, Tourism Minister, R.S. Chib, resigned. Among the reasons Chib gave for his resignation were the "directionlessness of the Government" and the "unprecedented chaos and corruption in the administration". He said that all the three regions of the State were in turmoil and methods of recruitment had made the State Government infamous amongst the people.

The National Conference was also suffering deep erosion due to a spate of resignations of the party's rank and file and declarations of dissociation from the party. Paid advertisements in this regard were appearing in local press, almost daily. On August 8, the subversive organisations issued a statement in which they asked the National Conference workers and members to resign from the party or face the consequences. To prove that this was not an empty threat, bombs were exploded near the houses of National Conference leaders. On August 12, there was an explosion near the house of Abdul Salam Deva, president of Kashmir province of National Conference, and on August 13, near the house of Ghulam Ahmed Mir, a prominent party worker of Ganderbal. On August 15, there were two such explosions, one near the house of Abdul Samad Teli and the other near the house of Ghulam Rasool. Both were senior leaders of the National Conference. On August 21, the terrorists, as noted earlier, shot dead Mohammad Yusaf Halwai, president of Zaina Kadal bloc of the National Conference. In October, Sheikh Rashid, a senior leader of the National Conference and a cousin of Dr. Farooq Abdullah, resigned soon after there was an explosion in the compound of his house. In his resignation letter, Sheikh Rashid assailed Dr. Farooq Abdullah and the National Conference for abandoning its basic principles.

Propaganda Blitz

Violent attacks–firing, shoot-outs and bomb explosions–were accompanied by 'hartals' and propaganda blitz. In August, for instance, a 'hartal' was observed for 13 days, even when no political party gave any call for it. A shopkeeper of Srinagar ruefully told a pressman on August 25: "We have had more 'hartals' and 'bandhs' than working days this year."

Violent incidents and 'hartals' were continuously fed by an underground propaganda machinery. No counter-measures were taken by the State Government to contain the highly deleterious effect of this machinery.* Consequently, the flood of pamphlets, posters, wall papers and cassettes and other propaganda material swept the public mind in its own channels. The subversives virtually established control over the thoughts of a large section of the people of the Valley.

Elections and Boost to Terrorism

By the end of October, it should have been clear to all concerned that there was not a sphere of State polity which had not been affected with the critical malady, and to hold Lok Sabha elections in the prevailing circumstances would provide a big boost to forces of subversion and terrorism in the State.

The superficiality and shallowness of those who took the decision to hold Lok Sabha elections in Kashmir was, indeed, amazing. What did they expect? Did they think that after hundreds of bomb blasts, scores of killings, repeated attacks on the security forces in broad daylight, recurring 'hartals' and a spate of resignations of party workers, the public would come out and vote? Could the voter have confidence in the set-up whose Deputy Commissioners were not willing to do their elementary duty of signing the 'transfer warrant' and whose Advocate-General and advocates were refusing to make even a token presence in the High Court?

The decision-makers had no understanding, no grasp, of the ground-level reality. They were living in a world of delusions. Their infinite capacity to deceive themselves stood thoroughly exposed. On the polling day, November 22, the cities looked deserted and villages somnolent. The subversives declared civil curfew for the day and blackout for the night. In a tantalising gesture, TV sets were placed

*See Chapter X: 'Nature and Pattern of Subversion'.

near some of the polling booths with placards reading: "Anyone who will cast his vote can take this as a gift." Near some other booths, coffins were placed with the cryptic note: "Anyone who will cast his vote will get this." Authority had eroded to such an extent that the State Government could be made fun of in this manner.

The extremely poor turn-out demonstrated to the whole world that the Valley was in turmoil, and that the National Conference and Congress(I) were nothing but corpses.

Sopore is the hometown of Ghulam Rasool Kar, who was at that time a Cabinet Minister in the State Government. It is also the hometown of the chairman of the Legislative Council. Hakim Habibullah, and also of former National Conference M.P. and Cabinet Minister, Abdul Ahad Vakil. Yet only five votes were cast in Sopore town. Not a single vote was polled in the main section of Baramulla town. The same was the position in numerous other polling booths.

In Srinagar town, from where, because of boycott, Mohammed Shafi Butt was declared elected unopposed, JKLF flags fluttered over a large number of buildings. The whole exercise turned out to be a farce, as also a tragedy. Both the National Conference and the Congress(I) put up a pathetic show. No election meetings were held, no mobilisation was done, and even the candidates did not stir out of their houses.

The description of the polling day–November 22–as given by the press, should leave no one in doubt about the total sway of the subversionists and also about the total casualness of the ruling alliance. The correspondent of *The Hindustan Times* wrote, "The fact remains that this correspondent was unable to meet even a single voter inside any polling station which he visited in the rural areas of Baramulla and Anantnag constituencies of the Kashmir Valley today. Nowhere any election agent of any candidate, including the sitting M.P., Prof. Saifuddin Soz, the National Conference nominee, was seen. The State Capital which has already returned the National Conference nominee uncontested observed a complete bandh today. The presence of staff in Government offices was negligible." The *Indian Express* reported that there were no queues, no polling agents, and much violence. It said: "Instead of being a day of hectic public activity, November 22 was a totally paralysed day in Kashmir Valley, with a total bandh in towns and most villages. At polling booths in both Baramulla and Anantnag constituencies, no queues of voters could be seen. At most of the booths, polling agents, even of the ruling National Conference, were absent. In Anantnag, the second big town in the Valley and in other centres like Baramulla, Sopore and Shophian, the polling was only around 1 per cent. As the 'finale' to the boycott call, lights were put off in most of the localities of Anantnag, Baramulla, Srinagar and other towns." The *Patriot's* comments were equally telling. It said, "It is the militants who call the shots in Kashmir and their success in enforcing the poll boycott underlines the extent of erosion suffered by the NC-Congress combine during the last three years."

The farce and the tragedy were compounded by the fact that, immediately after being elected to the Lok Sabha, both Mohammad Shafi Butt and Saifuddin Soz made statements which were prejudicial to national interests. Butt said, "The Centre and the Congress(I) are responsible for the prevailing turmoil in Kashmir. The situation is the outcome of the 'misdeeds of the Centre' which is treating J&K as its colony. The people living here are treated as second class citizens. The Centre has not fulfilled the promise which it made to the people of Kashmir in 1947." What does this promise of 1947 mean? Obviously, reference here is to plebiscite. Soz also made a similar statement.

Double-Facedness

The above facts speak volumes about the outlook and the representative character of Shafi Butt and Saifuddin Soz. And yet these are the persons who sit in the Indian Parliament on behalf of the people of Kashmir, make loud noises, spread disinformation, and propagate false notions. They complicate the Kashmir problems from both the ends. They annoy the nationalists by talking obliquely of plebiscite and pre-1953 position. They irritate the Kashmiri youth by their hypocrisy. No one is taken in by their stance. Their double-facedness only serves to multiply their own delusions and reinforce the general atmosphere of artificiality and cynicism. They do not realise that they have already overplayed their card of deception and duplicity.

With the impotence and irrelevance of National Conference(F) and Congress(I) fully exposed to public view during the Lok Sabha elections in the Valley, the wave of subversion further swelled. The terrorists struck a grievous blow on the already shattered morale of the

State Police by brutally assassinating* Saidulha, Station House Officer, Maisuma bazaar police station, on December 1; his dead body remaining unattended for hours in the market. The Capital was paralysed with terror and the administration rendered immobile and impotent. Even Saidulha's comrades in police seemed to have lost not only courage but also compassion. Leaderlessness and consequent panic had taken away even the frozen tears from their eyes.

On December 5, the birthday of Sheikh Mohammad Abdullah, the subversionists caused total 'hartal' in Srinagar and 'blackout' in the night. When Sheikh Abdullah's name mattered, a large number of roads, institutions, buildings, and places were named after him. It was often humorously remarked that everything in the State was 'Sher-e-Kashmir'–the food we ate, the air we breathed, the road we walked on, the highway on which we drove, the hospital to which we went, the park and garden in which we strolled. But on December 5, 1989, not a single National Conference worker or leader stirred out to frustrate the 'hartal' or 'blackout'. Where was the commitment of National Conference to 'Baba-e-Quam', the father of the nation? Its sham, its hypocrisy, was evident. And so was the decline of National Conference.

Eagle Swoops–Dr. Rubaiya's Kidnapping

One success after another acted as a strong tonic to the eagle. His eyes became sharper and his claws more venturesome. His wings grew fast and he spread them freely, traversing a larger span of the horizon. He gained greater confidence and soon chose for its prey the roof-garden of the palace of power itself.

On December 8, 1989, the terrorists of JKLF kidnapped Dr. Rubaiya Sayeed, daughter of the Union Home Minister, Mufti Mohammad Sayeed, stunning the whole nation with its suddenness. For five days, the pall of fear and anxiety hung over the nation. The state and the Central authorities groped in the dark. The blinkers that they had put on their eyes in the past, despite warnings,** had rendered them incapable of getting any clue. The Chief Minister, Dr. Farooq Abdullah, was abroad at the time of kidnapping and his cabinet colleagues prevaricated. About 20 prominent Muslim

---

* See Chapter XIV: 'Acquiring an Upper Hand'.

**See Chapter III: 'Warning Signals'.

organisations condemned the kidnapping. Some leaders of Pakistan, including Maulana Fazal-ul-Rehman, Chief of Jama'at-i-Ulme Islami, termed the kidnapping as un-Islamic. Mirwaiz Maulvi Farooq also called it anti-Islam. All this had no effect. On the contrary, on December 12, the Chief of Pakistan-based J&K Liberation Front, Amanulla Khan, renewed the threat to kill Dr. Rubaiya Sayeed. Ultimately, the State gave in to the terror tactics. Five top terrorists–Hamid Sheikh, Sher Khan, Javed Ahmed Zargar, Mohammad Kalwal and Mohammad Altaf Butt–were set free to secure the release of Dr. Rubaiya Sayeed from captivity.

The eagle had attained yet another telling success. He became the master of all he surveyed. He hovered ominously over the Valley of Fear.

Dr. Rubaiya's case, the details of which are given in Chapter XIV, titled 'Acquiring An Upper Hand', demonstrated the total ineffectiveness of the State machinery. The enthusiastic welcome that was given to the released youth by the milling crowds, who celebrated the victory, confirmed the impression that the ascendency of the terrorists was total and the people had gone over to the side about whose victory they no longer had any doubt.

As was bound to happen, the incidents of terrorism increased both in frequency and intensity. On December 17, the security forces were fired upon even during the curfew period. The Residency Road branch of the United Bank of India was looted on December 20, and, on December 21, a security guard of Allahabad Bank was shot dead in the heart of the town. Five more persons were injured in two bomb blasts. Two policemen were killed and seven seriously injured on December 24. A powerful bomb was blasted in the compound of Mrs. Aisha Amin who had condemned kidnapping of Dr. Rubaiya Sayeed. On December 25, a constable of the J&K Armed Police was shot dead at Khaniyar. Prem Nath Butt, a noted journalist of Anantnag, was killed on December 27. A Deputy Superintendent of Police was also shot at and seriously injured near the Kashmir University. On the same day, five bomb blasts occurred in the Valley. On December 28, the building of the Handicrafts Department, Anantnag, was badly damaged in a bomb explosion. On December 30, two police officers were shot at. One, a Sub-Inspector, died; and the other, a Deputy Superintendent of Police, was critically wounded. On the same day, an ex-serviceman was shot dead in Kupwara, and five bomb blasts occurred in different cities of the Valley. A hand-grenade was also thrown on the Earth Satellite Station at Hari Parbat. The year 1989 closed with a rising tide of bloodshed and violence.

A powerful bomb blast which seriously injured seven persons, signalled the dawn of the year 1990. In the disturbances which took place on January 2, two persons were killed and nine injured. On January 3, the Inspector of Intelligence Bureau, R.N.P. Singh, was shot dead. January 5–the day on which the first batch of UN officials arrived at Srinagar–was observed as 'self-determination day'. During the curfew, explosions and disturbances occurred in which one person was killed and several others were injured. On January 6, violent clashes occurred and the Valley was rocked by four explosions, injuring thirty persons. Another fifty persons were injured in the disturbances on the following day in Srinagar, Baramulla, Sopore and Badgam.

January 8 saw new heights of violence in the Valley in which thirteen persons, were killed and one hundred injured. An Embroidery Centre was set ablaze near the Idgah. In an attempt to intensify the impact of terrorism, a police official was blindfolded, gagged, brutally tortured and then hanged from a tree in Hyderpura. An Imam of Saller village mosque was also tortured in the same manner and hanged.

Non-existent State and Deaf Centre

Lest anyone should feel that I am portraying a dismal picture, I would let a few of the independent observers of the time speak. I have selected one or two contemporaneous opinions of every reputed national daily. The unanimity of views expressed should leave no one in doubt that Kashmir had been practically lost to the nation before my arrival on the scene, on January 19, 1990.

Sanjeev Miglani of *The Statesman* reported on November 6, 1989, as follows:

> The Kashmir Valley has been effectively left at the mercy of the militants. As it exists now, Kashmir is very nearly lost to the nation. The administration ceased to exist several months ago. But the damage is that it formalizes the delicate arrangement. The message to the militant is: "All right, we are leaving. Do what you want".
>
> To the people, the absent administration and a totally deaf Centre are the last straws. If earlier sympathy for Mujahids was out

of fear, it is now out of trust. The people are ready to do battle for the gunmen, now accepted as freedom fighters.

If you ask ordinary woman what does she expect the Centre to do, the immediate reaction is one of incredulity. 'You still think we want anything from them', she counters.

It is not even the Centre any more: 'It is India and Kashmir is a separate entity. The message is frequently reinforced in the mind of a visitor.'

In the Valley, everyone will point out that nobody from the Centre has ever come. Or, maybe things have reached such a pass that nobody dare step in. Somebody would tell them of the collapse of the administrative machinery. Not all the CRPFs of the world can do anything. It is now an open secret that the top level of the Kashmir Police are torn apart.

If the law and order machinery has collapsed, it is because the political masters are dead. There is no one to tell the officers what to do. Meetings are held only when absolutely necessary and seldom a firm decision has emerged.

The political masters are themselves playing out the battle of survival. The Rajiv-Farooq Accord has eaten up the two parties. The National Conference, always a mass-based party, stands totally discredited. In fact, Sheikh Abdullah, synonymous with the National Conference too, has become a victim. His grave has been defaced because the people think that Sheikh Sahib took them for a ride for 25 years. In his son, Dr. Farooq, they see nothing less than evil.

In effect, north of the Banihal, it is virtually a partyless State. The Opposition parties have thrown up their hands admitting that they are irrelevant. The Congress, never a party of substance, has been tarnished with the same brush as the National Conference.

No wonder then, that the militants have stepped in. They control the streets. It won't be long before they control the State. It may then be too late for Kashmir to return to the mainstream.

Earlier, on August 26, 1989, in a despatch from Srinagar, M.L. Kotru, Resident Editor, *The Statesman,* remarked:

If you decide to observe things for yourself, unaided by the fantasies of the day-dreamers who constitute the ruling elite at the Centre and the State of J&K, the conclusion you will come to is that no one really wants to face the challenge thrown by the militants.

The Hindustan Times observed on August 25, 1989:

> The people, including the die-hard followers of the ruling National Conference, are losing faith in the administration's ability to either govern or give protection to those who are prepared to stand up. The current state of affairs is the biggest vote of no confidence in Dr. Abdullah's administration.

The *Patriot,* in its commentary of October 24, 1989, lamented:

> Unknown to the rest of the country, Kashmir is heading towards a crisis. Srinagar is daily rocked by bursts of explosives aimed mainly at Central Government offices, installations and officials. There is a leadership vacuum in the Valley. The main crisis which manifests is the disquieting hold the Pakistan-based Kashmir Liberation Alliance has gained on the Valley.

In the issue of November 23, 1989 *The Times of India* commented:

> There seems to be a strange conspiracy of silence about the reign of terror, subversion and lawlessness in the once happy and now apparently helpless valley of Kashmir. For the daily outrages by Pakistani-trained militants, starting long before the announcement of the election, have gone on without evoking even a semblance of concern from New Delhi and nothing more than a few thundering speeches by the State Chief Minister, Dr. Farooq Abdullah.

In *The Hindustan Times* issue of December 17, 1989, this is what its special correspondent reported:

> The all-powerful National Conference, which claims to have its cadres in every village of the Valley, has miserably failed to fight terrorism and militancy over the last two years. Over the last two years about a hundred people have been killed in the Valley by the militants and the police. Even before the 1983 elections in J&K there were allegations against the Government that it had recruited a number of Kashmiri youth in police who had connections with Al Fateh, a militants' organization.
>
> Today in Kashmir the cult of violence is spreading very fast. Since there is not even a semblance of the Government in the Valley, particularly these days when the Government has moved to Jammu, the Valley has been left free to the militants. 'There is no rule of law but the rule of the bullet', a tourist who returned from the Valley remarked.

The editor of the *National Herald,* A.N. Dar, in his article of December 16, 1989, said:

> Innocent people have been killed; there have been bomb blasts and there have been bandhs galore.

On January 10, *The Times* of *India* editorially commented:

> It comes as no surprise that the situation in J&K has taken a turn for the worse. The latest bout of violence comes in the wake of decision by the militants to organise rallies outside the United Nations military group headquarters to launch a 'Quit Kashmir' movement. What is tragic and ominous is the fact that over a dozen people have died in the act of defying authority. It is National Front government's misfortune that it inherited a situation close to a boil. As V.P. Singh has said on more than one occasion, he is truly appalled by the problems left behind by the predecessor regime in Kashmir, even more so than in Punjab.

In its editorial comments, *The Hindu* of January 11, observed:

> Secessionists and subversives have been working havoc for several months now in the Kashmir Valley and the law and order situation has never been so bad as it is today. The imposition of curfew in almost the entire State some days ago–quite an extra-ordinary step–and its continuance now in Srinagar, Anantnag and Sopore, among other important towns, is a measure of the danger the State is facing. The State administration has been unable to restore even a semblance of normality. In the police firing that took place in Srinagar, following bloody incidents early this week, eight persons lost their lives. The obvious conclusion is that the Government has no clue as to how to control the situation; the Farooq Abdullah administration seems to grow over a long period beginning from last year's Independence Day when Pakistani flags were hoisted in a number of places right in the heart of Srinagar and a call was given to organise a bandh. Even as the curfew is on, the saboteurs have succeeded in exploding bombs in various parts of the Valley and setting fire to public buildings. These acts bring to sharp focus the utter impassivity of the administration. Dr. Abdullah's failure has not only been administrative but also political.

Writing about the conditions prevailing during Dr. Farooq Abdullah's regime, the noted journalist Nikhil Chakravartty, in his political commentary of March 11, 1990, said:

> From personal experience borne out by two visits to the Valley in that period, this correspondent gathered the very disturbing impression that behind all the high-visibility political impetuosity and exhibitionism on the part of Farooq Abdullah, his Ministry emerged as the symbol of utter corruption and maladministration. It was this very phase which saw the growing activity of the secessionist groups emerging out in the open.
>
> This account of the past in the Kashmir Valley has been necessitated by the patently distorted account given by Mr. Rajiv Gandhi in his letter to the Prime Minister on March 6. One would like to remind both Mr. Gandhi and Dr. Abdullah as to what happened on the Independence Day, August 15 last, when the secessionists coming out in the open had forced a blackout in Srinagar with Pakistani flag flying at many places. Was it an example of their 'maintenance of political contact with the people' or that 'at no time was the administration alienated from the people' as has been claimed in Mr. Gandhi's letter?

The chaotic conditions were noted by the Pakistan press also. In December 1989, the *Nation*, a well-known daily of Pakistan, editorially commented twice on the Kashmir situation. One comment said:

> The message from Srinagar is loud and clear. New Delhi's writ is no longer operative in the Valley and Dr. Farooq Abdullah has more glamorous pursuits to chase than putting the act of his crumbling administration together.

And the second comment was:

> Two things have emerged clearly from one week of dramatic developments in the Kashmir Valley. There is a virtual uprising against the Indian rule and nothing short of a military crackdown can cope with the situation. The Kashmiri Muslims' struggle for freedom is at crossroads and a historic opportunity awaits them to transform it into the decisive assault for breaking the shackles of Indian bondage.

The Jamaat Islami mouthpiece, *Jasarat*, also observed: "The wave of violence raging throughout Kashmir these days has reached its zenith." Another daily–*The Muslim*–exhorted the Pakistani Government "not to foreclose any option with reference to the inter-twined dynamics of the Sikh and Muslim movements in the areas adjoining Pakistan".

Even foreign press had noted the sad state of affairs. In the last week of January 1990, *New York Times International* reported:

> A resurgence of secessionist sentiment began nearly two years ago in J&K, the only State with a Muslim majority in predominantly Hindu India.
>
> 'Brave Kashmiris,' came the summons from loudspeakers in minarets throughout Srinagar, summer capital of the Indian State of J&K, 'the time has come to lay down your lives'. V.P. Singh has conceded, however, that the Kashmiris have many justified laments. Two weeks ago, he appointed as governor Jagmohan, an efficient administrator who governed the State from 1984 to 1989, thereby prompting Farooq Abdullah, the unpopular chief minister of J&K, to resign in protest. Eager to demonstrate his goodwill, Jagmohan has distributed food during curfews, created new jobs and offered nearly $3,000 each to the families of three civilians killed by Indian guards. But tempers in Kashmir are still too hot to be soothed by token measures. Other factors have also crept in. The general cry is: 'We will go and do as the Germans have done. We will destroy the wall and cross over.'

Not only press and political commentators but also a number of prominent leaders were bewailing the chaotic conditions. For instance, on August 25, 1989, Mir Qasim, former Chief Minister, who cannot be taken as unfriendly to Abdullah family, said: "If no protection is given to the people against violence, the situation may become irretrievable." At about the same time, V.P. Singh, who was then Jan Morcha Chief, also observed, "What is causing even more anxiety is the sight of an ineffective and unpopular regime which is neither able to effectively meet the challenge of a secessionist group nor is able to protect the life and property of the peaceful citizens."

On my arrival on the scene, I had asked both of my advisers–Ved Marwah and Jamil Qureshi–to make a brief assessment of the situation. The relevant portion of Ved Marwah's report has already been quoted in Chapter I. Here is what Qureshi, inter alia, reported:

> The people, almost the whole lot of them, believed that Kashmir was going to be either independent or become a part of Pakistan in

January 1990 itself. In fact, January 26 was promised by the militants to be a day of supposed deliverance when the new People's Republic of Independent Kashmir was going to be declared and foreign correspondents invited to be witnesses to the birth of the new State. The writ of the Government did not run beyond and generally outside the confines of their own command room circles. The morale of the police was in their boots and there was a revolt right within the police when the J&K Armed Police surrounded and held their own seniors to ransom at gunpoint. Far from going after the extremists, the policemen themselves were aiding and abetting them.

The events and observations recounted above clearly show that before January 19, 1990, frenzied chaos and savage anarchy had gripped Kashmir. In fact, even prior to the day (December 8, 1989) of Dr. Rubaiya Sayeed's kidnapping, when the eagle of terrorism swooped on the state with full fury, 1,600 violent incidents, including 351 bomb blasts, had taken place in the year 1989. The Valley had been stricken with violence, bloodshed and brutality. The 'ceremony of innocence' had been fully drowned. The huge administrative apparatus resembled a sprawling but lifeless octopus. The Kashmiri terrorist had become the real ruler. The ground had been yielded to him to such an extent that he dominated the public mind. It is, indeed, unfortunate–and it is a measure of the nation's general malaise–that notwithstanding hard facts and figures indicated in this chapter and the chapter on 'Nature and Pattern of Subversion', a section of the public is taken in by the false assertions of the 'Lords of Misrule' and their trumpeteers and apologists. Could there be anything worse than the conditions of death? The tragedy of Kashmir lay in the deafness of those who ruled either directly or through remote control; they could not hear even its death rattles.

CHAPTER IX

Approach, Attack and Counter-Attack

My only prayer is that I may feel the pain of others as if I were residing within their bodies and that I may have the powers of relieving their pain and making them happy.

–Bhagwatam

While formulating my approach to deal with the critical situation that prevailed in Kashmir, I had to take into account all the facts and forces that I have discussed in the preceding chapters. There were deep and ugly scars which its unkind history had left on its mindscape. There were wild and anarchic crops which had sprung up all over the Valley from the poisonous seeds which had been planted with impunity in the past. There were, then, hard and cruel realities of terrorism and subversion* on the ground with strong and many-directional roots.

Alongwith these, there existed sharp and ruthless spears of selfish and narrow politics, which showed no hesitation or compunction in wounding and bleeding to death any sincere and honest effort that might be made to salvage the position and carve out a new path.

I had little doubt that superficiality had seeped deep into the soul of contemporary India. The moral structure of our politics, the poor motivation of our institutions, the shallowness of the leaders that came to dominate the scene, had rendered the nation incapable of solving any serious problems, much less a problem of Kashmir's dimension

*See also Chapter X: 'Nature and Pattern of Subversion and Terrorism'.

and complexity. Could a country aspire to be great and yet ignore the emerging storm which I have sketched in the 'Warning Signals' and also remain oblivious of the dangers inherent in softness and permissiveness and in the politics of deception and duplicity and in spurious democracy and secularism? Nations with vision or even with the moderate objective of national reconstruction do not act in a casual and callous manner as has been displayed in Kashmir.

All along, I remained painfully aware of the country's atmosphere of moral chaos and collapse of its will to reform and regenerate. Nevertheless, the attempt, I thought, was worth making.

After frustrating the 'sinister design' of the subversionists for January 26, 1990, and overcoming the immediate crisis emanating from the virtual take-over of the Valley by them, I had to immediately attend to two grave problems. One was to meet the intensified onslaught of the terrorist campaign which Pakistan intended to fan vigorously by organising 'solidarity week' from February 5 to 12 and also by the decision of all the terrorist organisations to fully exploit Maqbool Butt Day on February 11. The second was to acquire a foothold from where I could commence my plan of rolling back the terrorists.

I set about the task of resurrection. The entire edifice had to be rebuilt. The authority of the State had to be re-asserted. What was still more important and crucial to the whole exercise was to provide a healthy motivation to the reconstructed machinery. Without activisation of the underlying spirit of work, I realised, the physical structure of the administration would not yield worthwhile results. A motivational impulse had, therefore, to be imparted. A higher purpose had to be indicated. An inspiring leadership had to be provided–a leadership which would not only reconstruct the administrative machinery but also infuse it with new life.

The Model

After a great deal of deliberations, I decided to follow, in the first phase, the model of the Governor's Rule of 1986. What was that model? What was done at that time? What was my motivation? What was the public reaction to what I did? And why was it relevant in the conditions that confronted me then?

I think, the best way of answering the above questions and making clear the entire background is to reproduce a few notes recorded by me in my diary at that time. These notes have a flavour of freshness of the time and speak for themselves.

March 7, 1986

Today, I have dismissed G.M. Shah's Ministry. His regime was another sad chapter in the unfortunate history of Kashmir. The task before me is truly awesome. The communal passions are running high. The minorities are fear-stricken. The Government machinery is rudderless. The officers are demoralised. Indiscipline has made deep inroads into the State Secretariat. Fundamentalists and obscurantists are nursing their own designs. Malpractices, corruption and intrigues are rampant. The economy, already in a poor shape, is further sliding downward. The judiciary is wayward. Regional tensions are mounting.

Late in the evening, while having my usual lonely walk in the vast complex of Jammu Raj Bhavan, I reflect on not only the formidable problems that confront me but also on the ends of power. For what purpose does one need power? Is it merely for administering the State better, or for demonstrating a higher and nobler purpose and also translating that purpose into a concrete reality? Power can corrupt. But it can also ennoble. It can elevate the wielder to a higher pedestal and transform him into a nobler creature. His scope for being good and doing good gets enlarged. In one way, the tragedy of contemporary India has been that power has largely remained in the hands of those who were seldom inspired by a nobler purpose. And those who have that purpose do not get the opportunity; rather, the system denies it.

I feel the burden of the challenges. But I am a bit elated, too. I have an opportunity to show the nobler, the purer, the more radiant face of power. I can now demonstrate how Government should function in a poor and developing country, how a person, inspired by a higher purpose can serve as a model administrator, how domination of the elites can be done away with, how power-brokers can be eliminated, how exploitation by communalists and obscurantists can be prevented, how youth can be weaned away from fundamentalism, how justice can be established as a new religion, and the vicious circle of underdevelopment and exploitative democracy can be sniped. I can also show that administration is not merely pen, pencil, paper and red tape; it is much more than this. It is imagination. It is vision. It is creativity. It is commitment. It is compassion. It is catharsis. It is sympathy. It is tact. It is Napoleonic precision, speed, timing and leadership. It is also hard work, sweat and blood. It is an ideology–an ideology of being an effective instrument of social, economic and cultural change. Am I not demanding too much of myself? How can a single individual, howsoever inspired and motivated, change the landscape dominated by the cowards, the corrupt, and the 'quisling' and bring in a new vision? History has known persons who, almost single-handed, changed its course. But were not such persons more gifted, more fortunate to secure or occupy positions which provided them with immense opportunities and wider scope for action? How can a mere administrative job enable me to bring about fundamental changes and to give new shape and colour to our polity? What, moreover, could be achieved in a short period of six months? How can muck and filth, scattered in so many nooks and corners, be cleared? Even to touch the decomposed filth is risky. Nevertheless, I must try. Satisfaction lies in the effort. Anyhow, something worthwhile will come out of it. Sharing the suffering of the victims of callousness and indifference will at least make a better individual–more compassionate and sympathetic.

I have made a modest beginning in the afternoon by making a public statement which, *inter alia*, says: 'My emphasis will be on peace and productivity, even-handed justice to everyone, eradication of corruption and service to the poor, the sick and the needy. I will devote special attention to reorganise and reform the administration and make the government machinery clean, dynamic, result-oriented, humane and enlightened in outlook, and responsive to the needs and aspirations of the people. The cities, lakes, streams, tourist spots, gardens and parks will be cleaned up, and numerous benefits which conservation and environmental upgradation can provide to the State will be demonstrated.'

April 7, 1986

A distinguishing feature of my 'action plan' is that service is now being rendered at the points where it is most needed and where it touches the people at the grassroot–the people in the streets, lanes, by-lanes, in the slums and shacks, in the villages and hamlets, where at present there is either no water or only muddy water to drink, where roads are merely an apology for slushy path, and where even rudimentary sanitation and civic services do not exist.

April 30, 1986

New orientation to the Administration has stirred the imagination of the people and they are often heard saying that no one had looked after them earlier, no one had come to their streets, lanes and by-lanes and no one had taken any steps to take care of their day-to-day problems of health, sanitation and upkeep. This bestirring, this transformation is evident everywhere–in villages and towns, and even amongst the student community who have been generally hostile to the Government. An instance of this is afforded by the Srinagar Medical College students who, on my appeal, not only went out to the villages to provide medical relief to the flood-affected families but also collected a substantial amount as donation to the Governor's Welfare Fund.

May 15, 1986

In a sense, a revolutionary change is being witnessed. The Central authority here has always been like a red rag to the bull, but now the rule of the Central representative is being hailed everywhere and the Governor is respected and shown all affection and cooperation.

May 30, 1986

The weekly public hearings and the dynamism that has been lent to the grassroot administration have helped create an atmosphere wherein the common man has come to acquire a feeling that his voice is heard and he can share the benefits of planned development equitably.

There is a perceptible impact of the changes effected and measures introduced by me after the imposition of Governor's Rule. If the response continues to be as favourable as it is at present, the Kashmir politics and Kashmir administration may undergo a fundamental change, and the distressing problems which have beset the State for years might no longer stare us in the face. A correct path is being found and an atmosphere for honest, clean, efficient, dynamic and service-oriented administration created.

However, extraordinary caution, vigilance and vision, besides hard work, are required to keep the points of the compass in the right direction.

June 30, 1986

In the background of the current speedy and spectacular development, the performance of the leaders of the yester-years, who have so far successfully posed as champions of the poor Kashmiris, especially Kashmiri Muslims, is becoming suspect. In other words, they are getting exposed. A substantial section of the people is beginning to ask such questions as these: Why such a development did not take place earlier, why roads were not repaired, why lanes and by-lanes remained full of garbage and silt, why lakes were not cleaned, why most of the schools were housed in dark, dingy and insect-ridden structures, why the general educational standard in schools and universities remained so poor, why a major portion of the important cities like Srinagar and Jammu remained without potable water supply, why a substantial section of the villagers were drinking muddy water from the streams, why a few doctors were allowed to monopolise the medical profession and mulct the poor people and at the same time pay no taxes, why the High Court facilitated non-payment of taxes which are paid by other citizens of India, why the Executive and the Judiciary have enabled the forest lessees to hold crores of rupees worth of royalties, why the influential political elements and higher bureaucracy subserved each other's interests at the expense of the common man, why recruitment depended not on merit but on the whims and predilections of the political and administrative elites? This process of questioning and this process of exposure of the vested interests need to continue. It will help the pro-Union forces. The bogey of Kashmiris being enslaved would wither away. Truth will begin to be gleaned from underneath the debris of false propaganda.

July 31, *1986*

The State has been bled white by the vested interests. The resources have been cornered by them and they have not paid taxes and other dues. They take advantage of the so-called pro-autonomy stance. A number of measures like gift tax, wealth tax, restriction on the size of the urban land, have not been allowed to become operative in the State. The High Court which comes from the same ruling elites, keeps on lending support to the pro-autonomy forces and stays or negates even the taxation measures which are designed to raise resources for the State and bring about economic equilibrium.

The vested interests of a few families had acquired a stranglehold on the social, economic and political framework of the State. These interests controlled the politics, dominated the administration, the High Court, the Judiciary, the Bar, the business and the industry. The vested interests of the small coterie of the ruling elite had been the biggest obstacle in bringing the State to the mainstream and to weld it with the Union–administratively, constitutionally and legally. Fortunately, under the impact of the current changes, the stranglehold on the vested interests is loosening and their influence is on the decline. The recent tax raids and the inability of the vested interests to raise a hue and cry and whip up mass hysteria, as it was able to do during the 1981 raids, is an illustration of this phenomenon. The levers of manipulation and exploitation are slipping out of their hands.

If the current reform and reorganisation continue and if the new institutional framework gets into shape, then the State would be permanently freed from the vice-like grip of the vested interests who, on the one hand, have kept the State away from the Union, while on the other, exploited the poor and the ignorant by fomenting sectional and communal differences and playing up the bogey of 'Indian' domination.

August 31, 1986

The peace and tranquility that prevail throughout the State and the positive impact of the changes introduced by me during the last few months is widely visible. For the first time in many years, Janam Ashtami processions have been taken out in some cities and towns of the Kashmir Valley with pomp and gaiety. The tempo of development activities has also received a fillip and a new environment has been created for the State's smooth economic transformation.

As long as Kashmir stands aloof and Central laws are not extended to the State, the isolationist, parochial and separatist forces would remain strong and the vicious circle of vested interests and pro-autonomy trends would never be broken. If the present set-up had not been there, much noise would have been made over the extension of Article 249 of the Indian Constitution to the State. Advantage of the current conditions should be taken to extend more Central laws to the State. The present set-up, the mood of the people, and the general favourable environment provide an opportunity for fuller integration which would never arise again. Vision demands that this opportunity should be boldly, though deftly, seized, the vicious circle of the separatist forces and traditional ruling elites broken, and, at the same time, the common man made to realise the truth that the Central Government and the general masses of the country are solicitous of their welfare.

These notes, recorded in my diary, indicate the impact of the 1986 model on the psyche of the people of the State. This would be evident from the comments of a number of observers. Here. I would invite attention only to a few.

V.N. Narayanan, Editor-in-Chief of the *Tribune,* after touring the Valley for three days in June 1989, wrote three articles on 'J&K Today'. In the last article, Narayanan said:

> Out of curiosity I put the question to everybody I met in Srinagar, Anantnag and Pahalgam recently: 'Who do you think would give the best government to the State?' It was not a surprise that without exception the answer was: 'The Governor.' 'Any Governor?' 'No, the present Governor–Jagmohan.'

This is what A.N. Dar, Editor of the *National Herald* observed in his article of April 1989, 'What is wrong in Kashmir':

> It has to be admitted that the last two years in Kashmir have been administratively sterile. The coalition has not been a shining example of purposeful administration. This is sad indeed, more so because it had the example before it of what the Governor, Jagmohan, did during Governor's rule. Jagmohan, a bureaucrat and an outsider to the Kashmir scene who had two governments dismissed, showed that it was possible to win the goodwill of the people through fair-minded, selfless and effective administration. Even the fundamentalists and the anti-nationals accepted that he was fair and efficient.

In its issue of April 6, 1989, *The Hindu* reported as follows:

In fact, a large number of youth indicated that they would be more than satisfied if the Governor, Jagmohan, were once again allowed to take over the administration.

Nikhil Chakravartty, the noted political analyst, in his Sunday column of October 30, 1988, wrote:

> One finds common people in many parts of the Valley getting bitterly disenchanted with the Chief Minister, and in contrast praising Jagmohan's period of Governor's Rule.
>
> This raises serious implications as it shows that an elected ministry is losing out to a competent Governor in the eyes of the public over whom it presides.

The widely circulated Urdu daily of Kashmir, *Srinagar Times,* in its issue of July 8, 1988, editorially commented:

> What Governor Jagmohan did during the six months of Governor's Rule, to set right the deteriorating conditions in the Valley and improve its environment would never be forgotten by the people of Kashmir.*

The purpose of citing these comments and observations is not to draw attention to my personal achievements but to bring home the point that the model of the Governor's Rule of 1986 was extremely relevant and also to expose the treacherous, almost treasonable, role of those elements in national and State leadership who moved heaven and earth to portray me as anti-Muslim and anti-Kashmiri and in the process scuttle the great effort to rescue the State from the jaws of death and destruction.

That much was achieved in concrete terms would be clear also from the note which I have added as Appendix XIII. The higher purpose of renovating society and bringing about fundamental attitudinal changes that could act as a pace-setter for social, cultural and administrative reforms was also realised to some extent.

I realised that in the changed circumstances and in the terrorist-infested environment, the pattern and pace of 1986 could not be brought about immediately. But the same underlying spirit, the same motivation had to be the guiding star.

*Translated from Urdu.

Farooq Abandons the Valley

The Farooq Government had practically abandoned the Valley and left the Srinagar Commissioner and Deputy Inspector-General, Police, to fend for themselves. In the circumstances in which they were placed, it was but natural that they would play a passive role and follow the line of least resistance. They and their staff had personal problems, too. Most of them, and also their relations, lived in the interior of the city. They could not think of causing even the slightest annoyance to the terrorists and invite trouble for themselves and their kith and kin.

A strong and high-level leadership, with a great deal of initiative and courage, was required in the Valley. But here even an ordinary leadership was not available. Someone had to become a symbol of resistance to subversion and terrorism. The bull had to be taken by the horns. I, therefore, decided to stay at Srinagar and set up a regular winter Secretariat there.

Public Interviews

Separately, I had decided to throw open the gates of Raj Bhavan and revive the system of public interviews of 1986. A large number of persons came to see me. I made it a point to redress their genuine grievances there and then.

The system appeared to be clicking. On January 31, 1990, about 300 persons met me. Another 700 persons came on the following day (February 1). Some of them came from as distant areas as Kupwara and Baramulla. I spent almost the entire day listening to their grievances. Most of the grievances were genuine. Casualness appeared to have become a part of the system built by the erstwhile regime. For instance, a deputation of a dozen staff members of the Islamia College for Women, Sopore, told me that sixty employees of the college had not got their salaries for the last 10 months. Likewise, a sizeable section of the junior staff of the Horticulture and Marketing Corporation had not been paid for three months. After speaking to the officials on the phone, I got these grievances redressed straightway. Quick response from the highest in the State dispelled a part of the frustration. The atmosphere became a bit relaxed.

A very large number of complaints pertained to unfair recruitment to subordinate services, particularly teachers. To redress the grievances in this regard, I made a general announcement that all recruitments would be entrusted to the Statutory Subordinate Service Selection Board which I set up by promulgating an Act, using my legislative powers, under Section 92 of the J&K Constitution. In respect of engineering works, too, complaints were galore. Various works had been ordered by the political elements without any financial sanction. Rupees fifteen crore was being demanded by the contractors, though hardly any work was done at the site. About 6,000 persons, who seldom came to the work site, were shown as appointees. For bringing about some order in the chaotic conditions, I immediately put a stop to the procedures and practices which facilitated robbing of the public exchequer. And for dealing with the complaints and for stemming the rot effectively in this respect, I declared that, in due course, a high-powered independent Committee would be appointed to look into all cases of corruption, favouritism, nepotism and squandering of public money. I also introduced austerity measures. I began with myself. I did not draw any salary. I gave up one post of A.D.C.

During the public interviews, a number of youth sought employment. I advised the able-bodied amongst them to apply for posts in the Border Security Force. Earlier, on January 24, I had announced Government decision to raise five battalions of the BSF from amongst the Kashmiri youth–5,000 in the constabulary and 2,000 in ancillary jobs. This force was to be raised and trained in Srinagar. This was done in view of the marked reluctance of the Kashmiri youth to move out of the Valley. A few other measures were also announced. Three thousand teachers were to be recruited through the Statutory Services Selection Board. Manual de-weeding of the Dal Lake was also started to attain the twin objective of cleaning the lake and providing employment to boatmen.

Apart from establishing direct contact with the people and redressing the accumulated public grievances, I went on renewing my appeal to the youth to abandon the path of violence and join hands with me in tackling the basic problems of poverty and under-development. Time and again I reminded them that nowhere in the world had terrorism yielded worthwhile results; and that our country's destiny lay not in barbarism, but in compassion, not in fractured cultural fabric, but in unity amidst diversity.

Counter-attack

All these measures seemed to have a salutary effect. The general tension eased a bit. Despite disruption of transport and other difficulties, more and more people started pouring into Raj Bhavan to meet me. All the time, however, I was conscious of the fact that January 1990 was not March 1986. The spirit of the latter could not be transplanted in the body infected by terrorism. Subversion had gone deep into the organs of the power structure. Tools for implementation did not exist. And powerful forces, both internal and external, were operating, at various levels, to frustrate whatever I was doing, or intended to do.

From the point of view of the elements inimical to our country, it could be understood that they would do everything within their power to defeat my strategy. They knew that they would never again get such an opportunity to wrest Kashmir from India. Internal subversion was at its peak; administrative machinery was at its weakest; and Indian leadership was divided, somewhat confused, and caught in the slushy web of its petty power politics, having neither the perception nor the time to understand the root causes of the problem.

Pakistan was all set to intensify its campaign. It was expecting dramatic developments to take place on January 26, 1990. On that day, nothing was allowed to happen. The preventive measures taken by us held the ground. Frustrated, Pakistan decided to put more punch in the 'Solidarity Week' which was to be observed from February 5 to 12, 1990.

During the Solidarity Week, a joint session of the two Houses of Parliament was held to evolve a national consensus and pass a resolution expressing full support of the people of Pakistan to the people of Kashmir. Attempts were also made to cross the line of control at four places–Suchet Garh, Abdullian, Nawapind and Budhwar. Crowds were brought to these places in buses from Sialkot and Suchet Garh. Provocative speeches were delivered and a 'show' of crossing the border was made. About one hundred of them actually crossed. But they retreated in the face of firm action by the Indian armed forces. The basic objective of these measures was to heighten tension, cause armed skirmishes here and there, whip up emotions on grounds of Islamic brotherhood, and attract attention at international level. Earlier, on January 31, Pakistan Foreign Minister, Shahibzada Yaqub Khan, in a radio broadcast aroused public passions and justified Pakistani support to the Kashmiri terrorists, calling them, of course, freedom fighters. He bemoaned: "I went to India with a bouquet of flowers, but returned with a basket of thorns." In her speech in the National Parliament, Ms. Benazir Bhutto was all venom and fire.

Amanulla Khan, 'Chairman', 'Jammu & Kashmir Liberation Front', also started pouring more oil on the fire. His bellicosity became more virulent. He threatened to send 10,000 commandos from Azad Kashmir to cross the border.

Though a bit chastened by their inability to carry out their 'plan' on January 26 and somewhat concerned about the Administration's bid to wrest the initiative, almost all the terrorist and subversive organisations were determined to cause a big upheaval on Maqbool Butt day, February 11, the date on which he was hanged in Tihar Central Jail. The 'J&K Liberation Front' even announced that scores of police officials, particularly those belonging to the Intelligence Bureau and the State C.I.D., would be kidnapped and hanged on that day. Repeated 'firmans' were also issued to the people not to meet the Governor. To raise the tempo of terrorism, the terrorists looked for soft targets.

A Treacherous Murder

On February 2, Satish Tikoo, a young Kashmiri Pandit, was murdered near his house in Habba-Kadal. He was a social worker, an activist, who helped the people of his community secure redressal of their grievances. He was equally popular amongst the Hindu and Muslim youth of the locality. Early in the morning, two Muslim youths, whom he apparently knew, called at his residence. His sister responded to the call. Sensing something sinister, she told the visitors that Satish was not at home. They went away, but lurked around the adjacent lanes. After a while, Tikoo came out of his room. His sister mentioned to him about the youth who had come to see him. He got a bit annoyed, and reprimanded his sister for being extra suspicious. He could not imagine that someone had planned to kill him. He stepped out of the house and peeped into the adjoining lanes and by-lanes. In a moment, a dreadful pistol shot was heard. The family rushed out. They found Tikoo in a pool of blood, motionless.

The brutal murder of Satish Tikoo was another blow to the already shattered morale of the Kashmiri Pandit community. This was bound to accelerate the pace of their migration which had been going on since the assassination of N.K. Ganju, Tikka Lal Taploo and P.N. Bhat.

To generate some confidence in the community and to offer condolences to the bereaved family, I decided to visit Tikoo's house the following day. Accordingly, on the evening of February 3, I went to Habba-Kadal, an old and congested locality in the interior of the city. By that time, the curfew relaxation period was over. Except for the long row of our vehicles, nothing was to be seen on the streets. The afternoon rain appeared to have soaked the houses with depression. The few windows that were open were without even the usual dim light. The dark clouds overhead completed the picture of gloom, "It is very unwise on our part", said a companion officer, "to move out like this in narrow lanes; a well planned grenade attack can finish us all." I nodded in agreement. But my mind was elsewhere–the slush and muck on the road; the threatening clouds above; the mute and dingy houses by the side of the road, and the overpowering silence all around.

The house of Tikoo was like a shattered nest. Everything lay scattered. I sat on the ground with the family members. An old lamp had been lighted. It pierced the darkness only around me. Satish's father narrated the tragedy in a slow, halting, voice. I thought it was unnecessary. The grim atmosphere around told the tale more vividly.

As I was about to leave, all the friends and relations of the family gathered there, demanded with one voice that they should be settled permanently outside the Valley. Satish's uncle, who was a bit vociferous and assertive, insisted that I should go upstairs and see the family deity. I agreed.

A calm majestic figure was soon visible. It looked so imposing even in the darkness. The man, his voice quivering with emotion, said: "Here we have lived for centuries under the benign grace of this deity. This house, this street, this lane, and this by-lane, where we have lived since our birth, we can leave, but not this deity. You must provide us with suitable accommodation." I remained silent. This, I thought, was not the occasion to discuss such demands. With tears in their eyes, the family members thanked me and the accompanying officers. We were all moved by the sad plight of the family.

Looking at the compact and enmeshed houses, and the by-lanes which acted like fine threads of a well-knit fabric, I wondered how these families, who had all their gods and goddesses here, and had deep roots in the soil, could leave and settle in distant and unfamiliar lands. Sometimes life is unaccountably cruel. And we human beings have, perhaps, no option but to suffer–suffer in silence, or wail.

Late in the evening, we had our usual daily meetings at Raj Bhavan to take stock of the situation and to consider further measures to meet it. In this meeting, one of the items discussed was the advisability or otherwise of making such visits. The general consensus was that these should be avoided. Too much strain was caused on the limited security forces that were available, and their attention was diverted from saving other human lives.

An Avoidable Tragedy

Four days later, on February 7, another tragic incident occurred. A bomb had been planted in the office of an assurance company in the Lal Chowk commercial area. It exploded soon after the office was closed. This was followed by a huge fire which engulfed the neighbouring shops. One of the adjoining shops had a number of cylinders stored in it. These started exploding, with loud bangs, almost at the same time. The BSF picket posted at Lal Chowk mistakenly thought that the terrorists had started firing after putting the shop ablaze. The 'jawans' started firing in the direction of the shop in which cylinders were exploding. Two innocent young men, Bhupinder Puri and Shabir Ahmed, were killed. Scores of shops were gutted.

It was a shocking incident. Immediately, I ordered a magisterial inquiry by Ghulam Abbas, District Magistrate, Srinagar. But the decision could not calm my inner turmoil. I was so upset that throughout the night I pondered over the tragedy. Was it an act of God, or a sheer accident, or a panic reaction, or a by-product of surcharged, violence-ridden, atmosphere, or a sad reflection on the training and upkeep of our para-military forces? Or were terrorists primarily responsible for creating a situation in which tragedies of this nature could not be avoided? In the morning, I somewhat unburdened myself emotionally by writing the following letter to Dr. Mohammad Yousaf Khan, father of Shabir Ahmed:

Raj Bhavan,
Srinagar
February 8, 1990

Dear Dr. Khan

I am deeply shocked to learn of the tragic death of your son, in the last evening incident near Lal Chowk. Your loss as well as the loss of your family and friends is indeed immeasurable. But ours is no less. We all share your grief.

Believe me, I could not sleep last night. Such was the imprint of the tragedy on my mind. Human dimensions of the incident should haunt all sensitive souls. It is not the blood of the individual but of all of us that flows–the blood of our brothers and sisters, our sons and daughters. It is the blood that would stain the fair name of Kashmir. It would congeal and leave an ugly mark on the inner as well as the outer landscape of the beautiful Valley.

Let us pray to God Almighty to make us see the path of peace and sanity. Let us create a situation in which no policeman is seen on the streets and they remain full of tourists and thriving people. Let us impress once again on our young brothers to see the futility of the cult of the gun and understand the magnitude of all-round misery that it has caused. Let us assure them that if they abandon the path of violence we would treat them with care and compassion. Let us remind them that our Constitution guarantees justice to all, and we would ensure that the same is given both in letter and spirit.

Let no more Shabirs die. Let no one feel the permanent loss of our near and dear ones.

With sincerest condolences and prayers for peace to the departed soul,

Yours sincerely,
(Sd.) Jagmohan

Precision Killing

On February 8, at about 8 o'clock in the morning, two unarmed BSF constables were shot dead by the terrorists, near the BSF headquarters, at Srinagar. The officials were off duty and making private purchases from a nearby shop. The killers, apparently, knew the identity of the victims. They chose their timing carefully. The shopkeeper, Abdul Majid Sheikh, also received bullet wounds and died subsequently in the hospital.

Planning, precision, confidence and the calmness with which the killings were carried out, suggested the hand of regular Pakistani soldiers or ISI/FIU agents masquerading as Kashmiris. The presence of Afghan Mujahideen in disguise could not also be ruled out. A number of terrorist outfits operating in the Valley drew inspiration from the Afghan rebels, particularly those who were votaries of Islamic fundamentalism. They even named their organisations after Afghan rebel groups, like Hizbulla and Hisbe-Islam. The video tapes of fiery speeches made by Afghan rebel leaders were circulated. Azam Inquilabi, chief of a local terrorist group, called 'Operation Balakote', issued a statement to the press in which he claimed that he was trying to bring about effective coordination between the Afghan rebels and the Kashmiri militants, and that in this connection he had visited Afghan camps both in Pakistan and in Afghanistan.

Maqbool Butt Day

Our next major worry was Maqbool Butt Day–February 11, 1990.

Maqbool Butt was born in 1939 in village Trehgam, district Kupwara. In 1958, he migrated to Peshawar in Pakistan, where he got his M.A. (Urdu) and LL.B. degrees. He had a brief stint with journalism. In 1965, he became Secretary of the Jammu and Kashmir Plebiscite Front at Sialkot. In 1966, he infiltrated into the Kashmir Valley. In one of his terrorist acts, he killed a State CID official, Amar Chand. For this crime, he was sentenced to death. But, in 1968, he escaped from Srinagar and went back to Pakistan. Suspected to be an agent of Indian Intelligence, the Pakistani authorities detained him for a short period. In 1971, the Pakistani authorities again arrested him, believing him to be an agent of India. He was, however, released under the orders of a Pakistani Tribunal.

After the Kashmir Accord of February 1975, Maqbool Butt again infiltrated into Kashmir and indulged in terrorist acts. He committed a bank robbery at Langet and killed the manager. He was arrested and tried in the court of the District and Sessions Judge, Srinagar, N.K. Ganju. He was sentenced to death. He was transferred to Tihar Jail, Delhi, as he was considered too dangerous to be kept in the Valley. The Government of India, perhaps, did not intend to execute him, and there was a move by an influential section of Kashmiri politicians to get his death sentence commuted to imprisonment for life. At about that time, Ravindera Mhatre, was murdered in London. This led to the speedy execution of Maqbool Butt.

Was Maqbool Butt an adventurer, or a spy, or a terrorist, or a genuine believer in Kashmiri freedom? It is difficult to give a definite answer. His career was a chequered one and full of contradictions. Apparently, he was not above intrigues and double dealings. At one stage, both Indian and Pakistani authorities considered him a double agent.

There is evidence to suggest that Maqbool Butt became a victim of faction-fighting in the Kashmir Liberation Front. Amanullah Khan and a few of his friends manoeuvred to kidnap and kill Mhatre, an Indian diplomat attached to the Indian High Commission. Their objective was two-fold: to secure publicity for the Kashmir Liberation Front and simultaneously to ensure elimination of their rival within the organisation, namely, Maqbool Butt.

After the execution of Maqbool Butt, the Kashmir Liberation Front and allied organisations and other pro-Pak outfits have been observing February 11 as Maqbool Butt Day. This gives a convenient rallying point and also an opportunity to embarrass the Government and get publicity.

Serious and extensive terrorist activities were apprehended on February 11, 1990. Declarations to this effect had been made by various subversive organisations. They had even threatened to hang a minimum of one hundred police officials. A large number of posters and wall papers had been distributed. Repeated announcements and appeals were also made from the mosques. Past experience showed that the so-called 'martyrdom' of Maqbool Butt had become an effective instrument in the hands of the militants to whip up public emotions. Inaction on the part of the State Government during the observance of 'Maqbool Butt Day' during the last three years had further sharpened that instrument. On February 11 of 1987, 1988 and 1989, widespread disturbances were caused with impunity, and the State Administration looked the other way. Dr. Farooq Abdullah even absented himself from the State on February 11, 1989.

This time, we in the State Administration were determined to prevent the terrorists from doing anything dramatic. Throughout the Valley, a strong vigil was exercised and strict curfew imposed. Instructions were issued to officials of the State and Central Governments to avoid movement and stay in the tourist reception centre for a few days. The idea was not to give an opportunity to the terrorists to pick up soft targets. With these and similar other measures, all the declarations of terrorists, all their plans of kidnappings and killings, all their attempts to boost the tempo of terrorism and thus keep control over the components of the power structure, came to naught.

Success of January 26 repeated

The success of January 26 was repeated. On both these occasions, the reassertion of the State authority was demonstrated in no uncertain way. And this helped in regaining ground in the administrative arena. It was a psychological victory, too.

This fact was noted by the national media. For instance, *The Hindustan Times* said the next day: "The Valley used to witness violence during the last two years and this year too there was widespread speculation of recurrence of violence but tight security prevented that." *The Times of India* reported, "Although militants had given a call for 'black day' today, not a single black flag was visible on any house or Government building in Srinagar. The militants' plan to emerge from their houses in large numbers in the afternoon was also foiled."

Two Gruesome Assassinations

The successful reassertion of authority and the confidence-generating actions were, however, undermined by two gruesome and well-planned assassinations on the following day and the day after. On February 12, an official of the Intelligence Bureau, M.L. Bhan, was murdered and on February 13, Lassa Kaul, Station Director, Srinagar Doordarshan, was done to death.

Bhan, in accordance with general instructions on the subject, stayed in his office campus. Unfortunately, the incident-free Maqbool Butt Day made him somewhat incautious and he decided to visit his parents in the downtown area of Srinagar city. On the morning of February 12, while he was returning to his office, someone came close to him, walked alongside for two or three minutes, took out a pistol from under his 'pherin' and shot upward from underneath Bhan's armpit into his neck, blasting his mouth and head. Bhan was wearing a bullet-proof jacket. The killer, obviously, knew it. That was why he avoided shooting into the chest and adopted the strategy of walking shoulder to shoulder and shooting through the neck upward, ensuring his instantaneous death. The incident once again demonstrated the depth and the extent of infiltration into various departments of the Government.

On February 13, late in the evening, Lassa Kaul was fired upon at the door of his house in Bemina Colony. Apparently, the assassins were waiting for him. They knew that he had left office at about 7 p.m.

Someone from Kaul's office was in touch with the assassins, directly or through some intermediary. Kaul had incurred the wrath of the terrorists by showing on television programmes which they termed as un-Islamic and forming part of what was labelled as cultural aggression by India. He had also tried to assert himself in the office. Quite a few of his subordinates were acting at the behest of the terrorists, either out of fear or by way of connivance. Some of the news and pictures telecast were dictated by the terrorists. Kaul's attempt to check and correct the distortion further annoyed the terrorists and they went ahead with their diabolical plan of silencing the voice of sanity and striking terror amongst the few officials who were still sincere in their duties.

The brutal murder of a thorough gentleman and a senior officer in the key position was a terrible shock to us all. It had a definite demoralising effect on our set-up. While, on the one hand, the terrorists claimed that they had eliminated an enemy, on the other, their collaborators in Doordarshan office blamed our administration for pressurising Kaul, thus indirectly bringing about his death.

Terrorism has its own stratagem of attaining the twin objective of killing and causing dissensions and demoralisation in the opposite camp. The Union Home Minister, Mufti Mohammed Sayeed, and the Union Information and Broadcasting Minister, P. Upendra, flew from Delhi to hold discussions with us and also to express condolences to the bereaved family. I myself thought that the security police had not done all that it should have. But on inquiry I found that factors other than security arrangements were also responsible. To give the complete background, I reproduce below the letter dated February 15, 1990, which my adviser Jamil M. Qureshi, wrote after discussions with me, to Suresh Mathur, Secretary, Ministry of Information and Broadcasting:

> I am writing to you with reference to our discussions last evening in the office of the Governor regarding functioning of the TV and Radio and the unfortunate and tragic killing of Lassa Kaul.
>
> Earlier, the viewpoint of the State Administration was placed before the Home Minister and Minister for Information and Broadcasting. Both the Director-General, Police, and Inspector-General, CID, were present. They stated that neither of them had received any request from late Lassa Kaul, for personal security or attachment of guard. Inspector-General, CID, added that he

personally advised Kaul not to go alone at odd hours. He cited an instance when he saw Kaul walking alone late in the evening and dropped him at his home in his own car.

In this connection, I would suggest that any officer receiving threat or feeling the need for personal security should immediately inform the Director-General of Police in writing, with a copy to Inspector-General, CID, who would examine the threat perception in the light of the principle and procedure evolved in this regard. This would eliminate any subsequent controversy on the subject.

Late Kaul and his staff had been given safe accommodation in the Tourist Reception Centre. Twelve beds in room Nos. 15 and 16 had been allotted to them. The keys of these rooms still continue to be with the staff of the Doordarshan Kendra. In this connection, I am enclosing a copy of the note received from the General Manager, J&K Tourism Development Corporation. This note, *inter alia*, states:

'On the night between 24th and 25th January, 1990, at about 8.00 p.m. Lassa Kaul requested the undersigned on phone that some rooms in the Tourist Reception Centre complex may be allotted to Doordarshan Kendra for occupation by its staff. He informed the undersigned on phone that he may also stay in one of the rooms. He also wanted to know about the tariff etc. of the accommodation on which the undersigned informed him that regarding rent etc., they could decide separately for which bills shall be forwarded to him and in the meantime the rooms could be occupied by them.

Accordingly, the undersigned issued instructions to the staff at the Tourist Reception Centre, Srinagar, that the required number of rooms be alloted to the Director, Doordarshan. The staff was also instructed to take proper care of Kaul in case he also stayed in the complex.

Today, on an enquiry, it has been learnt that 12 Nos. of beds in Room Nos. 15 and 16 of Tourist Hostel at TRC, Srinagar, have been allotted to Doordarshan Kendra, Srinagar, The keys of both the rooms continue to be with the concerned staff members of the Kendra. I have been informed that Kaul did not stay in TRC, Srinagar, and some persons stayed in the rooms for a few days and subsequently they did not. However, the keys of both the rooms continue to be with them.

It may be mentioned here that on 26.1.1990 Kaul again made a written request for allotment of two suites and rooms in the hostel in addition to the accommodation already allotted to Doordarshan. However, subsequently these rooms are reported to have not been occupied.

Arrangements for night stay in Kaul's office also existed. I learn that he even stayed there for a few nights. His wife and children were not here. Unfortunately and tragically, it was sheer bad luck that goaded Kaul to go to his house in a comparatively isolated locality in darkness. If even at that time he had asked for security or personal guard from any senior police officer, I am sure either he would have been given a guard or persuaded not to undertake the journey at odd hours for which, on the face of it, no compelling reasons existed.

So far as the functioning of the local TV and AIR is concerned, we have already explained at length our viewpoint. In this connection I would cite example of a news telecast of 23.1.1990. A draft letter was also prepared by the Chief Secretary on the subject. However, this was not issued.

Foolproof Security

Foolproof security can seldom be provided. This is specially so in the present time, when lethal and sophisticated weapons are easily available. In the Valley, the 'pherin', the traditional Kashmiri dress, made things easier. Weapons like pistols, Kalashnikovs and even grenades could be hidden under it.

Another important fact that I noticed was that the gravity of the situation had not fully dawned upon the people in general and officers in particular. Neither was it realised that there was subtle and deep-rooted infiltration in almost all the Central and State Government offices, nor was it appreciated that instructions on the subject had to be taken with utmost seriousness. Had the instructions been followed, the Indian Air Force Officers* would have waited for the van, with guards, to pick them up from their houses; the Border Security Force officials would not have ventured out to make purchases at odd hours; Bhan would not have gone all alone to see his parents in the heart of the troubled area; and Lassa Kaul would have stayed in his office or in the Tourist Reception Centre.

*See Chapter I: 'My Frozen Turbulence'

Terrorism is a ruthless phenomenon. The terrorist is the craftiest person going around. He or she strikes at a point where the strike is least expected at a given moment. Full advantage is taken of any laxity or weak link in the security armour. This is what happened in all the above three cases. And it was to happen in the subsequent tragedies involving Mushir-ul-Huq, H.L. Khera and others.

Destructive Role

While we were battling against heavy odds and dealing with the manifold problems of internal subversion and external conspiracy, Dr. Farooq Abdullah and his partymen were playing a highly destructive, even unpatriotic, role and continuously stabbing me in the back. The more I seemed to be succeeding, the greater were the efforts they put in. Presumably, some elements from Delhi were egging them on. At no cost they wanted me to succeed, because my success would also imply the exposure of their past indifference, casualness and even betrayal of the nation on Kashmir.

The National Conference and its leaders did not enjoy any respect at all. They were not in a position to do anything positive. But they could inflict damage. They could float rumours; they could incite the public through unscrupulous means. They could even pose as collaborators of the subversionists. They could whisper into their ears: "Please don't misunderstand. What you have been doing from outside, we have been doing from inside." They could even champion the cause of the terrorists. For instance, Ali Mohammad Sagar, former Minister of State in Dr. Farooq's Ministry, issued a statement on Maqbool Butt day itself, demanding withdrawal of the para-military forces to avoid 'repression', conveniently forgetting that it was the National Conference(F) Government that had called those forces. On February 2, ten legislators of the National Conference(F) issued a statement* in which they said, "We demand withdrawal of para-military forces from Kashmir, as they have let loose a reign of terror which is unheard of even in South Africa." One of these MLAs, Abdul Rashid Dar, supplemented the above statement by calling upon his party, the National Conference, to join the freedom struggle. He declared that he was placing his services at the disposal of the J&K Liberation Front.

**Indian Express* (Chandigarh), February 2, 1990.

What do these statements reveal? Do they not show that the commitment of the National Conference to India is only a ruse, a stance, to secure power and rule? As soon as power goes, loyalty to the Indian ideals goes. Withdrawal of security forces, which their Government itself had summoned, is asked for. They allege that the Security Forces have unleashed terror comparable to that in South Africa. Not a word is said against terrorists and their crimes. And some of them like Abdul Rashid Dar advocate participation in the so-called freedom struggle.

The process of cutting the ground from underneath my feet had commenced right from the word go. A tendentious statement was issued by the National Conference on January 20, 1990, itself. Another virulent statement was given by Dr. Farooq Abdullah at Srinagar immediately after his meeting with the Central leaders and return from New Delhi on January 29. These statements I have already dealt in Chapter I. Here, I would discuss what he said on February 15 in a written statement to the press. It really takes the cake in regard to the efforts that were being made to scuttle my drive to roll back the terrorists and bring back the country from the brink of disaster. This statement has been reproduced in original* and its English translation is as under:

> The entire Kashmir is writhing in pain due to continuous acts of barbarism and brutality by the army and para-military forces. Here, after January 20, 'holi' is being played with the blood of the innocent and unarmed people. This bloody holi is going on for the last 25 days. Different regions of the Valley, particularly Srinagar city, have been converted into Nazi camps. It appears that the Governor, in the personification of 'Hallaqu' and 'Chengiz Khan', is bent upon converting the valley into a vast graveyard. On account of continuous curfew since January 20, it is difficult to say how many hundreds of people have become victims of the bullets of the army and para-military forces, and in this general slaughter how many hundreds of houses have been destroyed. It is a matter of deep regret that those responsible for this critical situation are trying to make people believe that the conditions in Kashmir are returning to normal. At this moment, when Kashmir's situation is very grave and the Kashmiris are witnessing their beloved country

*See Appendix XIV.

being converted into a vast graveyard, I appeal to the national and international upholders of humanity to intervene in Kashmir and have an international inquiry made into the general slaughter of Kashmiris at the hands of the army and para-military forces.

Here is a 'patriot' calling Kashmir as 'Aziz Watan', the beloved country, suggesting a separate entity. Here is a 'national leader' asking for an international inquiry into the general slaughter of the Kashmiris by the Indian Army and para-military forces. Here is a 'responsible person' speaking about the continuous curfew for twenty-five days in the Valley and his consequent inability to find out as to how many 'hundreds of innocent and unarmed Kashmiris' have been massacred and how many hundreds of Kashmiri houses razed to the ground, although he knew perfectly well that there had been a number of days when there was no day-curfew, partial or complete, and the authorities had brought out the list of casualties, which totalled about 40 up to February 16, and were daily asking the public to give additional names, if they had any, so that correction could be made in our list. Here is an erstwhile Chief Minister who does not care to explain how 'innocent and unarmed people' were ruthlessly shooting down IAF officers, BSF Jawans, senior officers of the Television and Telecommunication Departments and young men in the streets; and how, while inciting the people through lengthy and fiery statements, he does not find a single word to condemn such brutal murders.

What was the real provocation for the aforesaid statement of Dr. Farooq Abdullah? The provocation was that nothing happened on Maqbool Butt day (February 11). The provocation was that the Governor's administration was acquiring an upper hand. And this was not palatable to him, his mentors in New Delhi and his collaborators. He, therefore, proceeded to arouse passions of the Kashmiris and pour oil on the diminishing flame in the Valley.

Stabbing me in the back at personal level, perhaps, did not matter. What really mattered was that, in the process, Dr. Farooq and his mentors stabbed the national effort to wage a successful campaign against terrorism and subversion. By keeping the pot boiling, they prolonged the agony of Kashmir and caused many more deaths and much more destruction and also losses to the national and State exchequer. The more I showed determination and resilience, the stronger became the thrust of their spears. The politics of narcissism and nastiness was brought to its lowest depth and played in its cruelest and crudest form. Against all facts, against their own past pronouncements and declarations, and against irrefutable evidence, some of which I have cited in the earlier portion of this chapter, they went ahead with all sorts of falsehood and fabrication.

While the prospects of my success rattled leaders like Dr. Farooq and his mentors, who apprehended exposure of their past misdeeds and lapses, it caused equal worry to the Pakistan authorities, including Ms. Benazir Bhutto and her agencies like the ISI. They realised that I could not only set the administrative machinery right, rid it of internal subversion, and secure loyalty and cooperation from a sizeable section of the bureaucracy, but also remove the grievances of the people by launching a drive against corruption, and reviving the tenor and tempo of the development of 1986. They, therefore, mounted a special campaign against me. That also explains Ms. Benazir Bhutto's hysterical outburst against me personally on Pakistan television and in her public speeches. Otherwise, there was no reason why she should be picking on a Governor of a State and not Prime Minister or Home Minister or other functionaries. She knew that I was aware of the deeper currents of Kashmir polity and administration and my approach was bound to be effective and fruitful. Ms. Bhutto also knew that Pakistan had benefited immensely from the shallowness and superficiality of the approach of the earlier regime. How could she and her officers of the ISI allow their years of labour to go waste when they had almost attained their objective?

All those who are the well-wishers of the nation need to ponder over, without any political or personal bias, a basic question. How is it that Dr. Farooq was calling me Hallaqu and Chengiz Khan, Rajiv Gandhi was travelling all the way to Srinagar to 'expose' me as anti-Article 370 and anti-Kashmiri and anti-Muslim, and how at the same time Ms. Benazir Bhutto was vowing to tear me to pieces—"Jag-Jag-Mohan ko Bhag-Bhag-Mohan Kar Denge"?*

---

*She used such expressions, with slight variations, in her public and television speeches. 'Newstrack' of *India Today* incorporated a portion of one of her speeches in its cassette.

Author, Farooq Abdullah, Rajiv Gandhi and Sonia Gandhi at Jammu (December 1986).

President Giani Zail Singh with the author and his family members at Srinagar Raj Bhavan during the President's farewell visit to the State. On extreme right is the President's elder brother.

Author, Farooq Abdullah, Rajiv Gandhi and Sonia Gandhi at Jammu (December 1986).

President Giani Zail Singh with the author and his family members at Srinagar Raj Bhavan during the President's farewell visit to the State. On extreme right is the President's elder brother.

Author attending to public grievances at Srinagar Raj Bhavan in February 1990.

Author at Zojila Pass with staff members, July 1985.

CHAPTER X

Nature and Pattern of Subversion and Terrorism

Connivance, Collusion, Conspiracies

When the foundation is made of spurious material which is infested with white ants from within, a gale of low intensity is sufficient to bring the edifice down; a hurricane is not needed.

—Author's diary, January 24, 1990

The more I proceeded with the approach indicated in the preceding chapter and the more I was subjected to counter-attacks, the more clearly I saw the nature and pattern of subversion and terrorism. It was like looking underneath the debris, not of the building that had collapsed during an earthquake, but of the building in whose rotting crevices tiny but deadly elements had made their nests to operate in all directions and multiply and penetrate into more and more crevices and widen the cracks and ultimately reduce the entire structure to rubble.

Questions

Who were these elements? What was their motivation? From whom did they get encouragement? What was their overall plan and modus operandi? How did they breed, multiply and make deeper inroads? Why were they allowed to function unchecked from their nests? How were these nests rendered safe and why were they not destroyed at the initial stage? And why no anti-termite treatment was undertaken when it had been known that the area was infested with termites?

In this chapter, I intend dealing with all these questions. In the process, the manner in which various components of the power-structure were seized, and intimidation, collusion and conspiracies effected, would also be revealed. The role and the stimulus provided by outside agencies and forces would also be brought out. The contours of a massive propaganda machinery would also be laid bare.

The tragic irony of the situation was that I, who had been persistently pointing out that poisonous seeds were being planted, had to come back to face a thick and thorny harvest. It was I who had tried hard in 1986 to humanise the Kashmiri landscape, and had to return to confront a wholly brutalised one.

Terrorist Organisations and their Training Centres

I soon found that there were at least 44 terrorist organisations operating in the Valley at that time. A list of these organisations is given in Appendix XV.* Important amongst them were the Jammu and Kashmir Liberation Front, the Hizab-ul-Majahedeen, the Students Liberation Front, the People's League, the Allah Tigers, the Hizbi Islami, the Hizbullah, the Operation Balakote and the Al Khomeni. An apex body, coordinating the activities of eleven major organisations, under the chairmanship of Mian Qayyum, a local advocate, also existed. But the real guidance and direction to almost all these organisations came from Pakistan-occupied Kashmir and Pakistan. The main leaders of the Jammu and Kashmir Liberation Front were Amanullah Khan, Raja Muzaffar and Farooq Hyder. They operated openly and made frequent declarations. The leaders of other organisations largely acted in a clandestine manner.

After the imposition of Governor's Rule on January 19, 1990, and the launching of an intensive drive to collect information, especially from the border-crossers and other arrested persons, it came to be known that there were at least 39 training centres in Pakistan-occupied Kashmir and Pakistan. There were some training centres in the Valley itself. But they functioned for very short durations and were quickly shifted, leaving no evidence, rendering the task of apprehending the trainers and the trainees difficult. A large number of guides and motivators had also been enlisted and were woven into a well-knit

*New training camps have been added since then. The latest list of 105 camps is given in Appendix XV-A.

organisation imparting training, facilitating border-crossing and indulging in acts of terrorism and allied activities.

The hold that these terrorist organisations had acquired was evident all over the Valley.* The people had been asked to surrender their passports because they described the passport-holders as Indians. The shopkeepers were ordered to paint their hoardings green, hoist flags, write slogans and observe 'hartals' whenever calls in this regard were given. Their 'diktat' was law, and the punishment was stoning, arson or even a bullet.

The public were also instructed not to pay taxes. They were only too happy to obey. The State machinery was incapable, and even unwilling, to collect even routine taxes like entertainment tax and excise duty. By the end of the year, the arrears on this account alone amounted to ₹ 24 crores.

To terrorise the non-Kashmiris, particularly those in key positions, intimidatory letters were sent. A typical letter which came to my hand, is reproduced below:

> We know you have been staying in Kashmir for a long time. You have a flour mill in Barbarshah and houses in Lalmandi. You are told to leave Kashmir immediately; otherwise we will blast your factory and houses in Kashmir. We will blast your home and hotel of Delhi also.
>
> We order you to leave Kashmir immediately, otherwise your children will be harmed; we know where they study. We also know one of your daughters has got married last winter. Close your business and leave immediately.
>
> We are not scaring you. But this land is only for Muslims, as it is the land of Allah. Sikhs and Hindus cannot stay here. If you do not obey, we will start with your children.
>
> Kashmir Liberation Zindabad.

In the same strain, warning was given to the landlords to eject all non-Kashmiri, non-Muslim tenants. Immediately thereafter, ejection notices were issued by the former. This fact was publicised through paid notices in the local newspapers to let it be known to the "militants" that their instructions had been complied with.

---

*See also Chapter VII: 'Conditions Before My Arrival'.

Subversion in Services and Other Components of Power Structure

The extent to which the rot had set in the vital components of the State's power structure and intrusion had taken place in them, was truly depressing. The police, the general services, the hospital administration, the press, the Bar and the Bench–all had been infected.

Police

I found that, notwithstanding the enormity of the crimes committed, the local police stations did not have even photographs of the wanted terrorists. How could any terrorist be spotted or arrested? How could surveillance at airport or bus stands be kept? Hardly anyone was able to answer such queries. When I called for the files of cases pertaining to serious crimes, I was appalled by the indifference and ineffectiveness. There was no investigation at all. Apart from recording the first information report, practically no action was taken. Even in the case of Dr. Rubaiya Sayeed's kidnapping, which had shaken the entire nation and received world-wide publicity, there was only a one-line investigation: "Accused are not known and no witness is forth-coming."

The local police had been so infiltrated that quite a part of it had become a hindrance and a drag. There was hardly any doubt that IB officials killed* during the period were betrayed by the infiltrators in the local police and their identity and whereabouts were made known to the terrorists either directly or through contacts. For instance, one of them, Krishan Gopal, who was living in the quarters attached to the police station, was murdered soon after he left the police station on January 9, 1990. Brutal murders of IB officers, followed by practically no action to apprehend the culprits, not only caused demoralisation amongst the ranks of the organisation, but also had the effect of drying up all sources of information.

Even the police driver of my own pilot car had deep links with the subversives. The wireless set of this jeep had been passed on to them. The driver conveniently reported to his officers that the wireless set had been stolen when he had parked the jeep outside his house at night. No wonder, there was once an explosion in this jeep.

A head constable of J&K police, working as a wireless operator at a joint interrogation centre, was working in close cooperation with the

*See Chapter VII: 'Conditions Before My Arrival'.

top terrorist Abdullah Bangroo and was passing all messages and incriminating documents from one subversive group to another. Another police constable of Anantnag was working as an associate of top terrorists, such as Mushtaq Waza and Bilal Ahmed Beg.

The Batmaloo area of Srinagar was badly infested with terrorists. Some of the most brutal crimes were committed there. The dead bodies* of the former Independent MLA, Mir Mustafa, and HMT General Manager, H.L. Khera, were found in this locality. Later on, it was found that a middle-level officer of this area was hand in glove with the terrorists. Two members of his staff were actively involved. The driver of the SSP, Srinagar, was in league with the subversives. He sometimes used the SSP's vehicle for moving them from one place to another. Quite a number of officials acted as guides and informers of the underground organisations. Another middle-level officer of Baramulla, too, was involved. Hameed Sheikh, who was released in exchange of Dr. Rubaiya Sayeed, had in his possession a very large number of curfew passes, apparently supplied by the officials who were concerned with the issue of such passes.

How some elements in the local police assisted the subversionists in accordance with a pre-conceived plan, would be evident from an incident that occurred on January 22, 1990. At about 4.30 p.m., a white ambassador car was spotted near Lal Bazar by a small contingent of CRP jawans. On suspicion, they signalled it to stop. But it did not; instead, it speeded up. The jawans fired. The car was hit slightly, injuring one of the occupants. All of a sudden, a local police jeep of the Soura police station appeared on the scene, blowing the siren furiously and continuously. This diverted the attention of everybody. In the confusion, the ambassador car escaped, virtually led by the jeep with siren. After about ten minutes, however, the same jeep of the local police station was seen and stopped by the CRP in the nearby locality of Hawal. On search, a person belonging to the border village of Uri, district Baramulla, was found sitting by the side of the police driver. When he came out, he left a blanket on the seat, covering some material. On removing the blanket, a loaded .38 revolver, a Chinese made grenade, a dagger and a toy pistol were recovered. Another person of Baramulla and three constables of the J&K Armed Police, who were involved in the conspiracy, were also apprehended.

---

*See Chapter XIV: 'Acquiring an Upper Hand'.

Release of 70 Hardcore Terrorists

Despite the fact that the situation as was prevailing in the State was extremely grave and needed deft handling, the administration was trifling with such matters as release of terrorists. When, on the one hand, the police set-up was getting rapidly demoralised, when intelligence was fast drying up, when infiltration in the services was becoming deeper and deeper, when terrorism was spreading at a phenomenal speed, when the press was bringing out stories of subversive plans like Topac,* when the nation was expressing serious concern about the rapidly deteriorating situation, and when the conspiratorial pattern was clearly coming into view, the State Government decided to release a large number of terrorists. Between July and December 1989, it released 70 hardcore terrorists.** I stumbled upon

---

* For particulars of Topac plan, the last section of this chapter may be seen.

**At the time such irresponsible decisions were being taken by Dr. Farooq Abdullah government, particularly in the period, from July 1989 to January 1990, the Intelligence Bureau unit in Kashmir was headed by A.S. Dulat. His superficial way in looking at the incidents of 'subversions, collusions and conspiracies', analyzed in this chapter, proved disastrous. He did not take any worthwhile initiative, either himself or through the Government of India, to prevent Chief Minister Farooq Abdullah from releasing 70 hard core, motivated, trained and pro-Pakistan militants, with high-level contacts on the other side of the Line-of-Control. He let the ground-level situation slip out of the Intelligence Bureau's hand to such an extent that his own field Intelligence Officers, such as R.N.P. Singh, Kishen Gopal and M.L. Bhan, could be killed with impunity. He himself records in his book, Vajpayee Years (page 63): "During that killing spree of IB officials there came a day when I was sort of gheraoed in my office. The staff came out and told me that they were insecure".

Tragically, a seven decade old, tried and effective institution, which had seen such redoubtable and far-sighted leaders, such as B.N. Mullik, stood emaciated. Dulat could not see beyond a few personalities, notwithstanding their proven record of unreliability. He failed to realize that to contain, and finally cure, critical maladies, it were the deep-rooted infections in the vital organs of the system that needed to be attended on priority. By being permissive to the spread of these infections, a brutal environment were allowed to come about in which Union Home Minister's daughter could be kidnapped and released only on the terms of the terrorists.

As analyzed in Chapter VIII, titled *Conditions Before My Arrival,* (for the second term, on January 19, 1990), the State Government at Srinagar had been rendered non-existent and Dulat's Intelligence Bureau Kashmir-Unit had been turning a deaf ear to the daily bomb blasts caused by the subversives in the valley–there were as many as 50 such bomb blasts in the month of October 1989 alone.

The agreeable and positive atmosphere created during the Governor's rule was soon set at naught. Likewise, the highly appreciative comments made about my contribution

Contd. on next page

these cases accidentally. What I found was truly amazing. I give below a brief description of five typical cases.

Mohammad Afzal Sheikh, a resident of Trehgarn, crossed over to Pakistan and stayed in the house of his brother-in-law, Ghulam Mohammad Wani, who had settled at Athmuqam in Pak-occupied Kashmir. In Muzaffarabad, he met Javed Maqbool Butt and Showkat Maqbool Butt, sons of Maqbool Butt, with the help of Amanullah Khan, 'Chairman', Jammu and Kashmir Liberation Front. He also came across Abdul Ahad Waza, a top leader of the JKLF. He took an oath of allegiance at Muzaffarabad and filled up a form in which he affixed his thumb impression with blood. He went to Kachi Ghari, Peshawar, for training. On return, he caused bomb blasts in buses. He was detained, and his detention was confirmed by the Advisory Board headed by the Chief Justice, J&K High Court. Yet he was released in July 1989 by the Farooq Abdullah Government.

Rafiq Ahmed Ahangar went to Pakistan after crossing the border clandestinely on August 22, 1988, via Leepa. He met Raja Muzaffar Khan at Muzaffarabad. He was given training in the handling of arms and explosives to create Punjab-like conditions in J&K. On return, he blasted a number of bombs in the Valley. He was arrested and detained. An Advisory Board headed by the Chief Justice of J&K High Court confirmed his detention. But he was released in July 1989 by the National Conference Government.

Farooq Ahmed Ganai went to Pakistan under the code name of Khalid. He was given to understand that the aim of the Liberation Front was to create chaotic conditions in the J&K State. He was told to

---

to the stability and development of the state during my first term of five years, by a number of reputed and independent political analysts, such as Pran Chopra, Nikhil Chakravartty, V.N. Narayanan, A.N. Dhar, Arun Shourie, Prem Bhatia were intentionally relegated to the background and erased from the public memory.

And it took little time for Dulat and company to fall back to their familiar political game of 'money and manipulation'. The charge that Dulat was throwing money too freely in Kashmir is not without validity. He himself mentions it in the aforesaid book (page 157): "People in the Intelligence Bureau, my former organization and higher-ups, apparently told the Kashmiris that Dulat had spoiled them".

Dulat also betrays ignorance of the plethora of unassailable documents and data cited by me in various chapters of *My Frozen Turbulence in Kashmir*, and makes imprecise and incorrect observations, based largely on hearsay. For instance, he does not take into account my letter of July 2, 1984, to the President requesting for imposition of Governor's Rule, and not replacement of Dr. Farooq Abdullah Ministry by G.M. Shah's.

make the Army, the Police, the CRPF, the BSF his special targets and also to kill important leaders. He was trained in Pakistan. He had meetings with Amanullah Khan, Chairman, Jammu and Kashmir Liberation Front, and Dr. Farooq Hyder, General Secretary, in the house of Raja Muzaffar Khan at Muzaffarabad. He was involved in bomb blasts and cases of looting, firing, etc., in the Valley. He was detained under the Public Safety Act. His detention was confirmed by the Advisory Board headed by the Chief Justice. But he was released in July 1989.

Ghulam Mohammad Gujri accepted the programme of the JKLF and went to Pakistan clandestinely in August 1988 via Bungna Bala for receiving training in the handling of sophisticated arms and ammunition. After crossing the border in the company of two Pak-occupied Kashmir guides, Ghulam Nabi Wani and Mamaji, he stayed for the night in the house of one Ghulam Mohammad Wani who was originally a resident of Kupwara but settled at Athmuqam (POK). This house was being used as a transit camp for different groups going to Pakistan for training. Gujri was issued one Kalashnikov gun, two magazines, and 200 rounds and detonators. He was caught in a bomb blast case. His detention was confirmed by the Advisory Board headed by the Chief Justice of J&K High Court, and yet he was released in July 1989 by the Farooq Government.

Farooq Ahmed Malik went to Pakistan with the help of Abdul Ahad Waza, *via* Rashanpur, for training in the handling of arms and explosives. During his stay in Pakistan, he had a meeting with Amanullah Khan. He was involved in a bomb blast in the Telegraph Office, Srinagar. His detention was confirmed by the Advisory Board headed by the Chief Justice of J&K High Court. But he was released in July 1989, by the Farooq Government.

These were persons who were highly motivated subversives. These were the persons who were trained in the handling of dangerous weapons. These were the persons who had contacts at the highest level in Pakistan-occupied Kashmir. These were persons who knew all the devious routes of going to and returning from Pakistan. These were persons who had practical experience of all aspects of terrorism–border-crossing, bringing weapons from Pakistan, and committing terrorist crimes. These were persons whose detention had been approved by a three-member Advisory Board presided over by the Chief Justice. Yet these were the very persons who were released, and that too at a time when the forces of subversion needed to be rooted out with an iron hand.

The fact that in none of these cases release was merited stood proved by the inability of the police to trace and apprehend any one of them when I ordered the re-arrest of all the 70 terrorists in question. Apparently, they had all gone underground and resumed their terrorist activities, causing more deaths, more bomb blasts, more acts of arson.

Since these terrorists were experienced in their activities, they established contacts across the border easily, and also served as guides, thereby causing an immense increase in cases of border crossing and smuggling of arms. They motivated more young men to join their ranks. By way of persuasion, they could very well point to their own cases and say: "Look what has happened to us. We have been to Pakistan. We have met the top leaders. We had the adventure of blasting bombs. And we have lost nothing. Here we are again."

Thus, the release of the 70 terrorists not only further demoralised the few police officers who were still discharging their duties with a modicum of loyalty, but it also swelled the ranks of the terrorists, made them more audacious and removed whatever little fear of authority they might have had earlier.

What was most unpardonable was the almost simultaneous release of these 70 terrorists. This enabled them to occupy key positions in the network of subversion and terrorism and complete the chain which took them again to Pakistan to bring arms to indulge in killings and kidnappings and other acts of terrorism. For example, one of the released persons, Mohammad Daud Khan of Ganderbal, became the Deputy Commander-in-Chief of a terrorist outfit, Al Bakar, and took a leading part in organising a force of 2,500 Kashmiri youth. Another released youth, Abdul Ahad Bhat enlisted a large number of youth for Jammu and Kashmir Liberation Front and Hizbul Mujahideen for training in Pakistan.

General Services

What was happening to the services other than the police? I found that a large number of Government servants were involved in subversive activities. Some of them even acted as organisers and group leaders. The manner in which the government servants took part in such activities would be clear from the five typical cases described below.

An Inspector in the State Electricity Department, Pulwama, functioned as an area commander of Hizbul Mujahideen. Though the official was working, almost openly, as an area commander and had been absent from his office for quite some time, he remained on the pay roll of the State and got salary and other perks. He was also using facilities of the electricity department, such as telephone and vehicles, for subversive activities.

A class IV employee of the Hospitality and Protocol Department had been functioning as an active member of a subversive organisation. He was involved in a case of arson. From his house and the house of his father, 13 bombs were recovered. Even when he remained underground, no serious notice of his absence was taken.

Ahmed Afzal Sheikh, a teacher, while remaining in service, went to Pakistan-occupied Kashmir. He even met top leaders like Amanullah Khan and Raja Muzaffar. After he returned, a bag containing pistols and loaded magazines was sent to him through another subversionist.

Irshad Hussain, while remaining on the pay roll of the State Government as Junior Engineer, acted as a motivator. He sent two groups of youth for training to Pakistan-occupied Kashmir. He also caused a number of explosions, including those in the Kashmir Club and Srinagar Zero Bridge. He kept arms and ammunition illegally on behalf of the top terrorists like Ahmed Sheikh and Bilal Ahmed.

Another employee, Mohammad Akram, remained in touch with top terrorists such as Yasin Malik and escorted a group of youth, from Rajouri side, to Pakistan-occupied Kashmir.

From the five cases narrated above, a few pertinent questions arise. How is it that so many government servants became instruments of subversion? How is it that they continued with their activities for such a long period and some of them even went to Pak-occupied Kashmir? Is it possible that such activities would have remained undetected, unless there was encouragement from influential quarters and unless the government servants had some political godfather or the other? After I had some heinous crimes detected, I found that quite a few Junior Engineers of a particular department were involved in such cases. I called the Chief Engineer concerned and asked him why this was so. He said that these Junior Engineers and the like of them hardly bothered about their senior officers. They had direct approach to Ministers and other political elements in the power structure and, more often than not, it were the Chief Engineers who were answerable to the Junior Engineers rather than the other way round.

Conspiracies

The extent of infiltration even in sensitive departments can be gauged from the cases relating to the escape of 12 dangerous detenus from the Srinagar Central Jail. The escape took place on March 27, 1990, but plans for its execution were made beforehand. Those who were responsible for the custody of the detenus had themselves made the escape possible.

Almost all the employees concerned, whether gazetted or non-gazetted, whether belonging to the Jail or the Police or the Electricity Department, were infected with the virus of subversion. Some conspired, some connived, while some others just looked the other way. Every facility for the escape was made available. There was a hack-saw for cutting the nails and the grills. There was wooden material in the adjoining abandoned barracks for fabricating ladders. The detenus were permitted to the barracks, ostensibly under the pretext of playing cricket. Conveniently, the noise of driving the nails in the ladder was taken as noise emanating from the contact of the bat with the ball! Long bedsheets had been given to the detenus so that they could be tied together to serve as a rope for suspension in the courtyard of the quarters of the Deputy Superintendent of the Jail who, conveniently, again, took permission from the Superintendent to leave station for the night. From the courtyard they could open the door and take a route which was outside the line of vision of BSF sentries. After crossing one or two fields the Nagin Lake could be reached, where small boats were already stationed to row the detenus away. When all these arrangements were made, the transformer of the jail got 'hot' and the electrician, who was normally not on duty at night, was available right on the spot to switch off the transformer. Every link in the chain played its role and established some alibi or other.

Such was the game plan that the right persons were available at the right spots. Quite a few invisible hands were operating in the administration to pull the levers of subversion. If anyone was questioned, a rueful face could be presented, complaining that the locals or members of a particular community could not be trusted. And if no attempt was made to detect the 'invisible' hands, they started moving with greater speed and alacrity.

The conspiracies were deep-rooted; they were extensively spread. There was hardly any link in the chain which could not be made to do the assigned job. Fear of authority was non-existent. One could enjoy the salary and perks and also act as a hero for the 'liberation struggle'. The bread for them was buttered on both sides. No wonder, the tempo accentuated and the pace of subversion accelerated.

State Hospitals as Centres of Collusion

Some influential doctors in the Valley constituted a powerful caucus for anti-national work within the government machinery. The hospitals in Srinagar, particularly SKMI, SMHS and Lal Ded, became, in course of time, centres of collusive and conspiratorial activities. Practically all the facilities of these hospitals were available to the terrorists. They ate the hospital food; they slept on the hospital beds; they used the hospital stores far hiding their weapons; they sneaked into the staff quarters whenever necessary; and they escaped from the backyards through secretly-charted routes, for instance, in the SMHS hospital, the outer compound wall had been breached at carefully chosen points from where one could easily move into the narrow lanes and by-lanes of the congested localities. The escape of top terrorists such as Hameed Sheikh and Yasin Mulick, the kidnapping of Dr. Rubaiya Sayeed, the killings in and around Soura Medical Institute Complex, were all connected, in one way or other, with the hospital administration. Dr. A.A. Guru who had over the years used his position and influence with the political bosses to secure a tremendous hold over the local medical community, was the key figure in all such cases. These cases have been narrated and analysed in Chapter XIV. Here only one example would suffice.

About the goings on in the Soura Institute, I received a letter dated February 3, 1990, from a doctor, the relevant portion of which is reproduced below:

> I am a Muslim doctor working in Sher-e-Kashmir Institute of Medical Sciences, Soura, Srinagar. I want to bring to your kind notice the dirty role of Dr. A.A. Guru, as far as subversive activities in the State are concerned.
>
> Sir, Dr. Guru is the Head of the Department of Surgery. But he is quite distant from his profession. Politics seems to be his field. He is the person who made Sheikh Abdul Hameed, Kashmir Liberation Front Area Commander, escape from the interrogation of the police. Had Hameed Sheikh come under interrogation, many

things would have been revealed to the police. Sir, here is what happened in brief.

Hameed Sheikh got injured. He was rushed to SMS Hospital, where he was operated upon by Dr. Ashaq Hussain and Dr. Peerzada. Dr. Ashaq Hussain has been a colleague and good friend of Dr. Guru.

Dr. Guru went to SMHS Hospital on his own and contacted Dr. Ashaq Hussain. He told Hussain to write a call for consultation to him so that he could help Hameed Sheikh. As a consultation note, Dr. Guru wrote that Hameed Sheikh's condition is serious, and he should be shifted to Sher-e-Kashmir Medical Institute. This was a crucial decision which helped Hameed in the long run.

Hameed got shifted to Sher-e-Kashmir Institute amidst tight security. Allah Baksh, SSP, accompanied him. Here Dr. Guru rebuked CRPF personnel and asked them to stay away from Hameed's ward. He made it look to the police as if his condition was very serious. Days passed. Dr. Guru used to tell the police that Hameed was not well. This was all done in consultation with other KLF boys who were in contact with Dr. Guru.

After a month, the police stressed through Home Ministry that Hameed should be handed over to them. For this, Dr. Guru played another big drama. He talked to Hameed. He told him that he would order his chest X-ray next day. He told Hameed that he should simulate breathlessness at the time of X-ray. Meanwhile, Dr. Guru informed Allah Baksh, SSP, and told him to come to X-ray Department as he had to get X-ray of Hameed's chest done. If the X-ray was clear, he would discharge him and hand him over to the police. Allah Baksh arrived. Hameed was shifted. He did what Dr. Guru had told him. He feigned breathlessness. Allah Baksh was told that X-ray could not be done. So Hameed was shifted back to the ward. It was falsely shown to Allah Baksh that the condition of Hameed was serious. Police was all the time informed that Hameed could not walk. It would take him months to do so. This was done in consultation with the KLF boys.

Dr. Rubaiya Sayeed was kidnapped. Her release was made conditional upon Hameed's release. As Dr. Guru knew that his release was imminent, he was made to get up from his bed and walk in the ward. How come! He began to walk all of a sudden when his release time got nearer. In order to deceive Mufti Mohammed Sayeed, Dr. Guru gave a ring to Manzoor who was a resident doctor in Sher-e-Kashmir Institute and son-in-law of Home Minister and told him that he felt bad about Rubaiya's kidnapping and was ready to help. In fact he was helping militants. He became a mediator, and his contacts with KLF were obvious. He told the Chief Secretary that he must release the militants; otherwise the kidnappers would kill Rubaiya. This was to create a fear psychosis in Government's mind and secure Hameed's release. Sir, the Institute is backing militants through Dr. Guru. Kindly set an inquiry against him.

Yours
One Muslim doctor

Subsequent inquiries made by me revealed that what had been stated in the above letter was substantially correct. Four days before Dr. Rubaiya Sayeed was released, the strong and earnest request of the police to allow a few minutes' interrogation of Hameed was vehemently turned down on the grounds that he was too critical to speak even a few words. How was it that, after a few days, the same Hameed was kicking around and showing 'V' signs all over Srinagar and asking 'Indian dogs to go back'?

Unfortunately, against normal practice and procedure, the Srinagar Medical Institute was allowed to function, on the insistence of Sheikh Abdullah, through a Trust controlled by him and his close associates, though all the funds for it were provided by the Union Government under the Five-Year Plans. Over the years, a pro-Pakistan caucus came to have a dominant say in the affairs of the Institute, particularly in respect of appointments and purchase of equipment. Thus, ironically, and thanks to its lack of vision, the Government of India brought into existence, with its own resources, a strong centre of subversive activities in the Valley.

Infection spreads to the Courts

Terrorism and subversion had taken a toll of the judiciary too. The courts at the District and Sub-Divisional level had practically ceased to function. In some of the towns such as Shopian some advocates gathered to constitute an Islamic court and the local leader of the Jama'at-i-Islami advised the public to refer their disputes to this court.

The environment also affected the State High Court. The two judges who functioned from Srinagar started passing orders for the correction of which we had to frequently move the Supreme Court.

Even when action was taken against the offenders who used 'Pakistan standard time', instead of Indian standard time, these judges intervened and stayed action. Similar was the position in respect of the newspapers against whom we proceeded for publishing criminal threats under the cloak of news story.

Another example of the manner in which the State High Court was functioning from Srinagar, was the formation of the Division Bench by the two judges on their own. Under the rules of the High Court, it was the Chief Justice alone who could constitute the Division Bench, but the two judges themselves constituted the Division Bench, thereby forcing us to go to the Supreme Court with regard to every order passed by them. Had there been an order of a single judge, we could have filed an appeal in the Division Bench of the same High Court, functioning at Jammu, the winter capital of the State.

A few other orders passed by the Srinagar Bench need to be noted. These orders related to: issuance of stay orders without giving an opportunity of hearing to the State Government; imposition of restrictions on the legal powers of the authorities to impose curfew; and granting of virtual anticipatory bails in cases in which detention of terrorists and subversionists was to be effected under the Public Safety Act. Aggrieved by these orders, we moved the Supreme Court which reversed the decisions of the High Court expressing surprise.

The Bar

Srinagar Bar had come under the control of elements who made it a powerful instrument of disseminating subversive thoughts. It would often pass resolutions and give wide publicity to them. For instance, in the memorandum submitted to the local office of the UN it said,

> "After the passing of the Indian Independence Act, 1947, the British suzerainty over the State of J&K came to an end and consequently J&K became an indepen-dent sovereign country under the International Law after the 15th of August 1947. The Dogra Maharaja of the country failed to realise the aspirations of the overwhelming Muslim majority of the State and started conspiracies in connivance with Indian leaders to manipulate the accession of J&K to India against the aspirations of the people of J&K. As a result of this conspiracy more than 2.5 lakhs of Muslims were massacred in Jammu Province and a large number of them were made to flee to the neighbouring area of Pakistan. Against this

threatened fraud and massacre of Muslims of Jammu Province, the inhabitants of the State supported by some tribesmen decided to foil the attempts of the Maharaja to accede to the State of India against the aspirations of its overwhelming Muslim majority. However, before the State could be liberated from the tyrannical rule of the Maharaja, Maharaja Hari Singh executed a sham Instrument of Accession of the State of J&K to India."

Under the guidance of Mian Qayyum, the Kashmir Bar Association also urged the lawyers to set their watches "half an hour behind" to protest against the "excesses of the security forces" and not attend the courts on Friday. The intention was obvious: to do what is done in Pakistan.

Subversion through Press

Terrorism relies heavily on propaganda by deeds and declarations. It attempts to demoralise the opponents and sap their will to fight and in the process creates a psychosis of fear. Kidnapping and killing of eleven Israeli athletes in September 1972 by the Black September terrorists, which was seen by 500 million television viewers all over the world, is the most telling example of this phenomenon.

As the shadows of terrorism lengthened over the Valley, the vernacular press, with negligible exception, became its willing instrument. A part of it was afraid of the terrorists' bullets, a part was not otherwise disinclined to play the subversive role, and a part merely whipped up its foundational motivation of propagating the Islamic fundamentalist ideology. The end result of all this was that the entire vernacular press became a mouthpiece of the subversive elements. It virtually abetted, incited, rationalised and even glorified terrorism. It was indirectly responsible for gruesome murders of innocent and upright men.

Under the guise of publishing the press notes of the terrorist organisations, their declarations, statements, and programmes were given wide publicity with banner headlines. The designations of the area commanders, chief commanders, military advisers, etc., were used as if they were real designations. The threatening postures, intimidatory language, and inflammatory expressions and phrases, couched in Islamic militancy, were reproduced.

The 'message' of subversion couched in fundamentalist terminology, with all the salt and spice, was taken to every nook and corner of the Valley. As the authority of the State further declined by November-December 1989, the vernacular press became more hostile, more aggressive, more venomous in its reporting and comments. By the time I landed in the State, hardly a word could be said in favour of India or anyone representing it. Derogatory and contemptuous expressions like 'Brahmin Imperialism', 'Delhi Darbar', were freely used. *Chattan, Wadi ki Awaz*, were prominent in this regard. Others soon followed suit. And the entire local press became, a monolithic spear daily stabbing the mainland and inflicting deep wounds on its links with the Valley. Tragically, while all this was happening, the State was providing them liberal help in the shape of advertisements, newsprint and loans. Could there be a worse example of a permissive State? Did it make any sense to fill the hands that were daily pouring oil on the fire ignited by the subversionists?

Some newspapers virtually acted as mouthpieces of the top terrorist organisation, the Hizbul Mujahideen. One newspaper published the threat to execute the senior functionaries of the Government, while another published a warning to Kashmiri Pandits and other non-Muslims to leave the Valley within 48 hours failing which they would be killed. These news items created fear and panic among the minorities and some of them started packing up for moving out of the Valley immediately.

On March 29, *Wadi ki Awaz* highlighted the statement of Azam Inquilabi, chief of 'Operation Balakote' that "they would not rest content till Governor Jagmohan was assassinated and Kashmir was liberated from the Indian clutches." The daily *Aftab* of April 1 carried the statement of Ul-Umar Mujahideen in which non-Kashmiris, including IAS and IPS officers, were directed to leave the State by April 15. Through the same statement, the people were instructed to consume beef.

On April 15, the *Srinagar Times* in its report stated that a special meeting of Hizbul Mujahideen was held on April 14. All the leaders of the organisation participated. In this meeting, Governor Jagmohan was characterised as Hitler. It was said that Hitler had challenged a nation which believed in 'La-Ilaha Illalah Mohammad Rasool Allah' and this was the nation which had put everything at stake for the establishment of Nizam-e-Mustafa. It was resolved that the time of warning given to the agents of Indian imperialists, informers and IB officials had expired and they were advised to expedite fulfilling their last wishes before their death. On the same day, the same newspaper, in another report, said that the J&K Students Liberation Front, in its emergent meeting, held under the chairmanship of its Chief Area Commander, Hilal Ahmad Beg, appealed to the people to remain on the roads even after the curfew relaxation period was over so that the Governor could be fully challenged.

What was the intention of this type of reporting? First, effective publicity was given to the Hizbul Mujahideen, and it was shown as an organisation with a large number of leaders. Secondly, the Governor was given a bad name and he was shown as having challenged the Kashmiri 'nation'—the nation which was inspired by Islam and whose aim was to establish Nizam-e-Mustafa, thereby stirring the religious emotions of the ignorant masses. Thirdly, threats of assassinations were conveyed to the so-called agents of imperialists and informers. Fourthly, the public was incited to defy the curfew.

What better instruments could the terrorist organisations find to attain their aims and objectives of terrorising the public and establishing control over their minds? How else could the terrorists get such wide-ranging free publicity of their programmes and policies? Any unsigned press note, with all its subversive and criminal implications, was sufficient to get into the media.

A note was issued by the employees of the CID Wing of the Police Department. It was published as under, in the *Srinagar Times* of April 6, 1990:

> Who will be the wretched man, who will oppose the Mujahids? We once again appeal to the Mujahid Organisations that no CID personnel are involved in working as informers and none takes part in effecting arrests by wearing veil. We assure the Mujahid organisations that we are not involved in any such actions which would harm the pious cause of Kashmiris.
>
> Employees CID Department

What could be the intention in giving publicity to this note without checking its authenticity? Is it difficult to see that the objective was to cause misgivings, plant suspicions, and demoralise the services and boost the cause of the subversionists?

The unfortunate behaviour of the local press was also noted by other observers of the scene. On February 10, 1990, the Editors' Guild of India deputed a team of two senior journalists, S. Sahay and K. Narindra, to study the state of the press at that time in J&K. During the visit of the team to Srinagar and Jammu, three senior correspondents of the national dailies and agencies submitted a note to it. This note made the following observations:

> Some of the local journalists had been quite irresponsible about the reporting of terrorism-related news. A local daily, with a sizeable circulation in Srinagar city, had indulged in a vilification campaign against Saidulha, an upright Station House Officer of Maisuma police station in downtown areas of Srinagar city and Justice Neelkanth Ganjoo, the judge who sentenced Maqbool Butt to death, till both of them were gunned down by the suspected terrorists. The police officer was shot dead when he was coming out from a mosque after offering morning prayers.
>
> P.N. Bhat, a prominent advocate and social worker of Anantnag used to write for various local and outside publications on issues related with Kashmir. A local journalist did a whisper campaign in Anantnag town that Bhat was an RSS man and was writing for Hindu fundamentalist publications. Following this campaign, Bhat was shot dead in broad daylight in Anantnag.
>
> Most of the local dailies used to act willingly or unwillingly, on the handouts of the terrorists. They used to give ideas to the terrorists by announcing new programmes of subversion, in the name of one or another outfit, and indulged in exaggerated reporting about the anti-India protests, publish sensational interviews claimed to have been given by underground leaders, and also splash highly sensational photographs of anti-India activities. Arranging bogus interviews of underground leaders and supplying enacted photos to visiting Indian and foreign journalists was also a big money-spinning business for some local journalists.

The note also pointed out how irresponsible had been even some of the visiting journalists. It stated:

> Many visiting journalists expect from Kashmir juicy, sensational and anti-India incidents to happen for reporting and photography during their sojourn of two or three days. If nothing happens, many of them try to manufacture stories and photographs with the help of the local aids who wait in the wings for such opportunities.

In regard to the January 21 incidents in which subversives, some of them armed, were killed in the firing resorted to by the Security Forces to quell the widespread disturbances, the note commented:

> Regarding the January 21 incidents, the *Sunday Observer* carried a report by a visiting correspondent in which it was stated that 200

persons were killed on that day and machine guns were reportedly used against civilians. The same correspondent who also wrote another story about the curbs on the press, too, might have listened to Pakistan Radio and watched Pak Television which have a big clandestine network in the Valley and are always in the forefront of the anti-Indian campaign. The Pakistan Radio had reported that so far 100 persons have been killed in Kashmir. But our *Sunday Observer* put the figure of casualties at 200 and *Sunday Mail* at 150. These are some instances of petty efforts of sensationalism and unhealthy competition among journalists.

In regard to the manner in which honest reporters were subjected to intimidation, the note said:

> The news agencies also receive telephone calls from anonymous callers claiming to represent various terrorist outfits. They often threaten that if their version is not carried in the press, the journalist would be in trouble.
>
> The atmosphere of fear and threats, developing in Kashmir before Governor's Rule could be gauged from the fact that some newspapers had started calling the subversives as 'mujahideens', others as 'freedom fighters'. The national dailies also shifted from the word 'terrorists' to 'militants' after the local Doordarshan and Radio, where infiltration of terrorists is no less, started using the more respectable word.

What to speak of local press, even the Srinagar Television Station was virtually acting as a mouthpiece of subversive elements. I was shocked to see, during the first week of my arrival at Srinagar, that in the local Kashmiri news, versions of the militants, false and highly exaggerated as these were, were being telecast as news. Even the 'Namaz-e-Janaza' allegedly performed in Anantnag, Baramulla and Sopore, were being shown.

One of the least expensive, and yet the most lethal weapon in the armoury of the subversives was rumour mongering. The Kashmiris have a special weakness for rumours, embellishment and exaggerations. More than 100 years ago, Walter Lawrence, the author of *The Vale of Kashmir*, noted:

> The Zainakadal, or the fourth bridge of the city, used to be the place where false rumours were hatched, but now the newsmakers

have moved to the first bridge, the Amira Kadal. Though the wise know that 'Khahri-Zainakadal' was false, the majority are not wise, and much misery is caused to the villagers, by the reports that emanate from the city.

This weakness for the rumours was made use of by the followers of Sheikh Abdullah in weaving a halo around him and proping up a personality cult. During the thirties, for example, rumours were deftly spread that some leaves of Chinar trees had Sheikh Abdullah's name imprinted on them. The subversives, too, fully exploited the Kashmiri's disposition to resort to rumour mongering. In fact, one of the items in their strategy was dissemination of concocted stories to cause revulsion against the State and the Central Government. The instruction on the subject said, "Spread rumours, to demoralise the enemy and undermine his image in the public." For instance, in the second week of April, 1990 when food packets were being distributed by the army on behalf of the State Government, during the curfew hours in Srinagar city, rumours were floated that these packets contained material which, when consumed, would cause frigidity amongst women and impotency amongst men, and that this was part of the overall conspiracy to reduce the population of the Muslims in the Valley. The basic objective of the subversives in coining such rumours was to prevent the State administration from coming close to the people. Another rumour suddenly floated one night in almost all the localities of the down-town area was that the security forces had mixed poison in the main water reservoirs of the city, and that the people should not drink water and come out in the mosques to protest. The whole exercise was intended to goad the public to defy curfew restrictions *en masse*. We countered such rumours by instructing the police and members of the para military forces to eat from the food packets and drink from the municipal taps in the presence of the people in the streets.

A Massive Propaganda

Apart from securing wide publicity from the local press, the subversive organisations brought out a lot of propaganda and motivational literature in the shape of slogans, songs, stickers, pamphlets, posters, periodicals and radio and video cassettes. The typical slogans and stickers are reproduced here.

It would be noticed that these stickers and slogans are fanatically anti-India, and incite the Kashmiris to burn all Indian camps and depots and obliterate all signs of Indian presence in the Valley. 'Jihad' is fervently advocated and the freedom of Kashmir is linked with Islamic faith and the will of Allah.

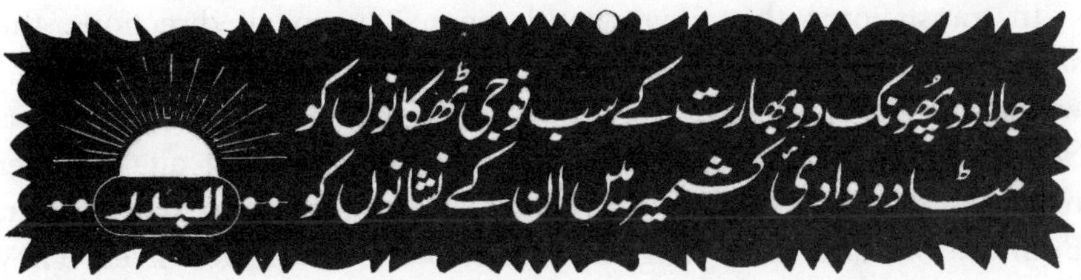

Use of Symbols and Metaphors of Islam

A notable feature of the motivational literature of the subversives is the extensive use of symbols and metaphors of Islam. Allusions are frequently made to the heroic deeds of the Seventh and Eighth Century Islamic history. For example, 'Badr', which is the name of the spectacular victory won by Prophet Muhammed over Arab pagans of Mecca, is extensively referred to. The attempt is to manipulate the mind of the Kashmiri Muslim, particularly of the unlettered, and to subject it to a heavy dose of religious emotionalism. An example of this phenomenon is what is called 'Kashmir's song of freedom'. This goes as under:

غلغلہ ہر چار سو ہے نعرہ تکبیر کا
جاگ اٹھا ہے مسلماں وادی کشمیر کا
جراءت فاروق و حیدر، حوصلہ شبیر کا
موت کا کچھ خوف ہے دل میں نہ دار و گیر کا
یا شہادت پائیں گے یا ہوں گے اب، ہم فتح یاب

لائیں گے کشمیر میں اسلام کا ہم انقلاب
سر فروشی کے لئے تیار ہیں پیرو جواں
نغمہء توحید لب پر، عزم چہروں سے عیاں
رائفل اک ہاتھ میں ہے، دوسرے میں ہے قرآں
پھر سے دہرانے کو ہیں بدر و احد کی داستاں
فتح و نصرت ساتھ ہے اور کامرانی ہم رکاب
لائیں گے کشمیر میں اسلام کا ہم انقلاب

In translation,* this song would mean: "From all directions, the slogans of 'takbir' are being heard. The Muslim of the Valley has woken up. He is as brave as Farooq and Hyder and as courageous as Shabir. He is not afraid of death or torture. We will attain either martyrdom or victory. We will bring Islamic revolution in Kashmir. Both the old and the young are ready to lay down their lives. They have the verse of 'tauheed' on their lips, and determination is writ large on their faces. The history of the battles of Badr and Uhud is going to be repeated. Victory is with us. And we will usher in Islamic revolution in Kashmir."

Clearly, the attempt here is to fan religious frenzy. The militant strands of Islamic history are carefully picked up. The language used is highly poetic and the phrases are coloured with images of martyrdom.

The same pattern of arousing emotions through Islamic terminology and impassioned verses was followed by the leaders of various organisations. For instance, most of the appeals, posters and pamphlets written by Shabir Ahmed Shah, 'Chairman' of the People's League, began with the following verse of Iqbal:

فضائے نو ہویدا کر، فرشتے تیری نصرت کو
اتر سکتے ہیں گردوں سے، قطار اندر قطار اب بھی

The main refrain of Shabir's speeches was "The enemies of Islam are uniting on all fronts to frustrate its mission. An example of this is the occupation of Kashmir. But now the Kashmiri 'nation', inspired

*Translated by the author.

and guided by Islam, has woken up. The sun of Islamic revolution is rising. The children of faith should now unite and come to the forefront to secure freedom from Bharat. Allah's will is our guide; Quran is our constitution, 'Jihad' is our strategy; and martyrdom is our aspiration."

A distinction is sometimes drawn between the Jammu and Kashmir Liberation Front and the Hizbul Mujahideen. The former is described as secular in outlook, and the latter fundamentalist. But this is not quite correct. The difference between the two is one of degree. The Jammu and Kashmir Liberation Front has assumed the posture of an organisation of quasi-religious crusaders and the Hizbul Mujahideen that of fanatic religious crusaders.

Three Major Mouthpieces

The three major mouthpieces of subversive organisations were three weeklies–*Sada-i-Huriyat, Sada-i-Huq,* and *Sada-i-Kashmir*–published by them. I will take one example from each of them to show what they were up to.

The *'Sada-i-Huriyat'* of February 9, 1990, carried a brief sketch of Hilal Ahmed Baig, 'area commander' of the Kashmir Students Liberation Front, praising his sacrifices, his disposition to see the correct path, and his dedication to the cause of Kashmir's freedom. The objective was to attach such qualities as may serve as inspiration to other young men, thereby attracting them to join the ranks of the 'freedom fighters'. This issue also carried Hilal's interview in which he said, "The strongest weapon of the Muslim is his faith–Islam. The examples of the people of Palestine and Afghanistan are before us. If the hearts of the Kashmiri Muslims were warmed by the light of Islam, I am confident that we would soon be free. Because our confrontation is not with a brave, but a coward, nation. And, besides that, we are not alone."

The aim, obviously, is to whip up emotions of the Kashmiris in the name of Islam and also paint the adversary as spineless and gutless.

Dispelling the impression that the Jammu and Kashmir Liberation Front was secular, Hilal Baig drew attention to the recent statement of Amanullah Khan in which he said, "Islam is our soul, our faith. We do not believe in any other ideology. We are dedicated only to the cause of Islamic republic. We want to bring about Nizam-e-Mustafa in toto."

The same issue of *Sada-i-Huriyat* published a report about killings in Kowdara, a locality of Srinagar. It said, "On February 6, the activists of the Kashmir Liberation Front fired upon a CRP truck in Kowdara, killing four army men and injuring several others. In fact, this area has become hell for the barbarous Indians. They have been attacked four times. 150 of their men have died. An agent of the 'Indian imperialism', Satish Kumar, has also been sent to hell." All these figures were concocted. This was intentional, because the underlying objective was to convince the public of the strength of the subversives and enlist support of more people.

In regard to the second weekly–*Sada-i-Huq*–I am taking the issue of February 23, 1990, as a sample. It carried an article which started with the following verse:

اٹھ کہ آزادی ہی تیرے خواب کی تعبیر ہے
اب ترا عزم جواں ناقابل تسخیر ہے

In translation it would mean, "Awake. Freedom alone is the manifestation of your dreams, your aspirations. Now your determination is really invincible."*

This article stated: "Of all the sins to which mankind is subjected, the worst is the sin of slavery. It can never be forgiven. On the day of 'Qayamat', some sinners would advance the plea of being helpless. But this plea would not be accepted. And the sinners would be punished. They would be told that, according to the dictates of Allah, it was their duty to attain freedom at all costs, even by risking their lives. If they did not have the courage to do so, could they not leave their land of slavery, go to a free country, and equip themselves for attacking the enemy and freeing their land from the clutches of the enemy?"**

It is evident that, as a part of the overall strategy of subversion, the design was to tell the poor, ignorant Kashmiri Muslims that if they did not fight for 'freedom of Kashmir', they would incur God's wrath, and they would be punished on the Day of Judgement. Inherent in this design is the suggestion, in the name of Islam, to go to Pakistan, get trained, and come back to fight.

The third weekly–*Sada-i–Kashmir*–in its issue of February 25, carried a commentary under the title 'Forty-two years of Kashmiri struggle for independence'. It said, "After the Indo-Pakistan War of

* Translated by the author.

**Translated by the author from Urdu.

1965, India employed every stratagem to fully integrate Kashmir. Freedom fighters were shot or rendered imbecile in prisons and interrogation centres. The Indian imperialists were convinced that as long as the values of Islam remained intact in Kashmir, this 'country' could not be enslaved. They, therefore, spent crores of rupees to remove the influence of Islam. The television was put to extensive use to spread the message of Brahminism. Easy virtues and atheism were propagated. Loans and banking were made part of public life. Cinemas, video-halls and radio-shops were encouraged. Drinking was made common even in Government-established liquor shops. In the name of tourism, Kashmir's honour and character were torn to pieces."

Is it difficult to see the purpose behind it? India, notwithstanding the provisions of its Constitution, was equated with 'Brahminism' which had mounted cultural aggression through television and other means, to destroy Islamic values and Kashmir's personality. The phantom of India strangulating the social, religious and cultural life of the Valley was raised.

From the above three examples, one from each of the weeklies in clandestine circulation, the features of the massive propaganda machine of the subversives become clear.

Mosques

Besides subverting almost all the organs of the State power structure, establishing complete control over the local press, and setting in motion a vast propaganda machine of their own, the subversives used mosques extensively for rearing, nursing and fanning their activities. In fact, one of the 'instructions' issued through pamphlets, posters, wall papers and weeklies, by various subversive organisations to the people, was that they should make mosques 'centres of revolution' and ensure that their management and control came into the hands of the 'mujahids'. From the mosques, fitted with numerous powerful loudspeakers, came the exhortations, slogans, declarations, announcements, and programmes. They became effective channels of information, coordination and crowd-collection. The religious functions held in the mosques were fully exploited and the masses indoctrinated in the name of Islam and freedom. In the event of death of any 'freedom fighter', special funeral prayers were held in big mosques and the occasion was used to make inflammatory speeches to whip up mass hysteria.

From the Other Side of the Border

From the other side of the border, the Pakistani leaders and the press launched a frenzied campaign to whip up Kashmiris' emotions. They eulogised and applauded their 'freedom struggle' and thus boosted the tempo of subversion in the valley.

At the end of 1989, an eleven-party alliance was formed in 'Azad Kashmir' to help the 'freedom struggle' in Kashmir. In January 1990, the Islami Jamhoori Ittehad set up a cell of its own for the same purpose. Not to be left behind, the Pakistan People's Party also started playing the Kashmir card. The most venomous part was, however, played by Jama'at-i-Islami. Its chief, Qazi Husen, strongly advocated intervention in Kashmir. On July 5 he said: "We are a small power but a Muslim country. We live in an ocean of Muslim brotherhood. The Hindus are not like us. The Brahmins and the 'Achoot' can never form a nation like Ummate Muslima. The people in Kashmir have carried the Pakistani flag. It is our religious duty to support the Muslims of Kashmir."

Simultaneously, the Pakistani press started raking up the Kashmir issue. In its article of January 8, the *Dawn* commented: "What New Delhi needs to recognise is that Kashmir is no longer just a simmering dispute between India and Pakistan; it is a rebellion by the indigenous population, much in the manner of the Palestinian 'Intifada' in the Arab West Bank." It further said, "The Kashmiris are drawing their inspiration not from the stumbling, faltering, Pakistani people, but from the valiant Afghan Mujahideens who have driven out the world's mightiest military power from their homeland."

On January 16, Nawaz Sharif, Chief of Islami Jamhoori Ittehad, appealed to the public to observe January 19 as a prayer day to express "firm solidarity with Kashmiri freedom fighters". He also called upon the Ulema to offer special prayers for the success of Jihad that was being waged by the Kashmiris.

Throughout Pakistan, strike was observed on February 5 to express solidarity with the Kashmiris. It was a government-sponsored strike in which all political parties participated. Huge placards were displayed. These placards read: 'KASHMIR WILL BE IN PAKISTAN'. Public rallies were held in almost all major towns of the country and fiery speeches were made. At one such rally at Lahore, the Jama'at-i-Islami leader thundered, "Indian forces have cordoned off Kashmir. But they do not know that a weapon which could suppress the spirit of Jihad has still not been invented in the world."

Active Help

Pakistan provided not only moral, political and propaganda support to the subversionists in the Valley, as it itself admitted, but also actively helped them in training in guerrilla warfare and techniques of contemporary terrorism. Batches after batches of the Kashmiri youth were trained in POK and Pakistan. Sophisticated weapons and finances were made available. A strong underground network for motivation, recruitment and guidance was set up. Besides the houses of Ghulam Mohammad Wani at Athmuqam and Raja Mazaffar at Muzaffarabad, the barracks of the Field Intelligence Unit of Pakistan at Kalamulla Chakothi, Tilwari, Nausheri, Dudbnial, Kel, Kamri and Minimarg were used as launching pads for the purpose. An overall strategy was also worked out to ensure that in the long run Kashmir fell like a ripe apple in the lap of Pakistan. The operation was largely conceived, controlled, and directed by the Inter Services Intelligence* of Pakistan which virtually functioned as a 'state within a state'.

Coordination

Training camps were set up both in Pakistan-occupied Kashmir and in Pakistan. But the fulcrum of subversive activities remained in Pakistan-occupied Kashmir. This was done to hide the evidence of Pakistan's direct hand in subversion and terrorism. Amanullah Khan, Dr. Farooq Hyder, Raja Zafar Ali and other leaders of the Jammu and Kashmir Liberation Front were allowed to operate freely. It was made to appear as if weapons were being purchased from 'clandestine arms market' and even from the Afghan Mujahideens. The services of official and semi-official agencies of the Azad Kashmir Government were also made available.

All the 44 subversive organisations, particularised by me earlier in this chapter, could be divided into two broad groups. One group worked for independent Kashmir and the other for its accession to Pakistan. The main organisation in the first group was the Jammu and Kashmir Liberation Front and in the second group the Hizbul Mujahideen. In the words of Amanullah Khan, Chairman, JKLF, the aim and objective of the Front was: "We firmly believe, on the basis of sound reasons and undeniable facts, that re-unification followed by complete independence of the forcibly divided, trodden, and

---

*See Appendix XXIII.

subjugated J&K State is the best, most honourable, most equitable and perhaps the only practicable solution of the Kashmir issue. This solution is in the best interests not only of the Kashmiris but of India and Pakistan as well."

The ISI of Pakistan naturally leaned towards the Hizbul Mujahideen and like-minded organisations. The youth who came through them were given more liberal assistance, more intensive training and more sophisticated and lethal weapons. While, for reasons of overall strategy, the youth coming through the Jammu and Kashmir Liberation Front were also given substantial help, the intention was to ultimately build up the ascendancy of pro-Pakistan, rather than pro-Independence organisations. The immediate priority, however, was to take Kashmir out of the Indian Union. In any case, Islam was the common factor in both the sets of organisations. One set wanted an independent Islamic Republic of Kashmir and the other desired Kashmir to be a part of the Islamic Republic of Pakistan.

At one stage, the ISI of Pakistan succeeded in persuading various groups to unite and coordinate their activities under the overall leadership of Jama'at-i-Islami leader, Syed Ali Shah Geelani. That was the reason why a number of posters, issued jointly by the Jammu and Kashmir Liberation Front, the Hizbul Mujahideen and the Allah Tigers, appeared stressing the need for Muslim unity.

The constitution of a coordinating agency of eleven secessionist organisations under the banner of Tehrik-e-Huriyat-e-Kashmir (Movement for the Liberation of Kashmir) was another step towards unification of the various bodies. Mian Qayyum, President of the Kashmir Bar Association, was chosen its convener.

Operation Topac

I had come across reports as well as newspaper stories about what was called Operation TOPAC.* The conception of this operation was attributed to the President of Pakistan, late General Zia-ul-Huq. Its execution was entrusted to the Field Intelligence Unit (FIU), Pakistan Army. The basic objective of Operation Topac was to make Kashmir a part of Pakistan. What Pakistan could not achieve through the wars of 1947-48, 1965 and 1971 had to be achieved through an amalgam of subterfuge, subversion, force and religious fundamentalism.

*This operation was named after Topac Amin, an Inca Prince, who fought a non-conventional war against Spanish rule in 18th century Uruguay.

The Operation Topac had to be carried out in three phases. In Phase I, all the components of the power structure had to be infiltrated and subverted from within. A friendly, permissive or collusive political regime had to be brought into being. Infiltration in police, general services and other organs of the administrative machinery had to be carried out extensively but deftly. Care had to be taken to ensure that Central intervention did not take place till the time was ripe for total internal subversion and armed intervention by Pakistani forces. Special attention had to be paid to involve the students. The peasants had to be motivated by exploiting their religious feelings.

In Phase II, pressure had to be mounted on the Indian Army in Siachen, Kargil and other vulnerable areas so that the Army remained engaged on the border and had no spare capacity to deal with internal subversion or low-level insurgency. In Phase III, preparations had to be made for armed conflict and military exercises such as Zarb-e-Momin. Finally, possession of Kashmir Valley had to be secured by intensified internal subversion and attack from across the border.

This is what General Zia is believed to have told his select band of Army Commanders and senior functionaries of the Intelligence Unit:

> Gentlemen, I have spoken on this subject at length before. Therefore, I will leave out the details. As you know, due to our pre-occupation in Afghanistan in the service of Islam, I have not been able to put these plans before you earlier. Let there be no mistake, however, that our aim remains quite clear and firm–the liberation of the Kashmir Valley–our Muslim Kashmiri brothers cannot be allowed to stay with India for any length of time now. In the past we had opted for ham-handed military options and, therefore, failed. So, as I have mentioned before, we will now keep our military option for the last moment as a *coup de grace*, if and when necessary.

In regard to the general traits of the Kashmiris, General Zia made the following observations:

> Our Kashmiri brothers in the Valley, though with us in their hearts and minds, are simple-minded folks and do not easily take to the type of warfare to which, say, a Punjabi or an Afghan takes to naturally against foreign domination. The Kashmiris, however, have a few qualities which we can exploit. First, his shrewdness and intelligence; second, his power to persevere under pressure; and the third, if I may so say, he is a master of political intrigue. If we provide him means through which he can best utilise these

qualities, he will deliver the goods. Sheer brute force is in any case not needed in every type of warfare, especially so in the situation obtaining in the Kashmir Valley.

General Zia referred to the special circumstances of Kashmir and dwelt upon the need of demoralising and defaming the Indians. He said:

> We must adopt those methods of combat which the Kashmiri mind can grasp and cope with–in other words, a coordinated use of moral and physical means, other than military operations, which will destroy the will of the enemy, damage his political capacity and expose him to the world as an oppressor.*

This is how General Zia explained the central core of the strategy:

> In the first phase, which may, if necessary, last a couple of years, we will assist our Kashmiri brethren in getting hold of the power apparatus of the State by political subversion and intrigue. Power must apparently remain with those whom New Delhi favours. We must therefore ensure that certain 'favoured politicians' from the ruling elite be selected who could collaborate with us in subverting all effective organs of the State.**

Delineating clearly the three phases of his plan, code-named Operation Topac, General Zia said:

> *Phase 1*
>
> A low-level insurgency against the regime, so that it is under siege, but does not collapse as we would not yet want Central rule imposed by Delhi. We plant our chosen men in all the key positions; they will subvert the police forces, financial institutions, the communication network and other important organizations. We whip up anti-Indian feelings amongst the students and peasants, preferably on some religious issues, so that we can enlist their active support for rioting and anti-Government demonstrations. Organize and train subversive elements and armed groups with capabilities, initially to deal with para-military forces located in the Valley. Adopt and develop means to cut off lines of communication between J&K and within Kashmir and Ladakh by stealth, without

* See *Indian Defence Review,* July 1989, pp. 35-48.

** *Ibid.*

recourse to force. The road over Zojila up to Kargil and the road over Khardungla should receive our special attention. In collaboration with Sikh extremists, create chaos and terror in Jammu to divert attention from the Valley at a critical juncture and discredit the regime even in the Hindu mind. Establish virtual control in those parts of the Kashmir Valley where the Indian Army is not located or deployed. The Southern Kashmir Valley may be one such region.

Phase 2

Exert maximum pressure on the Siachen, Kargil and Rajouri-Poonch sectors to force the Indian Army to deploy reserve formations outside the main Kashmir Valley. Attack and destroy base depots and HQs located at Srinagar, Pattan, Kupwara, Baramulla, Bandipur and Chowkiwala by covert action at a given time. Some Afghan Mujahideens by then settled in Azad Kashmir, will then infiltrate in selected pockets with a view to extending areas of our influence. This aspect will require detailed and ingenious planning. The fiasco of Operation Gibraltar (1965) holds many lessons for us here. Finally a Special Force under selected retired officers belonging to Azad Kashmir, with the hard core consisting of Afghans, will be ready to attack and destroy airfields, radio stations, block Banihal Tunnel and Kargil-Leh Highway. At a certain stage of the operation Punjab and adjacent areas of J&K will be put under maximum pressure internally by our offensive posture.

Phase 3

Detailed plans for the liberation of Kashmir Valley and the establishment of an independent Islamic State in the third phase will follow.*

It would be noticed that the 'Plan' was comprehensive, well-thought out, and made a lot of sense, military as well as political.

Not much success could be achieved by the Pakistani authorities, so far as the implementation of phases II and III was concerned. No worthwhile pressure could be exerted on the Indian military positions in Siachen, Kargil and other sensitive and vulnerable areas. Nor could base depots of the Army and vital installations be touched. This shows

**Ibid.*

that the Indian Army was vigilant and could not be easily trifled with. But in the civil administration the position was entirely different. Here, the 'Operation Topac' succeeded even beyond the imagination of its formulators. The entire government apparatus was systematically subverted. As I have explained in this chapter and also in the Chapter VIII pertaining to 'Conditions Before My Arrival', it was the writ of the subversionists that ran in all important departments of the government. This subversion was facilitated–rather abetted–by the sympathetic and permissive elements in the political and administrative structure. Some of these elements were openly pro-Pakistan; some were clandestinely so; some were indifferent and some were playing the role similar to that of double agents–they would go over to the side which appeared to be winning. Hardly anyone was inclined to work and fight to prevent internal subversion. Seeds of subversion had been planted over the years, and their roots, as demonstrated in Chapters III to VI, were deep. The environment was conducive. General Zia-ul-Huq and, later on, Ms. Benazir Bhutto took full advantage of the situation.

A doubt has been expressed in certain quarters whether 'Operation Topac' was at all formulated by the Pakistan authorities. The Pakistan Government has, of course, denied its existence and alleged that it was a handiwork of the Research and Analysis Wing (RAW). But it is immaterial whether such a plan was conceived and executed by Pakistani agencies or it was merely a model or scenario worked out by the Research and Analysis Wing or any other branch of the Indian Government. The Central issue was that the nature and pattern of such subversion was known to the then Union Government. And yet it did nothing. Its inaction was unpardonable. The present turmoil, the present sufferings, the present bloodshed, and the dangers to which the country's integrity is exposed today, could have been avoided by a modicum of vigilance and timely counter-moves. But the country, unfortunately, was in the hands of those who had no vision, and whose mental blindness was matched only by their conceit and arrogance of power.

Kashmir Terrorism A Distinct Alloy

In many ways, Kashmiri terrorism is not very different from other brands of contemporary terrorism. Yet it has acquired special features of its own. The amalgam of different elements from diverse sources has produced a distinct alloy.

The most quoted definition of the term, terrorism, is the one given by the State Department of the USA. It says terrorism involves "the threat or use of violence for political purposes by individuals or groups, whether acting for or in opposition to established governmental authority, when such actions are intended to shock, stun or intimidate a target group wider than the immediate victim".

But this definition does not cover all aspects of Kashmiri terrorism. Here, terrorism is largely sponsored by the neighbouring State of Pakistan and fanned by the forces let loose in the region by the developments in Afghanistan. The traditions of Islamic militancy are selectively used and doctored to subserve the overall design. So far as the techniques of operation on the ground are concerned, the concepts formulated by Mao Tse tung and Che Guerara are liberally borrowed. The models of the Iranian and Algerian Revolutions and the struggle of the Palestine Liberation Organisation are also kept in view.

As an illustration of this proposition, I would take a "Pamphlet of Guidelines" issued by the J&K Liberation Front to its members. It has been authored by Raja Mohammad Muzaffar. It is titled 'Freedom or Martyrdom'. It contains comprehensive instructions to the 'freedom fighters' and exhorts them to follow them strictly. These instructions, so far as they pertain to guerrilla or underground activities, are in general, the Urdu translation of Mao's well-known dicta, such as, "the enemy advances, we retreat; the enemy camps, we harass; the enemy tires, we attack; the enemy retreats, we pursue"; and also Che Guevara's formulation, "each guerrilla or 'freedom fighter' must show impeccable moral conduct and strict self-control and teach the local population the guerrilla band so that they see the advantage of aiding the insurgency". The cue for extensive use of the clergy and the mosque is taken from the Iranian Revolution. From the same source comes the propaganda line of painting the ruling elites as leading a luxurious and un-Islamic way of life and the masses as steeped in poverty and subjected to all kinds of social, economic and administrative injustices. But the pre-eminent place is accorded to the idiom and ideology of militant Islam.

It should be evident that Kashmiri terrorism was a subtle mix of various strands. The pattern of subversion and terrorism was carefully woven after study of the experiences elsewhere. A whipped-up fundamentalist fury was regularly injected in it to sustain the morale of the activists and arouse mass support for them. This pattern was put into operation with military precision, unobtrusive subtlety and uncanny sense of timing, taking full advantage of an effete and ineffectual adversary who had neither any commitment nor any capacity to learn from repeated setbacks.

Thus, on the one side was a well-conceived and well-executed plan of subversion and terrorism, while on the other side there were closed minds and bloated heads who were living in a 'paradise' of their own make-believe when the other paradise on earth was practically slipping out of their hands.

Contrasting Outlook–Zia and Rajiv

In 1983, I had occasion to meet General Zia-Ul-Huq, President of Pakistan, when I went to Karachi to attend a UNEP-aided Conference on Housing and Urban Development. He invited me for personal discussions regarding the problems of the metropolitan cities in general and old and historic cities in particular. He struck me as a cool and calm tactician who had all the time in the world to understand in depth any major problem and follow it up with some plan of action. Before discussions with me, he had apparently read at least a few pages of my book, *Rebuilding Shahjahanabad: The Walled City of Delhi.* He persuaded me to talk to senior officers of the Karachi Development Authority and also visit the walled city of Lahore. On the other hand, whenever I had the opportunity to discuss even the most critical problems of the State of J&K with Rajiv Gandhi, he always seemed to be in hurry, displaying a marked tendency to be patchy and superficial and inclined more to rely on hearsay and whispers in the ears than on any well-documented note. His whole approach was based upon his assessments of a few personalities and not on currents and under-currents which were really shaping the new political and social landscape of the Valley.

The contrasting outlook and dispositions of the two men at the helm of affairs in Pakistan and India were evident from what happened in Kashmir, particularly after March 1987. While Zia and his aides in the Inter-Services Intelligence were diligent, sound and practical in devising and implementing a comprehensive strategy of subversion, Rajiv Gandhi and the small political coterie around him showed no inclination to understand its nature, much less to evolve measures to encounter it. Any suggestion or warning was either smiled away or lulled with false assurances. Rajiv's man in the Valley,

Dr. Farooq Abdullah, was empty both in beliefs and action. And it was this emptiness that was as disastrous as indifference of the ruling clique at New Delhi.

To me, all this was exasperating. There was hardly any rational explanation for what Rajiv Gandhi and his coterie and collaborators were doing. I had, in fact, started nursing grave doubts–and there was circumstantial evidence to support these doubts–that they were deliberately allowing the situation to drift so that adequate justification could be later advanced for some strong action at the Indo-Pak border* or in the Valley itself near the Parliamentary Elections scheduled for January-February, 1990, the basic objective being creation of a "wave" in favour of the Congress(I). But certain developments overtook them. The election dates were advanced. And the 'likely action' remained only with the realm of calculation.

Unfortunately, the "wave phenomenon" is turning out to be a curse of the Indian polity. Reliance is being increasingly placed on artificially-created situations rather than on honest, sincere and dedicated service to the nation.

Sometimes, I wondered whether Rajiv Gandhi and Dr. Farooq Abdullah were really at fault. Both of them, after all, were the

---

*In his article, entitled "On the Nuclear Edge", published recently in the New Yorker magazine, Seymour Hersh, asserts that in early 1990, India and Pakistan were on the brink of a nuclear conflict on Kashmir. According to him, Pakistan had gone nuclear. President Ghulam Ishaq Khan and General Mirza Aslam Beg were "keeping their hands on the button", and India was also ready to retaliate.

Hersh's contention is speculative. It is, at best, based upon stray conversational remarks. Hard facts and circumstantial evidence point to the contrary. As I have shown in the earlier chapters with the help of contemporaneous records and factual data, the Indian government at the Centre was so casual in its approach that even collapse of administration and wide internal subversion in the valley during Dr. Farooq Abdullah's regime, did not spur it to action. Such could not be the attitude of a government that is contemplating war, let alone nuclear war. So far as Pakistan was concerned, why should it have risked a holocaust when its objective was being achieved through low cost proxy war in which the Kashmiri youth was serving as its cannon fodder?

Even at the worst of the Kashmir crisis (November 89 to March 90), most political parties in India were concerned more with their vote banks than for preventing Pakistan to close its jaws on Kashmir. On the other hand, they were, albeit unwittingly, aiding and abetting Pakistan's efforts. What, for instance, happened in Srinagar on March 7, 1990 (Chapter XII) was in tune with Benazir Bhutto's rabble rousing against me (Chapter IX).

In early 1990, neither administratively nor politically, India showed any signs which suggested a war mentality.

embodiment of superficiality that had gripped the Indian political psyche. For those who followed Rajiv Gandhi in the seat of power at New Delhi after November 1989 were no better. They were also products of the same pysche, though their superficiality, took them in another direction. They created whirlpools of confusion and contradictions, not only for themselves but also for those who were willing to lend a helping hand in extricating Kashmir from the intricate web of subversion and terrorism.

CHAPTER XI

Dissolution of the Assembly

In the name of God, go!
—Cromwell

By the end of January 1990, I had put the item of dissolution of the State Legislative Assembly at the top of my agenda for action. It became quite clear to me that, unless this step was taken, the number of casualties in securing back the reins of administration, and controlling the general situation, could be very large.

An overwhelming majority of the people believed that the Assembly elections of March 1987 had been rigged. The issue that I faced was not whether the allegations in this regard were correct or not, or whether these were partly correct and partly false, but what were the consequences of the strong feeling among the masses that large-scale rigging had taken place and that political aspirations of others had been bottled up by Dr. Farooq Abdullah's regime.

On account of these consequences and other factors which I have analysed in the earlier chapters, there was anger on the faces of the people, fire on their lips, and frenzy in their hearts. I was convinced that a good part of this anger, fire and frenzy would be taken away by the dissolution of the Assembly. It would take away the justification for the cult of the gun; it would take away that spark that causes upsurge as distinct from individual acts or group acts of terrorism.

I made no secret of my thoughts on the subject. As early as on January 30, 1990 I made my intentions quite clear to the President, the

Vice-President, the Prime Minister and the Home Minister. In my letter of that date to the President, with copies to others, I indicated six measures to deal with the crisis. One of these measures was:

> Dissolve the State Assembly immediately and hold elections after six months or so. By that time some of the subversive elements would be eliminated and some would prefer to participate in the elections. And various groups would balance each other out. A new leadership may emerge, which, besides looking to the Union, would enjoy real support of the people, particularly the youth, and would not be so corrupt and callous as the previous State Government.
>
> It would be wrong, if not suicidal, to resort to short-cuts or temporary solutions. Infection has gone deep into the vital organs. Unless this infection is first exterminated, we would stumble from one critical situation to another.

In my interview with *India Today,* which was in circulation from February 14, 1990, I had said in reply to a question that the Assembly should be dissolved. A copy of the interview is added as Appendix XVI.

My views on the subject were also published in other sections of the press. For instance, in its issue of February 10, *The Kashmir Times,* a daily which is widely read in the State and the editor of which is a personal friend of Mufti Mohammad Sayeed, former Union Home Minister, published under banner headlines: "Governor for Dissolution of J&K Assembly". It was stated:

> Jagmohan is believed to have said that an early dissolution of the Assembly would contribute in restoring people's confidence, severely shaken by the irregularities committed during the March 1987 Assembly elections, in the possible restoration of democratic order in the State.
>
> Besides tackling the problems faced at the law and order front, an immediate task before the Governor's administration was to restore respect for the constitutionally established authority. Adequate time was required also for evolving and implementing a broad economic package and reorganising the recruitment pattern which had become highly suspect during the coalition rule.

The Hindustan Times of February 13 carried the following news:

JAGMOHAN FOR HOUSE DISSOLUTION

J&K Governor Jagmohan has recommended the dissolution of the J&K Legislative Assembly.

The Assembly is under suspended animation as recommended by the predecessor of Jagmohan since January 19 when Dr. Farooq Abdullah resigned as the Chief Minister of the State.

In a communication to President R. Venkataraman about 12 days ago the Governor is also understood to have recommended holding of Assembly elections within the next few months after the situation returns to normal.

On February 19, 1990, I notified the following order:

In exercise of the powers conferred upon me by Clause (b) of Sub-section (2) of Section 53 of the Constitution of J&K, I hereby dissolve the Legislative Assembly.

(Sd.) Jagmohan

The aforesaid Sub-section of Section 53 reads as under:

The Governor may from time to time
(a) prorogue the Houses or either House,
(b) dissolve the Legislative Assembly.

Simultaneously, a press note was issued giving a brief justification for my decision. Relevant portions of this note were:

Jagmohan described this decision as the most firm and positive step in the direction towards the goal of attaining complete normalcy in the State. It would knock out the very basis of the complaint that certain elements had taken to guns because of rigged election in 1987. This would also curb the machinations of some other elements.

Jagmohan said: 'The events of the last one or two years have clearly demonstrated that the Assembly could not even pretend that it had a representative character. As regards the working of the State Government, its catalogue of maladministration was unending.'

Jagmohan specially appealed to the youth to see the futility of the cult of the gun. He said terrorism was a hydra-headed evil which usually consumed its own propagators. He advised the youth to play a positive role in building a strong and just State by making use of enlightened and liberal provisions of the Indian Constitution, the cornerstone of which is justice to all sections and communities.

At the same time, Jagmohan made it clear that no vested interest, no unpatriotic element, could be allowed to trifle with the national integrity and sovereignty and hoodwink the people by negative and subversive slogans. He said: 'Let us make a new beginning and move from the unreal to the real, from darkness to light.'

As was expected, the dissolution of the Assembly attracted considerable public notice. It was applauded by the press with unanimity. But in some circles, particularly those around the Central Government, I was criticised for what was stated as "not taking the Central Government into confidence". In view of my letter to the four top functionaries of the Union Government, my interview to *India Today,* and the news item published in *The Kashmir Times* and *The Hindustan Times,* I failed to understand how it could be said with any justification that I kept anyone in the dark. In fact, all the time I was signalling, if not shouting from the roof top, that the Assembly would be dissolved.

As *The Statesman* put it in its editorial "Only the First Step", of February 21, the dissolution of the Assembly can hardly be described as a step that was totally unexpected. "Even at the time of Jagmohan's appointment, the general belief was that not only would the Farooq Abdullah Ministry be dismissed but the Assembly, too, would be dissolved." *The Times of India,* in its report of February 20, pointed out that dissolution of the Assembly was "merely a constitutional rite that Jagmohan envisaged to perform way back". It said: "In a letter to the then Prime Minister, Mr. Rajiv Gandhi, in April 1989, the J&K Governor, Jagmohan, said: 'The Chief Minister, Dr. Farooq Abdullah, stands isolated. He has fallen politically and administratively; only constitutional rites remain to be performed.' By dissolving the State Legislative Assembly yesterday, Jagmohan has actually performed that constitutional rite." The *Indian Express,* in its editorial of February 21, commented: "The dissolution of the Assembly fits in with the logic of the situation in the troubled State." *The Tribune* observed: "The 78-member J&K Assembly has looked moribund for so long now that it is hard to understand what its dissolution on Monday meant. Only what is alive can be killed, and, for all practical purposes, the Assembly died even while Dr. Farooq Abdullah was Chief Minister but militants called the shots."

The Hindustan Times, in its report of February 20, said: "Though the step was on the cards since the imposition of Governor's Rule in the State one month ago, the vitriolic statement* of Dr. Farooq Abdullah, made five days ago, seems to have expedited the move."

It should be obvious from the above that there was nothing unexpected in what I did. Nor did I keep anyone in the dark. The decision lay embedded in the logic of the situation. Obviously, I could not have allowed politicians to put me in the firing line and simultaneously keep the arsonists active, as they might need them at a later stage, for their own little game of politicking. Incidentally, that this apprehension was not misplaced was proved by the events that took place at the end of May 1990.

Nevertheless, there was some lack of understanding about my decision. The Union Home Secretary, Shromani Sharma, spoke to me late in the night and said that the Prime Minister, who was on tour, wanted to know whether the notification in regard to dissolution had been issued at the instance of the Home Minister or on my own. I told him that the latter was the case. During the course of our talk, he observed once again: "Your decision is sound and correct but you might have waited till the State elections were over." I told him that the issue of elections was far from my mind. I was more concerned with having a grip over the situation and abating mass fury. I indicated to him once again in detail the rationale of my decision and its timing. I told him that the earlier the emotional anger was taken out of the minds of the people, the better. The Union Home Minister, who was on tour to Ahmedabad, also spoke to me early next morning. He said that he was feeling a bit embarrassed. I apprised him of my talk with the Home Secretary and also reminded him about my letter of January 30.

Unfortunately, few understood the correct legal position. Under the J&K Constitution, the actual act of dissolution has to be done by the Governor. He alone has the power to do so. His position under the J&K Constitution is different from that of the Governors in other States. To further clear the position, I wrote to the Home Minister, with a copy to the Secretary to the President, as follows:

February 20, 1990

*This statement has been discussed in Chapter IX: 'Approach, Attack and Counter-attack. It has been reproduced in Appendix XIV.

Dear Home Minister,

I am writing to you with reference to our telephonic talk regarding my decision to dissolve the State Assembly.

I do not think there is anything to be unhappy about. In this connection, I wish to make the following points clear:

(i) The J&K Constitution empowers the Governor, and no one else, to dissolve the State Assembly.

(ii) Under the Constitution, the Governor is required to act in his own good conscience and exercise his judgement and take the decision independently.

(iii) Without dissolution, there was no moral legitimacy for the use of force on an extensive scale. Nor was it possible for me and the Advisers to secure the obedience of our orders from the local officials who were constantly being fed with the impression that Dr. Farooq Abdullah and his colleagues were coming back after the role of 'butcher' has been played by the Governor.

(iv) The statements issued by Dr. Farooq Abdullah, asking for inquiry at the international level and comparing Kashmir with a Nazi camp, were inciting the people to create more and more violence. A verbatim copy in Urdu (with English translation) of one such statement issued by him is enclosed.* A note setting out the implications of this statement is also enclosed.

(v) As far back as January 30, I had clearly indicated my views in regard to the dissolution. If there were any reservations in this regard, I could have been clearly told so beforehand.

The other points in regard to the justification of my decision are contained in the press note on the subject. A copy of the said press note is enclosed.

I have no doubt that my decision is administratively, morally and constitutionally correct and would considerably help in removing misgivings of the people and restoring peace and normalcy in the State. Some relaxation of tension in the atmosphere is visible even today. The Constitution, to the faithful allegiance of which I have

*See Appendix XIV.

taken oath, precludes me from taking into consideration any extraneous factor.

Yours sincerely
(Sd.) Jagmohan

Shri Mufti Mohammad Sayeed
Home Minister
Government of India
New Delhi

I also sent another note to the press in which I reiterated my position and elaborated it further. Before issuing the notification in question, I had informally consulted the two Advisers and the Chief Secretary and also the officers of the intelligence agencies. All of them agreed with my assessment that the Assembly should be dissolved. In this connection, I reproduce below the note dated February 19, 1990, which I sent to the Secretary (G):

Subject: *Dissolution of the State Assembly.*

The above cited subject has been engaging my attention for quite some time.

I have informally sounded the two Advisers and also talked to the Chief Secretary earlier. It is agreed by all that it is necessary to dissolve the Assembly as it is wholly unrealistic in the present circumstances and is a formidable obstacle in normalising the situation.

After considering all aspects of the case, I have decided to dissolve the State Assembly forthwith. The order placed below should issue. The rationale of my decision is contained in the press note which should also issue simultaneously.

(Sd.) Jagmohan

While misgivings were being voiced in certain quarters of the Janata Dal Government at the Centre, the Janata Dal as a political party supported my decision. Jaipal Reddy, General Secretary, Janata Dal, said: "The dissolution of the Assembly was part of the political initiation since it paved the way for the fresh elections after normalcy was restored." The BJP welcomed the decision. The General Secretary of the BJP, Krishen Lal Sharma, said: "The decision of the J&K Governor should be appreciated as in the given situation the step became inevitable for ending the state of suspense and speculation." The Congress(I) and the National Conference(F), as expected, criticised my decision. The Congress(I) called it 'disastrous' and the National Conference(F) described it as 'political gimmickry'. Moulvi Farooq, Chairman, Awami Action Committee, however, welcomed it. He said that this was long overdue. The Left parties labelled it 'arbitrary'. Their grievance related more to the fact of not having been consulted than to the merit of the decision.

The press supported my decision with near unanimity. The *Indian Express* said, "The Assembly has ceased to have any relevance." *The Times* of *India* observed: "The dissolution is a logical step in the scheme of things which Jagmohan appears to have planned on the basis of his understanding that the political leadership in the State, provided by the National Conference and the Congress, was completely alienated from the people because it was corrupt and inefficient. Now, by dissolving the State Assembly Jagmohan seems to be appealing to those sections of the public which have often complained against the alleged large-scale rigging in the 1987 Assembly elections." The well-known political analyst, Nikhil Chakravartty, noted in the *Sunday* column of February 25, 1990:

> The inevitability of the dissolution of the J&K Assembly was writ large when Jagmohan was sent as Governor exactly a month before on January 19. The fact that neither the former Governor nor the then Chief Minister and his Ministry could manage the menacingly critical situation that had been developing in the Kashmir Valley was acknowledged on all hands and the need for a competent, go-getting, head of the Government in the State was widely felt. The utter incompetence and rampant corruption that marked the Government of the National Conference-Congress coalition under the Chief Ministership of Dr. Farooq Abdullah provided a happy hunting ground for the pro-Pakistan infiltrators to openly exploit the growing discontent among the people in the Valley. Instead of providing a baffle wall for the Centre, the Farooq Ministry during the last two years proved more and more a liability for the Central Government. In the average Kashmiri mind, the anti-India sentiment spread by pro-Pakistan elements was reinforced by the misdeeds of the Farooq Ministry which in the eyes of the Kashmiris had emerged as a symbol of an effete and corrupt regime foisted from New Delhi upon the Kashmiri people.

From the very beginning, the Congress(I) seemed to have adopted a policy of spreading 'disinformation' about me. The party was hell bent on ensuring that I did not succeed in J&K, for my success meant the exposure of its past misdeeds and miscalculations. Someone was having a guilty conscience–someone who had ignored* or had not applied his mind to my forceful pleas for corrective intervention, when the giant of subversion was deftly extending its sway over all the components of the power structure of the State.

In accordance with its strategy of disinformation, a slanted version of what I stated before the all-party delegation on March 8, 1990, in regard to the dissolution of the Assembly, was intentionally given to the press. To prevent wrong impressions from being created in the minds of the President, the Prime Minister and others in authority, I immediately sent the following message to the Secretary to the President, with a copy each to the Principal Secretary to the Prime Minister, the Cabinet Secretary, and the Home Secretary:

> I was assured, my briefing to the all-party delegation to Srinagar on March 8, 1990, was meant only for the members of the said delegation. But I find that a deliberately twisted version has been given to the press by Congress(I) Party, particularly in regard to the dissolution of the Assembly. I had, *inter alia*, indicated to the delegation that the decision to dissolve the Assembly was taken in the totality of the circumstances. One of its reasons was that it would knock out the very basis of the complaint that certain elements had taken to guns because of the alleged rigged elections in 1987. It was also evident from the Parliamentary Elections of November 1989 and the events† of the last two years that the Assembly had lost its representative character. I had also made it clear that the dissolution of the Assembly would provide the much needed opening of the alienated people to join the mainstream and the electoral process. And after giving that opening, there could be moral legitimacy for the use of force; otherwise, I would look like a butcher who had come to prop up an oligarchy which had brought the State to the brink of disaster. The other points explained by me were more or less the same as contained in my letter of February 20. Kindly inform the President of the correct position as stated above.

* See Chapter III: 'Warning Signals'.

† See Chapter VIII: 'Conditions Before My Arrival' and Chapter X: 'Nature and Pattern of Subversion'.

I gave reasons to the press and the public. I explained the correct position to those quarters in the Central Government who chose to express some misgivings, not on the merit of my decision, but on the grounds of not having been consulted. But I had much stronger motivation for doing what I did. Because of the position I held and other circumstances, I could not articulate that motivation at that time. I was quite clear that a new beginning had to be made. The path earlier followed had led to a precipice from which the State had to be pulled back seconds before it was to roll down to extinction.

There were other questions as well. What was our ultimate purpose? What did we intend to achieve? Why were we running on the stony and thorny path, bleeding and gasping, to pursue those who were about to push the body down the precipice? For whom were we undergoing the risk of being sniped and ambushed? Why had we put ourselves in such a situation when we were even afraid of putting our hands in our pockets lest we should be bitten by the scorpions therein? For whom were we exposing ourselves and our families to all types of risks? For whom did the jawans of the BSF and the CRP stand all night in dark and dingy lanes, in snowy mire, and frosty winds? For whom were millions being spent? For whom were these curfews, these searches and many other unpleasant tasks? Were all these sufferings, all these casualties, all these expenses meant to bring back the old, corrupt, callous, and compromising oligarchy? Were we to put back the same horsemen on the saddle? Or were we looking for something else–something new, something more lasting, something that would not waylay us once again?

These were the fundamental questions in my mind. And I was quite clear about them. If I did not dissolve the Assembly, I would look a bit deferential, a bit obtuse, or a mere agent for those who were really responsible for the mess. And there would be no moral justification for the use of force which was, in any case, needed. If, on the other hand, I dissolved the Assembly, and provided an opportunity to all to elect their representatives, through fair and free elections, within the framework of the Indian Constitution, and if I used force after providing the said opportunity, then I would look like fighting for the defence of the Union, for preserving and protecting the integrity of the country, for fulfilling a higher purpose, for realising a vision in which all communities and creeds, all races and religions, could live under the gentle shade of the great Indian tree, with its branches of truth, justice, love, compassion and human brotherhood extending to all.

Who were essentially responsible for all the kidnappings and killings, for all the murders and mayhem, for all the destruction and dislocation? They were not only the terrorists but also all those who shut their eyes to the reality. It is not only the Kalashnikov that kills; it is also the indifference, casualness and neglect that destroy without being visible.

It is not difficult to see that my motivation could not be understood or appreciated by those for whom narrow political machination had become second nature. They could not look beyond their little game of putting the old and discredited actor on the stage. They thought that dissolution of the Assembly had made one weapon less in their armoury of political manipulation. The talk of reviving the Assembly was, therefore, started. Uncertainty was again injected into the public mind. A writ petition, challenging the constitutional validity of my order, also got filed by the vested interests.

Surprisingly and, perhaps without fully realising the implications of what he was doing, the Union Home Minister, Mufti Mohammad Sayeed, made a statement in Parliament to the effect that the revival of the Legislative Assembly was being considered. He forgot that he had himself, as a leader of the Janata Dal, demanded the dissolution of the J&K Assembly. In a press statement on August 29, 1989, he had said, "Fresh election in the State is the only solution to the present situation."

The legal and constitutional position on the subject was absolutely clear. The Proclamation of Governor's Rule had been issued under Section 92 of the J&K Constitution, and it was done with the concurrence of the President of India. This Proclamation declared as under:

> *P-1/90 of 1990:* Whereas I, Jagmohan, Governor of the State of J&K, am satisfied that a situation has arisen in which the Government of the State cannot be carried on in accordance with the provisions of the Constitution of J&K (hereinafter referred to as the State Constitution);
>
> Now, therefore, in exercise of the powers conferred by section 92 of the State Constitution and of all other powers enabling me in that behalf, and with the concurrence of the President of India, I hereby proclaim that I

(a) assume to myself all the functions of the Government of the State and all powers vested in or exercisable by any body or authority (other than the powers vested in or exercisable by the High Court) in the State; and

(b) make the following incidental and consequential provisions which appear to me to be necessary or desirable for giving effect to the objects of this Proclamation, namely,

  (i) the operation of the following provisions of the State Constitution is hereby suspended, namely, sections 35 to 41 (both inclusive), so much of section 43 as relates to the allocation among the Ministers of the business of the Government of the State, section 44, so much of section 53 as relates to the stipulation of a maximum intervening period of six months between the last sitting in one session of the legislature and the date appointed for its first sitting in the next session, sections 51 to 57 (both inclusive), clauses (b) and (c) of section 58 and the first proviso thereto, sections 59 and 60, sub-section (2) of section 61 so far as it relates to clause (c) of and the first proviso to section 58 and to section 60, sections 65, 66, 67, 71 and 72, 74, 75 and 76, sub-sections (3) and (4) and (5) of section 79, sections 80, 81 and 82, sub-section (2) of section 83, sections 84 to 88 (both inclusive) and so much of section 187 as relates to the laying of the report with a memorandum before the Legislature of the State;

  (ii) in the exercise of the powers of the Legislature to make laws under or by virtue of this Proclamation, I shall prepare such bills as I deem necessary and declare in respect of any bill so prepared that I assent thereto;

  (iii) in the exercise of the powers of the Legislative Assembly to make grants under sub-section (1) of section 83 of the State Constitution, I shall, as often as I may deem it necessary and pending due appropriation of law,

    (a) make, by notification in the official Gazette, grants in advance in respect of the estimated expenditure or grants in respect of supplementary or additional expenditure for the period during which this Proclamation may be or is in force,

    (b) make by notification in the official Gazette grants for meeting any expected demands, and

(c) make by notification in the official Gazette exceptional grants which form no part of the current service of the financial year, and

(iv) any reference in the State Constitution to Acts or laws of or made by the Legislature of the State shall be construed as including a reference to Acts or Laws made in exercise of the powers of the Legislature of the State by me under this Proclamation and the J&K General Clauses Act, 1977, as in force in the State shall have effect in relation to any such Act or Law as if it were an Act of the Legislature of the State.

Place: Jammu (Sd.) Jagmohan,
January 19, 1990 Governor, J&K

It is clear that, after Section 92 had been invoked and the Proclamation issued, the Governor could perform all acts which the State Government or State Legislature could perform. He assumed, for a period of six months, the role and functions of the State cabinet and also the role and functions of the State Legislature, in addition to his own role and functions. The only restriction and prohibitions related to specific matters, mostly concerning the High Court. All powers and functions under other sections of the J&K Constitution could be exercised by the Governor.

Clearly, the powers to dissolve the Legislative Assembly vested in me. In fact, the concurrence of the President to the issuance of the Proclamation implied that the President himself intended that these powers should be exercised by me, if I so chose. If the President intended otherwise, it could have been mentioned in the Proclamation itself that the powers under clause (b), subsection 2 of section 53 would not be exercisable by me or these would be exercisable with the concurrence of the President. Since nothing of the sort was stipulated, it should be crystal clear that the aforesaid powers were to be solely exercised by me as powers under many other sections of the J&K Constitution. If no questions or doubts were raised with regard to the sole exercise of powers by me under other sections of the J&K Constitution, how could any question or doubt be raised with regard to the power under clause (b) of sub-section 2 of section 53? If I could amend laws and promulgate new laws, during the period of Governor's Rule, on the strength of the aforesaid Proclamation, why could I not dissolve the Assembly by invoking the powers which the

Proclamation, issued with the concurrence of the President, itself placed under my sphere of authority? If dissolution is unconstitutional or illegal, then all other acts and decisions taken under the 'non-prohibited' sections of my Proclamation of January 19, 1990, are also illegal and unconstitutional. Would it not lead to a wholly untenable and absurd situation?

In regard to the powers of the Governor during Governor's Rule under Section 92 of the J&K Constitution, the Government of India itself took the same position in the writ petition filed in the Delhi High Court by Dr. Mohammad Amin Andrabi against my decision vide which I had conveyed the concurrence of the State Government in 1986 to the extension of Article 249 of the Constitution of India to the State of Jammu and Kashmir. An Affidavit was sworn by Ajoy Chaudhuri, Deputy Secretary, Ministry of Home Affairs, on behalf of the Union of India. In this Affidavit it was affirmed that during the pendency of Governor's Rule, the Governor assumed all the functions, and exercised all the powers of the State Government.*

When a plain and straightforward reading of the provisions makes the position clear, no side or collateral issue can be considered. The Governor had the powers. He exercised them. And that should be the end of the matter. To use the words of the Punjab and Haryana High Court,† "There is neither room for intentment nor equity nor presumption."

My order of dissolution is, in fact, not at all justiciable. No court can substitute its opinion for that of mine. The law in this respect has been clearly laid down by the Supreme Court in the Rajasthan case (AIR 1977 SC 1361). This judgement declares beyond any doubt that the powers to dissolve the Legislative Assembly may be exercised by the Constitutional Authority on any ground which, in his opinion, is based on objective facts and consideration and is relevant to or necessary for the exercise of his constitutional powers. Whether another course of action would have been more suitable or justified cannot be examined by the court, or form a valid basis for challenging the constitutional validity of the impugned action. The court will not doubt the authenticity of the facts or the *bona fides* of the conclusion drawn by the constitutional authority, upon which the impugned action has been taken. Nor can the court compel the constitutional

* Para 5 of the Affidavit sworn by Ajoy Chaudhuri in writ petition No. 1865 of 1988 filed.

† Writ petition No. 2886 of 1989, para 102.

authority to disclose the material on the basis of which the impugned decision has been taken.

The Supreme Court has also held in Sat Pal's case (AIR 1969 SC 903) that members of the Legislative Assembly have no legal right to claim a full term as the Legislative Assembly can be dissolved even before the expiry of the full term, as clearly envisaged in the Constitution.

In the Affidavit filed by the State Government in the High Court on July 8, 1990, that is, quite some time after I demitted office, the same position, as enunciated by me above, has been taken. In para 9 of this Affidavit, it has been affirmed:

> Once the Proclamation under Section 92 of the State Constitution is issued and the Governor assumes to himself the powers of Council of Ministers, especially after suspending operation of Section 35 of the State Constitution, there is no question of the Governor acting on the aid and advice of Council of Ministers.

And, in para 13, it has been stated:

> The Governor of J&K has absolute powers vested in him by the State Constitution to dissolve the Legislative Assembly. The powers vested in the governor to dissolve the Legislative Assembly are total and absolute and are not amenable to challenge in a court. The order of dissolution of the Assembly is not justiciable.

There is no provision in the Constitution or any law which enables any authority to revive the dissolved Assembly. Nor has there been even a single case in which the dissolved Assembly has been revived. After the dissolution, the Assembly is dead. Can anyone revive something that is dead?

The above view stands reinforced by the recent judgement of the Punjab and Haryana High Court in the Punjab Assembly dissolution case. The court observed that even if it is "assumed that the dissolution of the Assembly suffered from any infirmity, no provision under the Constitution or in any Statute empowering the respondents (President/Governor) to revive it has been pointed out."* The Court, therefore, ruled that "to grant a declaration that the dissolution of the Assembly was void, would be futile". In the concluding portion of the

---

*Writ Petition No. 2886 of 1989, para. 108.

This Writ Petition has since been dismissed by the J&K High Court.

judgement, the Court said that since "the respondents have no jurisdiction to restore or revive the Assembly, no direction can be given to the respondents to revive the Assembly in exercise of the writ jurisdiction as it would amount to giving a futile direction or a direction to act in a manner not permissible under the Constitution".

As elaborated above, the courts cannot go into the facts which prompted me to dissolve the Assembly. That is the position in law. That is what the Constitution lays down. But, so far as I am personally concerned, I would very much like to have all the aspects examined by unbiased observers, be they in legal, academic, administrative, or journalistic profession. My larger purpose has to be understood. My justification has to be evaluated in the context of the facts indicated by me in other chapters, particularly in those dealing with the 'Nature and Pattern of Subversion' and the 'Conditions Before My Arrival' on the scene.

In conclusion, it is best to repeat what I stated in reply to a question by a pressman in 1990. I said: "My decision to dissolve the Assembly was taken in the totality of the circumstances. The basic objective was to make a new beginning and create an environment in which the people of Kashmir acquire the conviction that the new set-up would be fair and just, and would not do anything to prop up a corrupt and callous oligarchy which had brought the State to the brink of disaster. This decision is administratively, morally and constitutionally correct and would considerably help in restoring peace and normalcy in the State, unless it is made a victim of disinformation by the vested interests."

In reply to question about the judicial challenge, I said, "The Courts are as much answerable at the bar of History as anyone else."

CHAPTER XII

Whirlpool of Confusion and Contradictions

I wake and feel the fell of dark, not day
What hours, O what black hours we have spent. . . .
—Gerard Manley Hopkins

By the third week of February, 1990 I had been able to put the derailed Administration back on the track, though the bogies of the train were badly battered and the track was still, uneven and treacherous, over vast patches. By way of dissolution* of the State Assembly, I had opened new avenues for the aspirants of political power, be they in old political parties or new groups. I had also started various development works and launched a drive against corruption—measures which were bound to make the administration more agreeable with the people. In a wider perspective, I had started implementing, albeit quietly, a strategy that would not only isolate the hardcore pro-Pakistani elements but also help in reducing the impact of the forces that had pulled a large section of the public towards the subversives and terrorists. The objective, as indicated in Chapter IX could be attained by displacing their general appeal in respect of social norms and political and administrative injustices.

While I was creating a new environment and appealing to the estranged youth to move from the "unreal to the real, from darkness to light", V.P. Singh's Government took an extraordinary step to subject my little candle of realism and light to the nasty winds which

*See also Chapter XI: 'Dissolution of the Assembly'.

had the potential of extinguishing the light and blowing off the candle itself. It first set up an All-Party seven-member Advisory Committee; and, as if this was not sufficient to knock off the base of the candle, it designated the Railway Minister, George Fernandes, as Minister of Kashmir Affairs. These two steps took Kashmir back to confusion and contradictions.

Wrong signals were again sent to the Services. My position was again undermined. Misgivings about the fairness of Government were again planted in the minds of the youth. What was most damaging, however, was the absence of the *bona fides* of at least two constituents of the Committee, namely, the Congress(I) and the National Conference. As will be demonstrated hereinafter, their approach was destructive. They were bent upon creating all types of hurdles. It soon became evident that the Union Government was not only a bundle of contradictions but also wholly impractical in its approach and oblivious of the fundamental principles of governance.

Before discussing what George Fernandes and the All-Party Advisory Committee did, it is necessary to deal briefly with a few other aspects of the situation. One relates to initiation of action against public corruption, second to the policy during the period of festivities connected with Miraj-e-alam and the third to reducing the impact of five factors which favoured the subversives.

Action Against Corruption

The Bourbon of the National Conference and the Congress(I) were so insensitive to public feelings that they indulged in corrupt deeds unashamedly. They did not realise that the revulsion of the masses to corruption was strengthening the forces of subversion and terrorism.

The improprieties that were being committed could be seen from the case of allotment of seventy-four plots to the Ministers and Members of the Legislative Assembly and Legislative Council. The allottees included Dr. Farooq Abdullah, his younger brother and Minister, Dr. Mustafa Kamal, Urban Development Minister, Attaullah Suhrawardy, Finance Minister, Abdul Rahim Rather, ex-Revenue Minister and Member of Parliament P.L. Handoo and Congress(I) Cabinet Ministers Mangat Ram Sharma, Ghulam Rasool Kar, Moulvi Iftikhar Hussain Ansari, etc. The case strongly supported the widely held view that the National Conference(F)-Congress(I) Ministry had merely joined hands to feather their own nests.

I reproduce below my orders of February 23, 1990, which speaks for itself:

> Subject : Allotment of' seventy-four (74) plots to Ministers and MLAs/MLCs in Roop Nagar Housing Colony.
>
> I am dismayed to see this case. It shows how self-serving certain sections of the power structure have become. Almost all the MLAs/MLCs, including the Ministers, have decided to give unto themselves a plot each. And that, too, in a manner which shows no respect for fundamental principles of public administration and justice.
>
> The plots were meant for auction. By one stroke, they were taken out of auction by the Ministers for allotting these pots to themselves as well as to those (MLAs/MLCs) whose duty it was to act as a watch dog of the public interest.
>
> There is no resolution of the Jammu Development Authority, changing its decision to auction the plots in question. The statutory provisions of J&K Development Act have been flouted.
>
> I understand that the 'agreements' have also been executed with a speed wholly alien to the erstwhile regime. During the last week, I have come across a number of cases in which salaries have not been paid to the employees for the last 10 months. The cases of Sopore College and Sopore School are relevant in this regard. Likewise, the employees of the Notified Area Committees have not been paid. Only yesterday I had met a widow whose husband was killed in terrorist violence in December. She is still knocking the door from one office to another without getting even an iota of relief. In this case, however, decision was taken with unprecedented speed, allotment orders obtained and agreements executed after securing concessional method of payment of money.
>
> After considering all aspects of the case, including the *mala fide* nature of the transaction, I have come to the conclusion that it would be in the public interest to rescind the order which in any case was *ab initio* void. I, therefore, order that allotments should be cancelled and all concerned informed individually and amounts collected refunded.
>
> The case not only involves question of legality and impropriety but also mental attitude of those exercising power. Talking about the Municipal Councillors, Gandhiji once said that they should work as unpaid scavengers and road cleaners. This was the

motivation which he wanted the people's representatives to possess. And what motivation does this case show?

The order had a salutary effect. The common Kashmiri and the common Jammuite were happy that justice was being done and the State resources which had been cornered by oligarchs would now be available for development and welfare activities. In this case, an indirect subsidy of at least ₹ 3 lakhs, at the State expense, would have been available to each of the allottees. Since the total number of allottees was seventy-four, the State would have been deprived of over ₹ 2 crores.

The exasperation of the people over corruption could be gauged from the editorial* comments in all the local dailies. As an illustration, I would cite one such comment. It read:

> There has been general appreciation of the prompt action of Governor Jagmohan in rescinding the order allotting 74 plots to former ministers and legislators. The plots were allotted by the erstwhile Farooq ministry in most arbitrary and irregular manner just before it went out of office. The allottees who were aware of the fishy nature of the allotment got these registered in their names in hush hush manner using their political influence. The Chief Minister who himself was one of the beneficiaries of this open loot managed to secure the certificate of permanent residentship which he did not possess, having lost the citizenship right after he acquired the citizenship of United Kingdom, from the district magistrate in violation of all norms and in most irregular manner. Already the Farooq Government had misused its power in sanctioning loans worth several lakhs for construction of houses or purchase of cars to each of the legislator. In most cases, the amount was neither spent on constructing houses nor on the purchase of cars.
>
> The revelation about the allotment of these plots to the ministers and legislators in violation of norms and rules only highlights the stinking affairs of the coalition ministry which had set new records in corruption, nepotism and other acts of misuse of power. What has been revealed is not even the tip of the iceberg.

Here, it may not be out of place to invite attention to the case of Saifuddin Soz, M.P. On the face of it, the matter may look trivial.

*The *Kashmir Times* of March 9, 1990.

But, in the larger context, it explains one of the reasons of the tirade of the National Conference and the Congress(I) leaders against me. My drive against corruption, which was needed for winning the goodwill of the people and blunting their sense of alienation, involved clashing with deep-rooted vested interests of the elites and the oligarchs who retaliated.

Like the Chief Minister and Ministers, Soz also got a plot allotted in Roop Nagar colony. But he was not contented with it. He wanted the allotment to be changed to the still more lucrative colony of Gandhi Nagar. At this stage, I took over charge and the file was put up to me. I rejected Soz's request. I also raised the question as to how plots had been allotted to the political elites, as the usual policy all over the country was to make allotments, at fixed rates only to individuals falling in the low or middle income groups and that, too, on the basis of the draw of lots. It may also be noted that grant of Soz's application would have conferred upon him a monetary gain of five to seven lakhs.

I intended to drive home the advantage of the favourable atmosphere created by the dissolution of the Assembly and commencement of action against corruption in high places. I gave a brief idea of my thinking to the people on TV and a radio broadcast on February 18, 1990:

> I remind you that the Indian Constitution guarantees justice–social, political and economic. I promise you this justice both in letter and spirit. I request you to help me in creating conditions in which I will give practical shape to my promise.
>
> Already in a short span of three weeks or so, 7,000 posts in BSF, 3,000 posts of teachers, 4,300 posts of Home Guards and hundreds of other posts have been created and are being filled through an Independent Selection Board. The administrative machinery has been put on the rail. Two separate Commissioners have been created for Baramulla and Anantnag and civil supplies and communication restored. We have already drawn a blueprint of reforms, reorganisation and for implementation of welfare and development programmes.
>
> For the last several days, there has been no day curfew, but it appears that some elements are intentionally creating trouble to frustrate efforts of all law abiding citizens to attain peace. Let us not be taken in by these elements.

Miraj-e-Aalam

The Muslim festival of Miraj symbolises the commencement of the journey of the human soul towards better and higher spiritual life. 'MIRAJ' means 'ascent'. The main celebrations are held on the night between 26th and 27th of the month of 'Rajab' and then on the Friday that follows. In the Kashmir Valley, great significance is attached to these celebrations, and large congregations are witnessed at the mosques, especially at Hazrat Bal, where the holy hair of the Prophet is shown to the devotees at the time of 'Namaz'.

In the year 1990, the religious functions connected with the Miraj-e-Aalam were to be held in the third week of February. After a great deal of deliberations, I decided to give full relaxation during this period. I did not want to give any opportunity to the subversionists to carry out propaganda that the Governor's administration was causing hindrances to the traditional religious celebrations.

Two other important cosiderations weighed with me. First, I wanted to provide a relaxed atmosphere in which the accumulated steam of the past could be let off, and larger numbers of people could approach me directly with their grievances and suggestions. Secondly, I wanted to weaken the hold of the fanatics and the fundamentalists, and also of the pro-Pakistani groups by facilitating the ascendency of those elements in the J&K Liberation Front who had the latent disposition to be moderate and whom I could subsequently tackle to accept my idea of securing real freedom for the Kashmiri masses, within the larger framework of the Indian Constitution. I could thus relieve them of the incipient tyranny of the oligarchs and simultaneously provide them wider opportunities for expression of their political aspirations and also for their economic, social and cultural advancement.

Up to March 1, things moved not very differently from what I expected, except that Jammu & Kashmir Liberation Front blatantly misused the facilities provided for the religious festivals and organised a very large number of processions to the office of the United Nations Observation Group. From these processions and related activities, however, it was evident that the Jama'at-i-Islami, Hizb-ul-Mujahideen and other pro-Pakistani organisations were being relegated to the secondary, and even insignificant position. Obviously, this was not to the liking of these organisations. Most probably, it was they who, directly or indirectly, caused the two serious incidents on March 1, 1990.

The hand of the National Conference in these incidents could also not be ruled out. Its agents, too, were always on the look-out for an opportunity to spoil the congenial atmosphere. An army school bus carrying school children was attacked by a violent mob near Rawalpura bypass. The guards opened fire to save the children. At another place, Zakura, about 20 kms away from Srinagar, a mob tried to snatch weapons from the guard who was looking after parked army vehicles. The armymen following in other vehicles in the convoy saw the guard being overwhelmed. They opened fire. In these two incidents, unfortunately, seventeen persons lost their lives.

The above facts were established as a result of an inquiry which I had advised Lt. General M.A. Zaki, Corps Commander, to conduct on the same day. But the usual exaggerations were resorted to. The BBC gave the figure of twenty-one fatal casualties. Our own Radio Kashmir, however, slanted and exaggerated the news to say that the security forces fired at a passenger bus and thirty persons were killed. Dr. Farooq, without any verification alleged that over a hundred persons were killed, and held me responsible for the killings, ignoring the obvious fact that the civil administration was not connected with either of the two incidents which occurred in two distant suburbs of Srinagar primarily because of the bellicosity of some members in the crowd at both the places. Three MPs* of the National Conference, always staying away from the Kashmir Valley and busy in New Delhi only with their designs of frustrating my efforts to acquire full grip over the near hopeless situation, sat in dharna at the gates of the Parliament House, demanding my recall–and securing wide publicity in the national and international media.

Five Factors

To me, it was quite clear that there were five major factors that tilted the balance heavily in favour of the subversionists. My attention at that point of time was riveted to reducing, if not eliminating, the impact of these factors.

First, the subversionists had convinced the public that their victory was certain. This conviction had to be replaced by counter-conviction

*These were Saifuddin Soz, Mohammed Shafi Butt and Ghulam Rasool Mattoo.

that it was the State administration that was going to succeed, and succeed rapidly. After demonstration of the strong will and determination from the third week of January, 1990 onwards, the wind had slowly started changing its direction. The intensity of the pressure had to be maintained, and even increased. I had no doubt that with continued show of firmness and fairness, the wind would change its course completely and start blowing in favour of the administration.

Secondly, for the young and politically-ambitious youth, no healthy outlet for expression of their political aspirations existed. For most of them, subversion and terrorism had become "mere extension of politics". To remedy the position in this regard, a clear outlet and line of retreat had to be provided. The dissolution of the State Assembly was a move towards attainment of this objective. Now efforts had to be made diligently and unobtrusively, to point out that line of retreat to all except pro-Pakistani fanatics.

Thirdly, the core of the Kashmiri society was still conservative. The puritanical role which most of the subversive groups projected for themselves had an innate appeal for the commonfolk, particularly when they were fed up with corruption and accumulation of wealth in certain hands. Special emphasis had, therefore, to be given to clean and honest image of the new set-up.

Fourthly the Inter-Services Intelligence of Pakistan was trying hard to unite all the groups of subversives under the leadership of pro-Pakistani elements like Syed Ali Shah Geelani and Mian Qayyum. It was necessary to proceed in such a manner that this did not happen. Dominance of Jama'at-i-Islami and Hizbul-Mujahideen and other groups which were fundamentalist and pro-Pakistani in outlook had to be prevented by mounting a relentless pressure on them and blocking the avenues, such as schools, through which they acquired special influence in the society.

Fifthly, there were a number of background operators who fanned the subversive activities and who, if proceeded against, could raise, by virtue of the influential positions they held, a lot of hue and cry. Such elements existed in the bar, the medical profession, the press, and the business. A lot of propaganda dust could also be kicked up by them through writ petitions, resolutions and publication of slanted versions in the press. Some of these elements acted in the manner they did to 'buy' protection of the terrorists or divert attention from their ill-gotten wealth or past misdeeds. It was necessary to bring it home to these elements that their tactics would not go unnoticed, and they would have to face the consequences of aiding or abetting the subversive activities.

Thus, within the overall motivation and approach indicated in Chapter IX, the five planks which I had constructed, at that point of time, for re-erection of the fallen structure were: (i) demonstration of sustained firmness; (ii) provision of line of retreat for the subversives; (iii) the displacement of subversionists' appeal as moral and social reformers; (iv) prevention of emergence of unified body under the leadership of pro-Pakistani fanatics; and (v) proceeding against the background operators.

Visit of All-Party Advisory Committee

As things cooled down after the two unfortunate incidents of March 1, and as I once again proceeded firmly on my chartered course, it was suddenly decided at a meeting held at the Prime Minister's house on March 7, 1990, that a team comprising some Ministers and representatives of political parties, would visit Srinagar the following day. The decision-makers did not realise that the time was not at all opportune for the visit. They were so ignorant of the ground-level realities that they thought that the State Administration could make fool-proof security arrangements for so many VVIPs at a short notice.

It was almost midnight when Shromani Sharma, Union Home Secretary, contacted me on phone. He told me that an all-party committee would be landing at Srinagar early next morning in a special plane and suitable arrangements for security and accommodation would have to be made. He did not know any details about the composition of the team. He said that the meeting of all-party representatives, chaired by the Prime Minister, had ended a few hours earlier and the decision in regard to the visit had been abruptly taken. The Home Secretary was profusely apologetic. I could understand his predicament. He himself did not appear to be convinced either about the soundness of the decision to visit Srinagar or about its timing. But he was reluctant to put the decision-makers wise.

I was aghast at the superficiality of the approach to a highly complicated situation. What advantage was sought to be obtained by the visit? How could it help in evolving the 'national consensus'? Why could not the advice of the Governor or his Advisers or his Director-General, Police, or the state and central intelligence agencies be sought and considered before arriving at the decision? What was the use of having so many field organisations if decisions were to be taken without ascertaining their views even with regard to explosive issues? What would have been lost if the visit had been fixed a day or so afterwards? Had there been any advantage in the immediacy of the visit, all the dislocation and connected trouble would have been worthwhile. Unfortunately, exactly opposite was the case. Not only the entire administrative and security machinery was thrown out of gear for nothing but also both the long-term and short-term problems were compounded.

The hotel managers had to be pulled out of their beds, safe vehicles and drivers had to be located at the dead of the winter night, the raids planned for the early morning had to be abandoned and security personnel diverted to new assignments. The route from the airport to Centaur hotel was vulnerable to sniping and grenade attack. Even huge crowds could gather and block the way of the team, necessitating use of force, which in the circumstances of the case, would have attracted a lot of national and international publicity.

I was sad at the manner in which the serious affairs of the State were being handled, sad at the absence of mature and incisive thinking, sad at the unconcern shown by political parties about the real problems and their roots. Could a system that reared such superficialities, really fight the grim battle of terrorism whose fangs had spread as far as shown in Chapter X on 'Nature and Pattern of Subversion and Terrorism'?

It was well past midnight when Shromani Sharma rang up again. He told me that Rajiv Gandhi might also be coming. But even at that time, the Home Secretary was not aware of the precise composition of the team. Anyhow, we had to raise the level of security and make other arrangements.

In the morning, at the airport, an unexpectedly large team arrived. It comprised, besides Deputy Prime Minister, Devi Lal, two Cabinet Ministers–Railway Minister, George Fernandes and Law Minister, Dinesh Goswami. A second plane-load of pressmen and TV team accompanied them. When the party was on its way to the Centuar hotel from the airport, I was informed, through a wireless message by my adviser, Ved Marwah, about the composition of the team and also about the arrival of Devi Lal. Soon thereafter, I went to Centaur hotel to meet the Deputy Prime Minister and other members of the team.

News about the arrival of the team spread like a wild fire. In fact, quite a few persons had come to know about it the previous night itself. National Conference(F) leaders had contacted their friends on phone. They were trying to work out their own plans for the day–how to bring some groups before the Committee, how to embarrass the Governor's administration, how to cause more complications, how to appear as champions of those under 'repression' and how to stage dramas to prove their trumped up charges.

What I apprehended happened. The entire Srinagar city started reverberating with provocative slogans from numerous loudspeakers, fitted on the mosques. The people were goaded to come on the roads and tell the "Indian dogs to go back". Tension mounted. A serious law and order problem was at hand. Large-scale violence could erupt at any time. Curfew had to be clamped and enforced vigorously.

I met the Deputy Prime Minister in his hotel suite. I briefed him for a few minutes. But he did not seem to be interested except in a few broad issues. Understandably, he had little knowledge of a very complex problem. He could, like many other political leaders of the day, think only in terms of a few personalities. Nevertheless, his robust common sense could not but be appreciated. Dinesh Goswami came in the room and listened to my briefing. He, too, asked a few general questions. George Fernandes went somewhere without telling anyone. Strange, I thought, was the method of his operation.

What saddened me was that no one knew what was intended to be done. Some Ministers and members of the team said there would be briefing by the Governor, while the others said they would be receiving deputations from the public. A few others said that they would like to visit the city. The high-level confusion further dismayed me.

I suggested to the Deputy Prime Minister that the Governor should not be asked to brief the Committee, particularly in regard to matters which impinged on politics. I told him that it would be better if I briefed him and the Cabinet Ministers first, and they could later on talk to the members of the political parties. But no decision was forthcoming. Everyone was talking to the other without arriving at any decision. In the chaos that prevailed in the hotel, I was just ushered into the Conference Room.

The number of participants was quite large for the type of meeting that was to be held and the nature of the subject to be discussed. The contingent of the Congress(I) party was abnormally large. Besides Rajiv Gandhi, there were Shiv Shankar, M.L. Fotedar, G.N. Azad and Mani Shanker Aiyer. The National Conference group comprised

P.L. Handoo, and Mohammed Shafi Butt, M.Ps. They were obviously at the beck and call of Congress(I) team. Their approach was identical. Dr. Farooq Abdullah did not appear. This, I thought, was characteristic of the man. He would announce something and do exactly the opposite. I learnt he came to the airport at New Delhi but did not accompany the party. Saifuddin Soz, MP came to Srinagar but went away separately. Presumably, he and George Fernandes were operating simultaneously on another plan. The atmosphere was thick with dusty confusion. And contradictions were galore.

After an experience in December 1987, I had inwardly formed an unpleasant opinion of the human element that Rajiv Gandhi was made of. His obstinacy, his scant respect for rules of safety, had come to light vis-a-vis his attitude towards the officers of the Air Force, Civil Aviation, Border Roads Organisation and local police etc. I wondered whether this was the stuff of which the Prime Minister of a great country like India should be made of. This had disturbed me for days. His behaviour on March 8, 1990, at Centaur hotel, equally shocked me.

That a former Prime Minister of the country, Rajiv Gandhi, could behave in such an irresponsible manner and display such antics spoke as much about him as about the country which allowed itself to be dominated by persons of his outlook and values.

Incidents that betrayed Rajiv's real intentions

What happened at the beginning of the meeting may best be told through the reports of the pressmen who were present. The *Indian Express** said:

> Sharp and acrimonious exchanges marked the visit of the high-level multi-party delegation to this curfew-bound city on Thursday as the purpose of the exercise 'to meet the people and discuss the situation' in the valley was nearly lost.
>
> First, there was an angry verbal duel between the former Prime Minister, Rajiv Gandhi and the Bharatiya Janata Party leader, Jaswant Singh, triggered off by the former's repeatedly sarcastic remarks against Governor Jagmohan. Then there was a verbal clash between Gandhi and Jagmohan. Gandhi started making

*The *Indian Express,* New Delhi, March 9, 1990.

snide remarks against the Governor from the moment he entered the conference hall of the hotel. He told the Governor that he wanted to invite a few persons and that arrangements should be made for bringing them from the city. Gandhi, apparently seeking to score a point, then said: 'local press is not to be seen....' 'Jagmohanji, kya Kashmir main paper nahin chhapte (Jagmohanji, are newspapers not published in Kashmir?)'. Mohammed Shafi Butt, the local National Conference MP, shouted from his seat: 'The Governor has brought to a halt every activity'.

Unable to control himself, the usually cool Jaswant Singh virtually shouted at Gandhi: 'You are teaching us about the press; if you want, you can go and talk to the press'.

Gandhi did not stop at that. He objected to the manner in which the Deputy Prime Minister, Devi Lal, was made to sit on the left of the Governor and not on the right side as in accordance with the protocol. Gandhi: 'At least the Deputy Prime Minister should be shown due courtesy. It is a question of dignity of the nation'. Jaswant Singh: 'The prestige of the nation is not only your concern; having damaged so many institutions, you should be the last person to talk about the honour of the nation.' Gandhi: 'I take objection to the manner in which the Deputy Prime Minister has been allowed to sit on the wrong side. The Governor did not even go to the airport to receive him. He is my Deputy Prime Minister. He is the nation's Deputy Prime Minister.'

Jagmohan explained that he did not know about the composition of the delegation till the flight landed here. He said: 'When I came to know that Deputy Prime Minister had come here. . . .' Gandhi (interrupted): 'Ved Marwah, who is your adviser, told me at the airport that you had been apprised about the arrival of the Deputy Prime Minister three minutes before the landing.' Ved Marwah, who was present there: 'What I said was arrival of the Deputy Prime Minister was not known to me. That is why the Governor is not here (at the airport)'.

The CPI(M) MP Biplab Dasgupta, intervened at this stage to say: 'We cannot have this type of debate when the press is here. It is unfortunate and irregular.' He maintained that discussions at the meeting with a Governor was supposed to be 'confidential'.

Newsmen were then asked to withdraw from the conference hall. At the closed door meeting later, there were again bitter exchanges.

Gandhi reportedly told the Governor: 'When I was the Prime Minister, you were the Governor even at that time. Should I disclose what you told me on Article 370'? Jagmohan: 'I can also speak out what you had told me then.'

Gandhi later told newsmen all that Jagmohan had said at the meeting would lead to a 'dangerous path'. The Law Minister, Dinesh Goswami, expressed the opinion that no member of the delegation should have sought to disclose to the press what had been discussed in the 'camera meeting'. The Governor too was unhappy. He said: 'Whatever I said was for the members of the delegation'. Interestingly, when local persons, some of whom were described as leaders of social bodies whom Gandhi wanted to see, turned up, the first thing that they did was to shout at Mohammed Shafi Butt, the National Conference MP, whom they described as a stooge.

The other reports were similar in content. *The Tribune** observed:

The leaders, especially Rajiv Gandhi and those representing the National Conference made consistent efforts to score debating points over their rivals at the conference. When newsmen offered their curfew passes to Rajiv Gandhi for visiting various parts of the city and to meet the people, he did not respond. Minutes earlier he had expressed his disappointment that he was not being allowed to meet the people.

The local daily, the *Kashmir Times*, reported:

The trouble began when Jagmohan had just started briefing the leaders on the situation in the valley. Gandhi alleged that the Governor had treated the Deputy Prime Minister, Devi Lal, shabbily and had violated the protocol. He agitatingly said: 'The nation's honour is at stake.' This provoked Jaswant Singh to retort, 'Every one knows your concern for the nation's honour.'

When Gandhi said, 'I want to put on record' the treatment meted out to the Deputy Prime Minister and violation of protocol, Jaswant Singh shot back: 'Let us forget about the protocol at the moment. We are here for a more serious business and should not waste our time in such trivial matters.'

**The Tribune*, Chandigarh, March 10, 1990.

I have not described the incident in my own words lest I should be accused of any conscious or unconscious bias in recording exchange of words in which I was personally involved.

I leave it to the reader to decide whether Rajiv Gandhi's talk of consensus was not a sheer hypocrisy, a mere ruse. Do the above narrations of the incident leave any doubt about his *mala fides*? He came with predetermined objective of creating difficulties for my administration, running me down and undermining my image amongst the Kashmiri masses. His *mala fides* were compounded by the fact that he persisted with his course even when Ved Marwah flatly contradicted him in the presence of a large number of VVIPs. He went ahead with his diatribe without bothering to indicate or quote which item of the protocol the Governor had violated. He did not even care to find out from the Home Secretary, Shromani Sharma, or Devi Lal, what the actual facts were. Seema Mustafa, reporting in the *Sunday Observer* (of March 11 to 17, 1990), recorded:

> Devi Lal said that the Governor came to the airport to 'send us off' and behaved with propriety throughout. According to Devi Lal, he was asked by the Prime Minister to go to Srinagar at 12.30 a.m., and there was every likelihood that the Governor had no information about this. As for sitting on the left and not on the right, Devi Lal said, 'We were all sitting and talking when the governor came. He asked me to sit on the other chair but I, being so heavy, did not want to make the effort, and told him to sit down; it is not an official meeting. The matter has been unnecessarily distorted.'

Here, I would once again invite attention to a fundamental issue which I have briefly touched in Chapter IX and elaborated in Chapter XV. Notwithstanding all the risks and almost terminal malady in whose snares Kashmir had been pushed in, I accepted the assignment for the second term with the belief that, because of the excellent rapport that existed between me and the Muslim masses of the valley, I should not shirk the responsibility of extending a helping hand in tackling the grave situation. This is what the report of *The Hindustan Times* of January 19, 1990 said:

> The people of Srinagar have welcomed the return of Jagmohan as the Governor who is popularly known here by many fond names such as 'Jagwatal and Sarakram'.* These names have been given to

*Some one who cleans up things.

him out of sheer affection for his utmost zeal to improve the lot of the Kashmiri people. No wonder in the downtown last night, crackers were burst when the people heard about his appointment as Governor for the second term.

Then, what went wrong? Who blasted that popular image? Who ruined the mood of happiness? And who injected poison in the congenial atmosphere? The pro-Pakistani elements had their hand, but the real damage was done by the extremely narrow and nihilist approach of Rajiv Gandhi, Dr. Farooq Abdullah and their coterie and collaborators.

The Opposition leaders have legitimate right to find faults with the Government in power. But in the case of Kashmir, and particularly in the context of the conditions then prevailing, Rajiv Gandhi's actions were irresponsible. They caused much harm to the national interest. His behaviour at the all-party meeting was a part of the pattern which he set for himself after V.P. Singh's government took over, and particularly after my appointment was announced.

The earnestness of Rajiv Gandhi could be seen from the sarcastic remarks which he started making even before the visit of the all-party team to Srinagar. On March 6, 1990, he said to the press that he had written to the Prime Minister, V.P. Singh, to tell the officers of the State Government to issue curfew passes to him and other Congress(I) leaders, so that they could visit Srinagar. He also commented that V.P. Singh was dozing when Kashmir was being discussed at all-party meeting. Such utterances were hardly reconcilable with consensual spirit, which, parrot-like, was being advocated by many leaders without any regard for stark realities of the Indian political scene.

The press generally condemned Rajiv Gandhi's stance at the Srinagar meeting. *The Statesman**, for example, observed:

> Touche, Rajiv Gandhi. First, you create the mess. Then, you and your allies try to be the martyrs. Then you, with the support of the Trojan horses, within and without, force the Government to take a second look at the crisis of your own creation.
>
> At the prolonged all-party meeting yesterday, you and your cohorts were insistent that all-party team must go to the Valley. You were only seeking a cover-up for something that you single-

**The statesman,* March 9, 1990.

handedly created while you were at the helm of affairs in the country and of course in Kashmir.

Your feigned concern for Devi Lal's position as Deputy Prime Minister and the lack of courtesy supposedly shown by the Governor, only confirms doubts that your insistence on all-party initiative in Kashmir is nothing short of gimmickry. I am sure the people across the border and some of their sympathizers in the Valley must be having a whale of a time hearing the former Prime Minister mouthing inanities. When will you grow up, Gandhi? Or alternatively, why don't you suggest to the present Prime Minister, his deputy and his Home Minister, to make a gift of the Valley to anyone of your choice.

While briefing I was anxious to avoid controversies. But some of the members, particularly of Congress(I) and National Conference were determined to raise controversial questions. I was reluctant to answer. I once again pleaded that I would separately explain the matters to Deputy Prime Minister and Cabinet Ministers who could, later on, discuss in appropriate manner with the representatives of the political parties. It appeared that neither the Ministers nor the officials of Home Ministry accompanying them, were clear as to what would be the parameters of my briefing. Nothing my reluctance almost all the team members, including the Union Ministers, assured me that the briefing was for understanding all the issues involved, and what was said, would not go out of the room.

On the above assurance, I analysed the nature and potency of the political, social, economic, religious and regional forces that were operating both on the surface and underneath it. I explained to them the need for encouraging those traditions and forces which made for catholicity and eclecticism and dealing firmly with fanatical and fundamentalist groups which drew inspiration from Jama'at-i-Islami and pro-Pak elements. I also provided a glimpse of the options that may become available for chalking out future course of action. In regard to the reasons that prompted me to dissolve the Assembly, I stated, albeit briefly, what I have stated in Chapter XI.

The meeting became somewhat hot on occasions. Rajiv Gandhi, presumably on the advice of his accompanied aides, such as Mani Shankar Aiyar, had come with the diabolical idea of portraying me as anti-Muslim. The game plan was that I should not succeed in establishing old rapport with the Muslim youth with whom my rule of

1986 was very popular. He even went to the extent of saying as to what I had recommended in regard to Article 370 during my first Governor's Rule. This was a highly sensitive subject. His idea was to ensure that the Muslims of the Valley should know that I was not in favour of retention of Article 370. He did not want, at the same time, to divulge my thinking which I had indicated to him at that time. This thinking was based on entirely different consideration and was connected with my proposals for overall reform and reorganisation of the political and administrative structure of the State. I had argued that Article 370 was being misused by vested interests to build their own nests of power and also to secure unmerited financial benefits for the ruling elite. I had emphasised that it was in the interest of the poor Kashmiris that this Article should go. But Rajiv Gandhi was not interested in the truth. His objective was to lower my standing amongst the Kashmiri masses. And in this he succeeded. The vernacular press soon brought stories about my 'allergy' to Article 370. And tendentious versions and rumours went around, weakening my position when it needed to be strengthened.

The meeting continued till 3.45 p.m. Most of the talking had to be done by me. I was disappointed by the patently partisan approach of some of the participants who had come to Srinagar in great hurry for supposedly evolving national consensus. To what level, I reflected within, were we descending? Petty politics was destroying all scruples and regard for truth, justice and well-being of the nation. The irony was that it was happening in the land of Mahatma Gandhi who believed that "politics bereft of principles were like death traps; they killed the soul of the nation."

The lunch was taken at 4 p.m. in which pressmen also joined. Everyone saw that they were being talked to by Rajiv Gandhi. I learnt, this was about the meeting. It was against the assurance given only a few hours ago. What appeared in the press the following day confirmed my apprehension. Practically, everything was leaked out with slant.

Ghulam Nabi Azad and M.L. Fotedar were sitting on a side table and having their lunch. I wished them. We started talking. Azad said: "We pity your lot. You ended your first innings on such a glorious note. People fondly remembered you. They considered you a messiah of the poor and swore by your name. But, today, they are after your blood". "You are right", I said, "It was my misfortune to land in a situation in which there was no option for me to act except in the manner I did. Kashmir had to be saved first. Reputation, if damaged, could be salvaged later. The crucial question, moreover, is: Should I work for a certificate of popularity or for pulling back Kashmir from the edge of a precipice? I do not understand why your team is indulging in body-line bowling and throwing all type of vicious and unfair bumpers at me. You and your party know me very well. Then, why are you hurling all type of false allegations? With you, I was 'hero', a star performer on all kinds of sticky pitches, be they in Delhi, Goa or Kashmir. But you have now suddenly discovered that I am good for nothing, and that I am anti-Muslim, anti-Kashmiri. And look at CPI and CPI(M). Neither of them spoke a word against me from 1986 onwards. When I was Lt. Governor of Delhi for two terms (1980-84) their workers used to flock around me, and their newspapers were all praise for me. I distinctly remember how they praised me when I acted firmly in favour of the poor peasants who were deprived of their right by the powerful landed interests in village Mandi.* But now they have suddenly discovered that I am controversial. I am more pained by these false allegations than by anything else. Calumny is like oil that spills; it leaves its ugly marks even after it is washed. If you had any real objection to my appointment**, you should have telephoned me, the moment it was announced. I would have thought twice before accepting it. Now that I am here, now that I am aware of the extreme gravity of the situation, now that I know what would have happened but for my timely and determined intervention on January 26 or thereabout, now that I have undergone all risks and performed all unpleasant and unpopular tasks, I would not leave till Kashmir is fully secured and weaved in the national fabric, not with a weak thread, but with a strong and unbreakable one. I have no other motivation. I am not drawing any

* This is what Ms. Primila Lewis writes in her book: *Social Action and the Labouring Poor : An Experience* at page 139:

... From this point, until his departure for J&K in 1984, Jagmohan proved to be a man who was not only invariably accessible to the workers, but also one who sized up the essence of their problems and found solutions to them which he then had implemented as speedily as possible. He was one of the few officials who always addressed us in Hindi and would question the workers directly rather than through us. This so endeared him to all the workers in Mehrauli that when he left Delhi a large representation from the Union, consisting of delegations of farm, quarry and village people, went to Raj Niwas to say farewell and to express their gratitude for all that he had done for them.

** This refers to my appointment for the second time.

salary. Threats are piling up. Normal life of everyone in the family is disrupted. Nothing is the same any more." "Let us see", Azad said, visibly embarrassed. We all smiled and parted.

Rajiv Gandhi, presumably prompted by National Conference MP, Mohammed Shafi Butt, insisted that I should call the trade union leaders. Myself and my colleagues in the State Administration told him that it was not possible to do so at a short notice. There was curfew. The offices were closed. No name had been given of any office bearer. The Governor or his advisers were not supposed to know the present office bearers and their residential addresses. If Rajiv was so keen to meet a particular group, why could not we be told about it in advance? But the unreasonableness of the demand was not realised. It was persisted. The idea was to embarrass us. In sheer exasperation, we said that we would try. I asked a few local police officers to do whatever they could in the matter.

While I was still in the dining hall talking to officers, Additional Chief Secretary, Mahmud Rehman, came and said, "They are going to have a press conference. They want you in the Committee room".

The conference commenced soon after I entered the room. Apparently, neither the Union Ministers nor the Press Adviser to the Government of India, Ram Mohan Rao, had held prior consultations in regard to what was to be told to the press. After brief introductory remarks, the Press Adviser started making stray observations which showed how difficult it was to grasp the complicated Kashmir situation in a short time. Then, Dinesh Goswami took over. He, too, tied himself in knots. He happened to say that the Union Government was not averse to holding talks with the militants. This, I thought, was an unfortunate observation, and showed how poorly organised was the Government of India in dealing with the Kashmir problem. While the Union Home Minister was all the time declaring that no talk would be held with the militants, here was the Law Minister coming to Srinagar with two other Central Ministers and saying exactly the opposite.

The Law Minister, perhaps, realised his mistake. He also found it difficult to answer the extra-inquisitive queries of the pressmen. His experience and robust common sense made him pass on the mike to me.

I seized the opportunity to put the press conference on the right track, and end all questions. I simply said, "The briefing was only for the members of the all-party team. The objective was to acquaint them with the realities of the situation. For their benefit alone, I had analysed the political, social, economic and religious forces that were operating in the Valley. I had also indicated the need for having a fair and just administration and people-oriented development. The details could not be disclosed at this stage. In fact, I had briefed the team on the assurance that what I stated would remain with the members and the contents would not be parted to anyone else."

The press took advantage of the statement of the Law Minister and brought out banner headlines about the Union Government's intention to hold talks with the militants. Since this had an all round depressing effect on the administration and reflected the confused thinking on the subject, denial had to be issued by the Government of India the following day.

I was sitting in a corner of the hotel lobby, talking to officers. Suddenly, we heard loud slogans from another portion of the hotel. We went in that direction and found that Rajiv Gandhi and his party colleagues and National Conference MPs Butt and Handoo were being shouted upon. On inquiry, it was gathered that Butt had brought to Rajiv Gandhi a group who, he thought, would favour him. Instead, they turned hostile and poured their wrath on him. They said to Butt: "How have you become our representative? We never elected you. Who do you think you are? You cannot face anyone here. You sit in your cosy bungalow in New Delhi. You issue statements. You think our problems are solved like that. Is that your task? Whom do you think you are fooling." "And you, Mr. Rajiv Gandhi, you never came here when you were at the helm of the affairs at New Delhi. You thought, your prince, Farooq, was ruling in your name. He is a nut, a pleasure seeking, golf playing monarch. He fooled us, he tricked us. He butchered us when he wanted to do so. Today, he and his mentor, namely you, Mr. Gandhi, are shedding crocodile tears. Just go away. Get lost. We do not want to meet you or this clumsy man, Butt." This was followed by a chorus of slogans: "Indian dogs go back." The hotel staff also joined the group and shouted similar slogans.

The account given by the press was on similar lines. For instance, this is what the *Kashmir Times* reported:

> When Mohammed Shafi Butt wanted to say something to the persons, they interrupted him saying, "You cannot speak on our behalf. You have cheated us. We have never elected you to Lok Sabha."

At this stage Rajiv Gandhi started explaining that he had entered into an Accord for the good of the people of Kashmir. The visitors interrupted him to say: "You had entered into accord only with Farooq Abdullah."

When Makhan Lal Fotedar, Ghulam Nabi Azad and P.L. Handoo tried to pacify the agitated members, they hit back: "How do you know the situation in Kashmir and plight of the people while sitting in air-conditioned rooms in Delhi. You have multiplied corruption during your rule. There had been no development. Only few families had amassed wealth. What do you want us to talk about?

The members of the delegation then started raising slogans: Indian dogs go back. We want independence.

A deputation of Kashmiri Pandits also came to see the Deputy Prime Minister and Union Law Minister. Two of its prominent members were H.N. Jattu and J.N. Sapru. They narrated their tales of woe, "For the last one year, we have been living constantly under the shadows of fear and death. Since September 1989, we are being slaughtered and exterminated, under a diabolical plan. Members of our community have been fleeing. Neither the Central nor the State Government listened to our cries." Emotions often overwhelmed Jattu and Sapru. And they wept openly, adding to the agonising atmosphere around.

Two waiters of the hotel were serving tea at that time. I noticed their extraordinary keenness in listening to what leaders of the Kashmiri Pandits were saying. I realised the danger to which they had exposed themselves. I advised the Director-General, Police, to look to their safety. Subsequently, the Director-General Police told me that the intelligence reports indicated that both Jattu and Sapru would be killed if they did not move out of the Valley. In fact, Sapru had been badly beaten on the same night and admitted to the civil hospital from where, in the interest of his safety, we shifted him to army hospital and then to Jammu. In Kashmir, to complain or even express grief or sorrow meant an invitation to death.

Devi Lal wanted to meet the Corps Commander, Lt. General M.A. Zaki. I arranged the meeting. The General intimated the Deputy Prime Minister how grave the situation had earlier become, how the terrorists had totally crippled the civil administration before the Governor rule was imposed and how thereafter a vigorous and effective coordinating machinery of the civil and military authorities had been built.

Early next morning–March 9–I went to Centuar hotel to accompany Devi Lal and other members of the Committee to the airport. When I approached the portico of the hotel, I saw a sizeable crowd there. It was extremely tense. I noticed that the National Conference MP, Shafi Butt, was attempting to stage another drama. A driver, who was supposed to have been beaten, almost to death by CRP, was brought to the hotel with the twin objective of showing to Devi Lal and Rajiv Gandhi the atrocities of the para-military forces and causing a strike of the drivers of the State Government vehicles. When the matter was put up to me, I said that it would be inquired into. I did not want any heat or argument to be raised about it. The CRP officers were agitated over the feigned pain of the driver but I advised them to remain calm and not to argue with anyone. My concern was to avoid ugly situation from developing.

Sudden Change

As the party members were about to get into the cars, the Union Home Secretary told me that the Committee was not going to Jammu. Instead, it would be flying direct to Delhi. This, I thought, would irritate the people of Jammu. They would feel hurt and believe that the team was not bothered about their sentiments in the matters.

When I enquired as to what were the reasons for this sudden change, the Home Secretary told me that he did not exactly know but there was some talk between Rajiv Gandhi and the Deputy Prime Minister and thereafter it was decided to cancel the programme of flying to Jammu. Subsequently, I learnt that the most probable reason for the change was the hostility which Rajiv Gandhi, his Congress colleagues and the National Conference members of the team would have encountered at Jammu. Some party leaders had rung up Rajiv Gandhi and advised him not to come to Jammu as his views had annoyed the people of the entire Jammu region. In any case, Rajiv's purpose was to create problems for me and cause embarrassment to the National Front Government, and that purpose had been achieved.

Whatever the reason, the sudden change in the programme, without intimating even the Governor or his Advisers or Officers, was unfortunate. It annoyed the people of Jammu and caused serious law and order problem for Jammu authorities. The Kashmiri migrants termed it as an act of cowardice and marched on the roads denouncing Rajiv Gandhi and Dr. Farooq Abdullah. Over a hundred lawyers issued an angry statement condemning the indifference of the team towards Jammu. Tension mounted. I got in touch with Jammu officers immediately and advised them to ensure peace and also appeal to the people on my behalf not to get agitated. The situation was not allowed to get out of hand.

One of the most important, and yet the least understood and appreciated, contribution that I thought I made to the State at its most dangerous phase was that I was successful in preventing Jammu and Ladakh from exploding as a reaction to the happenings in the Valley. Because of the old rapport, affection which the people of the two regions bestowed upon me, and the speedy action I took in regard to various matters pertaining to Jammu, including its development, I was able to keep surging tensions under control. For instance, on January 20, when bad weather over Banihal prevented my helicopter from flying to Srinagar and I had to stay at Jammu, I made it a point to visit a number of localities to recommence old development projects which had been initiated by me in 1986 but subsequently neglected by the Ministry. These projects included 'Tawi river front', 'airport road' and 'Mahamaya city forest'. The Jammuites were convinced that speedy development would once again take place in their region. They were filled with hope, and their inner irritation over Srinagar's happenings in December, 1989 and early January 1990, abated. If all the three regions had become disturbed at the same time, the consequences would have been disastrous, not only for the State but also for the entire country.

The attitude of the Congress(I) and National Conference annoyed their own rank and file. Major General (Retd.) B.N. Dhar, a leader of the National Front and President of its ex-servicemen wing, resigned. He held the National Conference and Congress(I) responsible for the situation in the Valley, forcing the Kashmiri Pandits to leave the homes in distress. He described my role as the only silver lining in the prevailing situation.

Even at the Srinagar airport, we were not free from trouble. When the entire party of VIPs had reached the airport and the Deputy Prime Minister and Rajiv Gandhi and other members of the team had boarded the plane, I found that all the pressmen who were in a separate bus, had not arrived. Due to reasons of security, we had so arranged that all vehicles would form part of one convoy and escorted strongly. Non-arrival of the bus worried me. When it was delayed beyond reasonable time, my worry turned into anxiety and fear. Myself, the Director-General Police, and other senior officers made frantic efforts to trace the missing bus on the route. After quite a few agonising moments, it was learnt that the bus was stopped at the hotel because George Fernandes abruptly decided to hold a press conference. Everything was being done without any coherence and mutual discussions.

We all heaved a deep sigh of relief when the two special planes were taxied to the runway and roared into the sky towards New Delhi, though they left behind a trail of confusion and contradiction and also George Fernandes who, again without telling anyone, suddenly changed his programme.

Consequences of the Visit

The visit of all-party team was a disaster. It largely nullified the advantages that I had secured by dissolving the State Assembly, by repairing the administrative machinery, and by demonstrating to the people our honest intentions to carve out a new line based upon fairness and firmness. It united pro-Pakistan and pro-independence forces and enabled them to consolidate their position. The emotions, the drama of shouting slogans together against an imagined or real foe, gave them a strong fillip. It dampened the spirit of the youth who was entertaining the ideas of responding to my scheme of things. All the five planks, which I had constructed, as indicated earlier in this Chapter, were cut to pieces. The atmosphere in which we were acquiring an upper hand was vitiated.

The visit also demonstrated to the Kashmiris that I did not have the solid backing of the Union Government which was willing to be jostled around. It showed a confused and fragmented national will. It exposed the hypocrisy of the declared aim of consensus. It also showed how little most political parties understood the ground-level realities and how little they cared to learn from the past mistakes and go to the roots of the problem.

The damage done by Rajiv Gandhi's behaviour was the maximum. He virtually played the game of the subversives. The overall impact of his comments, as the *Statesman* report* pointed out, was to 'bolster'

*The *Statesman,* March 10, 1990.

the militants' anti-Jagmohan campaign. Nikhil Chakravartty in his commentary of March 11, 1990, condemned what he called Rajiv Gandhi's blatantly anti-national posture. In his write-up in the *Sunday Mail*, Girilal Jain described Rajiv Gandhi's attitude as "utterly deplorable". *The Indian Express*, in its editorial of March 14, also minced no words to point out the irresponsible conduct of Rajiv Gandhi. It said:

> The conduct of at least two of the parties which have been included in the Committee–the Congress(I) and the National Conference–has been nothing but undiluted and crass opportunism. It testified to a mind-set which places personal and political advantage, and that too of the moment, above the interests of the country. Will they now not use the committee for their own purposes and hinder the efforts that are being made to somehow or the other save the valley?

Rajiv Gandhi's attitude was deplored by the leaders of other political parties who came to Srinagar as members of the committee. On March 10, in a joint statement, Saifuddin Chaudhary and Biplab Dasgupta(CPM), M. Farooqi and A.S. Malhotra(CPI) and Jaswant Singh and Kedar Nath Sahani (BJP) said: "Rajiv Gandhi broke the consensus and briefed the Press on issues discussed confidentially at the meeting. He frustrated one of the main objectives of the visit, that is to demonstrate the common national concern, cutting across political boundaries. We deplore such kind of attitude on his part."

The editorial comments and statements of the political leaders were, however, of no help to me in Kashmir. The deed had been done. Hostility had been aroused, suspicion created, and my image of a sympathetic administrator, planted deep in the minds of the common Kashmiris on account of my earlier service, shattered. This, in substance, was the contribution of Rajiv Gandhi and his fellow-travellers in the Congress(I) and the National Conference. This was their way of bringing about consensus and tackling the gravest of the challenges that the country faced of its integrity and well-being. Stabbing me in the back or in the chest, perhaps, did not matter, though the act was wholly unjustified, immoral and irrational. What really mattered was the deterioration they caused in the Kashmir situation; they virtually poured oil on the diminishing flame.

George Fernandes

The following day, George Fernandes came to see me at Raj Bhavan. At the time of discussions, he showed a lot of sympathy and described my stand as courageous, clear and correct. In fact, before he became Minister for Kashmir Affairs, his comments to the press about me were laudatory. He earlier told the pressmen that the Governor had a very formidable task to handle and nobody could envy his job. According to the report of the *Indian Express* of March 10, 1990, Fernandes appreciated the work the Governor was doing in the situation he faced. He said: "The Governor has a very tough assignment. I do not think that any person in the country has as tough an assignment as Jagmohan is facing." The other media report also quoted Fernandes as saying: "Governor Jagmohan was doing the best in the circumstances." He termed Rajiv Gandhi's attitude as irresponsible. He accused Congress(I) of spreading disinformation about me. He disclosed:

> That at the multi-party meeting held in Delhi, a member of the Congress(I) delegation sought to sell a story which showed Governor, Jagmohan as one having hatred against the Muslims. The story, Fernandes recalled, was that four young Muslims disguised as Hindus met Jagmohan and complained to him about the harassment of Hindus at the hands of the armed militants in the Valley. On hearing this, so went the story, Jagmohan got wild and shouted that he would teach the Muslims a lesson and made disparaging remarks against them. After the meeting, the boys went back and rang up the Governor at his private telephone number given to them at their request and told him they were actually Muslims and had met him only to tape-record his observations against the Muslims. This tape-recorder, Fernandes recalled the Congress(I) leader having told the multi-party meeting was being played at every crossing in Srinagar.
>
> Fernandes was the only member of the multi-party delegation to have ventured out of the hotel and meet a few officials and civilians who said the charge made by the Congress(I) delegation was blatantly wrong. Question: Did Gandhi make the charge at the multi-party meeting in Delhi?
>
> Mr. Fernandes: The man who led the delegation was Mr. Gandhi.

I told George Fernandes all that was in my mind–how I planned to carve out a new path and how, after eliminating the pro-Pakistan and hard-core fundamentalists, other elements could be won over and woven into a really democratic, fair, just and corruption-free set-up, and how a few local officers could be of great help to us in attaining our objective. Little did I realise at that time that he would pick up threads from my line of thinking, twist them to suit his political game, and, what would be worse, apply them imperfectly and prematurely.

It would have been all right if George Fernandes had worked on the above ideas in consultation and collaboration with me and that, too, at the appropriate time. But George's personal and political ambition took the better of him. As soon as he became the Minister of Kashmir Affairs, he started working independently, surreptitiously and even at cross purpose. He thought that he should corner all the credit for solving the Kashmir problem and this would enhance his national image. He wanted to present me as a hardliner, as an uncompromising 'Hindu chauvinist' and himself as a healer and humanist, a progressive and liberal who would bring political process to immediate fruition. I was shocked at his approach and tactics. In the process, he harmed me immensely. What is worse, he harmed the country a great deal.

A Minister for Kashmir Affairs

On March 10, 1990, Mufti Mohammed Sayeed, rang me up in the evening. He said that the Cabinet Sub-Committee meeting at the Prime Minister's house was going on, and that it was thinking of appointing a Minister for Kashmir Affairs and also two or three advisers, including a political adviser. I could not fully understand what it all meant. Nor was it made clear whether it was a mere intimation or my views on the proposal were being asked for. But I was in no mood to argue or seek clarification. The all-party team had upset me and thoughts of tendering resignation were already crossing my mind. I merely replied, "Please do what you consider appropriate." Anyhow, it struck me as another by-product of high-level confusion and contradictions, something that would undermine the position both of the Home Minister and the Governor and also create host of problems of coordination and coherence.

The following day, March 11, the decision to designate a separate Cabinet Minister for J&K was announced. No details in regard to his role and functions were spelt out. It was also announced that he would be assisted by an advisory committee comprising representatives of all political parties. Later on, on this advisory committee, Janata Dal nominated Surinder Mohan, Congress(I), Ghulam Rasool Kar, the BJP, Kedar Nath Sahani, CPI(M), Saifuddin Chaudhary, the CPI, M. Farooqi and the National Conference, P.L. Handoo.

The genuine spirit of co-operation was not, however, forthcoming. The National Conference and the Congress(I) did not intend to play a fair game. Whenever opportunity came their way, they embarrassed the Government. For instance, on March 13, when the Home Minister, Mufti Mohammed Sayeed, rose to speak on Kashmir situation in the Lok Sabha, National Conference MP, Saifuddin Soz, objected. He said that, since George Fernandes had been appointed Minister-in-Charge of Kashmir Affairs, Mufti had "no business to speak." Soz knew that any Minister could speak on behalf of the Government. But his objective was to lower the standing of the Home Minister, particularly amongst the people of Kashmir.

The nominees of the Congress(I) and the National Conference on the advisory committee made the matters worse. Ghulam Rasool Kar and P.L. Handoo were anathema to the people both of the Valley and Jammu region. The Jammuites were infuriated over the appointment of George Fernandes and the constitution of the advisory committee. Processions were taken out in support of my actions and decisions, and a totally free hand for me was demanded. Presence of Kar and Handoo on this committee added to their fury. This was evident from the very first visit of the advisory committee to Jammu on March 17. The people demonstrated against it. The other members of the committee soon thought it necessary not to take these two members with them during their visit to the camps of the Kashmiri migrants.

The Kashmiri migrants staged a 'dharna' and resolved* "We don't recognise this advisory committee, as it was meant only to create hurdles in the way of Governor Jagmohan, who had accepted the challenge of restoring peace and normalcy in Kashmir Valley." A large number of associations of traders, industrialists, academicians and lawyers and social organisations told the advisory committee that the idea of "political process" in the prevailing circumstances was ill-conceived and would cause hindrances in the way of restoration of authority in the Valley.

*Report of *Excelsior*, March 18, 1990.

Another Front

Thus, another front was opened for me to take care of. V.P. Singh virtually surrendered the initiative and allowed himself to be pushed around by Rajiv Gandhi and Dr. Farooq Abdullah. Nor could he prevent the Left from playing its game of going after me merely because the firm and practical line that I adopted to acquire hold over the power structure of the State was in harmony with the thinking of the BJP on the subject. The issue that confronted me at the moment was not whether the BJP or the Congress or the Left parties were right or wrong but whether only those measures should be enforced which brought the desired results in the shortest time with minimum cost and least human misery. V.P. Singh also did not read correctly the mind of George Fernandes who moved in deftly to occupy the centre of the stage.

After George Fernandes acquired the designation of the Minister of Kashmir Affairs, I found him a different person from the one who came to Srinagar with the all-party team. His actions injected many more complications in the already complex situation. His approach was impractical, unrealist and even self-contradictory. Given to a sense of drama, he showed no sensibility to the administrative requirements and attached little significance to the timing of a measure. He ignored the fundamental features of the Kashmiri terrorism. He gave no consideration to the fact that as long as the pro-Pakistani elements, intoxicated by past successes, had faith in their guns and bombs, no worthwhile political process could be initiated and those who responded to it, were most likely to be eliminated.

The Inter-Services Intelligence Agency of Pakistan and the local fundamentalists and the fanatics were not playing ordinary game. They had undertaken a ruthless venture. They had almost succeeded. Their deep penetration into the organs of power structure before January 19, 1990, had given them a sense of confidence and also wherewithal to know who was doing what. Premature move for the so-called political process could do nothing but harm. It gave opportunity to the hard-core pro-Pakistan terrorist organisations like Hizb-ul-Mujahideen to eliminate those who could be of real help at a later stage, when the public in general and those occupying the seats of power in the local police and other services, at the operational level in particular, were left in doubt about the complete ascendency of the State administration and para-military forces.

The manner in which George Fernandes proceeded was still more damaging. He would frequently come to Srinagar, without taking me in confidence, talk to a few persons on phone with the help of some BSF or CRP officials, seek interviews with un-responsive elements in the subversives' camp, such as Dr. A.A. Guroo, advocate Mian Qayyum and Jama'at-i-Islami's Abdul Ghani Bhat, and then go back to New Delhi and claim, through inspired press reports, success of his mission in establishing contacts. His modus operandi not only resulted in misleading the public opinion at the national level about the nature and efficacy of the so-called political process but also made the pro-Pakistani terrorist organisations extra inquisitive about the persons whom George Fernandes spoke or met. It was his premature action and talk of having established contacts that, in part, was responsible for the assassinations of Mir Mustafa, former MLA, and Mirwaiz Maulvi Farooq. Even if he had talked to anyone, he could have done so unobtrusively and without arousing suspicions of the pro-Pakistani terrorists.

George Fernandes also did not see the contradictions in what he was doing. On the one hand, he was working as friend of Dr. Farooq Abdullah, on the other he was trying to cultivate those elements whose suspicions were aroused by the very mention of the name of Dr. Farooq. These elements entertained deep suspicions about the attitude of the Union Government towards Dr. Farooq Abdullah. They thought that he would, somehow or the other, be brought back to power. Frequent talks about the revival of the State Assembly strengthened their suspicions.

Whenever I tried to put some practical sense in regard to the timing of the political process or the manner of going about it, I was projected as someone who was against the political approach. The following day headlines would appear in the press: "bullets no answer to the Kashmir problem", insinuating as if I was advocating that approach. Little respect was shown to the truth. The basic fact was that by dissolving the State Assembly I had taken the most important step towards the initiation of healthy political process through which honourable line of retreat was available to the subversives and all parties and groups had a fair opportunity to capture political power, the essential pre-requisite being the elimination of the instruments of terror.

The term, political process, was no magic wand, and harsh and cruel realities of terrorism and subversion would not melt away by any gimmickry. A sound and silent approach, with five lines of action, spelt out earlier in this Chapter, would have actually diminished the flow of bullets from both the sides.

Administrative Complications

Direct involvement of George Fernandes in Kashmir affairs caused a number of administrative complications, and also baffling diffusion of authority. The Prime Minister attempted to clarify the position. Intervening in the Debate in the Rajya Sabha on 14.3.90, he said*, "In the allocation of business of the minister, no minister has been divested of any power. Fernandes has been designated to coordinate with all the ministries regarding J&K. He is not displacing any minister." But such clarifications had little meaning at the operational level. Nor did it take into account George Fernandes's interventionist and amazingly mysterious style of functioning. A host of problems pertaining to coordination and decision-making arose.

The Central Intelligence agencies were under the Home Minister and the State Intelligence agencies under me. While on the basis of their reports and other evidence, we proceeded against certain background operators, George Fernandes tried to have meetings with them, causing embarrassment to the officers who were entrusted with the task of implementing instructions. Sometimes, we had to experience the funny, yet agonising, spectacle, of the same official receiving contradictory messages from two different sources of authority.

In quite a few cases, myself, George Fernandes, and Mufti Mohammad Sayeed had different perceptions. For example, I wanted to proceed against a senior doctor of Sher-e-Kashmir Medical Institute. Mufti Sayeed agreed with my view. But George Fernandes, without bothering to counter the hard evidence in our possession and the recommendations of the intelligence agencies, asked me not to do so. The vague cliche of political process was his only justification. In the highly complex situation in which I found myself, I did not want to make an issue of it. I regretted it later. Had the intended action been taken, much of the subsequent trouble in the Sher-e-Kashmir Medical Institute, including kidnapping and killing of some innocent nurses and liftmen, would have been prevented.

**Indian Express*, March 15, 1990.

In local administrative matters having bearing upon law and order, too, George Fernandes's intervention was not infrequent. What was worse, he would intervene at the lower level without talking to me or the Home Minister. For instance, on March 30 Ashfaq Majeed Wani, a top terrorist, and 'chief area commander of Srinagar', was killed when a grenade exploded in his hand as he was preparing to throw it on a BSF party. According to the general instructions issued by the terrorist organisations to their field units, every 'martyrdom' had to be used to arouse mass frenzy and arrange mass gathering. Our settled policy, based upon past experience, was to permit only low-key burial. Provocative speeches and demonstration had not to be allowed. This policy was followed by the Director-General of Police and other officers concerned. Everything proceeded according to our way of thinking till George Fernandes landed at the Srinagar airport.

It was our experience that George Fernandes's visits to Srinagar and the manner in which he functioned during these visits not only caused unnecessary strain on the administrative machinery which we were trying to rebuild but also gave rise to problems which were avoidable. On March 19, 1990, for instance, he went to Bij Behare. This visit merely provided an opportunity to the subversive organisations, including splinter groups, to get together and put up a solid anti-Indian show. A total hartal was brought about and black flags were put on the houses. A problem that need not have arisen, arose. George's untimely visits virtually put fans in the hands of the leaders of subversion to rekindle the dying flames. A well-known local English daily, *Excelsior*, ruefully observed that George Fernandes appeared "determined to sabotage the State administration's efforts".

Contrary to what was stated by the Prime Minister in the Parliament, George Fernandes set up a parallel organisation. A whole-time Secretary of Kashmir Affairs, Bhaskar Ghosh, was appointed. Two Joint Secretaries, Syed Rizvi and B.R. Singh, IAS officers of J&K cadre, were also appointed. B.R. Singh was believed to be close to Dr. Farooq Abdullah. His unusual actions, taken at the behest of the Chief Minister, were the main causes of the resignation of R.S. Chib, a well-meaning Minister in Dr. Farooq Abdullah's cabinet.

George Fernandes created a nucleus of his own in the higher services of the State through Ashok Jaitley, an IAS of Kashmir cadre, in whom he always evinced special interest. When George Fernandes was Minister in the Janata Government, he had appointed Ashok Jaitley as his Special Assistant.

During the first few days of my taking over for the second term, George Fernandes used to talk to me practically every day about Ashok Jaitley, suggesting his appointment as Chief Secretary. Obviously, I was embarrassed by such requests. My own preference was for an outsider. I had nothing against any local officer but thought that in the prevailing circumstances only an outsider would be effective and act fearlessly. Mufti Mohammad Sayeed wanted R.K. Takkar to take over as Chief Secretary. The latter was senior to Ashok Jaitley and had worked as Chief Secretary for a short while during the last few months of G.M. Shah's regime. The then Cabinet Secretary was upset about the appointment of Takkar, as he considered him too junior for the assignment, at that time. When the Governor's rule came on March 7, 1986, I did not mind continuing Takkar as he was doing fairly well. At the same time, I did not want to stand in the way of the Cabinet Secretary. Takkar, I thought, nursed a grievance on that score. When Mufti came to know about the pressure being exerted on behalf of Jaitley, he suddenly sent Takkar to me. As I was keen to get along with the job, I appointed him. Unfortunately, Jaitley, though an intelligent officer, became a focal point of activities which caused problems of its own type–problems in which I need not go into here.

Mufti Mohammad Sayeed's position as head of the Home Ministry also created some administrative problems, as local officers who knew him could easily approach him for what they considered as their grievance in respect of transfers and other administrative matters. But in comparison to Fernandes, Mufti Sayeed was far more practical and rooted to the ground-level realities. He understood the need for removing the sway of terrorism and violence first. He was also unhappy about the way in which George Fernandes was weakening the authority of the State administration.

It was often stated on behalf of the Union Government that tasks being performed by the Governor and the Minister of Kashmir Affairs were complementary; one was concerned with the administrative action and the other with the political process. This proposition, in theory, could not be faulted. But the real issue was what happened in practice. The political process was undertaken in such a manner that it scuttled executive action and maimed the administrative machinery–whatever of it we had been able to reconstruct from the fallen debris.

Constitutionally and legally, the Governor alone had the authority and the responsibility. After the imposition of the Governor's rule under Section 92* of the J&K Constitution, all the powers and functions of the State Government vested in him. In other States, when the President rule is promulgated, the powers and functions of the State Government are taken over by the President who, in turn, delegates them to the Governor, subject to his overall control and superintendence. But in the case of J&K, the powers and functions of the State Government fall directly in the lap of the Governor by virtue of the provisions of Section 92 of the J&K Constitution. No one else has these powers and functions, not even the Home Minister.

Legal and constitutional position apart, dictates of administrative effectiveness required that there should be only one clear and strong line of command. The critical conditions prevailing in J&K compounded the need for such a command.

The Union Government, if it so desired, could certainly appoint another Governor. But to keep me and simultaneously create parallel and over-lapping organisations was administratively unsound, legally unsustainable and morally indefensible. Was I needed only for unpleasant tasks? Or did the Government have no clear perception of the reality, no idea about its direction or purpose?

At one stage, in sheer desperation, I did draft a letter of virtual resignation, suggesting to the Prime Minister that, if he considered George Fernandes was the person who could deliver the goods in Kashmir, he should be appointed as Governor of J&K.

The draft, which explains the rationale of my suggestions and also reflects the state of my mind, is reproduced below:

Raj Bhavan

Dear PM,

I am writing to suggest in all humility that you may consider appointing George Fernandes as Governor of J&K. In view of the prevailing conditions, it would be catastrophic, if not suicidal, to blur the focus of the drive that I have launched to recapture fully the authority of the State and pave the way for the lasting recovery. Let this drive be pursued with single-minded devotion and unflinching determination till the primary goal is first attained. If you think George Fernandes can perform this task better, I would be happy to step down at a few minutes notice.

*See Chapter XI: 'Dissolution of the Assembly'.

Let there be only one operational commander. Let both power and responsibility vest with him. Let him deal with subversion, terrorism, political process and whatever else he may choose. Let him tackle his old personal friends and also the new ones that he claims to have contacted. The nation should be concerned with the end-product. He should deliver the goods. You cannot have one commander holding the bloody and treacherous front and the other commander or commanders whistling to the troops from distance and disturbing, intentionally or un-intentionally, the rhythm of their march.

I mean no offence to anyone. But I would not hesitate to say that the whirlpools of confusion and contradictions that are being created around me and the new fronts that are being opened for me to attend to and the thunderbolts of disinformation* that are being regularly hurled through cleverly-planted stories and statements in the press would result in total undoing of what has been done so far after so much of pain, labour and risk.

With kind regards,

Yours sincerely,
(Sd.) Jagmohan

I scribbled this letter, late in the evening, in my own hand and put it in my briefcase to get it typed the following day by my private secretary. But by the morning, the surging turbulence within me had frozen in my mind. The long walk around the Raj Bhavan garden strengthened the encasing around this turbulence. The cool, crisp and gentle breeze had done the trick. The letter was neither got typed nor posted.

Subconsciously, perhaps, I did not want to see frittering away of the advantages that had accrued from my having acquired an upper hand** in many arenas and to make use of the times that were clearly coming to enable me to unfold a bold new blue-print† of reform and development–a blue-print that would have reoriented the Kashmiri ethos in favour of the Union and led to a new era of lasting peace and national cohesion.

---

* See Chapter XIII: 'Frightened Pigeons and Forsaken Community–Kashmiri Pandits' and Chapter XV: 'A Deluge of Disinformation and Distortion'.

** See Chapter XIV: 'Acquiring an Upper Hand'.

† *Ibid.*

CHAPTER XIII

Frightened Pigeons and Forsaken Community—Kashmiri Pandits

And the truth could be hid
Somebody chose their pain
What need not have happened did.
—Auden

Hall of Crooked Mirrors

In reply to a question at the Press Conference held by me, after the Congress(I) party did not allow me to speak in the Rajya Sabha on the subject of Kashmir on May 30, 1990, I said: "India does not require outside enemies; we are our own worst enemies." The truth of this assertion is borne out by the highly biased and tangential 'report' by a Committee called 'Initiative on Kashmir'.

The report virtually rationalises and justifies terrorism in Kashmir and provides indirect encouragement to it. It is a highly manipulated exercise in deception, distortion and disinformation. Even the worst enemies of India could not have produced more harmful propagandist material than this report. No wonder it was quoted time and again on Pakistan Television and Radio and also extensively used by it and other detractors of India at the international level.

The inner savagery of the report was matched only by its superficiality, its aggressiveness by its obstinacy not to see the truth. In the name of human rights, it butchered all basic human rights—the right to secure justice; the right to be heard before being condemned;

the right not to have reputations built over years of hard and honest work to be sullied by false and motivated accusations and the personal grudges and prejudices of a few individuals.

Could any agency calling itself a human rights body torment a forsaken community like the Kashmiri Pandits? Shorn of its verbiage and progressive veneer, it was really an 'inhuman report'. It did not matter to it if 'Y' was hanged for the fault of 'X'.

There were some good persons in the 'People's Union of Civil Liberties' Group. But how did their goodness matter if due to their preoccupation or other causes they allowed themselves to be blindfolded by 'clever' elements like Inder Mohan who had their personal scores to settle?

The report was a product of compulsive bias. It did not take into account any of the concrete facts and documents cited by me in the preceding chapters. The Committee accepted hearsay evidence of interested parties as authentic, and doctored the statements of persons interviewed to fit into predetermined conclusions. The tragic irony was that in the name of human rights, it did maximum damage to human rights. It forgot that truth is a human right, too. Nor did it appreciate that by providing indirect encouragement to the terrorists and by presenting them and their supporters as victims, it caused more kidnappings, more killings, and more violations of the human rights of the wholly innocent.

The report helped the terrorists ease their conscience and made them feel that they were 'more sinned against than sinning'. In that frame of mind, they thought that their acts were not unjustified. And they continued with their nefarious deeds–more kidnappings, more killings. *Sadai Kashmir,* the underground publication of the terrorists, the role of which I have already indicated in the chapter 'Nature and Pattern of Subversion and Terrorism', quoted extensively from this report to whip up emotions of the Kashmiri youth and to wean them over to terrorism. This was the service rendered to humanity by the 'human rights body'. Was it an initiative to help in resolving Kashmir's problem or an initiative to complicate it by arousing revulsion against the authorities?

The report, in its introduction, said:

> A four-member team on behalf of the Committee for Initiative on Kashmir, during a visit to J&K from March 12-16, 1990, obtained detailed information from a large number of sources, including

victims, eye-witnesses as well as senior govern-ment officials, about indiscriminate killings, arbitrary arrests, unlawful searches, unprovoked assaults on peaceful demonstrators and a complete dislocation of normal life due to imposition of indefinite curfew for months together with rare breaks of a few hours. The team found, in the course of investigation, that these abuses have been carried out by the official law-enforcement personnel–the CRPF (Central Reserve Police Force), the BSF (Border Security Force) and, in certain cases, by the Indian Army. That these cases of blatant violation of human rights were not isolated instances of aberrations, but operative extensions of an official policy was evident to the team members when they met senior administrators who justified such actions on the ground that they were necessary to contain 'terrorism'.

The conclusions are so sweeping, so vague, that the inbuilt bias of the Committee becomes self-evident to a discerning mind. These conclusions, moreover, are drawn with such an air of authority that it would appear that they have been arrived at after months of painstaking research. But what was the time span of this 'research'? It was four days and that, too, during the time when the shadows of the terrorists' guns were looming large over the Valley and no common man or so-called disinterested intellectuals would dare say anything except what the terrorists and their supporters wanted them to say.

What was the standard of objectivity in attributing statements to those whom the team met? Here is a telling example.

In regard to the discussions with the Chief Secretary, the report recorded:

He felt that during the last three years under Dr. Farooq Abdullah the State administration had become excessively corrupt. He, however, pointed out that the All India Services personnel in the State were the only people who were not corrupt. In other words, except IAS most of whom were outsiders, according to Takkar, all Kashmiri employees and politicians were corrupt.

It was clear that R.K. Takkar did not trust the people of Kashmir. But the bias became very clear when we discussed the Chhanpora incident on 7th March. He said, 'Chhanpora is a trouble spot. The people are with the terrorists. They will do anything to spread disinformation.' The last point that we raised was the migration of non-Muslims from the Valley. We told him that people of all communities had told us that government transport was provided to Hindu families to leave the Valley. He denied it.

When the Chief Secretary was requested to comment on this report by the Home Department, in the usual official routine, this is what he said in writing: "Many wrong statements have been attributed to me. I did say that the high level of corruption and nepotism that obtained during the three years of Dr. Farooq Abdullah's Government was one of the major contributory factors to the present trouble in the State. I am not so stupid as to believe or suggest that all members of All India Services are honest and all other public servants are corrupt. It is mischievous to suggest that I do not trust the people of Kashmir. In fact, I emphasized that most of the news analysis on the present crisis in Kashmir had failed to discount the elements of fear. In regard to migration of non-Muslims from the Valley, I had stoutly challenged their assertion that the State Government had sponsored it. Members of the Committee promised to send me the details of such vehicles but have failed to do so till date."

It is an elementary principle of justice that if any statement or view is attributed to any person on sensitive issues like the ones in question, the statement or the view should be in writing; in the alternative, the gist of the discussions should be sent to that person for confirmation before it is incorporated in any report. It is both unfair and unethical to put words into the mouth of certain persons to suit the conclusions which the team had, perhaps, already drawn. The Chief Secretary was fully justified in complaining that the report did grave injustice to what he had stated. Nor was he wrong when he attributed mischief to the Committee. The fact that the team was bent upon presenting predetermined conclusions would be evident from its unfulfilled promise of giving particulars of the government vehicles allegedly used by the migrants.

The other senior functionaries concerned also furnished their comments on the report. This is what Mahmud Rehman, Additional Chief Secretary (Home), said in his comments:

> It is also wrong to allege that the first day of Governor's rule was marked by raids and searches conducted by the security forces with the ostensible objective of flushing out the terrorists. 'These raids*

*See Chapter I: 'My Frozen Turbulence' and Ved Marwah's report quoted therein.

were already planned according to the security needs and intelligence reports and no orders on this subject were issued by the new Governor.

It is difficult to appreciate as to how the Committee has come to the conclusion that the common man in the Valley is prepared to have a dialogue with the Central Government.

In his comments, Amar Kapoor, Additional Director-General, Police, pointed out that the facts and figures given in the report were not correct. He asserted that from December 1989 to May 15, 1990, 134 innocent persons were killed by the militants. The killings of 71 Hindus during this period created fear among the minority community and accelerated the pace of migration of Kashmiri Pandits. "There is no truth", emphasised Kapoor, "that the State Government extended help to the Pandits to leave the Valley."

Jamil Qureshi, Adviser to the Governor, incharge of Law and Order remarked:

> I don't know how the PUCL has given such a preposterous version without even caring to meet the Adviser incharge Law and Order.
>
> In respect of the Chhanpora incident, Qureishi said:
>
> Apart from the fact that this was the scene of the cold blooded murder of four IAF officers, Chhanpora has been a hideout of militants where they have not only been finding support, but where they have been assiduously cultivated to foster and execute a network of safe houses.

It should be evident from the above comments that the committee's report was a virtual fabrication. All norms were violated by the champions of human rights. The doings of the terrorists were supported. Peaceful disposition of the mob was taken for granted, while the administration and the security forces were presumed to be cruel and callous in their behavior.

The haughty yet hollow assertions of the Committee stand thoroughly exposed by the school bus incident leading to firing at Tengpora on March 1, 1990. The report of the Committee reads:

> Following widespread protests against the killing of bus passengers at Tengpora, the Army conducted an inquiry into the incident under the directions of the government. The report of the inquiry sought to justify the killings on the ground that the people had pelted stones at an Army vehicle carrying school children of

> military personnel. Local people whom we interviewed dismissed the inquiry report as blatantly false, since all the schools in the Valley were closed at the time for winter holidays. Incidentally the J&K government issued an order on February 20th asking schools, colleges and other educational institutions to remain closed till March 15.
>
> Attempts by the army authorities to justify their killing of bus passengers at Tengpora on that day, by inventing a false story, are a further blot on the country's defence forces who are required to be a highly disciplined cadre dedicated to the task of protecting our people.

Just note the tone and tenor of the accusation about inventing a false story and the air of moral rectitude that is assumed. But what are the facts? The boot is on the other leg. It is the team which has invented the false story that all schools were closed. The army school was open. The students were taking their examinations during the period. The committee's team did not care to contact the headmaster of the school or any of the students or parents or army officers concerned. Why? The lapse is intentional. Had the team contacted the persons concerned, it would have found the truth. But then, how would it have drawn the predetermined conclusions?

I reproduce below the letter dated April 25 of S.N. Drabu of New Delhi which was published in the *Indian Express* of May 1, 1990:

> Sir, Apropos Ms. Suhasini Mulay's letter (IE, April 19). I want to put the record straight for the benefit of your readers and for Ms. Mulay's benefit also.
>
> Ms. Mulay is the Executive Secretary of the Committee for Initiative on Kashmir and she is naturally sore because the Governor of the J&K State, Mr. Jagmohan has dismissed the report of the Committee as 'totally incorrect'. She has tried to cover her embarrassment and indignation by posing smart and quoting 'just one instance' to pinpoint and expose 'inconsistency' in Jagmohan's argument. She writes, 'As a matter of fact, the much circulated allegations of an attack on an army bus carrying school children referred to by Jagmohan as a reason for firing by army guards (in Tengpora on March 1) turned out to be false, as our inquiries revealed and there was no question of any school bus plying on that day since all the schools in the Valley remained closed till March 15 under government orders.'

But there is nothing incorrect or incongruous in the 'allegation'. The bus in question was carrying children of the Army Public School, situated in the cantonment area of Srinagar. This school, unlike other schools of the Valley, reopened after winter vacation as scheduled on February 19. So the government notification extending winter vacation in the educational institutions of the Valley beyond March 1 (the usual date of reopening after winter break) did not apply to this school. The annual examinations in the school started towards the end of February and on the fateful day of March 1, it was the second day of examination. The army bus that was bringing children from Barzulla, Hyderapura, Peerbagh and other areas to the school situated in the Badamibagh cantonment, was attacked at Tengpora by a frenzied mob comprising the subversive elements and their supporters. And it was precisely after the mishap that the Army Public School too was closed for an indefinite period like other educational institutions in the Valley. Ms. Mulay can get these facts verified from the parents of the children reading in that school, army personnel or civilians, Hindus or Muslims.

Another letter dated April 20 of Thakur Dass of Jammu which appeared in the same newspaper on the same date, was equally revealing. It said:

> Sir, This refers to the letter of Ms. Suhasini Mulay, Executive Secretary, Committee for Initiative on Kashmir (IE, April 19). It is correct that all State government schools in the Valley were closed till March 15 (they will remain closed till May 1, according to a subsequent order) but the Srinagar Army School in question opened on February 20 after the winter vacation. The examinations for various classes started from March 1 and it was on this day that the army bus carrying students of the Army School, mostly wards of the defence personnel, was attacked by some anti-India demonstrators near Tengpora. These are undiluted facts which could be verified from the terrified students or their parents.
>
> If members of the Committee had gone to the Valley, they were under moral obligation to cross-check the facts before casting aspersions on our Army, much less arriving at conclusions which are detrimental to the national interest. If they have any doubts, they are welcome to check the facts from the defence authorities who run this school, or from the Principal of the school, Chaturvedi.

These intellectuals and so-called champions of civil liberties, in their eagerness to run down Jagmohan and the Indian Army, have provided enough material for anti-Indian propaganda in the foreign media. Pakistan made full use of these reports to build up anti-India feelings in Muslim countries.

The people, at least of J&K, would like to know which senior government officer and the officers of the security forces they have met and depend on for their assessment. Propriety demands that the names of such officers be disclosed.

The Committee restricted itself to the local people whom it supposedly interviewed. Who were these nameless people? What were their affiliations? In the opening paras, I pointed out that the Committee relied upon hearsay. But it was not only that; it relied upon the hearsay of the unknown.

The false allegations against the Army and the State Administration for having invented the school bus story, made with such cocky aggressiveness, did immense damage to national honour and the country's international standing. There was not a single correspondent, foreign or local, who met me and did not make adverse observations about it. While the report of the Committee was published in the world media, thanks to the resources and contacts of the PUCL, the letters like those of S.N. Drabu and Thakur Dass, published in some inconspicuous corners of a newspaper, were hardly noticed.

There are many other false observations in the report which call for comments. For want of space, I will give below only a few of them.

On page 23 of its reports, the Committee says:

> When we asked our Muslim interviewees why, in spite of their assurances of protection to their Hindu neighbours, the latter were leaving the Valley, they came out with an explanation which need to be gone into. We were told that the Administration, and Jagmohan in particular, had encouraged the migration by advising the Hindus to leave and by arranging government transport for their departure.

Who arranged for the trucks? Which department of the Government was concerned? On which date or dates were these trucks moved? Who were these nameless Muslim interviewees? And what was the basis of their saying that Jagmohan in particular encouraged the migration of Hindus? The Committee's team did not bother about such questions. Nor did it show its face to the Chief Secretary again when he asked about the precise details. It could not, because the allegations were sheer concoctions.

The Committee intentionally suppressed written evidence to the contrary. As an instance, I would invite attention to the press note issued on March 7 by the State Government. It said:

> Jagmohan, Governor, J&K, has appealed to the members of Kashmiri Pandit community not to leave the Valley even temporarily. He said that law and order machinery was being rebuilt. With the appointment of Special Commissioners and Special DIGs for the newly created Divisions of Baramulla and Anantnag, the authority at the State was being re-established. The senior officers have been specifically charged with the duty of giving protection and safeguarding the minorities and restoring confidence amongst them.
>
> Jagmohan also appealed to the members of the community who have temporarily migrated to Jammu to return to the Valley. He offered to set up temporary camps at four places, namely, Srinagar, Anantnag, Baramulla and Kupwara for those who will return from Jammu. In these places Rest Houses or some other suitable buildings would be requisitioned.
>
> Jagmohan said that accommodation in these camps would be free and arrangements for food and other facilities would also be made. Necessary medical cover would also be provided in each camp. For going to their houses occasionally, a pool of vehicles will also be provided in each camp so that the members of the community could go to their houses with escort. For administering these camps and for attending to the problems of these camps, a separate Relief Commissioner would be appointed.
>
> Jagmohan requested the President and the Secretary of All State Kashmiri Pandit Association, who called on him today, to persuade those who have migrated to Jammu temporarily to return to the Valley.

This omission, apparently intentional, confirms the view that the Committee saw and heard only what it wanted to see and hear. The Committee's compulsive bias of finding fault with me becomes too glaring to be missed.

Real Cause: Blood-Chilling Face of Terrorism

Since the Committee and the like of them did not look to the real cause–the blood-chilling face of Kashmiri terrorism–let me show it to them.

B.K. Ganju. A 'friendly neighbour' of B.K. Ganju, a telecommunications officer and an old resident of Srinagar, told him that he had seen in the nearby mosque a list of persons to be 'finished', and that the name of Ganju was included therein. He and his wife were frightened. They did not really know whom to turn to for help. They apprehended that approach to local police might hasten their end. They spent the night looking at each other with vacant expressions. Sometimes, tears would involuntarily roll down their eyes. In their feverish imagination, they would hear knocks at their doors. And yet, for a few moments, they would hope against hope. Why should they be killed? What wrong had they done?

The night of their agony, which seemed never to end, ultimately gave way to a cold and chilly dawn. Mrs. Ganju went to her prayer room, but did not dare to switch on the light. Then, she went to the kitchen to prepare tea in semi-darkness. While they were taking tea, the telephone rang. They dared not pick it up. It would ring again and again. And their hearts would miss more and more beats. Even their tea seemed to have frozen with fear. They simply could not feel its warmth.

At about 9 a.m. came the knock at the door. "Where is Ganju Sahib? We have an urgent work with him", came the voices from outside. "He is not at home. He has gone to office", Mrs. Ganju replied. "It cannot be. How can he go to office so early? Please open the door and realise the urgency of the matter", pleaded the visitors from outside. She refused. She even stopped responding to the voices. Then, the knocks were no longer there. The callers had apparently left.

Mrs. Ganju opened the upper window a bit and peeped outside. No one was to be seen. But this did not give her any relief. She advised her husband to ring up the police and his own officers. He did. Hardly had he done so when they heard a terrible pounding upon a jammed wooden plank and a sort of old window which gave an opening to Ganju's house from the neighbourhood. Someone was trying to break into the house. They froze with fear. But, somehow or the other, Mrs. Ganju was able to persuade her husband to go to the roof and hide himself in one of the old vacant drums with heaps of gunny bags around.

Within minutes, the two intruders were inside the house—one with a Kalashnikov and the other with a pistol. They looked for Ganju in every nook and corner of the house. They found that one small room was locked from outside. They thought that Ganju was inside. They asked for the key. She pleaded that it was with her brother-in-law who had gone out of station. They were furious. They smashed down the little door but found no trace of Ganju. They left saying, with blood-thirsty eyes, "how long can a rat escape?". Mrs. Ganju never understood why her husband was being called a rat.

At the corner of the street, the two visitors received a signal from one of the neighbouring houses. They ran back, climbing the stairs of Ganju's house with lightning speed. Mrs. Ganju stood motionless, with her legs paralysed. She knew where the intruders were heading for. She soon heard a burst of bullets and slumped down to the floor. Her husband lay dead on the roof, with the gunny bags soaking up his blood. The drum had rolled over towards the stairs. Nothing seemed to affect the intruders. Quietly and smoothly, they walked away. This time they did not even look at Mrs. Ganju, a half-dead woman. They paid no heed to her anguished sobs.

The Committee's members and the like of them did not even attempt to see any of the hundreds of frightened pigeons like Ganju in the cruel cages of Kashmiri terrorism. Nor did they have the time or the inclination to hear the sobs and anguished cries of their widows and other dependents. They had their predetermined streets to visit, predetermined class of persons to interview, predetermined conclusions to draw, and the predetermined target to assail and ask for his recall.*

Prof. K.L. Ganju. Ganju was a venerated lecturer in the Sopore Agricultural College. His scientific sense told him that Sopore had become a snake-pit and he and his family members could be stung by the poisonous fangs anytime. But his inbred Kashmiri sentiments led him to the contrary conclusion. "Why should anyone harm him; after all, he had not even hurt a fly in his lifetime; he had served the local community well and had a number of Muslim friends and admirers", he would argue within.

*See the section dealing with Inder Mohan in this chapter.

On May 2, 1990, when K.L. Ganju, his wife and his cousin 'Pista' were having dinner at about 9 p.m., four armed men, one with a Kalashnikov and the others with pistols, appeared at the door and ordered all the three to come out with them.* Even the sheep, when taken to the slaughter house, moan and make attempts to escape. But these, the three hapless individuals, pale, aghast and with their blood curdling in their veins, must walk to their chamber of death in silence. Almost all the neighbours in the locality saw them being taken away. Some of them recognised the armed intruders who belonged to the known local terrorist group of 'Luskar Ayub'. But none of the neighbours moved an inch, not even to plead for mercy. They just kept watching. Even after the captives and their likely slaughterers had moved away from the scene, no neighbour took the trouble of informing the nearby CRP picket. Informing the local police, of course, would have been a mere formality; they, perhaps, knew about it. But even that was not done.

K.L. Ganju and his two companions were taken to the assigned place of their execution near a mosque on the bank of the River Jhelum. From a point-blank range, six bullets were pumped into his body. When the first bullet was about to be fired, his hands moved involuntarily diverting the aim of the shooter. The bullet hit Pista on the tip of his heels, injuring him slightly. He jumped into the river and somehow or other managed to swim to safety. After a couple of days of fearsome hiding in the Valley, he escaped to Jammu.

For some unaccountable reason Ganju's corpse was kept in the mosque for the night and then thrown into the river. According to one of the assassins, who was arrested later, Mrs. Ganju, too, was ruthlessly killed and her corpse was tied with stone and thrown into the Jhelum. But her dead body was never recovered.

So much for the neighbours whose empty words and ineffectual assurances the Committee's team considered relevant.

From Srinagar and Sopore, let me take you to the rural Kashmir and show you how pitiless the monster of terrorism could be.

'Premi'. Premi's tragic story is the story of a poet–a poet who was a messenger of love, compassion, truth and justice, a poet who had translated Bhagwad Geeta into Kashmiri language, a poet who had

*These narratives are based upon the disclosures made by the assassins after their arrest and also upon the statements of the survivors.

kept a copy of Quran reverentially in his house for regular study, and a poet who, in his long career as a government teacher, had illumined many minds and given them the most precious of all gifts, education. It was this noble soul that was done to death, along with his 27-year-old young son, in a most treacherous and brutal manner.

After retirement, Serwanand Koul 'Premi' lived with his family in his village Shali in District Anantnag. He spent most of his time writing articles for local newspapers and magazines and in academic pursuits.

Some of the members of his family often expressed apprehensions about their safety in the remote village and suggested migration. But Premi would invariably overrule them, saying that migration from the soil in which he was so deeply rooted was unthinkable. Did he not, moreover, have a number of old students and friends in the area to take care of him and his family?

But the fact that the world of his poetic beliefs and sensibilities had ceased to exist and old loyalties and friendship had become powerless in the face of the fierce assault mounted by the forces of fundamentalism and fanaticism, dawned upon him and others around on the late evening of April 30, 1990, when three armed men, like hungry wolves, anxious to trap their prey by fair or foul means, appeared at Premi's door. They herded all the inmates in one room and asked the 67-year-old Premi to accompany them to their 'camp' for answering a few questions.

Some Muslim neighbours appeared on the scene and interceded on behalf of Premi. But their mild protests had no effect. The messengers of death, moreover, were trained in the art of deception. They swore in the name of their religion that no harm would be done to Premi. His son, Virender Koul, however, insisted that whatever questions had to be asked could be asked in a separate room in the house. But the intruders did not agree. How could they? They had to take him to their torture cell. They also took Virender Koul along.

No one reported the matter to the police, not even his relatives and lifelong Muslim friends. The climate of fear had numbed all old attachments.

After two days of painful anxiety came the dreadful news. Two dead bodies had been found hanging with their limbs broken, hairs uprooted, and portions of their skin slit open and burnt.

I am personally aware of many other blood-chilling incidents* of the type described above. But considerations of not merely being objective but also appearing to be objective require that I should prefer to invite attention to the experiences of Kashmiri Pandits as narrated by them to a team of the *Illustrated Weekly of India*.** These narratives bring out the compulsions which led to the flight of the Kashmiri Pandits from the Valley.

The following is the experience of Sudesh Kumar, a law student of Kashmir University.

> T.K. Razdan, an intelligence officer, was killed right in front of my eyes. We were travelling in the same Matador when some militants stopped it, pulled out their guns and fired at him from close range. They then dragged the body out and took it to the nearby mosque. They checked his pockets, took out his identity card and nailed it to his body, then laid out his body on the open road. It was only later that the police came and carried it away. The body was cremated by the CRPF. The relatives were so terror-stricken that they were afraid to even come out for the cremation. His murder really shook me.
>
> Again, one day in February, I ran into a 'jaloos'. To avoid being identified, I too joined them, shouting slogans. I also called for 'azadi' for Kashmir that day. I hailed Pakistan and condemned the 'Indian dogs'–there was little else that I could do if I had to live that day.
>
> Then we received a threatening letter from the militants. They had slipped in under our door. The letter ordered us to leave Srinagar, otherwise they would do to us what they did to A.K. Raina.† Our neighbours tried to pressurise us and promised to protect us but we decided not to take any chance. My father who works in the education department, my mother, a sister, two brothers and my grandfather escaped at 3 a.m. one-night in a hired truck with some luggage.

Here is another aspect of the Kashmiri reality as seen through the eyes of Jai Bhagwan, a Telephone Operator at the Institute of Medical Sciences, Srinagar:

---

* Those who wish to look at the face of Kashmiri terrorism still more closely, may turn to the pages of Chapter VIII and Chapter IX wherein the cases of Taploo and Tikku have been dealt with.

** In the last week of March.

† Deputy-Director, Civil Supplies, who was shot dead in his office.

Today we are suffering and living like dogs because we are Indians and stood for India. Had we changed our religion and raised pro-Pakistan slogans we would have been safe in Srinagar and our future would have been secure. . . .

The militants took control of my institute. Their task became easier because they had the tacit support of the hospital authorities. Meanwhile, killings by the terrorists became more and more indiscriminate.

One evening when I was returning home, two young men asked me the time. When I replied, they started beating me up. They told me to adjust my watch according to Pakistan standard time. The same evening the house of a Kashmiri Pandit in the neighbourhood was burnt down. On the following nights our area was pelted with stones and bottles filled with petrol. When we lodged a complaint the police officers refused to provide us guards, pleading that they did not have enough men. Their attitude completely demoralised us. After these incidents the Kashmiri Pandit families in our area, Nai Sark, started migrating.

In the Institute, the schism between us and the Muslim employees increased. Some of them were so close to the terrorists that they had prior information about bomb blasts and killings. One day they asked me to change my religion or leave Srinagar. That really scared me and that night, along with my wife, two children and father I left our three-storeyed house in search of security. A couple of days later four of my colleagues, including a nurse, were killed by militants. Two of them were kidnapped while on duty. Their dead bodies carried marks of severe torture. Their eyes were gouged out, their limbs broken and chests spotted with burns. Now in New Delhi I am left with no money. In Srinagar no one wants to buy our house. Who will buy it?

This is what Dr. Agni Shekhar, a writer, has to say:

I have done a Ph.D. in Hindi from Kashmir University and published three novels. A few months ago I received a note from some of the militant outfits saying that Hindi was the language of kafirs and I should stop writing in Hindi, otherwise I would be exterminated. . . . Soon enough I learnt that I was not the only one. My brother, too, who has been a TV artiste received threats. . . . And one day some men came to my house asking for me. My mother told them that I was not at home. . . . I noticed that there

> was a man seated at some distance under a street lamp and could see his gun. They had come to kill me! I wasted no time and escaped through the backyard. I hid in a friend's house for 10 days, and at the first available opportunity came away to Jammu. My brother who had received death threats had already run away to Madhya Pradesh.

And this is the narrative of a young staff nurse, Seema Raina, about her experience:

> I fled that Valley along with my family in January. But soon I mustered up enough guts to go back to collect my pay on February 1. All went well till I had collected the cash token from the Institute's branch of the Jammu and Kashmir Bank; then, all of a sudden a huge procession came. They were raising anti-national slogans along with the usual fundamentalist ones like 'Kashmir mein agar rehna hoga Allah ho Akbar kehna hoga' (If you wish to live in Kashmir you have to say 'Allah ho Akbar') and 'Dil mein rakho Allah ka khauf haath mein rakho Kalashnikov' (One must have the fear of Allah in the heart and a Kalashnikov in his hand).
>
> My pulse was racing. Just then I heard gun-shots and within a few minutes a group of gun-wielding militants barged into the bank. They asked everyone to leave and threatened the manager with dire consequences if he dared to make any more payments. This was the first time that I had come face to face with armed militants and was trembling with fear. I said to hell with the salary, it is not more valuable than my life. I got out of the bank, mingled with the demonstrators and then disappeared. I took the first available transport to Jammu and have not even thought of returning to the Valley.

Another aspect of human tragedy unfolds itself through the words of a poor driver of Srinagar Radio Station, Triloki Nath Kaul:

> My whole life was destroyed, laid waste. But for what was happening in the Valley, my wife would not have died. My wife was ill with shock and constant fear that the terrorists would kill us all. They didn't kill her directly, but indirectly they did. . . .

Astounding Proposition

What can you say of a Committee which comes out with a proposition that it is not the fearsome environment, it is not the brutalised landscape, it is not the ruthless Kalashnikov of the marauders, it is not the bomb explosions and fires, it is not the threatening telephonic calls, it is not the hysterical exhortations for 'Jihad' from hundreds of loudspeakers fitted on the mosques, it is not the 'Tirana-e-Kashmir' of having Quran in one hand and a rifle in the other, it is not the fall-outs of grave human tragedies of Ganjus, Tikkus and Premis, it is not the sinister design of 'killing one and frightening 1,000', but the inducement of the trucks that have impelled the Kashmiris to abandon their homes and hearths in the cool and crisp Valley and to move to the hot and inhospitable camps of Jammu. What can you say of the judicial attributes of ex-High Court judges who allow their names to be stamped on such propositions! And, if old-age casualness or stubbornness is not the cause, what can you say of a country's legal system, where such judicial luminaries could throng the State's highest courts at some point of time or other!

Call it disinformation or deception, superficiality or shallowness, carelessness or casualness, subjectivity or bias, the fact remains that a good section of the country and the world was misled about the so-called 'induced migration' of the Kashmiri Pandits. Such was the damaging effect of the Committee's report which in essence was nothing short of a cruel joke on the victims of a grave human tragedy.

Where, incidentally, are the truck numbers which the Committee promised to supply to the Chief Secretary? Why did it not publish these numbers in the report itself? And where are the plots, their numbers and their localities which are supposed to have been allotted to Kashmiris as inducements by Jagmohan's administration?

What will be the verdict on a nation which allowed its people to be divided and its international image to be undermined by such banalities and superficialities as were churned out by the likes of Inder Mohan and Miss Sohali under the benign umbrella provided by 'eminent' persons?

The 'Save Kashmiri Pandit Campaign Committee' poignantly says in an appeal issued by it: "Is it not an exhibition of heartlessness to impute motives to our decision of migrating from the land of anarchy and violence or to allege that the migrants left at the biddings of the highest-up in Srinagar. Must we tell these partisans that nothing is more distasteful to a Kashmiri Pandit than even the remotest thought of leaving the land which he loves only as a son would love his mother." The appeal emphasised:

The choice was forced on us by Pakistan-led terrorists who have imposed their writ on Kashmir, taken an unending toll of innocent human lives, wrought death and destructions, bombed and blasted residential as well as public buildings, not sparing even the schools.

We did not want to migrate. We love our land, our Kashmir, every inch of its bounteous soil which has nourished us all; we love every drop of its cool and clear water, every blade of its greenest grass. For us, bidding farewell to the soil we have sprung from is too traumatic an experience to be conveyed in words. Will you believe the symbol of wedlock of Kashmiri Pandit womenfolk 'DEJIHORU' (a kind of mangalsutra generally made of gold) changed hands, enabling our loved ones to get a lift in goods-laden trucks bound for Jammu? Many village folk from Southern Kashmir, men, women, and children, old and young, sick and infirm, trudged on foot the long stretch of the hazardous, snow-bound mountain terrain from Verinag to Jawahar Tunnel only to come out of the range of fire of the terrorists' deadly Kalashnikovs.

The Kashmir Migrant Forum, in its statement issued on May 1, 1990, expressed similar views on the Committee's report:

What can be more cruel, more insulting to the people who have been made to flee their ancestral land through tactics of terror and subversion, killings and kidnappings, bomb blasts and arson, and forced to live a miserable life in some rotten refugee camps in tropical heat. Do these self-styled champions of human rights consider the highly intelligent and educated Kashmiri Pandits to be so naive as to abandon their homes, property and jobs all for the sake of rumour? Or do they think that they are away on a collective picnic in Jammu, Delhi and other places of the country?

V.M. Tarkunde and his friends had gone to Srinagar with a pre-set mind, eager to buy the militants' line lock, stock and barrel, pick up fault with the Jagmohan administration and blame the security forces for all sorts of excesses.

What the Kashmiri Pandits stated in their "Appeal to the People of India", is equally incontestable:

We migrants were forced to abandon our homes and hearths, our jobs and business enterprises, our fields and orchards, because the armed militants killed many of our loved ones brutally, in broad daylight, without any reason, without our having ever given them the slightest provocation now or in the past. History is witness and the majority community will acknowledge that we have stood by them at all times of trials and tribulations and contributed our mite to the peace and well-being of our homeland.

The militants warned us, our families, our children through posters, that no one was going to protect our lives and property. They stoned our houses especially during dark nights, day in and day out, breaking window panes, hurling abuses and invectives; they forced many of us at gun point to join anti-national demonstrations which they used as cover for firing at security personnel inviting counter-fire, thus endangering our very lives; they yelled at us through loud-speakers fitted in each mosque: 'Death to infidels; Kashmir shall become an Islamic State; those who do not accept it will be pronounced traitors; death to minorities–the agents of India.'

Tragic, very tragic, is the story of our forced migration. But far more tragic is the story of how the armed militants came to impose their Nazi-like dominance over entire Kashmir, over every sector of its life. How could those openly dubbed 'agents of India' continue living in violence-torn Kashmir when the State administration, until the arrival of Jagmohan on the scene as the new Governor, had melted away completely, so much so that the militants forced, in the fundamentalist style, closure of all cinema halls, video and beauty parlours, wine shops, bars; held an armed parade on Pakistan's national day in Srinagar stadium and defiantly unfurled a Pakistan flag; bombed branches of Indian banks, post offices, Central Government offices; coerced them to have the word 'Indian' erased from their front entrances; received salutes from senior Kashmir police officers, imposed at gun-point what came to be called 'civil curfew', total bandh, violation of which by some led to bombing of their establishments and also brutal killing of the owners; flew atop public and private buildings, even State and Central offices, secessionists' flags; ordered on pain of death switching off of electricity at times of important national telecasts.

Acute scare had gripped the Kashmiri Pandits from September 1989 onwards. At that time, the community had started feeling what it felt when it was hounded out by the Afghans in the second half of the eighteenth century:

O heart, there is fear
And dread in the city
Prepare for journey
Disorder is dominant in this city.*

In a memorandum dated January 16, 1990, submitted to my predecessor General K.V. Krishna Rao (Retd.), the Kashmiri Pandit Sabha, Jammu, and other organisations, said:

> The ineffectiveness of the State Government has not been able to check loot, arson and killing of innocent people. Instead of the Government, it is the militants who are the *de facto* rulers in the Valley today. The ruling political forces are solely concerned with their own survival avoiding the wrath of the secessionists. Happenings in Anantnag, Sopore, Baramulla, Tral, Murran, Pulwama, Ishber, Vicharnag, Shopian and other places in the Valley are indicative of the fundamentalists' designs regarding their planned targets of attack on the minorities. On 15th December 1989, in Shopian, men, children and old women of the minority community were mercilessly attacked and women-folk molested. The murder of Mahant Keshav Nath, Tikka Lal Taploo, N.K. Ganjoo, Prem Nath Bhat, Ajay Kapoor and others, was to create scare and awe among the minority community to force them to leave the Valley. The pace of exodus has further accelerated now.
>
> It is a sad commentary on the present administration that not even a single assailant of the minority leaders and others has either been identified or apprehended by the Police till now. The fully Pakistan-trained underground elements who are armed with modern weaponry openly engage in battles with the Security Forces, which unmistakably speaks of the inefficiency of the State Government and alleged involvement of some of the high-ups in the State Government itself. The statement made by Ali Mohammad Sagar, Minister of State, as appeared in the Press on 13.1.1990, suggesting setting back the clock to 1953 position is indicative of the working of the minds of the National Conference political bosses.

In fact, for quite some time, Kashmiri Pandits had been feeling extremely insecure. I vividly remember their fear-stricken faces when

*Quoted from Anand Kaul, *Kashmiri Pandits,* Calcutta. 1926.

I visited various villages and towns of Anantnag District after the riots of February 1986. In this regard, I can do no better than reproduce the letter which I wrote on March 5 to the Home Minister, S.B. Chavan, with a copy to the Prime Minister, Rajiv Gandhi:

> I have toured almost all the affected areas of the four districts—Anantnag, Srinagar, Baramulla and Doda. I have visited practically every damaged building, religious or private, in villages/towns of Wanpoh, Lukbhavan, Fatehpur, Gautamnag, Salair, Akoora, Sopore and Doda.
>
> The damage done to individual property—houses and shops—and temples of Kashmiri Pandits is substantial. But much greater damage has been done to the psyche of the Kashmiri Pandits. They are now living like frightened pigeons. In some villages like Wanpoh or Bonigund, Akoora and Salair, their terror-stricken faces reminded me of the picture of the war-time German Jews slated for the gas chambers. On seeing me, they started weeping and bewailing loudly, and demanded immediate evacuation from the Kashmir Valley. They did not want monetary or any other kind of relief. They argued that, since their property, honour and lives were not safe, relief was meaningless for them. To the best of my ability, I assuaged their injured feelings. But it would take a long time for their wounds to heal, if they heal at all.
>
> It is unfortunate that inaccurate reports were sent by the State Government and District and Divisional Administration to me and the Central Government. What I saw at the site was vastly different from what was reported to me. For instance, the damage done in village Bonigund, which suffered the most grievous attack on February 20, 1986, has not been indicated in the report of the State Government sent to the Central Government as late as March 4, 1986. Here, 7 houses were totally burnt, 8 partially damaged and looted, 3 temples and one shop demolished burnt. This village is not even 3/4 km away from the District Headquarters. This fact alone demonstrates the many-sided infirmities of the present set-up in regard to which in depth analysis has been done in my monthly reports from time to time.

Kashmiri Pandits and the Quirks of their History

Ever since I saw the plight of the Kashmiri Pandit community from close quarters in February 1986, I have been pondering over its curious fate. It is a community whose history generates envy at their achievements as well as sorrow at their plight. In one way, its members have played a dominant role in ruling India after August 1947. In another way, it has been hounded by a deep sense of insecurity in the Valley. In one way, again, it has been a well-knit community, and in another way hopelessly divided and leaderless. Its long history* has been one of triumphs and tragedies–steady and silent triumphs and tumultuous and terrible tragedies. Like Kashmir's weather, its bright, sunny, cool and crisp days have been punctuated by those of floods and famines and of grey and depressing clouds.

The antiquity of the Kashmiri Pandit community and its Aryan origin are well established. As noted in Chapter II, except during Harsa's time, when the Kashmiri 'purohits' were persecuted, they constituted a powerful elite group during the reigns of Hindu kings. Their material needs were mostly met by the royal families and establishments. Such was their influence on society that, by resorting to collective fasting, they could virtually force the monarch to concede their demands, reasonable or unreasonable.

After the establishment of the Muslim Sultanate, the community underwent its most tragic phase during the regime of Sultan Sikander (1389-1413) and his fanatic Chief Minister, Suha Bhatta who, ironically, was himself a Kashmiri Brahmin before his conversion. Persecution and forcible conversions knew no limits. As Ferishta recorded, "Many Brahmins, rather than abandon their religion or their country, poisoned themselves; some emigrated from their native homes, while a few escaped the evil of banishment by becoming Mohammedans." *Rajtarangini* of Jonaraja portrayed the same tragic reality in these words: "The Brahmins fled to foreign countries, the son left the father and the father the son. The difficult terrains through which they passed, the scanty food they ate, the painful illness and the torments they suffered during their lifetime removed the fear of hell from their minds. Only eleven Pandit families were left."**

Maybe the number of eleven is only symbolically true; but the fact remains that at the end of Sultan Sikander's rule, the Kashmiri Brahmins were reduced to a microscopic minority largely through conversion, persecution and consequent migration. As narrated in

---

* See Chapter II: 'Survey of History'.

**Anand Kaul, *Kashmiri Pandits,* Calcutta, 1926; *Cambridge History of India,* Volume III, and Walter Lawrence, *Valley of Kashmir.*

Chapter II, Sultan Zain-ul-Abidin (1420-1471) reversed the policy of religious persecution and allowed the migrants to return and the local converts to reconvert. In the end of the fifteenth century, however, under the influence of Shams-ud-Din Iraqi, the Kashmiri Brahmins were once again persecuted.

The fifteenth century, thus, turned out to be one of the most fateful periods in the history of Kashmiri Pandits. Before this century, the community was intact and divided into 199 exogamous 'gotras',* the members of which claimed descent from the 'rishi' whose name the 'gotra' bore. To these 'gotras' were now added the distinction between the Kashmiri Pandits who withstood the persecution and stayed in the Valley and those who migrated and later on returned. The former were known as 'Malmasis' and the latter 'Bhanamasis'. In popular parlance, those who stuck to their faith were known as 'suchi-haddi' (pure bone) and those who reconverted as 'jhuti-haddi' (already tasted bone).

By the time the Mughal rule commenced in Kashmir, the Pandits had regained their poise and position. They identified themselves with Mughal manners and modes of administration. Their proficiency in Persian, the court language, proved a great asset. The Pandits became the backbone of the structure of governance at the middle level. Their prestige in society was also enhanced by Emperor Akbar's visit to the Martand Temple and offering a cow, with garlands of gold and jewels, as a gift. From the insignificant figure of 11, their number also increased. Their number was estimated by Abul Fazal, during Akbar's regime, at 2,000.†

With the decline of the Mughal Empire, misfortune once again visited the Kashmiri Pandits. Some of the Mughal Governors were fanatics and resorted to forcible conversion. The story of Kashmiri Pandits approaching Guru Tegh Bahadur, which has already been recounted in Chapter II, is revealing in this regard. The Afghan rule occasioned another period of terror for them, as it was for other Kashmiris.

Over the years, Kashmiri Pandits migrated to different parts of northern India. This was largely due to the combined effect of

---

* Brahmanical *gotra* 'may be defined as exogamous patrilineal sibship, whose members trace their descent back to a common ancestor' *(Dictionary* of *Hinduism,* Margaret & James Stutley).

† Abul Fazal, *Ain-e-Akbari.*

occasional persecution at home and opportunities available in the Mughal Court at Delhi, the Sikh Darbar at Lahore, the kingdom of the Nawab of Avadh, and the native States of central India and Rajputana. Destitution, consequent upon the famine of 1831,* which resulted in reduction of the population from 800,000 to 200,000 in the Valley and the famine of 1878, in which three-fifths of the population perished, played not an insignificant part in their migration. The tradition of going on pilgrimage was another factor, though the pilgrims moved from the Mandir to the Darbar at the first available opportunity. Pandit Kishen Das, the great-great grandfather of Raja Narendra Nath, for example, "went from the temple along the Ganges to the fort along the Jamuna and ended at the Mughal Court".

In respect of Kashmiri migration, Dhanavanthi Rama Rau, in her memoirs, *An Inheritance*, observes:

> They (Pandits) arrived and learned to live in what was almost a different country to them. They were obliged to alter their dress from the loose robes and distinctive headcovering of Kashmiris to the Hindu saris for women and pajamas and long coats for men, or to the trousers and tunics dictated by the Muslim Mughal Court. They had to learn a new language, adopt a new cuisine and get used to the flat, dry landscape of the North Indian plains. However, they continued to cling to their names and the customs, rites, and ceremonies that belonged particularly to their community.

The Kashmiri Pandits who migrated had little in common with the Brahmins of northern India. While the latter were highly conservative, strictly vegetarian, and, with a few exceptions, deficient in learning and true knowledge of religion, the Kashmiri Pandits were meat-eaters, scholarly, well versed in Persian, and both adaptive and traditional. They were also liberal in their thoughts and beliefs. While the menfolk took to social norms of the rulers, composed Persian and Urdu poems, and participated in and attended Court 'Mushairas', poetry, symposia, the womenfolk strictly observed all the rituals of religion and sang 'bhajans' (devotional songs) at home. The migrants also developed a tendency to be somewhat self-centred. They kept few contacts with friends and relations at home. They developed a hybrid culture which had some invisible roots in the Valley and some fresh ones in the new soil of their settlement.

*Walter Lawrence. *The Valley of Kashmir* (Srinagar, 1895).

Forsaken by All on a Rough Sea

Whatever be the vicissitudes of their history and whatever unkind quirks their fate might have brought to them in the past, these all pale into insignificance when we reflect on what of late has been happening to them.

When viewed in all its dimensions, the current phase of Kashmiri Pandits' misfortune is the most calamitous. The grim tragedy is compounded by the equally grim irony that one of the most intelligent, subtle, versatile, and proud community of the country is being virtually reduced to extinction in free India. It is suffering not under the fanatic zeal of mediaeval Sultans like Sikandar or under the tyrannical regime of the Afghan Governors, but under the supposedly secular rule of Rajiv Gandhi, V.P. Singh and the like whose unabashed search for personal and political power is symbolised by the callous and calculated disregard of the Kashmiri migrants' miserable plight and the uncertain future that stares them in the face. And to fill their cup of sorrow, there are bodies like the 'Committee for Initiative on Kashmir' which are over-anxious and over-active to rub salt into their wounds.

P.N.K. Bamzai, in his three-volume *Cultural and Political History of Kashmir*, in the section titled: *Jagmohan Saves Kashmir for India* (Chapter 8, pages 274-276) has underlined:

> The Kashmiri Pandits were hounded out of their homeland by the Islamic Fundamentalists who receiving unlimited financial and arms aid from Pakistan and Arab countries,.... When Jagmohan took over he found the situation very grim. On every housetop fluttered either JKLF or Pakistan flag.... The JKLF had planned to declare Kashmir as an Islamic Republic on the occasion of the Indian Republic Day in the presence of foreign journalists... Every day, while peeping out of their windows, the Kashmiri Pandits saw hundreds of gun toting terrorist walking fearlessly on the streets and in many cases being saluted by the local police.... The fear of death, the danger to the honour of their women-folk prompted them to flee... The work of Jagmohan in suppressing terrorism was hampered by the loose methods employed by the Centre in handling the Kashmir problem.... But it must be said to his credit, Jagmohan faced this polity single-handed and mostly ignored the conflicting signals from the Centre.... By 15th April 1990, he was able to assert that the current drive to root out militancy and

subversion was yielding encouraging results. It was apparent from the last Friday of Ramadan prayers which passed off without any untoward incident....

In a recent interview, January, 2018, to the *Trauma of Kashmir–The Untold Story,* the veteran journalist, Ghulam Mohammad Sofi, Editor of The Kashmir Times, has also affirmed:

> One has to appreciate the January 1990 situation in the Valley. Jagmohan stayed in Jammu for one night. He took a flight from Jammu and arrived in Srinagar Raj Bhavan the next day. He called some of his friends. He called me too. Had I known that the situation was as bad as it later turned out to be, frankly, I would not have gone to Raj Bhavan. There were just three people in the room when I arrived in Srinagar Raj Bhavan. He offered a cup of tea to me but there was nobody to bring one. I saw him go towards the kitchen three times; presumably, he made the tea himself. There was no administration worth the name anywhere in the state, I mean in the Valley. The police stations all over the Valley were centres of operation for the militants.

With equal candour, Sofi reacted to the allegations that Governor Jagmohan had encouraged flight of Kashmiri Pandits:

> "It is total lie. It was a part of the systematic propaganda. The exodus was a sequel to a plan worked out in advance. It had nothing to do with Jagmohan. The conditions were too bad when he assumed office on January 19, 1990 for the second term."

As indicated in the footnote of the section titled: Release of 70 hard core terrorists, of Chapter X, A.S. Dulat admitted that he was unable to protect even his own field Intelligence Officers belonging to Kashmiri Pandit community. He was categorical: "Pandits were dead scared, because there had been targetted killing of them. They had started escaping before Jagmohan was appointed as Governor on January 19, 1990 (for the second term)".

Tragically the migrants' own kith and kin, their own high-placed stalwarts, too, have forsaken them. Where are those influential Kauls, Sukhdars, Nehrus and Dhars? Why have they not come forward and provided solace and meaningful leadership to the resourceless migrants? I have seen tears flowing from the eyes of these hapless migrants and also perceived the imprints of terror permanently etched on their minds. I have no doubt that had 'the celebrated and distinguished' sons of the Valley taken the trouble of flying even for a few hours to Jammu and seen the true face of Kashmiris in the migrants' camps, they would not have remained mute spectators of the tragedy or contented themselves with sterile discussions at seminars sponsored by the interested parties. If nothing else, they could have helped in countering the disinformation spread by them. And if, during the course of this endeavor, they could assuage the sufferings of these unfortunate people, they would have earned something for the life to come.

Perversion

The deep crisis through which the Kashmiri migrant, or for that matter the entire Kashmir, is passing is really the crisis of Indian values–the perversion, in practice, of its constitutional, political, social and moral norms. If you visit the camps of the refugees and try to extend the hand of justice to a community in distress, if you instruct that, instead of cash doles, the migrant Government servants should be given leave salary, and if you concede the demand of the widow of a person brutally killed by the terrorists for allotment of a house on payment, you become communal, a 'known anti-Muslim', about whom concocted stories would be published in the press, and who would, even when an opportunity comes to expose the blatant falsehood in Parliament, not be allowed to speak, and would be obstructed by members from different corners of the House. If, on the other hand, you falsely accuse the Indian Army and Governor's administration of inventing stories as in the case of the school bus incident narrated above, if you assail the Administration and 'Jagmohan in particular' for giving inducements through provision of plots and trucks, without giving particulars either of the plots or of the trucks, your accusations get published in the press, your reports are flaunted in national and international forums and are copiously quoted in Parliament, and you are labelled as secular and progressive and a champion of human rights and what not.

A few other basic questions in regard to the plight of Kashmiri Pandits have often cropped up in my mind. How are these unfortunate victims of avoidable tragedy connected with the commissions and omissions pointed out by me in the chapters titled 'Roots', 'Nature and Pattern of Subversion and Terrorism', and

'Warning Signals'? Why do they have to suffer the consequences of the treacherous sabotage of my Operation Rescue as detailed in the chapters titled 'Approach, Attack and Counterattack' and 'Acquiring an Upper Hand'? The only answer that I can find to these questions is that, perhaps, it is another quirk of the Kashmiri Pandits' destiny that they have to suffer for the sins committed by others.

Another Web of Distortion

Let me now turn briefly to another web of distortion–"Kashmir Imprisoned"–the second report of the Committee for Initiative on Kashmir. For want of space, I would lay bare, as illustrations, only a few thick threads of this foggy jumble.

At page 38 of the report, one Ghulam Hassan Mohju, 65, narrates his tale of torture by the Central Reserve Police. In the concluding portion of his narrative,* he says:

> The doctor came and some medication was provided. When I was asked about the weapons, I said that I had lied to save my life. Again the beatings started. Again I said, 'Yes I have weapons" and fell unconscious. A three-star officer came in and I told him, 'If I tell you lies you stop and at the truth you beat me.' Then, they made me wear a uniform. I was put in a jeep and was brought back to Baramulla around 5 a.m. They dug the grounds and searched my house, and took me back. Again the beatings started. Then they handcuffed me and threw me in a rubbish heap, thinking that I was dead. Two days later, finding me still alive, they took me to Sopore police station and left me there.

This concoction is writ large on the face of the story. Just imagine a man being 'considered' dead by the CRP, instead of having it ascertained from the doctor who was available. Just imagine the CRP being so foolish as to throw the 'dead' man on the rubbish heap of Baramulla–the man whom they are supposed to have picked up from his house in the presence of his people. Just also imagine a 65-year-old man severely beaten and handcuffed lying on the rubbish heap in Baramulla for two days and nights, without being noticed by anyone in a town where even a fly cannot buzz in your ears without the whole town coming to know about it. Just imagine further, the CRP team

*Except for correction of 'he' and 'I' jumble, this narration is a reproduction from page 38 of the cyclostyled report.

coming again after two days to the same spot, and, without being noticed by anyone, picking up the 'dead' man and taking him, of all places, to Sopore police station.

"He lies like an eye-witness." Does this Russian proverb not fit perfectly to the above narrative of Mohju? And what can one say about the perception and *bona fides* of a Committee which accepts this narrative and records it in its report without asking obvious questions? The Committee does not stop at mere recording. It assumes the posture of a High Court and observes: "What was very disturbing was the casualness with which the Security Forces could perpetrate violence."*

At page 33 the report records, and obviously accepts as true, the following allegation of a group of women lawyers:

> Women BSF tell us to say 'Jai Mata Ki' and threaten to take the girls to Delhi and make them prostitutes or to take them to 'mandirs' (temples) and put tilak on them. Is this secularism?

To any knowledgeable person, the fabrication is too glaring to be missed. The BSF had no women's wing. The *mala fide* of those making the allegation as well as those accepting them are evident. The sinister design also betrays itself. Expressions like 'Jai Mata Ki' are coined to convey a particular kind of impression. The allegations are made not by ordinary folks, but by lawyers who are well versed in law and are otherwise active in public affairs. It also becomes clear that the Committee is ignorant even with regard to elementary matters and yet it has the audacity to speak with an air of great authority on the subject.

On page 62, the Committee refers to the allegation made by Abdul Ahmed Safi of Kanthbagh, Baramulla. He says, "On the night of April 24-25, the Army picked me up at random along with 49 others, and we were made to eat faeces and drink urine in public." Stray references to Baramulla searches are also made in other portions of the report.

When a complaint containing the above and similar other allegations, signed by a number of lawyers of Baramulla, arrived at my desk, I had it immediately sent to Baramulla's Special Commissioner, C. Phonsog, and Corps Commander Lt.-General M.A. Zaki. This is what Phonsog said in his report:

---

*Opening para of the Section in question, page 37.

> On request of the security forces, the District Administration placed at disposal of the former four magistrates and four police parties by 6.00 a.m. Searches were commenced simultaneously between 6 and 8 a.m. and carried out in broad daylight and were concluded by 6 p.m. A large number of people, both men and women from different areas affected by the search, met me during the following days. None of them made any mention of molestation of women, stealing of valuables, outrage to religious shrines or scriptures, damage to property, extortion or confession under pressure, tying of people to trees, forcing them to drink dirty water or smearing of face with human night-soil. All those whose houses were searched mentioned, without exception, that there was not a single instance of even as much as a needle having been lifted from any of their homes. They found the officers supervising the searches generally kind and understanding.

General Zaki's report corroborated the facts stated by Phonsog, a senior IAS officer hailing from Ladakh.

From the above-quoted reports and other inquiries made by me, it became clear that no allegations were really made by the residents affected by the searches on April 25, 1990. The allegations were subsequently concocted by a group of lawyers of Baramulla who were Jama'at-i-Islami's activists and included in the memorandum sent three days after the incident to the authorities and the press. The Committee goes by these concocted allegations. Even otherwise, could anyone, aware of the outlook and disposition of our civil and military officers, believe that such misbehaviour, as alleged, would be permitted by them?

Methodology of Suppression and Omission

A characteristic feature of both the reports under discussion in this chapter is their methodology of suppression and omission of material facts. Let me cite a few examples.*

At page 26, the report titled 'Kashmir Imprisoned' says:

> Governor Jagmohan amended this section by deleting the words 'in the State'. As a result of this amendment anyone detained under the Act in J&K can be transferred to any part of the country.

*These examples are in addition to the school bus incident and other matters pertaining to the migration of Kashmiri Pandits, cited earlier in this chapter.

Significantly, the Committee omits to indicate the rationale of my decision. It also suppresses a vital fact. The Supreme Court of India accepted the rationale of the amendment and upheld it.

The laws of all other States as well as the Central laws provide for detention in States outside the State to which the detenu might belong. What is valid and justified in regard to other States should be equally valid and justified for the State of J&K, particularly when it is in the savage grip of subversion and terrorism.

The Committee alleges that, except in the case of Kashmiri Pandits, no compensation was offered to the dependents of those killed in the State. Here again, the Committee suppressed material facts. Compensation was offered to all innocent victims of terrorist violence. The widows of Mushir-ul-Haq and Abdul Ghani were paid Rupees two lakh each–one lakh from State Government and one lakh from the University. The son of the latter was also given a job in the University as a lecturer. The family of the young Muslim government servant; who was killed in the Jammu disturbances, was also paid Rupees one lakh. His brother was given a job in the State Government. Compensation was also offered to the Muslim families whose two relations were killed in the firing by the security guards when a UN jeep was attacked. But they were afraid of accepting the amount, as the terrorists had held out a threat that anyone accepting compensation from the Government would be suitably dealt with. Of course, no compensation could be offered in cases where a person died while indulging in terrorist activity and challenging lawful authority by violent means.

In its obsession to condemn the Governor's Administration and to paint it as devil incarnate, the Committee suppressed all the humanistic elements upon which my approach was really built. It intentionally ignored my policy statement* of January 19, 1990, in which I had declared:

> Constitutionally, I would be a Governor. But, for all practical purposes, I would function like an orderly–a nursing orderly–to help the patient with love, compassion and service to regain his health.

The Committee also made no mention of my radio and television broadcasts in which I fervently reminded the Kashmiri youth that our

*For the full text of this statement see Chapter I titled 'My Frozen Turbulence'.

country's destiny lay not in barbarism, but in compassion, not in fractured cultural fabric, but in unity amidst diversity.

The Committee's compulsive bias also led it to make contradictory observations in regard to the registration of complaints of alleged excesses. The police were given instructions to register all complaints against the security forces even if such complaints appeared to be motivated, doctored or false. During the period January 19 to May 26, 1990, twenty-four complaints were registered as listed in Appendix XVII. In regard to the incidents of firing by the BSF on February 7, 1990 I even ordered an inquiry by the Srinagar District Magistrate, Ghulam Abbass. But the Committee suppressed these hard facts. Instead, it took a queer stand. If a case was registered, it was taken as an admission of guilt. If there was no registration, the administration was accused of being so callous as not to even register complaints. The Committee's dictum appeared to be: "heads I win; tails you lose".

The Committee was unfair to our valiant para-military forces. It did not appreciate the fact that our jawans, hailing from such hot regions as Bihar and West Bengal, had to stand for hours together in chilly winds, with heaps of snow around, and suffering surprise and swift attacks from Pakistan-trained guerrillas who showed no compunctions of conscience to use the non-combatant population as their shield and camouflage.

Inder Mohan and his Unclean Hands

Inder Mohan's role in weaving the webs of distortion needs to be specially mentioned. It would, apart from making known how the affairs of organisations like PUCL are being run, reveal why 'Governor Jagmohan in particular' was being blamed and associated, without any evidence whatsoever, with alleged lapses and excesses of security forces.

The cat came partly out of the bag when the *Indian Express* published a letter jointly written by Inder Mohan and George Mathew. Ironically, this letter got published in the same issue of the paper in which the two letters of S.N. Drabu and Thakur Dass, exposing the perjuries of the Committee in regard to the Army school bus incident appeared. The letter, *inter alia*, stated:

> Jagmohan has come to be identified in popular perception as a symbol of repression with shades of an anti-Muslim bias. We are not surprised. The Governor's recall is in our opinion a

> precondition to build the confidence of Kashmir in its common destiny with India.

It should be evident to a discerning mind that the real objective of Inder Mohan and the likes of him was to manoeuvre my recall. Their methodology was to carry out false propaganda at a high pitch, making use of the resources and the forum of the PUCL, and then ask for my recall on that false propaganda.

The unclean hands of Inder Mohan, are seen in another letter of his published in *The Hindustan Times* of May 16, 1990. This letter was in response to a report which appeared in *The Hindustan Times* of April 30 under the caption 'PUCL Report Flayed'. After questioning the validity of the observations made in the report about the encouraging results achieved by the Governor and after claiming that the PUCL report was based on "first-hand direct knowledge acquired by the team members", Inder Mohan wrote in the aforesaid letter:

> Why was Jagmohan so keen to oblige his Home Minister by releasing five hardliners in exchange for his daughter?

Inder Mohan knew perfectly well from his first-hand knowledge that I was not the Governor of the State at the time of Rubaiya Sayeed's kidnapping (December 8, 1989) and her release (December 13), and that one of the reasons for my being sent to the State again on January 19, 1990, was the total collapse of the Kashmir Administration and its virtual take-over by the subversives. But Inder Mohan's expertise in the art of disinformation impelled him to make the accusation, believing that a large segment of the Indian populace would not be remembering, in mid-May 1990, the true position of the case. His game plan, obviously, was to level false allegations after spicing them with seemingly acceptable slants of "first-hand knowledge" and hope that a sizeable section of the people would take it.

As Trotsky once observed, the modern tragedy, in essence, lies in the wider conflict between man's 'awakened mind' and his 'constricting environment'. The more motivated a person is to do something creative, the worse he is likely to be treated by his compatriots. This, unfortunately, has been the experience, in post-Independence India, of practically all those who have tried to set the moorings of public affairs right by way of deeds and solid work, instead of harping on mere words and empty rhetorics.

During my fairly long innings in the Delhi Development Authority, I had to undergo a similar experience, when I attempted to bring some order in the chaotic conditions and ensure planned development of the metropolis. I came into conflict with a number of vested interests. A part of my experience has been narrated in my books–*Rebuilding Shajahanabad: The Walled City of Delhi; Island of Truth;* and *The Challenge of Our Cities.*

In Jama Masjid-Red Fort complex,* in the improvement of which I was specially interested, I came into conflict with Inder Mohan who, supposedly, was doing some social work in the area. After the lifting of Emergency in March 1977, Inder Mohan spread a number of incorrect stories about me, intentionally and knowingly and with a design. Some of these stories found place in some post-emergency books–'instant histories' written in haste by journalist-writers with whatever 'material' they could lay their hands on, as everyone was keen to beat the other in the race for early publication. Persons like Inder Mohan got ample opportunities to pass on their motivated stories to these journalists. Consequently, a number of glaring inaccuracies crept in, particularly with regard to the city's clearance programme.

So far as the Emergency, its imposition in June 1975 and its operation till March 1977 was concerned, I had nothing whatsoever to do with it, being the Vice-Chairman of Delhi Development Authority at that time. But the post-Emergency period, in its early phase, was swayed by a persecution mania. I was unjustly pilloried, primarily because I refused to step out of my *Island of Truth* and shift the alleged blame on Mrs. Indira Gandhi or Sanjay Gandhi. All the schemes executed by me during the Emergency were part of the Delhi Master Plan and the subsidiary projects envisaged under it. These were approved by the Union Cabinet and Parliament or other competent authorities much before the imposition of Emergency. Undoubtedly, the work pertaining to the 'planned development of Delhi' attained tremendous acceleration during the period; but this was largely due to the hasty retreat of vested interests who earlier caused some obstruction or the other.

In my book, *Island of Truth,* published in early 1978, I pointed out all the inaccuracies in the post-Emergency books and also referred to the vicious atmosphere in which contributions of persons like me,

*For my blueprint of the complex, see Chapter VI of my book *Rebuilding Shahjahanabad.*

instead of being appreciated, were condemned. The truth of my assertions was so unassailable that I swore the whole of the book as affidavit and filed it in the special Court of Justice M.L. Jain in which Mrs. Indira Gandhi was being prosecuted on the basis of the Shah Commission's findings.* The then Government, or anyone else, did not muster, enough courage to file counter-affidavit to challenge any of the facts recorded in the book.

In Chapter VI titled 'Lies, Half-Truth and Convenient Conscience' and Chapter VII titled 'Untold Story of Turkman Gate', I laid bare the true position and also briefly referred to the role of Inder Mohan. The *Sunday* magazine published excerpts from the former chapter in its two issues of July 30 and August 6, 1978. Inder Mohan was stung. Truth annoyed him. Instead of appreciating my motivation, he resorted to browbeating tactics and accelerated his campaign of spreading false stories. He crossed all limits of villainous concoctions, when he goaded a correspondent of the Indian Express to publish an item under the caption: *The Day of Bullets and Bulldozers,*** on the front page of the newspaper in its issue of April 18, 1977. Since the item was a product of a highly crafty and conspiratorial mind, I thought, to let it pass would not only mean my own moral capitulation but also result in swelling the ranks of wrong doers and run counter to my belief in the old saying: 'For evil to prosper, all that good men have to do is nothing'.

After days of agonizing deliberations, I decided, whatever be the cost and whatever be risks of undergoing further harassment, to expose the sordid net-work of calumnies by filing a criminal defamation complaint in the Metropolitan Court having jurisdiction in the matter.

---

* The findings of the Shah Commission were subsequently declared null and void by the Delhi High Court.

** For the chequered background of the Turkman Gate episode and the historic importance of the massive Clearance-cum-Resettlement-cum-Redevelopment projects, executed in 1976, the reader may go through my book, *Triumphs and Tragedies of Ninth Delhi,* (Allied Publishers-2015) particularly its Chapter titled: *Clearance of Turkman Gate Slums: Facing An Inexhaustible Arsenal of Lies.* I have no doubt that he would find it highly rewarding. It would show in ample measure how dirty and diseased are the mental slums of Indian polity, how vicious is the grip of falsehood on the nerve centres of our social system, how a terrible deluge of disinformation and distortion could be brought about by a vengeful caucus and a section of media who specialise in relying more on hearsay and concoctions than on documents and concrete evidence.

In view of the total exposure of their fabrication, the accused had really no defense. All that they could do was to cause delay by repeatedly raising flimsy issues and then going in for revision to the High Court if their plea was rejected by the trial court. My cross-examination covered about 50 pages. The intention was to tire and harass me. But I did not give up.

After 13 years, the verdict was pronounced. The Metropolitan Court was so incensed by the outrageous concoction that it awarded four months' imprisonment to the reporter who wrote the story. Inder Mohan's conspirational game of story weaving stood exposed. In its order, the Court observed: "His (Inder Mohan's) evidence is self-contradictory, full of material contradictions. He is not a trustworthy witness and no reliance can be placed upon his evidence."

Should a person of Inder Mohan's mental frame have been allowed to use, PUCL to carry out false propaganda against me and in the process undermine the national effort to free Kashmir from the clutches of savage terrorism? I would leave this question for consideration to the general public and well-meaning persons in the PUCL. Already, some discerning persons, such as M.V. Rama Murty, Vice-President, PUCL, Andhra Pradesh, have expressed their sorrow over what the 'Committee for Initiative on Kashmir' has done. This is what Rama Murty wrote in his letter of May 5 published in the Indian Express in May 1990:

> I read the report of the PUCL team published in your paper with anguish in my heart. It has departed from the accepted policies of PUCL.
>
> The militants among the terrorists by their conduct infringed upon the civil liberties of the people. This point was not prominently brought out in the report. It should not be the concern of PUCL to canvass support for the militants indirectly on the ground that the demand of the people of Kashmir is for independence and not for joining Pakistan. It is not given to PUCL to assess the minds of the people of Kashmir when there is no known method of gauging public opinion.
>
> It is beyond the purview of PUCL to suggest reconciliation. One wonders whom the team had in mind. Is it the section of militants that must be appeased or the leaders of public opinion in Kashmir who did not raise their little finger to condemn violence on the part of militants?

The PUCL team erred in not drawing a lesson from the fact that some Hindus have taken shelter in camps at Delhi also. The team should not have opined that setting up of camps was not necessary.

In sum, the report is highly subjective and not supported by facts.

Dimensions of the Hall of Crooked Mirrors

These, then, are the dimensions of the hall of the distorted mirrors which the "Committee for Initiative on Kashmir" built on the foundation of deception, suppression, casualness, prejudices, personal vendetta, and arrogance. No one could have done greater injustice under the pretensions of justice. No one could have violated more craftily the fundamental human rights in the name of human rights. No one could have danced with greater ecstasy to the drum-beats of subversives and their agents. No one could have embraced more enthusiastically the sinners and slaughterers. No one could have overlooked the blood-thirsty laws of terrorism that consumed innocent persons like the Ganjus, the Premis and the Tikoos.* And no one could have resorted to a greater degree of suppression and intentionally turned a blind eye to hard facts and data, such as the occurrence of about 2,000 violent incidents, including 500 bomb blasts, in a year before the imposition of Governor's Rule.

All crimes were ignored by the Committee if the cry was for 'azadi' and not for merger with Pakistan. All activities became non-communal if, along with Kashmiri Pandits, some Muslim 'informers' and 'traitors' were also killed, even if the decision to pronounce them as such were taken by the murderers themselves. The Committee did not see any of the propaganda and motivational literature,† soaked in blood and dagger terminology and the battle cry of Quran in one hand and sword in another. Nor did it come across even a single case out of the scores of cases of connivance, collusions and conspiracies, including the well-publicised case of Srinagar Jail break in which twelve hard-core terrorists escaped after weaving deftly the chain of conspiracy in which practically every official concerned got involved.

---

* See Chapter IX also.

† This propaganda and literature have been cited in detail in Chapter X: 'Nature and Pattern of Subversion and Terrorism'.

The Committee intentionally glossed over the known written instructions* of the leaders of the subversives operating from Pakistan which said: "Continue your propaganda both inside and outside your houses and localities. Keep also in full swing the propaganda campaign against the security forces, and false and reckless allegations** should be made."

The Committee wove a pattern which was similar to the one woven by Goebbels during the Second World War. No wonder, it succeeded for a while and played its part in seeing me out of the State. But history does not rest in the lap of such manipulators for long. Truth soon tears the veil of falsehood and the guilty either sink into oblivion or get buried under the debris of their own 'hall of crooked mirrors'.

A few journalists like Balraj Puri and Kuldip Nayar, who show an amazing capacity to sacrifice truth to propitiate their one-eyed goddess of 'secularism', have, taking advantage of their easy access to the press, been persisting with the untruth, initially spread by the aforesaid 'Committee on Kashmir', that I was responsible for the 'migration' of the Kashmiri Pandits from the Valley. They, too, stand thoroughly exposed. Exasperated by their false propaganda, H.N. Jattu, President, All India Kashmir Pandits Conference, sent a letter/ 'write-up' to *The Tribune,* Chandigarh, *The Excelsior,* Jammu, and a few other magazines. This letter/'write-up', citing documents and concrete evidence, effectively demolishes their castle of concoction. It is reproduced in Appendix XXVI.***

---

* There were written instructions contained in the booklet written by Raja Mohammad Muzaffar Khan of 'J&K Liberation Front'.

** There are a number of cases in which false allegations were intentionally coined. A touch of authenticity was imparted by procuring helpful statements from local officials who were either part of the subversive network or too terror stricken to refuse. One such well-publicised case was of "rape of 23 women of Kunan in the Valley on February 23, 1991". After a thorough enquiry and spot visits, the Press Council of India concluded: "The Kunan rape story on close examination turns out to be a massive hoax orchestrated by militant groups and their sympathisers and mentors in Kashmir and abroad, as a part of a cleverly contrived strategy of psychological warfare and as an entry point for reinscribing Kashmir on the international agenda as a human rights issue. The women of Kunan have been tutored or coerced into making statements derogating their own honour and dignity. This cruel exploitation of simple women through demeaning self-abuse is itself a deplorable human rights violation."

*** The letter was published in *The Tribune* of October 28, 1993 and the 'write-up' in The *Excelsior* of November, 1993.

CHAPTER XIV

Acquiring an Upper Hand

Who dares, wins.
*Let us dare. We will win.**

Notwithstanding all the whirlpools of confusion and contradictions that were set in my course and the vicious attacks of the sharks of disinformation, I went on swimming, taking all the wounds and scratches with stoic forbearance. There was hardly any shore to look to, hardly any moment to slow down and gasp for breath. Quite a few dangerous points of turbulence had been successfully crossed by me. But the moral vacuum that existed in the psyche of most of the political parties, was continuously creating new centres of turbulence. The hollowness of the system, its void, was causing conditions in which new tornadoes were sure to be formed and sucked in the rarefied atmosphere in which I found myself working. I had, however, decided to go on and put my faith in Marti's words: "A true man does not seek the path where the advantage lies, but rather the path where the duty lies."

Firm Message

Let me first narrate how, against heavy odds, an upper hand was acquired. Our first and foremost objective was to wrest the initiative from the subversives and assert the authority of the state. A firm message had to go to the people that, no matter what the cost, no matter what the sacrifices, Kashmir would not be allowed to remain at

*A variation of the British S.A.S. motto.

the mercy of the subversionists, terrorists and fundamentalists. Our resolve, our will, had to be made clear.

If a government servant crossed the border for receiving arms training and then returning to indulge in overt or covert subversive activity, he had to suffer summary dismissal. If electricity was switched off from the mains at a particular time to prevent the viewing of some programmes, the Chief Engineer had to account for it. If newspapers served as vehicles for criminal intimidation by the terrorist organisations, they could not take cover behind freedom of the press. It had, in brief, to be conveyed to all concerned, in no uncertain terms, that lapses would no longer be overlooked and no soft belly of the state would be offered to punch or fool with.

Innovations

But no assertion of authority, however vigorous and determined, could alone suffice. It had to be supplemented by creativity in administration and an innovative and imaginative approach.

The situation, too, was very different from what the administrations are usually confronted with. There was subversion; there was terrorism; there was fundamentalism; there were external propulsions like TOPAC and Pakistan Solidarity Day; there were also factions, intrigues, wooden-headedness, clogging of the mind and the inability to go beyond 'stock responses'. And, above all, there were the sins of the past–the sins of others–the burden of which I had to carry on my shoulders. The rotten apples in my bag, howsoever foul and insufferable, could not be thrown away.

I had to pick up the debris, add fresh material to it and rebuild. I had to generate confidence. I had to inject drive and dynamism. I had to gather the broken threads and weave a new pattern, a new fabric. I had to locate old threads which still had some life, some tenacity left in them, and bind them with new threads.

Besides the two Advisers, I picked up the right elements from the local civil service, the Army, the BSF, the CRP, and the IB and spun them into a vibrant group. Lt.-General M.A. Zaki, Corps Commander, represented the Army. He was a strong pillar of the new edifice. He acted with exemplary patience and warmth. Solid, sound and enthusiastic, he carried out the assigned work speedily and with quiet precision.

Like all other dedicated and determined men, Lt.-General Zaki, too, was made a target of false propaganda. He was even accused of being communal. An instance that was cited in support of this charge was that he was distributing Army ration-packets to the Muslim inhabitants during the curfew hours. The false charge was even believed in some quarters. It was at this stage that the Defence Secretary and the Cabinet Secretary came to see me when they casually talked to me on the subject. I told them that it was under my instructions that the General had distributed the ration packets for which the payment had been made by me to the Army. The objective was to make the distribution of milk and other necessities to the needy people from the Army Store which could be replenished with the funds provided by me. Since the civil administration at that stage was not functioning, it was not possible to arrange rations through normal channels in a short time. Earlier, distribution of essential commodities to the needy people of Srinagar had virtually been taken over by the subversives under the garb of relief committees.

I removed speedily all the operational difficulties of the officers. I personally attended to their problems and put the entire machinery in top gear. I brought about a change of emphasis, a change of mood. I slashed the unproductive channels of work, relegated the paper work to the background and strengthened the field agencies. I assigned specific tasks to each group and then personally coordinated the working of all these groups. I used my powers to settle the issues straight away and dictated notes and orders forthwith. This besides raising the morale of the officers, gave sharp focus to all our activities and prevented narrow or sectional views being taken.

I won complete loyalty of the Army, the BSF, the CRP, the IB and the core-group of the local civil and police officers. Their response was enthusiastic, sometimes overwhelming. Even a midnight telephone call from me evoked prompt response. A report in *The Tribune* noted this aspect of the situation. It said, "A well-known security expert felt surprised over the way the environmentalist and bureaucrat in Jagmohan have given way to the soldier in him who has secured cent per cent loyalty from the jawans of the Army and the para-military forces."*

**Tribune,* May 21, 1990.

A series of innovative decisions were speedily taken to give a new shape and direction to the administration, particularly at the ground level.

Special Commissaries

Three special Commissaries were created–one for Baramulla and Kupwara Districts; the second for Anantnag and Pulwama; and the third for Rajourie, Poonch and Doda. The measure helped in establishing the authority of the state in the outlying areas. It also provided a high-level coordinating and supervisory agency to ensure that field organisations functioned properly and did not act according to the dictates of the subversives. It also restored the shattered system of civil supplies.

Five-Kilometre Belt

On my arrival, one of the priority items on my agenda was to effectively stop crossing of the border from Pak-occupied Kashmir. The presence of a large number of trained youth in the Valley and the accumulation of huge dumps convinced me that clandestine crossing from across the border had been taking place on a fairly wide scale.

I found that ineffectiveness at the border was mainly due to the fact that, in actual practice, very little help was forthcoming at the border from civil and political authorities. As a senior Army officer put it on my arrival: "Orally we get everything; in practice, nothing." Despite repeated requests by the Home Ministry and also by the BSF and the local level, no powers to search and arrest were conferred on the BSF. Consequently, the BSF officials were powerless and they could do nothing even if they suspected that an infiltrator was hiding in a village. By the time they approached the local police, the suspect would disappear. In some cases, even connivance was apparent. A very large number of persons, moreover, moved even at night in the area very near the line of control on the pretext of attending to the fields.

In the absence of any effective restriction, border crossing took place with impunity. Persons in political authority opposed the idea of imposing night curfew along one or two-kilometre belt. Whenever any proposal in this regard was mooted, theoretical issues relating to Article 249 and Article 370 of the Constitution were raised. It was never explained how the rationale of creating a security belt to stop infiltration was irreconcilable with the special status of the State.

I removed these handicaps of the Army and the BSF. I communicated the consent of the State Government to the Union Government to confer police powers of search and arrests on the BSF. There was no danger of misuse of authority, because even the BSF and other para-military forces operated under the guidance of the Director-General of Police and the Governor. I also issued instructions to District authorities to impose dusk-to-dawn curfew in the five-kilometre belt along the border.

These measures had an electrifying effect. Things started happening on the border. The intruders began to be arrested in this belt and arms seized. For instance, on a single day, May 2, 1990, huge quantities of arms and ammunition were intercepted. It included eight AK-47 rifles, one multi-purpose machine gun, one rocket launcher, four rockets, fifty hand-grenades, eleven pistols, and fifty packets of explosives. Simultaneously, four contractors, who were connected with a political heavy-weight, were arrested. They were believed to be part of the network which brought arms from Pak-occupied Kashmir, hid them at odd sites near the border, and then took them, at a suitable time, to other places in trucks of the contractors by keeping them underneath other material.

The interceptions demonstrated that wherever there was a will, there was a way. Earlier, the will was lacking and the way was never found. Within a short span of three months, 64 infiltrators were shot while crossing the border and 268 arrested in areas close to the line of control. The weapons seized were: 155 AK-47 rifles, 149 pistols, 724 hand-grenades, 23,000 rounds of ammunition and 244 kilograms of explosives. Just imagine what would have happened, what terrible havoc would have been caused, if all these infiltrators and weapons had also flowed into the Valley.

State Security Board

Another step taken by me to bring about more effective and speedy coordination between civil and army authorities and to give sharp teeth to the machinery against terrorists was to revive the State Security Board, which I had set up in 1986, during the first Governor's Rule in the State. This Board had proved extremely useful at that time. In the prevailing circumstances, I thought it would be still more useful as it would help in not only day-to-day coordination but also in imparting sharper focus to the activities of the various agencies that were operating at the border and also in the disturbed areas.

The Board comprised, besides myself as Chairman, the Army Commander, Northern Command, Lt.-Gen. Gobinder Singh; Corps Commander Lt.-Gen. M.A. Zaki; Corps Commander, Nagrota, Lt.-Gen. Harwant Singh; two Advisers to the Governor; Director-General of BSF and Director-General of CRPF; Director-General of Police, J&K; and other senior civil and army officers.

The contribution of the Board, as I expected, proved beneficial. Information was exchanged at the highest level. Lists of guides and suspects were prepared and updated, and coordinated action enforced to achieve quick results without any overlapping of efforts and diffusion of responsibility.

Special Initiative Squad

One great advantage that the terrorists enjoyed was the element of surprise and swiftness. They could choose their own time, place and mode of operation. The initiative invariably rested with them. After striking, they could disappear into the lanes and by-lanes or into some obscure place among passive supporters,–to use Mao Tse-tung's well-known dictum, "just swim like a fish in the sea", or "melt into the crowd".

I had been thinking how to counter this advantage. To catch the mice, cats had to be set after them, and not a large contingent of police or para-military force. A tiny group of experts, with a capacity to strike rapidly, and with an element of surprise, was considered by me to be the best. After some thought, I issued the following order which is self-explanatory:

> I would like to organise 'Special Initiative Squads' to surprise and apprehend the terrorists who may be gathering at a corner or at odd places or on the roadside or planning to strike at the innocent individuals in any other way.
>
> My objective is to turn the element of surprise and suddenness in our favour and not to allow the terrorists to easily choose the victims as well as points of attack.
>
> Fifteen teams of specially trained personnel will be organised. Each team will have 3 to 5 armed personnel dressed in day-to-day clothes and travel on foot or in vehicles which may not be easily

identifiable from a distance. These teams would be on the lookout for suspicious-looking persons or groups of persons and surprise them and check them suddenly.

The move yielded very good results. A number of arrests were made through these operations. What was still more beneficial, it confused the terrorists. They were not sure when and where they would be spotted by the Special Initiative Squad. Gone for ever was the calm assurance and confidence with which they used to plan and execute their kidnapping operations in the cities. The terrorist groups were so bamboozled that they issued their 'orders' banning the use of light vehicles by the general public. This, in turn, led to wrangling amongst these groups. The JKLF did not want this 'ban' to continue. It thought it was inconveniencing the public. On the other hand, the Students Liberation Front wanted this ban to continue.

My purpose was served. The subversives and terrorists came under strain. They got exhausted. Divisions appeared amongst them.

Banning Subversive Organisations

From the interrogation of the persons arrested, the ruthless manner of operation of the subversive organisations became still more clear. To undermine their operational effectiveness, I decided to declare unlawful some of the more dangerous organisations.

On April 16, 1990, I issued orders under the State Criminal Law Amendment Act, declaring eight organisations unlawful. These were: Jama'at-i-Islami, J&K Hizbul Mujahideen, J&K Liberation Front, Students' Liberation Front, Mahaz-e-Azadi, Islami Students' League, Peoples' League, and Islamic Jamait-e-Tulba.

I made it clear to the public that the organisations in question had been banned because of their secessionist and terrorist activities, for which ample proof existed. These organisations, I further pointed out, were building up a general atmosphere of subversion and terrorism and were sowing the seeds of the disintegration of India.

One immediate and significant result of the orders was that the offices and bank accounts of Jama'at-i-Islami were sealed and their cadres scattered. Publicity material could not also be easily produced and distributed. The Friday gathering could not also be addressed from the mosques by the Jama'at-i-Islami's leaders who either fled or were arrested.

One of the root causes of the current turmoil in Kashmir was the role played by Jama'at-i-Islami and its auxiliary agencies like Falah-i-Aam. As brought out in the earlier chapters, these bodies had been laying the seed-bed of fundamentalism and fanaticism through the numerous schools and 'madrassas' run by them. Narrow ideas were planted in the impressionable minds of children. The present crop of fundamentalism in Kashmir which has weakened the indigenous Kashmiri Islam is largely a result of unchecked activities conducted through the schools and 'madrassas' run by Jama'at-i-Islami and Falah-i-Aam Trust. While discussing the Kashmir issue in the Pakistan Press and Parliament, the Chief of Pakistani Jama'at-i-Islami has often been boasting that it was due to Jama'at-i-Islami's influence that Kashmiris had woken up and understood the true meaning of Islam and resorted to 'Jihad' against India.

I, therefore, decided to immediately plug the fountain-head of subversion and fanaticism in Kashmir. I also banned the Falah-i-Aam Trust and declared its activities unlawful. The closure of 157 schools run by the Trust was the obvious consequence of this decision. For 15,000 students of these 157 schools, arrangements were simultaneously made for admission to the Government-run educational institutions where normal education was imparted. A difficult task was smoothly and speedily performed.

Surgery on Infected Portions

As indicated in Chapter X titled "Nature and Pattern of Subversion", a larger number of public servants were involved in subversive activities but, practically, no action had been taken against them. Consequently, the infection went on spreading. When I undertook the task of restoring the administrative organs back to health, surgery on the hopelessly-infected portions was the only effective cure available. The extent of the rot became strikingly visible when it was found that in the kidnapping of the Union Home Minister's daughter, a number of public servants played key roles.

Public servants involved in serious cases, such as border-crossing or working as office-bearers of terrorist organisations like Hizbul Mujahideen, were summarily dismissed by me by resorting to my constitutional powers under Article 126 of the J&K Constitution. This provision enables the Governor to dismiss or remove public servants without holding any formal departmental enquiry, provided he is satisfied that in the interest of the security of the State it is not expedient to hold such an enquiry. This constitutional provision, obviously, would have no meaning or significance if it cannot be used even in cases involving treason and terrorism.

In this 'surgical drive', 121 public servants were dismissed from service. Each case was decided on its merits, after considering the reports of all concerned. Another 101 police officials, involved in subversion and insubordination, were dismissed by the Director-General of Police under his own powers.

A close study of these cases also indicated a pattern which linked subversion, corruption and political patronage. In some cases, huge amounts were recovered from government servants involved in terrorist activities. These amounts had been collected through corrupt means. Apparently, these government servants had political godfathers. For instance, from the house of a Junior Engineer who was an active member of Hizbul Mujahideen, a sum of rupees two lakhs was recovered in cash, besides ₹ 50,000 in fixed deposits. He had also been maintaining a car and living in great style.

Detention outside the State

The Public Safety Act was amended to provide for detention outside the State. When the local High Court stayed the operation, the matter was swiftly taken to the Supreme Court which reversed the decision of the High Court. Consequent upon this, about 100 terrorists, subversives, and leaders of unlawful organisations who could cause further violence through their links, were speedily transferred outside the State.

Dynamic Coordination

It was quite clear to me that dynamic coordination, thrust and initiative were needed to detect and prevent serious crimes and to unravel the techniques and methods employed by the terrorists. I, therefore, made it a point to ensure that the useful information obtained by any of the agencies operating in the field, was quickly made use of by all concerned and immediate follow-up action taken. I virtually assumed the role of the chief investigating officer. This, I thought, was absolutely necessary. Unusual circumstances required this unusual approach. Apart from the involvement of the Army, which required careful handling at my level, speedy information, speedy investigation, speedy coordination and speedy follow-up action was the crying need of the hour.

As a result of dynamic coordination, boosting of morale and other measures described above, almost all the heinous crimes were worked out in a short time. It is both revealing and instructive to know what happened in these cases, how the main culprits were arrested and what was achieved as a result.

Searches and Arrests of Top Terrorists

The house to house searches, which were started vigorously from April 7, yielded, as I expected, extremely useful results. On April 8, when intensive searches were being made to apprehend the kidnappers of H.L. Khera, Mushrul-Huq and Abdul Ghani, a BSF party raided the house of a businessman Hafizulha Bhatt. Four suspects were located. After a brief and bloodless encounter, three were straightway arrested. They were Iqbal Gandroo, 'military adviser' to JKLF, Javed Zargar, a top terrorist who was one of the persons released in exchange of Dr. Rubaiya Sayeed, and Hafizulha Bhatt, the harbourer of these terrorists. The fourth suspect tried to escape. He jumped from the window of the roof of an adjoining house, which was at a lower height. He was injured. Some blood came out of his nostrils. The BSF party picked him up and took him to SMS hospital. After formally arresting him, the party left the injured person in the custody of two local police officials and the doctors on duty.

Yasin Malik

The BSF party, unfortunately, did not know that they had arrested the top-most terrorist of the State, the 'Commander-in-Chief' of JKLF, Yasin Malik. Apprehensive of false accusations of excesses that are generally made against security forces, the party wanted to get away from the scene as early as possible. The BSF officials thought that if the injured man died they would be accused of causing death by excessively pursuing the suspect, and the accusation would be so orchestrated in the local press and other circles that no one would accept the actual fact that the suspect had himself jumped from the window.

The doctor on duty played foul. The local police officials on guard duty played foul. The officials of the police station, in whose jurisdiction the incident took place, played foul. So did the officials of the police station in whose jurisdiction the hospital was located. The local doctor on duty and policemen identified the injured person as Yasin Malik, and immediately set about the task of plotting his escape. A rumour was intentionally spread that the injured person was so critical that there was hardly any hope of his remaining alive. An ambulance, which was taking a female patient to the Sher-e-Kashmir Medical Institute, was stopped and Yasin Malik put in it for being transported to the said Institute. The doctor at the SMS hospital informed the doctors at the Institute as to who was coming. The staff at both the ends spun the threads of conspiracy quickly.

As soon as the van arrived at the Institute, Yasin Malik was taken on a stretcher to the hospital lift from where he was made to disappear with a small group of doctors and supporters. Simultaneously, a rumour was floated that the injured man had been waylaid by his supporters and he was most probably dead. This was done to deceive us and lull the pursuing parties into complacency.

It was a perfect escape. It once again showed how formidable our task was, how deftly conspiracies were hatched, how watchmen had themselves turned betrayers, and what psychological damage was being caused to the security forces by falsely accusing them of excesses.

I was disappointed over the escape of Yasin Malik. His arrest, with three other top 'commanders', would have dealt a near fatal blow to the Jammu & Kashmir Liberation Front. It would have demoralised their supporters. It might have put my critics of house to house searches on the defensive. It might have enabled me to quietly talk to Yasin, through an intermediary officer, and point out to him and other top functionaries of the Front, the escape route from militancy to elections and the road to power through legitimate means. It might have also helped me in isolating more fundamentalists, more ruthless pro-Pakistani groups like Hizbul Mujahideen and Students' Liberation Front. But that was not to be, at least for the moment.

I accepted the escape with stoic calmness but proceeded with added vigour to clean up the infected wards of the hospital and corridors of police stations. It was soon brought home to the caucuses of the professionals like doctors and members of a disciplined force like the police that no conspiratorial behaviour, howsoever cleverly camouflaged, would remain undetected and unpunished.

The escape of Yasin Malik notwithstanding, the arrest of three other top terrorists–Iqbal Gandroo, Javed Zargar and Hafizulha Bhatt–was a highly significant success. It served as a device by which many a plan of the subversives was thwarted. Even before these arrests, substantial successes had been achieved by the new machinery. Fazal-ul-Haq Qureshi, a prominent figure of Hizbul Mujahideen, had been arrested and valuable information obtained from him. A large number of bombs were recovered from a hideout in Soura, a suburb of Srinagar, and a good part of the network with which Qureshi was connected was smashed. Rangrez, a top terrorist, had been killed in a shoot-out at Khanyar. Ashfaq Mujeed Wani had died when a bomb exploded in his hand during the course of his attack on a Border Security Force party. There were many other moderate successes. Taken together, they mattered a lot.

Shaukat Bakshi

House to house searches also yielded many vital clues. Shaukat Bakshi, another top terrorist, fell into our net on April 8. His interrogation provided extremely useful information and led to a number of arrests, including the arrest of those involved in the kidnapping of the Union Home Minister's daughter, Rubaiya Sayeed.

Information given by Shaukat Bakshi and other arrested persons was supplemented by information provided by a young man named Sherazi. The house of his father, Abdullah Sherazi, was raided as he was known to be a staunch pro-Pakistan subversionist. A pistol was recovered from the possession of the young man, and he was arrested. He was extremely intelligent, alert, and full of information. It was he who disclosed particulars of the Maruti van which belonged to Ali Mohammad Mir. From his accurate descriptions the car used for kidnapping Dr. Rubaiya Sayeed was identified, traced, and its owner arrested.

Subsequently, Mrs. Abdullah Sherazi came to see me in one of my public hearings. She said, "My son is innocent. My husband's whereabouts are not known. He does not bother about us. He has his own circle of friends. Some of them have become 'martyrs', and some have gone to Pakistan. I do not know whether he is also now sleeping forever in the lap of God or staying in Pakistan comfortably. He has not even cared to have his name broadcast over Radio Pakistan in the listeners' choice programme.* Earlier he used to send money; now he

*The pronouncement of the name in this programme was a code-signal indicating that the person concerned had reached Pakistan.

does not do that. But all my worries would be over if my son is released. He is very young. He is wholly blameless. He cannot account for his father's wrong actions." I was touched by Mrs. Abdullah Sherazi's pleadings which showed how her mind had been subjected to confusing and conflicting emotions. She talked of her neglect, her family problems, her son's innocence, and also of her husband's friends and their 'martyrdom'. I wondered whether the likes of Abdullah Sherazi realised how many disturbed homes they were creating and how they were being fooled by certain interests. Purely on compassionate grounds, I asked the police officer concerned to see whether the young Sherazi could be released after taking due precautions.

From the arrests and interrogations of persons responsible for Dr. Rubaiya's kidnapping it became clear that the top leadership of the Jammu and Kashmir Liberation Front, emboldened by the ineffectiveness of the State administration and its own deep infiltration into the Government apparatus, decided to strike in a telling way. The objective was to do something sensational, something that would demonstrate its strength and secure wide national and international publicity. To attain this objective, what could be better than kidnapping the daughter of the Union Home Minister, Mufti Mohammed Sayeed, who also happened to be Kashmiri and whose role in Kashmir's politics was bound to increase with the assumption of a very high office at the national level!

A conspiracy was hatched under the overall guidance of Yasin Malik. To work out the details of the plan, a meeting was held at the Chhanpura residence of Mushtaq Ahmed Lone. This meeting was attended by Yasin Malik, Ashfaq Majeed Wani, Javed Ahmed Mir 'Nalka', Shaukat Bakshi, Iqbal Gandroo, Ali Mohammed Mir and others. It was decided to assign different roles to different individuals and groups.

On the afternoon of December 8, Dr. Rubaiya Sayeed came out of Lal-Ded hospital. As soon as she boarded a mini bus for going home, as usual, Gulam Hassan, Mushtaq Lone, Iqbal Gandroo, Mehrajuddin Mustafa and Salim alias 'Nanaji' also got in.

Before the last stop at Nogam, the bus was hijacked. The driver was forced to drive to a secluded place at Natipura. Here, Dr. Rubaiya was made to come out of the bus and sit in a blue Maruti Car.

Yasin Malik, Ashfaq Majeed Wani and Gulam Hassan sat in the car. It was driven by Ali Mohammed Mir, Technical Officer of SIDCO. The car proceeded to the house of another Government servant, Javed Iqbal, Junior Engineer, at Sopore. Dr. Rubaiya was kept there for a day. On December 9, she was taken to the house of Mohammed Yaqoob, an industrialist of Sopore. This house had been arranged by two other industrialists of Sopore, *viz*. Zaman Mir and Abdullah. She was kept at this house up to December 14, 1989. This house was continuously guarded by Iqbal Hassan and Iqbal Gandroo.

While Dr. Rubaiya Sayeed spent five agonising days of confinement, sobbing and suffering in silence, and occasionally wondering whether she was living in a condemned prisoner's cell or being thrust on the worldwide stage of publicity in a drama which would end merely as a cruel prank, two of her tormentors, Yasin Malik and Ashfaq Majeed Wani, remained at Srinagar negotiating with the representatives of the State Government through intermediaries. Yasin Malik used his friendly contacts with Ajaz Kar, son of Congress(I) Minister, Ghulam Rasool Kar, to have an easy access to the house of a top businessman from where some of the telephonic talks were carried out. The Government, broken, boneless and infiltrated as it was, crawled in confusion and ultimately conceded the demand of the captors to release five top terrorists to secure freedom for Dr. Rubaiya.

Working out of Rubaiya Sayeed's case brought out facts of crucial significance. It showed how easily and confidently conspiracies of far-reaching consequences could be hatched, how fear of authority had totally disappeared, and how government servants and persons in business and industry often joined hands to help, and even participate, in terrorist activities. It also confirmed that quite a few government officials and middle-range industrialists had perfected the technique of cornering, through corrupt practices, resources provided by the Government of India for development purposes, and of securing mutual benefits and also extending operational and financial support to the subversionists to buy protection or non-exposure. For instance, Ali Mohammad Mir in whose car Dr. Rubaiya Sayeed was driven to Sopore, was illegally helping the two industrialists whose houses were used for confining Dr. Rubaiya, and Mir himself was living much beyond his known means.

*Lassa Kaul Case**

Working out of Lassa Kaul's case was another notable success of the new set-up. As indicated in Chapter IX, Lassa Kaul had been targeted for killing. He was accused of carrying out national programmes which, according to the terrorists, were un-Islamic. They were also unhappy with him for not fully complying with their instructions about the contents of news telecasts. They had already intimidated the subordinate staff; some of them were, in any case, their sympathisers and collaborators. That is why the news telecasts from Srinagar Doordarshan were heavily loaded in favour of the subversionists. Some of the new items were virtually based upon the hand-outs of the terrorists' organisations. Even publicity was given to their programmes. For instance, sometimes it was announced that 'namaz-e-Janaza' of 'martyrs' would be held on a certain date at a certain time. Shots of such 'janazas' were also shown on the T.V.

Kaul wanted to correct the imbalance. This was not to the liking of the subversive organisations. They believed, "if you are not willing to serve as our tool, you are our enemy, and have to be eliminated."

The arrest of Shaukat Bakshi brought to light the manner in which the crime was planned and committed. Kaul stayed in his office on the night of February 11 and 12. Having come to know that he was likely to return to his home on the evening of February 13, to meet his handicapped father who was living there all alone, his family having gone to Delhi earlier, Shaukat Bakshi and Hanif hid themselves near his house in Bemina. When Kaul alighted from his car, Shaukat Bakshi fired at him from a pistol, which Ashfaq Majeed Wani had given to him, killing him almost instantaneously.

Shaukat Bakshi's arrest and his interrogation proved useful in another way. He disclosed that Kaul was killed on the instructions of Amanullah Khan, conveyed through Ashfaq Majeed Wani. At that time, Khan was in the USA, and from there had launched virulent anti-India propaganda about Kashmir. Every day he would give out one damaging press statement or another.

The confessional statement of Shaukat Bakshi, implicating Amanullah Khan, enabled us to obtain from the High Court a warrant for his extradition. We worked hard to collect correct and convincing

*Information about all the cases given here is of as all the cases are subject to further investigation.

evidence. Our objective was to move the courts in a short time. It was believed that even if we did not succeed in securing his extradition, the warrant itself would serve an important purpose. It would put a stop to his poisonous propaganda from US soil as he would go away from that country. This was exactly what happened. As soon as warrants of extradition* were obtained, Amanullah Khan slipped away from the USA.

Here I may say a word or two about the conduct of the Chief Judicial Magistrate, Jammu, Avtar Krishan Kaul. Shaukat Bakshi wanted to make a statement under Section 164, Criminal Procedure Code. This statement was of great importance to us. The time for recording the statement was fixed. The Magistrate told the police and other officers concerned that he would record the statement at the specified time. But when the police reached the Courtroom with the accused, a huge crowd was there but not the Magistrate. He quietly slipped away, giving an application for casual leave.

I was shocked at the irresponsible behaviour of the Magistrate. It was apprehended that Shaukat Bakshi might change his mind and we would lose the opportunity of securing warrants for the extradition of Amanullah Khan. Fortunately, on the following day, the statement was recorded by another Magistrate and Shaukat Bakshi did not change his stance in regard to Amanullah Khan. However, he cleverly omitted a few items to weaken the prosecution case.

The episode once again demonstrated the growing infirmity of the institutions of governance. While the challenges with which the State is faced are increasing, both in magnitude and complexity, the State institutions are getting weaker and weaker and persons in key positions of authority are acting with less and less responsibility, and, what is worse, getting away with it.

Working Out the Mushir-ul-Haq Case

The arrest of the main accused in the case relating to the kidnapping and killing of Professor Mushir-ul-Haq and his Special Assistant, Abdul Gani Zargar, was another significant achievement. On May 11,

**Patriot*, May 1, 1990. It was on the basis of the warrant of extradition that Amanullah Khan was arrested by the Belgium authorities when he landed in Brussels to attend the Round Table Discussion on Kashmir organised by the Socialist Group of European Parliament on Oct. 18, 1993. However, he was subsequently released on what was given out in the press as political grounds.

a brief announcement to this effect was made to the press. On May 15, the red Maruti car used in the kidnapping of the Vice-Chancellor and his Special Assistant was recovered.

The arrests revealed that after Professor Mushir-ul-Haq and Abdul Gani were kidnapped on April 6, 1990, at the gate of the Kashmir University, they were kept in the house of one Sabir at Natipora for two nights. Thereafter, they were moved to the house of Ghulam Qadir Mir, retired constable, Kashmir Armed Police, and resident of Baganday, Lasjan. They were kept there for one night. Thereafter, they were moved to the house of Ghulam Mohammad Dar, resident of Baydhopra, Pandhrathan, Srinagar. On April 10, 1990, they were moved out to the field by Salim Ahmed Zargar alias Fiaz, resident of Jamia Masjid, Nowhatta.

At about 4.30 p.m., Hilal Ahmed Beg came to the field in Padshahi Bagh and ordered killing of the hostages. Late in the evening, they were asked to go with their hands raised. They thought they were being set free. But within seconds they were shot in the back and left to die in the field.

Another person arrested was Mushtaq Ahmed Sheikh alias John alias Kachru, resident of Soweteng, Lasjan. Later on, Javed Ahmed Shalla was also arrested. Mushtaq was one of the three accused who overpowered the driver of the Vice-Chancellor and drove the vehicle to Lal Bazar where the kidnapped persons were put into a Maruti van. Mushtaq Ahmed also got into the van. Earlier he had arranged for the house of Ghulam Qadir Mir and Ghulam Qadir Dar where the kidnapped were kept.

Why Killed?

Why was Professor Mushir-ul-Haq killed? Was it because he was non-Kashmiri and belonged to a comparatively liberal school of thought? Had the internal intrigues of the University, or matters pertaining to certain appointments, or the extension of his term as Vice-Chancellor, anything to do with it? Or did the local terrorists simply carry out the instructions of Amanuallah Khan and the Inter-Services Intelligence of Pakistan? Was Amanullah Khan himself tricked by the ISI? Why was a local Kashmiri officer of middle-level rank, Abdul Ghani Zargar, done to death?

Answers to these questions were not available from the interrogation of the persons arrested, as they merely followed someone else's instructions. In this connection, what Professor Wani of the Kashmir University told me on the night intervening April 9 and 10 needs to be briefly narrated.

At about 11 p.m. on April 9, I was told by my adviser Jamil Qureshi that he had received a telephonic request from Professor Wani to send some senior Police Officer, Director-General or Deputy Inspector General, to the house of the Vice-Chancellor where he would like to talk to them in the presence of the family members of Professor Haq and Abdul Ghani. These officers were accordingly sent. They were told by Professor Wani that at about 7.30 p.m. he received a telephone call from the captors of Professor Haq and Ghani and they wanted him to tell the police authorities in the presence of the families of the hostages that Government was not doing enough. Later on, from the same telephone, Professor Haq also spoke to say that he was well. I asked Qureshi to arrange to bring all the persons concerned to Raj Bhavan.

We all met at 1 a.m. on April 10 for detailed discussions. We asked Professor Wani to secure the precise modalities of release and ensure extension of time. But Professor Wani was unable to give any assurance. Nor did he know how to get back to the captors or their representatives. He said he was not even sure whether anyone would telephone him again. We were a bit baffled. If he could not establish any contact with the kidnappers, directly or indirectly, how would any meaningful negotiations take place? The meeting ended at about 2.30 a.m. We told Professor Wani that he should get in touch with us the moment any further telephone call or message was received. Surprisingly, whatever discussions took place at Raj Bhavan at well past midnight, appeared the following morning in the local Urdu daily, *Alsafa*. Someone in Professor Wani's camp was in touch with the editor of *Alsafa*, and both of them were keen to tell the Kashmiri public about the entire matter. Could it be that the background for something was being prepared?

The aforesaid meeting was followed by our own internal meeting in which we reviewed our strategy in the light of our discussions with Professor Wani. By that time thousands of houses had been gently searched in four days by scores of parties. Such an intensive combing had never taken place before. Quite a number of terrorists found themselves bottled up in Srinagar city. The sudden, strict and continued curfew completely upset their plan of moving out of the city and spread into small towns and villages. While we apprehended about half a dozen top terrorists, such as Shaukat Bakshi, and met with spectacular success in other areas, we could not locate the kidnappers involved in this case. Luck was not on our side. At one point, we later learnt, our search parties missed the premises of confinement by a few yards.

We could conclude our deliberations at 4 a.m. Hardly had three hours passed when frantic telephone calls from Delhi and from the Vice-Chancellor's house started pouring in. These were about the lead story published in *The Times of India**, on the basis of a PTI report from New York, which stated that Amanullah Khan had announced at a press conference at the UN Headquarters that the Vice-Chancellor of the Kashmir University, Professor Mushir-ul-Haq, the HMT general-manager, H.L. Khera and two others had been "executed". Amanullah even indicated the mode of execution: "Shot dead".

The news item was a mystery. How was it that Amanullah Khan had on April 9 pronounced the hostages dead, when they were actually alive? Or was it Amanullah Khan's way of telling his local followers to kill them? Why did Professor Wani make it a point to say in the presence of the families of Professor Haq and Ghani that the government was not doing enough? Was he, or someone else through him, trying to blunt the edge of public resentment that would follow the killing? Was some sort of justification being built for the brutal murders?

It soon became clear that the decision to kill the hostages was taken by Brigadier Imtiaz of Inter-Services Intelligence, and a temporary lecturer in Baramulla Government College, who went by the name of Professor Ashraf Saraf, and had crossed over to Pak-occupied Kashmir, and who had a personal grudge against Professor Mushir-ul-Haq. He played a nefarious role in this tragic event. A press note issued by the J&K Liberation Front on April 20, 1990, from its Rawalpindi headquarters, provided fairly reasonable explanation for the statement made by Amanullah Khan on April 9. It said:

> We have received a large number of letters, messages and telephone calls from freedom-fighters and our well-wishers expressing their shock over the recent kidnapping and execution of Mushir-ul-Haq, Vice-Chancellor of Kashmir University and his aide

**The Times of India,* April 10, 1990.

Abdul Ghani. Our attention has also been drawn to the fact that Abdul Ghani was a son of Kashmir and that his father died of shock on coming to know of the execution of his son. Our friends and well-wishers have also stated that this execution has been exploited by the Indian authorities for depicting the JKLF as a terrorist organisation and for starting a campaign of calumny against it and Amanullah Khan.

We agreed to support and participate in the operation on condition that no harm would be caused to the hostages. We were assured by Professor Ashraf Saraf and Shafi that no harm would come to them. . . . The JKLF was completely taken by surprise at the news of the execution of the hostages which was completely in violation of the agreement reached. On making inquiries, we were shocked to learn that Imtiaz had, on his own, used the name of Amanullah Khan and conveyed instructions to the freedom-fighters through Ashraf Saraf and Shafi for the execution of the hostages. At the same time he (Brig. Imtiaz) informed Amanullah Khan through a Pakistani diplomat in New York that the freedom fighters had, on their own, without consulting him and Prof. Ashraf Saraf and Shafi, executed the hostages.*

The facts of the case once again demonstrated that there were wheels within wheels and we were up against a ruthless adversary who would not hesitate to execute one of the finest followers of Islam, namely Professor Mushir-ul-Haq, under the pretext of serving Islam. No mild options were really available to us. We had to mount relentless pressure if further kidnapping and killing of innocent persons like Haq, Ghani and Khera had to be prevented.

We had an excellent opportunity to break the back of terrorism in the Valley. Almost all the top terrorists had been cornered. The continued pressure would have placed more of them in our net. But the trumpeters of the disinformation campaign, such as Saifuddin Soz, were continuously at my throat. They misrepresented facts about my decision to impose curfew and conduct house to house searches in the badly affected areas. Arrangements for free distribution of food packets to the needy, and for taking the seriously sick to the hospital, through local police stations, and curfew passes, existed. But who bothered about the facts? Propaganda, false alarms and hysterical

*Reproduced from facsimile published in the *Blitz* of September 22, 1990.

noises mattered. Mufti gave in. He stated in Parliament that the Governor was being asked to lift or relax the curfew. As feared, the period of relaxation was used by the terrorists to scatter, and even slip away from the city.

No killing could be more sad, more sinful, more devious and dastardly, and, at the same time, more pointless, than that of three hostages whose families, friends and well-wishers remained in unbearable suspense and agony for four days. But fate and the follies of the past had made us helpless. All that we could do was to provide some succour and solace to the bereaved families. Our approach in this regard was reflected in the letters that I wrote to three widows. One such letter to the wife of the murdered Abdul Ghani Zarger, which speaks for itself, is reproduced below:

Raj Bhavan
Srinagar

Dear Mrs. Hafiza Begum,

As I mentioned in my condolence message, the brutal and inhuman murder of your noble husband sent shock waves throughout the country. The entire nation condemned it, and we all shared your grief.

One cannot really understand what the ruthless terrorists got out of their brutal deed. Some persons even tried to give a wrong picture to you. But, I assure you, the killers would have to soon answer for it. During the days of kidnapping, we in the State Administration did our best to trace the kidnappers. Thousands of houses were searched in four days. Fate, however, willed otherwise.

I fully realise that no amount of relief can diminish your agony and the agony of your family members. Your loss is, indeed, irreparable. But the amount of ₹ 2 lakhs (one lakh from the State Government and one lakh from the University) and appointment of your son, Mohammad Afzal Zargar, as Lecturer in the Bio-Chemistry Department of Kashmir University, might help the family in standing on its own feet.

I send my sincerest condolences once again and pray for peace of the departed soul.

Yours sincerely,
(Sd.) Jagmohan

Working Out the Khera Case

The mystery of kidnapping and killing of H.L. Khera, General Manager, HMT, was also soon solved. Arrests and interrogations revealed that, as part of a diabolical design to strike terror amongst the public servants of Central Institutions, a conspiracy was hatched to kidnap and kill H.L. Khera.

The conspirators who belonged to the 'Kashmir Students' Liberation Front' hijacked Khera's car at about 9.30 a.m. on April 6, 1990, at Qamarwari Chowk. Four of the militants who were carrying Kalashnikov rifles and pistols, forced their entry into the car and pushed the driver aside. One of them took control of the steering wheel. Two of them sat on the rear seat, keeping Khera in between, and the other sat on the front seat with the driver and an unarmed security man. They drove the hijacked car towards Batmaloo where they dropped the driver and the security man and further drove to Aloocha Bagh where they had already arranged the house of Ghulam Mohammad Bhat to keep Khera as a hostage.

On April 7, 1990, Khera was shifted to another house of Ghulam Mohammad Dar, a shopkeeper in Madhopura Mohalla, Srinagar. On April 8, 1990, he was again brought to the house of G.M. Bhat at Aloochi Bagh from where he was shifted in a Maruti van to another house in Majid Bagh.

From the third hideout, Khera was taken by the militants in the same Maruti van to Batmaloo and killed. His body was found there near the fire station building.

About Khera we did not get even a vague message. His killing had, perhaps, been settled as soon as he was kidnapped. His case, too, was pursued vigorously. Hundreds of houses were searched. I did not even hesitate to get the premises of a former Minister searched when seemingly reliable information was received that he and other hostages could be kept there for the night, not necessarily with connivance but out of fear.

The Shalla Case

Another important case which involved the killing of C.L. Shalla, Inspector Police, was worked out. The pattern of the crime showed how personal grudges had combined with the internal subversion and militant fundamentalism.

In January 1990, Rafiq, a hard-core subversive, was arrested by the Border Security Force. He was handed over to the local police. During his detention, he was interrogated by C.L. Shalla. Thereafter he was let off.

On May 1, 1990, Shalla took a bus from Handwara to Baramulla. A constable named Habibullah came to see him off. At that time, Ghulam Mohammed, a resident of Handwara, was standing at the gate of the bus. He called one Abdullah from a nearby shop. He was wearing a 'phiran' and carrying an AK-47 rifle underneath it. Ghulam Mohammed touched the body of Abdullah to make sure that he was carrying the weapon. The conductor of the bus saw all this.

After about 10 minutes' drive, the bus stopped. Three persons boarded it. They were Yousuf, Rafiq and Riaz. They were all residents of village Heewan. After a few minutes, the bus stopped again. One of the three persons, namely, Rafiq, pulled out a pistol and asked Shalla to raise his hands. He was dragged out of the bus. Ghulam Mohammed, Abdullah, Yousuf and Riaz also got down. Shalla was most inhumanly tortured and then shot dead.

Other Cases

I have restricted myself to five cases, each having its own significance and indicating some contour, or the other of the general conspiratorial pattern. One related to a top political figure, Mufti Mohammad Sayeed, the second to an important functionary in the Information Department, Lassa Kaul, the third to the head of the University, Mushir-ul-Haq, the fourth to the Chief of a central public enterprise, H.L. Khera, and the fifth to the Police Inspector, Shalla. There were other important cases, such as the murder of four Indian Air Force officers, which were solved. Working out of all these cases created an immense impact on the public mind. It became clear to everybody that nobody could any longer get away with his crime or with any active or passive participation in it. In working out all these cases, Ashok Patel, a senior IPS Officer working as IG, BSF, and Additional Director (Coordination) made a remarkable contribution. In the annals of Indian police, his name deserved to be written in golden letters for his superb investigative skill and diligence.

Central Bureau of Investigation

To ensure that investigations were diligently and expeditiously completed and prosecutions launched in the Courts, I entrusted all these cases to the CBI. This had a further deterrent effect. Earlier the State Government was allergic to the CBI being brought in. The self-created bogey of Article 370 always haunted it. Its own investigating machinery had been so crippled that no one would entertain any fear of it.

Designated Court

I appointed only one designated court under the Terrorist and Disruptive Activities Act, and set up its headquarters at Jammu. I did so with important considerations in view. Apart from the fact that the work-load justified only one designated court, its effective functioning in the vitiated atmosphere of Srinagar was not possible. Public hysteria could be worked up and crowds gathered at the time of hearing. Moreover, almost all the accused apprehended in connection with the terrorist-related crimes had been kept in jails in the Jammu Division or in jails outside the State. I had also laid down that if any advocate of Srinagar or any other place wanted to come to Jammu for the defence of the accused, he could be given all facilities of accommodation etc. in Government Circuit or Rest House.

Shifting of the Secretariat

One of the most formidable challenges that I faced in the middle of April was the issue of shifting of the State Secretariat–a phenomenon popularly called 'Darbar Move'. If normal practice was followed, the Secretariat/Capital had to be shifted in the first week of May from Jammu to Srinagar. In the circumstances prevailing in the Valley, it looked almost an impossible task. Threats of kidnapping officials had been held out. A number of terrorist organisations had also announced that they would not allow the Secretariat to function from Srinagar. They did not want the seat of Union-State power to come in the Valley.

The Hindu employees of the State Secretariat and some Muslim employees belonging to the Gujjar communities also opposed the 'move'. They thought that they would be unsafe in the Valley. Their stand was supported by quite a few local leaders. On the other hand, the Kashmiri Muslim employees of the Secretariat wanted to shift to Srinagar at the earliest. They advanced the plea that they were unsafe at Jammu. They threatened to move to Srinagar even if the Secretariat was not shifted.

The matter was further complicated by the informal proposal of some top civil servants to set up a Summer Secretariat in Jammu. The idea was to keep as large a number of Hindu officials as possible in Jammu. Pressure began to be exerted on me for acceptance of this idea. Sponsored stories also appeared in the Press.

I was quite clear about the fundamentals of the issues involved. I was determined not to permit any deviation from the normal practice. It would have deep psychological and emotional repercussions. The setting up of a Summer Secretariat, I thought, would virtually imply a Hindu Secretariat at Jammu for Hindu employees and Muslim Secretariat for Muslim employees at Srinagar. Delay in shifting, or non-shifting of the Capital, was also not reconcilable with my overall approach to assert vigorously the authority of the State. Non-shifting would mean non-assertion; and delay in shifting would be still more damaging in this regard.

I took the initiative in my own hands and formulated a comprehensive plan for shifting. I explained, in a statement on April 15, the basic principles involved in the shifting. I appealed to the general public to let me do the right thing. I told them that for a short-term convenience we should not inflict long-term damage on the national psyche. I reminded the public in general and the employees in particular how in essence the situation had improved, how heinous crimes such as the murder of Lassa Kaul and that of Prof. Mashir-ul-Haq had been worked out and how the assassins would soon have to face the consequences of their brutal acts. I emphasised that the shifting of the Capital to Srinagar would result in further improvement of the situation. It would undermine the already sagging morale of the subversives. It would demonstrate to everyone that we were in command of the situation and were willing to take the bull by the horns. I appealed to the patriotic sentiments of the employees and exhorted them to rise above their personal conveniences. I assured the employees that adequate arrangements for their safety would be made. I also announced that the officials who preferred to leave their families at Jammu would be allowed to retain their government residential accommodation free of rent, and that at Srinagar they would be given hostel-type accommodation.

My appeal had the desired effect. After negligible murmuring, the Hindu employees of Jammu as well as Gujjar Muslim employees agreed to shift. The proposal of the setting up of a summer capital was also given up. It was reported to me that some employees were saying that they were shifting for Jagmohan's sake and not for the sake of the Government. It gladdened my heart. I had always felt that the Jammuites' patriotism and sacrifices for the nation had never been appreciated. The decision of the Jammu-based employees to shift won a great deal of respect from the inner recesses of my heart. They agreed to suffer the inconveniences; they agreed to live separately from their families; they agreed to expose themselves to risks for ensuring that the national will over the entire State was asserted. The nation, I felt, has been unjust and ungrateful to Jammu.

In the course of my statement, I once again advised the misguided youth to abandon the cult of the gun which had brutalised the situation and tarnished the image of the Valley and caused all-round social and economic miseries. I promised that those who voluntarily gave up this cult would be treated with care and compassion. I once again appealed:

> Let us all get together to rebuild and revitalise the Administration, to revive and rejuvenate the economy, and to repair and re-weave the social fabric. Let our streets be full of tourists this season and let this 'Darbar Move' help in bringing complete normalcy. I promise you clean, dynamic, just, fair and sympathetic administration.

I made Hamidulla Khan as overall incharge of the arrangements and personally monitored every detail. Hamid put in a superb effort. Because of his imposing personality and commanding voice, I used to call him, light-heartedly, Field Marshall. On this occasion, he truly behaved like one.

A week before the shifting I went round various places like hostels etc. where employees from Jammu had to be housed. On the day of shifting, I was on tenterhooks, anxious about their safety. Fortunately, everything went according to plan.

On May 7 the offices opened. I myself went to the Secretariat. I held a brief discussion with the officers. Earlier in the day, I issued the following letter to the Secretaries and Heads of Departments:

> May 7, 1990
>
> My dear. . . .
>
> With the shifting of the Secretariat and other offices from Jammu to Srinagar, we are entering an important phase of our efforts to normalise the conditions in the State. Our job is to remain cool and face the current challenge with courage and fortitude.

Civil services have a special responsibility to discharge. I expect everyone of you to put your best foot forward.

The inner spark of a Nation is tested only in times of difficulties. I have no doubt that you would demonstrate the potency of that spark and go ahead not only with the task of eliminating terrorism and repairing the brutalised landscape but also of implementing the new blueprint of development which I have drawn up and which I would soon place before you.

While the beastliness and malignancy of terrorism have to be rooted out with the unfaltering hand of a surgeon, we must not forget that our real fight is against the forces of poverty, backwardness and economic and administrative injustices. We must redress public grievances speedily.

Please remember that we are not scoring any point against anyone. In the entire State, we have only one family. Some of our brothers, who have gone astray, have to be brought back to the fold of this family. Care and compassion should be our watch word.

We have all to join hands, and solicit cooperation of all right-thinking people, to provide a clean, dynamic and result-oriented administration. Both our capacity and courage are under test. Let it not be said by posterity that we were found wanting in any respect.

I would request you to convey my feelings to all the staff members working under you.

Yours sincerely,
(Sd.) Jagmohan

My objective was to take officers to a higher plane, to remind them of the inner spark of the nation and to motivate them to adopt a dedicated and missionary approach to the numerous problems that faced the State. I knew that, over the years, the Indian bureaucracy had, in good part, become wooden, somewhat routine-minded and devoid of emotional and enthusiastic fervour. Without reminding them of the historic role that they could play, it might not have been possible for me to secure the best out of them.

Cumulative Effect

The cumulative effect of all the afore-discussed measures, coupled with the relentless pressure that was put on the subversives, was that by the first week of May 1990, an upper hand had been decisively acquired. The adversary was in retreat on all the fronts. It was getting increasingly demoralised.

By the middle of January an impression had been created that 'Azadi' had been practically achieved; only the formalities remained to be gone through. This impression melted away like a thick smog that begins to thin out and disappear as the wind blows and the sun rises. The landscape was not resplendent, but it was showing clear signs of light and hope.

No longer did the JKLF flag flutter on the houses, tree-tops and lamp-posts; no longer were 'V' signs exhibited on the streets; and no longer were the subversive slogans written on the walls and posters seen on them. On the other hand, the people were themselves erasing what was once written on the walls of private houses. Occasional shootings from street corners of congested colonies were a sign of frustration rather than of any assertion of supremacy.

That this impression was not merely an expression of a pat on our own back, would be evident from the press reports of well-known national dailies. *The Hindu* in its issue of May 15 said:

> All agreed that there was a perceptible change of atmosphere in the Valley in that the administration had begun to function effectively and the Government was visible, unlike only a few months earlier. This spoke of Jagmohan's success.

The *Indian Express,* in its issue of the same date, observed:

> Mosques in the Valley no more blare out the slogan 'azadi'. Flags of the secessionist organisations–Jammu and Kashmir Liberation Front and Hizbul Mujahideen–are not seen anywhere. The names of these bodies on the walls of the city have been erased.
>
> After a long time one sees signs of some life in the city. Little children going to private nurseries early in the morning present a soothing spectacle. One also comes across at times the sight of jawans of paramilitary forces exchanging pleasantries with local shopkeepers.
>
> An indication of improvement in the situation is that members of the all-party advisory panel in Kashmir are able to move on either side of the City–first to Anantnag and then to Baramulla–and talk to local people unlike a more powerful delegation led by the Deputy Prime Minister, Devi Lal, and including the former

Prime Minister, Rajiv Gandhi, which had to confine itself to its hotel during its visit to the Valley two months ago.

The Governor, Jagmohan, says with confidence: 'We are on the verge of restoring normalcy. He is immensely satisfied after the successful 'darbar move' (shifting of summer capital here from Jammu). The move has encouraged the Central Government to think of reopening its 25 offices which are closed at the moment of the total 44 it has in the Valley.

The Tribune, in its issue of May 17 commented:

Stringent measures taken by the administration have brought about a qualitative change in the situation during the past six to seven weeks.

Senior officials, including army commanders leading the forces deployed in the Valley, are believed to have told the all-party team that they were in sympathy with Jagmohan and would like the Centre not to interfere with the Governor's work. 'They are all admiration for the drive, dedication and courage of the Governor' a member of the team observed.

The team's impression is that the Governor has now a better grip over the administration. District officials listen to him, obey his orders and send regular reports of their activities to the State headquarters. This is described by the team members as the most important aspect of the qualitative change in the situation.

This observation may be a bit baffling for those not used to the situation on the ground in the Valley two months ago. When Jagmohan took over as Governor, it may be recalled, district police chiefs would refuse to issue warrants of arrest and would not take into custody even wanted men. Those were the days when even government servants would join anti-India demonstrations and defy orders of their seniors.

It is worth recalling that Rajiv Gandhi, who was a member of the high-level team led by the Deputy Prime Minister, Devi Lal, which visited the Valley on March 8, had to face a hostile crowd in the hotel and even senior members of the hotel staff joined the crowd in raising anti-India slogans.

But there is a change in the situation. Public send-offs which used to be organised for youth going to occupied areas for training are a thing of the past.

The team was pleasantly surprised to find that the attendance in government offices of Srinagar was normal. About 1,200 employees have, of course, been housed in hostels and are brought to their offices under strict security. But the fact remains that a majority of 2,200 employees living in the Valley are also attending offices.

The Statesman in its issue of May 15, pointed out:

> One did not come across the throng of men, women and children shouting 'Azadi' (freedom) on the streets as was the case about a month ago. Non-stop chanting of anti-India slogans using mosque loudspeakers had also come to an end.
>
> A heartening sight was the arrival of a group of tourists in this idyllic valley after a gap of eight months.

In its issue of May 17, the *Indian Express* again pointed out:

> Administration seems to have recovered some of its lost authority and established its credentials with the people who now approach them with their grievances.
>
> Pakistani flags and pro-Pakistani and pro-Independent Kashmir slogans are no more there. Pro-Pakistan graffiti are no more visible.

Similar observations were made by *Patriot, The Hindustan Times* and other national and regional dailies.

The members of the all-party committee also individually reinforced the impression gathered by the Press. In their meeting with me, they congratulated me for the great qualitative change that had been brought about in the situation. The Intelligence Bureau had also made the same assessment.

Too Good to Survive

A straight and clear line of action, a demonstration of determined will to succeed, innovations in the administrative set-up, dynamic coordination, and an intense and sustained pressure on subversive elements were too good to survive in our work environment. These were not the usual products of the current national ethos which breeds deviousness and almost infinite capacity to be destructive, rather than constructive, negative rather than positive.

If two persons are sitting on two chairs of equal height and one wants to raise the level of his chair, he could proceed in two ways.

One is to raise the height of his own chair and the other is to cut down the legs of the chair on which the other person is sitting. Our current national ethos rears the second approach. Hardly anyone is willing to put in honest and dedicated work to give a better performance; most of them try to run the others down, to show that they look better in comparison. Whenever and wherever any solid or sound work is done, the process of running down is immediately begun. My adversaries set about the task in right earnest. What they did, the next chapter would reveal.

CHAPTER XV

A Deluge of Disinformation and Distortion

وہ بات' سارے فسانے میں جس کا ذکر نہ تھا
وہ بات ان کو بہت ناگوار گذری ہے

The content which was not part of
my story was found fault with most
—Faiz Ahmed Faiz

It is a measure of our country's moral decline that the Republic which began its journey with lofty idealism and the adoption of the inscription *Satyameva Jayate* (Truth Alone Triumphs) on its national emblem today rears in its lap heaps of lies, half-truths and fabrications. A glimpse of this phenomenon, so far as it pertains to the case of the Kashmiri Pandits, has already been provided by me in Chapter XIII. In this chapter, I will show how a deluge of disinformation and distortion emanating from a number of denuded hills around—denuded practically of every tree of scruple—swept away my little valley of truth and swamped it with all the slush and stink of the highly polluted political psyche of contemporary India.

"Never has any administration achieved so much in such a short time with such a subverted machinery and in such a vitiated atmosphere", remarked a senior officer to me during his visit to Srinagar at the end of April 1990. And yet I was out of office by the end of May. How did it happen?

As brought out in the previous chapter, in the middle of May, almost all the reputed 'dailies' reported heartening improvement in the situation. Why had I, then, to leave barely a fortnight afterwards?

In his letter dated May 22, 1990, Lieutenant-General (Retd.) N.C. Rawlley wrote:

> You will be surprised to get this letter. I am writing to congratulate you on the excellent results achieved by you over the past several weeks.
>
> I have had a fair amount of experience of guerrilla operations. Two months ago, I was of the opinion that we had lost Kashmir. Since you adopted the present policy of cordons and searches, the whole position has changed. Now I feel that though we may not win over the locals for a long time, at least we would not lose Kashmir. For the sake of India I only pray that you can carry on without having to pull back due to pressures from outside Kashmir. It will not be in India's interest and will be a great pity if you are made to ease the pressure applied by you. I also hope, for India's sake you don't leave Kashmir.
>
> Once again please accept my sincerest congratulations on the outstanding work you are doing in spite of provocations and pressures on you.

Yet I left the State within four days of this letter being written.

M.K. Dhar, Chief of News Bureau, *The Hindustan Times*, in his personal communication of April 28, 1990, said:

> Without any hesitation I admire the efforts you are putting in to restore a semblance of order in the Valley despite carping criticism from interests within and outside the State. You enjoy a fund of goodwill among the people and you have to isolate the secessionists and attend to the miserable living conditions of the people in the Valley.

Why was not this fund of goodwill allowed to be encashed?

H.N. Mota, an old Kashmiri freedom fighter and President of the Indian Society for Social Democracy, in his letter of April 18, 1990, wrote:

> While I am not interested in party politics, I have been pained to find that certain vital aspects of the recent Kashmir situation, including your appointment as the Governor, was viewed by some political parties from a very narrow angle and some of them are still indulging in partisan politics for their own selfish reasons. I sincerely believe that you are doing a great job for the country, and

> it is the moral duty of every patriotic Indian and every true son of Kashmir to render whatever assistance he can in furtherance of the plans and programmes you may undertake to free Kashmir from the scourge of terrorism and to restore peace and tranquility in the State.

How was it that such patriotic sentiments were not given any weight?

An independent observer, Brigadier Rai Singh, in his article "Kashmir–Learn from Errors" noted as follows:

> The rulers of Pakistan had assumed that the Rajiv Gandhi-Farooq Abdullah duo would remain in power after the November 1989 Lok Sabha elections and that Pakistan would have all the time in the world to perfect its subversion assault mechanism to finally achieve its cherished objective of getting hold of the Valley, not necessarily militarily. The assumption of office by the National Front Government at the Centre, resignation of Farooq Abdullah and appointment of Jagmohan as Governor, completely unnerved Pakistan vis-a-vis Kashmir: they panicked, redoubled their subversive activities and let loose a reign of terror with the hope that they might succeed in their nefarious aims before the new Government had time to settle down. Their hopes were belied because they had failed to reckon with the Jagmohan factor.
>
> Within a short span of some three months, Jagmohan, the great doer, sorted out the messy situation. The Durbar-Government moved to Srinagar from Jammu, schools and colleges reopened, and things started looking up generally. In short, the worst was over and behind us. The country heaved a sigh of relief. Then, lo and behold, the most inexplicable event took place. Jagmohan was removed. L.K. Advani has termed his removal as a 'monumental blunder'; very few Indians will disagree, Jagmohan was doing a yeoman service. He had a successful gubernatorial innings at Delhi, Panaji and Srinagar. Even then, he accepted the call of duty, subordinating his personal ease and comfort, to the nation in its hour of need.

Why did "the most inexplicable" event occur?

The answer to all the above questions, in the main, is the aforesaid deluge of disinformation and distortion.

From the first to the last day of my stay, I had to face not only the most grim and critical battle of terrorism and subversion but also an equally extensive and dangerous battle of disinformation and distortion. I could hold my own, and even win the first battle, but not the second. Such were the dimensions, frequency and fury of the avalanches of insinuations and concoctions.

Anti-Muslim—Who?

Before I deal with the various features of the disinformation deluge, let me deal briefly with the question as to who is anti-Muslim. It is, indeed, tragic, and also a reflection on the nation's current ethos of superficiality, that those who are really the well-wishers of the Muslims are portrayed as anti-Muslims and those who have used them for their own selfish purposes by injecting a fear psychosis in the community and playing the politics of religion under the garb of protecting minorities have succeeded in posing as its champions. I would illustrate my point by a living example.

In the late sixties and early seventies, first as Commissioner, Implementation, Delhi Master Plan, and then as Vice-Chairman of Delhi Development Authority, I worked out a major scheme of clearing the areas of slums and shacks around historical places. The two main objectives were to protect the architectural legacy of the Capital and also to resettle the squatters in newly-developed areas to enable them to become healthy and productive units of society and expand their business and industry in future and also attain higher productivity by taking advantage of the infrastructural facilities.

I persuaded hundreds of squatters around Idgah, who were mostly Hindus and Sikhs, and also the squatters around Jama Masjid, who were entirely Muslims, to shift to Naraina and Rewari-Line areas by taking plots which were offered at highly subsidised rates and on easy instalments. But, so far as Muslims of the Jama Masjid area were concerned, my persuasion was torpedoed by the so-called well-wishers of the Muslims; for their own selfish interests, they imputed communal motives to the scheme.

The result is for everybody to see. Today, almost all the Hindu and Sikh resettlers have become progressive and modern entrepreneurs, owners of properties worth lakhs of rupees in the Capital, living and working in clean environment, and with assured future for themselves and their children, while the Muslims around Jama Masjid are still huddled in their slums with ever-deteriorating conditions and with no prospects for improvement either for themselves or for their increasing number of children and grandchildren.

Who, then, is anti-Muslim? One who gave the Muslims an opportunity to carve out a new life of progress and prosperity, away from the grooves of dirt and disease, or those who perpetuated their poverty and kept them in virtual serfdom of obscurantist forces? One who treated all slum-dwellers as slum-dwellers and wanted to facilitate their economic and social integration in the city's overall fabric or those who thought only in terms of Hindus and Muslims and wanted to keep the latter in separate ghettos?

Deluge–Points of Origin

The disinformation deluge did not emanate from a single source. It had quite a few points of origin. The principal source of the deluge was Rajiv Gandhi and his coterie. Later on, another source–George Fernandes and his associates–made their contribution and added to the intensity of the deluge. Yet another source was the unimaginable ignorance about the fundamental reality of Kashmir. The personal and communal biases of critics like Shahabuddin and Imam Abdullah Bukhari also played their part in swelling the tide of the deluge.

Most of the disinformation was *mala fide*, intentionally coined, against the facts known to the framers of the accusations. The allegations of Rajiv Gandhi and Dr. Farooq Abdullah largely fell in this area.

An Open Letter to Rajiv Gandhi

Incensed by the false accusations of Rajiv Gandhi, particularly those made at the election meetings, I wrote an open letter to him, laying bare various facets of his design of disinformation and distortion. A shorter version of this letter was sent to the Press on April 21, 1991. The Press, I thought, would not have the space to publish it in toto. But the matter received attention much beyond my expectations. It appeared that a large section of the public was itself resentful of the falsehood that was being spoken against me and my letter had touched its inner chords. This section was very eager to know what I had to say.

There was wide demand for the letter in full. Obviously, I could not meet this demand through individual communications. I have therefore decided to reproduce it. In this chapter as originally planned, the letter did not find place, as it had not been written then.

Now, to meet the demand, I have included it here after omitting facts which were given in the original draft of this chapter. This has been done to avoid repetition. However, a few points made in the earlier chapters, such as those pertaining to Article 370 and the Kashmiri Pandits, have been retained with the twin objective of maintaining the continuity of thought and exposing to the view of the readers all the facets of Rajiv Gandhi's disinformation at one place.

The full text of the aforesaid letter is as follows:

New Delhi
April 21, 1991

Dear Shri Rajiv Gandhi,

You have virtually forced me to write this open letter to you. For, all along, I have persistently tried to keep myself away from party politics and to use whatever little talent and energy I might have to do some creative and constructive work, as was done recently in regard to the management and improvement of the Mata Vaishno Devi shrine complex and to help in bringing about a sort of cultural renaissance without which our fast decaying institutions cannot be nursed back to health. At the moment, the nobler purposes of these institutions, be they in the sphere of executive, legislature or judiciary etc., have been sapped and the soul of justice and truth sucked out of them by the politics of expediency.

You and your friends like Dr. Farooq Abdullah are, however, bent upon painting a false picture before the nation in regard to Kashmir. Your senior partymen, like Shiv Shanker and N.K.P. Salve have, apparently at your behest, been using the forum of the Parliament for building an atmosphere of prejudice against me. The former raked up a fourteen-year-old incident of Turkman Gate and the latter a press interview–an interview that I never gave–to hurl a barrage of accusations of communalism against my person. Mani Shankar Iyer, too, has been dipping his poisonous darts in the columns of some magazines. I, however, chose to suffer in silence all the slings and arrows of this outrageous armoury of disinformation. Only rarely did I try to correct gross distortions by sending letters to the editors of newspapers and magazines. My intention was to remain content with a book, an academic and historic venture which, I believed, I owed to the nation and to history.

But the other day some friends showed to me press clippings of your comments in the election meetings in Rajasthan. That, I thought, was the limit. I realised that, unless I checked your intentional distortions, you would spread false impression about me throughout the country during the course of your election campaign.

Warning Signals. Need I remind you that from the beginning of 1988, I had started sending 'Warning Signals' to you about the gathering storm in Kashmir? But you and the power wielders around you had neither the time, nor the inclination, nor the vision, to see these signals. They were so clear, so pointed, that to ignore them was to commit sins of true historical proportions.

To recapitulate and to serve as illustrations, I would refer to a few of these signals. In August 1988, after analysing the currents and undercurrents, I had summed up the position thus: "The drum-beaters of parochialism and fundamentalism are working overtime. Subversion is on the increase. The shadows of events from across the border are lengthening. Lethal weapons have come in. More may be on the way." In April 1989, I had desperately pleaded for immediate action. I said: "The situation is fast deteriorating. It has almost reached a point of no return. For the last five days, there have been large-scale violence, arson, firing, hartals, casualties and what not. Things have truly fallen apart. Talking of the Irish crisis, British Prime Minister Disraeli had said: 'It is potatoes one day and Pope the next.' Similar is the present position in Kashmir. Yesterday, it was Maqbool Butt; today it is *Satanic Verses*; tomorrow it will be repression day and the day after it will be something else. The Chief Minister stands isolated. He has already fallen—politically as well as administratively; perhaps, only constitutional rites remain to be performed. His clutches are too soiled and rickety to support him. Personal aberrations have also eroded his public standing. The situation calls for effective intervention. Today may be timely, tomorrow may be too late." Again, in May, I expressed my growing anxiety: 'What is still more worrying is that every *victory* of subversionists is swelling their ranks, and the animosity is being diverted against the Central authorities.' But you chose not to do anything. Your inaction was mystifying. Equally mystifying was your reaction to my appointment for the second term. How could I suddenly become communal, anti-Muslim and what not?

When I resigned in July 1989, there was no rancour. You wanted me to fight, as your party candidate, election for the South Delhi

Lok Sabha seat. Since I had general revulsion for the type of politics which our country had, by and large, come to breed, I declined the offer. If you had any serious reservation about my accepting the offer of J&K governorship for the second term, you could have adopted the straightforward course and apprised me of your views. I would have thought twice before going into a situation which had virtually reached a point of no return. There would have been no need for you to resort to false accusations.

Maybe you do not consider truth and consistency as virtues. Maybe you believe that the words inscribed on our national emblem–*Satyameva Jayate*–are mere words without any meaning and significance for motivating the nation to proceed in the right direction and build a true and just India by true and just means. Perhaps power is all that matters to you–power by whichever means and at whatever cost.

Reality. In regard to the conditions prevailing before and after my arrival on the scene, you and your collaborators have been perverting reality. The truth is that before the imposition of Governor's Rule on January 19, 1990, there was a total mental surrender. Even prior to the day (December 8, 1989) of Dr. Rubaiya Sayeed's kidnapping, when the eagle of terrorism swooped on the State with full fury, 1,600 violent incidents, including 351 bomb blasts, had taken place in eleven months. Then, between January 1 and January 19, 1990, there were as many as 319 violent acts–21 armed attacks, 114 bomb blasts, 112 arsons, and 72 incidents of mob violence.

You, perhaps, never cared to know that all the components of the power structure had beer virtually taken over by the subversives. For example, when Shabir Ahmed Shah was arrested in September 1989 on the Intelligence Bureau's tip-off, Srinagar Deputy Commissioner flatly refused to sign the warrant of detention. Anantnag Deputy Commissioner adopted the same attitude. The Advocate-General did not appear before the Court to represent the State case. He tried to pass on the responsibility to the Additional Advocate-General and the Government Counsel. They, too, did not appear.

Do you not remember what happened on the day of Lok Sabha poll on November 22, 1989? In a tantalising gesture, TV sets were placed near some of the polling booths with placards reading: 'anyone who will cast his vote can take this as a gift'. Near some other booths, coffins were placed with a cryptic note: 'anyone who will cast his vote will get this'. No one in the Administration of Dr. Farooq Abdullah took any step to remove such symbols of defiance of authority.

Let me remind you that Sopore is the hometown of Ghulam Rasool Kar, who was at that time a Cabinet Minister in the State Government. It is also the hometown of the Chairman of the Legislative Council, Habibulla, and also of the former National Conference MP and Cabinet Minister, Abdul Ahad Vakil. Yet only five votes were cast in Sopore town. In Pattan, an area supposedly under the influence of Iftikhar Hussain Ansari, the then Congress(I) Minister, not a single vote was cast. Such was the commitment and standing of your leaders and collaborators in the State.

And you still thought that subversion and terrorism could be fought with such political and administrative instruments.

Around that point of time, when the police set-up was getting rapidly demoralised, when intelligence was fast drying up, when infiltration in services was becoming deeper and deeper, when the press was bringing stories of subversive plans like TOPAC, your protege, Dr. Farooq Abdullah, was either going abroad or releasing 70 hard-core and highly motivated terrorists who were trained in the handling of dangerous weapons, who had contacts at the highest level in Pakistan-occupied Kashmir, who knew all the devious routes of going to and returning from Pakistan and whose detention had been approved by the three-member Advisory Board presided over by the Chief Justice. Their simultaneous release enabled them to occupy key positions in the network of subversion and terrorism and to complete the chain which took them again to Pakistan to bring arms to indulge in killings and kidnappings and other acts of terrorism. For example, one of the released persons, Mohammad Daud Khan of Ganderbal, became the Deputy Commander-in-Chief of a terrorist outfit, Al Bakar, and took a leading part in organising a force of 2,500 Kashmiri youth. Who is to be blamed for all the heinous crimes subsequently committed by these released 70 terrorists? I would leave this question to be answered by the people to whom you are talking about the 'Jagmohan factor'.

The truth, supported by preponderance of evidence, is that before January 19, 1990, the terrorist had become the real ruler. The ground had been yielded to him to such an extent that he dominated the public mind. He could virtually swim like a fish in the sea. Would it matter if the sea was subsequently surrounded?

Labelling Anti-Muslim. In your attempt to hide all your sins of omission and commission in Kashmir and as a part of your small politics which cannot go beyond dividing people and creating vote banks, you took special pains to demolish all regards and respects which the Kashmiri masses, including the Muslim youth, had developed for me during my first term from April 26, 1984, to July 12, 1989. Against all facts, unassailable evidence, and your own previous pronouncements, you started labelling me as anti-Muslim.

Turkman Gate. As a part of your overall design, the leader of your party in the Rajya Sabha, Shiv Shankar, on March 14, 1990, reminded the 'House' about my so-called anti-Muslim leanings as reflected during the slum clearance operation of Turkman Gate in April 1977. This was the most foul, the most cynical, thing to do. Neither Shiv Shankar nor you nor anyone in your coterie had the mental alertness or depth to realise that in the process it was the memory of your late mother and your late brother that was being sullied. None cared to ascertain that with regard to this case, too, large-scale disinformation was resorted to in the post-emergency period, and it was primarily directed against Mrs. Indira Gandhi and Sanjay Gandhi. I was roped in because I refused to step out of my 'Island of Truth' and put all the blame on them, as most of the bureaucrats and your partymen of the time did.

If you had taken the trouble of glancing through the chapter titled 'Untold Story of Turkman Gate' in my book, *The Island of Truth*–a book which your mother had read and recommended to all those who were interested in knowing the truth about the city's clearance-cum-resettlement project–you would have discovered that the Turkman Gate area had been declared unfit for human habitation as far back as 1938, that, as was tragically demonstrated by eight subsequent deaths due to house collapses, the slum dwellers lived under constant fear of death, and that, after clearance of 120 houses, about 1,000 alternative allotments were made, including 200 flats in the most attractive colonies of Ranjit Nagar and Shahdara. You would have also come to know that the incident of April 19, 1976, was due to incitement and rumours connected with the family planning programme and that none of the six persons who died as a result of the action taken by the District authorities and the DIG (Police) was affected by the clearance of the slums, and five of them came from distant localities.

In this regard, I may remind you that this book was filed as an affidavit by me in the special court of Justice M.K. Jain, wherein Mrs. Indira Gandhi was being prosecuted, and no one dared to file even a counter affidavit–so much of solid and unalloyed truth it contained.

Incidentally, do you know that there was not even a scratch on anybody's head during the course of resettling 7 lakh squatters, and the slum-dwellers of Turkman Gate did not even constitute 0.07 per cent of this population? Now on the site cleared, 480 flats have been constructed and the erstwhile slum-dwellers have moved therein. Is it not ironical that those who provided them with new habitation with modern civic amenities were projected as anti-Muslim, while those who virtually forced them to live in death traps assumed the role of their saviours?

You took pride in the successful holding of the Asiad (November 1982). But do you know that not a single project of Asiad could have been undertaken if the massive clearance-cum-resettlement programme had not been successfully carried out in 1976? No land would have been available for Nehru Stadium, Indraprastha Stadium, flyovers, bridges, expansion of roads, parking lots and other infrastructural facilities.

May I, in this connection, also invite your attention to three of the important suggestions made in my book, *Rebuilding Shahjahanabad: The Walled City of Delhi.* One pertained to the creation of the green velvet between Jama Masjid and Red Fort; the second to the construction of a road linking Parliament House with the Jama Masjid complex, and the third to the setting up of a second Shahjahanabad in the Mata Sundri Road-Minto Road complex, reflecting the synthetic culture of the city, its traditional as well as its modern texture. Could such suggestions, I ask you, come of an anti-Muslim mind?

Forum of Parliament. How you and your associates used the forum of Parliament to undermine my standing amongst the Kashmiri Muslims, was also evident from what N.K.P. Salve, M.P., did in the Rajya Sabha on May 25, 1990.

Referring to the so-called interview to the Bombay weekly, *The Current*–an interview which I never gave–Salve chose wholly unjustified expressions; "There was a patent and palpable attitude of a very disconcerting communal bias and, therefore, he (Governor) was happy under the garb of eliminating the terrorists, the saboteurs and the culprits, in eliminating the whole community as it were; now the Governor has himself given profuse and unabashed vent to his malicious malignity, hate and extreme dislike, branding every member of a particular community as a militant."

I know Salve. I do not think, if left to himself, he would have done what he did. Clearly, he was goaded to say some thing which was against his training and background. But the elementary precaution which any jurist, at least a jurist of Salve's eminence, would have taken, was to first check up whether any such interview to the *Current* weekly had been given by me, and, if so, whether the remarks attributed to me were actually made. The unseemly haste was itself revealing. The issue was raised on May 25, while the weekly was dated May 26-June 2, 1990. You yourself rushed a letter to the President on May 25 on the basis of the 'interview' that in reality did not exist. You explained that V.P. Singh had appointed a person with "rabid communalist opinion as Governor".* You also got your letter widely publicised on May 25 itself.

Since your partymen did not allow me to have my say in the Rajya Sabha, even when an opportunity came my way to speak on the subject, I was left with no other option but to file a ₹ 20 lakh damages suit against the *Current* weekly in the Delhi High Court. The case may take a long time and I may donate the damages, if and when awarded, to charity, but I intend sparing no effort to expose all those who have played dirty roles in the disinformation-drama.

Article 370. You created a scene on March 7, 1990, at the time of the visit of the All-Party Committee to Srinagar, and made it a point to convey to the people that in 1986 I wanted to have Article 370 abrogated. At that critical juncture, when I was fighting the forces of terrorism with my back to the wall and beginning to turn the corner after frustrating the sinister designs of the subversives from January 26, 1990 onwards, you thought it appropriate to cause hostility against me by tearing the facts out of context. Whether this act of yours was responsible or irresponsible, I would leave to the nation to decide.

*In *The Hindustan Times,* May 26, 1990.

What I had really pointed out in August-September 1986 was: 'Article 370 is nothing but a breeding ground for the parasites at the heart of the paradise. It skins the poor. It deceives them with its mirage. It lines the pockets of the "power elites". It fans the ego of the new sultans. In essence, it creates a land without justice, a land full of crudities and contradictions. It props up politics of deception, duplicity and demagogy. It breeds the microbes of subversion. It keeps alive the unwholesome legacy of the two-nation theory. It suffocates the very idea of India and fogs the very vision of a great social and cultural crucible from Kashmir to Kanyakumari. It could be an epicentre of a violent earthquake in the Valley–an earthquake, the tremors of which would be felt all over the country with unforeseen consequences.'

I had argued, 'The fundamental aspect which has been lost sight of in the controversy for deletion or retention of Article 370 is its misuse. Over the years, it has become an instrument of exploitation in the hands of the ruling political elites and other vested interests in bureaucracy, business, judiciary and bar. Apart from the politicians, the richer classes have found it convenient to amass wealth and not allow healthy financial legislation to come to the State. The provisions of the Wealth Tax, the Urban Land Ceiling Act, the Gift Tax etc., and other beneficial laws of the Union have not been allowed to be operated in the State under the cover of Article 370. The common people are prevented from realising that Article 370 is actually keeping them impoverished and denying them justice and also their due share in the economic advancement.'

My stand was that the poor people of Kashmir had been exploited under the protective wall of Article 370 and that the correct position needed to be explained to them. I had made a number of suggestions in this regard and also in regard to the reform and reorganisation of the institutional framework. But all these were ignored. A great opportunity was missed.

Subsequent events have reinforced my view that Article 370 and its by-product, the separate Constitution of J&K must go, not only because it is legally and constitutionally feasible to do so, but also because larger and more basic considerations of our past history and contemporary life require it. The Article merely facilitates the growth and continuation of corrupt oligarchies. It puts false notions in the minds of the youth. It gives rise to regional tensions and conflicts, and even the autonomy assumed to be available is not attainable in practice. The distinct personality and cultural identity of Kashmir can be safeguarded without this Article. It is socially regressive and causes situations in which women lose their right if they marry non-State subjects and persons staying for over forty-four years in the State are denied elementary human and democratic rights. And, above all, it does not fit into the reality and requirement of India and its vast and varied span. What India needs today is not petty sovereignties that would sap its spirit and aspirations and turn it into small 'banana-republics' in the hands of 'tin-pot dictators' but a new social, political and cultural crucible in which values of truth and rectitude, of fairness and justice, and of compassion and catholicity, are melted, purified and moulded into a vigorous and vibrant set-up which provides real freedom, real democracy, and real resurgence to all.

I must also point out that when other States in the Union ask for greater autonomy, they do not mean separation of identities. They really want decentralisation and devolution of power, so that administrative and developmental work is done speedily and the quality of service to the people improves. In Kashmir, the demand for retaining Article 370 with all its 'pristine purity', that is, without the alleged dilution that has taken place since 1953, stems from a different motivation. It emanates from a clever strategy to remain away from the mainstream, to set up a separate fiefdom, to fly a separate flag, to have a Prime Minister rather than a Chief Minister, and Sadar-i-Riyasat instead of a Governor, and to secure greater power and patronage, not for the good of the masses, not for serving the cause of peace and progress or for attaining cultural unity amidst diversity, but for serving the interests of the 'new elites', the 'new sheikhs'.

All those aspiring to be the custodians of the vote-banks continue to say that Article 370 is a matter of faith. But they do not proceed further. They do not ask themselves: what does this faith mean? What is its rationale? Would not bringing the State within the full framework of Indian Constitution give brighter lustre and sharper teeth to this faith and make it more just and meaningful?

In a similar strain, expressions like 'historical necessity' and 'autonomy' are talked about. What do these mean in practice? Does historical necessity mean that you include, on paper, Kashmir in the Indian Union by one hand at a huge cost and give it back, in practice, by another hand on the golden platter? And what does autonomy or so-called pre-1953 or pre-1947 position imply? Would it not amount to the Kashmiri leadership saying: 'You will send and I will spend; you will have no say even if I build a corrupt and callous oligarchy and cause a situation in which Damocles' sword of secession could be kept hanging over your head'?

Kashmiri Pandits. You and the like of you have made India a country which has lost capacity to be true and just. Anyone trying to be fair is dubbed communal. The case of the Kashmiri Pandits bears eloquent testimony to this fact.

Whatever be the vicissitudes of the Kashmiri Pandits' history and whatever unkind quirks their fate might have brought to them in the past, these all pale into insignificance in comparison to what is happening to them at present. The grim tragedy is compounded by the equally grim irony that one of the most intelligent, subtle, versatile, and proud community of the country is being virtually reduced to extinction in free India. It is suffering not under the fanatic zeal of mediaeval Sultans like Sikandar or under the tyrannical regime of Afghan Governors, but under the supposedly secular rule of leaders like you, V.P. Singh and others whose unabashed search for personal and political power is symbolised by calculated disregard of the Kashmiri migrants' current miserable plight and the terrible future that stares in their eyes. And to fill their cup of pain and anguish, there are bodies like 'Committee for Initiative on Kashmir' which are over-anxious and over-active to rub salt into their wounds, and to label anyone who wants to stand by them in their hour of distress as communal.

In a soft, superficial, permissive and, in many ways, cruel India which has the tragic distinction of creating over one lakh refugees from its own flesh and blood and then casting them aside like masterless cattle to fend for themselves on the busy and heartless avenues of soulless cities, chances for Kashmiri Pandits to survive as a distinct community are next to nothing. Split, scattered, and deserted practically by all, they stand today all alone, looking hopelessly at a leaking, rudderless, boat at their feet and extremely rough and tumultuous sea to face before they can reach a safe shore across to plant their feet firmly on an assured future.

The deep crisis through which the Kashmiri migrant, or for that matter, the entire Kashmir, is passing is really the crisis of Indian values–the perversion, in practice, of its constitutional, political, social and moral norms. If I visited the camps of the refugees and tried to extend the firm hand of justice to a community in pain, if I instructed that, instead of cash doles, the migrant Government servants should be given leave salary, and if I conceded the demand of a widow of the person brutally killed by a terrorist, for allotment of a house on payment, I became communal, a 'known anti-Muslim', about whom concocted stories were planted in the press. If, on the other hand, someone falsely accused the Indian army and the Governor's Administration, if he assailed 'Jagmohan in particular' of giving inducements through provisions of plots and trucks, without giving particulars either of plots or of trucks, his accusations got published all over the press, his reports were flaunted in national and international forums and were copiously quoted in Parliament by the members of your party and he was labelled as secular and progressive and champion of human rights and what not.

Hard Evidence about 'Jagmohan Factor'. I do not like to refer to anything that looks like indulging in self-praise. But not to let you get away with your calculated campaign of disinformation, about Jagmohan/communal factor, I must invite attention to some hard evidence about what the people of the valley actually thought about me before you and your proteges started the smear campaign on my appointment for the second term.

Writing in the *Indian Express's* issue of July 30, 1987, under the caption 'The Alliance in Kashmir', Pran Chopra, reputed political commentator, noted:

> But there is a recent example from which Farooq Abdullah can learn much; despite the same limited resources and the same administration to work with, but through sheer diligence and application, Governor Jagmohan accomplished so much during the recent spell of Governor's rule that everyone I met was full of praise for it. I had not expected to see so much affection shown for Governor's rule in a State so highly politicised as Kashmir is, especially because the present Governor is also thought wrongly as I now learn, to have been responsible for foisting G.M. Shah's rule on the State. But diligence and application are not qualities which people have detected much in the Chief Minister yet.

V.N. Narayanan, Editor-in-Chief of the *Tribune*, after touring the Valley for three days in June 1989, wrote three articles titled 'J&K

Today'. In the last article Narayan said: "Out of curiosity I put one question to everybody I met in Srinagar, Anantnag and Pahalgam recently: 'Who do you think would give the best government to the State?' It was not a surprise that without exception the answer was: 'The Governor.' 'Any Governor?' 'No, the present Governor–Jagmohan.'"

This is the scene as depicted by the noted journalist Kum Kum Chadha at the time of my departure from the State in the second week of July 1989:

> Tears, emotion, poetry, sentiment, adjectives and smiles marked the farewell of Jagmohan who relinquished charge as Governor of J&K last week. Perhaps no other Governor has, in recent times, got the kind of tribute from the people as Jagmohan did. For them, he was a 'messiah', an architect, a crusader, a reformer, a revolutionary and a visionary. The nostalgia of Governor's rule still lingers. Even its bitterest critics admit its achievements. As Ritu Jeetendra, a lecturer in a women's college told Jagmohan: 'As a student of political science I am totally opposed to Governor's rule but I liked your rule, Sir!' Described as a 'legend', State Minister P.L. Handoo said: 'On April 26, 1984, Jagmohan took the oath as Governor. On July 7, 1989, he lays down office. Between these two dates, he has written the contemporary history of J&K.' Even Ruskin was quoted: 'The value of a thing is not known until it is lost.' . . . Perhaps no other Governor generated the kind of emotion that Jagmohan did.

Earlier, on February 27, 1987, Prem Bhatia, in his editorial comments in the same paper, said:

> In J&K itself, many of those who opposed the imposition of Governor's rule following the fall of the G.M. Shah Ministry did not take long to praise Jagmohan who showed a rather uncommon responsiveness to the people's problems.

This is what A.N. Dar, Editor of the *National Herald*, observed in his article, 'What is Wrong in Kashmir', of April 15, 1989:

> It has to be admitted that the last two years in Kashmir have been administratively sterile. The coalition has not been a shining example of purposeful administration. This is sad indeed, more so because it had the example of purposeful administration. This is sad indeed, more so because it had the example before it of what the Governor Jagmohan did during Governor's rule. Jagmohan showed that it was possible to win the goodwill of the

people through fair-minded, selfless and effective administration. Even the fundamentalists and the anti-nationals accepted that he was fair and efficient.

The widely circulated Urdu daily of Kashmir, *Srinagar Times*, in its issue of July 8, 1988, editorially observed: "What Governor Jagmohan did during the six months of Governor's Rule, to set right the deteriorating conditions in the Valley and improve its environment, would never be forgotten by the people of Kashmir." The same newspaper, in its issue of February 19, 1987, published an editorial–Memory of Governor's Rule is coming to mind* and stated:

> During Governor's Rule the administration became alert and development and construction work got speedily executed. Whatever work was done was done properly and in a neat and clean manner. The important roads like Maulana Azad Road, Dal Gate Road, Boulevard and many other roads which were earlier being repaired and damaged every year, were made with such solid and sound material that in spite of grave winter and continuous snow-fall, the roads remained in excellent shape. Even when heavy bulldozers were put on the road for removing the snow, they remained as strong and smooth as they were before snow-fall and not even a single rubble or stone came out.
>
> The offices functioned in a disciplined manner and everyone attended office in time. The Governor listened to the grievances of the people personally, high or low, rich or poor, man or woman, urban or village folk. He passed some order or the other on every application. He followed up the matters and ensured that his orders were complied forthwith. Now, no one is attending to the grievances of the people and they are seen waiting for days in the Secretariat.**

Nikhil Chakravartty, the noted political analyst, in his Sunday column of October 30, 1988, wrote:

> One finds common people in many parts of the Valley getting bitterly disenchanted with Chief Minister, and in contrast praising Jagmohan's period of Governor's rule.

In its issue of April 6, 1989, *The Hindu* reported:

* This is a translation of the caption to the editorial written in Urdu.

**Translation from Urdu by the author.

In fact, a large number of youth indicated that they would be more than satisfied if the Governor, Jagmohan, were once again allowed to take over the administration.

On my demitting office on July 12, 1989, the reporting of *The Hindustan Times* from Srinagar was as under:

The news of the exit of Jagmohan from the Kashmir scene has created a mood of shocked disbelief and quiet anger of a kind which the Valley had not felt before.

Fed up with the prevarication of Chief Minister Farooq Abdullah, the people always had a ray of hope in Jagmohan. During Governor's Rule, the bureaucracy was tamed and developmental work proceeded at a feverish pitch. New roads were constructed and old ones repaired almost in every corner of the State. People were bewildered as they had rarely seen an elected government function at such a furious pace. For the people, it was like a dream come true.

Even today when people travel along a pot-holed road, they call it a 'Farooq Abdullah Road', but a well-metalled road is known as 'Jagmohan Road'.

An able administrator, Jagmohan cleared all pending cases and took on-the-spot decisions, expediting development work.

Tourists still fondly remember the time they spent in the city forest. On the slopes of Shankaracharya-Zaberwan hills, descending to the shores of the Dal Lake, the city forest was created during Governor's rule. Tourists descended in hordes on the 907 hectares of the city forest to delight in the peace and serenity of its exquisite foliage and lush greenery. It was also given the status of a national park, but with the installation of the Farooq Government, thousands of trees were felled to convert the area into a golf course.

Jagmohan had also introduced "district merit system" in the selection of candidates. He was of the opinion that merit should be the only criterion for selection. Jagmohan had also banned private practice by doctors employed in public hospitals. Dr. Abdullah has allowed doctors to go in for private practice. Jagmohan had stopped construction of hotels around Dal Lake to restore it to its pristine beauty. Jagmohan looked upon Dal Lake as a historical legacy of the people of the State to be protected at all costs. But now encroachments and construction of hotels have again commenced in the area.

A 21-year-old Kashmiri youth, Javed, went to Pakistan for training. While returning in a group of 85 trainees, he was apprehended at the border by the Indian Army. In an interview to the press and television, Javed gave an account of his experience. Describing the conditions in Pak-occupied Kashmir, he said, "They have only outdated suspension bridges. The roads are as bad as these were in Srinagar before Jagmohan came to the State." Despite turning militant, the Kashmiri youth nursed a latent respect for the welfare and development work done by me in Kashmir.

The purpose of citing these comments and observations is not to draw attention to personal achievements but to expose the treacherous role of those elements in national and State leadership who moved heaven and earth to portray me as anti-Muslim and anti-Kashmiri and in the process scuttled the great effort to rescue the State from the jaws of death and destruction. I could have tapped, for the good of the State and the country, the regards and affections which existed for me in the inner layers of the Kashmiri mind. But you were bent upon strangulating everything and denying me the opportunity to make use of the goodwill.

Your principal prop of current politics of Kashmir, Dr. Farooq Abdullah, was not to be left behind in the drive launched to create an 'anti-Muslim' image of mine. In his interview published in *The Times of India* of August 3, 1990, he said, "A known anti-Muslim was appointed as Governor of a Muslim majority State". How untrue, how unfair, was the propaganda, should be obvious from the fact that on November 7, 1986, at the time of his swearing-in ceremony, Dr. Farooq Abdullah, in a public speech, for which the records exist, said: "Governor Sahib, we would need you very badly. It is, indeed, amazing that such remarkable work could be done by you in a short time through an imbecile and faction-ridden bureaucracy. If today three ballot boxes are kept–one for the National Conference, one for the Congress and one for you, your ballot box would be full while the other two ballot boxes would be empty."

The misfortune of our country is that we have leaders like Dr. Farooq Abdullah who have no regard for facts or truth and whose superficiality is matched only by their unprincipled politics.

Incidentally, did it not strike you that Dr. Farooq was virtually accusing your late mother of being anti-Muslim because she was the Prime Minister when, in April 1984, 'a known anti-Muslim' was appointed, for the first term, as 'Governor of a Muslim majority State?'

Apparently in consultation with you, Dr. Farooq Abdullah, on February 15, 1990, issued a written statement to the press in Urdu in which he, *inter alia*, said, "The Governor, in the personification of 'Hallaqu' and 'Changez Khan', is bent upon converting the Valley into a vast graveyard. On account of continuous curfew since January 20, it is difficult to say how many hundreds of people have become victims of the bullets of the army and para-military forces, and in this general slaughter how many hundreds of houses have been destroyed. At this moment, when Kashmiris are witnessing their beloved country being converted into a vast graveyard, I appeal to the national and international upholders of humanity to intervene in Kashmir and have an international inquiry made into the general slaughter of Kashmiris at the hands of army and paramilitary forces."

Here is your 'patriot' calling Kashmir 'Aziz Wattan', suggesting a separate country. Here is your 'national leader' asking for an international inquiry into the general slaughter of the Kashmiris by the Indian Army and para-military forces. Here is your 'responsible friend' speaking about the continuous curfew for twenty-five days in the Valley and his consequent inability to find out how many 'hundreds of innocent and unarmed Kashmiris' had been massacred and how many hundreds of Kashmiri houses raised to the ground, although he knew perfectly well that there had been a number of days when there was no day-curfew, partially or wholly, and the authorities had brought out the list of casualties, about 40 up to February 16, and were daily asking the public to provide with the additional names, if they had any, so that correction in the official list could be made. Here is an erstwhile Chief Minister who did not care to explain how 'innocent and unarmed people' were ruthlessly shooting down I.A.F. officers, B.S.F. jawans, senior officers of the Television and Telecommunications Department and young men in the streets; and how, while inciting people through lengthy and fiery statements, he did not find a single word to condemn such brutal murders.

Is the nation not entitled to know why you have not disowned such unfortunate behaviour on the part of Dr. Farooq Abdullah? And how do you account for his recent statement as published in *The Times of India* of February 7, 1991: 'I directed my partymen to lie low, go across the border, get training in arms handling; do anything but do not get caught by Jagmohan'?

Stabbing me in the back at personal level, perhaps, did not matter. But by keeping the pot boiling, you and your proteges prolonged the agony of Kashmir and caused many more deaths and much more destruction. The politics of unscrupulousness was brought to its lowest depth.

Roots. You once said, 'I do not read history; I make history.' Apparently, you do not know that those who happen to make history without reading it, usually make bad history. They cannot understand the undercurrents and the fundamental forces that really shape the course of events and determine the ultimate destiny of a nation.

In the absence of historical perspective, you and the like of you never perceived the roots and tendrils which gave rise to the current crop of separatism and subversion in Kashmir. Poisonous seeds were persistently planted in the Kashmiri psyche. And these were liberally fertilised. Those of you whose obligation it was to stop these plantations and their fertilisation, were not aware of even the elementary lesson of history: to compromise with the evil was only to rear greater evil; to ignore the inconvenient reality was only to compound it; to bow before the bully was only to invite the butcher the next day.

I could cite scores of cases to support my contention. Here, I would restrict myself to only two examples.

Softness and Surrender. On October 2, 1988, Mahatma Gandhi's birthday, his statue was to be installed in the new High Court complex at Srinagar. The function had been announced. The Chief Justice of India, R.S. Pathak, was to do the formal installation. But a few Muslim lawyers objected. They threatened to cause disturbance at the time of the function. The Chief Minister gave in, almost willingly, to the bullying tactics. The function was cancelled.

What were the implications of what happened? A secular Kashmir, part of a secular India, could not have, even in its highest seat of justice, a statue of the Father of the Nation, of a sage who laid down his life for communal harmony. Who was the person spearheading the move against the installation? It was none other than Mohammad Shafi Bhat, an advocate of the J&K High Court and an active member of the National Conference, who was later on given party ticket for Srinagar Lok Sabha seat in the elections held in November 1989 and with whom you kept warm company during your visit to Srinagar on March 7, 1990, to create as many difficulties as possible for Governor's Administration.

At that time there was National Conference(F)-Congress(I) Ministry in office. Such was its lack of adherence to principles, such was the character of Congressmen who formed part of the Ministry and such was its disposition to cling to power that not even a little finger was raised when the function was cancelled.

The bully's appetite could not have been whetted better. Intimidation could not have secured better results. The trouble-makers could not have perceived a more casual and non-committed adversary. Was it not natural for them to nurture higher ambitions and think that more spectacular results could be achieved by deploying a more aggressive and threatening strategy? Only a naive would believe that in the context of the Kashmir situation, softness and surrender on basic principles would not act as an invitation to terrorism and militancy.

The Union Government enacted the Religious Institutions (Prevention of Misuse) Act, 1988. It was made applicable to all the States of the Union except J&K. Because of Article 370, concurrence of the State Government was needed for extension of this law to the State. But the same was not given. Why? Because J&K is different. What an argument for not having a law which aimed at eradication of misuse of religious premises for political purposes!

Nowhere was this law needed more than in the State of J&K. Nowhere were religious places misused more than here. Nowhere were seeds of fanaticism and fundamentalism sown every Friday more assiduously than from the pulpits of mosques here. Nowhere was it preached more regularly than here that Indian democracy was un-Islamic, Indian secularism was un-Islamic, and Indian socialism was un-Islamic. And yet, neither the State Government which was ruled by two supposedly secular parties, nor the Union Government took the matter seriously. What intrigued me most was that the law which was considered good for 100 million Muslims in other parts of India, was not considered good for 40 lakh Muslims of Kashmir.

What was the use of the nationalist forces ruling the country when they would not act in national interest at all; when they remained mental slaves of the politics of communalism; when they were inclined to place reliance on words and not on deeds; when they did not lead, but succumbed; when they encouraged, and not defeated, separatist elements; when, instead of building a new society, strong in human and spiritual values, they did everything, wittingly or unwittingly, to repair, renovate and strengthen the old, decaying and smelly citadel of obscurantism; and when they invariably gave precedence to expediency over the basic goals and principles of our Constitution? What could be the result of all this? Did it require any unusual insight to understand where such spurious forces would take us?

A Basic Question. While the prospects of my success rattled you and Dr. Farooq, as both of you apprehended exposure of your past lapses, it equally caused worry to Pakistan authorities, including Mrs. Benazir Bhutto and her agencies like ISI. They clearly understood that I could not only set the administrative machinery right, get it rid of internal subversion, and secure loyalty and cooperation from a sizable section of the bureaucracy, but also win over public support by speedily redressing the grievances of the people, launching a drive against corruption, and reviving the tenor and tempo of the development of 1986. They, therefore, mounted a special campaign against me. That also explains Mrs. Benazir Bhutto's hysterical outburst against me personally on Pakistan television and in her public speeches. Otherwise, there was no reason why she should be picking on a Governor of a State and not the Prime Minister or the Home Minister or any other high Central functionary. She knew that I was aware of the deeper currents of Kashmir polity and administration and my approach was bound to be effective and fruitful. Mrs. Bhutto also knew that Pakistan had benefited immensely from the shallowness and superficiality of the approach of the earlier regime. How could she and her officers of the ISI allow their years of labour to go waste when they had almost attained their objective?

I leave it to the well-wishers of the nation to consider, without any political or personal bias, a basic question. How was it that Dr. Farooq was calling me Hallaqu and Changez Khan, and you were travelling all the way to Srinagar to 'expose' me as anti-Article 370, anti-Kashmiri and anti-Muslim, and, at the same time, Ms. Benazir Bhutto was vowing to tear me to pieces–Jag-Jag-Mohan ko Bhag-Bhag-Mohan Kar Denge'?

There are many other facets of Kashmir's truth which lie buried underneath the heaps of disinformation and also of superficiality and shallowness. These days I am busy in an attempt to remove some of these heaps. One day, I hope, the country will acquire the true perspective of the problem. The Kashmiri masses would also realise that I was their greatest well-wisher. I wanted to save them permanently from the exploitative oligarchs and also from the machinations of religious 'Czars' and forces of obscurantism.

You have already committed the sin of letting down the Bharat Mata in Kashmir. Now do not add to it another sin of letting down the other Mata also. There is, after all, some power above. Be conscious of Her. She may condone your negligence. But She would not condone your sin of blaming an innocent person for what were your own faults, particularly when he had been persistently reminding you of your obligations.

So far as I am concerned, I am content with my gloomy pride of having done the correct thing in Kashmir. True, I seemingly and, perhaps, temporarily, lost the goodwill of some of the locals. But I was not seeking a certificate from anyone. I had gone for the second term to do a national duty.

The country's polity and administration have assumed such a character that it has become incapable of solving, from its roots, any serious problem. Elections have virtually lost all meaning. And these would continue to be meaningless until and unless Indian democracy and its constitutional structure acquires a healthy cultural base, a pure soul and soil, from which the seed of justice, truth and selfless service could sprout and blossom into a Great Tree providing shade and shelter from Kanyakumari to Kashmir. Currently, the inner light is gone, and we are being led virtually by blind men with lanterns in their hands. We stumble from one crisis to another. As a poet says:

It has happened
and it goes on happening
and it will happen again.

With best wishes,

Your sincerely,
(Sd.) Jagmohan

National Conference Campaign

The disinformation campaign of the National Conference was practically at the same wave length as of Congress(I). The objective was to raise the pitch of the propaganda and cause a crescendo in which the voice of truth would be lost. Saifuddin Soz, MP, played a major role in this regard. Using the forum of the press and the Parliament, he frequently resorted to gross exaggerations. An example may be given.

In the last week of March 1990, Soz started saying that, since I took over on January 19, 450 persons had been killed in the State. On March 28, when I saw in the newspapers that he had mentioned this figure in the Lok Sabha, I drafted an official letter and asked Secretary, Information, N.R. Gupta, to issue it. This letter which speaks for itself is reproduced below:

> Our attention has been drawn to your statement in which you have indicated that 450 persons had been killed in Kashmir, after the imposition of the Governor's Rule in the State. We would be grateful if you could kindly furnish to us the detailed particulars of the persons allegedly killed, including their names and addresses, because there is a wide variation between what you have stated and what exists in records and the reports of the Police Department and other authorities concerned.

Soz never replied. What was worse, he created an impression that all the "450" persons were killed on account of the action of the security forces.

The truth was that during this period, there were 137 casualties. Out of these, 43 innocent persons had been killed by the terrorists; 61 lost their lives when security forces acted in self-defence or in discharge of their duty to enforce public order or in warding off attacks of terrorists and also in consequence of cross firing; 31 died due to firing by the Army guards when subversionists attacked army convoys or school bus carrying children of the Army personnel; and two were shot by the security staff attached to the United Nations officials when their vehicle was attacked.

By way of comparison and contrast, I would quote what the noted columnist, Tavleen Singh wrote* after her visit to the Valley just four days before my appointment for the second term was announced:

**Economic Times*, January 1990.

> In the past year, nearly 150 people have lost their lives in Kashmir. Of these, around 30 are policemen and officials and the rest are civilians killed in what the security forces call 'crossfire'.
>
> Not a single terrorist has been killed. And yet the Kashmir government, if it can be called that any more, claims that its main aim is to protect innocent lives.

The Members of Parliament, belonging to the National Conference, sitting in their secure and sheltered houses in New Delhi, made it a practice to issue, almost daily, a statement or two condemning the Governor and demanding the withdrawal of para-military forces. But what they would always conveniently forget was that it was their party and Dr. Farooq Abdullah who had brought the para-military forces. I give below a few more extracts from the above-cited write-up of Tavleen Singh:

> Srinagar today resembles a war zone. There are more troops at the airport than passengers. Their presence in the empty, silent streets is even more ominous and pervasive. The situation is very, very bad. The politicians, however, sit in the safety and warmth of Jammu so that you feel that there is no government in Kashmir at all.
>
> A chorus of complaints rises against the CRPF, against India and against Farooq Abdullah. "They treat us like animals." "And where is Farooq Abdullah", asks Imtiaz's sister Rubaiya. "Where are his daughters? They are in London for their safety while we are attacked here by the police. He is in Jammu. His son studies in Shimla or somewhere else. What does Farooq Abdullah care about what happens in Kashmir". The complaints turn into a tirade of abuse from the men while the older women weep quietly. Everyone praises the mujahideen for being the only ones who have distributed food and other necessities, house to house, during the week of curfew.

And this is what Tavleen Singh said in the second instalment of her piece written after the imposition of the Governor's Rule:

> So Delhi is left with no option but to come down with a heavy hand. Already senior Janata Dal leaders are talking privately in terms of crushing the insurgency even if it means a spell of martial law in the Valley. This is unlikely to be easy despite the new governor's fabled administrative abilities.

His task is going to be complicated by the fact that Farooq Abdullah is already showing signs of trying to win back his lost political base by siding with the militants and shrieking about the 'repression' that has been unleashed since the governor took over.

He has clearly forgotten that the violence began with an attack on him in May 1987 in which he narrowly escaped with his life. A couple of months later the attacks on the police began and there was the first appearance of the Kalashnikov. By the time Farooq Abdullah resigned, the Valley was being virtually ruled by the militants.

Equally hollow and hypocritical were their allegations with regard to press. On February 9, for instance, five National Conference M.Ps. accused me of illegally banning the publication of the newspapers in the Valley. Many a time I publicly asked them to show me any notification or order or regulation under which I had banned any publication or put any restriction on the press. They would not care to give reply in concrete terms, but go on repeating their general allegations after short intervals with the sole purpose of causing prejudice against me. Suddenly, these M.Ps. became champions of the freedom of the press, forgetting that it was their leader, Dr. Farooq Abdullah, who had only three months earlier brought the infamous legislation to impose virtual censorship on the news, and it was the nation-wide agitation that forced him to drop the measure. After due cautioning and after showing to the two-member committee of the Editors Guild, which visited Srinagar in the second week of February, the type of reporting that was being done by some newspapers, I proceeded, in the month of March, against individual newspapers which had blatantly violated specific provisions of law and indulged in gross criminal intimidation.*

George Fernandes's Style

George Fernandes's modus operandi was, by comparison, more subtle, indirect and complex. The Kashmir situation at the moment demanded a wholly objective, apolitical and practical approach. But George Fernandes was not able to rise above the deep-rooted reflexes which he had acquired as a trade union leader. Nor could he give up

*See Chapter X: 'Nature and Pattern of Subversion and Terrorism' and Chapter XIII: 'Frightened Pigeons and Forsaken Community–Kashmiri Pandits' for details.

the temptation to carve out for future a larger political niche for himself, particularly amongst the Muslims, by making use of his position as Minister for Kashmir Affairs. By nature, moreover, he was possessive and somewhat meddlesome; inclined to be more destructive than constructive in administrative matters. He could not shake off past predilections, particularly in regard to persons like Dr. Farooq Abdullah and Ashok Jaitley. He had little practical insight into the nature and pattern of internal subversion in Kashmir and the emergence of new forces and personalities. But it was his overpowering desire to look liberal and progressive, and his method of undermining the image of his opponents through planted and slanted news stories in the press, that did the greatest damage.

As indicated in Chapter XII, George Fernandes's stance and method of operation contributed a great deal to the whirlpools of confusion and contradictions. I, therefore, decided that I would not any longer suffer, without protest, any interference from him in administrative matters of the State. I did not want to go on attempting to fill the empty bucket of Kashmir's administration and at the same time allow someone else to puncture its bottom. I thought that if Prime Minister truly believed that George Fernandes was better equipped to fill the bucket, he should be asked to take over as Governor of the State. Why could not our political leaders, I wondered, be more forthright and straight? Why should the Prime Minister cause conditions in which one functionary of his set-up thought that he could succeed in his objective only by under-cutting the other functionary of the same set-up.

On May 2, I came to know that George Fernandes was planning to visit Srinagar with the members of the Advisory Committee at the time of shifting the capital from Jammu to Srinagar. He had nothing to do with the decision. Nor did he know anything about the arrangements. Yet he, along with a large contingent, wanted to be there from May 5 onwards merely because he wanted to be at the centre of the stage. I would have let it pass but for the fact that his presence and presence of the Advisory Committee would have caused unnecessary distraction to the administrative machinery which would have its hands full with an extremely complex and onerous task. It would have also, as experienced on March 7*, impelled the subversives to put an extra effort to cause some incident or the other

*See Chapter XII: 'Whirlpool of Confusion and Contradictions' for details.

to secure publicity on a wider scale than would have been normally available.

As was the practice with George Fernandes, he did not inform me about his intending visit. But as soon as I got an inkling of it, I sent him the following telex message:

> I understand that the Committee on Kashmir is planning to visit Srinagar from fifth May onwards. I would strongly recommend that the proposed visit be postponed. The presence of the Committee would affect the rhythm of the administrative machinery which should remain wholly geared to deal with the problems of shifting of the Secretariat and opening of the educational institutions. The Committee could visit after the current crucial stage is over.

I also sent a copy of this telex to the Principal Secretary to the Prime Minister, advising him to inform the Prime Minister about my recommendations in the matter. Apparently, the Home Minister and the Prime Minister agreed with my views. George Fernandes's intended visit did not materialise.

On May 9, George Fernandes used the forum of Aligarh Muslim University to resort to disinformation in his own special style. Though the meeting was supposed to be closed-door, certain observations made by George Fernandes to the students with a set purpose were leaked through a friendly correspondent. The *Daily Telegraph* of May 10 reported:

> "When are you going to recall the J&K Governor, Jagmohan?" Though Fernandes always wriggled out saying, "I will not debate such things publicly", his sympathy with the demand was evident. Fernandes made it clear that what he favoured was political process, while Jagmohan and the Mufti were in favour of further repression.

Against this wholly unjustified insinuation of George Fernandes, I wrote to the Prime Minister as follows:

> May 16, 1990
>
> Dear Prime Minister,
>
> I am enclosing a press cutting of *Daily Telegraph* dated May 10, 1990, which speaks for itself. I would request you to kindly consider whether this type of projection of mine in the press/public will help me in effectively tackling the Kashmir situation. After all, I am

merely following the government policy of firmly rooting out terrorism from the State.

Incidentally, the aforesaid report has not been publicly denied.

Yours sincerely,
(Sd.) Jagmohan

Earlier, in the middle of April, George Fernandes had brought Syed Shahabuddin to Srinagar. Immediately thereafter, Shahabuddin issued a virulent statement* against me. Without even a shred of evidence, he alleged that "Jagmohan was being used as a tool to implement a diabolical plan to demolish the secular State and establish a Hindu Rashtra." Just to run down my administration which was otherwise securing public applause from a large section of the countrymen, he alleged, without checking facts with anyone in the State Government, that there was acute shortage of essential commodities in the Valley. The actual position** at that time was that I had built up a stock for two months. There were 57,461 metric tonnes of rice, 16,826 metric tonnes of wheat, and 3,183 metric tonnes of sugar in our stores. The position, in fact, was so easy that I had sanctioned additional quota of 575 grams of sugar per head for the holy month of Ramzan.

The Muslim League leaders were not to be left behind. Their statements spoke as much about their mind as that of the person at the back of such statements. On May 8, when there was wide public appreciation of my success to shift the capital from Jammu to Srinagar without any incident, Sulaiman Sait and Banatwala issued a statement† in which they said, "Jagmohan was thwarting the efforts of George Fernandes to start a dialogue with various politically influential people in the troubled Valley. Fernandes must be allowed to create the right atmosphere in Kashmir and for this it was imperative that Jagmohan be recalled. Jagmohan had been sent there under pressure from Bhartiya Janata Party." Neither they nor other instruments of disinformation cared to address themselves to the obvious questioning: Was I also sent to J&K in April 1984 and kept there for over five years under the pressure of Bhartiya Janata Party?

* PTI release, April 14, 1990.

** These facts were stated by the Secretary, Civil Supplies, Qazi Mohammad Amin in a letter to the *Patriot* of April 6.

† *Hindu,* May 9, 1990.

And in what manner was I preventing George Fernandes from opening dialogue with anyone?

By the beginning of May, I had started doubting whether George Fernandes's subtle and indirect propaganda against me was not also due to psychological and political reasons. Substantial improvement in the situation was, inwardly, not palatable to him, as it had been brought about through measures with which he was not connected. Equally unpalatable, perhaps, was the impression in certain quarters that credit for this improvement was going to the BJP. Whether my doubts were valid or not, the fact remained that George Fernandes's activities and stray observations had generally negative and unsettling effect upon the situation.

It was experienced by us that whenever the State Administration acquired an upper hand, George Fernandes came to Srinagar, talked to a handful of saboteurs and their collaborators whose sagging morale got a boost and they re-started their subversive activities with a renewed vigour. This, for instance, was what exactly happened during George Fernandes's visit of May 14-15. We had attained a definite ascendency on the security and law and order front. Serious cases had all been worked out. With blitzkrieg of searches and raids on the hideouts, the subversives were demoralised and on the run. The formidable task of shifting the offices to Srinagar had been successfully completed. From Tuesday to Friday, the attendance in the offices was full and vehicles and traffic functioned normally. This would be evident from the attendance registers and the figures of sales from the government depots and open markets. Anantnag had no demon-stration, no firing on security forces.

In came George Fernandes and his team. An entourage of 40 vehicles went to Anantnag. The visit was premature. Fear still lurked in the public mind. No one came to see the Minister, except the known subversives who greeted him with the slogan of 'Azadi'. The visible leadership of the area once again slipped into the hands of the secessionists. The following day, the exercise was repeated for Baramullah. In the evening, Fernandes went on television, indirectly suggesting to the people to make complaints against the excesses of the security forces.

The net result of all this was serious psychological setback to the State Administration in its fight against terrorism. The legacy of the visit was three days of hartal in Srinagar and upswing in terrorist activities, particularly in Anantnag which again saw firing and cross firing.

What was most unfortunate was that an impression was calculatedly created in the public that the State Administration was repressive while George Fernandes was nothing but flowing with milk of human kindness. Just imagine, the Minister saying at the Hindustan Machine Tools factory*: "Great sin is not to give bread and butter. Greater sin is to snatch it. In Kashmir, we are doing both the things." What were these observations meant to convey?

George Fernandes also resorted to untimely gestures. He spoke to Srinagar Radio and Doordarshan, and said: "The Prime Minister, Vishwanath Pratap Singh, has agreed that in local news bulletins the Prime Minister can be addressed as "Wazire-e-Azam" and the President as "Sadar" instead of general policy of using the expressions like "Pradhan Mantri" and "Rashtrapati". The Prime Minister has also agreed that these bulletins can be wound up with the expression 'Khuda Hafiz'. The *Indian Express* rightly observed, "Infinitely worse in its implications is the decision to allow the bulletins to end with "Khuda Hafiz"–a term which many Indians other than Muslims would willingly use and do use, but one which in the current context of Kashmir cannot but be seen as pandering to fundamentalist whims, with all its dangerous repercussions."

New Technique

Despite extra efforts and all kinds of subterfuge, the campaigners of disinformation were getting a bit desperate. They found that it was not easy, in the face of visible results, to demolish my image. The country generally was appreciative of what had been done in a short time. The Union Home Minister, Mufti Mohammed Sayeed, voiced the view of the Government of India as a whole when he forcefully lauded in the Parliament on April 25, what he called "tremendous work" done by me. Mufti said, "Jagmohan had to function in a vacuum, in a situation where there was no respect for law or authority of the State government. He braved terrorists, instilled courage in government officials who had almost given up the situation as a lost case. It is very unfair for anyone to criticise Jagmohan for what he has done for the country."**

* *Indian Express,* May 16, 1990.

** *Times of India*, April 26, 1990.

But George Fernandes and the like of him knew the technique of turning my very successes to their advantage. They started playing upon the mind of V.P. Singh to exploit his inner weakness for the Muslim vote bank. They understood that the long-term political strategy of V.P. Singh was to build a strong base upon the Muslims, including the obscurantists, and curtail the influence of the BJP. They, therefore, concentrated on planting an idea in him that the credit for whatever improvement had taken place in Kashmir situation, was going to BJP and not to the Janata Dal.

Moulvi Farooq's Assassination

These elements got their opportunity in the unfortunate and unexpected assassination of Moulvi Farooq–a tragedy in which they had themselves played, albeit unwittingly, no small part by initiating the so-called political process prematurely and creating an impression amongst pro-Pakistani terrorist groups like Hizbul Mujahideen and Hizbulla that the Moulvi was having talks with George Fernandes or his emissary. The noise about my ouster, linking it with this unfortunate incident, was unjustified. It was a part of the disinformation campaign. That is why when, after demitting office, I demanded an inquiry into the whole gambit of Kashmir events by a panel of the Supreme Court Judges, neither the Government nor the noise-makers responded. Truth would have exploded in their face and blown the trumpets of disinformation out of their hands.

On May 21, Robert Gates, special envoy to President Bush, was to arrive at New Delhi for holding discussions on Kashmir with the Prime Minister. A day earlier, he was to be in Islamabad for discussing the same matter with the Pakistan Prime Minister. We apprehended that on May 21 the subversive organisations in Kashmir would create disturbances by organising hartals and demonstrations with a view to securing wide publicity.

In my usual evening-meeting of the "high-level core-group", I gave clear and firm instructions to the chiefs of the police and para-military forces to ensure that, even in face of grave provocation, restraint should be shown, and resort to firing or any other extreme measure should be avoided to the maximum extent feasible.

May 21 was my public hearing day. Call for "civil curfew" notwithstanding, over a hundred persons turned up to meet me with their grievances. While I was busy in public hearing and everything seemed to be peaceful in the city, I got at noon a message from Director, Sher-i-Kashmir Institute, that Moulvi Farooq had been shot, critically wounded and was being operated upon in the Institute where a huge crowd had gathered and banging the hospital doors and even pounding at the operation theatre. Immediately, I tried to get in touch with Director-General Police. He, I was told, was on the way to the Medical Institute. The Additional Director-General, Sabharwal, was reported to have already arrived there and he was being located to speak to me on phone. Within a few minutes, I got another message, intimating that the Moulvi had passed away and the crowd had virtually snatched his body and was proceeding towards the city. After frantic efforts, DIG Azhar Alam could be contacted. He told me that there was firing at Hawal and one person had died. Hardly had I put the receiver down than DIG, CID, A.K. Suri rang me up in response to my message. He told me that the casualties were more and that he was further checking up the position. I was upset. But by that time the worst had happened.

I reproduce below the report which J.N. Saxena, Director-General Police, sent to me about the incident:

> At about 1000 hours on May 21, two visitors came to meet Moulvi Farooq, Chairman, Awami Action Committee, at his residence at Nageen. When these visitors were still with the Moulvi, three youth in the age group of 18-25 reached there and told the Moulvi's chowkidar, Ghulam Qadir Sofi, that they had a prior appointment with the Moulvi. They waited for about 15/20 minutes after which they were allowed to go in. When these youths went in, the earlier two visitors left. At the time, these youths went in, the Secretary of the Moulvi, Syed Rahman Shamas, and another chowkidar, Mohd. Maqbool, were in a separate room. The youth stayed with the Moulvi for about 15/20 minutes whereafter the Moulvi was fired at by 7.65 pistol. The Moulvi sustained injuries in the head, shoulders and the abdomen and was removed in a critical condition to the Sher-i-Kashmir Medical Institute of Sciences at Soura. The Moulvi was operated upon but succumbed to the bullet injuries at 12.20/12.25 p.m.
>
> According to Ghulam Qadir Sofi, the chowkidar, all the youth were Kashmiris and were wearing trousers, shirts and jogging shoes. They were stoutly built, of medium height, and fair complexioned. Sofi caught hold of one of the assailants who was

able to throw the chowkidar and got himself released from his grip. He chased the assailants upto the University gate where they disappeared.

On hearing of the news of the injury and the subsequent death of the Moulvi, his supporters poured out in the streets and scenes of mob frenzy were seen. To keep the situation under control, curfew was imposed at about 12.30 p.m. in the affected localities and order was restored.

A frenzied mob attacked the CRPF picket at Rajouri Kadal and destroyed it at about 1300 hours. A CRPF Commandant and 8 of his men were injured. The CRPF had to open fire resulting in one fatal casualty and injury to another person.

A procession of about 20/25,000 people coming from Soura side and proceeding to Rajouri Kadal was stopped by the CRPF at Hawal, near Islamia College. The processionists pelted stones at the CRPF and some militants opened fire with AK-47 rifles from three sides and attacked the CRPF picket at Hawal. The CRPF had to return the fire and in the cross firing and the stampede, several persons sustained injuries. The tally of fatal injuries is 24. The injured were shifted to the Sher-i-Kashmir Institute and order was restored.

Simultaneously, pro-Pak elements spread rumours in a big way that the assailants were non-Kashmiris and not militants. This was intended to disturb peace and incite communal violence on a large scale. Effective steps were taken to rebut the propaganda and the situation remained under control due to the vigil of the security forces.

A free English translation of the statement of the chowkidar is as under:

My name is Ghulam Qadir Sofi* son of Salam Sofi, resident of Sazgirpora. I am employed in the house of Moulvi Sahib. I was watering the roses with a pipe in the house since the gardener had not come. While Mohd. Maqbool was going out three persons opened gate. Mohd. Maqbool enquired from them their names, purpose of visit. In reply, they stated that they had come the day before and Moulvi Sahib had given an appointment for the said date; they wanted to meet him–with this motive they entered.

*Ghulam Qadir Sofi understands and speaks only Kashmiri.

Maqbool asked me to accompany them but I stated that since I was busy he himself should accompany them. Nevertheless, I went in. They were disclosing their identity to the Secretary after which the Secretary gave me a slip which I took inside. I was asked to wait. After 5 to 10 minutes I went outside. As I came out I heared a 'bang' sound which was followed by repeated shots. I caught hold of the person having the revolver, which was of black colour. He tried to fire at me but I swayed towards my right side. Two persons following him pushed me on one side and ran away. I chased them upto the University gate where I fell down because of giddiness. I was shouting 'Oh God, Moulvi Sahib is dead'.

The Moulvi had repeatedly refused to accept security offered by the State Government and the same is on record.

This report speaks for itself. Where does the Governor come in! A preliminary administrative inquiry by the two I.Gs.–I.G., BSF and I.G., CRP–was also ordered. But immediate task was to avoid further bloodshed and to control the situation which had suddenly and unexpectedly become highly explosive. That this task was successfully performed and burial took place without any incident was not taken note of by anyone.

In connection with the incident, a few specific points also need to be highlighted.

First, I had instructed all the senior officers to ensure that utmost restraint was exercised, as the pro-Pakistani subversive groups were likely to cause trouble on the day of Bates's visit to New Delhi. Secondly, everything happened suddenly and in a couple of hours. No opportunity came my way to assume charge of the situation. Thirdly, the crowd which clashed with the CRP was not really a funeral procession. It snatched the body of the assassinated leader, rather irreverentially. The confusion and violence were engineered, under a pre-conceived design, by the terrorists who infiltrated into the crowd by posing as the Moulvi's followers. Fourthly, both the Director-General of Police, J.N. Saxena, and Additional Director-General, M.N. Sabharwal, had reached the hospital complex. The latter was at the spot when the motley crowd took possession of the body. Unfortunately, he quietly slipped away. Had he gone with the crowd or sent a strong contingent of police under the charge of a senior police officer to move with the crowd, the incident might have been averted, and if firing had to be resorted to by the CRP to return the firing by the terrorists who were in the crowd, the casualties could be kept to the minimum. His conduct, to say the least, was highly irresponsible, particularly in the context of my instructions mentioned above. An officer of his seniority was expected to provide leadership and show initiative on such occasions. Fifthly, it was on record that security had been offered to the Moulvi but he had persistently refused the same. In fact, only a few days earlier, the Moulvi had himself spoken about the turmoil in the Valley and said, "It is a peoples' movement. I am a public man. I do not want anybody's security." About a month before the incident, I had received a report about the likely kidnapping of Qazi Nissar of Anantnag. At that time, I had sent a written note to the Director-General of Police advising him to provide security to him even if he did not want it. The Director-General explained to me his difficulties in the matter. How could the security officials accompany the person to be protected if the latter refused to have them in his vehicle? What stand could the authorities take if the person concerned accused the police of 'spying' on him in the guise of security or thought that provision of security was actually exposing him to graver risk as he would be reckoned as someone who was close to the Government? Sixthly, the assassins, apparently, knew the Moulvi; otherwise his Secretary would not have sent their slip and the Moulvi would not have called them to his room. Seventhly, shooting took place after about ten-fifteen minutes of talk.

All these points were known to the noise-makers. On no point, I could be faulted. But they were not interested in merit or truth of the case. Their sole purpose was to get together, twist facts, concentrate attack on me alone, and beat their drums so loudly that the Government, which was dependent upon so many crutches, lose their nerves and yield. Chandra Shekhar intentionally embarrassed the Government. He criticised me for "having marred the solemnity of the burial ceremony." The slant was deliberate. There was no burial on the day of the incident. The seven facts, stated above, which reflected the true position, were ignored. Imam Abdullah Bukhari mounted his own pressures.

One more wrong impression need to be corrected. In an interview to *India Today*, Mufti Mohammad Sayeed said that he had advised me to take Moulvi Farooq in 'protective custody'. This is not quite correct. Mufti had been occasionally discussing with me the Kashmir situation on telephone. During one of these discussions, he suggested that Moulvi Farooq who had been making provocative speeches could be arrested. I, subsequently, broached the subject with my officers. The general opinion was that it would be inadvisable to do so, as it would amount to opening another front and bringing the Administration in direct conflict with his aggressive followers. Instead, it was thought that Moulvi Farooq should be proceeded against for violation of foreign exchange regulations for which the Government of India had been pressing the State Government for the last three years to prosecute him. I called for the file. I was surprised to find that the State Government had taken no action on the request of the Union Government. I passed the order that prosecution should be launched as advised by the Government of India.

It is also not clear as to what is meant by 'protective custody'. Does the law permit arrest of the person merely because he apprehends harm from others? Moreover, if Mufti knew that there was a grave threat to the life of Moulvi Farooq, he should have strongly advised the Moulvi to accept security from the State Government and also advised the State Government suitably in writing.

Guillotine

In the afternoon of May 24, I was rung up by the Home Secretary, Naresh Chandra, to say that the Home Minister wanted to discuss a few points with me in connection with the debate in the Parliament about Kashmir situation, and for that purpose I could come in the evening to New Delhi by a special plane. I told the Home Secretary that I was too preoccupied, and if the matter to be discussed pertained to the holding of judicial inquiry into the firing incident at Hawal, my concurrence could be recorded. But the Home Secretary said that he did not know what the Home Minister had in mind. I sensed something unusual.

I reached New Delhi in the evening. At the airport, the Resident Commissioner of J&K Government met me. He had no intimation about any meeting with the Home Minister. I felt someone was trying to delay the proposed meeting. I could contact the Home Minister on phone only at about 10 p.m. The meeting was fixed for the following morning at 8 o'clock.

B.G. Deshmukh, Principal Secretary to the Prime Minister, rang up at about midnight. My wife, Uma, picked up the phone. Deshmukh told her that he wanted to call on me. Uma informed him that I was asleep but could be woken up if the matter was urgent. He said he would come early next morning.

As I got up, I saw the *Times of India** which carried the lead story under the caption: "Jagmohan asked to step down". It was the unkindest cut of all. The injury was still more painful by these words in the news story: "In fairness to Jagmohan, it must be said that he had made it clear that he would not like to continue as Governor in the changed circumstances." I had given no such indication to anyone.

The contents of the exclusive story left me in no doubt that it was a calculated leak. The intention, perhaps, was to forestall any second thought on the matter.

I rang up Deshmukh. I told him that he might not take the trouble of calling on me, and that I would myself drop at his residence on my way to the Home Minister's house. When we met, Deshmukh tried to deal with the matter in a rather diplomatic way. "What about accepting President's nomination to Rajya Sabha?" I understood. I told Deshmukh that I had seen the *Times* of *India.* Further discussions became unnecessary.

Why could not such matters be handled by the Government in a more straightforward manner, I wondered. When Rajiv Gandhi's Government, in pursuance of the 'game' which he intended to plan near the Lok Sabha Elections, wanted me to leave the State, he said that I should fight elections from South Delhi as his party's candidate, and when V.P. Singh's Government found it opportune to appease certain interests he showed me the way to the Rajya Sabha. In both cases, political expediency determined the approach. In our current national ethos, a straightforward and honest outlook has become a rarity.

As I proceeded to the Home Minister's house, I was seething with a sense of betrayal. Only the other day, I reflected, the Government was saying that the nation could not forget the services rendered by me in the most difficult and trying circumstances, and now the same Government was dealing with me in such a devious and shabby manner.

The Home Minister was apologetic and said that he was helpless. His words did not register anything on my mind. I dictated to his stenographer a one-line letter of resignation to the President and handed over its copy to him. My mood at that moment was similar to the one in which one would put one's "head on the block" and say: "Here is it; do your worst, heathen."

**Times of India,* May 25, 1990.

I was, undoubtedly, wronged. But that was of little consequence. After all, individuals do sometimes suffer on account of betrayals and unfair decisions. But it was the wayward nature of the Indian State that stood thoroughly exposed. In the process, the appetite of negative, nasty and nihilistic forces in the Indian polity was whetted, thereby creating more serious and formidable problems for the future.

CHAPTER XVI

Prolonging the Agony

Removal of Jagmohan
raised our hopes.
Thanks to V.P. Singh's
decision. For the next
fifteen days, we managed to
reinforce and strengthen
*ourselves.**

—A top terrorist

Festering Stalemate

In regard to Kashmir, India has repeatedly displayed a strange, almost a suicidal, knack of converting successes into festering stalemates. These were the first few words that I recorded in my diary when, within three hours of submission of my resignation, I was airborne again for my return journey to Srinagar.

The special plane was an old Avro. Besides three members of the staff, my wife, Uma, was the only occupant. All along, she had been opposed to my taking up the assignment. She thought that I was taking too much upon myself. But today she did not say: "I told you so". She remained engrossed in her own little world. She symbolised

*This is what Manzoor, a top terrorist of Anantnag said in an interview to the magazine, *India Week* (August 24, 1990). The exact wordings are:

"Here, a change of tack: Did the removal of Jagmohan raise hopes?" Manzoor laughs: "Yes, for the next 15 days, we managed to reinforce and strengthen ourselves. Thanks to V.P. Singh's decision."

some of the finest traditions of Indian womanhood–total attachment and almost an infinite capacity to suffer for the dear and near ones. I persistently advised her to stay in Delhi with our dutiful children–Deepika and her husband Rajiv and Man Mohan and his wife Nutan. But she preferred to spend four agonising months of loneliness, looking at the vacant walls of the Raj Bhavan on the first floor while I practically spent all the time downstairs in my office. It is, perhaps, such values that keep our society going even in troubled times.

The sheer emptiness of the plane's space weighed upon the mind. The inner conflict was equally oppressive. Though I had nodded my consent to being a member of the Rajya Sabha, I was not sure whether I had done the correct thing. Should not I have made my protest more explicit? Should not I have made it clear that, after being stabbed in the back, I could not relish the plate of salad being placed before me?

What depressed me more was the thought that truth had lost and propaganda had won. The observation of John Stuart Mill, "That truth always triumphs over persecution is one of those pleasant falsehoods which men repeat but which all experience refutes", sailed before my eyes. But it is not a part of my nature to get overwhelmed by feelings of despondency or cynicism. I tried to shake off the mood and concentrate on looking at the unending horizon outside, punctuated as it was with the grey, foamy, clouds and almost blinding sun. Alternating shades had a message of their own.

The movement of the plane appeared to be painfully slow. The journey did not seem to end. A member of the crew walked up to my seat and said, "Sir, we cannot proceed to Srinagar. The weather over Banihal has turned bad. Visibility is poor. This plane cannot fly very high. We have to divert to Jammu."

After about half an hour, we landed at Jammu airport. A wireless message had been flashed from the plane to the Divisional Commissioner and other officers concerned. They were at the airport. Their mute expression indicated that they knew what had happened. None broached the subject. Silence spoke more than words could convey.

The officers sought my permission to take me to Raj Bhavan, through a much longer route that skirted the city instead of the usual straight one that passed through it. I was told that the shops and other establishments had been closed, and the people had come to the streets shouting slogans against V.P. Singh and George Fernandes, and saying that they would not let the Governor go.

I was very tired. My wife was almost sick. The slow and stuffy journey had taken its toll. Mental pressures bend even nerves of steel. Fifty minutes of extra drive, I thought, would be another torture. But I was anxious to avoid any embarrassing incident. At the moment, the crowds did not know that I had landed in Jammu. If they saw me passing through the city, they were likely to stop me. They might get worked up and pour their wrath against the Central Government in some violent form or the other. I, therefore, took the longer route. But it had its compensation. Our convoy moved along the Mahamaya city forest, a creation which gave me immense pleasure and solace. Thousands of trees and shrubs were greeting us with the gentle swing of the evening breeze–a cool, brisk, and refreshing breeze which is peculiar to the Tawi river front.

Later, in the evening, Mufti Mohammad Sayeed spoke to me on phone. He said that there was very strong reaction to my resignation in the entire Jammu region. He suggested that I should use my personal influence to pacify the people and tell them that I was going to a position of considerable public importance. Though embittered by betrayal, I told Mufti not to worry. I would use all my resources to maintain peace. At the same time, I apprised him of my firm resolve to demit office the next day.

On the following morning, I went to Vaishno Devi shrine. It was a sentimental journey and in sharp contrast to the depressing experience of the first one. The smiling faces of the pilgrims and their gracious gratefulness expressed through the sudden sparkle in their eyes, was elevating and inspiring. No solid work done, I thought, could be destroyed by all the intrigues and betrayals of the world.

I returned from Vaishno Devi just in time to catch the flight for New Delhi, dispensing with ceremonial functions. These would have been out of place in the sullen environment around. The city was observing a complete *hartal*.

An idea about the reaction in Jammu region could be gathered from the following three press reports of the local daily, the *Kashmir Times*, of May 26, 27 and 28:

May 26

There was widespread condemnation of the Central Government's decision.

A flood of statements of political, social, trade, religious and other organisations deluged the newspaper offices here. All of them were highly critical of the Government decision.

They termed it as a 'reckless decision taken by the government oblivious of the ground realities in J&K, particularly the Valley, where terrorism has paralysed life.'

'Jagmohan was making vigorous attempts to restore normalcy and had neared his goal when an indefatigable soldier in Jagmohan has been pulled back from the front under the pressure of forces hostile to the nation's integrity and unity', the statements said.

These statements highlighted the role of Jagmohan in curbing terrorism reaching to the culprits responsible for the killings of various innocents in the Valley. 'It was a preposterous decision at this moment', it was remarked.

May 27

As major towns of Jammu region overwhelmingly responded to the bandh call given by various organisations to protest against the recall of Governor Jagmohan, police had to open fire and lob teargas shells in one locality in the city.

Shops, business establishments and industries remained closed in almost all the major towns of the six districts of Jammu region. At most of the places, passenger, commuter and private vehicles remained off the road. Particularly affected were the office-goers, which accounted for comparatively low attendance in the offices and other public institutions. Schools, colleges and university remained closed.

Work was also struck down in all the courts in Jammu city and other towns. Lawyers abstained from the work and joined the bandh, saying that the National Front Government had committed a 'blunder' by recalling Jagmohan.

May 28

Major towns of Jammu region observed complete bandh for the second day today on the call given by various organisations to protest against the recall of Jagmohan by the centre.

The report of the other daily, *The Excelsior* of May 29, 1990 said:

Jagmohan's resignation spread like a wildfire in the State and the moment people heard this news, all commercial establishments were closed. The people have called for an indefinite strike to bring back Jagmohan.

Even a senior leader of the National Conference criticised the Union Government. According to the press reports:

> Babu Parmanand, former minister and central executive member of the National Conference, today criticised the removal of Mr. Jagmohan as State Governor saying the step will prove counter productive.
>
> In a statement here today, Babu Parmanand described as 'unfortunate' the decision to recall Jagmohan. The removal has been done on the basis of 'erroneous feedback, misrepresentation of facts, and failure to understand ground realities' by the Central Government, he said.
>
> He asserted that the change of Governor was fraught with dangerous tendencies, the immediate fallout of which, he said, has been a joint statement of 137 State Government officials, who have alleged 'atrocities on Kashmiri Muslims'.
>
> Such an anti-India statement by people with 'pro-Pak leanings' is likely to give a new dimension to the militant and separatist activities, the veteran NC leader said.

As I sat in the plane pondering over the turn of events, I regretted having found myself in a position wherein I had to demit office without touching Srinagar–the city whose inhabitants, only a year or two ago affectionately called me Jagwatar and Sarakvam*. But what purpose would the visit, even if it had materialised, have served in the changed circumstances? The terrorists were happy to see my back. And the commonfolk had been overwhelmed by the propaganda blitz, terror and intimidation. I had no means of convincing them about the real facts. A radio or TV broadcast would have also seemed out of place. I, therefore, decided to repose my trust in future. I scribbled an open letter to the Kashmiris, which, after filling a few gaps of words and phrases, I am reproducing below:

An Open Letter to the Kashmiris

May 26, 1990

Dear Kashmiri brothers and sisters,

I do not know why I feel like writing to you when I am leaving the State. Today, you may not understand my motivation. But one day you would.

*It means one who cleans up things.

You would recall that on the very first day of my arrival for the second term, I advised you* to remember that new routes are discovered only from points at which the caravans lose their way. Unfortunately, even before the new pathway could be charted by me, made safe and shown to you as a way to a happy future, it was submerged by a flood of intentional falsehood.† There were persons at work, who were hell bent to misrepresent the facts and subvert my efforts.

At the oath-taking ceremony itself, I declared that I would function like a surgeon to stitch the bleeding wound and also work as 'nursing orderly' to serve the patient with care and compassion and put him on the way to full recovery. But they made the surgeon look like a butcher and the nursing orderly a heartless sweeper of the blood-splattered floors of a slaughter house.

I appealed to all to remember that one basic principle of all religions was to relieve human pain and to consider service to the needy as service to God. On the day of Id-ul-Fitr, I specially pleaded, 'Let us honour the spirit of this auspicious day and work as saints of service.' They propagated that I was a communalist.

Time and again I warned that we should not ignore the real India–the India of synthesis and assimilation. And yet they called me a Hindu chauvinist.

On the death of a young man, I wrote to his father, Dr. Mohammad Yousaf Khan: "Let no more Shabirs die, and let us create a situation in which no policeman is seen on the streets and they remain full of tourists". They shrieked that I had the outlook of 'Hallaqu' and Hitler.

I dissolved the State Assembly to give everybody a fresh opportunity to secure power through ballot. Instead of acknowledging that this was the fairest and the healthiest initiation of the political process, they went on adumbrating that I was advocating only a law and order approach.

I proceeded in right earnest to analyse the nature and pattern** of terrorism and snap its chains and links, and also eliminate its by-products. They were bent upon hiding the maladies and preventing

---

* See Chapter I: 'My Frozen Turbulence'.

† See also Chapter XV: 'A Deluge of Disinformation and Distortion'.

** See also Chapter X: 'Nature and Pattern of Subversion and Terrorism'.

me from treating these maladies from their roots and dealing with the various infections that had invaded the body.

They knew that I had nothing to do with the searches conducted on January 20 or with the firing on the so-called funeral procession of Moulvi Farooq. Yet they went on with their calculated campaign of spreading lies.

You would, sooner or later, understand the machinations of these persons and regret having fallen prey to them.

You see your own history, both recent and distant. In the recent past, who were the custodians of your political destiny? Were they not your own people? It were they who turned out to be fake guides and inadequate leaders in whom the malady of political degeneration made quick inroads. In their search for uninterrupted power and glory and establishment of personal rule in the guise of democracy, they manipulated your minds and never allowed you to adjust to the reality. As long as they remained at the helm of affairs, accession was final and India was a haven of secularism, but as soon as power slipped out of their hands, they brought out green handkerchiefs from their pockets, with the salt of Pakistani brothers wrapped in between, and India became an imperial power out to destroy the identity of Kashmir. They extended their legs to both boats and kept you in the disturbed water in between. As was bound to happen, you got hurt frequently. But that did not matter much to them. They continued with their power game.

How much service did they render to you and how much to themselves? You know the answer. Most of you have read the 'Red Book'* and the 'Black Book'. Was it not one of the dissatisfied youth amongst you who wrote: 'What to speak of others, it is our own people who are treating us like sheep and plucking our wool mercilessly.'

For all the ills of unemployment and deprivation, they found the Central Government a convenient whipping boy. They misused** Article 370 to misappropriate the resource-base of the State and built a self-serving nest of power. They got more than average share of the Union funds. But they misapplied them. Did you not notice that in 1986, with the same scale of funds, roads were laid, lakes and streams cleaned, cities made beautiful, environment improved and

* See Chapter V: 'Roots: Hidden Veins' (Section: Public Corruption).

**See Chapter VI: 'Roots: Article 370'.

rural development works executed with such speed and effectiveness that the State's rating† in this regard jumped from the 25th position to the tenth? I request you to consider dispassionately who is your real well-wisher and who is not.

You need to learn from your long history as well. Today, some of you are leaning towards Pakistan and inclined to accept its hug. It would turn out to be the bear's hug, I am sure. Remember that in the mid-eighteenth century some of you felt the same way towards Afghanistan and invited Ahmed Shah Abdali. You never had it so bad. Once you place yourself in the fist of Pakistan, you would soon find how strongly it clenches on you. In fifty years or so, your identity would be diluted, if not lost. In the name of Islamic brotherhood, there would be inter-marriages and large-scale settlement in the Valley. The Punjabi-dominated military junta and landed aristocracy which really rule Pakistan would not show any sensitivity or compunctions in this regard. You would find yourself being swept away. But then it would be too late. Even your voices would be stifled.

Remember that the worst form of tyranny is one which is established through the combination of a narrow interpretation of religion and military might. Everything is thrust upon the people in the name of God. That is what the mediaeval monks did. And this is what cliques in Pakistan are doing.

And where is the viability for an independent entity? Hard facts of geography, history, defence and resources are against it. What to speak of any future development expenditure. The government would not be able to pay salaries to about half of its existing staff. Would Pakistan leave you alone? And would not dreams soon turn into nightmares?

You are obsessed with the notion of identity without fully understanding what it really means. Do you realise that, at the moment, your identity is collapsing? The cancerous culture of the Kalashnikov is eating into its vitals. No trace of it would be left, unless remedial measures are taken straightway.

Some of you, with incitement from across the border, are trapping the youth by weaving a myth of immortality or presenting a vision of a grand future. There is no such immortality, no such

† This rating is done by the Planning Commission and the Min. of Programme Implementation, Govt. of India.

future. How can anything good come out of a perverse philosophy of crime? A person is dubbed as a police informer or his style of life is labelled as un-Islamic and he is slaughtered. Who decides the issue? It is the accuser himself. I know of a case of a poor young girl who was shot dead for allegedly leading what was called an un-Islamic way of life. The accuser pronounced the judgement. The poor father was made to say in public that the allegations against her were true. What else could he do, unless he himself wanted to meet the same fate as that of his daughter? How many such crimes would you allow to be committed?

When the current phase of fury and frenzy has boiled over, you would find yourself having been tricked. If you think calmly and in depth, you would understand the parameters of the hoax to which you are being subjected. You would realise that you have been imagining an enemy that does not exist, and you have been made to run towards mirages where 'kafirs' are supposedly hatching conspiracies against you.

The hour of tiredness would arrive. But by that time the self-inflicted torture would have taken its toll. Exhaustion would linger on; it might even debilitate you.

It is not the artificial affinity brought through a narrow interpretation of religion, but an enlightened polity and inspired spirituality that would provide real scope for amelioration and herald an era of true freedom and true progress. The soiled pages of our past history point to the urgent need for a reformed and rejuvenated Kashmir prospering within a reformed and rejuvenated India. If this does not come about, both will sink into third rate existence.

Against the prejudices of time and malignancy of the past, I tried to create a just situation wherein all of you would have got a fair opportunity to evolve new leadership or choose the old one after chastening it, and work for a new pattern of development and a humane and balanced order based upon spiritual secularism–real secularism which derives ethical values from the fundamentals of religion, fundamentals about which Nud Rishi and Lal Ded had spoken in these words: 'There is one God with a hundred names; there is not a single blade of grass which does not worship Him.'

But the times were 'out of joints'. The poisonous darts of a soulless Indian polity repeatedly attacked me. Wounded and bleeding, I am leaving the State. This may be a minor crime of the forces of disruption and distortion. But what is unpardonable is their crime of prolonging the collective agony of the people–the agony which I was confident of ending within a couple of months.

In this letter, I cannot pen all that has happened, is happening, and might happen in future. One day, I would write all about it. You may read and judge the truth.

Wishing you early peace and recovery from the current malady,

Yours sincerely,
Jagmohan

After demitting office from New Delhi, I had separate meetings with the Home Minister and the Prime Minister. Both of them assuaged my hurt feelings, appreciated my services and thought that I could do useful work in Rajya Sabha.

I had a poor opinion about the state of our polity. Even then I was shocked to see the press statement of Prime Minister V.P. Singh, saying that "Jagmohan had resigned on his own". I had done nothing of the sort. Did he have some political compulsions? Or was he trying to soften the resentment of some of his cabinet colleagues and also a sizeable section of the people, particularly the people of Jammu region? Later on, Arun Nehru, Union Commerce Minister said, "Jagmohan did a very good job. Everything that we in the Cabinet do may not be right".* V.P. Singh also performed his characteristic balancing act by dissolving on May 26 the special cell of Kashmir Affairs, under the charge of George Fernandes, and the all-party advisory committee.

About Rajya Sabha membership, I was in two minds. Finally, I decided to go ahead with it. Apart from security, the consideration that weighed with me was that I could fight the battle of truth through its forum. But disappointment in this regard, too, was in store for me. I had not fully realised that the soul, the underlying motivation, of the Indian institutions had gone dry at the source. All were experiencing conditions of drought. The Rajya Sabha was no exception.

Rajya Sabha: Interruptions

On the morning of May 30, I got permission of the Chairman of the Rajya Sabha to make a "special mention" in regard to "intentional disinformation on Kashmir situation", I started thus:

**The Sunday*, June 24-30 (page 24).

I* have to submit that a lot of disinformation is being intentionally spread about Kashmir. I hope this country is not going to be run by planted stories in the press and by disinformation techniques. If you want to know the truth about Kashmir, I would suggest that there should be a panel of Supreme Court Judges who should go into all aspects of the Kashmir situation . . .
(Interruptions).

Perhaps, anticipating what was coming, R.K. Dhawan and some other members of the Congress(I) interrupted me again and again. After a great deal of effort, I resumed my statement:

What I am submitting is that in view of the disinformation that has been going around about Kashmir, a panel of Supreme Court Judges should be appointed to look into all aspects–the background, the circumstances and the facts, and even after I have taken over, whatever things have gone right or wrong, should also be subjected to that enquiry by that Commission. Nothing could be more fair than this. The Moulvi's murder or the subsequent events or the incidents prior to that, all should be looked into by the Commission so that the truth may come out.**

I was interrupted again. The repeated and determined interference did not stop even when the Presiding Officer observed, "You are not even allowing him to complete a sentence." Sensing that even the "House of Elders" had acquired a new culture of interruptions, and the power of the lung mattered more than the power of reason, I gave up the attempt with these words:

I am not going to speak (Interruptions).† You do not want any Member to speak. I withdraw (interruptions).

I strongly protest. They are not hearing me. Therefore, I sit down (interruptions).

On the same day (May 30), S.A. Salaria, National Conference MP, made a "special mention" about the complaint of 137 officials of the State Government to the "World Forum" against the "excesses" of the Security forces. He made all sorts of unsubstantiated observations. No one interrupted him. No one asked him why the officials had

* Rajya Sabha Proceedings, May 30, 1990 (p. 546).
** Rajya Sabha Proceedings, May 30, 1990 (p. 572).
† Rajya Sabha Proceedings, May 30, 1990 (p. 574).

approached an international forum and not the Union Government or the Parliament or any other national institution. No one questioned Salaria's motives, and motives of the officials in playing to the tune of Amanullah Khan who had also issued a similar appeal to the "World Conscience".

What came out of the above events was not only the poor state of health of our parliamentary institutions, not only the exhibition of political permissiveness and double standards, but also a deep-rooted disinclination to face the bitter truth and meet the challenge of grim reality.

In the evening, I held a press conference to communicate my views which I wanted to express in the Rajya Sabha.

Disinformation Continues

The agents of disinformation did not leave me alone even after I demitted office. I will give only one example. On August 3, Dr. Farooq Abdullah made a highly inaccurate observation in an interview to the *Times of India.* I wrote a letter to the editor indicating the correct position. This letter was published in the daily. In view of the irrefutable evidence cited by me in support of my contentions, no reply could be given by Dr. Farooq Abdullah. Instead, Mrs. Jaya Jaitley came into the picture. In her letter to the *Times of India,* she resorted to gross disinformation to injure my public standing. I give below a few excerpts from my reply of September 8 which shows the nature of her allegations and also the extent of her distortion:

> Mrs. Jaitley's letter is nothing but an exercise in slant and slander and a deliberate attempt to hide the truth by causing confusion in the public mind. She is the wife of a senior officer of the State Government. She has, knowingly and intentionally, stated false facts about the revision of my salary. In 1987, the Union Parliament passed a law, raising the pay of the Governors, with effect from April 1, 1986 from ₹ 5,500/- per month to ₹ 11,000/- per month. I got the benefit of this revision of salary like all other Governors in the country. The question of my pressing anyone did not arise. Moreover, for passing any bill in the State Legislature about the Governor's salary, approval of the President of India is necessary. Does she mean that the President was pressurised? Similar revision was done for judges and Chief Justice of J&K High Court. There should be some limit to disinformation. During my second tenure

as Governor, I did not draw any salary. I was quite clear in my mind that I was going to Kashmir not for the second term but for lending a helping hand in resolving a grave national crisis. I thus left a substantial sum to the State Exchequer. And this is the way that I am being repaid. False allegations are being made and that, too, with regard to the decision taken in 1987 for all Governors.

To confuse the issue in regard to the release of 70 hardcore terrorists by Farooq Government,* she has falsely stated that I had released one Irfan Chisti and 25 others. To be doubly sure, I checked up the position today on phone from Director General (Police) and Addl. Director General (Police-CID), J&K. Both have confirmed that no such releases were ordered by me.

Just for the sake of finding fault, she has raked up the issue of extension of Article 249 of the Indian Constitution to J&K. This extension was agreed to by me in 1986 at the request of the Union Government. And there was nothing wrong in doing that. Incidentally, after March 1987, there was Dr. Farooq Abdullah's Ministry in the State. Why did he or Rajiv Gandhi not muster courage to reverse my decision of 1986? The plain fact is that criticism against me was only a false propaganda.

Mrs. Jaitley is also wrong in saying that I have now become a politician. I have not joined any political party even after entering Parliament. I am only propagating the truth.

The modus operandi of the agents of the disinformation campaign was that, whenever I rebutted their baseless allegations with incontestable evidence and they found it difficult to persist with these allegations, they fabricated fresh ones and raised extraneous issues to confuse the public and undermine my image. For instance, in the case cited above, Mrs. Jaya Jaitley coined false allegations in regard to the salary-case, release of Irfan and other terrorists, and Article 249.

This modus operandi was repeated with respect to my open letter to Rajiv Gandhi. For three weeks, there was no response. Thereafter, to confuse the public mind, Dr. Farooq Abdullah was made to reply. He indulged in wild allegations. He did not have even an iota of concrete evidence. The following extract from my reply of May 9, 1991 would serve as example:

Dr. Farooq Abdullah's statement that I did not sleep in the Raj Bhavan but in the Cantonment is sheer concoction. The truth of the

*See Chapter X: 'Nature and Pattern of Subversion and Terrorism'.

matter can be ascertained from the Army Commander, from the Corps Commander and any officer of the Army, Security and Raj Bhavan staff. Would Dr. Farooq Abdullah and his guides in the art of disinformation spell out the house number, place, date or any other specific information about my alleged stay in the Cantonment?

Peculiar Aspect

A peculiar aspect of the situation was that some elements in the Union Government had acquired a vested interest in letting untrue impressions continue, as they had themselves been a party to incorrect allegations. When they came to hold office, they found that documents on government records showed how hollow were their allegations. For instance, I wrote several letters to Subodh Kant Sahai, Minister of State for Home Affairs, and Prime Minister Chandra Shekhar to disclose the findings of the administrative inquiry which the two Inspectors-General had conducted in regard to the incident of firing on the so-called funeral procession of Moulvi Farooq. As the findings did not at all fit into the allegations which Chandra Shekhar had himself been making earlier, my letters were never replied. In this connection, I reproduce below my letter of September 25, 1990, which speaks for itself:

Dear Shri Subodh Kant,

You will kindly recall that during the discussions on Kashmir in the last session of the Parliament, one Janata Dal M.P. had pertinently raised the issue about the firing on the so-called 'funeral procession' of Moulvi Farooq. He had said that there were two versions and the Government should indicate the correct version, particularly when an administrative enquiry into the matter had already been held.

While replying to the debate, you could not reply to the aforesaid question. I shall be grateful if the correct position in this regard is indicated to me and also made known to the public. This would help in curbing the disinformation campaign that is going on in regard to Kashmir.

Yours sincerely,
(Sd.) Jagmohan

Time and again, I requested the Prime Minister as well as the Minister of State for Home Affairs to give a point-by-point version of the Government with regard to the allegations made against the security forces and my Administration in the reports of Human Rights Bodies such as "Kashmir War" and "Kashmir Imprisoned". I also raised the issue in the Rajya Sabha and also in the Home Ministry's Parliamentary Consultative Committee of which I became a member. In one of the Committee's meetings, I illustrated my proposition in regard to intentional falsehood of the reports by citing the example of firing by the Army guards to protect the children in the school bus. The Prime Minister, promised to have a note on the subject prepared. This, again, turned out to be promise which was never fulfilled; perhaps, it was never intended to be. The Prime Minister, when not in office, had himself been basing his allegations on these spurious and motivated reports.* In this connection, I reproduce below my letter of January 31, 1991, the contents of which are self-explanatory:

> Dear Prime Minister,
>
> You will kindly recall that in the last meeting of the Consultative Committee I had suggested that Government should communicate the correct facts in regard to the various incidents of alleged excesses and atrocities committed by Government Agencies. including CRP, BSF and Army in Kashmir which have been mentioned in the Human Rights Bodies' reports, such as 'India-Kashmir War', 'Kashmir Imprisoned', 'PUCL' and 'Citizens for Democracy' and 'Kashmir Bleeding' etc. You had very kindly agreed to have the facts placed before the Consultative Committee. I hope this would be done in the next meeting to be held on February 5.
>
> Yours sincerely,
> (Sd.) Jagmohan

Careless Reporting

Carelessness and ignorant reporting in the press has been another cause of misinformation about Kashmir. Leave alone biased scribes, there are quite a few correspondents who do not know basic facts and yet write with an air of authority. For instance, in a weekly, Ms. Shiraz Sidhva wrote a piece on Kashmir. In this piece, she betrayed her

*See Chapter XIII: 'Frightened Pigeons and Forsaken Community–Kashmiri Pandits'.

ignorance even with regard to elementary matters. She did not know that the State Assembly was not dissolved on the day of my arrival in Kashmir. This happened much later. Nor did she know that the imposition of the Governor's Rule was asked for by my predecessor, and the President's concurrence in this regard was given before my arrival on the scene. And yet Ms. Sidhva had been lent the hospitality of the press columns quite liberally to write about Kashmir and thus spread wrong impressions in the minds of the public.*

An unfortunate tendency has also developed amongst some of the correspondents to rely upon hearsay or interested interviews even in respect of cases where documents and written records to prove the contrary exist. Journalism is supposed to be a 'first draft of history'. With the type of reporting that is taking place in a section of our press, I do not know whether it should be called instead the first attempt to waylay the infant child of history! Most of the commentaries written by political analysts were based upon incorrect facts, careless reporting, interviews of interested parties, and even totally concocted stories.

Damage

After my head had been chopped off by sharp weapons of disinformation and distortion, nothing new, except damage to the morale, could be achieved either by the V.P. Singh or the Chandra Shekhar Governments. On the contrary, the advantages secured by me in asserting the national will in no uncertain way were squandered.

Manzoor, the Anantnag terrorist, made an understatement when he thanked V.P. Singh and said that my removal gave the militants time to regroup and reorganise themselves. It was not only regrouping and reorganisation but also the tremendous psychological boost that mattered. The retreating adversary had been presented with the head of its enemy commander. He could hold it aloft and proclaim to his followers and others around him: "We have got him. Do not lose heart. Victory is going to be ours". The battered groups of terrorists, with their morale rapidly sagging, suddenly got a fresh lease of life. The dying flames were oxygenated. The problem of terrorism which could have been solved within the next couple of months with much less cost, both in men and material, was allowed to linger on.

---

*A few other typical cases of ignorant and superficial reporting have been given in Appendix XIXB.

The public mood that the militants had no chance of success in face of Administration's determination to assert itself, disappeared. The sizeable section of the bureaucracy, which was leaning towards the Administration, beat a hasty retreat. This section, in fact, became over-anxious to ingratiate itself with the militants to escape harm. The 'appeal' of 137 officers to the 'World Forum' was a direct outcome of the new atmosphere that came into being soon after my departure. While officials whose undesirable activities had been kept under check, got emboldened, others who had responded to my administration got panicky and thought it expedient to sign the appeal. They, in fact, demonstrated extra sympathy with the militants' cause to make up for their 'lapse' in cooperating with the administration earlier. Such was the psychological and environmental damage done.

In the atmosphere of uncertainty and low morale, the administration did not show its a firm hand on the very first day. This emboldened other officials who joined the recalcitrant group. The Governor belatedly dismissed five officers and State Government officials went on strike on September 14. After 74 days, the Governor retraced his steps under political pressure of Chandra Shekhar Government. The disastrous consequences of this event hardly need to be spelt out.

Pertinent Questions

More than a year has passed since I left the State. Where is the political process? Had I been the obstacle, as was insinuated, the political process should have started and fructified long ago. The false impression which George Fernandes and others were creating stands thoroughly exposed. The line which they were planting in the mind of the nation did not actually exist on the ground. They knew it. Yet they persisted with it. Their game really was to undermine my image. And in this they succeeded. Today–such unfortunately is the state of our superficial society–no one is asking them where is the political process which Jagmohan was supposed to have been obstructing. Again, why is no one raising the question: If Jagmohan had induced the Kashmiri Pandits to move out of the Valley, how is it that they have not been persuaded to return even after one year has passed since he left the State?

Chandra Shekhar was continuously playing to the tune of political processes and finding fault with me. What did he do when he became the Prime Minister? The ground level conditions gave him no other option but to follow the line that I had adopted. By his earlier tactics, incorrect accusations and in causing my exit, he had even impaired the efficacy of this line.

Current Conditions

And what are the conditions now? It may not be necessary to outline here all the incidents* relating to terrorism and subversion. To drive home my point, however, I would pick up only a few recent events.

On March 31, two Swedish engineers, Jan Ole Loman and Joh Jansson, working for Uri Hydel Project, were kidnapped, when they were travelling on Srinagar-Gulmarg road, by the Muslim Janbaz Force, a militant outfit of the People's League. They remained in captivity for 96 days. The Government could not obtain any clue and had to face considerable embarrassment at the international level and before the Swedish authorities. On the 97th day, taking advantage of relaxed vigil, the two engineers escaped. According to another version, they were let off after an understanding had been arrived at between the Swedish authorities and the militants through some contacts in Pakistan.

On April 11, an attempt was made to kidnap Srinagar Divisional Commissioner, Wajahat Habibullah. In the process, Ghulam Hassan Shawl, Deputy Superintendent of Police, was shot dead.

On June 20, two BSF officials, who fell into the hands of the terrorists at Bandipur, were done to death in the most inhuman manner. Bombs were tied around their waists. One was pushed out of the moving autorickshaw in the downtown area of Nowhatta and the other at Nai Sarak. Seconds after being pushed, the bombs were detonated and the bodies of the two officials blown to pieces.

On June 24, three young Probationary Officers of the Life Insurance Corporation of India were kidnapped and locked in a small rest house. The building was then set on fire, burning two of the officers in the most gruesome manner, bringing to mind the harrowing picture of Auto De Fa. The third officer, though critically injured, escaped.

On June 27, seven Israelis and one Dutch woman, all tourists, were kidnapped from a house-boat by Pasadaran Inqulabi Islam, a terrorist

*These incidents relate to the period upto September, 1991. For the period from September, 1991 to January, 1994, see Chapter XVII.

group linked with Ikhwanul Muslimeen. The woman tourist was released. But the Israelis were tied with ropes and lined up for being shot. In a rare act of courage and presence of mind, they managed to get themselves released from their rope-handcuffs and attacked their would-be executioners with bare hands. They snatched two Kalashnikovs and killed two terrorists, the remaining having fled. One Israeli, Erez Kahana, lost his life and the other took refuge in a nearby house whose inmates handed him over to members of the Jammu and Kashmir Liberation Front. He was later released.

On June 27, K. Doraiswamy, Executive Director of the Indian Oil Corporation, who was on an inspection tour of Srinagar, was kidnapped. After fifty days of the incident, he was still in the captivity of Ikhwanul Muslimeen.

Earlier, in December 1990, 88 years old, Maulana Masoodi, was brutally assassinated. On March 8, Mrs. Nahida Imtiaz, daughter of Saifuddin Soz, M.P., was kidnapped. She was let off only after the kidnappers secured the release of five terrorists, including the dangerous terrorist, Mushtaq Ahmed Khan. On April 9, Mohammad Shaban Bhat, former MLA, was killed. Peer Hissam-uddin Bandey, ex-Minister in Sheikh Abdullah and G.M. Shah ministries, was gunned down at his house on June 4. On June 17, a Station House Officer and his four body-guards were kidnapped.

What do these horrible incidents reveal? Is it not clear that the advantages secured earlier by putting tremendous pressure upon the various terrorist organisations were sacrificed at the altar of political expediency and the abominable campaign of calumny? Crores of rupees have gone down the drain, and valuable lives have been lost. In the first five months of the current year (1991), there were 361 attacks on the security forces, killing 70 jawans. In January, 21 civilians were killed by the terrorists; 29 were killed in February, and 46 in March. The number of terrorist organisations has increased to about two hundred.

What is more pertinent than casualties and the horror of burning, kidnappings and killings, is the negative atmosphere and the general impression that the Government could be bent to agree to anything; as was done through the government servants' strike and by way of release of terrorists involved in heinous crimes. In a number of areas, the militants have regained the capacity to dictate orders to the government departments. There are reports that quite a few terrorist organisations are cornering, directly or indirectly, 33 per cent of the

Government finances and passing virtual orders on behalf of the subordinate officers. Their writ runs in respect of such matters as appointments and promotions in government jobs, admission to professional colleges, and grant of loans etc. They even arrange for mass copying in examinations and securing favourable results from the teachers and examining bodies.

On March 23, 1991, 'Pakistan Day' was celebrated and Pakistani flags hoisted at various places.* No less a person than the Director-General of B.S.F., H.P. Bhatnagar, observed,† "In Kashmir, the militants seem to be getting bolder. They are engaging the security forces in gun battles even in the rural areas where such incidents did not take place in the past."

From June 1990 onwards, even Kashmiri Muslims started migrating to Jammu and New Delhi. About 20,000 Muslim families are believed to have so far moved out of the Valley. *The Hindu*, in its editorial of July 9, 1991, rightly commented, "The absence of definitive policy in relation to Kashmir in the past several months has for sure promoted anarchy in the State."

Far more serious incidents, involving allegations of excesses against the security forces, have also occurred. These include burning of 361 buildings and killing of 17 persons in Handwara on October 1, 1990; burning of 150 houses and killing of 30 persons on October 6/7 in Srinagar downtown area; burning of the entire Iqbal Market in Sopore on October 12; and burning of about 500 houses in Anantnag district in the last week of the month. The allegations in respect of such incidents might be false or highly exaggerated, as they were during my tenure. But there was a crucial difference. While, earlier, the propagandists assailed me personally, in the subsequent phase the attack was directed mainly against the security forces. Further, whereas I was criticised for conferring powers on BSF and CRP under ordinary criminal law–the powers which these forces enjoyed in the rest of the country–extraordinary powers were conferred on the security forces under the Armed Forces (J&K) Special Power Ordinance, 1990 which was promulgated on July 6, 1990.

What do all these facts show? The casualties have gone up. The expenses have mounted. Kidnappings have increased. And the kidnappers dictate terms. The impression that the authorities could be

* *The Times of India*, March 24, 1991.

† The *Indian Express*, June 30, 1991.

bent to agree to anything, including acceptance of defiance by its employees, has generally dawned upon the public. Psychological advantage has passed on to the militants and their writ counts with the officials, particularly at the lower level and the middle level. A substantial portion of the Union funds and the financial help extended to the general public in the shape of subsidy, flows into their hands.

In the prevailing circumstances of Kashmir, the primary obligation of the Government and the political parties is to be practical and earnest. Unfortunately this obligation has been submerged in gimmickry and hypocritical pretensions. By being liberal before establishing authority and dispelling the fog created by disinformation, virtual help has been extended to the subversionists to prolong the agony of Kashmir and its common people. The problem which could have been resolved through a practical and sound approach has unnecessarily been allowed to drag on and become a festering stalemate–a stalemate, the advantage of which, psychologically as well as in practical terms, would rest with the forces of destabilisation, their temporary period of fatigue or respite notwithstanding. Prolongation of the problem would also provide greater opportunity to Pakistan to internationalise the issue.

As indicated in Chapter IV, Sardar Patel once remarked: "If we cannot have confidence in our strength we do not deserve to exist as a nation." To me it is quite clear, we cannot exist as a cohesive nation unless we refuse to live with festering sores, and learn to control fully the steering wheel of history.

CHAPTER XVII

Tyranny of Shallowness

I wish someone had invited President Clinton's attention to what Senator Jackson said when safety of the American citizens was itself under terrorists' threat. Jackson had observed: "The idea that one person's terrorist is another's freedom fighter cannot be sanctioned. Freedom fighters or revolutionaries do not blow up buses containing non-combatants; terrorist murderers do. Freedom fighters do not assassinate innocent businessmen or hijack and hold hostage innocent men, women and children; terrorists murders do. It is a disgrace that democracies should allow the treasured word 'freedom' to be associated with acts of terrorists.

–From the author's reply given at a function in Bombay on January 11, 1994, to a question about President Clinton's letter to Ghulam Nabi Fai, of Kashmiri-American Council.

Talking to John Gunter, Churchill once described Soviet policy as "a mystery in a mystery in a mystery". With a little turn of phrase, the Government approach towards Kashmir could be labelled as "a confusion in a confusion in a confusion".

–From the author's newspaper article on Hazratbal Imbroglio (Oct-Nov, 1993).

They drink sea-water
and cry–
Lemonade.

–From a Czechoslovakian poem.

Inner Malignancy

From my intense ground-level experience of about six years and earnest reflections on the general health of the Indian polity, I had come to the firm conclusion that the current turbulence in Kashmir had been caused as much by the negative forces in the Indian political, social and moral order, as by the individuals who were the products, and in some ways, also the creators, of these forces. It was the inner malignancy of the overall eco-system that had brought into being the petty politics of disruption, even in the gravest of the emergency, caused the whirlpools of confusion and contradictions, set in motion the deluge of disinformation and distortion, bled the country white of its resources and prolonged the collective agony of the people.

I had, therefore, soon after demitting office, set myself the task of making the nation fully aware of the aforesaid malignancy and urge the national leadership to tackle it with a sense of mission. The struggle that I had waged in performing this task and the menacing forces that I had encountered in the process have been delineated in the pages that follow. Whether, and to what extent, I succeeded or failed in my venture, is not for me to judge. My effort to lay bare the truth, in all its manifestations, has been a reward in itself.

Deepening of Tyranny of Shallowness

In my very first interaction, at the India International Centre, with a group of intellectuals, after publication of the first edition of this book, a young student asked me to reply in one line to his question: What went wrong in Kashmir? I said, "Truth went astray, rather it was waylaid."

The stark and grim realities, as they exist on the ground, have to be fully recognised and tackled by a pure, positive and practical frame of mind; otherwise, truth would continue to hit us in the face and leave us with a bloody nose. As Emile Zola puts it bluntly, "While truth is buried underground, it grows, it chokes, it gathers such an explosive force that one day it bursts out, it blows everything up with it."

The events from June 1990 to February 1994, with which this chapter largely deals, underscore once again that we cannot look ahead with hope unless the country learns from its past errors and develops inner and outer strength to shake off the 'tyranny of shallowness'. Unfortunately, this 'tyranny' has not merely continued, it has deepened and assumed a more serious form. This would be clear from the documented facts and data set out hereinafter.

I reproduce below my Parliament Question No. 1094 and the reply given in writing by the Minister of State for Home Affairs on March 3, 1993:

> Q. (a) How many times, during the period from January 1, 1992 to January 31, 1993, the security forces in J&K were attacked by the militants/terrorists?
>
> Q. (b) How many casualties were suffered by the security forces in these attacks and how many attackers were killed or injured in these attacks?
>
> A. (a) & (b) There were 3,647 attacks by the militants on the Security Forces from 1.1.1992 to 31.3.1993 in which 185 personnel of the Security Forces were killed. During the same period, 805 militants/attackers were killed and 93 injured."

In another reply, given to my question (No. 742), on December 8, 1993, the Home Minister said that during the period from January 1 to October 31, 1993, the militants attacked the security forces on 2,103 occasions, killing 176 members of these forces. According to the figures given by the State Government to the UNI, the year 1993 saw 2,240 attacks on the security forces.

The above figures speak for themselves and show the increasing frequency and ferocity of the terrorists' activities. A telling example of this phenomenon was the attack on January 11, 1994 on the radar station, serving Avantipur Air Force base, in which 9 officials of the Defence Service Corps were killed and four seriously injured. The deadly incident of Ashudhar, Doda, in which the BSF lost 15 personnel is another example of the same phenomenon.

In 1992, there were 4,971 cases* of terrorism-related violence, giving an average of 14 incidents a day. 183 persons were kidnapped, including 43 civil officials, 30 members of the security forces and 26 political workers. 2,312 private houses, 200 shops, 65 government buildings, 57 educational institutions and 28 bridges were burnt. 1,909 people were killed as compared to 1,393 in 1991 and 1,177 in 1990, showing a rising graph of violence. To bring home the nature of this violence, a few revealing incidents of 1992 may be briefly narrated and analysed here.

*The figures quoted here are according to official records.

In the middle of March, a friend, agitated and furious, thrust in my hand a *Newstrack* cassette. "See, to what a low level we have sunk as a nation. See, how a self-proclaimed killer describes, with obvious relish, the murder of an innocent vice-chancellor, and nothing happens to our government and spineless people." A few moments later, I saw and heard on the screen Javed Shalla* saying with a heartless voice: "We asked the hostages like H.L. Khera to walk, and then we shot them in the back. They were dealt with for serving the Centre. We are able to bend the authorities. You know the extent to which we did so in the case of Doraiswamy."

On January 24, 1992, there was a powerful bomb explosion in the Srinagar office of the Director-General of Police itself. In this incident, besides the Director-General, J.N. Saxena, four top police officers– Additional Director-General, Ashok Patel, the Inspector-General, CRP, N.K. Singh, the Inspector-General, Kashmir Range, V. Aivelli, and the Deputy Inspector-General, Kashmir Range, R. Bakshi, were seriously injured. I saw these officers at the All India Institute of Medical Sciences soon after they were flown to Delhi. It was a painful sight. Their extensive injuries and heavily-bandaged bodies clearly showed that it was one of those cases wherein survival could be attributed only to the grace of God. The orderly, Head Constable Mohammad Amin, was not so lucky. He died on the spot. The incident brought home dramatically the depth of internal subversion about which I had been crying hoarse from the very commencement of my second term as Governor.

On January 21, Hafiz Ullah Dar, Deputy Inspector-General, Security, was kidnapped. For about three months, no one knew where he was. Earlier, on September 28, 1991, Puran Anand, Deputy Superintendent of Police, was kidnapped from the premises of Kashmir Armed Police, Srinagar, and was kept as hostage for a long time. Tassaduq Deva, the brother-in-law of Ghulam Nabi Azad, Union Minister, and M.S. Khan, brother of Hamid Ullah Khan, Advisor to the Governor, were kidnapped on September 22 and November 7 respectively. They were released after long captivity, on January 17, 1992, in exchange of three detenus. In the month of March 1992 alone, there were 30 cases of kidnapping. As the

*Javed Shalla was arrested on the charge of murdering Mushir-ul-Haq and Khera under a drive launched by us. He was one of the persons released in exchange of K. Doraiswamy, Executive Director, Indian Oil Corporation.

Times of India reported on April 8, "Taking hostage has become a favourite ploy of the militants."

On February 4, there was a serious bomb blast in Srinagar Television Centre. In the preceding fortnight, there were 1,300 grenade attacks on the security forces by the terrorists. On February 21, Madina Tul Uloom Library, attached to the Hazarat Bal Shrine, containing valuable books, was burnt down in circumstances that have not become clear so far. On February 28, a powerful blast in a bus, near Wampo, killed three persons, including the Assistant Sub-Inspector of Police, Dewan Singh. On April 1, the following news item appeared in the national dailies:

> Militants barged into the house of Sohan Lal and killed him. They also killed his wife and daughter. In their dying declarations, the women said that they were raped and then shot.

Terrorism increased both in scale and intensity in 1993. The year began with a macabre incident* at Sopore in which at least 50 persons were killed and the entire central market gutted.

In this year, the casualties mounted to 2,560, registering an increase of about 600 over the figure of 1992. 745 innocent persons were killed by dubbing them as informers. The Valley saw 120 hartals–one every third day of the year (1993). In Doda district of Jammu, too, terrorists made deep inroads. There were 425 serious incidents in which 200 persons were killed, including 21 personnel of the security forces.

The scale of militants' activities could be seen from the number and nature of the weapons recovered. During 1993, the recovery included 5,000 grenades, 2,170 AK rifles 69C pistols-revolvers, 35 rocket-launchers, 2,940 Kgs. of explosives and 300,000 rounds of ammunition.

A few cases which provide a true picture of the conditions that had been prevailing throughout the year 1993 may be dealt with here. (Some more cases of 1993 and January 1994 have been dealt with in the subsequent sections of this Chapter.

Dr. A.A. Guru** was murdered on April 1. He was kidnapped a day earlier. At his funeral, there was firing which resulted in the death of his brother-in-law, Ashiq. At the time of his death, Dr. A.A. Guru

---

* A judicial inquiry has been ordered into this incident. But so far there has been no indication of Sopore's public cooperating with the Inquiry Commission.

**See Chapter X on the NATURE AND PATTERN OF SUBVERSION AND TERRORISM.

was a member of the 'supreme revolutionary command council of JKLF'. His propensity to incite terrorism shows that those who play with fire are ultimately consumed by it. Of late, the pro-Pakistan outfits like Hizbul-Mujahideen had started suspecting him about his links with those who had started talking, albeit prematurely, about a political process. They promptly removed him from the scene, as they had done earlier in the case of Moulvi Farooq and Mir Mustafa. The subsequent (December 31, 1993) kidnapping and killing of Dr. A.A. Wani, Head of the Law Faculty, of the Kashmir University, also fall in the same category.

On April 9, a contingent of BSF which was in occupation of Sanatan Dharam Sabha building in Lal Chowk, moved out. The following morning, a crowd, led by a few militants, sprinkled oil on the building with impunity and set it on fire. Soon the centre of Lal Chowk turned into an inferno, consuming 260 shops and 50 houses. When the para-military forces rushed to the site, there was a prolonged exchange of firing. According to the *Hindustan Times* report of April 12, "10,000 gun shots were fired in this area in less than four hours." In this and other terrorism-related violence in the Valley, 124 persons were killed in three days–36 on April 9, 50 on April 10 and 38 on April 11.

On April 14, Captain V.H. Sahay and three jawans of the Indian Army were killed in an ambush near Sopore. Eleven others died on the same day. The Deputy Commissioner's office at Anantnag was also set ablaze by a rocket attack. Earlier, on April 8, an Assistant Commandant of BSF and three of his officials were done to death. An HE-36 grenade exploded in the police headquarters on April 21, when A.K. Suri, Inspector-General Police, and other senior officers were present in the headquarters. Luckily, the officers escaped. A CRP jawan on duty died.

The same day (April 21), on the basis of disclosures made by an arrested militant, the Army cordoned off the Hazarat Bal mosque complex, where a number of terrorists were hiding. It was a golden opportunity to inflict a grievous blow on terrorism in the Valley. The arrest of a number of terrorists at one go would have considerably weakened their groups. But, curiously enough, the Army was withdrawn after a few hours, thereby enabling the dreaded terrorists to escape. The orders for withdrawal, it is gathered, came from above.

On April 23-25, 1993, news about the police revolt in Srinagar poured in. All the national dailies reported that the policemen have virtually mutinied. K. Rajendra Kumar, Senior Superintendent of Police, in the police control room, was detained and there was an exchange of firing between the personnel of Kashmir armed police and para-military forces. The following day, the policemen took out a procession from police headquarters to the U.N. Observer's office. They marched in uniform and carried their weapons and vehicles. To stop the procession from proceeding beyond a point, a barricade of empty trucks was set up. But it was meekly lifted when the processionists 'cocked' up their rifles. At the U.N. Observer's office, demonstration was held for about an hour. Senior police officers like M.N. Sabharwal* had no clue how to handle the situation which their dithering had caused.

The ostensible cause for this unprecedented act of indiscipline was the death of a constable of Kashmir armed police, Riaz Ahmed, in the Army's custody. But the real cause is embedded in the infection of internal subversion. The authorities' version is that the constable, who was on leave, died in the cross firing between the militants and security forces. They have also ordered an inquiry into the matter. But this has not satisfied the policemen. Next day, they gathered in still greater strength–10,000 according to the report of the *Times of India.* Some of them guarded the police armouries to ward off any action by the para-military forces. In support of the policemen, a general strike was observed throughout the Valley. The government servants also abstained from work. The policemen violated the prohibitory orders and took out a procession again. This is what the *Tribune* of April 25 says: "Demonstrations by armed policemen continued in Srinagar on the third consecutive day today with the State government still undecided. . . . All police stations and other establishments have been

---

*Sabharwal is the same officer who had quietly slipped away from Soura Medical Institute when the crowd virtually snatched Moulvi Farooq's body from the operation table and moved towards the city and clashed with CRP pickets which resulted in the tragedy of May 21, 1990. The true facts are reiterated in my recent letter of March 23, 1993 to the *Times of India* which, *inter alia*, states: "The documented facts–the Home Minister's statement made in Parliament, wireless messages recorded on the police network, the inquiry report of the two Inspectors-General of Police, CBI's investigations, etc.-clearly unfold the sequence of events. . . . All these points were known to my detractors who, in pursuit of their narrow ends, were hell bent in seeing me out of the State. Chandra Shekhar intentionally embarrassed the government. He criticised me for "having marred the solemnity of the burial ceremony". The slant was deliberate. There was no burial on the day of the incident. The 'disinformers' finally won."

virtually deserted by the agitating policemen. Most of the middle-rung police officers were forced to remain inside their homes for neither their escorts nor their subordinates would listen to them. . . . Agitating policemen manhandled certain senior police officers on Friday and snatched away weapons from one of their bodyguards. . . . "We will never be able to work with our subordinates after this armed mutiny", remarked most of the non-Kashmiri police officers. They allege things were allowed to drift by the police brass for inexplicable reasons on the first day of the agitation". . . . Ultimately, an effective action had to be taken by the army to disarm the policemen.

Price of Evading Truth

The data and the few typical cases that I have cited above raise some basic questions. Why has the scale and intensity of terrorism increased? Why is there irritation amongst the security forces? Why do incidents like those of Lal Chowk and Sopore take place? Why have policemen virtually mutinied? How could powerful bombs explode in police headquarters and DG's office, and how could D.I.G. (Security) himself be kidnapped?

The answer to these and allied questions is that truth has never been, and is still not being, faced in Kashmir. The truth is that there is large-scale subversion from within. The truth is that no one is trying to rebuild the collapsed structure of civil administration. The truth is that small minds are holding the stage when constructive, courageous and committed leadership is needed. The truth is that some senior officers are indulging in gross indiscipline and getting away with it. Some of them made representations about the alleged atrocities not to their own government, their own Parliament, or their own courts, but to the 'World Forum'. And they are still enjoying cosy jobs, drawing huge salaries, and, to cap it all, feeding foreign journalists and 'human rights activists' with slanted, and sometimes totally fabricated, stories. Should it, therefore, surprise anyone that Kashmir's policemen are behaving in the manner they do today?

What is happening now is the inevitable consequence of not facing the truth, and encouraging quacks and quislings to have a field day. It has been said: "Those who make revolutions by halves dig their own graves." The same is, perhaps, true of those who are inconsistent and irresolute in their approach and refuse to call a spade a spade. The pity is that such people are not only digging their own graves but also of united India. Their myopic vision is crippling the nation and imperilling its future.

Internal Subversion

From the very commencement of my second term, I had pleaded for recognising the harsh realities and for adopting a clear, consistent and firm line of action to tackle them. *First and foremost*, I had pointed my finger to the serious problem of internal subversion as it existed on the ground. I had started taking action to weed out subversive elements from the services, particularly the police and jail. Only the worst cases such as those involving border-crossing and facilitating escape of terrorists from jail, were taken up. A little over hundred officials were dismissed.* This had a deterrent effect. Attendance in offices improved dramatically.

Realisation soon dawned that price would have to be paid for acts of disloyalty and indiscipline. To let the realisation disappear like mist in thin air after I left the stage was an act of grave miscalculation and short-sightedness. Emboldened by my departure from the scene, a couple of subversives from the top rung of administration persuaded 137 officials to make a representation to the UN World Forum about alleged atrocities in Kashmir. This representation was practically on the same lines as Amanullah Khan's appeal to the "world conscience". It gave no specific details of any of the so-called 'atrocities'. Nor did it speak of the horrible crimes that were being committed by the terrorists. The government's reaction to this and similar other acts of gross indiscipline and unpatriotic behaviour was unbelievably confusing and cowardly.

When there was a 74-day strike of a section of government officials, the Union government and Governor Girish Saxena, under the pressure of quacks and hand wringers, yielded to the most unreasonable demands and, thus, gave further impetus to the forces of indiscipline and disloyalty.** It became a normal practice with most of the government officials and officers of public undertakings to absent themselves from duty whenever any call for hartal or 'bandh' was given by Hizbul Mujahideen, JKLF or any such outfits.

Now new recruitments to subordinate services are being made virtually on the dictates of the militants. The lists of their proteges are

* For details, see Chapter XIV: ACQUIRING AN UPPER HAND.

**See Chapter XVI: PROLONGING THE AGONY.

prepared by them and handed over to the recruiting officers for formal selections and appointments. Likewise, contracts for public works are awarded, mostly on work-charge basis, to the supporters of the militants and amounts collected without doing any real work. Thus, not only is infiltration in services regularly taking place, but funds are also freely flowing to the subversives. And this is providing sharper teeth and longer staying power to militancy in Kashmir.

Political Process

Secondly, with regard to the so-called political process, I had emphasised that premature moves in this direction would cause more harm than good. I was painted as a believer only in the 'law and order' approach. But cheap antics of posing as a progressive could not and did not pay. The tragic incidents, like the murders of Mirwaiz Moulvi Farooq and Mir Mustafa, could have been prevented if the militants had not gathered the impression from the political gimmickry of a central minister that those leaders were in touch with him. Recent murders of Dr. A.A. Guru and two close relations of Ghulam Rasool Kar were fall-outs of similar gimmickry. To simulate progressive posture to attain personal political ambitions, thereby exposing certain individuals to the risk of death, is an act of callousness, if not a crime, of its own kind. It also damages the cause of the political process, the chances for revival of which recede further.

Subsequent inability to make my headway in regard to 'the political process' by any of three governments–V.P. Singh's, Chandra Shekhar's and Narasimha Rao's–has shown, if any proof was needed, how hollow and totally irresponsible was the claim about such a process. An essential prerequisite is the establishment of authority on the ground. In fact, a grave mistake was committed in November 1989 by holding Lok Sabha elections without realising that Dr. Farooq Abdullah had absolutely no hold over the administration and all the components of power structure had been practically taken over by subversives. When this stark reality came dramatically to the surface, militancy received a tremendous psychological boost in the Valley and the morale of the activists rocketed sky-high and fence-sitters went over to what they believed was the winning side. All moves towards 'liberalisation', without first establishing control at the field level, are bound to misfire. For instance, as soon as the news about the appointment of Sheikh Ghulam Rasool, a Kashmiri officer of the State I.A.S. cadre, was published, his son was kidnapped. Likewise the release of five leaders* of the erstwhile Muslim United Front proved pointless. Immediately after their release, they jointly issued a statement in which they ruled out any settlement within the Indian Constitution. They asked for the U.N. intervention and the right of self-determination.

Human Rights Bodies

Thirdly, I protested against the deception and distortion** of the so-called human rights bodies like People's Union of Civil Liberties. I was not listened to; rather I was run down by the members of the ruling party who cited false and motivated reports of these bodies in the Parliament. Now, Prime Minister P.V. Narasimha Rao and Home Minister S.B. Chavan, are saying, almost verbatim, what I used to say in March-April 1990. Recently, the former spoke of the "stunning silence"*** of the human rights bodies about the atrocities committed by the terrorists, and the latter condemned them, in the Rajya Sabha****, as anti-national.

It is sad to note how members of the present ruling party used the highly tendentious reports of these 'bodies' to serve their narrow ends at the cost of national interest. The diametrically opposite† stands taken then and now also show the extent to which hypocrisy and cynicism have seeped into the body-politic of the country.

Fourthly, I had warned against the confusing and contradictory signals that were being sent by different authorities in the Central Government. The situation in this regard, too, had not materially changed. The Union Home Minister S.B. Chavan spoke about Rajesh Pilot, who was then Minister of State for Communications, thus:

> In spite of the fact that he should not go there, he has been going. It is a sensitive area. He should not say or do anything which runs

* These leaders are Syed Ali Shah Geelani of Jamaat-e-Islami, Abdul Gani Lone of People's Conference, Qazi Nissar Ahmed of Umat-i-Islami, Prof. Abdul Gani Bhat of Muslim Conference, and Moulvi Abbas Ansari of Itihadul Muslimeen.

** See Chapter XIII.

*** In the speech at National Integration Council, held on December 31, 1991.

**** Rajya Sabha proceedings, February 27, 1992.

† Also refer to attitude towards Dr. Farooq Abdullah (Chapter IV).

contrary to my view. His action is very undesirable. Still he is persisting.

Strangely enough, instead of straightening the position, Prime Minister Narasimha Rao had virtually institutionalised the confusion by appointing Rajesh Pilot as Minister of State for Home Affairs in the Cabinet reshuffle of January 18, 1993. For 18 days, the Ministry was in disarray. Even the distribution of work between the two Ministers of State could not be decided. One of the sufferers of this policy of drift and inertia was the Union Home Secretary Dr. Madhav Godbole, who resigned in disgust. The entire matter has become a symbol not only of government's inconsistency with regard to Kashmir but also of its disregard for the basic principles of good governance.

Web of Lies

Finally, I had protested against the web of lies that was so craftily woven by vested political interests to undermine my image amongst the Kashmiri Muslims–the image that had emerged during my first five-year term, particularly during the Governor's Rule (1986). After the publication of the first edition of this book and the documentation contained therein, truth began to dawn on the public. With facts now becoming still more clear, the pure gold of my truth shines like the one that has been through a heated furnace. But the damage done to the national cause in Kashmir cannot be undone.

Take, for instance, the case of the Bombay weekly, *Current*, the particulars of which are given in my letter* to Rajiv Gandhi and which has since been decided through court proceedings. Both the correspondent and the editor have tendered unconditional and unqualified apologies. This is what Soumitra Bose, correspondent, who wrote the front-page story of my being anti-Muslim, submitted:

> I hereby tender my unconditional and unqualified apology for having wrongly written in my report, which was published in the weekly issue of May 26–June 1, 1990 of 'Current' to the effect that you talked to 'Current' at Raj Bhavan in Srinagar and stated, inter-alia, "Every Muslim in Kashmir is a militant today. All of them are for secession from India. I am scuttling Srinagar Doordarshan's programmes because everyone there is a militant", although, in fact, you had not talked to Current/me at Raj Bhavan in Srinagar

*See Chapter XV.

> and you had not uttered/stated the aforesaid words or any other words to that effect.
>
> I repeat that I am extremely sorry for having done so. Kindly accept my this unconditional and unqualified apology for the same.

And this is what Ayub Syed, editor, printer, publisher, of the *Current* stated:

> I have made enquiries in the matter and have found that you had not stated, "Every Muslim in Kashmir is a militant today. All of them are for secession from India. I am scuttling Srinagar Doordarshan's programmes because everyone there is a militant", or any other words to the said effect. I have fully satisfied myself that the aforesaid words, as printed and published in the weekly issue of May 26-June 1, 1990 of *Current* on its front page, have been falsely attributed to you by Shri Soumitra Bose, who at that time was the Special Correspondent of *Current.* . . . I express my sincere regrets to you for printing and publishing the aforesaid words, which have been found by me to have been falsely attributed to you, in the said weekly issue of *Current.* I shall print and publish on the front page of the next following weekly issue of *Current* my sincere regrets for having printed and published the aforesaid words in the said weekly issue of May 26-June 1, 1990 of *Current,* as the same have been found by me to have been falsely attributed to you by Shri Soumitra Bose. I trust that this would satisfy you that there was no malafide intention on my part in this matter and that I had acted bonafide at that time, and also that it is only Shri Soumitra Bose who is to be blamed in this matter.

After the aforesaid statements have been put on the records of the Delhi High Court and after my costs for filing the 20 lakhs damages suit have been met by the Weekly, my position stands totally vindicated and the network of conspiratorial lies thoroughly exposed. But larger and more fundamental questions still remain. What about the Rajya Sabha proceedings of May 25, 1990, which created a wrong impression to be spread throughout the country? What about late Rajiv Gandhi's letter to the President of India–the letter which was based upon the concocted story of the *Current* and which was released to the press before it found place on the President's table? And, to cap it all, what about the nexus that was built amongst the vested interests to destroy my standing and thus undermine the national efforts to overcome the unprecedented crisis in Kashmir?

A social and political order, which gives precedence to petty interests over fundamental issues of national integrity and which butchers truth so cynically, cannot escape terror and turmoil which it is experiencing today.

Disinformation Abroad

During my lecture tour of the United States in May-June, 1992, I saw the most ugly aspects of disinformation to which India was being subjected abroad. The Pakistani propaganda machinery was operating in top gear and exploiting to the hilt false stories, written by Indian journalists, like the one of the *Current* described above. Some Congressmen, Senators and other opinion makers were naturally influenced by this propaganda, particularly because there was very little attempt by the Indian side to explain that these stories written by the Indians and quoted by the Pakistanis were fabricated or highly tendentious. It was painful to note that quite a few Indians, posing as 'progressives' and 'humanists', smeared the face of the country with the dirt and mud of their own mind. A senior officer of the J&K cadre who had special contacts abroad was particularly active in spreading false impressions amongst the foreigners.

I made special efforts to retrieve the situation. The following extracts from a press interview which I gave, in question-answer form, to a local daily* would best indicate what I did:

Q. What places did you visit and what subject did you speak on?

A. Besides attending an international symposium on terrorism in Kashmir, I visited New York, Boston, Los Angeles, Houston, Chicago and Detroit. I spoke mainly on Kashmir in the context of its history and contemporary developments. At a few places, I addressed the Indian community exclusively and dealt with what I consider to be a fundamental issue: the need for imparting a creative impulse and reformative thrust to the Indian political, social and cultural scene. I outlined the role which the Indians settled abroad could play in this regard.

Q. The media reports also spoke of your discussions with various groups and officials. Whom did you meet?

A. I called on the senior officials of the State Department, Mrs. Schafer and Mr. James Bishop; advisors to the Senators and Congressmen;

**Daily Excelsior*–July 20, 1992.

members of the editorial boards of *New York Times, Newsweek* and *Washington Post;* and representatives of the Amnesty International.

Q. What was the main motivation of your visit? What objective did you have in view?

A. My primary purpose was to smash the network of lies which Pakistani and pro-Pakistani propaganda machinery had spread and also to undo the damage done by the writings of the so-called human rights bodies and a few Indian journalists whose superficiality is matched only by their inner propensity to look progressive.

Q. How far were you successful in your mission?

A. For me, the fruits lay in making sincere efforts. From the audience reaction, of course, it was apparent that response to my assertions, which were largely based upon documented facts, was extremely warm and encouraging.

Q. Did not Congressman Dan Burton lash at you?

A. Yes, he did. When, after my very first exposition at the Washington Symposium, Pakistani and pro-Pakistani outfits found that their citadel of disinformation and distortion was collapsing under the pressure of concrete evidence, they sought the help of the known India-baiter, Dan Burton. He obliged them by resorting to plain vituperation without showing any respect to actual facts.

Q. How did it affect your tour?

A. His general denunciation carried no conviction. Ironically, he helped my mission. Larger number of people came to hear my subsequent lectures. They realised that truth had upset the elements hostile to India.

Q. You spoke of the damage done by some Indian 'human rights bodies' and a few journalists. How did you undo the damage?

A. By citing contemporaneous records and documented facts. For instance, in regard to their insinuations that the Kashmiri Pandits were induced by me to move out of the Valley, I invited attention to the following pieces of hard evidence:

(a) Much before I went to the State for my second term, a number of eminent leaders of the Pandit community, such as Tikka Lal Taploo, N.K. Ganjoo, P.N. Bhat, etc., were brutally murdered. Terror had struck, and the exodus of Pandits from the Valley had begun.

(b) In a memorandum dated January 16, 1990, submitted to my predecessor, General K.V. Krishna Rao (Retd.), the Kashmiri Pandit Sabha referred to broad-day killings and consequent scare among the minority community. It said, "The pace of exodus has further accelerated now."

(c) Written warnings were administered by terrorist organisations like Hizbul Mujahideen, through publications in *Aftab* and *Alsafa,* asking the Pandits to leave the Valley within 48 hours or face the consequences. (I showed these publications* to the audience.)

(d) For a long time, continuous threats were given in frightening tones through hundreds of loudspeakers fitted on the mosques.

(e) The State Government's Press Note of March 7, 1990, which was duly published in the newspapers, speaks eloquently of the efforts made by me to keep the Kashmiri Pandit community in the Valley. I read out this note.

Q. How did your audience react?

A. When I drew attention to such unassailable facts, the people simply marvelled at the extent to which falsehood could be carried. They noted that India's image abroad had been damaged as much by Pakistani propaganda machinery as by some journalists and 'activists' of the so-called 'human rights bodies'.

Q. Did you speak of 'Kalashnikov for Kalashnikov' approach?

A. No. All that I said was that human ingenuity had yet to evolve a method other than the mechanism of security forces for tackling contemporary terrorism or violence on large scale. I pointed out how the Federal Government in the United States brought in national guards and issued shoot-at-sight orders to check killings and arson in Los Angeles. I also invited attention to the fact that I secured back the reigns of power from the terrorists with minimum of casualties—no 'Tiananmen Square' tragedy, no 'Blue Star', no deaths in police encounters.

Q. What do you think was the overall impact of your visit?

---

*See Appendix XXIV.

A. I trust, I was able to establish the sway of the truth. A strong motivation was also imparted to the Indian community to wage a campaign against Pakistani propaganda machinery on the basis of concrete facts.

Increasing Terrorism

Terrorism has been with us for quite some time. Telangana became 'red hot' soon after independence. In the late sixties, the Naxalites appeared like 'spring thunder' over West Bengal and Bihar, seeking 'power through the barrel of the gun'. At about the same time, in the North-East, insurgency, which had shown its fangs as early as August 1947, started making deeper inroads. Assam, Punjab and Kashmir followed suit, staging the most heinous drama of Indian terrorism. The jungles of Godavari, Terai, Bastar and many other areas have often been ignited by its spark.

Despite experiences, no lessons have been learnt and no comprehensive strategy evolved to prevent or combat terrorism.

While terrorists are not generally pathological lepers or products of narcissistic rage, and they are applauded by their supporters as 'freedom fighters' and 'commandos for justice', the fundamental reality is that terrorism is a bloody and brutal phenomenon which is saturated with criminality and which shows a total disregard for basic human values. No grand design for human freedom, no moral quibbling or relativism can hide the inherent bestiality of a terrorist act.

I had been emphasising that the savage nature of terrorism, as briefly described above, and its pattern in Kashmir, as unfolded in Chapter X, should be fully understood. But the ruling leadership remained as casual as before. Experience the world over demonstrates that while inflexibility may not be feasible or practical in all circumstances, a clear policy-line helps. "If your policy changes from incident to incident, then you have already lost." In India, unfortunately, the government is doing exactly that. It has no real policy. It vacillates between softness and sternness, having in the process the worst of both. It results in nothing but frequent falls between the two stools.

Unfortunately, in Kashmir, India never set its moorings right. It showed a marked tendency to compromise even on basic principles. For instance, most of the culprits apprehended in serious terrorist crimes were dealt with in a manner which produced a negative impact on the situation. Most of the kidnappers of Mufti Mohammad Sayeed's daughter and killers of Vice-Chancellor Mushirul Huq, Assistant Registrar Abdul Ghani, HMT General Manager H.L. Khera, Station Director, Srinagar Doordarshan, Lassa Kaul, and four IAF officers were arrested during my stay, and for their speedy and effective prosecution, a 'designated court' was set up in Jammu.* Unfortunately, after I left, another 'designated court' was allowed at Srinagar, under the pressure of 'political and administrative quacks', by Governor Girish Saxena. This had an adverse psychological impact, and the tempo of prosecution was lost. Three years have now passed, and nothing worthwhile has happened. Half hearted action is worse than no action. It only helps in raising the morale of the adversary. Had the above prosecution cases proceeded, as originally planned, it would have not only proved a deterrent but also enabled the country to show to the world the cruel and crafty hand of Inter Services Intelligence† in organising terrorism and subversion in Kashmir.

The soft underbelly of the Indian State has proved tempting to the ISI and it has spread its tentacles far and wide. The 13 simultaneous bomb blasts in Bombay on March 12, 1993, killing about 300 people and injuring about a thousand, show the depth to which it has penetrated. The police investigations reveal that about 500 AK 47/56/57 rifles and about 15,000 kg. of explosives–6,000 kg. RDX and 9,000 kg. ammonium nitrate–were smuggled into India during the short period from December 3, 1992 to March 12, 1993, and that this quantity could trigger off about 300 Bombay-type explosions. From Thane creek alone, about 2,380 kg. of RDX, was recovered on April 2. Ahmedabad and Surat, too, have experienced a series of bomb blasts. All this shows how a power-structure based on smuggling, land racketeering, bootlegging and corruption has come into being in our metropolitan towns.

According to a document** prepared by a 'task force' of US House of Representatives, titled: "The New Islamist International", about 20,000 Kashmiri youth have been trained and equipped by the ISI.

---

* See Chapter XIV.

† See Chapter X.

** The document was released on January 16, 1994.

The document says: "The mere size of Pakistani training programme is telling. In 'Azad Kashmir' alone, there are 13 permanent, 18 temporary and 8 joint training camps. Islamist indoctrination is provided by Jamaat-i-Islami of Pakistan. . . . Highly trained terrorists of the Jamiat-e-Tulba, then operating in Kashmir, were sent in to establish a countrywide support system. They developed a professional infiltration and exfiltration route for their operatives via Nepal and used that nation as a site for their meetings and consultations with Pakistani and Arab terrorism and subversion experts. While in India, the terrorists relied on support from members of such organisations as the Indian Student Islamic Movement."

Over the years, the ISI has become the most dangerous and powerful intelligence organisation in the Third World. It has an uncanny knack to exploit the forces of fundamentalism and their capacity for 'blind terrorism'. It has also manipulated the huge supply of lethal and light weapons which were sent by US to Pakistan for the Afghan Mujahideens. According to a US Congressional report, about 60 per cent of the sophisticated weapons were diverted by the ISI for its own use. So was the position with regard to funds. In 1987-88 alone, it sliced away about 35 per cent of $ 1.2 billion American aid to the Afghan refugees. Drug money was also laundered for the smuggling* of arms and for recruitment and training of terrorists. It has been estimated** that in 1992 "the landed value of the drugs from Pakistan" was about $ 13 billion which is equal to its defence budget for five years.

The ISI has also been conspiring with drug barons to raise resources for financing terrorist activities. It has been particularly active in the 'unpatrolled, lawless frontier' of 1,400 miles between Afghanistan and Pakistan which has the potential to produce about 800 tons of opium and 80 tons of heroin a year. Here, the drug trafficking and arms smuggling go hand in hand, providing ideal ground for spread of narco-terrorism. The area also provides a safe sanctuary and training ground for Mujahideens operating in Sudan, Egypt, Kashmir and even in the US, as the recent blast (February 16, 1993) in the New York World Trade Centre suggests.

---

* *Times of India*, April 3, 1993, Means of Terrorism, Jasjit Singh.

**India's difficulties are compounded by the fact it has 6,800 kms of coast line to guard.

The US document† quoted above significantly observes: "The ISI programme is based on experience that was acquired while supporting the Afghan Mujahideen. Special attention is paid to the recruiting, training, and organising of young Kashmiries 'on militant lines' to serve as the cadres of the 'long-term intelligence offensive' against India. Even Muslim countries like Egypt, Algeria, Tunisia and Saudi Arabia have complained that Islamic radicals are using Pakistan-Afghanistan border for organising terrorism in these countries and subverting their governments."* *The Times* noted that "the war in Afghanistan had left behind what one described as a virtual band of Islamic mercenaries, highly motivated, militarily hardened and ready to take action almost anywhere in the cause of Islam".

The increasing activity** of the ISI could be seen from the fact that in Kashmir alone, during 1990-92, 455 rocket launchers, 474 machine guns, 8,048 grenades, 7,851 AK series rifles, 1,625 mines, 2,616 pistols/revolvers and 9,04,329 ammunition items were recovered. The rocket attack on the State Secretariat in the highest security zone of Srinagar on May 12, 1993, which killed two employees and caused widespread panic, is another indication of ISI's alarming success in spreading terrorism. In this, it has been helped by India's hesitancy, illogicality and refusal to see the danger inherent in its divisive and vote-bank politics. Pakistan, on the other hand, continues to stoke the fanatics' zeal. For example, Prime Minister Nawaz Sharif said on May 3, 1992, "The victory of Mujahideens in the Afghan Jehad, after fourteen years of struggle, is the success of Islam. It will pave the way for the liberation of Kashmir which will become part of Pakistan. Thanksgiving prayers will be offered by me in the mosque of Srinagar like the one I offered in the mosque in Kabul."***

JKLF March

An event of considerable significance that occurred during the period (June 1990–February 1994) under discussion in this Chapter related to the 'march' of Jammu and Kashmir Liberation Front across the 'line of

† The latest US State Department report, "Patterns of global terrorism, 1995" clearly accuses Pakistan of sponsoring terrorism in Kashmir and refers particularly to the activities of Harkat-ul-Ansar and Al Faran.

* *The Hindustan Times,* March 15, 1993.

** For up-to-date (June, 1996) data, see Appendix XXIX.

*** The *Nation*, Pakistan.

actual control'. In the month of December 1991, the Front announced its plan to cross the line on February 11, 1992, which happened to be the 'Maqbool Butt Day'.* Extensive publicity was given to it. At the initial stage,** the Pakistan government and political parties encouraged the plan and helped in building up an atmosphere hostile to India.

The reaction of the Government of India appeared to be a bit panicky. It called the Ambassadors of the five permanent members of the Security Council, and apprised them of India's concern in the matter.

Later on, the Pakistan government found it expedient not to allow the 'march'. But Amanullah Khan, Chairman of the Front, decided to defy the government. On February 11, when the procession of JKLF, led by Amanullah Khan, was stopped near Chakothi, violent clashes followed. Three or four persons*** were killed. The 'march' was suspended. But subsequently, Amanullah Khan announced that the Front's followers would make another attempt to cross the 'line of actual control' on March 30, 1992.

This development had two important aspects. One pertained to India's reaction to the 'march' and the other to Nawaz Sharif's statement to the BBC on February 18, 1992, that "if Kashmiris were given their right of self-determination, they could decide their own future by either joining India or Pakistan or remaining independent".

Did not India react unwisely to the 'march' on February 11? And would not fall-out of this reaction cause problems for India in the international arena?

There was nothing new in what Amanullah Khan did. As particularised in Chapter X, he had done exactly the same in January-February 1990. A stage-managed strike was organised with the full backing of the Government of Pakistan and political parties, and Amanullah also boasted that he would cross the border with 10,000 'commandos'. Even batches were brought in scores of buses at Suchet

* See Chapter IX.

** Amanullah Khan, later on, ruefully remarked that uptill February 6, Sardar Abdul Qayyum Khan, the 'Prime Minister' of 'Azad Kashmir', supported the 'march', but suddenly changed the stand on February 7.

*** According to the statement of Sardar Mehtab Khan, Minister for Kashmir Affairs, in the National Assembly, on February 13, 1992, only three persons were killed on the 'line of control' but none died of firing. According to another Federal Minister, four persons died.

Garh, Abdullian, Nawapind and Budhwar. But the 'volunteers' beat a hasty retreat as soon as the Indian security forces fired a few shots.

In contrast to the quiet and confident action taken in January-February 1990, this time, highly exaggerated publicity was given to the issue. A simple and straight declaration that no crossing of the 'line of actual control' would be tolerated, and a clear warning to Pakistan, at diplomatic level, would have been sufficient. By calling the Ambassadors of five permanent members of the U.N. Security Council, India made an error of judgement. The British newspaper, *The Independent** commented: "The apparent loss of political nerve by New Delhi has reversed its decade long policy of keeping U.N. out of Kashmir's affairs." Pakistan, on the other hand, acted cleverly. Its spokesman, in an ironical gesture that subserves his country's diplomatic purpose, "accused India of internationalising the Kashmir issue unnecessarily".

While, on the one hand, Nawaz Sharif went to Pakistan-occupied Kashmir and thundered that Pakistan was working to materialise the dreams of the Kashmiri people and would not disappoint them, on the other, he created an impression among the international community that Pakistan was a 'good guy' and was preventing, and not instigating, intrusion in J&K State.

What was equally important was that, in the process, Pakistan did not lose a single chip from the foundational planks of the movement which aims at wresting Kashmir Valley from India by playing upon the issue of Muslim identity. In our country, it has not been fully realised that, so far as the whipping of religious frenzy is concerned, there is little to choose between the hard core of JKLF and pro-Pakistan groups. In an interview to *Sada-i-Huriat*, one of the three mouthpieces of subversive organisations, on February 9, 1990, Hilal Baig, the then chief of J&K Students Liberation Front, made it clear that basic inspiration of JKLF was Islam. He quoted from Amanullah Khan's statement in which he said: "Islam is our soul, our faith. We do not believe in any other ideology. We are dedicated only to the cause of Islamic Republic. We want to bring about 'Nizam-e-Mustafa' in toto." On February 25, 1992, Amanullah himself declared** "While my 'political kalma' is 'Kashmir Banay Ga Khud Mukhtar' (Kashmir would be independent), my 'religious kalma' is Islam."

* *The Independent*, February 8, 1992.

** Amanullah Khan's address to 'Jang Forum'.

The crucial fact is that the pro-independence groups like JKLF and pro-Pakistan-merger outfits like Hizbul Mujahideen have anti-India minds and anti-India motivation. Both rely heavily on terrorism. Both draw sustenance from the forces of Islamic fundamentalism. Both get training, arms and funds from Inter Services Intelligence, nick-named the 'Invisible Soldiers of Islam'. The replacement of Major General Assad Durrani on March 3, by Lieutenant General Javed Nasir, belonging to Tableeghi Jamaat,* as head of the ISI, also showed in which direction the wind was actually blowing.

Unfortunately, when the international community, by and large, was generally expressing the view that the Kashmir issue should be settled on the basis of Shimla Agreement, India, in continuation of its tradition of bungling and blundering, took another false step. Too much publicity was given to JKLF. Its adverse repercussions soon emerged on the scene. For instance, the Parliament of European Community, in its meeting held at Strasbourg, on March 12, 1992, adopted a resolution, calling upon the U.N. Security Council to "re-examine the volatile situation in Kashmir and use its influence with India and Pakistan to resolve the situation". The Parliament also talked about the right of self-determination.

In view of its potential for publicity, 'marches' were organised by other political groups also. For example, the leader of the PoK unit of the Peoples Party of Pakistan and former 'Prime Minister' of PoK, Mumtaz Hussain Rathore, led 'Safr-e-Shahadat' (journey to martyrdom) to Sehri, a village near the 'line of actual control' on April 4, 1993. Rathore, along with his 102 followers, was arrested and the 'march' proved abortive. Earlier, on October 24, 1992, the J&K Democratic Alliance undertook a similar venture.

Third Option

Too much, perhaps, need not be read in Nawaz Sharif's remarks about the 'third option'–option for 'independent Kashmir'.** Nawaz Sharif spoke about this 'option' in Tehran in a BBC interview on

* This Jamaat is an association of missionaries who propagate a rigid interpretation of Islam.

**Maharaja Hari Singh, Sheikh Abdullah and 'Anglo-America bloc' had all, at one stage or the other, flirted with the idea of independent Kashmir. From their very inception, the JKLF and its allied outfits have also been propagating it. (See Chapter II: Survey of History; and Chapter IV: Roots.)

February 18, 1992, but, a day later, at Islamabad airport, he virtually wriggled out of it.

When the Pakistani government realised that, from the point of view of international opinion, it would be advantageous not to allow the JKLF supporters to proceed to the 'line of actual control', it decided to stop the 'march'. At the time of taking this decision, government did not visualize that a serious incident would occur. It was, perhaps, to mollify the enraged feelings of Kashmiris that Nawaz Sharif talked about the 'third option'. Amanullah Khan applauded the statement. But it caused considerable annoyance to Jama'at-e-Islami. That was why the Pakistan government clarified its official position soon thereafter.

On February 22, 1992, Mehtab Khan, Minister for Kashmir Affairs, denied that Islami Jamhuri Ittehad Government was changing its stand on Kashmir. Sardar Sikandar Hayat Khan, 'President' of 'Azad Kashmir', charged that the 'issue of third option' was a conspiracy of those who were opposed to the Nawaz Sharif Government and its programme of Islamisation and nuclearisation. Further, on February 23, Ghulam Ishaq Khan, President of Pakistan, said, "Everybody wants a solution to the Kashmir problem within the framework of U.N. resolution."

In pursuance of the official stand of Pakistan government, effective measures were taken to foil the JKLF's 'march' of March 30. Amanullah Khan was arrested on March 25. Arrests of his supporters followed. Despite tall claims by the JKLF leaders on both the sides of the 'line of actual control', few volunteers turned up. And the 'march' proved a flop. According to Sardar Abdul Qayyum, the 'Prime Minister' of 'Azad Kashmir', the detention of about 130 persons for a couple of days was sufficient to meet the situation.* To demonstrate that JKLF had no solid backing in 'Azad Kashmir', Pakistani flags were hoisted on a large number of buildings on March 30.

Earlier, Qayyum had denounced the 'march' in these words: "It is apparent that JKLF is not independent in its move to cross the 'line of actual control'. Certain elements are endeavouring to destabilise 'Azad Kashmir' and Pakistan to further their vested interests. The aim of such attempts is to fan infighting." Later on, Qayyum sarcastically commented: "Amanullah Khan has qualified himself for a letter of

*Statement to the press on March 31 at Muzaffarabad.

congratulation from the BJP leader, Dr. Murli Manohar Joshi."* Pakistan Minister of State for Foreign Affairs, M.S. Khan Kunju said, "Talk of third option is malafide."

A large section of Pakistani press has also condemned Amanullah Khan for playing what it calls a dangerous role. A fairly representative comment** was: "Those Kashmiris who have been led away by the dubious idea of a 'third option', should realise that without Pakistan's active support and sacrifices, there would have been nothing like Kashmir as it is. Alienation from Pakistan would be suicidal for them. Their separate existence as a truly independent and prosperous entity, is politically, geographically, economically and strategically a fake and wishful idea. After all, why are anti-Islamic outside forces favouring this idea? Why is their media so anxiously supporting it?"

A small section of the press as well as leadership has, however, taken a different line. It has posed the question: "If there is a ban on independence, what is the meaning of the word, self-determination?"

May be, Amanullah Khan is receiving encouragement from some quarters whose geo-political interests might be better served by an independent Kashmir. A few days before his arrest on March 25, he wrote a letter† to U.N. Secretary-General Boutros Boutros-Ghali, suggesting that the United Nations should take over, for five years, the entire State of Jammu & Kashmir, as it existed on August 14, 1947, and then hold a plebiscite, giving all the three options. He claimed that he had the support of 200 U.S. Congressmen, and also of a number of British Members of Parliament. About the same time, the *New York Times* came out with an editorial asking for the U.N. settlement on Kashmir, though the Secretary-General had made it clear that the "U.N. had no role in territorial disputes unless both the claimants want one to be assigned to it."

Some Western politicians and academicians have also been feeding Amanullah Khan's ego. For example, Lord Avebury, Chairman, British Human Rights Group, in his Foreword to Amanullah's autobiography, *Jehad-e-Musalsal*, says: "The international community is listening to the voice of the 12 million people of Kashmir, who are the only legitimate arbiters of their own political destiny. Representatives of the people are turning up at United Nations

* *The Hindustan Times*, February 20, 1992.

** *Frontier Post*, April 4, 1992.

† *News,* March 29, 1992, Lahore.

forums, at meetings of Islamic leaders, and at great rallies and seminars in the capitals of the world. In Kashmir itself, the 'intifada' continues unabated, and now gets some of the moral backing accorded to the Palestinians or South Africans. If the legitimate freedom struggle of the Kashmiris prevails, as it must do one day, Amanullah Khan will be remembered as the leader who articulated their demands, persuaded them to make great sacrifices that gained their freedom, and led them to victory." In U.S., Congressman Dan Burton has been talking in the same vein, using harsher words against India.

It is difficult to say with certainty whether Nawaz Sharif's remark about the 'third option' was a calculated one or a slip of tongue. To me, it appears that he happened to show, albeit inadvertently, Pakistan's last card with regard to Kashmir. Whatever be its repercussions in Pakistan–whether or not separatist movements like 'Jea Sindh' and 'Pakhtoonistan' would get a fillip†–for India, the propagation of the idea of an 'Islamic' republic of Kashmir would be no less harmful than the attempts to secure merger of the Valley in Pakistan. It will also be suicidal for the Kashmiris themselves.*

Fourth Option

Of late, some old proposals are being floated with slight modifications. One of them is what has been called the 'fourth option'–establishment of a "co-confederation between two closely interacting autonomous units". This proposal, in essence, envisages a quasi-independent state on the Indian side of the 'line of actual control', with internal autonomy granted to its three main regions of Kashmir, Jammu and Ladakh, and a similar quasi-independent state on Pakistan's side with internal autonomy available to 'Azad Jammu-Kashmir' and Northern Territories of Gilgit and Baltistan. It also envisages conversion of the 'line of actual control' into a soft international border with a free flow of people and trade.

---

† That is why the new Prime Minister of Pakistan, Ms. Benazir Bhutto, has firmly opposed the demand for "Independent Kashmir". In June 1996, elections in Pakistan-occupied Kashmir, 34 candidates were debarred from contesting as they refused to affirm that the territory was an integral part of Pakistan.

* On June 18, 1990, Amanullah Khan even announced the formation of a provisional government of independent State of J&K comprising the entire area of the princely State. See also my 'Open letter to the Kashmiris', Chapter XVI.

A recent report of the joint American-Russian Study Mission sponsored by the Asia Society and Institute of Oriental Studies, puts forward a slight variation of this 'option' in these words: "There has to be a compromise. The most general form of such a compromise would be the sharing of responsibility by India and Pakistan for the situation in Kashmir, followed by joint control over the state."

The 'option' suffers from a number of infirmities and is clearly impracticable. It assumes that deep rooted animosities, particularly those engendered by the two-nation theory and partition of India in 1947, would vanish. History does not die so easily.

With regard to a similar proposal taken to the President of Pakistan by Sheikh Abdullah in May 1964, with the implicit approval of Jawaharlal Nehru, this is what Ayub Khan has recorded in his political autobiography, *Friends Not Masters*:

> Only those who had neither knowledge nor appreciation of history could think on these lines. India and Pakistan could never work as a confederation even if such an arrangement were to be brought about by force. And the reason is simple: Indian nationalism is based on Hinduism and Pakistan's nationalism is based on Islam. The two philosophies are fundamentally different from each other. Those who talk of confederation ignore the past history and temperament of the people, their whole ideology and philosophy. When Sheikh Abdullah and Mirza Afzal Beg came to Pakistan in 1964, they too had brought the absurd proposal of confederation between India, Pakistan and Kashmir. I told them plainly we should have nothing to do with it. It was curious that whereas we were seeking the salvation of Kashmiris, they had been forced to mention an idea which, if pursued, would lead to our enslavement. It was clear that this was what Mr. Nehru had told them to say to us. I did not blame them because they were obviously acting under the compulsion of circumstances but they left me in no doubt that their future was linked with Pakistan.

These observations reflect a frame of mind which is tightly held by forces of Islamic exclusivity and cannot accommodate principles of 'co-confederation'. Unfortunately, over the years, the frame of mind has acquired a deeper hue of fundamentalism and radiates sharper beams of suspicion and intolerance. If some sort of 'co-confederation' was unthinkable then, it is more so now.

Even if it be assumed, for the sake of argument, that the arrangements of the type envisaged here are brought about under international pressure, how long would they last? How much extra friction would they cause? And would not organisations like Jama'at-e-Islami subvert the loyalties of the people on the Indian side of the soft border and virtually convert it into an Islamic enclave of an Islamic Pakistan?

Practical considerations, too, rule out restricting free movement only to J&K. The visitor from the other side cannot be prevented from moving to other parts of the country. If, for instance, a person living on the Pakistan side of the 'soft border' crosses over to the Valley, he or she can easily move to other States and Union Territories. Free movement between the two parts of erstwhile princely State of J&K would really mean free movement between the two parts of pre-partitioned India. Are India and Pakistan prepared for it?

The idea of autonomy, too, is misplaced. As I have shown in Chapter VI with the help of budgetary figures and plan allocations, the State of J&K cannot even pay salaries to about half of its staff without large-scale financial assistance from the Centre. Nor can it undertake any development work. Presently, its entire plan expenditure and a good part of its non-plan expenditure are met by 90 per cent grants and 10 per cent loans from the Union government. In the budget of 1993-94, Central subventions amount to about ₹ 1200 crore.

The position in this regard is even worse on the Pakistan side which, with the exception of Muzaffarabad proper and plains of Mirpur, comprise one of the poorest portions of the erstwhile princely State of J&K. Its lands are rugged, uneven and unproductive. It is deficient in other resources as well. Without liberal Federal aid, it cannot sustain its current population of about two million. For example, in its budget of about ₹ 250 crore for the year 1987-88, 210 crore had to be provided by the Federal government.

Apart from the hollowness of the autonomy syndrome, votaries of 'fourth option' remain silent or vague about the Northern territories of Gilgit and Baltistan which have immense strategic importance. Gilgit has been described thus: "High above the snow line, somewhere midst the peaks and glaciers that wall in the Gilgit valley, the long and jealously guarded frontiers of India, China, Russia, Afghanistan and Pakistan meet. It is the hub, the crow's-nest, the fulcrum of Asia."

The Northern territories have been virtually annexed by Pakistan. They are administered directly by Islamabad through a commissionerate. The area (5,180 sq. miles) that has been illegally leased out by Pakistan to China as well as an area (37,555 sq. miles) that has been illegally occupied by it present another set of issues that are not touched by the 'fourth option'. Nor does it provide for the resolution of the Siachin conflict.

On the Indian side of 'line of actual control', the State of J&K has functioned for about four decades as an integral part of the Union. Any talk about grant of quasi-independent status, or restoration of pre-1953 position, is bound to create many more problems than it can supposedly solve. It would, apart from causing harm to the welfare and advancement of common Kashmiris and creating a mini-Pakistan with Indian tax-payers' money, pose serious threats to the unity and stability of the country. Any retreat from the existing position would have serious repercussions on Punjab, Assam and other States of the Union.

In Chapter IV, I have drawn attention to the 'spirit of Munich' and shown how disastrous it was for J&K and the rest of the country to let that spirit prevail. Jawaharlal Nehru, with all his insight into history, failed to appreciate that in J&K neither patch-work nor appeasement could yield any worthwhile result. Such an approach could cause only deeper ruptures and more intense pain and anguish in the years to come. Should not any lesson be learnt from the bitter experience of the past?

The notion of internal autonomy for the regions is fraught with equally serious consequences. As pointed out in Chapter VI, there would be too many claimants for separate identities and the claims and counter-claims would divert the limited talent and energy of the people into fruitless channels. New grievances would be dished out and existing ones exaggerated. Given the populist disposition of local political leaders, they would attempt to build 'separate mosques of one brick each' and carve out their own 'Imamats'. To prop up their leadership, some of them may not even hesitate to undertake ethnic cleansing in their little courtyards. Frictions generated in the process could badly singe, if not burn, the entire fabric of the State. While petty ethnic lords would fight over their petty autonomies, the poor would continue to wallow in poverty, the sick would continue to remain unattended and the homeless would continue to be without a roof over their heads. On both the sides of the 'line of actual control', the basic problems would be solved not by pandering to the ambitions of tin-pot demagogues, thriving on slogans of separate identities, but by building up higher motivation and giving priority to commonalities and using the resources, both human and material, to eliminate hunger, ignorance and disease among the masses.

The recent experience of Yugoslavia shows how murderous ethnic warlords could be and to what extent human mind could be demented by the drugs of ethnicity. If formation of new states on grounds of ethnicity or principle of self-determination is accepted, there would be 5,000 sovereign states, rendering the international system unworkable.

Only Option

Placed as it is, India has no second, third or fourth 'option'. It has one, and only one, option–the option of adopting earnestly, and implementing effectively, the concept of 'one state, one nation and one destiny'. That is the only way of construction without destruction, of democratisation without fragmentation, of humanisation without the blood-stain of ethnic violence. If India does not exercise this option, it will not only remain ill-equipped to heal the deep wound which history has inflicted upon it but also run the risk of stumbling over new ethnic minefields and blowing itself into oblivion. The challenge before us is to mingle and melt all the subsidiary strands into a Great Tradition of Indian Culture and create a new alloy–an alloy that is a reflex of our ideology of ONE IN ALL AND ALL IN ONE.

External Intervention

For lack of clarity and consistency on the part of ruling national leadership on Kashmir, not only terrorism increased in many directions at the ground level but also larger scope made available to the international groups to meddle in Kashmir affairs to serve their ends of power.

Some academicians who have a substantial say in the formation of American policy on South Asia had started advocating that "the road to accession to Non Proliferation Treaty runs through Kashmir", implying thereby that India's current difficulties with regard to the

Valley could be used to pressurise her to sign the NPT.* Even the report** of the 'Carnegie Endowment Study Group on US-India relations in a changing international environment' (1993), which is generally favourable to India, recommended (page 34): "The United States should seek both unilaterally and through United Nations, to promote multi-faceted Indo-Pakistan negotiations in which nuclear non-proliferation and other issues are addressed concurrently. Efforts to promote nuclear dialogue without parallel initiatives on other fronts are likely to prove futile. The Kashmir dispute, in particular, could become the flash point of a conventional war that could escalate to nuclear level." The message in between the lines is quite clear. It is to link India's stand on NPT with Kashmir.

India stands for a nuclear weapon-free world. The discriminatory nature of the present Non-Proliferation Treaty has been consistently pointed out by her. The country's position was once again clearly stated at the meeting of the United Nations Commission on Disarmament, held on April 2, 1993. Ambassador Satish Chandra said: "We do not believe that partial and unjust measures on punitive action on a selective basis will achieve the desired results. Nor can initiatives which in reality only preserve the monopoly of a few states over weapons of mass destruction, missile technology and export markets for conventional weapons contribute to prevention of proliferation. . . The real issue is how to put an end to proliferation and to eliminate nuclear weapons. Accordingly, there is need for an international dialogue to review the NPT to plug the existing loopholes and to make it an instrument for achieving the complete elimination of nuclear weapons." This stand of India was not to the liking of the United States and some other western powers.

The report of the 'joint American-Russian study mission' (1993), referred to briefly in the sub-section dealing with the 'fourth option',

---

*According to opinion polls, about 85 per cent Indians were in favour of keeping the nuclear option open.

**The central thrust of this report is best summed up in its own words: "American foreign policy should give increased priority to India as the world's largest democracy and as a potential partner in multilateral action to resolve global problems and maintain regional stability. The new post-Cold War emphasis on promoting democratic and secular values as a central American goal in world affairs has focused so far on helping authoritarian states to make the transition to democracy and market systems. This goal should also embrace support for the preservation of an already-functioning Indian democratic system with a vigorous private sector."

goes to the extent of saying: "Russia and the United States could initiate, in the UN Security Council, a resolution that would state their concern about the confrontation in Kashmir and appeal for a peaceful solution... We also suggest the convening of an international conference on Kashmir to which non-officials would be invited. Such a conference might address the agenda that would be appropriate for one or more official-level conferences or fora. Finally, it would be useful to assemble a multinational group that could examine developments in Kashmir and, on a permanent basis, track developments in the state. There is now global interest in the Kashmir problem. . . ."

It was obvious that through study-groups and discussions at non-official level, background for outside intervention in one form or the other was being prepared. In a seminar organised by American Institute of Peace at Washington in the middle of January 1993, informal parleys were held amongst the 'influential' non-officials of the United States, India, Pakistan, Kashmir Valley and Pakistan-occupied Kashmir.* The objective of the seminar, as subsequently explained by one of the Indian participants, was to have a 'basketful of ideas' and to provide 'an input into whatever Clinton Administration might formulate'. These ideas were, in fact, nothing but subtle variations of the 'third' and 'fourth' options which have been discussed above. The point to be noted here is that efforts were being made to prepare the Indian public mentally for a change in Kashmir.

At the official level also, unfavourable signals have started appearing. For example, John R. Mallot, US Deputy Assistant Secretary of State, soon asserted that "the view of the Kashmiri people will have to be taken into account". The British Prime Minister, John Major, during his visit to New Delhi in January 1993, also called for a "negotiated settlement under the framework of Shimla Agreement, keeping in mind the aspirations of the people of Kashmir and respect for their human rights".

For all these unfavourable developments which had led to strong pressures** being put on India on issues of vital concern to her, such

*The four Indians who attended this seminar were: Bhabani Sen Gupta, B.G. Vergese, Muchkund Dube and A.G. Noorani.

**Such pressures have also been put on India during the recent (June 1996) International Conference on Comprehensive Test Ban Treaty.

as NPT, 'missiles technology', 'intellectual property rights', 'special legislation 301', the country had only to blame itself. By its halting and unimaginative approach, the ruling leadership had not only prolonged the internal agony of Kashmir but also caused a number of problems for itself at the international as well as trans-national levels. For example, at the 89th meeting of the Inter Parliamentary Union, held at New Delhi in April 1993, Gohar Ayub, head of the Pakistani delegation, created an ugly situation by haranguing: "The Kashmiri people have been denied their inalienable right of self-determination for the last four decades despite the commitments made by Indian leaders to the United Nations and the people of Kashmir. On the contrary, the legitimate aspirations of the Kashmiri people have been met by armed force leading to widespread violations of human rights which have been amply documented by a number of international human rights organizations." Likewise, at the twenty-first Islamic Conference of Foreign Ministers, held in Karachi (April 25-29), Pakistan was able to have a resolution passed unanimously, "calling upon member States to take all necessary steps to persuade India to cease forthwith the massive human rights violations of the Kashmiri people and to enable them to exercise their inalienable right to self-determination as mandated by the relevant resolutions of the Security Council".

The OIC is a toothless body. Its individual members are generally weak. It has been said that zero plus zero is a zero and OIC is nothing but a big zero. Nevertheless, it was Government of India's dithering that gave Pakistan an opportunity to project Islamic solidarity in favour of Kashmiri militants and provide a great psychological boost to them. In the context of US threat to declare Pakistan a terrorist state, the OIC resolution also acted as a shot in the arm of Pakistan and made it more assertive. Pakistan's Prime Minister Bulkh Sher Mazari, proclaimed:* "We will continue to raise the Kashmir issue in all international forums and lend support to the secessionist movement in Kashmir."

At about the same time, the American Administration hinted at the possibility of declaring Pakistan a 'terrorist state'.** James Woolsey,

* Statement made on May 5, 1993 in the National Assembly of Pakistan.

** So far, six countries-Iran, Iraq, Cuba, Libya, Syria and North Korea–have been listed as States which sponsor terrorism. The States so listed are denied trade as well as bilateral assistance. Multilateral assistance from institutions like World Bank and IMF is also not given.

CIA Director, told the Senate Committee: "Sudan and Pakistan, while not yet on the State Department's list of state sponsors of terrorism, are on the brink. The Kashmiris and Sikhs found safe haven and other means of support in Pakistan while forcefully redressing grievances against New Delhi." Despite this hint and the fact that a Pakistan-based terrorist is suspected to be involved in the bomb blast at the New York World Trade Centre and a Pakistani immigrant fanatic shot dead two CIA employees on January 25, 1993 near the Agency's office, it was doubtful whether Pakistan would be branded as a 'state sponsor of terrorism'. The intention, perhaps, was to keep pressure on both India and Pakistan. The former had already been put on the priority list for punitive action under 'legislation 301'. It bad been asked to "take steps to curb the abuses of its security forces making them strictly accountable in Kashmir".* Obviously, US was playing its own game and was guided by its own global interests, particularly its interests in South Asia and Middle East.

The US objectives in South Asia were spelt out in a report sent to the Congress, under Foreign Assistance Act, by President Clinton on May 5, 1993. The report said: "The US seeks to prevent nuclear and ballistic missile proliferation in South Asia. Our objective is first to cap, then over time to reduce, and finally eliminate the possession of weapons of mass destruction (WMD) and their means of delivery." It goes to "underscore to India and Pakistan that non-proliferation is a global, not just a US, concern", indicating thereby that other western powers would toe the US line. The report also suggested to both the countries that certain tension-reducing measures should be immediately taken. These included: (i) Indo-Pak dialogue on Kashmir; (ii) demilitarisation of the Siachen glacier; and (iii) expanded Indo-Pak dialogue to cover not just nuclear weapons and ballistic missile delivery systems, but also conventional arms limitation.

United States' New Posture

In the last quarter of 1993, marked hostility towards India, with regard to Kashmir issue, was shown by the United States. Its inclination to lend its weight in favour of 'third' or 'fourth' option could be seen in between the lines. President Clinton, in his speech to the United Nations General Assembly on September 27, 1993, said:

*Statement of John Malott in New Delhi on May 19, 1993.

Bloody ethnic, religious and civil wars were raging from Angola to Caucasus to Kashmir.

On October 29, 1993, Ms. Robin Raphel, US Assistant Secretary of State, at a 'background briefing' for the South Asian journalists, made, *inter alia*, the following observations:

> We do not recognise the instrument of accession a meaning that Kashmir is for ever more an integral part of India. . . . We view the whole of Kashmir as disputed territory, the status of which needs to be resolved. . . . The people of Kashmir have got to be consulted in any kind of final settlement of the Kashmir dispute. We believe there is no way that any resolution can be stable and lasting unless agreed to by the people of Kashmir. . . . Whatever outside support there may be, there is a strong indigenous element to the insurgency. I can also argue that it is self-sustaining. . . . We believe that the Indians need to look at the underlying cause of insurgency and these are not limited to outside assistance. . . . Kashmiris have been unhappy vis-a-vis their status with India for a long time and in recent years this has become worse . . . . We have pressed India to clean up their act and try to restore some semblance of Government there. . . . The Simla Agreement is 21 years old and there have been very few discussions to resolve the Kashmir situation.*

Asked about the storm of protest in New Delhi over President Clinton's reference to Kashmir in his United Nations address, Ms. Raphel replied:

> It is very easy to create a storm in Delhi. Delhi enjoys storms. It was correct to say we saw Kashmir on the radar screen along with Yugoslavia and Somalia and lots of places in the former Soviet Union.*

A clarification, subsequently issued by the State Department, tended to confirm what was stated by Ms. Raphel. "It did not change the content of the dish but merely the manner of serving it."*

On December 27, 1993, President Clinton wrote to Dr. Ghulam Nabi Fai, 'Executive Director', Kashmiri-American Council, as follows:

**The Hindustan Times* and other national dailies: October 30-31, 1993.

Thank you so much for your kind words about my recent speech to the United Nations General Assembly.

I share your belief that, in order to face the dilemma of a post-Cold War global landscape, we all must look closely at our policies with regard to human rights. I am confident that we can bring about changes that are consistent with what the U.N. founders envisioned.

I look forward to working with you and others to help bring peace to Kashmir, and I appreciate your input.*

In reply to a letter from US Congressman Gary Condit and 15 other legislators, President Clinton observed:

I am aware of the chronic tensions between the Indian Government and the Sikh militants, and share your desire for a peaceful solution that protects Sikh rights.**

All these statements and letters, issued in a short span of about four months, clearly point to the direction in which the wind is blowing. President Clinton's address to the UN Assembly in which he virtually equated Kashmir situation with that of Yugoslavia and Somalia; his warm response to Fai, a self-styled interlocutor whose activities, everybody knows, are funded by Pakistan, and who is fuelling terrorism in the Valley; his reference to Sikh rights as if Sikhs were not like other Indian citizens; and Ms. Raphel's highly provocative observations, questioning even the validity of the Instrument of Accession, are all manifestations of US increasing disposition to ignore Indian sensitivities, lean towards Pakistan and indicate, in the process, a subtle preference for independent or semi-independent Kashmir.

There are other straws in the wind which point towards the same direction.

On September 27-28, 1993, the Kashmir Bar Association organised a "Lawyers Meet" at which a series of resolutions were passed. A text of these resolutions is given in Appendix XXVI. It would be clear that public opinion was sought to be built to secure modification of the UN resolutions and provide for the '*third option*', that is, independent Kashmir. Efforts of this nature, there were reasonable grounds to

* *Indian Express:* January 7, 1994.

***Indian Express:* January 23, 1994. President's letter was sent to the Congressman Gary Condit on December 27, 1993–the same date on which he replied to Dr. Ghulam Nabi Fai–it was released to the press on January 23, 1994, by the 'Council of Khalistan'.

believe, were being encouraged, behind the scene, by US policy-makers.

For the last two years, the US Institute of Peace, Washington, a 'think tank', which is funded by the US Congress, has been showing more than usual interest in Kashmir affairs. In continuation of the January 1993 meeting, to which reference has been made earlier in this section, another meeting was organised by the Institute in the second week of January, 1994. Fifteen non-officials from India, Pakistan and 'both parts of Kashmir', who are believed by the Institute to exercise influence over public opinion, mainly through media, were invited. The 'frame-work' papers and pattern of discussions, albeit informal, seem to suggest that the 'position of Kashmiris as central actors' need to be given a 'top slot'. The intention was clear. It was to prepare a background for a change in the thinking of both India and Pakistan. One of the Indian participants, in a newspaper article,* written after the Washington meeting, argued:

How long can India be indifferent to the status-damage it suffers as a result of the continuing bloodletting in Kashmir?

Taking an overall view of the situation and long-term interests of the US in the region, its policy-makers seemed to be seriously thinking that it would be best to have an independent or semi-independent Kashmir. Such a state could serve as an effective instrument for putting pressure on China, if the need for doing so arises in future. It could also help in acquiring a stronger foothold in five Central Asian Republics and manipulating events in Russia to prevent an unfriendly power-structure emerging there once again. Pakistan could become a client state to a greater degree and India's arm twisted more forcefully to sign the NPT.

At this juncture, the United States was seeing new opportunities for itself in the troubled waters of Kashmir and it was moving, albeit unobtrusively, to seize these opportunities. Its basic objective was to remain as the only super-power in the world. President Clinton, in his address to the UN General Assembly, on September 27, 1993, made it clear.

The United States intended to remain engaged and to lead.

An influential section of American academics have also been arguing that the "bear may be dead but snakes and scorpions still roam."

**The Hindustan Times:* Room for Dialogue: January 27, 1993.

If India encounters US moves on Kashmir with a determined stand and by mobilising strong opinion in its favour, the US might abandon or modify the course it has presently taken. After all, the US cannot afford to incur the hostility of a nation of 880 million people. In this connection, it is worth recalling that when the die-hard Tory members of the British Parliament, like R.A. Butler and Churchil, tried to browbeat India by espousing the cause of the Nizam of Hyderabad, the 'faithful ally of the empire', Sardar Patel firmly told them not to stand by the 'old world'. He made it clear: "It is only in goodwill spirit, and not on the malice and venom of Mr. Churchill's tongue, that an enduring relationship of friendship can be built between India and Britain and other members of the Commonwealth." He thus successfully prevented Hyderabad, whom he described as an 'ulcer in the abdomen of India', from becoming cancerous. Such a forthright and fearless stand towards US's new posture, I am sure, would help India in retrieving the situation, besides sending the right signals to the secessionists in the Valley".

Human Rights–International Power Politics

In the final analysis, it is the country's own internal strength and guts that really matter. At the Asia-Pacific Economic Cooperation Summit, held at Seattle in November, 1993, President Clinton asked for human rights reforms in China. In reply, Chinese President, Jian Zemin, not only made no concession but also repeatedly 'signalled that China would not be bullied". In the words of Washington press reporter, Ludwina Joseph, the Chinese President "lectured Clinton on the importance of not interfering in the domestic affairs of other nations. He (Jiang Zemin) was stiff, formal, and did not offer any promises. He did not blink, even once." Thereafter, President Clinton did not return to the subject. Contrast the Chinese stand with the meek and defensive posture of India at both official and non-official meetings at the international level. No wonder, she has come under increasing pressure on the human rights issue.

What India has not done is, first, to set its own house* in order and, secondly expose the hypocrisy and double standards of those who are needling her on the human rights issue. How is it that not much hue

*The incalculable damage done by some of the so-called 'human rights organisations' operating in India has already been brought out in Chapters XIII and XV and earlier sections of this Chapter. See also Appendix XIX.

and cry was raised when, on September 10, 1993, US/UN helicopters fired on unarmed crowds in South Mogadishu, Somalia, causing about 150 casualties? Why was the plea of action in self-defence accepted in such a case and not in the case of Indian security forces who have to daily face lethal attacks by trained militants equipped with sophisticated weapons?

There can be no two opinions about the protection of the human rights. What is disconcerting, however, is the intrusion of hypocrisy, double-standards and power-politics into this sphere.

United States
Forgetting its own History

While talking about Kashmir, quite a few Americans tend to forget their own history. During my visit to US, to which reference has been made earlier in this chapter, I was often asked: "If most of the Kashmiris wanted the State to secede, why do you not allow it?" My answer to this seemingly pertinent question was simple and straight: "You see your own history. A vast chunk of America–the Southern States–wanted to secede. You did not allow that. You fought a civil war. Both North and South suffered a great deal. There was hardly a household that did not undergo trials and tribulations. But you kept the country united. Today, you are a great power–world number one. You call Abraham Lincoln the 'father of the nation'. And rightly so. You take pride in your great melting pot. And there is every justification for doing it. How can then you of all the people suggest that we should allow a part of our territory to separate? Do you not understand the long-term implications of succumbing to the momentary pressures of forces of fanaticism and fundamentalism? Has the partition of India solved any problem? Has it served either the Muslims or Hindus? On the contrary, it has kept both in perpetual poverty. Old animosities have sharpened and new animosities created. Had India remained united, it would have, like US, become a great power–a model of dynamism, resurgence, a country in which hunger, ignorance and disease would have been forgotten like a bad dream.

Tyranny of Shallowness

Unfortunately, there was no deep thinking on the issue of building a principled, cohesive and truthful nation, and the tyranny of shallowness continued to exacts its heavy toll. So far as I was concerned, I tried my best to loosen the shackles of the tyranny, using every forum including the forum of Parliament, that came my way. But my efforts did not yield any worthwhile result. Everywhere the stone-wall of indifference remained as thick as before.

I give below a brief summary of the points that I had been making during the last two years in Rajya Sabha. I am doing so in the first person and in the form of a speech. This format is being used not only to keep the originality of the presentation made but also to emphasise how insensitive the government had become.

Parliament's Inadequate Response

Whenever the Kashmir issue comes up for consideration in the House, I ponder over the futility of speaking. The government has shown no inclination to look into the roots of the problem. Even to concrete and constructive suggestions, there is practically no response. For example, I have repeatedly pointed out that false propaganda is causing grave damage to India's image abroad and some effective action should be taken to contain it. I invite attention, as an example, to the following portion of an advertisement which appeared on January 28, 1993 in *The Independent*, London:

> Men, women and even children (in Kashmir) . . . . are beaten senseless, given electric shocks and have their limbs crushed by heavy rollers . . . . throughout the land, pain and indignity are deliberately inflicted by paid agents of the State. . . . Sexual torture, including rape, is common.

May I know from the government what specific action has it taken to undo the damage done by this sort of vicious propaganda? Has it issued a counter advertisement? Is it, on the other hand, not a fact that a large number of advertisements of the government and public undertakings; such as those of tourism and forest departments, regularly appear in the magazines* and newspapers, which espouse the cause of militants? Does it not amount to financing subversion and secession?

Several times, I have suggested to the government, through this august House, to circulate a tabular statement, listing each and every allegation of the so-called Human Rights organisations and of the self-styled progressive individuals along with the version of the

*See, for example, issue of August 1992 magazine *Mountain Valley* which contains two full-page (coloured) advertisement of Forest Department.

State and Central governments with regard to these allegations, so that the matter could be considered in specific terms and public could judge the reality for itself. For example, why has the government not made public the report of the two Inspectors General of Police about the incident that took place after the dead body of Moulvi Farooq was snatched by the crowd from the hospital?

If my suggestion had been accepted, I have no doubt that quite a few organisations and individuals would have by now stood discredited. In a typical case, at personal cost and labour, I took a Weekly to the Delhi High Court, wherein the party had admitted that the entire interview, in question, had been fabricated by it. Unfortunately, this 'fabricated' interview is still being circulated by anti-India propaganda machinery abroad without any agency of the government taking the trouble of telling the public that the interview has been held by the Court to be a fabricated one.

Likewise, I have time and again indicated, through this House, to the government how portions of an affidavit, sworn by Mufti Baha-u-Din, an ex-Judge of the J&K High Court, were being distributed in thousands by Pakistani propaganda machinery in the United States and UK. If Baha-u-Din had been prosecuted and falsehood of his affidavit established through a Court verdict, the pernicious nature of the Pakistani propaganda abroad could have been effectively countered.

Similar is the position with regard to concoctions about the "induced migration" of Kashmiri Pandits. The Government has taken no effective action to bring to the notice of the public irrefutable documentary evidence that exists; how, for instance, notices* were published in the leading newspapers, *Aftab* and *Alsafa*, asking the Pandits to leave the Valley within 48 hours or face death; and how pronouncements made from numerous mosques, fitted with loud-speakers, frightened the minorities?

Why is the present government not taking steps as suggested? Is it afraid that the untruth spoken in the past by its members would be exposed and they would stand condemned before the public and the Bar of history? Does the government apprehend that it would be accused of double standards? During my time, the Governor was blamed even when it was crystal clear that the terrorists were engineering violence; now for the same type of incidents, the blame

*See Appendix XXIV.

goes to the ISI. Earlier, what the 'human rights bodies' wrote was gospel truth and used against, and quoted in, Parliament; now what these bodies write is described by the government as concoction and exaggeration. Earlier, excesses, assuming that they occurred, were attributed to me as Governor; now these are being attributed to the security forces. Does not the intentional falsehood spread earlier stand out clearly? Why is the government keeping a Sphinx-like silence on the subject? Why does the government not make a clean breast of it?

The recent memorandum* submitted by the National Conference to the Governor, General (retd.) K.V. Krishna Rao, is typical of the brazenness and recklessness of the contemporary Kashmiri politics. This memorandum, *inter alia*, reads: "Ex-Governors let loose a reign of terror; anarchy, state terrorism became their fundamental policy which aimed at planned genocide of Muslims on the direction of the central government." Poor Governors, these days, do not count. Any wild allegation can be hurled against them. But what about the central government? Here, the National Conference has accused the central government of "planned genocide of Muslims"! It is a charge–political as well as criminal–not only against V.P. Singh's and Chandra Shekhar's governments but also against the present government, because the charge extends right up to the time Girish Saxena demitted office in March 1993. I ask the government whether it is left with any courage and respect for law, truth and justice or mere timidity and permissiveness have become its guiding stars? If it has any morality, principle, or commitment to the Constitution, or regard for the national aspiration of 'Satyameva Jayate', it should either prosecute the offender or accept the charge. Is not the government aware of the provisions of sections 153-A and 153-B I.P.C. which stipulate stringent punishment for those who promote enmity on grounds of religion, race, etc., or who do anything which is prejudicial to national integration? More importantly, does the government not realise that by coining out the charge of "planned genocide of Muslims, at the direction of the Central Government", the National Conference is causing deep revulsion and hatred amongst the Muslim youth and thus inciting them to join the ranks of the militants? Is there any difference between what Pakistan and OIC are alleging and what the National Conference is saying? You condemn the former but

*See Appendix XXV.

embrace the latter! Do you not think of the grave implications of your acts of commission and omission? What would history say? Would it not look with 'deep disdain' at your confusion, your contradictions and your infinite capacity to deceive yourself, and, what is worse, the nation?

The memorandum beats its own record of recklessness by alleging that Saxena was meeting Jagmohan whenever he visited Delhi and was getting directions from him. The truth is that during his entire tenure in J&K, Saxena did not meet me even once. I would have, in fact, never done what he did in regard to some crucial issues. For instance, I would have never yielded to the pressures at the time of the strike of the Kashmiri government servants in september 1990. Nor would I have abandoned the idea of keeping a sole 'designated court' at Jammu to prosecute the killers and kidnappers effectively and speedily. I would have concentrated, as I was doing, on the reconstruction of civil administration and never allowed the introduction of the Disturbed Areas Act and Armed Forces J&K) Special Power Act, 1990. I would have also ensured that not even a single rupee went to the terrorists or their supporters under the cover of purchasing carpets, handicrafts, apples and other items. Apart from effectively weeding out subversive elements from sensitive departments, no one with terrorist leanings could have been recruited or given any contract for civil work. I would not have talked at all about the political process or elections till the administrative control at the ground level had been fully established. Dr. Farooq and other 'paper leaders' would have been kept at bay, because giving them any leeway or prominence meant uniting all the militants. Clearly, Saxena's decisions were his own or taken under the dictates of the Central Government.

I would suggest to the Parliament to impress upon the Government that it should fully recognize the inconvenient reality, rise above the past reflexes and adopt the following *ten-point strategy*:

(i) put strong and sustained pressure on pro-Pakistani terrorists and their collaborators;
(ii) deal effectively with subversive elements within the services and take serious notice of the absentees from offices, particularly on the days when calls for *hartal* are given by the pro-Pakistani outfits;

(iii) eliminate indirect flow of aid, through civil works and recruitments on the 'diktats' of the militants;

(iv) expose the disinformers in concrete cases by moving the courts and prosecute speedily persons like Mufti Baha-u-Din whose propaganda, through affidavits, tend to acquire authenticity abroad;

(v) organise counter-guerrilla groups, such as GSG9 of Germany, SAS of UK and GIGN of France.

(vi) activise the 'designated court' at Jammu and hold, as far as possible, day to day hearings in cases involving heinous crimes;

(vii) concentrate first on rebuilding the civil administration and establishing ground-level control, so that the Disturbed Areas Act and Armed Forces J&K) Special Power Act, 1990, could be withdrawn;

(viii) bring home to the people of the Valley that Article 370 is not in the interest of the poor Kashmiris and give subtle indication about its abrogation if pro-Pakistani outfits are organised and encouraged solely on communal lines;

(ix) keep an honourable line of retreat and route to power, through fair and free elections, open to comparatively moderate elements amongst the militants and do not take any action which would have the effect of creating an impression that Government is pre-disposed to bring certain individual or individuals to power; and

(x) provide liberal relief to the Kashmiri Pandits and solve immediately numerous problems of migrant-employees.

Immediately after I went to the State for my second term and noticed the total take-over* of the administration by the militants, I chalked out a strategy on the above lines and implemented it with vigour and precision. I secured back control of the State machinery without any incidents like the 'Blue Star' and Tienanmen Square. Simultaneous to putting all-pronged pressures, I dissolved the State Assembly to provide an honourable line of retreat to the moderates amongst the militants. Things started looking up** when 'vote-bank' politics and other negative elements struck and the rug was pulled from underneath my feet on May 26, 1990. Whatever damage has been done by the drift and diffusion of the last three years has been

* See Chapter VIII, particularly.

**See Chapter XIV, particularly.

done. At least now, take the right course and pick up the strategy of January-May 1990 and pursue it firmly. I beseech this honourable House–Rajya Sabha–to persuade the government to do so.

National Integration Council

To other institutions, I approached with similar exhortations. For instance, in my open letter of December 30, 1991, I, *inter alia*, urged the National Integration Council:

> If the nation wants to wage a successful campaign against terrorism, it should treat the terrorists as what they really are. It must first eliminate their primitive savagery and their 'Kalashnikov' culture. Till this is done, no political formula would be relevant or capable of being implemented.
>
> You want to tackle the problem of terrorism in Kashmir. But have you studied the nature and pattern of subversion in the Valley? Unless you spot the real malady, the curative measures would remain misdirected.
>
> If you are really serious, you have to rid the country of its current culture of shallowness and give it a new mind and motivation–pure, positive and practical.

No change

Unfortunately, despite all efforts being made in the Parliament and other fora, no basic change in the attitude came about. And the wheel of history continued to move on a precarious path. The old pot holes were deepening and the new ones were appearing. The journey remained hazardous. What is still more disconcerting, those at the steering wheel were not even clear about where they proceeding.

Continued Canard: Kashmiri Migrants

The Government continued to be unkind to the Kashmiri migrants and their future remained uncertain. The feelings of the Kashmiri Pandits were poignantly brought out by Dr. K.N. Pandita, former director of Central Asian Studies, at a conference held on April 17, 1992 at New Delhi. He said, "The members of the National Integration Council could visit the debris of a religious shrine, but no one visited the refugee camps in Jammu where the Hindu migrants are leading life worse than animals."*

The sad plight of the migrants was also highlighted at the World Kashmiri Pandit Conference, held at New Delhi, on December 28 and 29, 1993.

What was still more unfortunate, the canard about the migration of the Pandits continues to be spread. This was nothing short of rubbing salt in their wounds and also rationalising the barbarous acts of those who had been writing a terrible history of blood in the Valley.

To hide the total collapse of Dr. Farooq Abdullah's Government and to underplay the human rights violations of the Kashmiri Pandits, some crafty disinformers have been suppressing all relevant documents. By their cunning techniques of converting hearsay into evidence, they have been propagating, through their network at the national and international levels, that Kashmiri Pandits moved out because of 'inducements'. They had been intentionally hiding the trained butcherous hand of terrorism that went on its killing spree from mid-1989 onwards. I have already narrated the facts of some of the victims (the tragedies of Satish Tikoo, B.K. Ganju, Prof. K.L. Ganju, Sarwanand Koul Premi, etc.) Herein I give in Appendix XIX up-to-date data of the most inhuman crimes which practically find no place in the catalogue of 'human rights bodies'.

Appendix XXVI, which is a reproduction of the letter of October 21, 1993 of H.N. Jattu, President, All India Kashmiri Pandits Conference, shows to what extent intentional misrepresentation** could be resorted to by the vested interests–politicians, their apologists and fake champions of human rights.

Human Rights of Kashmiri Pandits and President Clinton

It spoke volumes about the infirmities of the Union Government that it had created about 250,000 'refugees' in its own country, and that was not their human rights violations, but those of the terrorists, that were usually discussed at the national and international fora. President Clinton found time to respond personally to an ordinary functionary of PoK/Pakistani propaganda machinery. In a letter written on December 27, 1993, to Ghulam Nabi Fai, 'Executive Director,

* *The Times of India*, April 18, 1992.

** See also the resolution of *Panun Kashmir* and other pieces of evidence indicated in Part II of this Appendix.

Kashmiri–American Council', the President said that he shared Fai's belief and looked forward to working with him. It was a measure of India's failure that the US President remained oblivious of gross human rights violation of the Kashmiri Pandits* who had been hounded out of the Valley, *en masse*, and whose houses, about 5,000, were burnt down. I wish someone from our foreign office or the President's own circle had invited his attention to what Senator Jackson and Andrei Sakharov said when safety of the American citizens was itself under terrorists' threat. The former observed:

> The idea that one person's terrorist is another's freedom fighter cannot be sanctioned. Freedom fighters or revolutionaries do not blow up buses containing non-combatants; terrorist murderers do. Freedom fighters do not assassinate innocent businessmen or hijack and hold hostage innocent men, women and children; terrorist murderers do. It is a disgrace that democracies should allow the treasured word 'freedom' to be associated with acts of terrorists.

Sakharov echoed similar sentiments in these words:

---

*This community is a repository of a great human heritage. About 5,000 years ago, there existed a highly developed community, with a "profound spiritual culture", along the banks of River Saraswati, which, according to the Vedas, was the Mother of Rivers. The Rig Veda (II 41.16) speaks of it as "The best mother, the best river, the best Goddess".

Recent researches, particularly of Dr. V.S. Wakankar, conducted with sophisticated instruments, such as multi-spectral scanner, have clearly established that Saraswati was not a mythological river. It actually existed and flowed from the foothills of the Himalayas, through what is now the Thar desert, to the Rann of Kutch on the Arabian Sea. It dried up because its main tributary, Sutlej, changed its course, approximately at right angles, consequent to geological changes.

After the drying up of the Saraswati, the community, which developed on its banks, dispersed. A section of this community comprising Brahmins, Kshatriyas and Vaisyas, moved towards the mountains and finally settled in the Kashmir Valley. Amongst the settlers, the Brahmins soon acquired a pre-eminent position, largely because of their great learning in mathematics, philosophy, astrology and law. In course of time, they came to be known as Kashmiri Pandits.

The mother tongue of the Kashmiri Pandits was Sanskrit, and they made the Valley a great nursery of Hindu culture. Many schools of thought were developed, including the celebrated Trikka philosophy, popularly called Kashmiri Saivism. The tradition of *guru-shishya* was firmly established. Every Pandit student had to learn at least four Vedas, six Angas, besides astrology, music and sciences. All this has justifiably given the Valley the name of Saradapeeth–the seat of Sarada, the Goddess of Learning.

For their history, present plight and disinformation to which they are being subjected, see Chapter XIII titled "Frightened Pigeons and Forsaken Community" and Appendix XXVI (Part I and Part II).

> "No matter how high the aim predicated by the terrorist. . . . their activities are always criminal, always destructive, throwing humankind back to the time of lawlessness and chaos."

Most of the Kashmiri migrants had been staying, on scanty relief, in miserable camps in Jammu, Nagraota, Udhampur and other cities. The children had been going to badly maintained tented schools with hardly any furniture. The women had to cook in the open, even under the scorching sun or heavy rainfall. A study conducted by Miss Poongotha of Lady Irwin College, New Delhi, revealed that 84 percent of the women in Delhi's migrants camps suffered from anemia. Dr. Shakti Bhan, who had been working in the camps, noted: "Gone are the pink cheeks and fair skin; gone is the confidence and vigour of life. The Kashmiri woman is now pale, exhausted and harassed, not knowing the ways of life in new surroundings." Another study of Jammu camps by Dr. P.K. Haq and his associates found that a number of diseases, unknown or rare in the Kashmiri community, had cropped up.

That, during the four year period–June 1990 to February 1994, none of the Prime Ministers–V.P. Singh, Chandra Sekhar and Narasimha Rao–had felt the prick of conscience to visit any of these camps showed how compassion had completely dried up in the minds of the Indian rulers. For them, politics was everything, justice and truth nothing. Since the poor Kashmiri Pandits had no balance in their vote banks, they were not much bothered about. Not even simple problems, such as posting husband and wife at the same place, and giving 'out of turn' accommodation to Kashmiri Government servants to enable them to accommodate their aged parents and close relations who, like frightened pigeons, had to flee the Valley, were attended to.

World Kashmiri Pandit Conference

It was to the credit of the Kashmiri Pandits community that, even in such indifferent environment*, it had not lost heart. Its various associations had been voicing their grievances vigorously and trying to get across the barriers of Government apathy. A recent example of

*With Narasimha Rao talking of 'Kashmir: Short of Azadi', and Deve Gowda's United Front Government committing itself to 'maximum autonomy', the future of the Kashmiri Pandits has become all the more uncertain.

this phenomenon was the World Kashmiri Pandit Conference, organised in New Delhi, on December 27 and 28, 1993. Emphasis was not on singing the songs of despair, but on presenting the various facets of problems confronting "the community in exile" and putting forward concrete demands. At the conclusion of the Conference, a document named "Delhi Declaration", the main points of which are given in Appendix XXVII, was issued. Earlier, on September 14, 1993, in a unique gesture of gratitude and as a measure of evoking public response, a group of Kashmiri Pandits went in a procession to Gurdwara Sisganj and submitted a "plaint" which, *inter alia*, read:

> O True Master! Had you not listened to the plaint of the 500 representatives of Kashmiri Pandits who had come to Anandpur Sahib in 1675 under the leadership of Pandit Kripa Ram and given your great sacrifice that opened everyone's eyes, we would have been obliterated from the soil of India. . . .
>
> In these troubled times, divine and great men like you are nowhere to be found. . . . Finding no hope anywhere, Kashmiri Pandit refugees have come again, after 318 years, to Gurudwara Sisganj, to seek your blessings and divine inspiration.

*Another Crisis–Hazratbal**

On October 15, 1993, first the BSF and then the army, were abruptly asked to lay 'siege' around the Hazratbal Mosque, Srinagar. As subsequent events showed, that was done without much thought being given to the problem, though it was officially stated that that had been done to prevent the theft of the Holy Hair, apprehend a number of dreaded terrorists and seize huge dump of arms and ammunition.

After laying the 'siege', the Government started negotiating. The whole affair turned into a serious crisis, drawing worldwide media attention. The protracted negotiations and supply of sumptuous food to the besieged, first by the State Administration and then the orders of the Court, caused a serious national controversy.

On the 25th and 26th days of the 'siege', I wrote two articles for the *"Indian Express"*. One was published on November 15, 1993, under the title *"A confusion in a confusion in a confusion"* and the other, on

*More particulars about the authorities' 'defeatist' approach towards both the crises, one at *Hazartbal* and the other at *Charar-e-Sharief*, and the all round damage they suffered in consequences thereof, have been given in the next chapter in the section titled: *Charar-e-Sharief*.

November 16, 1993, under the title "*Hazratbal–What would have I done?*" These articles analysed the Hazratbal events in historical perspective and brought out their short-term and long-term implications. A few paras from these articles, which speak for themselves, are reproduced below.

A confusion in a confusion in a confusion

The current turmoil in Kashmir is embedded so deeply in the blunders of the past, it is linked so closely with the negativism of the present, and contains so much explosive material for the future, that a constructive leadership, with a new vision, alone can tackle it. The quacks who are holding the reins of the country's power structure or the 'one-eyed columnists' whose rusted intellect remains a prisoner of the old postures will only push it further into situations wherein a handful of militants can hold the entire nation to ransom, or a Mallot or a Raphel can treat it shabbily.

It is not only the government machinery, but also the psyche of India that her ruling elite have polluted and, in these circumstances, recurring crises are inevitable.

The Hazratbal incident does not surprise me. The Government has enmeshed itself so badly in a whirlpool of confusion and contradiction that what has happened was bound to happen in one form or the other. Talking to Gunther, Churchill once described Soviet policy as "a mystery in a mystery in a mystery." With a little turn of phrase, the present Government's approach towards Kashmir could be labelled as "a confusion in a confusion in a confusion."

Tragically for the country, at every crucial moment of Kashmir's contemporary history, the decision-makers were caught in the quagmire of their own shallowness.

In the long dark tunnel of confusion, the Hazratbal incident shows the Indian decision-makers at the worst spot.

- What was intended when the "siege" was laid? If the object was to ensure the safety of the Holy Hair, why was the "siege" continued when it came to be known within a few hours that the relic was safe?
- If the intention was to apprehend the "most dangerous militants", why was not surprise and swift action taken? The complications accruing from the "mix of common people and militants" were known before-hand. In any case, did it make any sense to shout from the house-tops that the authorities would not do this or that?

- Why were not the options kept close to the chest and negotiations, if any, conducted from a position of strength? Why was it not realised that by first laying the 'siege' and then providing wholesome food, not only was a new definition of the term being written in the dictionary, but also a pathetic spectacle of a gregarious and mindless State presented for days together? Why was it not visualised that this would undermine the morale of the armed forces?
- Could Pakistan's game of internationalising the issue be played better by anyone else? Was it not known to all intelligence agencies that some of the elements placed at the top echelons of the Kashmir administration were merely loud-mouthed, hollow men–no more than fake coins–who, till recently, were approaching the "world forum" (the UN), and also feeding foreign journalists and "human rights activists" with slanted, and sometimes, totally fabricated stories about "Indian atrocities"?

Hazratbal–What would have I done?

This question has often been posed to me these days. Here is my answer.

I must spell out my concept of administration, particularly at higher levels. Administration is not merely pen, pencil, paper and red tape. It is imagination. It is vision. It is ability to perceive a gathering storm, comprehend a situation in toto and take preventive action. It is also precision, speed, dynamism, courage and commitment.

It has always been my endeavour to bring these attributes into play. Had I been at the helm of affairs, I would have relied more on anticipation and crisis-prevention than on crisis-management after allowing events to overtake me.

When I went to the State for my second term on January 19, 1990, there was hardly any administrative machinery on the ground. Even at that time, one of the top-priority tasks that I set for myself was to ensure that the Hazratbal and Idgah did not become centres of action and counter-action. I strained every nerve, employed every stratagem that I could think of, to keep my options to myself and take swift and surprise action to prevent any gathering in and around Idgah on Friday, January 26, 1990, as was secretly planned by the subversives on the pretext of offering mass 'namaz'. There are certain events which are inherent in the logic of a situation. One has to set one's logic right if tragic events have to be avoided.

I must also make another basic point clear. No administration exists in vacuum. Even the most dynamic, the most imaginative and the most committed administration can do little if the environment around is suffocating. Political arthritis will cripple all administrative initiatives and sap all administrative actions. A constructive and courageous political leadership is a *sine qua non* of a confident and effective administration. The integration of 561 Princely States is an outstanding example of the phenomenon. A bloodless revolution, adding 86 million people and about 800,000 square miles of area to the Indian Union, was created. It was Sardar Patel's political foresight and firm leadership that enabled a band of dedicated civil servants to put their best foot forward and achieve something that has few parallels in history.

A weak and wooden political leadership, on the other hand, would give rise to only a divided and diffident administration which would only fret and fume and stumble from one mistake to another.

Subject to the above, I would say that, in the first instance, I would not have allowed accumulation of arms and ammunition in or around Hazratbal. This object could be substantially achieved by conducting surprise checks in an area of one hundred yards' radius around the Mosque, through the 'Special Initiative Squads', and by permitting entry and exit only through a dozen or so points at which sufficient number of metal detectors and other equipment could be installed, as is done at the airports. Such an arrangement would have sent a message to all concerned that nothing could be done with impunity in the Hazratbal complex. And if, even then, militants had been able to cause some problem, it would have remained within easily manageable limits.

The worst way of dealing with terrorism is to be soft and stern in patches. Its inevitable result is frequent falls between the two stools. A strong and sustained pressure is the only effective method of avoiding recurring crises.

If ill-winds or some conspiracy of circumstance had brought a crisis on my hand that occurred on October 15, 1993, I would have, like an architect who conceives his design in the totality of the requirements, viewed the situation in its entirety, assessed my strength and weaknesses, and taken whatever action had to be taken within a few hours. I firmly believe that lack of clarity about the objectives or procrastination at the time of such incidents invariably exacts a heavy price, as has happened in this case by putting the Kashmir problem under the gaze of international publicity continuously for 26 days.

I would have also speedily checked the authenticity of the information supplied to the control room that the lock of the enclosure in which the Holy Hair was kept had been tampered with. It could as well have been a trick of some internal saboteurs among the subordinate police force to create a situation which would serve the purpose of Pakistan and its collaborators at a time when certain meetings at the transnational and international levels were taking place.

If the Holy Hair was found to be safe, I would have called the custodians of the hair and offered them plainclothes Muslim members of the security forces for guard duty and simultaneously announced to the public that that had been done. If mischief was continued even then, I would not have allowed the Indian State to be blackmailed by the mischief-mongers. Mere apprehension that someone would blame the Government even if it did the correct thing, would not have been allowed to deter me from adopting the just course firmly.

As regards the other object of apprehending the 'dreaded terrorists' holed up inside, if I came to the conclusion that the Indian State or the Government of the day did not have the stomach or stamina to take hard decisions and to implement them with courage and clarity of purpose, I would have quickly moved away from the situation without anybody coming to know about it and have waited for some other suitable opportunity to strike. In any case, I would not have allowed the 'siege' in the manner it was done.

In no case, would I have allowed serving of food as was done. If, however, supply of food to common people trapped inside became unavoidable, I would have announced that the food would be available only to them in a special enclosure erected for the purpose, a little away from the Mosque, under the supervision of the security forces, and they would be allowed to go back to the Mosque, if they so wished, and their wishes would be ascertained in the presence of eminent public figures of unimpeachable integrity like Justice Krishna Iyer, Justice R.S. Sarkaria or jurist Soli Sorabjee.

If even then the militants did not allow the common people to come out, their savage inhumanity would stand thoroughly exposed and they would lose the public sympathy they enjoyed in the Valley and outside.

In the context of the Kashmir problem, Sardar Patel once remarked: "If we cannot have confidence in our strength, we do not deserve to exist as a nation". I would have, in brief, demonstrated that we fully deserved to exist as a nation; only the 'Chamberlains of the crisis' and impractical hand wringers had to be shown their way.

Post Hazrat Bal

After 32 days, just one day before the elections, to the U.P. State Assembly, 62 militants came out of the mosque between 2.30 a.m. and 4.30 a.m. No one from the media was present. The Government projected it as a victory. Both the Home Minister and the Prime Minister claimed that the militants had "surrendered without any condition". Two Srinagar citizens, Ghulam Nabi Dagg and Ghulam Mohammed Bakshi, however, rebutted this claim and issued a press statement in which they asserted that there was an 'agreement' between the authorities and the militants, and they were witnesses to it. Under this agreement, almost all the offenders would be let off in due course–first 'soft-core terrorists' and then 'hard-core terrorists' and two 'terrorists from Pakistan-occupied Kashmir' would be 'pushed back to the other side of the Line of Actual Control'. A local English daily* also claimed that it had interviewed the militants in which they made it clear that they "had finally come out under an agreement".

Both the State and the Union Governments claimed credit for resolving the crisis peacefully. A section of the 'progressive press' went to the extent of calling it a turning point. But nothing could be more hollow, more untrue. Subsequent release of all the militants on one pretext or the other showed that the Government had suppressed facts.

During the 'siege', the Government surrendered many of its options, including the one pertaining to the manner of serving food which I have discussed in the second of the two articles reproduced above. After the 'siege', it surrendered its laws. It virtually bought 'peace with dishonour' after putting the Kashmir issue under the international gaze for over a month. It humiliated the Indian army by agreeing to the militants' demand that they would not surrender to the army but 'place themselves only in the hands of Kashmir police'. Even the limited objective of effecting re-use of the mosque could not

---

**Kashmir Times*: November 19, 1993.

be achieved. Appeasement merely resulted in the level of demand being raised. An 'ultimatum' was given by all-party Hurriyat Conference to the State Government to remove the BSF bunkers from the neighbourhood of the mosque by November 26, 1993. On November 27, a general strike/protest day was observed. On the eve of Meraj-un-Nabi,* the Government further yielded by withdrawing BSF from four bunkers. But the problem remained unresolved. For the first time in 300 years, the usual functions, including 'deedar'/glimpse of the holy relic,** were not held at Hazratbal.

All these facts reinforce my views, expressed in the above two articles, that the Indian ruling elite are trapped in their own shallowness and have acquired habit of deceiving themselves.

How the conditions have further deteriorated after the 'victory' and the 'turning point' would be evident from what has been happening since then. To cite only a few incidents, the Doordarshan Station Engineer, R.P. Singh, was killed in a rocket attack on November 26, 1993. A day later, at least 15 persons lost their lives in Sopore. Major Sidhu was killed on December 23 and Prof. A.A. Wani was kidnapped and done to death on December 31. On January 11, 1994, nine officials guarding the radar station, near the Avantipur Air Force base, were shot dead in a swift attack, their building burnt and weapons taken away. January 16 saw a series of fierce clashes, and on January 18, Major Bhupinder Singh and his driver were kidnapped. The Major's dead body was found a day later. Eight BSF officials were killed in Doda on January 19. On the Republic Day, rockets were fired at the venue of the parade. In the closing days of January, serious incidents took place in Kupwara, causing the deaths of 23 civilians and three policemen. On February, 3, even a Doordarshan tower in Jammu region, at Soti Gandoh, was set on fire and costly electronic equipment destroyed.

It was once again proved that the Government was confused in its thinking and chaotic in its action. It has developed a sort of expertise in compounding its problems. Release of dangerous militants who had resorted to armed rebellion, in conspiracy with a foreign power,

---

* See Chapter XII.

**Because of the Prophet's Hair being kept here, Hazratbal is considered as one of the most sacred mosques of the country. The Prophet's Hair, the Holy Relic, is shown only on special occasions. It was brought from Medina by Mutwali Syed Abdullah whose son passed on the same to a Kashmiri merchant Nuruddin Ishhavi.

was another 'victorious step' in its 'march of folly'. It was in the same class as the release of 70 hard-core militants in September-December, 1989 by Dr. Farooq Abdullah's Government* which added more fuel to the fire. No wonder, after Hazratbal, bouts of violence increased and the environment became more turbulent.

India-Pakistan Talks: January 1-3, 1994

It was the compulsion of circumstances and the subtle pressure of the United States which made India and Pakistan resume Secretary-level talks, after a gap of sixteen months. Both sides agreed to change, albeit slightly, their earlier positions. India agreed to discuss Kashmir, while Pakistan held up its hand to move a resolution at the United Nations on 'human rights violations in Kashmir'.

As expected, the talks did not yield any worthwhile results. Only fine diplomatic postures were shown. Pakistan's Foreign Secretary, Shaharyar Khan, said: "In diplomacy, things move forward only in small steps". The Indian counterpart, J.N. Dixit, invited attention to Plato's observations: "It is not a sign of wisdom to be desperate about things". But diplomatic veneer was soon cast aside, particularly by Pakistan. On January 8, its Foreign Minister, Assef Ahmad Ali, said in a press conference at Tashkent, "Unless the Kashmir issue is solved peacefully on the terms of international law and UN resolutions, there cannot be lasting peace in South Asia and there is always the danger of a fourth war. And this time, it might become a nuclear war."** India was also accused, both by Pakistani spokespersons and media, of diverting attention from the 'core issue of Kashmir' and bringing in items of lesser importance, such as Siachin, Sir Creek and Wular barrage. Now, Pakistan has officially proposed a "one-point conditional agenda". The agenda is "modalities of holding a plebiscite" and the condition is "staying of India's hand in committing human rights violations". Ms. Benazir Bhutto further vitiated the atmosphere by her speech (February 2) at the U.N. Human Rights Commission, Geneva. She compared the condition of Kashmiris in the Valley with that of the Jews in Germany during the Holocaust."*** Her party has also joined the "all-parties strike" called on February 5 to support the 'cause of Kashmiris.'

---

* See Chapter X.

** The *Times of India*, January 9, 1994.

***The *Pioneer*, February 2, 1994.

India, on the other side, has commented that if Pakistan wanted to harp on Kashmir being a 'core issue', and restrict future bilateral talks only to 'the modalities of holding plebiscite', then talks would be 'non-starters'. Prime Minister P.V. Narasimha Rao also made it clear in Bonn on February 3 that India would like to "freeze the contentious issue of Kashmir" and make joint efforts to improve bilateral relations in economic, political and cultural fields.

On the same day, President Shankar Dayal Sharma, while speaking at a Jaipur school function, criticised Benazir Bhutto for raising the Kashmir issue at the world forum and commented that she had 'lost all touch with reality and history'.*

Thus, the temperature that was sought to be brought down, has returned to the pre-talk level. In fact, after the events of February 5, 1994, the temperature has even risen higher. On that day, both Pakistan and India saw public rallies. In the former, life was brought to a halt by the all-parties strike which aimed at 'pressing' India to agree to implement the United Nations resolutions on Kashmir. Even the Government offices were officially closed. In Karachi, the demonstrators tried to force their way to the Indian Consulate. About 30 effigies of P.V. Narasimha Rao were burnt. On the Indian side, about 30,000 youth held a noisy demonstration at the Wagha border to protest against 'Benazir raising the Kashmir issue at international forums and making a false case on human rights violations in the Valley'. Similar demonstrations were staged in Jammu and other Indian cities. Effigies of Clinton, Benazir and Nawaz Sharif were burnt. In Kashmir Valley, a militant-sponsored 'bandh' was observed.

The message of the aforesaid events is clear. Poisonous old seeds, implanted in the roots, cannot but yield a bitter harvest. As Ayub's observations, quoted under the section "Fourth Option", show, Pakistan continues to be a prisoner of the 'idea of Pakistan'** of Kashmir being its 'unfinished business', of India being a Hindu India and Pakistan being a Muslim Pakistan, and of the superiority of the latter, ideologically and culturally. Even after the inglorious defeat and loss of Bangladesh, Z.A. Bhutto, in a top secret memo of June 23, 1972, to the Chief of Army Staff, General Tikka Khan, observed:

> So neither a few years of arranged peace, nor the present situation can possibly permit us to ignore the reality that there must

* *Indian Express:* February 6, 1994.

**K.K. Aziz: *A History of the Idea of Pakistan:* Introduction.

inevitably, sooner or later, come another war. . . . In a new war the enemies around us will be depending largely upon material superiority and not the human factor, upon technique and not the force of an ideal. In this can lie their weakness and our strength.... Recent history has amply proved, in China, in Korea, in Israel and in Vietnam that a people's war can withstand innumerable ups and downs but that no force can succeed in altering its general march towards inevitable triumph. . . . In the remotest of our villages the humblest of our people possess a self-confidence, a ready willingness to march forward into India–a spirit the equivalent of which cannot be found on the other side. . . . Great and terrible scourges have come to India from this side . . . every invasion from this side has defeated India . . . . Thus the terror, fear and habit of defeat cannot be wiped out of their national memory overnight. . . . And we ourselves have ruled them for eight centuries. All this is not ancient history. It is current history–and the Indian masses are just now still struggling against the legacy of superstition, religious intolerance, caste system, racial animosities, . . . poverty, backwardness . . . ignorance, deceit and the unconquerable habit of submission and servility.*

It is this attitudinal framework that Pakistan refuses to give up. It has caused tensions in the past, is causing tensions at present and will continue to cause tensions in future, unless India abandons its soft and permissive attitude, both internally and externally.

US Game Plan

So far as the US is concerned, its 'game plan' seems to have been well laid out. It is to pressurise both India and Pakistan to talk and after some exercises, which are likely to be barren, suggest a formula informally; and in the event of that formula, too, being unacceptable to the two parties, intervene in the dispute through the United Nations or by other means.

Nuclear Conflict

It appears that fears about a nuclear conflict between India and Pakistan are being exaggerated and overplayed to suit the American

*Stanley Wolpert: Zulfi Bhutto & Pakistan, p. 186.

'plan', particularly in regard to the NPT.* The *India Today*, in its issue of February 15, 1994, has published excerpts from a forthcoming book *Critical Mass* by William E. Burrows and Robert Windrem. These excerpts, in brief, propound a central theme and a proposition. The central theme is that the fight for Afghanistan had turned both superpowers into losers and that, taking advantage of the situation, Pakistan had acquired–or at least acquired the capacity to assemble–the atom bomb while the United States looked the other way. The proposition is that Pakistan and India were on the verge of a nuclear war in May 1990 and in October 1984, Mrs. Indira Gandhi was planning to bomb Kahuta.

While the aforesaid central theme is supported by substantial evidence, the proposition about a nuclear war between India and Pakistan is based on conjectures. In the footnote at the end of Chapter X, I have referred to Seymour Hersh's assertion which is similar to that of Burrows and Windrem. What I have observed therein merits repetition:

> In his article, entitled "On the Nuclear Edge", published recently in the *New Yorker* magazine, Seymour Hersh, asserts that in early 1990, India and Pakistan were on the brink of a nuclear conflict on Kashmir. According to him, Pakistan had gone nuclear. President Ghulam Ishaq Khan and General Mirza Aslam Beg were "keeping their hands on the button", and India was also ready to retaliate.
>
> Hersh's contention is speculative. It is, at best, based upon stray conversational remarks. Hard facts and circumstantial evidence point to the contrary. As I have shown in the earlier chapters with the help of contemporaneous records and factual data, the Indian government at the Centre was so casual in its approach that even collapse of administration and wide internal subversion in the Valley during Dr. Farooq Abdullah's regime, did not spur it to action. Such could not be the attitude of a government that was contemplating war, let alone nuclear war. So far as Pakistan was concerned, why should it have risked a holocaust when its objective was being achieved through low cost proxy war in which the Kashmiri youth was serving as its cannon fodder?
>
> Even at the worst of the Kashmir crisis (November '89 to March '90), most political parties in India were concerned more with their

*See also the section "External Intervention".

vote banks than for preventing Pakistan to close its jaws on Kashmir. On the other hand, they were, albeit unwittingly, aiding and abetting Pakistan's efforts. What, for instance, happened, in Srinagar on March 7, 1990 (Chapter XII) was in tune with Benazir Bhutto's rabble rousing against me (Chapter IX).

In early 1990, neither administratively nor politically, India showed any signs which suggested a war mentality.

Burrow and Windrem's view that Mrs. Indira Gandhi was intending to bomb Kahuta in October 1984, too, is highly speculative. Five days before her assassination on October 31, 1984, Mrs. Indira Gandhi was in Srinagar with her grandchildren, visiting religious shrines. She had detailed discussions with me about the situation in J&K. There was nothing in those discussions which indicated any likelihood of confrontation with Pakistan or any other happening of significance occurring in the near future. After all, bombing of Kahuta could not have been without repercussions, particularly in the state of J&K which also includes the strategic area of Ladakh bordering China.

New Fault Lines

The events, the trends, the currents and the undercurrents, discussed in this Chapter, show one thing clearly. It is the tyranny of shallowness and casualness that is mainly responsible for all the new fault lines that have recently appeared on the scene, be it the new US posture or the talk of 'third/fourth' option or crises like the Hazratbal or increasing level of subversion and terrorism, etc. It is this tyranny, again, that is undermining all State institutions and rendering them wayward and directionless. The only thing that the present rulers seem to have decided about Kashmir is to remain undecided. The only resolution that they have drawn up is to remain irresolute. Their capacity to live with illusions and deceive themselves remains undiminished. In this sphere, they are aided and abetted by some 'intellectuals' who advocate, wittingly or unwittingly, that the best way of keeping Kashmir with India is to surrender it to others with Indian money and seeds for future troubles of many more hues and colours. They remain prisoners of their wishful illusions. Anyone who attempts to pull them out of the present narrow groves of thinking is soon berated with some derisive label or the other and hounded out by a campaign of calumny and disinformation and other propaganda techniques.

My Belief: My Doubts

Had I not been stabbed in the back by the most repugnant lies spoken in contemporary history and thrown aside by the hurricane of negative politics, I would have pursued my strategy relentlessly and built, during my second tenure, the same bonds of love and affection, through selfless service, as I was able to build during my first tenure. And the temporary confrontation which was neither due to me nor due to the large mass of the poor Kashmiris, but had been engineered by outside elements and local vested interests, would have turned out to be no more than a short lovers' quarrel. This is my belief. Equally strong, however, are my doubts. Am I not making too great an assumption? Am I not ignoring the fatal flaws of a system that has developed the habit of ignoring the roots of the problem and also forgetting that a serious malady, if not subjected to a speedy, sound and sustained treatment, would leave in its wake new complications? Am I not sub-consciously suppressing my inner voice:

> It has happened
> and it goes on happening
> and will happen again?

Now, perhaps, all that I can do is to plead with the nation:

> Consider the darkness and the great cold
> In this vale which resounds with misery.*

*Brecht, *The Three Penny Opera*.

CHAPTER XVIII

Hesitancy and Hollowness

(February, 1994 to July, 1996)

We are the hollow men
We are the stuffed men
Leaning together
Headpiece filled with straw.

–*T.S. Eliot*

Events after events in Kashmir show how perfectly the above lines of T.S. Eliot apply to the most of the post-1947 political leaders of India. Some of them, may be 'stuffed' with learning but they are hollow in commitment and clarity. The analysis of the currents and undercurrents, in the backdrop of history, presented in the previous seventeen* chapters, amply bear the truth of this assertion. In this chapter, I would take up significant events of the latest period (February, 1994 to July, 1996), elaborate my proposition and also show how more fault lines are being added to the already chaotic landscape of the Valley and how, even after paying a heavy price in men, material and money, a patch-work is being preferred to a lasting solution.

Charar-e-Sharief

From Hazratbal to Charar-e-Sharief, there is a continuity–a continuity that is the product of the same timid and befuddled mind and shows the same hesitancy and hollowness in action.

*These chapters cover events and attitudes up to February, 1994.

Both the cases are marked by the same lack of clarity about the basic principles of governance, the same absence of commitment to protect the sovereignty of our space and the same disregard for the fundamental need to ensure that the appetite of the subversive forces is not whetted.

Both the events go to show that the only strategy Government knows is to move one step forward or sideward and then start spinning on its toes, causing a whirlpool of confusion around itself and undermining, in the process, the nation's prestige and honour.

After what happened at Hazratbal in October-November, 1993, the occurrence at Charar-e-Sharief in December, 1994—May, 1995, was not at all surprising. Here, the terrorists exploited, to the hilt, all the timidity and hollowness shown by the Government during the Hazratbal incident.

The Charar-e-Sharief Dargah of Sheikh Nuruddin is one of the most sacred Dargahs of the country. It was built in 1808-1810 by the Afghan Governor, Atta Mohammad Khan, in honour of the Sheikh who founded the famous Sufi-Rishi Order of Kashmir at the end of the 14th Century. This Order, till recent years, has wholly dominated the mindscape of the Valley. It is because of this domination that Kashmir is often called Rishi Vaur—the abode of saints.

Some time in December, 1994, about 50 hard-core militants, led by an Afghan mercenary, Mast Gul, sneaked into the Dargah. The State and Central intelligence agencies remained ignorant or casual about their presence. The militants dug in and collected a large number of lethal weapons inside the complex. On March 5, 1995, the militants killed two BSF jawans in a nearby area. Only then, the seriousness of the situation dawned upon the authorities. On March 8, the Army was moved to lay a sort of siege from a distance of about two kilometres. Characteristically, the Government was quick to announce 'safe passage' to the militants. But the offer was spurned by Mast Gul. Both at the State and at the Central levels, indecision and confusion continued, while the militants called all the shots. Eventually, on May 11, 1995, the Dargah and the adjoining housing and shopping complex were burnt down.

As brought out in the preceding Chapter, in the section titled: *Another Crisis—Hazratbal*, by agreeing to practically each and every dictate of the militants, and by displaying woeful absence in the unity of command-structure of civil and army authorities, with Srinagar Commissioner Wajahat Habibullah, insisting on even serving sumptuous food at the venue of the militants' choosing, another tragic chapter of drift and demoralisation had been written. The 32 days of 'decisions' and 'revisions', spread their unsavory fall-outs all around.

The heightened tension and deployment of pressure-tactics by the militants and their collaborators all over the valley were bound to cause collateral damages as well. And these did come about on a fairly large scale. On October 22, a reckless crowd, led by armed militants, clashed with the security forces at Bijbehara, resulting in the death of 28 persons. In another militancy-driven incident at Fateh Kadal, Srinagar, four subversives lost their lives. Neither peace nor prestige could be attained.

The disgraceful succumbing to the intimidatory tactics of the militants and boosting, in the process, the forces of fundamentalism and fanaticism, could only render the conditions more critical. In fact, neither the incident of Hazratbal nor that of Charar-e-Sharief nor the current general turmoil in the Valley would have occurred if the Indian political leaders had a clear commitment to the ideals of their Constitution, and stood by their proclaimed principles at the time of their testing. Unfortunately, they have, more often than not, shown a weak and vacillating mind which merely emboldened the adversaries to undertake still more destructive ventures. Had the authorities withstood the bouts of bluff and blusters at Hazaratbal, burning of Charar-e-Sharief, and accompanying loss of life and property, would not have, perhaps, happened.

Indo-Pak Co-operation!

Physically, Charar-e-Sharief Shrine was burnt by the pro-Pakistani elements. But, on a different plane, it was burnt by the timidity and hesitancy of the Indian rulers. Pakistan and its terrorist outfits committed the 'crime' by commission. The Indian rulers committed it by omission. Who says there is no Indo-Pakistan 'co-operation'? One's commission and the other's omission often converge to the same end.

And was this 'co-operation' not in evidence even earlier, when Benazir Bhutto's harangue against me from the other side of the border was joined in by the most malicious disinformation campaign mounted against me on this side? While Ms. Benazir Bhutto, Prime Minister of Pakistan, was resorting to hysterical outbursts—**'Jag-Jag-Mohan ko bhag-bhag kar denge'**—a section of our press was working overtime to plant fabricated stories and some of the 'intellectuals' found it opportune to corner the limelight by posing as 'progressives' and virtually rationalising terrorism and subversion, and at the same time, berating the action taken to deal with the alarming situation with a firm hand.

While Pakistani terrorists had spread lethal mines around the shrine complex, the Government had planted its own mines of indecision in the strategy of the Army, making it look like a hesitant force without any initiative and freshness of approach. The result was a repeat performance of 'a confusion in a confusion in a confusion', with many more losses in men, material and morale. No less grievous was the mental injury suffered at the Dargah of Charar-e-Sharief–the injury which severely undermined the soft, syncretic and Sufi form of Kashmiri Islam and paved the way for its rapid replacement by extra-conservative and rigid form of Jamait-e-Islami and Wahabbi Islam.

After the great fiasco, Prime Minister Narasimha Rao's statement in Parliament on May 12, 1995 that burning down of the Shrine by mercenaries and militants was only going to steel our determination, sounded both hollow and pathetic. When did he ever show any determination with regard to Kashmir that could be steeled? As Brutus says in *Julius Caesar*.

There are no tricks in plain and simple faith;
But hollow men, like horses hot at hand,
Make gallant show and promise of their mettle;
But when they should endure the bloody spur,
They fail their crests, and like deceitful jades,
Sink in the trial.

All that was seen during the five-month long crisis of Charar-e-Sharief was the Prime Minister's famous 'do-nothing' posture. It was a case not of masterly inactivity, but of inexcusable irresponsibility.

Could there be a worse demonstration of ineptness and incompetence? The monumental mishandling resulted in total destruction of the historic shrine, burning of 800 houses and 200 shops, besides costing* millions of rupees to the poor country's exchequer and causing grave human misery and pain not only to the residents of Charar-e-Sharief but also to thousands of others who became victims of the fallout. What is still more deplorable, Mast Gul, the most wanted foreign mercenary, escaped and even held press conferences and TV interviews on Indian soil. Overnight, he became a cult figure,

*Soon after the incident, the Prime Minister announced Central assistance of ₹ 15 crores for rebuilding houses and shops.

providing another prop to subversion and terrorism in Kashmir. He returned to Pakistan-occupied Kashmir to receive a hero's welcome.

Unanswered Questions

Possessed as they are with their superficial thinking, the rulers are unlikely to draw any lesson even from this tragedy. Nevertheless, the nation is entitled to seek answers to quite a few unanswered questions.

How were the terrorists allowed to gather inside the 'dargah', accumulate lethal arms and ammunition and install scores of 'improvised explosive devices'? What were the Intelligence Agencies of the Union and the State Governments doing?

Should one assume that those in charge of Kashmir affairs were so ignorant about the methods deployed by terrorists that they allowed them and the foreign mercenaries to have a free run of Charar-e-Sharief and its adjoining areas? Why, for instance, could not a few metal detectors and other equipment be installed at the entry points to the 'dargah'? Why could not vigil be mounted at the initial stage and surprise checks conducted around the complex? Why was it forgotten that crisis-prevention, and not crisis-management, was the need of the hour?

What was the rationale of a 'distant siege' or cordon? Could it not be understood that such a strategy had the potential of having the worst of 'both the worlds'? And what was the point in keeping the Army unit in 'suspended animation' for as long a period as three months? Did this long and 'distant siege' or cordon not facilitate the escape of Mast Gul?

It was stated on behalf of the Government that the explosion which started the fire in the 'dargah' occurred at 2.30 a.m. on May 11 and the Army went inside the 'dargah' at about 5 a.m. What happened during the intervening period? Is it not clear that during this crucial period, there was no effective liaison between the civil and the Army administrations? Obviously, the Army was psychologically inhibited to put its heart into a job and its promptitude had been severely undermined by lack of clarity and courage of the political and administrative leadership of the Government.

The 'civil fire-brigade', which was stationed nearby, did not move in time to extinguish the fire. Knowing the attitude of the civilian staff–their frequent strikes, their non-cooperative attitude at the time of the Amarnath Yatra and preparation of electoral rolls–was it not incumbent on the authorities concerned to make alternative arrangements? Why was the need for having a second line of defence or action not visualised?

Where was the civil set-up when the terrorists and foreign mercenaries started moving freely in Charar-e-Sharief and laying mines and manufacturing explosives by setting up local factories? It was claimed that after the first fire, on the night intervening May 8 and 9, which consumed about 800 houses and 200 shops, but not the Shrine, Lt. General Zaki and the Director-General of Police, M.N. Sabharwal, visited the Charar Shrine. What did they do during this visit? Should they not have set up any senior civil unit to keep in touch with the Army unit?

Why did the Director-General of Police himself not stay near the Charar Shrine to provide effective coordination between the police and the civil administration on one side and the Army on the other? Is it not a fact that he is the same Officer who quietly slipped away from the hospital at the time of the assassination of Maulvi Farooq whose dead body was snatched by the crowd in which the terrorists had mingled and later on clashed with the CRP, causing a number of casualties? If such persons are kept in key positions, would tragedies like the one in question not be repeated?

Lastly, there is a larger question–a question ingrained in morality and justice. Is the nation today not paying for the sins of those who, for petty personal and political ends, mounted a vicious disinformation campaign, suppressing hard and concrete facts, to frustrate a well thought out ten-point strategy which had started yielding results by early 1990 and causing frustration amongst the Pakistanis and their collaborators in the Valley–a frustration which found hysterical expression in the shrieks of Benazir Bhutto against me? Now, instead of demoralising the adversaries, our own people are getting demoralised.

Inevitability of Recurring Crises

In this background of the ingrained disposition of Indian rulers not to set their faces firmly against destructive forces, and to appease them instead, recurring crises of the type witnessed at Hazratbal and at Charar-e-Sharief are inevitable. The forms of the crises may be different but their immediate impact and long-term consequences would be the same.

Contours of Concrete Reality

In-depth thinking and acceptance of facts, as they exist on the ground, by the present-day decision-makers are conspicuous by their absence. Let me here spell out briefly a few contours of the concrete reality which they have glossed over in the year 1995, while remaining obsessed with the issue of elections.

In 1995, 2,768 persons were killed. The security forces were attacked 2,570 times, that is, on an average, about seven times a day. The number of security personnel killed increased from 198 in 1994 to 234 in 1995. 211 more civilians were killed in 1995 than in 1994. On the other hand, 264 less militants lost their lives in 1995 than in 1994. In other words, while the number of casualties suffered by the security forces and civilians increased, those of the militants declined. The number of persons abducted also shot up from 368 in 1994 to 548. The number of houses set on fire, too, increased from 612 in 1994 to 1,814 in 1995, shops from 162 to 405, and schools from 119 to 133.

The year, 1995, commenced with the most serious and most revealing incident. It showed not only the depth of internal subversion but also the high level of sophisticated technique the terrorists in Kashmir could successfully deploy. At the time of the Republic Day Parade, on January 26, two bombs exploded near the saluting base and one at the entrance of the stadium. Eight persons, including a 'black cat commando', two Army jawans, two police constables and two officials of the State Information Department, were killed. 54 others were injured. The Governor himself had a providential escape.

On February 6, an Army vehicle carrying Army jawans from Jammu Cantonment, was blown up near Jorian by a powerful mine. Nine Army men lost their lives. In another similar landmine blast, near Khumriyal in Kupwara District, six Army jawans and a civilian were killed.

Several electricity towers and an electric sub-station were badly damaged in a series of bomb blasts in Bishneh and Chuhey Chak areas of Jammu District.

As briefly noted earlier, in an almost unbelievable act of negligence and casualness, the Government allowed about 30 hard-core militants and foreign mercenaries, led by one 'Major' Mast Gul, to occupy in January-February, 1995, the famous 550-year old Dargah of Kashmir's patron-saint, Sheikh Nuruddin Noorani, lay mines and other explosive devices therein and eventually burn it. Nothing could have had more traumatic, more tragic and more damaging effect upon the mental and physical landscape of Kashmir Valley than this incident. Nothing could also reveal better than this unfortunate occurrence the utterly confused, casual and incompetent ways of the Government.

In the wake of the Charar-e-Sharief incident, there was extensive violence in the State, particularly in South Kashmir and Doda District of Jammu. Within two days, 21 innocent persons were done to death. A large number of Hindu temples and vacant houses of Kashmiri Pandits in the Valley were burnt, thereby compounding the woes and anxiety of this unfortunate community–a community which, strange though it may sound, has become a refugee in its own country.

In the worst incident of communal killing since August 14, 1993, when 16 Hindu bus passengers were brutally put to death, eight Hindus were shot dead and about half a dozen others seriously injured by terrorists on May 13, 1995, in Bharat Village of Doda District–a district the mountainous regions of which virtually became a domain of pro-Pakistan militants and foreign mercenaries.

On July 5, four foreign tourists were kidnapped by a hitherto unknown terrorist outfit, Al Faran. On July 11, a Norwegian tourist, Hans Christian Ostro, was also picked up. For freeing the hostages, Al Faran demanded release of 21 hard-core militants in Government custody. Ostro was brutally killed and his body, with head severed, was found near Anantnag. One of the American hostages, however, managed to escape. Despite assistance obtained from the foreign specialists, a step which, in itself, raised controversy, albeit of a different kind, and despite heart-rending appeals from the families of the hostages, the other innocent hostages* have not been freed.

Even in the heart of Jammu, in its oldest and most popular market, Purani Mandi, the terrorists were able to effect, on July 20, an extremely high-powered RDX blast which took away the lives of 17 persons and caused grave injuries to about 50 others.

In a bid to disturb the Amarnath Yatra, despite massive deployment of security forces, the terrorists caused an explosion in a hotel at Pahalgam and subsequently another explosion at a camp site. These explosions resulted in the death of a Jammu official and serious injuries to five persons.

*Britons Paul Wells, 23, Keith Mangan, 33, American Donald Hutchings, 42, were kidnapped on July 4, 1995. German Dirk Hasret was picked up on July 8. Norwegian Hans Christian Ostro was kidnapped on the same day. He was killed in the first week of August.

There were two very lethal car bomb explosions on September 4 at the Residency Road, Srinagar, which killed on the spot 12 persons, including 8 officials of the security forces, and seriously injured 25 others.

Let alone co-operation, the Kashmiri Government servants continued to be hostile throughout the year with practically no fear of any disciplinary action or any other form of disability.

The Crux of 1995 Reality

Thus, apart from general increase in the killing and kidnapping of civilians and personnel of the security forces, the year 1995 saw the highest number of attacks on the security forces, the longest hostage crisis, the largest number of cases of arson, the worst incidents of car-bomb and landmine explosions, the most wanton destruction of the holiest of the holy shrines, the most glaring case of internal subversion, the most wilful defiance of discipline by Government servants and the deepest blow to the national prestige on Republic Day.

First Half of 1996

In the first half of 1996, practically, the same conditions continued. During the period January-May, 1996,* 1,183 persons were killed and 302 abducted. The security forces were attacked 775 times, and 333 private houses and 110 shops and public buildings burnt. There were 25 rocket attacks and 317 bomb explosions.

And what did the Government do all this time? Throughout, it hardly did anything else but to say repeatedly that elections would be held soon. Even the most savage and inhuman killings and kidnappings did not stir its conscience or arouse it to commit itself to a solid and sound plan of action.

Disproportionate Emphasis on Elections

Throughout the five years of Narasimha Rao's regime, a wholly disproportionate emphasis was placed upon elections as if they were an end in themselves. The basic problems of far more practical significance–the problems of internal subversion, of an imbecile civil

*For up-to-date figures, see Appendix XXIX.

administration, of gross indiscipline in a sizeable section of the State bureaucracy, etc.–were not attended to. Even repeated declarations to hold State Assembly elections could not be implemented due to uncongenial ground level conditions.

Now, after massive deployment of additional security forces (about 60,000) and appointment of almost the entire staff (about 10,500) for conducting the election from outside the Valley and incurring huge expenditure on hundreds of bullet proof cars, jackets and other extremely costly and sophisticated equipment, three members elected to Parliament, two of the Congress and one of Janata Dal, cannot carry conviction about their representative character. Though the reports describing these elections as sham and fraudulent are not correct, the salutary impact that was adumbrated is nowhere to be seen. Nor did these elections alter the terrorism-related situation. Blood is still being spilled. Killings and kidnappings are still going on. No official yet feels safe in moving out without heavy escort, and fear of landmines and sudden attacks looms large. For example, with regard to a single day–June 7, 1996–*The Tribune* reported the following in regard to terror related events:

> Ten persons, including four militants and a policeman, were killed and 10 others, seven of them security personnel, injured when militants fired a rocket, exploded bombs and engaged the security forces in encounters in different places in the Kashmir Valley since last evening...Two persons were also injured in the firing incident in Anantnag...Militants kidnapped and later shot dead two persons, constable Nazir Ahmad Shah of the local police and Mohammad Ramzan Ganai...They also gunned down two persons in their villages at Rampora Mattan and Bonagam-Qazigund.

The happenings on the other days of June have been no less gruesome. On June 8, five Army personnel were shot dead in Badgam district. On June 9, in village Kamari, Doda District, ten persons were massacred in the most savage manner. Some of them were cut to pieces by axes and knives. On June 15, five members of a family were beheaded in village Drungsu, District Kupwara. The total number of persons killed on this day was 18. On June 16, in a single day, 25 persons were killed in the Valley. All in all, elections have resulted in intensification rather than abatement of violence, the continued presence of a good number of additional security forces notwithstanding.

Core Issue

For militancy to decline, and then disappear altogether, elections, unaccompanied by basic organisational and attitudinal changes, would be of little avail. These could, on the contrary, prove counter-productive by imprinting forces of religious frenzy on the Kashmiri mindscape and turning the populace into permanent votaries of doctrinaire Islam. Unfortunately, since mid-1989, when militancy started attaining rapid acceleration, the Indian political leadership has not able to rise up to the grave challenges and do some fresh thinking. Already on a slippery road, with heavy burden of past errors and omissions in its baggage, the leadership has been unable to envision anything beyond offering one more item of appeasement after another.

In any case, the core issue in Kashmir is the creation of an environment in which seeds for a fundamental and lasting solution germinate and grow into a fruitful harvest. I have no doubt that qualitative change of a permanent nature would not come about unless the roots of the problems, which I have delineated in Chapter IV, V, VI and X are attended to with a new sense of mission.

Unfortunately, the political rulers of the country and the opinion-makers–columnists, self-proclaimed progressives and liberals–have shown little grasp of the basic issues involved and given highly exaggerated importance to the western spread notions of ethnicity, sub-nationalism, 'Kashmiriyat', etc. They have established–unwittingly, perhaps–a tyranny of shallowness on the common people, taking advantage of their hold on the mass media.

The superficial understanding of the Narasimha Rao Government was evident from the statement he made on May 17, 1995, in the Rajya Sabha. He said: "I can see some light at the end of the tunnel. By Azadi, the Kashmiri leaders may not mean total independence." Coming as it did in the wake of the Charar-e-Sharief incident (May 11, 1995), it was both cowardly and careless. It not only showed how hollow was Government's commitment to national integration but also betrayed an infirm mind–a mind which was so possessed by illusions that it was willing to see 'light' even in abject capitulation.

In the face of the criticism* that followed the aforesaid statement, Narasimha Rao subsequently toned down the pitch of his autonomy

*See, for example, my article titled: 'Short of Azadi' in the *The Hindustan Times* and also my speeches in the Rajya Sabha (May, 1995).

song. In his broadcast* to the nation from Burkina Faso on November 4, 1995, he spoke only in general terms. Nevertheless, confused thinking on the subject persisted. And the dangers embedded in the idea of strengthening autonomy and making Kashmir semi-independent remained.

Unfortunately, the Government of the United Front, without even studying the practical implications of the basic issues involved, has committed itself to grant 'maximum degree of autonomy' to the State. The 'Common Minimum Programme' of the Front said: "Respecting Article 370 as well as wishes of the people, the problems of J&K will be resolved through giving the people of the State maximum degree of autonomy". This declaration is hardly different from Narasimha Rao's ill-conceived statement on 'Kashmir–Short of Azadi'!

Hollowness of Approach

The background of the present constitutional relationship between Kashmir and the rest of India and the rationale of extensions of various provisions of the Indian Constitution to the State of J&K have already been discussed in Chapter II. The implications of Article 370 and the manner in which it has been exploited over the years by the vested interests have been brought out in Chapter VI. The infirmities of what are loosely called 'third option' and 'fourth option' have also been spelt out in the preceding chapter. All that needs to be pinpointed here is the utter hollowness of the approach to the problem of Kashmir through such notions as 'short of Azadi' or 'maximum degree of autonomy' or pre-1952/53 status. It makes no sense to ignore either the past experience or practical aspects of the working relationship.

Experience over the years has shown that, besides breeding a separatist psyche, provisions of Article 370 and the State Constitution have been misused, at the expense of the common Kashmiris, to establish a self-serving oligarchy whose interest is to prop up anti-Indian sentiments. These provisions also really emanate from the same base from which the two or three-nation theories have sprung

*In this broadcast, Narasimha Rao promised to strengthen Jammu & Kashmir's autonomy. He also said: "There would be no objection to changes in the nomenclature of Chief Minister and Governor to Wazir-e-Azam (Prime Minister) and Sadar-i-Riyasat (Head of the State) respectively.

up. About this Article, as early as August 7, 1952, Dr. Syama Prasad Mookerjee had significantly observed: "What you are going to do may lead to Balkanisation of India, may lead to strengthening the hands of those who do not believe that India is a nation but a combination of separate nationalities". Instead of removing the provisions that foment forces of disintegration, the notions now being flaunted by Narasimha Rao and the United Front would result in removing the few integrative links that exist. Even at the time of the Kashmir Accord (1975), when the impact of the separatist forces was not so acutely felt as at present, Mrs. Indira Gandhi refused to 'set the clock back'. She did not agree to scrap any of the essential links established over time. Parthasarathi and Afzal Beg, who reviewed these links on behalf of Mrs. Indira Gandhi and Sheikh Abdullah respectively, could not find anything worth changing.

In fact, no provision of the Indian Constitution has been extended to J&K which is not necessitated by practical considerations and which is not in the interest of common Kashmiris. What objection, for instance, could be taken to the extension of jurisdiction of the Election Commission or the Supreme Court or the Comptroller and Auditor-General of India? These extensions merely make available better justice and better accounting and audit arrangements. What fault, again, could be found with labour welfare laws? In what way do they militate against the identity or personality of Kashmir?

Nuts and bolts of Working Relationship

Those who demand the pre-1952/53 position seldom address themselves to concrete questions. They suppress the fact that, in the absence of full financial integration with the Union, J&K would be left with no resource at all for development. It is the Union finances that provide the entire funds for the State's Five-Year Plans and also for a substantial part of the non-Plan expenditure. According to the Reserve Bank Bulletin (October, 1994), the per capita central assistance for the year 1993-94 was ₹ 2,291 for J&K as against ₹ 192 for Bihar, ₹ 232 for Tamil Nadu, ₹ 304 for Rajasthan and ₹ 331 for U.P. In the case of J&K, 90% of this assistance is in the shape of grants and 10 per cent as loans; while for the four States mentioned above, it is 30 per cent grants and 70 per cent loans. Like-wise, the per capita non-Plan grants for J&K in the same year comes to ₹ 699 while it is ₹ 64 far Bihar, ₹ 26 for Tamil Nadu, ₹ 73 for Rajasthan and ₹ 20 for U.P.

All this shows the tremendous gains that have flowed to J&K State from the financial link with the Union. What will happen if this link is now ended?

Coming to the practical issues, take, as an example, the case of extension of Article 356 of the Indian Constitution which enables the President to bring the State under President's rule. It is often said that this extension constitutes an encroachment on the State's autonomy. But no one asks a connected question: if there is a breakdown of the constitutional machinery in the State or if the State refuses to comply with any direction concerning Defence, Foreign Affairs or Communication, what will happen in the absence of President's powers under Article 356? Suppose the Governor has the corresponding powers; then does it not mean that the President would have to submit to the decision of the Governor, his own appointee? Again, suppose the Governor is made 'Sadar-i-Riyasat' who is not appointed by the President, but is elected by the State Assembly, then would not granting the final say to the Sadar-i-Riyasat amount to subordinating the Union to the State?

It should be clear that neither Narasimha Rao's nor Deve Gowda's Government cared to take into account the 'nuts' and 'bolts' of practical relationship that needs to be maintained between the State of J&K and the Union of India. This carelessness typifies the attitude of successive governments of the Union since October, 1947 towards J&K.

I have no doubt that, if leaders like Narasimha Rao and Deve Gowda persist with their present approach, they would cause new complications and make the future of Kashmir more uncertain and troublesome. Both of them fail to make a distinction between autonomy that leads to efficiency in administration, speed in development and fuller realisation of creative potential of a community and autonomy that breeds separatism, subversion and secession and provides fillip to the forces of parochialism and chauvinism. Both of them also do not realise that it is not the absence, but the surfeit, of powers that has given rise to a number of maladies from which Kashmir is presently suffering. And these powers have been misused with impunity to set up a self-serving oligarchy which developed a vested interest to encourage pro-Pakistan and anti-India sentiments. In the process, the common Kashmiri–the deprived and disprivileged–has suffered. He, in fact, has been exploited and prevented from realising that his interest lay in development and removal of poverty, ignorance and disease, and not in Article 370 or contrived notions of 'identity', 'personality' or 'ethnicity'.

Specious Argument

Another disconcerting feature of the present position is that, instead of educating the public on the right lines, some specious argument or the other is generally advanced by narrow political interests to justify the retention of Article 370 and to enlarge the present area of Kashmir's autonomy. For example, Narasimha Rao, while participating in the debate on the 'motion of confidence' in the Deve Gowda Government, on June 12, 1996, said that Kashmir and Article 370 were inseparable. He also posed a few questions: "What about Articles 371A, 371G and the like? Do they not contain special provisions? Why no objection is being raised with regard to them? Why an issue is being made only of Article 370?"

It was surprising that a former Prime Minister and a leader of Narasimha Rao's standing and experience should be making these observations. No less surprising was the silence of others who got the opportunity to speak on the 'motion'.

The untenability of Rao's observation regarding 'inseparability of Article 370 and Kashmir' stands exposed from what I have analysed in Chapter VI*. Jawahar Lal Nehru himself, while making a statement on the 'Delhi Agreement' on July 24, 1952, had described Article 370 as "an unusual provision and by no means final". Sardar Patel was far more clear when V. Shankar expressed doubts about the wisdom of Patel agreeing, albeit against his better judgment, to the draft of Gopalaswamy. Regarding this Article, he pertinently remarked:** "Neither Sheikh Abdullah nor Gopalaswamy is permanent. The future would depend upon the strength and guts of the Indian Government and if we cannot have confidence in our strength we do not deserve to exist as a nation." In fact, as argued earlier in this book, the Union of India has a duty to discharge under Article 355 of the Constitution. This Article enjoins upon the Union of India to protect the States from external aggression and internal disturbances. Since

---

* See particularly pages 227 to 234. See also Nehru's letter to Pandit Prem Nath Bazaz (page 239) wherein he had observed: "Much has been done in spite of Article 370 which is supposed to give special status to Kashmir and gradually what little remains would also go."

**V. Shankar: *My Reminiscences of Sardar Patel.*

Article 370 is facilitating both internal disturbances and external aggression, one by way of breeding separatism and the other by way of causing proxy war, it is constitutionally incumbent upon the Union of India to abrogate the "temporary and transitional provision" of Article 370 or to reduce it to a nullity to enable it to fulfil its fundamental duty, under Article 355, of protecting the States.

Equally untenable is the parallel which Narasimha Rao sought to draw between the provisions of Articles 371A, 371G, etc. and those of Article 370. The provisions of the former Articles are meant to safeguard the customary laws and procedure and social and religious practices of the tribal communities–Nagas, Mizos, etc. By no stretch of imagination can the case of these communities be compared to that of the inhabitants of J&K. Do Narasimha Rao and the like consider the people of Kashmir as tribals who require special protection? Or do they think that the laws which are good for the Muslims living elsewhere in India are not good for those living in Kashmir? Or do they believe that Articles 25 to 30 of the Indian Constitution, which afford protection to religious, cultural and educational rights of the minorities, cannot provide similar protection to the rights of Muslims in Kashmir? They know that there is no valid answer to these questions. And yet they would not stop misleading the public on Article 370.

An Unhealthy Feature

Unfortunately, it is an unhealthy feature of the present-day Indian public life that even senior leaders like Narasimha Rao are ever willing to subordinate intellectual honesty to the compulsions of narrow politics. They are always on the look-out for an argument, howsoever laboured and far-fetched, to support a stand that can swell their account in the vote-bank. By resorting to slant and even suppression, they hope to prevent the public from seeing through their game. For example, while inviting attention to Articles 371A and 371G, Rao not only omitted the points brought out above but also suppressed the vital fact that, unlike J&K, neither Nagaland nor Mizoram had a separate constitution or a separate flag of its own. Nor did Narasimha Rao say anything about the place of* Pandits in

---

*See chapter XIII, Appendix XXVI (Part I & Part II).

'Kashmir with maximum autonomy'. He also conveniently kept silent on the regional sensitivities* of Jammu and Ladakh as well as the unworkability of regional autonomy.

Tragic

It is, indeed, tragic that to serve their ends of power, quite a few of our leaders are confusing the people, dividing them and indirectly facilitating the task of those who want to see a torn and tormented India, an India that is continuously at war with itself. When I hear such superficial expressions like 'Kashmir: Short of Azadi' being intentionally touted by these leaders with nauseating frequency, I get very much concerned about the future of the country in general and Kashmir in particular and feel like saying: Forgive them not, father, for they know what they are doing.

The atmosphere had been fouled to such an extent that even otherwise well-meaning Prime Ministers of 1990s, such as V.P. Singh, Chandra Shekhar, P.V. Narasimha Rao, H.D. Deve Gowda and I.K. Gujral, were unable to sail above their small ends of personal and political power. They would make use of any opportunity to run down political rivals, outside or inside their party, without caring whether their actions would have the effect of weakening the national will to fight unitedly the menace of terrorism. In this regard, I may give an example from personal experience of first few months of my second term of Governorship in Kashmir.

On May 21, 1990, Mirwaiz Moulvi Farooq was assassinated. By no stretch of imagination, any act of commission or omission could be attributed to the Governor. As would be seen from the documented narration in Chapter XV, in section titled: *Moulvi Farooq Assassination,* Governor or his personal office was no where in the picture. But this did not deter Chandra Shekhar, rival of Prime Minister V.P. Singh within the same party, from causing huge problems for the Central Government and Governor's administration. Without ascertaining even elementary facts, he blurted out a statement to the pressmen, criticising the Governor 'for having marred the solemnity of the burial ceremony'. The motivation was to undercut Governor's position among Muslim masses and cause acute embarrassment to the Prime Minister. Truth was soon brought out, detailing the sequence of events

*See chapter VI. (Regarding notion of regional autonomy.)

that led to the assassination of the Maulvi by terrorists of the Hizb-ul-Mujahideen. But, with swarms of pro-Pakistan elements and several groups of professional disinformers around, the damage done by the fulmination of Chandra Shekhar could hardly be retrieved, particularly when he chose not to make it clear to the public, even subsequently, that his initial statement was wrong. His politics of vote-bank inhibited him from correcting himself, thereby letting the vitiated atmosphere to gather more sound and fury.

For quite sometimes, the attitude of Chandra Shekhar, who even attained the office of Prime Minister soon after May 21, 1990 incident, mentioned above, rankled in my mind. I nursed a sense of revulsion against his hidden disposition to serve his ends of personal and political power by banishing the dictates of truth from the terror related case of murder of Mirwaiz Farooq. But this sense of revulsion underwent a dramatic change when I came in close touch with Chandra Shekhar after about ten years.

While working as Union Minister for Culture and Tourism in the Cabinet of Atal Bihari Vajpayee, I was entrusted by the Prime Minister with an additional responsibility of acting as a Member-Secretary of Jai Prakash Narain Memorial Committee of which Chandra Shekhar was the Chairman and L.K. Advani, Deputy Chairman. In connection with the work of this Memorial Committee, I interacted with Chandra Shekhar on a number of occasions, and also travelled with him to different places. I found him a leader with a golden heart, sharp insight into the happy as well as unhappy layers of Indian history, and ever keen to collect the dismembered threads of national fabric and weave them into a cohesive pattern.

Ever since this elevating and refreshing experience with Chandra Shekhar, I have often been asking myself: How is it that a leader with such positive attributes in his attitude and outlook and such a high motivation for nation building activities, could be driven to furiously fan the forces of disruption and disarray on May 21, 1990, and thereabout, when the menace of terrorism and subversion was at its peak in Kashmir? The only answer that I could think of was that the contemporary Indian leadership has, by and large, shown an extraordinary weakness for serving its personal and political ends of power; and this weakness is not only undermining its standing in the public but also rendering its positive contribution in other fields effete and uninspiring.

With so many formidable problems, both internal and external, facing the country, and with the burden of past tragedies, arising out of habit of discord and disunity, on its back, the Indian leadership cannot afford to continue with its current fatal flaw. It must get rid of it–sooner the better. It would do well to remember what Vaclav Havel said at the time of assumption of power in Czechoslovakia on January 1, 1990: "Let us teach ourselves and others that politics can be not only the art of the possible–especially if this means intrigues, 'deals' and manoeuvring–but also the art of the impossible, namely, the art of improving ourselves".

CHAPTER XIX

Decisive Phase

Terrorism is a persistent disease and so the fight goes on. Just as we acknowledge success today, we know that there will be new challenges and yes, some setbacks tomorrow.

*Colin Powell**

The fight against terrorism has reached a decisive phase.

*Atal Bihari Vajpayee***

Continuation of Fundamental Infirmities

The oscillation between sternness and softness and getting in the process the worst of both the worlds has been the dominant feature of the State's approach to tackle terrorism in Kashmir. Its unfortunate consequences are for everybody to see. From September 1989 to November 15, 2001, about 52,000 terrorism related incidents had occurred in Kashmir, resulting in the death of about 9,700 civilians, about 3,000 members of security forces and about 14,000 terrorists. And yet terrorism remained and subversion continued. If anything, its beastly and brutal claws had become sharper and acquired greater reach. The attack on the Indian Parliament on December 13, 2001, which could have caused one of the gravest tragedies in Indian history, is a proof of this phenomenon.

---

* This observation was made by Colin Powell, US Secretary of State, while releasing the annual report on Patterns of Global Terrorism in May 2001.

**Prime Minister's Address to the Nation on December 13, 2001.

Contrast the terrorism related situation in India with that arising from the 'pro-democracy movement' centred around Tiananmen Square, in China. Once the Chinese state came to believe* that what was happening would imperil the stability of the country, cause large scale public disorder and divert the attention and resources of the nation from development to internal conflicts, which could be further fanned by external forces, it moved, with great clarity and vision, keeping at bay the cacophony of the human-rights bodies and armchairs intellectuals and hand ringers. After a few days, China was wholly out of the woads. Today, it is a powerful and peaceful State, attaining unprecedented pace in economic development, earning applause and prestige all around the world. On the other hand, India has remained engulfed not only in bloody terrorism but also in a number of its internal and external fall-outs. The inherent disinclination of the State and its governing machinery to take the bull by the horn and tame or vanquish it and to adopt a strong, sustained and focussed approach, concentrating on the centrality of the issues rather than on their peripheries, has cost the nation dearly. What is no less disconcerting is that, despite all talks about reforms and reorganisation, no 'root and branch' measures are in hand to combat internal subversion and acquire a strong political will and also show a determined face of governance to the saboteurs and their ring-masters across the border.

In Chapter X, titled: '*Nature and Pattern of Subversion and Terrorism*–Connivance, Collusion, Conspiracies', I had observed: "When the foundation is made of spurious material which is infested with white ants from within, a gale of low intensity is sufficient to bring the edifice down; a hurricane is not needed". It speaks volumes about India's inability to learn lesson from the past events that, even after several years, the white ants, let alone being destroyed in Kashmir, have spread to the capital, and the gale is threatening to turn into a hurricane, engulfing the nation in more serious trials and tribulations.

Mind and Soul Relationship

Few in our country realise that Kashmir's relationship with the rest of India is based not merely on the Instrument of Accession and Articles 1 and 370 of the Constitution of India; it is rooted in far more potent

*What I am advocating here is not the Chinese methodology of dealing with the problem but the clarity and consistency of its approach.

and enduring forces whom neither the turbulence and tornadoes of the past nor the negativism and nihilism of the present-day politics can really destroy. It is a relationship of mind and soul that has existed from time immemorial and found ample expression in common avenues of intellect and emotions, poetry and literature, philosophy and outlook. Every green pasture that you walk around in Kashmir, every silvery peak that you watch from pleasurable distance, every stream that sings its song by your side, every enchanting lake that you come across now and then and every little town and city that you visit, has some signpost or the other of this deep and abiding relationship. Kalhana was not off the mark when he observed in the *Rajtarangini* that there was hardly any place in Kashmir that was not a *tirtha.* And Vincent Smith rightly pointed out that ancient India had nothing more worthy of its early civilisation than the grand ruins of Kashmir.

To understand in depth Kashmir's relationship with the rest of India, it is necessary to address ourselves to a few basic questions.

What were the forces that brought into existence, about 4,000 years ago, a quiet little temple on what is now known as the Sankaracharya Hill? What made the great Kashmiri Lalitaditya (721-761) to build the glorious temple in honour of Surya, the Sun Lord, at Martanda, and Avanti Verman (855-883) to construct equally splendid temples at Avantipura? What inner urges did these constructions symbolise? What philosophy, what temper of mind, did they represent? Were these inner urges, these tempers of mind, not products of the same cultural forces that prevailed in other parts of India?

How is it that for thousands of years, the learned Brahmins of South India have, on getting up from bed, folded their hands, looked northward and prayed: *Namaste; Saradadevi; Kashmira Mandala Vasini* (I salute the Goddess of Sarada who resides in Kashmir). Why is it that even now parents tell their children to seek the blessings of this Goddess of Learning who has her abode in North Kashmir in the Valley of Kishanganga?

What made Sankara, when he wanted to rejuvenate the spirit of India, to travel from a small hut of Kaladi in Kerala all the way to the distant hills in Kashmir? And what made him stay there for quite some time and compose his famous poem, *Soundarya Lahari*, propounding his philosophy of Shakti and Shiva? Why is it that Abinava Gupta, the great savant of Kashmir Shaivism, is also called 'Sankaracharya of Kashmir', and how is it that he draws his philosophic thought from the same cultural spring as that of Sankara?

What were the forces that attracted Swami Vivekananda from Calcutta to Kanyakumari and then to Kashmir? What made him, standing before the holy Cave of Amarnath, experience one of the highest stages of spiritual ecstasy? Why was he so captivated by the sight in the Cave that for days, to use the words of Sister Nivedita, he could speak of nothing else but the image of Shiva and proclaim that he had never been so greatly inspired as then?

What do the various landmarks on the route from Pahalgam to the Cave of Amarnath–Chandanwari, Pishu Ghati, Seshnag, Panchtarni–stand for? Are they not some of the most important symbols of Indian culture and beliefs?

How is it that Kashmir had always an innate attraction for Indian saints and sages, poets and philosophers, and provided them with perennial inspiration? What, in moments of poetic intensity, made Kalidasa see the 'laughter of Shiva' in the Himalayas and Subramania Bharati think of Kashmir as the Crown of Mother India?

The answer to all these questions is one and only one: Kashmir, for thousands of years, has been a part of the Indian vision–a silent and serene, yet solid and strong part; an integral and inseparable part.

Even when Islam came to Kashmir, it did not alter the ethos of the common folk. Most of the Islamic teachings were just grafted on Vedantic beliefs and thoughts. The central message of Kashmir's patron saint and founder of the Rishi Order, Sheikh Nuru'd-Din Noorani was: "There is one God/But with a hundred names/There is not a single blade of grass/Which does not worship Him".

Sheikh Nuru'd-Din himself was deeply influenced by Lal Ded who "saw Shiva and Shakti sealed in one" and whose outlook was permeated with some of the finest components of Indian thought and tradition.

Both Sheikh Nuru'd-Din and Lal Ded were endowed "with vision which increases the power of speech and with inspired speech that makes vision penetrating". It was their inspired speech and their penetrating vision, coupled with earthy sense and rub of life, that kept the Kashmiri ethos within the overall cultural mainstream of India even after a very large part of the Valley's population had been brought under the fold of Islam. The followers of the Rishi Order abhorred killing. Like the Jains, they were careful not to cause harm even to insects. Sheikh Nuru'd-Din went to the extent of refusing to walk on the grass lest it should be damaged. Poet Mohammad Iqbal, who was a Kashmiri by descent, also noted in one of his Persian couplets, the habit of Kashmiri Muslims to carve out 'moortis' even from the stones of graves.

The list of the living symbols and signposts of Kashmir's relationship with the rest of India is long and virtually unending. But for our policy-makers it does not exist. No mention of it is ever made either inside or outside the country. No child is taught a word about it. No pressman writes a line on the subject. All that is spoken of or written about, almost ad nauseam, is the special relationship, the need to continue and strengthen Article 370, and of giving more and more autonomy–'anything short of Azadi'–promoting thereby a separatist psyche and according a tacit approval to the 'two nations' or 'three nations' theory.

The Indian decision-makers have been going astray at every turning point of Kashmir's contemporary history as they have neither any clear idea about the true vision of India nor of Kashmir's place in that vision. The few who have, in the past, entertained such a vision have, for one reason or the other, not been able to project it effectively at the national and international scene or secure its materialisation on the ground.

India must bring its 'mind and soul relationship' with Kashmir to the forefront and assert it at every fora with unwavering conviction. Without this fundamental reorientation of its approach, developments connected with Kashmir, both internal and external, would not take the right course. There is, in fact, only one way to salvage the position. And that lies in the emergence of new political, social and cultural forces that could discover the true vision of India and outline its true destiny and assign Kashmir its rightful place in that vision and that destiny.

Killings–A Routine

As I was writing this chapter, my eyes fell on the front page story of a national daily of February 18, 2002, which reads: "Suspected Lashkar-e-Taiba terrorists gunned down eight Hindu villagers in the remote area of Kalakote in Rajouri district early on Sunday. Among the dead were five children and two women. Six people, including a pregnant woman, were critically injured... The dead children were aged between one-and-a-half and 13. The eighth victim was 20". The brutal events of this nature have been happening with such a chilling ferocity and frequency that they have now virtually become a routine part of Jammu and Kashmir's landscape and get noticed only in passing.

To recapitulate only a few of these dreadful incidents, 28 innocent persons were killed in cold blood at Prankote on April 19, 10 at Deesa on May 6, 25 at Chapnari on June 19, 17 at Thakraimhar on June 27 and 34 near Himachal Pradesh border on August 3, 1998. Twenty persons were done to death near Rajouri and Udhampur on February 19, 1999, that is, on the very day Indian Prime Minister, Shri Atal Bihari Vajpayee, was undertaking his 'Bus Yatra' from the Wagah border to Lahore. On December 24, 1999, the Indian Airlines Flight IC-814, Kathmandu-Delhi, was hijacked and one passenger, Rupin Katyal, was killed. The termination of hijacking and release of the hostages could be secured on December 31, 1999 only by releasing three top terrorists–Masood Azhar, Mushtaq Zargar and Omar Shaikh, who subsequently played a prominent role in organising such dreadful events as the blasting of World Trade Centre Towers and attack on J&K Assembly. On March 28, 2000, during President Clinton's visit to India, 35 Sikhs were brutally murdered at Chattisingpur. In the same bloody strain, 31 civilians were killed in Doda on July 21 and May 02, 2001. The State Legislative Assembly was attacked on October 1, 2001 killing at least 29 persons and seriously injuring 63.

Treacherous Drama: Kargil War

In all these heinous crimes, Pakistan's complicity was more than clear. In between, in early 1999, it enacted a treacherous drama in Kargil. While the Indian Prime Minister was taking a message of peace to Lahore, both the parties were committing themselves, through the Lahore Declaration, to share a vision of peace and stability between their countries and reiterating their faith in the Shimla Agreement, Pakistan was sending its troops, in the guise of Mujahideens, and occupying such strategic areas as Mashkoh, Daras, Kaksar and Batalik.

The nature of Pakistan's perfidy was brought out by the Kargil Review Committee which was set up by the Government of India on July 29, 1999. It has made the following observations at different portions of its report:

> It would appear that reconnaissance parties comprising officers started crossing the LOC in late January/early February 1999. They

> established a first line of administrative bases within a limited distance across the LOC in February. March saw heavy snowfall and so they could move further forward only in April... It is difficult to say whether the initiative for this move came from the Army or was politically driven. There was a heady combination of circumstances and personalities... The balance of probability suggests that Nawaz Sharif was fully in picture. This is borne out by the tapes of conversation between General Musharraf and Lieutenant General Aziz, Chief of General Staff. These tapes also revealed that expectation of Pakistani authorities was of early intervention by the international community and the likelihood of a cease-fire.

The Committee's overall conclusion was:

> The Kargil action saw the deployment of a limited number of troops and aircraft on a restricted front in response to a shallow Pakistani penetration across the LOC of no more than eight to nine kilometres at most. Nevertheless, given the terrain and political implications of an attempt to create a 'new LOC', and in the background of nuclear capability on both sides, *this was not a minor skirmish but a short, sharp war in which the Indian Army and Air Force suffered 474 killed and 1109 wounded.*

Poor Work-ethos

The inadequacies of the present-day Administration and its poor work-ethos, which I have highlighted in earlier chapters, were also noted by the Review Committee. It said:

> There are no checks and balances in the Indian intelligence system to ensure that the consumer gets all the intelligence that is available and is his due. There is no system of regular, periodic and comprehensive intelligence briefings at the political level and to the Committee of Secretaries. In the absence of an overall, operational national security framework and objectives, each intelligence agency is diligent in preserving its own turf and departmental prerogatives. There is no evidence that the intelligence agencies have reviewed their role after India became a nuclear weapon state or in the context of the increasing problems posed by insurgencies and ethnonationalist turbulences backed with sophisticated high-

tech equipment and external support. Nor has the Government felt the need to initiate any such move.

That such a situation should prevail even after more than a decade of experience of dealing with terrorism and subversion is a sad reflection on the culture of governance in this country.

Nuclear Factor

During the Kargil war and a decade old Pakistan's proxy war against India, the nuclear factor has all along remained in the reckoning. India, for once, showed courage and decisiveness and successfully exploded five nuclear devices on May 11 and 13, 1998. By doing so, India not only broke the monopoly of the 'five members nuclear club', but also established a credible deterrence *vis-à-vis* Pakistan which all along had been hinting at the use of the nuclear bomb, should India choose to wage conventional warfare to end the menace of terrorism from across the border. In August 1990, for example, India had received reliable information that, in the event of direct military confrontation between India and Pakistan, the latter would not hesitate to use the nuclear weapon as a first resort.

Peace Initiatives

Despite bitter experience, India undertook a bold step and announced a unilateral cease-fire on November 27, 2000. It was continued up to May 23, 2001. But the outcome was no different. Neither the killing of innocent persons abated nor was there any let up in other subversive activities. On the other hand, the number of civilian casualties increased and the terrorists re-equipped and re-organised themselves. During this period, there was also 79 per cent increase in the casualties suffered by the security forces, and the terrorists extended their activities even to Delhi. On December 22, 2000, an army garrison within Red Fort was attacked.

Subsequently, the Indian Prime Minister took another initiative and invited President, General Pervez Musharraf, for a Summit Meeting at Agra–July 14-17, 2001. The old story was repeated. During the three days of the Summit, the killings mounted and 84 innocent persons were massacred. In the first sixteen days of July 2001, 256 persons were killed. President Musharraf, moreover, used this Summit as an opportunity for putting the Kashmir issue on the centre-stage and attracting world-wide attention in the process.

Attack on World Trade Centre

On September 11, 2001, the world underwent what may turn out to be an epoch-making spin. It saw the world's most unexpected, most spectacular and most lethal terrorist attack on the fortress of the world's only super-power–United States. Two American planes, hijacked by the terrorists, rammed into the 110 storeyed World Trade Centre and reduced it to rubble, causing as many as 2800 fatal casualties–perhaps 'the largest conventional kill on a single day'. Another hijacked plane slammed into the Pentagon, causing a number of casualties.

As noted by Stephen Emerson, a specialist on Islamic terrorism, neither the United States nor its European allies took any serious notice of the menace of terrorism till it affected its own citizens. They took practically no notice of India's repeated warning that Afghanistan and Pakistan had become a new epicentre of 'Jehadi terrorism' which was being led by resourceful and fanatical leaders as Osama bin Laden and Mullah Omar. But the destruction of the World Trade Centre caused a fundamental shift. The international opinion was mobilised. A wide-ranging anti-terrorism resolution was passed unanimously by the United Nations Security Council on September 28, 2001. This resolution said that the States should "refrain from providing any form of support to entities or persons involved in terrorist acts; take the necessary measure to prevent the commission of terrorist acts; deny safe haven to those who finance, plan, support and commit terrorist acts".

Clearly, the United States and its allies have committed themselves to elimination of terrorism in all forms and from all places. For tactical reasons, however, they have not, at the moment, joined hands with India for mounting effective pressure on Pakistan. The compulsion of the Afghan situation makes it, perhaps, necessary for them to keep Pakistan on their side. But in the coming days, India would have to show its best diplomatic and strategic cards to turn the events in its favour and secure total elimination of terrorism, sponsored by Pakistan, from its soil.

Attack on Parliament

On December 13, 2001, in an audacious move, terrorists attacked the Indian Parliament. "This time", to use the words of Union Home Minister, L.K. Advani, "the terrorists and their mentors across the border had the temerity to try to wipe out the entire political leadership of India, as represented in our multi-party Parliament". The entire nation was outraged. The Indian troops were moved to the border, signalling both to Pakistan and the international community that India was no longer taking things lying down. It also asked Pakistan to hand over 20 most wanted terrorists hiding in that country.

Decisive Phase

In his address to the nation on December 13, 2001, Prime Minister Atal Bihari Vajpayee declared that the fight against terrorism had reached a decisive phase. But the Government had to do something more. It had to comprehend indepth the totality of the circumstances around and meet the challenges of decisive phases with determined action which had so far been absent from its approach. General Douglas MacArthur once observed: "The history of failure in war can be summed up in two words: Too late. Too late in comprehending the deadly purpose of a potential enemy; too late in realising the mortal danger; too late in preparedness; too late in uniting all possible forces for resistance; too late in standing up with one's friends." The relevance and significance of these observations, in the context of terrorism and subversion in Kashmir, have not so far crossed the mind of the Indian political rulers. Consequently, the country has paid, and is still paying a heavy price for its leadership's delayed, half-baked, narrow and inconsistent response.

Would the present Indian attitudes change in the 'decisive phase'? Would the political mindscape of India receive a new orientation? Would Kashmir's abiding link, with the rest of India, get projected both at the national and international level? Would the culture of governance undergo a 'root and branch reform'? The outcome of the 'decisive phase' would be determined by the new responses to these questions. It has to be kept in mind that 'there is always a tide in the affairs of men; if seized, it takes them across, if missed, it leaves them stranded on the wrong side of the shore'.

CHAPTER XX

New Era: New Response

The era does not reward those who struggle in vain; who redraw borders with blood... There is no military solution to Kashmir... There is a danger that Pakistan may grow even more isolated, draining even more resources away from the needs of the people, moving even closer to a conflict no one can win.

*–President Clinton**

Marx's opiate has become Islamists' Elixir.

–Lawrence Ziring

The struggle against current terrorism is not a clash between civilisations; it is a clash about civilisation.

–Tony Blair

Persistence of Old Attitude

Despite Prime Minister Atal Bihari Vajpayee's statement that the fight against terrorism had reached a decisive phase, India's old habit of not taking decisive action persisted. As an expression of national indignation and with a view to taking steam out of the rising criticisms of government's inability to end the menace of terrorism, a few seemingly strong measures were taken. The Indian High Commissioner was recalled from Islamabad, the road, rail and air links were snapped and troops were amassed at the line of control and

*These remarks were made by President Bill Clinton in his Television and Radio address to the people of Pakistan during the course of his five hours' visit to the country on March 25, 2000.

international border, in battle formations, under an operation code-named *Parakram*. But nothing concrete happened on the ground.

At that time, a swift but limited action to attack and destroy the training camps of the terrorists in Pakistan-occupied Kashmir (PoK) would have sent a strong message to all concerned that India's patience had been exhausted and it could no longer suffer serious threat to its security and brutal deaths of its innocent citizens. The international community on the whole would have understood India's predicament and its reaction against the move would not have been very strong. Even if its intervention had brought an immediate end to India's action, Pakistan support to terrorism would have been thoroughly exposed and President Musharraf would have come under much stronger international pressure to close the terrorists' camps and end cross-border terrorism.

Unfortunately, India remained indecisive, vacillating between 'to do or not to do'. The general impression that India was a soft state was reinforced. The *Operation Parakram,* which involved a huge deployment of forward troops and which cost the country about ₹ 6500 crore and lives of 798 soldiers, was called off after about ten months. If India had not the will to take result-oriented action, it need not have resorted to such a costly venture. It did not, as detailed in a subsequent section of this chapter, cause any meaningful reduction in the terrorism-related incidents in J&K or other parts of country.

As compared to India, Pakistan proved cleverer in playing its cards. On the one hand, President Pervez Musharraf ordered full deployment of armed forces, in battle formations, on the border, giving an impression to the international community that there was a danger of full scale war, including nuclear war, between India and Pakistan; on the other, he talked of measures being taken by him against the extremists and *Jihadi* organisations. In his televised address to the nation, on January 12, 2002, he announced a ban on two of the most dangerous militant outfits–*Jaish-e-Mohammad* and *Lashkar-e-Taiba.* He also declared that he would ensure that misuse of mosques was ended and affairs of *madrasas* regulated. A few days earlier, at Kathmandu, Pakistan had become a party to the SAARC Declaration which not only reiterated support to the UN Security Council Resolution no. 1373 but also emphasised: "Terrorism in all its forms and manifestations is a challenge to all states and to all humanity and cannot be justified on ideological, political, religious or on any other grounds and it constitutes one of the most serious threats to international peace and security in the 21st century".

By and large, through such measures, Pakistan was able to secure favourable reaction from the United States and the European powers, despite the fact that there was no decline either in the number or in the savagery of incidents of terrorism. To cite a few cases, on May 14, 2002, 36 family members of Army Jawans, residing in the cantonment of Kaluchak, near Jammu, were mercilessly killed. During the August–September 2002 elections to J&K Assembly, 34 political leaders and 168 civilians were killed by the terrorists.

Oscillation

The Indian leadership, typical of its attitude with regard to the Kashmir issue, oscillated between sternness and softness. After showing firmness at the initial stages, it soon exposed its softer side. In a newspaper article, written on new year's eve, Prime Minister A.B. Vajpayee reflected: "In our search of a lasting solution to the Kashmir problem, both in its internal and external dimensions, we shall not traverse solely the beaten track of the past. Rather we shall be bold and innovative designer of a future architecture of peace and prosperity for the entire South-Asian region". Addressing Pakistan, he added: "Shed your anti-India mentality, and you will find India willing to walk more than half the distance to work closely with Pakistan to resolve through dialogue any issue including the contentious issue of J&K".

Soon thereafter, however, at the SAARC Summit, held at Kathmandu in the first week of January, 2002, Vajpayee adopted a stiff posture. When, somewhat unexpectedly, President Pervez Musharraf came to the seat of Indian Prime Minister to offer greetings and extend what was termed as "a hand of genuine and sincere friendship", Vajpayee's response was rather cold. He reminded Musharraf, albeit in a faint tone, that India had been betrayed twice: Kargil witnessed infiltration of Pakistani troops in the guise of Mujahideen soon after India's Bus Yatra of Peace to Lahore, and attack on the Indian Parliament came in the wake of Agra Summit.

During the period of stalemate, as was, perhaps, calculated by President Pervez Musharraf, India came under pressure from the United States, European powers and even Russia, to ease tension and resume dialogue with Pakistan whom they had simultaneously advised to view the J&K Assembly elections positively and to take firmer measures against those who infiltrated into India and resorted to terrorist activities.

India went on reiterating that Pakistan must first ensure that the cross-border terrorism came to an end. But then, suddenly, on April 18, 2003, at a public meeting at Srinagar, Vajpayee announced that notwithstanding the failure of his earlier peace initiatives–Lahore Bus Yatra and Agra Summit–he would once again extend India's hand of friendship to Pakistan. The response of Zafarullah Khan Jamali, Prime Minister of Pakistan, to this announcement was warm. He invited Vajpayee to visit Pakistan. He also volunteered to come to India for talks.

De-escalation of Tension

De-escalation of tension was the natural outcome of these developments. The snapped links of road, rail and air were gradually restored, High Commissioners appointed and normal diplomatic activities resumed. Earlier, on October 17, 2002, India had withdrawn its troops from the border. Pakistan followed suit a day afterwards. On November 25, 2003, both India and Pakistan agreed to a cease-fire along the entire border.

On January 6, 2004, during the SAARC Summit held at Islamabad, President Pervez Musharraf and Prime Minister Vajpayee, issued a joint statement to the Press after their meeting. This statement, *inter-alia,* read:

> Prime Minister Vajpayee said that in order to take forward and sustain the dialogue process, violence, hostility and terrorism must be prevented. President Musharraf reassured Prime Minister Vajpayee that he will not permit any territory under Pakistan's control to be used to support terrorism in any manner. President Musharraf emphasised that a sustained and productive dialogue addressing all issues would lead to positive results. To carry the process of normalisation forward, the President of Pakistan and the Prime Minister of India agreed to commence the process of the composite dialogue in February 2004. The two leaders are confident that the resumption of the composite dialogue will lead to peaceful settlement of all bilateral issues, including J&K, to the satisfaction of both sides.

The change of government in New Delhi, following the Lok Sabha elections of April-May 2004, did not make any material difference to the above position. Dr. Manmohan Singh, the new Prime Minister, broadly followed the line adopted by A.B. Vajpayee. This would be clear from the joint statement issued by President Pervez Musharraf and the Prime Minister Dr. Manmohan Singh on September 24, 2004, after their meeting in New York. They reiterated their commitment to continue bilateral dialogue to restore normalcy and cooperation between India and Pakistan.

In pursuance of the two aforesaid meetings, a number of 'confidence building measures' were taken. Delegations of parliamentarians, businessmen, journalists and other non-officials had started visiting each other's country. The official talks at the level of Secretaries and experts have also been held to resolve various issues. During the cricket matches, arranged between the two countries, friendly atmosphere prevailed. This was in sharp contrast to what used to happen earlier.

Spanner in the works

Nevertheless, a spanner in the works had been thrown in by Pakistan from time to time. President Pervez Musharraf's reference to UN resolutions in his address to the UN General Assembly in September 2005 and his patronising attitude towards Hurriyat leaders had once again caused serious misgivings in India about his intentions. He had also been instrumental in getting a declaration made, on December 9, 2005, at the Conference of the 57-member Organisation of Islamic Countries, which called for "respect of the human rights of Kashmiri people" and agreed to provide all possible political and diplomatic support to representatives of Kashmiri people. Musharraf's attitude had, indeed, been baffling. Sometimes he looked friendly, at other times hostile. In her book on Pakistan, Mary Anne Weaver has said: "Musharraf had been described to me as a chameleon: a man who can be anything". The course of Indo-Pak talks shows that this description was not wrong.

Continuance of Terrorism

What was, however, most disconcerting was that, notwithstanding 'dialogues', 'joint statements', 'peace processes' and 'confidence building measures', there has been no let-up in the activities of the terrorists. The triple attack by them in Delhi on October 29, 2005 which butchered 62 innocent persons, including women and children, spoke volumes not only about their savage nature but also of the long reach that they still possessed.

In connection with the continuing menace of terrorism, what needs to be especially noted is that after the withdrawal of Soviet forces from Afghanistan, all the wherewithal needed for causing terrorism in Kashmir became available to Pakistan. By that time, its Inter-Services Intelligence (ISI) had become one of the most dangerous, powerful and resourceful intelligence organisations in the World. Thousands of well-trained, well-armed and well-motivated young 'mujahideens' were at its disposal. Earlier, the organisation had manipulated a huge supply of lethal and light weapons which were sent by US to Pakistan for the Afghan war.

According to a US Congressional Report, about 60 per cent of the sophisticated weapons were diverted by the ISI for its own use. So was the position with regard to funds. Drug money was also laundered for smuggling of arms and for further recruitment and training of 'mujahids'. It was estimated that in one year alone, 1992, the landed value of the drugs from Pakistan was about US $ 13 billion.

The soft underbelly of the Indian state, its partisan politics and its disposition to live in the world of make-believe facilitated the task of the ISI. Further, the United States and other western countries, instead of outright condemnation of militants' activities, placed disproportionate emphasis on alleged human rights violations and provided a massive puff of oxygen to them by way of publicity.

Neither the United States nor its European allies took any serious notice of the menace of terrorism till it affected its own citizens. They took practically no notice of India's repeated warning that Pakistan had become a hot bed of militancy which was being served, in diverse ways, by the ISI as well as by the private sectarian armies, the number of which was daily increasing.

Lapse of Historic Proportion

By not going all out to nip the evil of terrorism in the bud, the USA and its allies committed a lapse of truly historic proportion. It ignored the stark reality that the so-called 'freedom fighters' of Kashmir were a part and parcel of the network of terror that was emerging all over the globe to destroy the 'enemies' wherever they existed. By the time the

U.S.A. and other western countries woke up to the reality, the menace had spread far and wide. The militants could strike anywhere they chose, be it in New York, New Delhi, Madrid, Bali, Egypt or London.

According to a research study (2004) of the London Institute of International Security, about 18000 potential terrorists are functioning in about 60 countries, and "there has been terrifying jump in terrorist incidents–175 in 2003 to 651 in 2004". Terrorism is becoming mega-terrorism. Even 'cyber warriors' and 'computer hackers' are being trained.

Madrasas

In Pakistan alone, there are thousands of religious schools–'madrasas'–which are virtually serving as a continuous supply-line for the militant organisations. In 1947, there were 137 'madrasas' with a total enrollment of about 20,000 students. The number of these 'madrasas' has now swelled to about 10,000 and students to about one and half million.

In theory, these 'madrasas' are meant for providing free religious education, board and lodging to poor students with a view to preparing them for undertaking services in the religious sector. But, in practice, a large number of these 'madrasas', particularly those that are run, directly or indirectly, by extremist organisations, have become a vast breeding ground for orthodoxy, narrow sectarianism and militancy. They promote the culture of *Jihad* and inject fanaticism in young and impressionable souls. They have developed a capacity to collect large funds by way of alms. The extent of their collections can be seen from the fact that in a single year, 2002, they were able to muster finances to the tune of ₹ 70 billion from domestic sources alone. The donations made by the people of Pakistani origin, settled abroad, are also phenomenal.

Some of the institutions of this genre have acquired enormous powers. For example, the *Markaz-e-Dawa al Irshad,* a seminary located in Muridke, near Lahore, has set up a huge organisational network, with a number of subsidiary schools and training centres. It has created a military wing of its own–Lashkar-e-Taiba. This wing has been very active. It has caused hundreds of terrorism-related incidents in J&K and other parts of India. It also runs a vast publicity and propaganda machine. Its monthly publication *Majallah-al-Dawa* has a circulation of over 400,000. Its weekly–*Jihad Times*–has over 200,000 buyers. Through these publications and other publicity material, the *Markaz* is spreading its ideology far and wide and influencing the thinking of a sizeable section of the people.

Clearly, the 'madrasas' and the special institutions, such as the *Markaz-e-Dawa al Irshad,* are creating an overall environment which breed religious fanaticism and violence. No wonder, in 2001-2002, there were as many as 58 religious political parties and 24 religious militias in Pakistan. The International Crisis Group* has rightly observed:

> The crux of the problem comes down to the type of education that the madrasas impart. Education that creates barriers to modern knowledge, stifling creativity and breeding bigotry, has become the madrasas' defining feature. It is this foundation on which fundamentalism–militant or otherwise–is built.

The 9/11 Commission**, in its first part of the Report, has come to similar conclusion: "Some of the madrasas have been used as incubators for violent extremisms."

War on Terror

Immediately after '9/11', President George W. Bush declared war on terror and in pursuance of this war he has made it clear:

> We will make no distinction between those who planned these attacks and those who harbour them...You are either 100 per cent with us or 100 per cent against us...There is no grey area.***

Change of Stance

President Pervez Musharraf was one of those who got the message. He changed his stance quickly. In a televised address to the nation on

---

* The International Crisis Group is an independent, private multinational organisation with its headquarters at Brussels, Belgium. It has a high level Board which is chaired by the former Finnish President, Matti Ahtisaari. Its main objective is to strengthen the "capacity of the international community to anticipate, understand and act to prevent and contain conflicts." The Group produces regular analytical reports which contain practical recommendations for consideration of the decision makers at the national as well as international levels.

** This is a ten-member Independent National Commission set up by the President in November, 2002 to investigate into the matters connected with the Terrorists attacks upon United States.

*** Text of President Bush's speech on September 11, 2001.

January 12, 2003, referred to earlier in this chapter, he raised quite a few pertinent questions and denounced the 'extremist minority':

> Do we want Pakistan to become a theocratic state? Do we believe that religious education alone is enough for governance or do we want Pakistan to emerge as a progressive and dynamic Islamic welfare state?...Look at what this extremist minority is doing. They are indulging in fratricidal killings...Mosques are being misused for propagating and inciting hatred against each other's sect and beliefs...The extremist minority must realise that Pakistan is not responsible for waging armed Jihad in the world.

To curb the forces of fundamentalism and fanaticism, a number of measures were also taken by the government of Pakistan. An ordinance* asking all the 'madrasas' to get themselves registered under the Societies Registration Act and keep account of the donations received, was issued on June 19, 2002. Foreign pupils of the seminaries and 'madrasas', who did not fulfill prescribed conditions, were asked to leave the country. Under the latest Anti-Terror Resolution (September 2005) of the United Nations Security Council, Pakistan has committed itself to adopt tighter measures to check terrorism.

Half Measures

But, as has been a characteristic of President Musharraf's regime, all these measures have turned out to be half measures. Their ineffectiveness has been exposed by the independent media reports in Pakistan itself. For example, the prestigious magazine, *Herald,* in its issue of August 2005, has published the list of training camps** that are still functioning in Manshera complex. The banned organisations have merely changed their names and re-located the centres of their operations. Almost all the 15,000 members of these organisations, who were arrested when the drive against the extremists was first launched, were soon released. Even now more than a dozen private armies are functioning on the ground. The ordinance issued to keep a watch over the affairs of 'madrasas' has no teeth. Both registration of

* This ordinance is titled *Deeni Madaris* (Volunteer Registration and Regulation) Ordinance 2000.

**These training camps are: Pano Dheri, Jallo Sufaida, Ogi, Khewari, Jabba, Batrasi, Naradoga, Akherilla, Hisari, Boi, Tanglaee and Achherian.

the 'madrasas'* and making their accounts available to the audit are not compulsory. Consequently, in essence, the old order, with all its deleterious fall-outs, continues.

The International Crisis Group has rightly noted that "Musharraf's actions reveal a piecemeal, tentative and ad hoc approach to a complex problem". This Group has also remarked:

> It is doubtful whether the military government has the intent or the will to set Pakistani society on a sustainable course that would lead to political pluralism and religious tolerance. On a key test–reform of madrasas, Pakistani religious schools that breed extremism of many hues–the military government thus far has acted weakly.

The 9/11 Commission, in its third report, released on November 14, 2005, too, has underlined the inadequacy of the measures taken by President Musharraf against the forces that breed sectarianism, extremism and militancy. It says:

> Pakistan remains a sanctuary and training ground for terrorists. Musharraf does not appear to have lived up to his promises to regulate the madrasas properly or close down all those that are known to have links to extremist groups. Taliban forces still pass freely across the Pakistan-Afghanistan border and operate in Pakistani tribal areas. Terrorists from Pakistan carry out operations in Kashmir...Pakistan needs to enact terrorist financing legislation...We are disappointed that Musharraf has not done more.

A Two-Fold Strategy

With the passage of time, it is becoming increasingly clear that in regard to his new approach towards the issue of terrorism, President Musharraf had adopted a two-fold strategy. So far as the interest of the USA, UK and other European powers were concerned, he was taking action to keep them satisfied. He had extended full cooperation to the CIA and FBI in tracing and arresting the terrorists wanted by them.**

---

* In the first week of December, 2005, President Pervez Musharraf has issued another ordinance which prohibits the 'madrasas' from teaching or publishing literature which promote militancy, sectarianism and religious hatred. It is too early to assess its impact on the ground.

** Al-Qaeda leaders like Abu Zubaida and Khalid Sheikh Mohammad and many other members were handed over to the US. They had been detained in Guantanamo.

But he had his limitations.* Over the years the Pakistani society has been largely fundamentalised. “Propagation of Jihad and weaponisation of Islam have inflicted a permanent damage on civil society and state institutions of Pakistan.”** In view of this damage President Musharraf cannot stamp out extremism and anti-Americanism in a short time.

As regards India, President Musharraf did not seem to have even intentions to dismantle the infrastructure of terrorism. As indicated above, the militant organisations and the training camps have been functioning in Pakistan. Their activities are mainly directed against India. In addition to the outrageous events, referred to earlier in this chapter, there had been hundred of terrorism-related incidents which have resulted in death of about 700 persons, in 2005, in J&K alone. And organisations like Lashkar-e-Taiba, Jaish-e-Mohammad, Hizbul Mujahideen and Al Badr have been routinely claiming responsibility for these incidents.

Pakistan government has taken no tangible measures to stop such incidents. No militant has ever been intercepted by Pakistan’s military while crossing the ‘line of control’. In an interview to the *Herald* (September 2005 issue), Maulana Fazlur Rahman, ‘amir’ of Jamiat Ulema-e-Islam had said, “The Pakistani youth who support the cause of Kashmir go there to fight. Providing them with training, money, weapons and transportation is not a task which is cut out for you and me. In fact, it cannot happen without the government’s support”. That is why there had been a series of serious terrorism related incidents all over India.

To recount some of the these deadly incidents that ensued from these activities, sixty-five persons were killed on October 29, 2005, in a series of blasts that occurred at Delhi in Sarojini Nagar, Paharganj and Govindpuri. On December 28, 2005, the pride of the Indian science, the Institute at Bangalore, was attacked, causing the death of an eminent academician, M.C. Puri, Prof. Emeritus, Mathematics, Indian Institute of Technology, Delhi. Right on the bank of Ganga, in one of the most sought after Hanuman temples in the country, Sankat Mochan, Varanasi, were caused two powerful explosions on March 7, 2006, by way of bombs hidden in the pressure cookers. At about the

* There were several attempts on President Musharraf’s life by Jihadi elements.

**Khalid Ahmed: Islamic Extremism in Pakistan–Journal of South Asian Journalists (Vol. 2).

same time, another bomb was blasted at Cantonment railway station. Twenty persons lost their lives in these two incidents. On July 11, 2006, a horrible drama was enacted in the suburban trains at Mumbai, when 192 commuters were killed in a series of bombs lasted in the crowded compartments. On the same day, Srinagar witnesses a number of grenade attacks, specially targeting tourists. Eight persons were killed and 41 injured. After about two months, on September 8, Malegaon town, Maharashtra, became a hapless victim of bomb attacks, losing 34 of its innocent citizens. 68 persons were burnt to death, on February 18, 2007, in another inhuman act of bombing 'Samjhauta Express' near Panipat, Haryana. On March 30, 2007, at Thiriat village in Rajourie district of J&K, five Hindu labourers were segregated from their Muslim colleagues, lined up and shot in cold blood. The ease and confidence with which this brutal act was performed showed how strong is still the presence of terrorists in the State. They even stayed in the same house for the night, cooked and ate their food and left only in the morning. The grim ground-level reality was further reinforced by the broad-day killing of a senior Congress leader, Jan Mohammad Kakaroo, in Baramulla on April 1. At historic Mecca Masjid, Hyderabad, immediately after the Friday prayer on May 18, 2007, a powerful blast ripped through a large crowd at the gate, killing 11 persons.

Musharraf's 'Out of Box' Suggestions

Amidst all these happenings, President Musharraf had been talking of the possible lines on which solution of the Kashmir problem could be worked out. In the course of press conferences, interviews with individual journalists and inaugural speeches at seminars, he had been floating suggestions in respect of 'self-rule on both the sides' of 'line of control', 'demilitarisation', 'free movement between the two sides', 'joint management', 'splitting up of the state regions', etc.

The most charitable interpretation that could be put on President Musharraf's suggestions was that, like a good General, he was searching for a line of retreat. But a realistic interpretation, which was more in tune with Musharraf's past deeds, would lead to the conclusion that he was laying a trap for India and attempting to attain his objective which he could not attain by way of terror-tactics and proxy war. Let me analyse these suggestions, one by one, and expose their untenability.

*Self Rule**

President Pervez Musharraf has never cared to spell out his concept of self-governance, though he has been saying: "We need to define what is the maximum autonomy that you are talking of and what is the self-governance that I am talking of. We need to see how the people govern themselves".**

In a modern democratic state, the people do not rule themselves directly. They do so through their representatives whom they periodically elect. On the India side, such a self-rule already exists.

The Indian side of Line of Control

As in other states of the Union, people of J&K elect*** their own representatives to the Legislative Assembly, which has vast area of independent governance under its jurisdiction. Not only that, the state of J&K enjoys a special status under Article 370 of the Indian Constitution. It enjoys a workable autonomy, as has already been indicated in chapter XVIII****. To temper with this structure of self-governance, either at the instance of President Musharraf or on the demand of some politically ambitious local leaders would amount to nothing but fanning further the forces of subversion and secession and pushing the State in the lap of Pakistan.

Self-Rule: Pakistani Side of LOC

In respect of the Pakistani side of Line of Control, no serious discussion on the pattern of self-governance is really called for. Where is the question of any such governance, when the entire Pakistan itself has been ruled, for about half the period of its existence, by one

* The bulk of the Valley of Kashmir, Jammu region, Ladakh and a portion of Rajourie and Poonch fall on the Indian side of Line of Control. On Pakistan side are Northern Areas of Gilgit and Baltistan and also districts of Muzaffarabad, Kotli, Poonch, Mirpur, Bagh, Bhimber and Sudhnot.

** Frontline: August 25, 2006. President Musharraf in an interview given to journalist, A.G. Noorani.

*** The State Assembly elections, held in 2002, were recognised as fair by independent national and international observers. The turnout of voters was also impressive. The party in power, National Conference, was voted out.

**** See sub-sections: Short of Azadi: Maximum Autonomy, Hollowness of Approach; Nuts and Bolts of Working Relationship; Specious Argument and An Unhealthy Feature.

military dictator or the other? If no respect is shown to the democratic aspirations of the people of Pakistan, how could the military rulers entertain any idea about grant of autonomy in practice to the government of "Azad Jammu-Kashmir"? In fact, they did not make even pretence in this regard. For example, after General Zia-ul-Huq coup in 1977, the "Azad Jammu-Kashmir" Assembly was dissolved, Parliamentary system scrapped and Presidential form of government set-up. An army Brigadier was appointed its Chief Executive. This arrangement continued till 1985, when elections were held after amending the rules in such a manner that the opposition parties were marginalised. Even during the period of civilian rule in Pakistan, the conditions were manipulated to bring ruling party of Islamabad in power in Muzaffarabad. Throughout the period of its existence, the "Azad Jammu-Kashmir" government has virtually remained a proxy of the Government of Pakistan.

It is significant to note that under the Constitution Act, 1974, an "Azad Jammu-Kashmir" Council was set-up with Chief Executive of Pakistan as Chairman, "Azad Jammu-Kashmir" President, as Vice Chairman and Pakistan Minister of Kashmir Affairs and Northern Areas as Secretary. It had executive and legislative jurisdiction over 52 subjects, leaving little area for exercise of powers by the "Azad" government and Assembly. It was given out that the Council would act as a 'link' for coordination. But in practice it has always a decisive say. Its Chairman enjoys the sole power of declaring emergency and dissolving the Assembly. Further, the Act of 1974 stipulates that "Azad Jammu-Kashmir" Supreme Court has no jurisdiction over the decisions of aforesaid Council.

In the circumstances, the "Azad Jammu-Kashmir" government is nothing but an appendage of the Pakistan government, enjoying no independence in practice. Its financial powers, too, are limited. Nor can it make any key appointment. Its Chief Secretary, Finance Secretary and Inspector-General are appointed by the Central government. Whatever little sphere for exercise of independent power exists, it has all along been monopolised by a small clique of politicians–Sardar Abdul Qayyum Khan and his son, Barrister Sultan Mahmood, Raja Mumtaz Rathore etc. In respect of Central financial assistance, the 'Azad JK area' has also not been liberally treated. On the other hand, a sizeable section of its population has suffered displacement on account of Mangla Dam the benefits of which have largely gone to West Pakistan.

So far as Northern Areas are concerned, these have been virtually incorporated in Pakistan and are directly administered by the Ministry in Islamabad. A subtle demographic change is also being brought about by settling a number of Sunnis in areas where the Shia* and the Ismaili communities have majority at present. The legislative council of Northern Area, moreover, is merely an advisory body.

In legislative sphere, too, loyalty to Pakistan is a pre-condition to contesting elections. The Act of 1974 lays down that only those persons can contest elections "who are loyal to the cause of accession of the State of J&K to Pakistan". In the elections, held in 2001, the nomination papers of 32 candidates were rejected for not taking such a loyalty-pledge.

Demilitarisation

Equally untenable is President Musharraf's reference to human rights violations** and his proposals with regard to demilitarisation. The sizeable presence of the Indian army currently in J&K is primarily to deal with the deadly forces of subversion and terrorism that have been let loose in the State by Pakistan's ISI and its outfits–forces that have been equipped with and trained in the most lethal modern weapons designed for carrying out guerilla warfare. If operation of these forces is brought to a halt by the ISI and if the infrastructure of terror built by it, both within and outside the Valley, is dismantled, the Indian army would go back to its barracks and restrict itself to its routine duty of guarding the borders. Clearly, for bringing about demilitarisation in the State, the network of terror and subversion has to be removed first. The cart cannot be put before the horse. President Musharraf's idea of securing demilitarisation without creation of conditions that make the

* Baltistan and Nagar have Shia majority and Gilgit and Hunza etc. Ismaili majority. The Northern Areas comprise about 72,500 sq. km, which "Azad J&K" extends to about 13,300 sq.

** As a part of the propaganda by the terrorist-outfits, a number of concocted or highly exaggerated stories about human rights violations are circulated in the media. Quite a few overzealous human rights activists also fall into the trap of the anti-national forces. The army has the mechanism to deal with the violators. Out of the 890 complaints it received, during the period January 1990-April 2006, 854 were investigated. Only 24 were found to have some substance. 47 soldiers and officers were punished, some with even rigorous imprisonment.

presence of army unnecessary is not at all practical. It would merely result in spilling of more innocent blood*.

In this connection, it also needs to be understood that the auxiliary agencies of Lashkar-e-Taiba and Jaish-e-Mohammad, like Asiya Andrabi's 'Dukhtaran-e-Millat' (Daughters of Faith) and Mian Abdul Qayoom's 'Forum Against Social Evils' have been frequently intimidating the common Kashmiri to follow the 'true Islamic way of life'. The attempt is to fundamentalise the Kashmiri Islam which has been traditionally liberal in outlook and syncretic in practice. The cool calculation is to raise the tempo of religious frenzy, expel the liberal strand of Islam from the mindscape of the common Kashmiri, fill the vacated space with the rigid and virulent form of Islam and inject the ideological virus of extremism for ever in the body-politic of the State. In case this calculation materialises, pro-Pakistan elements would achieve what they have so far failed to achieve through the techniques of terror and subversions.

Joint Management

No less unconvincing is President Musharraf's idea of joint-management or joint control. Apart from its imprecision, the idea does not even deal with an elementary question: what would happen if there is difference of opinion or approach between joint managers or controllers? In this connection, a few other models, such as Andorra**, Trieste*** and Northern Ireland model have also been mentioned. None of these models or any other institutional arrangement can work as long as forces of fanaticism and fundamentalism

* Despite the presence of Army, the terrorist-outfits like Lashkar-e-Taiba, Jaish-e-Mohammad and Hizbul Mujahideen are able to terrorise the common people, particularly in the remote areas. On October, 4, 2006, for example, they mercilessly butchered a Dental Surgeon of Handwara with a barber razor because he was considered to have disobeyed their 'Islamic Instructions'. A day before, they killed another resident, Mohammad Shafi for having dared to join Territorial Army. For keeping mobile phones, hairs of the young ladies were cut in full public view. What would be the scale of terror if the Army is withdrawn?

** Andorra is a small land-locked principality, bordered by France and Spain. Its population is about 70,000. The languages spoken are: Catalan, Spanish and French.

*** Trieste is a small city, with a population of about 220,00, on the Adriatic sea. It is the capital of the autonomous region in north-eastern Italy. The population is an ethnic mix–Italian, Slovenian and German.

The analogy of these small territories with the case of Kashmir is misplaced.

continue to operate at the ground-level. Such forces would subvert the system from within and establish their hegemony. If any of their 'diktats' is not followed, they would revert to their old game and resort to terror-tactics. Free-movement across the 'Line of Control' is also not feasible. Anyone entering Kashmir Valley or Jammu Division from Pakistan could, later on, move to other parts of India as well.

Regionalisation

President Musharraf's suggestion to split J&K into regions–Jammu, Srinagar and Ladakh on the Indian side and Northern Areas and "Azad Kashmir" on the Pakistan side–is also vague. He has not even cared to spell out whether his suggestion includes grant of autonomous or semi-autonomous status to these regions. So far as the Indian side of Kashmir is concerned, none of these regions is a homogenous entity. For example, Jammu region has a substantial area of Muslim-majority. Likewise, Kargil district of Ladakh is dominated demographically by the Shia Muslims who are different from the Buddhists of the Leh region and the Sunnis of the Kashmir Valley. Gujjars and Bakarwals have their own distinct way of life.

There would be too many claimants for separate identities. New grievances would be dished out and existing ones exaggerated. Given the populist disposition of local political leaders, they would attempt to build 'separate mosques of one brick each' and carve out their own 'Immamats'. To prop up their leadership, some of them may not even hesitate to undertake ethnic cleansing in their little courtyards. Friction generated in the process could badly singe, if not burn, the entire fabric of the State. While petty ethnic lords would fight over their petty autonomies, the poor would continue to wallow in poverty, the sick would continue to remain unattended and the homeless would continue to be without a roof over their heads.

On both the sides of the 'line of actual control', the basic problems would be solved not by pandering to the ambitions of tin-pot demagogues, thriving on slogans of separate identities, but by building up higher motivation and giving priority to commonalities and using the resources, both human and material, to eliminate hunger, ignorance and disease among the masses. The experience of Yugoslavia shows how murderous ethnic warlords could be and to what extent human mind could be demented by the drug of ethnicity.

India's one billion people with about 400 languages and dialects and different religions and local identities are learning to co-exist and move towards the realisation of its overall belief –'One in all and all in One'. Let this movement be not disturbed by imprecise ideas rooted in superficial thinking. On account of its uncertain approach, India has already suffered extensive bleeding by what is called 'a thousand cuts'.

Improvements

At the same time, however, it cannot be said that relations between India and Pakistan have not improved in any respect. Some of the 'confidence building measures' have yielded concrete results. To a limited extent, the borders have been softened. The old travel routes have been revived and new ones opened. The exchange of prisoners between the two countries have been carried out. It has been agreed to provide advance information about each other's programme of missile testing. The Joint Economic Commission, which was dormant during the last sixteen years, has been reactivated.

But all such measures would soon lose substance if Pakistan does not take earnest and firm measures to dismantle the infrastructure for terrorism in all its shapes and forms. In any case, it is totally indefensible to butcher children, women and other innocent persons in the name of freedom or brainwash young men to blow themselves up as suicide bombers. In no circumstance, should savagery of this nature be tolerated by the international community.

Need of the Hour

The need of the hour, therefore, is that the entire international community should brace itself and mobilise all its resources–financial, military and diplomatic–to target terrorism in all its hues and colours. Lapses of the type that occurred in the past, when the phenomenon was viewed from a selfish and narrow angle, should not be repeated. When terrorism in Kashmir was being confused, intentionally or otherwise, with human rights or fight for freedom, whoever thought that the same forces that fed that terrorism would one day attack the World Trade Centre, New York, and cause deaths of over 3000 innocent persons! The present-day terrorism is like a plague which should be eradicated from every nook and corner of the world. If it is allowed to remain anywhere, it could erupt any time at any place and move in any direction to engulf even those who are watching the beastly show from the sidelines.

Apart from ensuring that President Musharraf's declarations are translated into deeds, the aid of the United States and international agencies to Pakistan must be linked with its commitment to destroy extremism from its roots. In this regard, the recommendations made by the 9/11 Commission are sound: "The United States should support Pakistan's government in its struggle against extremists with a comprehensive effort that extends from military aid to support for better education, so long as Pakistan's leaders remain willing to make difficult choices of their own". The Commission has also pointed out that what President W. Bush's administration has so far done to eliminate terrorism is not enough. "What is most striking to us is that the size of the problem still totally dwarfs the policy response."

Action on other Fronts

While the members of the international community, particularly the United States, United Kingdom and Russia should put their best foot forward to obliterate the menace of terrorism from the globe, in the shortest time, the need for action on a few other equally significant fronts should not be lost sight of.

War of Ideas

First, the war on terror should not be restricted to financial, diplomatic and military means. It must be extended to incorporate a more fundamental war, a war of ideas. It is generally not being appreciated that as long as the extremists' ideologies exist and as long as a large section of the Muslim mind remains hostage to these ideologies, terrorist activities would continue somewhere or the other. Lawrence Wright, a noted scholar of the subject, has rightly observed: "Al-Qaeda is seen as threatening not so much because of its famous leaders but as an ideological virus–a spore that floats invisibly across borders and replicates itself anywhere there are discontented young men and internet connections".

Ideological Virus

The task of dealing with ideological virus should be entrusted to UNESCO or a new specialised agency of UN, which could help in bringing about a positive change in the forces that are currently shaping the mindscape of large number of Muslims all over the world. The UNESCO or the specialised agency should formulate a comprehensive policy and programme to encourage enlightened leadership in Muslim countries to promote those strands in Muslim thought which are conducive to the growth of liberalism, humanism, and pluralism.

Harmonious Construction

This could be done by following what in constitutional law is called *the principle of dynamic and harmonious construction.* What it implies is that if there are two provisions in the constitution which, by way of their rigid interpretation, run counter to each other, they should be so viewed as to bring about a positive and harmonicus construction on them–a construction which is in tune with the spirit of the time.

By way of elaboration, let me take the two provisions of Quran:

(i) "To you your religion, to me my religion."(*Sura 109, verse 6*); and

(ii) "O mankind! We created you from a single pair of male and a female, and made you nation and tribes, that you may know each other, not that you may despise each other." (*Sura 5, verse 49*).

It is this genre of verses that need to be given prominence while harmonising them with other verses, which provide a scope for narrow and distorted interpretation of Islam. In essence, the issue boils down to interpretation–a task which is performed by the humans. As was rightly underlined by Ali Ibn Abi Talib, the fourth Caliph and son-in-law of the Prophet: "This is Quran, written in straight lines; it does not speak with a tongue; it needs interpreters; and interpreters are people".

Those who claim that all aspects of Islam are divine often forget that interpretation of these aspects is "thoroughly human and this worldly". In fact, every interpretation emanates from the social and political outlook of the interpreter. And ambitious and unscrupulous political leaders have, more often than not, resorted to interpretation of religion to suit their power-game and establish their rule over the people and make them do things in the name of God, even the most heinous crimes such as the killing of innocent women and children.

The Talibans' way of interpreting Islam in Afghanistan, for example, had led to the closure of all girls' schools and awarding of barbaric punishment even for minor crimes. In fact, the issue today is not of what is called Islamic terrorism but of a brand of terrorism that emanates from a negative, narrow and nihilist interpretation of Islam—an interpretation which is at variance with some of the basic formulations of the Prophet Himself and which violates the basic principles and provisions of the United Nations Charter and is wholly out of tune with the march of human civilisation. The fanatics and fundamentalists view Islam through a defective prism, collect a series of distorted images and present them to ignorant Muslims as the true ones. The problem, therefore, is one of the removal of ignorance and telling the Muslim masses what the extremists are propagating is not the true vision of Islam.

International Community and Enlightened Leadership

In the context of the conditions prevailing in most of the Muslim countries, it is necessary for the international community and enlightened leadership within these countries to take a vigorous initiative to rid the world of extremist elements and establish the hegemony of the forces springing from liberal Islam. Simultaneously, the schools of Islamic thought that are dominated by the ideologies of Mohammad Wahhab, Sayyid Qutb, Maulana Maudoodi, Osama bin Laden, al-Zawahiri and the like need to be discouraged. These schools of thought show an extraordinary narrowness and rigidity. They believe in the supremacy of what they consider is the social system of Islam. They view modernity as a cultural corruption and want the rule of *Sharia*, as interpreted by them, to be followed strictly both in private and public domains. Either out of misplaced fervour or on account of failure to do integrated thinking, they come to the wrong conclusions and float wrong theories. Sometimes, they even bend the divine revelations to fit into their pre-conceived notions. For instance, Sayyid Qutb looked at *Jihad* in a different way. While Quran lays down that a ruler, who is a perfect Muslim, alone could sanction *Jihad,* Sayyid Qutb declared that the people could themselves sanction *Jihad* and use it as an instrument to eliminate "culturally corrupt" regimes.

Enlightened Ideologues

The ideologues of the genre of Qutb, Wahhab and Maudoodi have introduced extreme rigidity in the Islamic thought. They have totally ignored the way the great Islamic scholars like Jamal al-Din al-Afghani and Muhammad Abduh, viewed Islam. These scholars had argued that Islam was not at all irreconcilable with modernity. They had propagated that the laws as embodied in Nature and Science were also the Laws of God, and rational and critical faculties were also the gifts of Allah. In other words, both the sets of Laws–Laws as expressed in *Quran* and *Hadith* and laws as embodied Nature–had emanated from the same source and were worthy of equal reverence.

United Nations

In the light of what I have analysed above, it is incumbent upon the international community–United Nations, UNESCO or any other specialised agency–to take, in the interest of international peace and security, a new initiative, and set up a mechanism to provide ways and means of encouraging those elements and schools of thought whose interpretation of Islam is dynamic, more in tune with the requirements of the current times and helpful to the growth of a global humanitarian order. I have often wondered why no effective action has so far been taken by the United Nations and its allied agencies, such as UNESCO, to end the tyranny of terror and spilling of innocent blood in a sizeable part of the globe. With what principles and purposes, after all, was the United Nations set up? Was it not the aim of UNESCO to orient the mind and motivation of mankind towards peace and pluralism? The international community should not remain content by passing a few resolutions or by asking the members states to take action. It must take concrete measures, both short-term and long-term, to ensure that extremist ideologies of the type propagated by the fanatics are dislodged from the minds of the people and the space thus created is filled with ideas and ideals that emanate from the enlightened and wholesome interpretation of Islam.

What I am arguing, I must clarify, is not interference in Islam but of extending help and encouragement to those enlightened sections within Islam who view it as a positive, rational and an accommodating force and who attempt to administer internal drug to root out the ideological virus that the extremists have planted in its body.

Forward-Look Group's Obligations

Unfortunately, so far, the international community and the forward looking groups in Islamic countries have not realised the importance of formulating a liberal Islamic ideology and waging a war of ideas against orthodoxy and bigotry with that ideology as a weapon.

The proponents of liberal Islamic ideology should also expose the 'Jihadi' leadership which has acquired a deep vested interest in terrorism. This leadership brainwashes young recruits to kill and get killed but itself remains in the background, accumulating in the process substantial wealth which flows as donations and alms. "It is quite certain", says the noted political analyst of Pakistan, Khalid Ahmed, "that at the level of the Jihadi leadership, the Jihad was motivated by financial gains. Almost all the Jihadi leaders came into possession of considerable wealth." From a recent Conference on counter-terrorism, held at Riyadh in December 2005, a clear message has emerged for the first time: "Money launderers, drug traffickers, makers of light weapons and other interests groups, including organisations that promote destructive thoughts and ideologies, are the main beneficiaries of terrorism. They exist on the blood of an unstable and divided world." Such a message needs to be repeated not only to expose the vested interests involved in terrorism but also to ensure speedy victory of liberal Islamic ideology in the war of ideas.

Redressal of Economic Imbalances

Secondly, serious attention needs to be paid to the economic, social and political order of the present-day world. This order is creating vast disparities in every sphere of life. "Fantastic fortune has been accumulated by a few as poverty in which many live has deepened." World unemployment, according to Juan Somavia, Director-General of the International Labour Organisation, is at the highest level ever, particularly among the youth. More than one billion people are unemployed or under-employed.

The power structure of the world, moreover, is dominated by the West. The noted American intellectual, Samuel Huntington, has rightly observed: "The West in effect is using international institutions, military power and economic resources to run the world that will maintain Western predominance, protect Western interests, and promote Western political and economic values." Earlier, it was said: "whatever is good for General Motors is good for the world." Now, this saying has been replaced by a new one: "American homeland is the planet".

Clearly, in the overall environment which is determined by current social and economic inequities, and unfair political dominations, frustrations and alienation would continue to grow and express themselves in irrational and inhuman behaviour like that of the militants. As early as 1968, the Pearson Commission had warned: "The world could not survive, half rich, half poor". Unfortunately, no one is listening to such warnings, not even after 9/11. "The American Self", it has been pertinently observed, "abdicates responsibility for contributing to the economic and political 'malaise' that has plagued the Middle East or, more specifically, the funding and training of those who now arm against us. In not recognising this complicity, we are doomed to reproduce the same conditions for murderous hatred that motivated 9/11. Instead, we propagandise 'globalisation' or 'regime change' when, in fact, America treats the world like a backyard, confusing others for our servants or acolytes".* It is time that the international community takes effective steps to redress the imbalances and aberrations which are rendering our world a dangerous place to live in.

New Era

Thirdly, in the new era and fast globalisation of the world in which the borders are becoming increasingly irrelevant, both India and Pakistan need to have a fresh look at their relationship. Pakistan must shed its obsession with Kashmir and understand that neither terrorism nor subversion nor military action can bring the Kashmir problem anywhere near solution. President Clinton, in his television and radio address on March 25, 2000, gave a clear message to the government and people of Pakistan:

> The era does not reward those who struggle in vain; who redraw borders with blood...I share your concerns about Kashmir. But a stark truth must also be faced–there is no military solution to Kashmir...I hope you will be able to meet the difficult changes. If you do not, here is danger that Pakistan may grow even more isolated, darning even more resources away from the needs of the people, moving even closer to a conflict no one can win.

The only sensible way to end the current conflict is to first end terrorism in all its forms and then enter into extensive dialogue to consider in-depth various proposals** that have been made from time to time by those who are engaged in what has been called 'back

* This has been culled out of the conversation between Chancellor Bill and Professor Lina on the 9/11 Commission Report.–Millennium Journal 2005 Vol. 33

** A brief note about these proposals has been added as Appendix XXX.

channel diplomacy'. As long as terrorists' net-works remain and the culture of violence prevails, no solution would be implementable in practice. Over the years, Pakistan authorities have created a 'Frankenstein'. Under its dreadful shadow, no move in the right direction can be made.

New Response

Once the monster is done away with and militancy and the accompanying bloodshed end, a congenial atmosphere would emerge. The borders could be made virtually non-existent. Tourism and culture exchanges could replace terrorism and exchanges of gun-fire. Economies on both sides could get a big boost. Unemployment could abate. Instead of being amongst the 15 largest spenders on defence, India and Pakistan could become the biggest investors of the world in programmes for poverty-removal.

At present, both India and Pakistan suffer from acute economic deprivation. In terms of Human Development Index (HDI), India ranks 127 and Pakistan ranks 132 in the descending order as per the UNDP Human Development Report. About 35 to 40 per cent of their population is still living below poverty line. About 9 per cent of their labour force is unemployed. Approximately 31 per cent of adult Indian males and 54 per cent of adult females are illiterate. In the case of Pakistan the corresponding figures are 42 per cent and 71 per cent. The public expenditure on health in both the countries is just 0.9 per cent of their respective GDPs. Likewise, public expenditure on education in India and Pakistan has been 4.1 per cent and 1.8 per cent of their GDPs.

In view of the above and in the light of the new realities emerging out of the fast shrinking world and the unprecedented technological revolution that it is witnessing, both India and Pakistan must evolve a new wavelength and concentrate on ending economic miseries of their common folks, reforming their societies and upgrading their cultures. They must also join hands to secure a better deal for the developing countries in an international order which is dominated by developed countries. With such a common approach, a mutual atmosphere of give and take would come about, and all differences could be sorted out. The two countries could, in fact, become one economic unit, while retaining their separate political entities. Their culture could mingle and produce a new brand of humanism and service to the poor.

Even if new response is not forthcoming from Pakistan, India should work for it. In no case, however, should it yield any quarter under threat of terrorism. It must learn from its past mistakes which I have brought out in this book. It must also shed its current culture of softness and shallowness and effectuate fundamental reforms in its machinery of governance wherein its true strength would lie. In my recent publication, *Soul and Structure of Governance in India,* I have provided a blueprint for reforms which, *inter alia,* incorporates the following four measures:

(i) Rekindling the power of the Indian mind;
(ii) Freeing the long suppressed soul of India;
(iii) Providing a new structure to enable the rekindled mind and reawakened soul to express itself in a most creative and elevating way; and
(iv) Building a powerful and committed leadership rooted in non-acquisitiveness and constructing an inspirational reservoir for the nation in general and leadership in particular.

If new attitudes are developed and if a new edifice of governance is built on the basis of above blueprint, I have no doubt that India would become a strong state, with courage, conscience and commitment of its own, and would soon acquire the capability and capacity of solving, within a short time, all its chronic problems, including the problem of Kashmir. Today, a truly historic challenge of the new era stares us in the face. Let our past timidity and superficiality not stand in the way. Let a new response emerge from all of us—a response that is rooted in the power of India's mind, purity of its soul and potency of its institutions.

CHAPTER XXI

The Stage: 2008-2010

The first decade of the 21st century will be remembered not only as the period when terrorism moved on to a new level of barbarity, but also as the time when it became a strategic threat to democracies....and, indeed, to the established world order.

–Peter Clarke

I do not believe in a fate that will fall on us no matter what we do but I do believe in a fate that will fall on us if we do nothing.

–Ronald Reagan

The need for a fundamental change in the outlook of individual nations and the international community, which I have underlined in the preceding chapter, is not being attended to at all. The war of ideas, as a part of war on terror, is not being waged. Some of the actors on the stage have, no doubt, changed. But the new actors carry with them the same attitudes, the same reflexes, as were possessed by their predecessors. And the net outcome is no different. Blood continues to be splashed on and around the stage, and the terror-smeared curtains continue to rise and fall virtually in the same manner as before.

The period of the last three years, terror, 2008-2010, with which this chapter deals, is crowded with events, both in India and Pakistan, which have a vital bearing on different aspects of the Kashmir issue. On the surface, these events may seem to belong to a different genre. But in no way have they altered either the nature or direction of the under-currents that have been pushing the basic problems towards larger and deeper complexities. To these complexities are being added a different set of problems that are arising out of the American policies with regard to Afghanistan and Pakistan, and also out of the general unwillingness of the international community to fight, on the ideological front the unprecedented challenge posed by the forces of extremism.

In Pakistan, President Musharraf first suffered a deep erosion in his standing, then lost power and eventually left the country. Benazir returned to Pakistan after about nine years of self-imposed exile and was soon consumed by its tumultuous politics. The General Elections of February 2008, brought in a new set of regime-managers on the political stage of the country. But neither the Army nor its ISI lost any of its controlling power. The various militant outfits, sponsored and reared by the ISI, too, remained as potent and ruthless as before. A few other terrorist groups, with agendas of their own, also cropped up. The sectarian violence extended its reach and intra-communal killings increased both in frequency and ferocity. Pakistan, to borrow the expression of Bruce Riedel, "became the most dangerous country in the world, where every nightmare of the 21st century converge, terrorism, government instability, corruption and nuclear weapons"*.

In India, the entire nation was traumatised by the most dastardly and dreadful terrorist attack on its commercial capital, Mumbai, on November 26, 2008. The state of J&K continued to be aggravated by turbulent weather. The turbulence was further menaced by two violent agitations, first in the Kashmir Valley and then in the Jammu region, on the issue of leasing land to the Amarnath Shrine Board. Soon thereafter, the State Assembly Elections were held. On January 5, 2009, a new coalition government of the National Conference and the Congress, headed by Omar Abdullah, assumed power.

After a short period of comparative peace and decline in the activities of gun-wielding and bomb-bursting militants, a new phenomenon emerged on the scene in the Valley. There were a series of 'protests' by way of stone-throwing mobs of youth whose Islamic frenzy and pro-'Azadi' sentiments had been aroused under a highly disruptive programme crafted by the ISI and its local supporters. The hesitant and somewhat confused approach of the State government compounded the problems created by the new mode of subversions.

*Bruce Riedel: *The Search for al-Qaeda*. p. 181.

And the Valley was soon engulfed in the worst kind of turmoil which is still continuing in one form or the other.

In the troubled region of Afghanistan-Pakistan, particularly its tribal areas on the Pakistani side of the border, the conditions did not improve, despite reinforcement of troops and the massive military and development aid by the United States to both Pakistan and Afghanistan. The former alone has so far got $ 16 billion. What is more problematic, Pakistan has been, and is still, using clandestinely a part of this aid to prop up terrorist outfits operating against Afghanistan as well as India. It has been double-crossing the United States. In its own way, Pakistan has perfected the art of biting the hand that feeds it, taking care not to take the bite beyond a limit.

An in-depth analysis of the above and connected events would be necessary to understand what has been going wrong, why Pakistan is sliding deeper and deeper into the snake-pit of violence, why Indians have to live under constant fear of terrorist attack, why Kashmir is frequently disturbed with impunity by subversion, why America is not winning its war in Afghanistan and why, years of bitter experience notwithstanding, the peace and democracy-oriented leadership at the international level is not evolving a new response and mustering a higher vision and stronger will to fight the menace that surrounds us all and which has the potential of deforming modern civilisations all over the globe.

Developments In Pakistan

Musharraf's Regime

Immediately after General Pervez Musharraf seized power on October 12, 1999, in a bloodless coup, he had declared: "The armed forces have no intention to stay in charge any longer than is absolutely necessary to pave the way for true democracy to flourish in Pakistan"*. But, like similar declarations made by the previous military dictators, this declaration was never intended to be followed.

In the beginning, the 'Musharraf' coup, though illegal, was accepted by the people in general. The preceding regimes of Benazir Bhutto and Nawaz Sharif had provided neither honest nor efficient governance. The common man in Pakistan had come to regard most politicians of the time as corrupt, crafty and incorrigible. In the

*October 17, 1999: Televised speech to the nation.

international arena, however, the replacement of a democratic regime by the military dictatorship was viewed with disfavour. For example, President Clinton, when he visited Islamabad for five hours on March 25, 2000, showed a distinct disinclination to even shake hands with General Musharraf before TV cameras.

It was only after 9/11, when Musharraf became an ally of the United States in its war on terror, that he was accepted by the West. Not merely that, he was made a 'buddy'* and his regime strengthened by way of liberal financial and military aid.

Musharraf also took care to present himself as a 'liberal autocrat'. By smoothly manipulating constitutional changes and a national referendum, he soon positioned himself both as a Chief of Army Staff and President of Pakistan. He virtually changed the parliamentary system into a presidential one and exercised unfettered powers for eight long years. In respect of Kashmir and the rest of India, without changing either the policy or pace of sponsoring terrorism and subversion, he continued, as detailed in the preceding two chapters, the process of India-Pakistan dialogue and kept the international community in good humour.

But with the passage of time, Musharraf, like all other dictators, grew over-ambitious and over-confident. A series of serious miscalculations followed. He clashed with what was called 'men in black' and 'women in black'. The first expression referred to the members of Bench and Bar, the judges and lawyers, who wore black jackets and who resorted to a vehement agitation against Musharraf's attitude towards the Supreme Court and dismissal of its Chief Justice Iftikhar Muhammad Chaudhry.

The other expression, 'women in black', referred to a set of fanatical women, attached to the Lal Masjid, Islamabad, who wore 'black burqas' and went around terrorising people and forcing them to adopt what they considered to be the dictates of true Islam. The mosque itself, under the leadership of two powerful extremist clerics, Abdul Aziz and Abdur Rashid Ghazi, had become a huge citadel of the Taliban type of militancy**. The two clerics virtually ran a parallel

* This word was used for Musharraf by no less a person than President George W. Bush.

**Lal Masjid, under the patronage, extended to it by the ISI and the military ruler, especially President Zia-ul Haq, had become an epicentre for breeding and disseminating culture of extremism in Pakistan. It also acted as a patron for such ruthless militant organisations as Harkat-ul-Mujahideen, Lashkar-e-Jhangvi and Sipah-e-Sahabah.

government. For a long time, President Musharraf hesitated to take action. After all, it was the ISI who had nursed the extremist forces and used them for carrying out terrorist operations in Afghanistan and Kashmir. Soon, however, lawlessness went totally out of hand. Even seven Chinese women were 'arrested' by the female Talibans on the alleged ground of running a prostitution racket. Musharraf was left with no other option but to order a strong commando action. In the bloody venture to clear the mosque, 88 occupants and nine commandos were killed.

These confrontations with two highly influential segments of the society, coupled with the 'dictatorial fatigue' that usually sets in the public after a few years of authoritarian rule, made Musharraf unpopular. While his action with regard to Lal Masjid had some supporters, the manner in which he dealt with the judiciary, particularly the Chief Justice, was condemned by an overwhelming majority of the people.

Realising that Musharraf's position was becoming untenable and at the same time recognising his pivotal role in the war on terror, the American and British diplomats, while remaining behind the curtain, brokered an 'agreement' between him and Benazir Bhutto who had been staying at Dubai/London for the last nine years. The 'agreement' envisaged the withdrawal of all corruption cases against her and her family members, her participation in the forthcoming elections and becoming Prime Minister for the third time*, if the strength of her party in the National Assembly so warranted. As a *quid pro quo*, Benazir Bhutto's Pakistan Peoples' Party agreed to help Musharraf for becoming President for the second term. Earlier, in 2006, Benazir and Nawaz Sharif had met in Jeddah and London on quite a few occasions and decided to work together for the restoration of democracy in Pakistan. A formal agreement, titled, *Charter of Democracy,* was also signed by them. It was in the context of these developments that President Pervez Musharraf issued the National Reconciliation Ordinance** in October 2007. All cases of corruption against leading politicians were withdrawn, paving the way for return of Benazir Bhutto and Nawaz Sharif to Pakistan.

* Earlier, President Musharraf had got the Constitution amended to prevent a person from holding the office of the Prime Minister for more than two terms. This amendment was repealed by Musharraf as a part of the deal he cut with Benazir Bhutto.

**In 2009, the National Reconciliation Ordinance was declared unconstitutional by the Supreme Court. Reopening of corruption and other criminal cases was also ordered.

The above arrangements appeared to suit all the concerned. A democratic facade could be provided to the governance machinery of Pakistan, while the United States' interests in its war on terror could remain safe in the hands of its indispensable ally, President Musharraf. Benazir Bhutto could rid herself and her family members of all the criminal charges, return to Pakistan, revitalise her party, and become Prime Minister for the third time. Nawaz Sharif, too, could rebuild his personal and political life. Nevertheless, quite a few grey areas remained, and uncertainty persisted about the fairness of the forthcoming elections* to the National Assembly and Provincial Legislatures. Nor did the long standing mistrust and misgivings about one another vanish. Many political analysts wondered whether the new arrangements, particularly the power sharing formula between Musharraf and Benazir, would work in practice.

Benazir's Return and Assassination

As things turned out, the occasion to test the new arrangements on the ground never arose. Benazir was assassinated. The bloody deed was done at Rawalpindi on the evening of December 27, 2007**, as she was about to leave after addressing an election rally at Liaquat Park– a park named after Pakistan's first Prime Minister who was shot dead at the same venue on October 16, 1951 in circumstances that have so far remained unclear***.

In the conditions prevailing in Pakistan, it would, perhaps, never be possible, to find out who conceived, ordered and executed the crime of killing Benazir Bhutto. But an underlying fact is amply clear. She had become a victim of those very forces of religious fundamentalism with which she had ingratiated herself during her years of power in Pakistan; first from 1988-1990 and then from 1993-1996. Instead of checking the rising tide of these forces, which had acquired a great

---

* There was a widespread impression in the public that the General Elections of 2002 had been rigged by Musharraf's regime.

** Immediately after the incident, the government came out with a version that there was first a shoot out and then a suicide bomber detonated explosives near Benazir's vehicle. Baitullah Mehsud's terrorist outfit of Tehrik-e-Pakistan was named as the sole culprit. In this incident, 24 other people were killed and 91 injured.

*** The assassin of Liaquat Ali was killed at the spot. Clearly, he was not acting on his own. Those who hatched the conspiracy to get rid of the then Prime Minister were never apprehended.

hold on the state and society during the regime of President Zia-ul-Haq*, she had exploited them for her own ends of power and used them without any scruple for causing terror and subversion in Kashmir.

It was during Benazir's rule in Pakistan that her ISI ordered, in 1989-90, the killing of innocent Kashmiri Pandits and such noble persons as Kashmir University Vice-Chancellor, Mushir-ul Haq, and his aid, Abdul Ghani. When she found that her agents in the valley were scattering under the impact of firm measures taken by me as Governor of the State, she herself came to Muzaffarabad and incited the Kashmiris against me. Made during the course of a televised speech, her shocking chopping gesture–striking her right hand on the palm of her left hand and ranting Jag-Jag-Mo-Mo-Han-Han**–showed the extent to which she could go in pursuit of her ambition.

In the years that followed, the extremist forces, coupled with other negative developments in the arenas of religion and politics, acquired much greater strength and made further inroads in Pakistan's power-structure. The Army became a state within a state. The ISI became an Army within an Army. Within ISI itself, ultra-conservative elements carved out an independent niche for themselves. A large number of non-state terrorist organisations, which enjoyed covert support of the ISI and virtually acted as its auxiliary agencies, also emerged on the scene. The overall atmosphere was thick with collusions and conspiracies.

No wonder, 2007–the year of Benazir's return–saw the highest incidence of violence*** in Pakistan. On the very day of her arrival at Karachi, October 18, the terrorists attacked her cavalcade, killing as many as 149 persons and injuring 402. About two months later, the pitiless conspirators succeeded in eliminating her.

---

* Commenting upon the background of Ms Bhutto's return to Pakistan in October 2007, the UN Inquiry Commission has pertinently observed: "Under the military dictatorship of General Zia-ul Haq from 1977 to 1988, a once secular military was aligned with political Islam, and jihad was used as a tool to recruit and support insurgents fighting against the Soviet-backed government in Pakistan. Similar tactics were used in Kashmir against India after 1989". For particulars of the Inquiry Commission, the subsequent footnote may be seen.

** The implication of what Benazir gesticulated was that Jagmohan would be cut into pieces.

*** In the arena of suicide bombing alone, there were 44 incidents which took away 614 innocent lives.

President Musharraf's administration did not appear to be very serious in providing effective security cover to Benazir. This fact was underlined by the Inquiry Commission* appointed by the United Nations, at the request of Government of Pakistan, to ascertain the facts and circumstances of the assassination of Benazir Bhutto. In its report, the Commission said:

> The Federal Government did not have a comprehensive security plan to protect Ms Bhutto...At Liaquat Bagh, on December 27, 2007, the security for her was ineffective, insufficient and passive...A range of government officials failed profoundly in their efforts first to protect Ms Bhutto and second to investigate with vigour all those responsible for her murder, not only in the execution of the attack but also in its conception, planning and financing.

Clearly, Benazir Bhutto had made a serious mistake in coming back to Pakistan without first securing a firm guarantee for her security from President Pervez Musharraf and his mentors in the United States and Britain. Her overpowering ambition, perhaps, drove her to an extremely risky venture.

Despite her earlier unenviable record** in office, Benazir's brutal assassination at a time, when she was attempting to turn a new leaf in her life and also in the politics of Pakistan, was a grim tragedy. Though she had harangued against me, *albeit* unjustifiably, I and many other well-wishers of Pakistan were deeply saddened by her death. She, it was thought, was a changed person after she had learnt her lessons in adversity. She was showing a promising potential for freeing Pakistan from stranglehold of religious extremism and terrorism. In her book, *Reconciliation*, published after her death, she has provided ample evidence of evolving a new agenda for Pakistan and for creating a pluralistic and modern Islamic society. But this

* This Inquiry Commission comprised Ambassador Heraldo Munoz, Chile's Permanent Representative to the UN, Mr. Marzuki Drusman, a former Attorney-General of Indonesia and Mr. Peter Fitzgerald, a former Deputy Commissioner of Irish Police. It started its proceedings on July 1, 2009 and submitted its report on March 30, 2010.

** During her two terms as Prime Minister, Benazir was accused of being sly, opportunistic and corrupt. In her first term, 1988-90, she accelerated the pace of ISI's sponsored terrorism and subversion in J&K. Her second term, 1993-96, saw the ascendancy of Talibans in Afghanistan. She was over ambitious. Her treatment of family members made her mother to bewail: "I had no idea I had nourished a viper in my breast."

agenda remained merely an agenda. Fate did not give her even a chance to try her hand at its implementation. On her death, a noted American commentator, Dan Rather, rightly observed: "The pendulum has swung towards the extremists. Benazir's murder is the biggest victory of the extremists since the murder of President Anwar Sadat of Egypt in 1980."

Musharraf's Exit

The assassination of Benazir Bhutto further lowered Musharraf's standing in the public. In the elections, held in February 2008, his supporting party, Pakistan Muslim League (Qaid-e-Azam), popularly known as King's party, did not perform as well as was expected by him. A coalition government, led by Prime Minister Yusaf Raza Gillani of the Pakistan People's Party, came into being at the federal level. Earlier, on January 22, 2008, he had handed over charge of the office of the Chief of Army Staff to General Ashfaq Parvez Kayani. A joint move of the Pakistan People's Party and the Pakistan Muslim League (N) to impeach him was also in the offing. Like a good general, Musharraf realised that it was time for him to retreat. On August 18, 2008, he announced his decision to resign. In his place, Asif Ali Zardari, Co-Chairman of the Pakistan People's Party, was elected as President. He assumed office on September 9, 2008.

Musharraf's stand on terrorism was marked by the Machiavellian duplicity. He repeatedly declared his total support to war on terror. But on the ground, there was only a pretence and little meaningful action. Almost all the terrorist organisations and their feeding centres remained alive and active, though they assumed different names and professed different objectives. When Musharraf departed from the scene, Pakistan was no different "from the biggest rogue of all the rogue states", a description of it as given by the famous French writer, Bernard-Henri Levy, in his much acclaimed work, *Who Killed Daniel Pearl?*

Zardari/Gillani Government

With Asif Ali Zardari as President of Pakistan and Yusaf Raza Gillani as Prime Minister of the coalition government, conditions could not take a turn for the better. The new government was in no position to go against the wishes of the Army. The old attitudes, the old double-dealings, that were characteristics of Musharraf's regime, continued.

And so did the wave of terrorism. On the very day of Presidential elections, there was a serious terrorist attack in Peshawar. Soon thereafter, on September 22, Marriot Hotel, in the heart of Islamabad, was savagely bombarded and burnt by way of an explosives-filled truck, killing 53 persons and injuring about a hundred others. In 2008, there were as many as 2,148 terrorist and sectarian attacks, indicating the increased strength with which the terrorist wind had started blowing.

Consequent to the negative development analysed above, Pakistan's landscape today is littered with a bewildering variety of terrorist organisations. Their number is so large and their objectives and motivations overlap to such an extent that it is extremely difficult to subject them to a clear-cut categorisation. Nevertheless, four broad categories are discernible. One, there is a set of 'non-state associations', such as Lashkar-e-Taiba and Jaish-e-Mohammad*, which have the patronage of the ISI and are largely used by it to carry out terrorism-related activities in Kashmir and other parts of India. Second, there are quite a few outfits, such as Afghan Talibans**, Mullah Omar's Quetta-Shura, Gulbadin Hikmatyar's Hizbe Islami and Haqqani's network which operate mainly against US and NATO forces in Afghanistan from their havens in the tribal areas of Pakistan and enjoy covert support of the ISI. Third, there is a formidable religious movement called Tehrik-e-Taliban whose objective is to 'Talibanise' the state and society of Pakistan and enforce strictly the holy law of Quran–*Sharia*. Fourth, there are a number of Sunni extremist organisations whose primary aim is to undermine or eliminate other sects of Islam, such as Shias, Sufis, Brelvis, Ahmedias, Ismailis etc. and ensure dominance of what, according to them, is a pure form of Islam.

All the above four categories of terrorist organisations have, however, a few things in common. They are all anti-America and anti-India. They are, in one way or the other, aligned with al-Qaeda. They are brutally violent in their approach, and have perfected the technique of motivating a number of Muslims to become suicide-bombers. Even their fellow-Muslims in acts of prayer are not spared if they belong to sects other than own. They are also making every

* Most of the recruits of these organisations come from Punjab. In popular parlance, they are known as Punjabi Talibans.

**The members of these outfits are mainly Pushtuns and are called Pushtun Talibans.

attempt to acquire weapons of mass destruction. According to the report, *World At Risk**, "al-Qaeda has strengthened its ties with Pakistani militants in the past year. It will continue to try to acquire and employ chemical, biological, radiological or nuclear materials in attacks".

The religious frenzy of medieval times, the organised skills of the modern army and sophisticated weaponry of the technological age have all combined to make Pakistan a hotbed of savage terrorism which imperils not only international peace and security but also human civilisation as a whole. The threat to India is particularly serious. If any confirmatory proof of this threat was needed, it was soon forthcoming in the form of a horrible attack on Mumbai on November 26, 2008 from Pakistan's soil.

Developments In India

Horrific Event: 26/11

The terrorist attack on Mumbai on November 26, 2008 must be reckoned as one of the most horrendous, the most tragic, yet ironically, among the most instructive events in the annals of the Indian Republic. Apart from causing huge loss of life and property, it exposed a number of wide chinks in the armoury of Indian polity and machinery of governance. A country, aspiring to be a super-power, stood before the entire world as nothing more than a huge tree with a hollow trunk. The event also brought to surface the inner shallowness of India's intellectual discourse which had shaped the outlook of its social and political elite and caused the emergence of a soft and superficial state.

In this case, ten young terrorists sailed on a Pakistani steamer from Karachi, hijacked an Indian fishing trawler on the high seas, landed quietly at a point near the Gateway of India, divided themselves in four groups and moved towards their pre-determined targets.

One group seized the Taj Hotel, the second entered the Leopold Café/Oberoi-hotel, the third proceeded to Chabad/Nariman House and the fourth went to the Chhatrapati Shivaji Railway Terminus. Everywhere, they resorted to a bloodbath with impunity, shooting innocent persons with the utmost savagery. They held the city in

---

* *World At Risk:* The report of the United States Commission on Prevention of Weapons of Mass Destruction, Proliferation and Terrorism.

terror practically for three days. Before nine of them were killed and one captured, they had butchered 166 persons and left many more wounded. It was a tragedy too deep for tears.

What was no less tragic was the incompetence that was displayed on the occasion. When the terrorist attack occurred, the clarity, cohesion and promptitude that was needed was nowhere to be seen. In sharp contrast to the military precision and speed with which all the four groups of terrorists went about their task, the security apparatus of both the state and central governments looked disjointed. It took quite some time for this apparatus to adjust itself for effective action.

The other components of the social structure did not cover themselves with glory either. For example, almost all the television channels vied with one another in showing live the operation conducted by the National Security Guard against the terrorists at the Taj Hotel. They did not care to consider that their coverage could be used by the Pakistani handlers* of the terrorists to convey fresh instructions and cause heavier loss of innocent lives.

All this happened despite the fact that India had seen a number of terrorist attacks in its metropolitan cities. In 2008 alone**, it saw such bloody and brutal attacks as eight serial blasts in Jaipur on May 13, which took away 80 lives; seventeen serial blasts in Ahmedabad on July 26, which left 53 dead; and eight serial blasts in Delhi, which killed 26 people. Unfortunately, India remained incorrigible, tempting its adversaries to take advantage of its soft underbelly again and again.

In the aftermath of the attack, there was a furious denunciation of the central and state government agencies by the social and intellectual elite whose mental attitude towards terrorism underwent a marked change. They experienced, first hand, the pain, agony and horror that the terrorist act caused. In the early phase of terrorism, when Kashmiri Pandits and other innocent persons were being killed like caged pigeons in the valley, these very elite, by and large, had

* As gathered from intercepts and other evidence, there were three experienced handlers of ten terrorists in Pakistan. They were Zakiur Rahman Lakhvi, Muzammil and Abu Hamza. While Lakhvi was the chief military commander, Muzammil and Abu Hamza had earlier conducted successful terrorist operations in India. Muzammil had organised attack on Akshardham, Gandhi Nagar, and Hamza on Indian Institute of Science, Bengaluru.

**For particulars of earlier attacks of serious nature, the two preceding chapters may be seen.

remained unsympathetic and did not come forward in any meaningful way to pressurise the authorities to end the misery of the victims. On the other hand, some of them rationalised terrorism, talked of alienation of Kashmiri youth, went to the extent of ignoring documented facts and other hard evidence and even blamed the Governor's administration for having induced the exodus of the Pandits. To be counted as progressive and to corner publicity in the media, flaunting of such postures had become the order of the day. It caused incalculable harm to the nation. While the terrorists slaughtered innocent people in the valley, the so-called progressives and liberal-intellectuals, who had no idea of ground-level reality, slaughtered truth, reputations and will to fight the menace and nip it in the bud. The stark reality dawned upon them only when the terrorists began to spread their tentacles and shoot people in cold blood in seven-star hotels and restaurants.

Since the mid-1980's, when the Indian diplomat, Ravinder Mahatre, was murdered by Jammu and Kashmir Liberation Front at Birmingham and a huge subversive drama was staged at Srinagar during the West Indies–India cricket match, I had been underscoring the sinister nature of the Pakistani plan under which terrorism was being injected in Kashmir by arousing religious frenzy and by diverting and deploying sophisticated weapons which the CIA was supplying to the ISI, ostensibly for use in Afghanistan War. But no one listened. In fact, those like me who wanted to incise away the cancerous cells when they were in process of growing, were pilloried and shown the door. Now that the cells have proliferated and started attacking the vital organs of the body politic of India, a very heavy cost and a long time would be required to bring back this body to health. Already about 50,000 lives and several thousands crore of public funds have been lost.

The interrogation of David Coleman Headley, an American citizen and a recruit of Lashkar-e-Taiba, has revealed how diabolical plans for future terrorist attacks* are being worked out, how even houses of our Prime Minister and Vice-President have been surveyed and how the so-called non-state-actors and the ISI are working in close collaboration for executing their bloody plans against India.

*313 Brigade of Ilyas Kashmir which has its base in North Waziristan, is believed to be planning for future attacks on India. Ilyas is a former commando of the Pakistan Army and was trained by the United States. He coordinates the activities of various terrorist outfits, such as al-Qaeda and Lashkar-e-Taiba.

After the tragedy of truly historic proportion, Government of India should have appointed a high-level independent commission of inquiry, on the lines of United States 9/11 Commission, to investigate the background and all other facts and circumstances pertaining to the case, and recommend measures to prevent such attacks in future. But it did not do so. Expediency and narrow consideration of politics seemed to have weighed with it. Nevertheless, some lessons seem to have been learnt. A National Investigative Agency has been set up and Unlawful Activities (Prevention) Act has been amended. The Coastal Security Scheme has been provided with additional funds to the tune of ₹ 1100 crore. A National Counter-Terrorism Centre is also in the offing. Undoubtedly, all these measures would give stronger teeth to the administrative machinery. But who would provide the will to bite? India so far has shown unpardonable hesitancy in acting firmly even in the face of terrible pounding it has received from the agents of the ISI.

Dialogue: Track II Diplomacy

The Mumbai attack and the ISI instigated plans for future strikes in India have also exposed the futility of the processes of dialogue, 'track II diplomacy'*, 'people to people contact' and 'confidence building measures'. In fact, when these processes were on, a new height of brazenness and barbarity had been reached in terrorist attacks on India. Even the Indian Embassy in Kabul was got savagely bombarded by the ISI through its protégé, Haqqani network. The revelations made by David Coleman Headley and Ajmal Amir Kasab**, during the course of their interrogation, should leave no one in doubt about Pakistan's subterfuge and perfidy.

All along, President Pervez Musharraf had been saying that Pakistan was not sponsoring terrorism in Kashmir or other parts of India. He had also given, in January 2004, a solemn assurance to the

* According to Khurshid Mahmud Kasuri, Foreign Minister of Pakistan from 2002 to 2007 in President Musharraf regime, track II diplomacy yielded some results. In February 2007, India and Pakistan were about to come to an agreement on demilitarisation and on a point between 'complete independence and autonomy'. But this agreement could not be finalised on account of Musharraf's pre-occupation with the Lawyers agitation against him. The above position was enunciated by Kasuri in an interview published in the *Times of India* of April 4, 2010.

**Ajmal Amir Kasab is the lone survivor of a ten-member terrorist group that attacked Mumbai. He was prosecuted and sentenced to death.

Indian Prime Minister, Atal Bihari Vajpayee, that the territory under control of Pakistan would not be allowed to be used to support terrorism in any manner. But now, in an interview, given in October 2010, to the German magazine, *Der Spiegel*, he has admitted that 'his country has been forming and training militant groups to fight in Kashmir'.

Pakistan has, indeed, earned world-wide notoriety for their deceptive behaviour and 'double-speak'. In his memoir, Mullah Abdul Salam Zaeef, a former Ambassador of Taliban to Pakistan, has observed: "Pakistan's authorities are so treacherous that they can get milk from a bull. They have two tongues in one mouth, and two faces on one head; they can speak everybody's language...They milk America and Europe in alliance against terrorism, and they have been deceiving Muslims around the world in the name of Kashmir jihad."

Unfortunately, despite Pakistan's known record of deception, Prime Minister Dr. Manmohan Singh was inclined to think that the process of dialogue had become 'irreversible'. The position in this regard was elaborated in the joint statement issued at the end of the meeting held on July 16, 2009 at Sharm El Sheikh, between Dr. Manmohan Singh and Yusaf Raza Gillani. Explaining his position a few days later, Prime Minister told the Indian Parliament: "Dialogue and engagement is the best way forward". Earlier, during the regime of the National Democratic Alliance, Atal Bihari Vajpayee had expressed similar views: "We cannot change our neighbour; we have to live with them."

The two Prime Ministers again met at Thimpu on the side-line of SAARC, April 27-29, 2010. They agreed to commence dialogue at the Foreign Ministers' level without any pre-conditions and remove what was called 'trust-deficit'. But a follow-up meeting of the two Foreign Ministers held at Islamabad on July 13-15, 2010, ended in a fiasco. At present, the process of dialogue is in 'suspended animation'. Even if this process is recommenced, nothing worthwhile is likely to come out of it.

Kashmir Scenario

Amarnath Shrine Land-Lease Row

About five months before the state Assembly elections, which were scheduled for December 2008, the Congress-Peoples' Democratic Party coalition government, headed by Ghulam Nabi Azad, collapsed. Ostensibly, the collapse was caused by the fall-outs from what is known as 'Amarnath Shrine land-lease row'. But this 'row', itself was caused by the vested interests who, in the tradition of Kashmir's exploitative politics, were out to secure electoral gains by whipping up communal and parochial frenzy among the masses.

To provide 'shelter cum civic facilities units' to the pilgrims against natural hazards on the route to the Shrine and to manage other affairs pertaining to the pilgrimage, a statutory board, named Sri Amarnath Shrine Board, was set up on the pattern of the Vaishno Devi Shrine Board*. After protracted efforts, the Board secured allotment of about 40 hectares of land from the State government. Soon thereafter, at the instigation of Mehbooba Mufti, President of the Peoples' Democratic Party, a virulent public agitation was started against the allotment. She cynically disregarded the fact that the two main Ministers–the Forest Minister and the Law Minister–concerned with the land allotment decision belonged to her party. The Peoples' Democratic Party walked out of the coalition government. Ghulam Nabi Azad resigned, and the state was placed under the Governor's rule.

In the meanwhile, the secessionists took control of the agitation and oriented it towards subversion and terror. It was vehemently propagated that a conspiracy had been hatched to change the demographic profile of the valley, though the propagators knew very well that neither could the 'non-state subject' acquire any property in J&K nor was it feasible to have a regular human habitation on the land which remained under snow for about eight months in a year. Strikes and street marches became a matter of daily occurrence. The conditions deteriorated to such an extent that Pakistan's flag was hoisted at the historic Lal Chowk.

Following public outcry, M.K. Narayanan, National Security Adviser, visited the State. Firm action was, thereafter, taken. In the clashes that ensued between the trouble-makers and the Security Forces, 20 persons lost their lives. Separately, the Governor, in his capacity as Chairman of the Amarnath Shrine Board, withdrew the request for allotment of land. The agitationists hailed the Governor's decision as their victory and terminated this agitation.

---

*The organisational features and other particulars of Vaishno Devi Shrine Board may be seen in the author's book, *Reforming Vaishno Devi and a Case for Reformed, Reawakened and Enlightened Hinduism.* The story of Amarnath Shrine and its cultural significance would also be found in the same book.

But this caused a wave of anger in the Jammu region. It was felt that the Government had allowed itself to be bullied by the exploitators. A movement was launched to secure restoration of land to the Shrine Board. Self-immolation by an activist rendered it too furious to be controlled. Ultimately, the government saw wisdom in making some concessions. The use of land by the Board and construction of temporary structures on it were allowed during the period of pilgrimage.

The consequences of the above two agitations could not be any thing but deleterious. The separatists and divisive forces acquired greater strength, rendering the resolution of the basic problems of the state all the more intractable. It is the unabashed proclivity of the so-called mainstream parties to exploit practically every issue to serve their narrow ends that constitutes the never-ending tragedy of the present-day Kashmir. Neither the loss of innocent lives nor the debilitating turmoil in public life has prevented the local leaders from persisting with their destructive politics.

Assembly Elections

As was calculated by the Peoples' Democratic Party, it received the tacit support of separatists' outfits in the valley, though they publicly boycotted the elections. Consequently, the Party whose prospects were not otherwise very bright, increased its strength in the Assembly from 16 in 2002 to 21. The overall votes polled by it also went up 6 per cent.

In Jammu region, the agitation brought electoral gains to the Bharatiya Janata Party. Its representation in the Assembly went up from 1 in 2002 to 11. The National Conference adopted one posture in the Valley, and other in Jammu and maintained its old strength of 26 in the Assembly, though its share of votes polled declined by 4 per cent as compared to 2002 Elections. The Congress, too, tried a balancing act. But it could achieve only a limited success. Its tally came down to 16 from 20 in 2002. The number of 'others' also fell—from 22 to 10. Clearly, the outcome of the elections was greatly influenced by unhealthy forces of separatism, communalism and regionalism.

A few other features of 2008 Elections need to be noted. As compared to the Assembly Elections of 1996 and 2002, these Elections were peaceful. In 1996, 61 political workers lost their lives and another 57 were killed in its aftermath in 1997. As the Elections of 2002 neared, 76 political workers became the victims of terrorists' bullets and another 100 were done to death in the course of Elections.

As is usual in India, the conduct and outcome of the 2008 State Assembly elections were viewed superficially. It was proclaimed that a new chapter in the history of the troubled State had been opened, and the new coalition government of the National Conference and the Congress, headed by young Omar Abdullah*, would usher in a period of normalcy. Undoubtedly, on the surface, the conditions looked bright. The average turn-out of the voters–61.5 per cent–was promising. In constituencies, such as Kupwara and Bandipur, which were considered to be strongholds of the separatists, the voting percentage was as high as 70. The fairness of the Elections was also certified by the independent observers, both national and international. But in all such reckonings, more fundamental issues were lost sight of. It was forgotten that the agenda of the two main political parties, the National Conference and the Peoples' Democratic Party, contained all those seeds which had caused the growth of a bitter harvest of subversion and terrorism in the valley and which would continue to push it towards semi-independence or independence.

The National Conference had declared that it was fighting the elections to gain power and manage day to day affairs of the state and that its goal was to secure the constitutional and administrative position as it obtained in 1952-53. Such a position would be hardly distinguishable from that of a virtually independent state which would have the additional privilege of being run with Indian money. The Peoples' Democratic Party's agenda had a still greater potential for undermining and then ending Kashmir's relationship with the rest of India. Its advocacy of self-governance, open borders, common currency, joint management etc., had all the paraphernalia of giving Pakistan a decisive say in the affairs of Kashmir and ultimately absorb it in its fold. In these circumstances, to believe that the Elections of 2008 could turn the tide of insurgency in Kashmir was nothing but another exercise in naivety which had been the hallmark of the Indian approach to the Kashmir issue from its very inception. One cannot avoid the inconvenient reality by looking the other way.

---

*Omar Abdullah was sworn as Chief Minister on January 5, 2009.

Shopian Rape/Murder Case

The reality of the Kashmir situation did not take long to show itself. After a short period of normalcy, one untoward event followed another. The first major event related to the alleged rape and murder of two young women of Shopian town. These women, who were sisters-in-law, left home, on the evening of May 29, 2009 for their orchards across Rambiarah rivulet. They did not return by the time they were expected to do so. A search was launched for them with the help of local police. After some time, their dead bodies were found near the rivulet.

Immediately thereafter, false stories were coined to allege that the two women had been raped and then murdered by the members of the Police/Security Forces. The High Court Bar Association, dominated as it was by pro-Pakistan elements, went to the extent of goading an 'obliging witness' to say: "I saw a dead body lying half naked on sand. Her clothes were torn, hair and body were dry. Blood was dripping from her nose. It appeared 'sindoor' had been thrown on her forehead".*

On inquiry, the local police found that the deaths had occurred due to drowning in the Rambiarah rivulet. A report was accordingly submitted to the State Government. On the basis of the report, the Chief Minister Omar Abdullah made a public statement indicating how the two women had died. At this, public protests were taken to a higher pitch. It was given out that the Chief Minister was involved in a 'massive cover-up'. In the intimidating atmosphere, no one dared to say anything which did not fit into the story woven by trouble-makers. The Chief Minister betrayed poor nerves and withdrew his statement. He ordered an inquiry by a Special Investigating Team and also set up a single-member Inquiry Commission, comprising Justice (retd.) Mohammad Jan. On the cooked up evidence, four innocent police officials were arrested. This further emboldened the subversives. They became more vociferous and violent. In the clashes that followed, 8 persons lost their lives and about 400 were injured. The matter was ultimately entrusted to the Central Bureau of Investigation (CBI) for a thorough probe.

---

*Quoted from a report published in the *Hindu* of December 28, 2009. Clearly, the element of 'Sindoor' was introduced in the concoction to suggest that the 'culprits' were Hindus. The 'scheme' was to incite the gullible masses.

The investigations conducted by the CBI revealed that a huge machinery for creation of witnesses, procurement of evidence on pre-determined lines and securing false medical reports under duress had been set in motion. For example, the husband of one of the deceased, who had earlier appreciated police help in carrying out search for the missing women, was subsequently made to say that his wife had told him on mobile phone that the Central Reserve Police personnel were chasing her and her sister-in-law. The CBI found that she carried no mobile phone.

The relevant medical facts pertaining to the deceased were subjected to a detailed scientific investigation at independent national institutes and laboratories. The reports of the Department of Forensic Medicine of the All India Institute of Medical Sciences, the Madhuban Forensic Science Laboratory, the New Delhi Central Forensic Laboratory and the Indian Agricultural Research Institute showed that there was no evidence of either rape or murder; that, on the other hand, there was ample evidence to support the view that the two deaths had been caused by drowning; and that the local doctors had, knowingly and intentionally, suppressed certain medical facts and invented others. The CBI also discovered that the rivulet Rambiarah occasionally and suddenly got large quantity of water, that around the time of incident it had flowed at its year-high flood and that in the periods 1999-2010, as many as 23 persons were drowned in it.

As a result of the aforesaid investigations, the CBI has filed a charge sheet against five lawyers of the Shopian Bar Association and two other persons for 'intimidating and inducing witnesses to make false statements'. Six local doctors have also been accused of fabricating evidence. The charge-sheet is now pending in the court.

I have considered it necessary to analyse this case at some length to show how pro-Pakistan elements and votaries of militant Islam, though in a minority in comparison to the silent majority of the Muslim masses, have created a vicious atmosphere and how in this atmosphere, a common Kashmiri, who wants to get along with his day to day work, thinks it expedient to join the processions and participate in the 'hartals' engineered by the subversives and trouble makers. Invariably, in all such cases, the authorities show a weak, uncertain hand and do not extend effective support to those who have no inclination to follow the militants' diktats. Consequently, a situation has come to stay in which practically every Kashmiri is afraid of the militants and no one has confidence in the protective capacity of the government.

If the Shopian case is taken to its logical ends, if the intimidators and fabricators of false evidence are sternly dealt with and if practice and pattern of inventing lies to create mass hysteria is thoroughly exposed, both at the national and international levels, the subversives and militants in the state would lose support and the 'pro-peace', 'pro-stability' and 'pro-integrity' forces would gain ground.

Mode of Falsification and Fabrication

I have, in a slightly different context, commented upon various cases of this genre in earlier chapters. Here, I would draw attention to a case which bears striking resemblance to the Shopian incident. This case pertained to the alleged rape of 26 women of village Kunan-Poshpora of Kupwara district in the Kashmir Valley in 1990 by men of the Indian Army, stationed at Trehgam. The allegations remained in circulation for several months, and filled the pages of the newspapers in India and abroad. A number of human rights bodies shed copious tears on the fate of the 'victims' and berated the Indian Army no holds barred.

The Press Commission of India thought it necessary to appoint a high-level Inquiry Committee, headed by George Verghese, to inquire into the matter. After a thorough investigation, which included visits to the spots and interviews and discussions with all concerned, the Committee recorded: "We were able to see a video cassette of the alleged Kunan Poshpora incident that had been passed on to us by a respected NGO, on behalf of the secessionist elements, who claimed they had shot the film after revisiting Kunan Poshpora and interviewing each of the women who had allegedly been raped, their parents and other villagers. It concluded with an impassioned political harangue by the kazi." The findings of the Committee were:

> The Kunan rape story on close examination turns out to be a massive hoax orchestrated by militant groups and their sympathisers and mentors in Kashmir and abroad, as part of a sustained and cleverly contrived strategy of psychological warfare, and as an entry point for re-inscribing Kashmir on the international agenda, as a human rights issue. The loose ends and contradictions in the story expose a tissue of lies by many persons and at many levels.

Unfortunately, despite a thorough exposure of the massive hoax, no action was taken against any one. No falsifier, no fabricator, no scheming mind, no agent of Pakistan-sponsored propaganda network, was effectively questioned or brought to book. No human rights body felt any compunction of conscience to publicly denounce all those who had trapped it to spread a concocted story as a genuine one. Nor was any media person who extensively publicised false allegations about the Army's atrocities, without any verification, was black-listed.

With such an attitude of mental surrender on the part of the authorities, both at the State and Central levels, no wonder the craft of concoction has become a powerful instrument in the hands of the subversives to cause frequent breakdown of public order in the valley.

Stone-Pelting Mobs

After a brief-spell of surface calm, Kashmir again found itself in deep turmoil in June 2010. Presumably, on the instructions of their masters in Pakistan and with huge finances already available to them, the subversives used the technique* of provoking police and other security forces by organising stone-throwing mobs of youngsters whose emotions could be easily aroused in the surcharged atmosphere obtaining in the valley. It all began with the death of a teenager, Tufail Ahmed Mattoo, on June 11. He was hit by one of the teargas shells that were lobbed by the police to disperse an unruly mob in down-town area of Srinagar. Tear-gassing is recognised as a non-lethal mode of crowd-control. But in this case, unfortunately, the shell fell on the head of Tufail, and proved fatal.

The tragedy was exploited to the hilt by the All-Parties Hurriyat Conference, particularly by the Syed Ali Shah Geelani's faction, Tehreek-Hurriyat, of which the Muslim League, headed by Masart Alam Bhat, is a constituent. For the next four months, practically every day, large groups of youngsters were made to gather at prominent points of major cities and to pelt stones, in waves after waves, on the local police and other security forces.** If the police/

* The technique of stone-pelting had been deployed earlier also. In 2008, there were 350 incidents of this genre, and in 2009, 250. About 1000 persons were injured, out of whom about 50 persons were policemen. On every Friday, practically, stone-throwing was resorted to at multiple locations. Cue for the mode of 'stone-throwing' seems to have been taken from the Palestinian Intifada.

**About 2000 personnel of the local police and other security forces were injured in the stone-pelting campaign from June to October 2010.

security forces withdrew, the mob indulged in arson and destruction of public property. If, on other hand, they acted, the pitch of provocation was raised to such a high level that, more often than not, firing had to be resorted to, causing one or two, sometimes more, fatalities. These fatalities, in turn, provided a handle to the leaders to pour oil on the raging fire and organise more aggressive groups of youngsters.

The disturbances of this phase reached their peak in the second week of September. On the day of Eid-ul-Fitr, September 11, permission was given impromptu by the Chief Minister to the Hurriyat leader, Mirwaiz Umar Farooq, to take out a procession after the prayers at the main mosque. Because of the presence of a number of extremists, it took little time for the procession to turn violent and set fire to public buildings* on the way. After two days, on the alleged desecration of the holy Quran in a little known American town, as shown on Tehran Television, almost all the major centres of the valley were engulfed in violent protests. To bring the situation under control, the police and other security forces had to open fire at several places, resulting in the death of 17 persons. Nowhere in the world, not even in the hard-core Islamic countries, any violent protest occurred on this issue. Clearly, there are a number of subversives in the valley who are out to keep it on the boil, no matter how much destruction was caused in the process. In the cycle of violent clashes, extending over four months, 105 lives, mostly of youngsters, were lost.

Throughout the period of disruption and disarray, from June to September, Chief Minister Omar Abdullah appeared rather indecisive and schizophrenic. While he wanted his police and other security forces to check stone-pelting, arson and destruction of public property, he would criticise them when they proceeded to take necessary steps to do so. He wanted to remain at the helm of affairs in the state, and yet ingratiate himself with pro-separatist forces. He, of late, has been demanding withdrawal of the Armed Forces Special Powers Act**, instead of taking a firm and clear line of action against the extremists and disruptionists.

---

* The public buildings burnt included the main office of Power Development Department and Traffic Police Post, government jeeps etc. The Clock Tower at Lal Chowk was also damaged.

**The allegations that the Armed Forces (Special Powers) Act generates a frame of mind which leads to a large scale violation of the human rights is not at all well-founded. The Indian Army observes strict discipline, and there is an internal control mechanism.

Old Approach in New Form

To devise a fresh strategy to deal with the situation, the Prime Minister convened an all-party Conference. Consequent to the deliberations in this Conference, the Government of India first sent in September a 39-member all-party Parliamentary delegation to the state and then appointed three interlocutors* to hold discussions with different shades of opinion. But these steps have not yielded any worthwhile results. By and large, the conditions have remained unaltered. The separatists have even refused to meet the interlocutors. Unfortunately, the successive Union governments have not been able to shake off their appeasement complex and have persisted with a few token measures here and there, turning a blind eye to the stark realities that emanate from the fundamentalist fury of terror-oriented minds.

Earlier, too, as a result of the Round Table Conferences, called by Prime Minister Manmohan Singh in 2006, in which representatives of all political parties were present, five 'Working Groups'**, headed by 'experts', were set up to suggest measures that could be taken in

---

Contd. 708

Since the enforcement of the Special Powers Act in Kashmir, 1514 cases of human rights violations were reported. Out of these, 1470 were found to be baseless. In 44 cases, involving 70 officers and ranks, which were found to be true, strict punishment was awarded to the offenders. In the matter of safeguarding of human rights, the record of the Indian Army is much better than that of the United States Forces in Iraq and Afghanistan.

* These three interlocutors are Dilip Padgaonkar, Radha Kumar and M.M. Ansari. It is not for the first time that interlocutors have been appointed. Earlier, in April 2001, K.C. Pant was assigned this task and in February 2003, N.N. Vohra, took over this work. But their efforts proved barren.

** These Five Working Groups were constituted consequent to the decision announced by the Prime Minister at the Round Table Conference held at Srinagar on May 24-25, 2006. The First Group was concerned with the 'confidence-building measures', the Second with 'strengthening relations across the Line of Control', the Third with 'economic development', the Fourth with 'ensuring good governance', and the Fifth with the 'Centre-J&K relations'. Most of the recommendations of these Groups were overtaken by subsequent developments in the State. Some of them were even too general to be of any practical value. For example, the recommendations of the Fifth Group on 'Centre-J&K relations, headed by Justice Saghir Ahmed, is thick in volume but thin in content. Its concluding observations are: "The question of autonomy and its demand can be examined in the light of the 'Kashmir Accord' or in some other manner or on the basis of some formula as the present Prime Minister may deem fit and appropriate so as to restore the autonomy to the extent possible". These observations, clearly, do not make any specific recommendations.

certain specified areas to meet the 'aspirations' of the people of the State. The recommendations made by these groups, after a considerable span of time, were essentially no different from the ideas which were already in the air, and were soon blown over by the nasty waves of violence unleashed by the extremists from time to time. Such measures, moreover, have not worked in the past, they are not working at present and they would not work in the future. Most of these 'aspirations' are neither legitimate nor rooted in practicality; they have been manufactured by the subversives and other vested interests and are designed to take away the state from the Union. If India has to solve multiple and chronic problems of Kashmir, it has 'to be real' and rely, not on appeasement, not on wishful thinking, but on fairness cum firmness and on sound and sustained action.

Accession/Merger

As if the raging controversies were not enough, Chief Minister Omar Abdullah thought it expedient to add another one to them. On October 6, 2010, he made a statement in the Assembly, asserting: "We had acceded to and not merged with India". Clearly, his attempt was to placate those elements who either favoured total separation or asked for autonomy that virtually meant a separate state to be run with Indian money. In quite a few quarters, eye-brows were raised. A number of protest meetings were also held in Jammu, Delhi and other places.

Apart from its intriguing timing, the statement was a typical example of 'half-truth, half-lies'. In the beginning, J&K acceded to India, like all other princely states. Every state executed the Instrument of Accession in the same form and with same content. But history did not stop with signing of the Instrument. With the coming into force of the Indian Constitution with effect from January 26, 1950, J&K became an integral part of the Indian Union by virtue of the provisions of Article 1 which defines the territory of India and includes J&K. The Constitution itself contains an absolute bar against the amendment of this Article, thereby making the integration of this state with the Union irrevocable. Article 3 of the Constitution of J&K also declares that "the state is and shall be an integral part of the Union of India".

In view of these constitutional provisions, it is pointless to draw any distinction between 'accession' and 'merger'. Omar Abdullah has done so merely to serve his ends of power. The true position with regard to the integration of J&K and its constitutional, administrative and financial relationship with the Union has been spelt out in detail in the earlier chapters*. All that need to be underscored here is that those who are asking for the restoration of 1952-53 position must address themselves a few basic questions. Do the Kashmiris not have all the fundamental rights which are available to individuals in modern liberal democracies? Has their identity, culture, religion or language been undermined by the constitutional arrangements that have been in existence for several years? Who, in the absence of financial integration, would provide the funds that are needed to the tune of 78 per cent of the State's annual expenditure? How would requirement of national security be met and how would certain other contingencies be dealt with if Article 356 is not applicable?

Unfortunately, hardly any one in position of authority today realises that one of the principal causes of the continuing Kashmir tragedy has been the marked disposition of the three Abdullahs to play the card of '1952-53 position', whenever they found that power was slipping out of their hands. This exploitation must end, and the Kashmiri masses must be educated about the true position. In any case, nothing should be done to weaken the bonds between J&K and the rest of India. These bonds are not merely constitutional; they are cultural and have persisted for thousands of years.

Kashmir's Identity–Real Threat

As the experience of the last several decades shows, the Kashmir identity is absolutely safe in India. Not merely that, it has full scope to creatively express itself further and develop in its own way. It has also ample opportunity to transmit its ripples all over the country. Kashmir is essentially the land of Nud Rishi, Lal Ded and many other venerable Sufi saints whose message is rooted in catholicity, compassion and inner elevation of man.

---

*For issues pertaining to accession and Delhi Agreement, sub-head, titled: *Delhi Agreement,* in chapter II may be seen. The analysis of Article 370 has been given in chapter VI. For comments on the ill-advised statement of Prime Minister Narasimha Rao–'Sky is the limit for autonomy'–sub-head, titled: *Short of Azadi: 'Maximum Autonomy',* in chapter XVIII, may be seen. The implications of the so-called Musharraf's formula pertaining to 'self-rule' on both the sides of LOC, 'joint management', regionalisation etc., Chapter XX may be referred to.

The threat to the cultural ethos of Kashmir–Kashmiriyat as it is loosely called–comes not from any provision of the Indian Constitution but from Sunni-Deobandi-Wahhabi extremist groups who interpret Islam in a very narrow way and who want to impose their interpretation on all other sects. What is worse, this imposition is sought to be done by force–not ordinary force but one that emanates from bullets and bombs.

To materialise their objectives, the Sunni-Deobandi-Wahhabi extremist groups have raised a number of militant outfits, such as Lashkar-e-Jhangvi and Sipah-e-Sahabah. The other sects are subjected frequently to terrorist attacks. For example, the Data Darbar, the most celebrated Sufi Shrine in Lahore, was ruthlessly bombarded on July 2, 2010, when the gathering was at its largest. 42 innocent persons were killed and 175 injured. Earlier, in March 2009, the historic shrine of Rahman Baba was blasted. Likewise, a huge Shia procession was brutally attacked in September 2009, killing as many as 37 processionists.

In the heat of the moment and amidst the brainwashing that the Kashmiris are currently undergoing by way of propaganda in the name of Islam, they do not seem to realise that fanaticism that is being exported to them from across the border or is being propped up locally by a group of insurgents, would one day destroy their identity, their Kashmiriyat, from its very roots. It is time that the responsible leadership in the state shows some vision, stop sloganeering about unworkable 'self-rule' or 'pre-1952-53 position' and devote its time, energy and talent for evolving a socially compact and culturally vibrant community–a pride of the Indian Union.

Signals From Obama's Visit

A significant aspect of the Kashmir issue is connected not only with the Unites States' policies towards Afghanistan, Pakistan and India, but also with its overall strategy to combat international terrorism. A considerable importance was, therefore, attached to President Obama's visit to India from November 6 to 8, 2010. Quite a few expectations were in the air. But in the course of his stay, Kashmir was mentioned only in passing.

At the same time, however, Obama said quite a few things that were pleasing to the Indian ears. He spoke of United States' support for a permanent seat on the United Nations Security Council for India, and underlined the significance of the 'shared vision', 'shared values' and 'shared security' of the two countries. He made an elevating reference to India's civilisational nobility and its abiding faith in peace and plurality. The two great apostles of humanism and universal brotherhood–Gandhi and Vivekananda–were especially mentioned. Obama also acknowledged India's contribution to the expansion of 'moral imagination' of America. In respect of terrorism, too, his observations were reassuring. In his address to the Indian Parliament, he said:

> Here in this Parliament, which was itself targeted because of the democracy it represents, we honour the memory of all those who have been taken from us, including American citizens on 26/11 and Indian citizens on 9/11. This is the bond we share. It's why we insist that nothing ever justifies the slaughter of innocent men, women and children. It is why we are working together, more closely than ever, to prevent terrorist attacks and to deepen our cooperation even further.

By making Mumbai his first halt and by staying at Taj Hotel, which had seen maximum horror and bloodshed during 26/11, Obama sent a clear signal to the terrorists about what he thought of their activities against India. He also reaffirmed his earlier commitment to ensure that the perpetrators of Mumbai's carnage were brought to justice.

But the real question is, whether all that Obama said and did during his visit would curb, or even weaken, the terror-oriented factors and forces that have been operating in Pakistan over the years? The answer to this question is plainly in the negative. There would be no transformative turn in the current conditions, unless the United States shows greater firmness in dealing with Afghanistan and Pakistan, and also takes a vigorous initiative to have a meaningful mechanism set up, at the international level, which would effectively wean away Muslim communities from the extremist ideologies which are being presented to them by way of a restricted and skewed interpretation of Islam. It makes no practical sense to allow fire-brand militants to be produced in large numbers and then pursue them all over the world. The unprecedented problem has to be tackled through an unprecedented mechanism* which must have a massive educational

*For my proposal in regard to the mechanism and war of ideas etc., see preceding chapter (XX), particularly sub-head beginning from 'Need of Hour'. A detailed analysis of these and connected issues would be found in chapter V, titled, 'Meeting the Challenges of Contemporary Terrorism', in author's book, *Shaping India's New Destiny*.

programme. The war on terror should not be restricted to financial, diplomatic and military means. It must be extended to incorporate a more fundamental war, a war of ideas, which is rooted in a positive and reformative outlook and which draws its strength from a creative and dynamic interpretation of Islam with a view to presenting its humane and enlightened face. Such a presentation, if disseminated effectively by governments in Muslim countries, would act as a bulwark against the tide of fundamentalism.

The strategy that the United States has so far been following to eliminate al-Qaeda and other militant organisations from the Afghanistan-Pakistan region has been of little avail. It has allowed Pakistan to run with the hare and hunt with the hound. Under the strategy, billions of dollars have been received by Pakistan, in the form of military aid, to eliminate camps of militants from the tribal areas on Pakistani side of the border. But the Pakistan Army and its ISI have been 'double crossing' the United States. They have been taking action here and there to provide a limited satisfaction to the United States; but at the same time extending monetary and material support to major groups amongst the militants to keep them active and strong. The members of these groups frequently sneak into Afghanistan to attack the forces of United States and NATO, and cause heavy damage. What it comes to in practice is that the United States is aiding Pakistan to get its own objectives in Afghanistan defeated.

The United States is aware of Pakistan's game of deception and duplicity. But it has persuaded itself to believe that, on balance of consideration, it should persist with its current strategy of 'disrupting, dismantling and defeating' all militant groups, including al-Qaeda and its affiliates. At the same time, a serious rethinking is being done. Of late, Pakistan is being told by the United States in no uncertain terms that 'terrorist safe-havens with its border are unacceptable'. After Faisal Shahzad's* abortive attempt to blow up an explosive laden car in New York Time Square, a stern warning was given: "The US can no longer tolerate Pakistan's *a la carte* approach to going after some

*Faisal Shazad is naturalised American of Pakistani origin. He turned a terrorist and received training in the camps run by al-Qaeda and Lashkar-e-Taiba in Pakistan's Tribal areas. On May 1, 2010 he attempted to explode a make-shift bomb placed in his SUV parked in the Time Square. He was prosecuted and awarded life-sentence.

terrorist groups and supporting, if not owning, others"*. It was also hinted that if any Pakistan-linked incident of terror occurred in the United States in future, "a retribution campaign of bombing up to 150 known terrorist safe-havens inside Pakistan**" could follow.

But Pakistan Army and its ISI are too shrewd, too hardened, to be influenced by such warnings and hints. They have, over the years, got accustomed to using the terrorist outfits as an instrument of state policy, both with regard to India and Afghanistan***. By doing so, they have reaped a huge bonanza. Their appetite now stands whetted, and they are unlikely to abandon these outfits and change the approach that has proved so rewarding to them. Pakistan should have been checked at the initial stage when, in 1989, it started organising terrorist groups and deploying them in Kashmir. At that time, the United States and other Western countries did not fully realise the dangers inherent in use of terror as a technique by Pakistan to secure its foreign policy goals. Nor did they ever think that this technique would one day be directed against them.

Now that the experience of the last decade or so has taught the United States and its Western allies a bitter lesson, they must undertake a comprehensive review of their on-going policies, both with regard to physical and ideological aspects**** of the problem. If Pakistan does not change its style of operation and if it does not disband or disable all its terrorist groups by a specified date, it must be denied all kinds of aid, and international sanctions should be imposed upon it.

China Factor

Unobtrusively, the Pakistan-China axis is sowing seeds of serious trouble for India in the future. Out of its illegally occupied

---

* Bob Woodward: *Obama Wars*. p. 365.

** *Ibid*.

*** Pakistan plans to use the militant groups to set up a regime in Afghanistan, friendly to it but hostile to India, after the United States and NATO forces leave that country and Karzai's government falls. The oft-repeated declarations by the United States that its forces would start leaving Afghanistan from July 2011 onwards had strengthened the belief of Pakistan Army and its ISI that all they had to do was to continue to prop up militant groups till the foreign troops leave.

**** For details in respect of ideological aspects, see the preceding chapter (XX).

area* of Gilgit and Baltistan, *de facto* control of a vast chunk of land is being given by Pakistan to China for creating rail and road links between Eastern China and Pakistani port-cum-naval bases at Gwadar, Pasni and Ormara. These bases are also being built by China. With the completion of these projects, China would be able to transport its goods for exports to and imports from the Gulf countries in two days instead of the present period of 22 days. The Karakoram Highway is also being extended and strengthened to provide an effective link between Sinkiang province of China and Pakistan.

All this is bound to establish stronger strategic and economic bonds between the two countries. Both of them may join hands to cause more difficulties for India with regard to the Kashmir issue and also for the United States *vis-à-vis* its interests in Afghanistan. Already, about 10,000 soldiers of the People's Liberation Army are working in Gilgit-Baltistan area on road, rail, irrigation and other development projects. Some of them are believed to be engaged in constructing scores of tunnels for providing a gas pipe line from Iran to China.

Ending the Turbulence

As I have said in the beginning of this chapter, the period, 2008-2010, is full of highly significant events. The analysis of these events has been done above. It shows how far reaching are they in their impact. But the analysis also shows that underneath all these events, flow the same currents that had, in the first instance, caused the Kashmir turbulence to freeze. The political culture of superficiality, softness and selfishness and poverty of governance persist. So do their fall-outs.

I have already spelt out in the last few paragraphs of the preceding chapter what fundamental reorientation of mind and matter, attitudes and outlook and civilisational norms and thought-processes, is called for. It is the warm breeze from this reorientation that alone could end the cold turbulence that has engulfed the Kashmir Valley for years.

*The total area of the erstwhile princely state of J&K was 222,236 sq. km. Out of it, Pakistan has illegally occupied 78,114 sq. km. 85 per cent of this area comprises what are called Northern Areas–Gilgit and Baltistan etc. These areas have been virtually annexed by Pakistan and are directly administered by the Federal Government. Only 15 per cent of Pakistan held area covers what is described as Azad J&K.

CHAPTER XXII

My Kashmir— Truth Speaks Again

While truth is buried underground, it grows,
it chokes, it gathers such an explosive force
that one day it bursts out, it blows everything with it.

–Emile Zola

Laser-like Focus

Almost all significant events of the period* (January 2011-July 2012) put a laser-like focus on Pakistan's** 'politics of deception and disinformation' and its accompanying military strategy of nurturing and deploying Jihad-oriented terrorist outfits to attain its goals with regard to Kashmir/India and Afghanistan. As brought out in detail in the earlier chapters, from the very day of my arrival at Srinagar for my second term in January, 1990, I had been pin-pointing the diabolical threads with which Pakistan, in pursuance of the said politics and military strategy, had woven a vast network*** of

* As indicated in the preface, the Ninth Edition of this book covered developments upto January, 2011. This chapter of the Tenth Edition analyses events that have happened thereafter, upto July 2012, and have direct or indirect bearing on the Kashmir issue.

** When I refer to Pakistani politics/strategy, it really means politics/strategy as worked out/approved by the Army/ISI. Because, even under the civilian rule, Army/ISI has a final say on key issues of foreign policy, national security etc. It remains 'state within a state'.

*** For detail, chapter X, titled: Pattern of Subversion and Terrorism in Kashmir and chapter VIII, titled: Conditions Before My arrival, may be seen.

subversion and terrorism in Kashmir. But neither the Indian nor the American authorities paid any attention. Both, in their own way, were led astray by their short-term approach.

The Indian decision and opinion makers were known for their soft and superficial outlook and their disposition to live in a world of their own make-believe. They woke up to the brutal truth* only when the terrorists' bombs started exploding in the busy streets of Delhi and seven-star hotels of Mumbai. But what was really astounding was that even the hard-headed leaders of America and its well-endowed 'think-tanks' of long standing, who were envisioning the 'end of history' and laying down a road-map for a New American Century, should have failed to read in time the dangerous potential of the sinister contours of the Pakistani game-plan. Today, 'my Kashmir truth'**, ignored by all concerned, speaks through the silent voices of about 50,000 dead Indians and also through the dilemma and discomfiture which American authorities are presently facing in Afghanistan after discovering that Pakistan had all along been serving as a breeding ground for frenzied terrorists and acting as a deceitful ally. Just look at what the veteran Californian Congressman, Dan Rohraba-cher, who was once a staunch supporter of Pakistan, said in mid-May 2012, while introducing the Pakistan Terrorism and Accountability Bill in the House of Representatives: "Pakistan helped to create the Talibans and Pakistan's Intelligence Services hid Osama Bin Laden from the US for years. Today, one of the most dangerous and sophisticated groups

---

* In this regard, my comments under Section, captioned *Horrific Events: 26/XI* of chapter XXI, titled: *The Stage 2008 to 2010,* may particularly be seen.

**From day one, it should have been clear to any dispassionate observer that the terrorist violence that started in the Kashmir Valley in mid-1989 could not have come about without being planned and directed by Pakistan's Inter Services Intelligence and without being supported by a massive training programme of Jihad-oriented Non-State-Actors in use of modern weapons and communication equipment. The data and documents available at that time (see chapter X) should not have left any one in doubt about it. But if we look at the latest data, we would be amazed at the extraordinary capacity of the power-wielders and opinion-makers of India not to see hard facts. The affidavit filed by the State Home Department in July 2012 before the State Human Rights Commission shows that since 1990, the Security Forces have seized 45,00,000 bullets, 11,431 pistols and revolvers, 1027 universal machine guns, 2,262 rocket-propelled grenade launchers, 2,830 rocket boosters, 391 sniper rifles, 79 carbines, 219 light machine guns and self-loading rifles and 295 .303 rifles. The weaponry on such a large scale could have been arranged and supplied only by Pakistan Army/Inter-Services Intelligence.

killing American troops is the Haqqani network which is closely operated by the Pakistan government."

In a similar tone of exasperation, a Senior Congressman, Gary Ackerman, told the House Foreign Affairs Committee: "Pakistan is like a black-hole for American aid. Our dollars go in, our diplomats go in, our aid professionals go in, our hopes go in and our prayers go in. But nothing comes out. We have, since 2004, already sunk a whopping $24 billion." A year earlier, an American 'think-tank', West Point Centre for Combating Terrorism, in its research study (2011), had shown how, during the 1980s, "Jalal-ud-din-Haqqani quickly rose to be one of the most favoured field commanders and how the support he provided had a significant impact upon Pakistan Security Establishment and the *Jihad* in Kashmir to follow."

Embittered and Distrustful

For quite some time, a section of the American Administration had held the view, that Pakistan was resorting* to 'deception and disinformation' on an extensive scale. This view gained near total acceptability amongst the American decision and opinion makers, when it was found that Al-Qaeda chief, Osama bin Laden, was hiding** in the garrison town of Abbottabad. He was killed in the early morning of May 2, 2011 by way of a commando action of the US Navy Seals. No one in the Pakistan establishment was informed, showing how distrustful had American authorities become even of the top functionaries of the Pakistani state.

Pakistan's perfidy became all the more glaring by the treatment it accorded to Dr. Shakeel Afridi who had helped CIA in verifying the identity of Osama bin Laden by way of an American sponsored scheme to vaccinate the residents of the locality against Hepatitis B and collecting their DNA in the process. Dr. Afridi was arrested, tried under a primitive Tribal Code of Khyber Agency, declared guilty of treason and sentenced to imprisonment for 33 years. It was not taken

* With regard to its planned and directed terrorism in Kashmir, Pakistan's ISI had largely got away with its lies. This had encouraged it to increasingly rely on its web of deception and disinformation to virtually trap the United States in Afghanistan.

**It is widely believed that Brig (retd.) Ajaz Shah, who had earlier held senior assignments in the Inter-Services Intelligence and the Intelligence Bureau, had the Abbottabad house built for Osama's safe stay, with the full knowledge and approval of the then President of Pakistan, General Pervez Musharraf.

into account that Doctor Afridi was acting against Al-Qaeda, and not against the State of Pakistan which in fact was an ally of the United States in its 'war on terror'.

The extremely harsh and legally untenable punishment awarded to Dr. Afridi and the unabashed violation of basic human rights and norms of natural justice by Pakistan have embittered the United States and caused further deterioration in the already tense relations between the two countries. A few other incidents have added sparks to this tension.

In November, 2011, 24 Pakistani soldiers were killed in a NATO strike at Pakistan's Salala military check post*. The killing** was unintentional and a result of confusion in the messages transmitted to each other by the parties. But Pakistan over-reacted, *albeit* with a calculated mind. It closed the only available land route for providing supplies to the NATO troops in Afghanistan. It also withdrew airbase facility, earlier granted to the Americans for flying drones from strategically located Shamshi Airfield in Balochistan. To cap it all, Pakistan demanded personal apology from President Barack Obama. Understandably, Obama refused. He also made his displeasure at Pakistan's attitude known to all concerned by cold shouldering President Zardari at the NATO Summit, held at Chicago in May 2012.

Though the United States badly needed Pakistan's cooperation for maintaining supply line to the NATO's troops in Afghanistan, without incurring heavy costs which the alternative route through the Central Asian Republics and Russia involved, it sent clear signals to Pakistan that there was a limit to its patience. It started curtailing aid*** and slashing Pakistan's claim for reimbursement from Coalition-Support

* The Salala incident, though serious in itself, could not be attributed solely to what Pakistan called American high-handedness. Nor was it of such dimensions as to provoke Pakistan to close supply-route to NATO troops in Afghanistan. In fact, it was a retaliatory move to settle scores with Americans whose unilateral action in Abbottabad killing of Osama had exposed the Army and ISI before the Pakistani public as well as international community as an incompetent organisation, unworthy of trust.

** A high-level military Inquiry, ordered by the NATO commander immediately after the incident, held that both the parties were at fault.

*** The US Senate Appropriate Committee resolved to cut aid to Pakistan by 58% for the fiscal year 2013. The American authorities also rejected a good part of Pakistan's claim for reimbursement from the Coalition Support Fund.

Fund. It also refused to consider Pakistan's demand for stopping drone attacks, and declared that the United States would undertake whatever steps were required to protect its forces in Afghanistan. It even increased the frequency of the drone attacks. In the month following the Chicago Summit, eight drone attacks were carried out, killing at least 30 members of Al-Qaeda, including Abu Yaha al Libi, who was believed to be next in command to Ayman al Zawahri.

Sensing that this time US was determined to rely more on stick than on carrot, Pakistan, after seven months of obduracy, thought it expedient to beat a retreat, under the cover of semantics, and reopen the land-route for transporting military supplies to NATO troops in Afghanistan. Referring to Pakistan's Foreign Minister Hina Rabbani Khar's telephonic talk, US Secretary of State Hillary Clinton said: "Foreign Minister Khar and I acknowledged the mistakes that resulted in the loss of Pakistani military lives. We are sorry for the losses suffered by the Pakistani military. We are committed to working closely with Pakistan and Afghanistan to prevent this from ever happening again." Earlier, it needs to be underscored, Pakistan was insisting on personal apology by President Obama. Its climb down shows once again that Pakistan understands the attitude of firmness better than the attitude of softness.

The resumption of supplies to the NATO troops in Afghanistan warded off the crisis and eased the tension between United States and Pakistan. But bitterness remained. And American mistrust of its 'difficult partner' has increased to such an extent that it is considering a fundamental reorientation of its policy towards Pakistan and subjecting it to 'malign neglect' or 'active isolation'.

L'affaire Fai

Another important event which is instructive for both US and India, though in different ways, pertains to what has come to be known as L'affaire Fai. For years, Ghulam Nabi Fai, an American citizen of Kashmiri origin, had been functioning as Chairman of the Kashmiri American Council. Taking advantage of the then pro-Pakistan tilt of American Administration and as one having large hospitality funds at his disposal, he had become an influential lobbyist for Pakistan's stand on the Kashmir issue. The extent of his influence could be seen from the letter which President Bill Clinton wrote to Fai on December

27, 1993 in the context* of what he had said about Kashmir in his address to UN General Assembly on September 24, 1993. But when Pakistan started playing the same sinister game of deception and disinformation with the American Administration in respect of its stand on Afghanistan as it had earlier played with India in respect of its stand on the Kashmir issue, the American officials decided to get tough with persons like Fai and started looking into their activities closely. The FBI soon found that, since mid-1989, Fai had virtually been functioning as head of a branch of Pakistan's Inter-Services Intelligence and had transgressed American laws in the process. He was prosecuted and sentenced to imprisonment. The message that Pakistan got was that it had to pay for sabotaging American strategy with regard to Afghanistan.

From the numerous e-mails and other documents, cited in the FBI's criminal complaint to the Court, it became clear that the operational and financial parameters of the Kashmiri American Council were tightly controlled and it was required to follow the agenda set by the Inter-Services Intelligence. Even the select-list of the Indian and Pakistani journalists, invited to the seminars held by it, was provided by the ISI. And this aspect of the matter had an Indian angle which was instructive in itself. It showed how some journalists and makers of public opinion in India, in their anxiety to appear as liberal at the national and international stage had, wittingly or unwittingly, acted as a tool of Pakistan in spreading, far and wide, its network of disinformation on Kashmir.

It is not possible to say with precision whether, or to what extent, the thinking of the Indian journalists and opinion makers was coloured by the free business-class air travel, stay in 5-star hotels and other items of hospitality provided to them by Fai's council. But one thing is quite clear. The views expressed by these journalists on certain significant matters pertaining to Kashmir were on the same wave length as those projected by the Inter-Services Intelligence as a part of its disinformation plan which itself was a key constituent of their overall plan of unleashing terror and subversion in Kashmir and simultaneously demonising those who stood against it. Let me

*For the context and other details in this regard, section, titled: *United States New Posture*, of chapter XVII may be seen.

elaborate by drawing attention to the case of mass exodus of the Kashmiri Pandits from the Valley in mid 1989-1990.

One of the objectives of the aforesaid overall plan of the Inter-Services Intelligence was to terrorise and drive out of the Valley all the 'infidels' and 'agents' of the Union. On September 14, 1989, the President of a pro-India political party, Tikka Lal Taploo, was brutally murdered in broad day light in front of his house in Srinagar. Soon thereafter, on November 4, Judge N.K. Ganjoo, who had tried Maqbool Butt, considered a revolutionary by his supporters, on charges of terrorist acts committed in 1966 and 1975, was done to death on the busy thoroughfare of Hari Singh Street. This was followed by the merciless killing on December 28, 1989 of Anantnag based journalist, P.N. Bhat, whose writings were not to the liking of the subversionists and terrorists. A number of other Kashmiri Pandits, living in small towns and remote areas, suffered similar fate. On January 16, 1990, a high-level delegation of All India Kashmiri Pandit Conference called upon the then Governor, General (Retd.) K.V. Krishna Rao and submitted a detailed memorandum which bewailed accelerating pace of Pandits exodus from the Valley.

Clearly, before the resignation of Dr. Farooq Abdullah government, imposition of President's rule in the state and my appointment as Governor for the second term on January 19, 1990, the terrorists, subversionists and other pro-Pakistan elements held the Valley virtually in their jaws. Before, however, they could close their jaws and swallow the Valley, it was pulled back by a series of measures taken by me.

As my multi-pronged strategy started frustrating the designs of the ISI and other forces of terrorism and subversion, and as these forces were even otherwise hell-bent on destroying my agreeable image which existed in the mind of the common Kashmiri on account of the welfare and development work that I had done from early 1984 to early 1989, they made me a special target of their disinformation plan. All kinds of concoctions were foisted on me.

One of the patent falsehoods, assiduously spread, was that it was I who had brought about the migration of the Kashmiri Pandits from the Valley. This disinformation resorted to by the ISI and its network was reprehensible. But what was far more reprehensible was that some of the 'eminent journalists', who have now been discovered to be on the 'select-list' of Fai's council, had been giving expression to the same fabricated allegations. They ignored all the documented and contemporaneous evidence*.

L'affaire Fai brings out the contrasting attitude of India and United States. The former has been diffused and weak in its approach and the latter clear and firm. United States has not hesitated to talk tough and act tough against its 'steadfast and historic ally', as Condoleezza Rice once described Pakistan. A clear indication has been given to Pakistan to behave in a straight-forward manner or suffer the consequences of its crafty designs.

Fall-outs

For Kashmir and the rest of India, there have been two significant fall-outs of the stand off between the United States and Pakistan. Practically, the entire energy, resources and attention of the Pakistan Army and Inter-Services Intelligence are currently engaged in dealing with plethora of problems that have arisen all along its western border and also with the terrorists violence that is caused, from time to time, by the ultra conservative outfits** who have got out of control and are intolerant of any opinion or act which, according to their interpretation of Islam, does not conform to *Sharia*. Secondly, it has now fully dawned upon the American authorities how deceptive and disinformative has Pakistan been about its real plan of wresting Kashmir through religion-propelled terror and subversion, and how unwise have they been in not foreseeing the dangers inherent in such a design for liberal democracies all over the world. Be that as it may, these two fall-outs have resulted in substantial reduction in terrorist violence in Kashmir, providing another proof that it was largely directed from the other side of the border.

---

* For details, chapter XIII., titled: *Frightened Pigeons and Forsaken Community-Kashmiri Pandits* and Appendix XXVII, may particularly be seen.

** A telling example of the inroads which ultra conservative Islamists have made in the Pakistani state and society is provided by the assassination of Punjab Governor Salman Taseer in January 2011 by his own body-guard who, while being taken to the Police-lock up, was showered with rose petals for acting like a true Muslim in killing a non-believer. Taseer's only 'crime' was that he had advocated changes in the blasphemy law. Two months later, Federal Minister for Minority Affairs, Shahbaz Bhatti, was murdered for expressing views similar to Taseer. That the radicalised Islamists had even infiltrated the Armed Forces was clear from the terrorists attack (May 2011) on Pakistan's Naval Base at Mehran. Such a serious attack could not be carried out without insiders' collaboration.

Will India be able to take advantage of the current conditions and proceed to solve the problem permanently by eliminating the basic shortcomings of its polity? These shortcomings and the approach to remove them have been exhaustively discussed in previous chapters* and need not be repeated here. Suffice to underscore, new vision and will would have to be mustered by the national and state leadership, if the past mistakes of taking wrong direction at every turning point of Kashmir's chequered history have to be avoided.

Interlocutors' Report

Unfortunately, even now, the old ethos, attitudes and outlook show no sign of going away. The recent Report** of the Group of Interlocutors bear ample testimony to the fact that culture of superficiality and wishful thinking still dominates the Indian political scene and intellectual discourse. Instead of suggesting any lasting remedy for the deep rooted infection in the body-politics of the State and the Union, it has injected a new viral in the form of a Constitutional Committee which would be mandated to draw up a New Compact for the People of J&K. The setting up of such a Constitutional Committee, it is easy to see, would only result in providing an additional avenue for fanning the disintegrative forces not only in J&K but also in other parts of the country. Could similar demands from other regions, such as North-East, for a 'new compact' through a new 'constitutional committee' be resisted?

The report is based not on indepth examination of precise issues, but on selective picking up of items from the demands of those who want either to secede from India or establish a virtual Sheikhdom*** of their own with Indian tax-payers' money. It refers to the 'deep sense

* The reader may particularly see chapter XX, titled: *New Era: New Response*.

** The Report of the Group of Interlocutors is titled: A New Compact with the People of J&K. For the backdrop of the constitution of this Group, section, titled: *Old Approach* of chapter XXI, titled: The Stage: 2008-2010, may be seen. The Report of Interlocutors was submitted to the Home Ministry and made public on May 24, 2012.

*** As early as 1951, one of the most perceptive journalists of the time, Frank Moraes, had noted: 'Even at that time, Sheikh Abdullah was moving towards independence for the Valley of Srinagar, with himself as the Kashmiri equivalent of the Grand Moghul'. *Witness To An Era*; p. 220.

of victimhood' in the Kashmir Valley, without realising that this 'sense'* is a manufactured one and is a product of an unprincipled exploitation of constitutional illiteracy of the masses by the extra-ambitious and power-hungry leaders of the State. By and large, the Report rearticulates the known position of different groups and different regions and sub-regions. With respect to every crucial issue that has to be faced in practice, it follows a convenient line by simply ignoring the inconvenient reality.

The Report does not care to make a distinction between an autonomy that leads to efficiency in administration, speed in development and fuller realisation of a creative potential of a community, and an autonomy that leads to separation, subversion and secession and provides a fillip to the forces of parochialism and chauvinism. Nor does it engage itself with a number of pertinent questions: Do the Kashmiris not have all the fundamental rights which individuals in modern liberal democracies enjoy? Has their identity, culture, religion or language been undermined in any way by the constitutional arrangements that have been in operation for the last several decades? How would a common Kashmiri be benefited by changing the nomenclature of Chief Minister to Prime Minister or of Governor to Sadar-i-Riyasat, or by ousting the jurisdiction of Supreme Court, the Election Commission and the Comptroller and Auditor-General of India? What would happen if the so called pre-1952 position is restored and only defence, foreign affairs and communications are kept within the jurisdiction of the Union Parliament/Government and all the remaining items are assigned exclusively to the State Legislature/Government? How would the State Government meet its requirements of finances which at present are provided by the Union Government to the tune of 74% of its needs? Could the 'nuts and bolts' of objective reality and the need to have smooth and workable relationship between the State and the Union be dispensed with?

---

*How does the so called sense of victimhood accord with one of the highest per capita assistance that the State receives from the Union, the special packages that are given to it from time to time and the huge development bonanza it has got from such projects as Jammu-Qazigund Rail Link, Srinagar International Air Port and various tunnels and Four-way National High Way? Is it not, on the contrary, a case of appeasement and pampering?

The Interlocutors have also not attempted to meet any of the solid arguments* advanced, in the historical context, in different parts of the book, for not encouraging too many claimants for separate identities. The national unity is already skating on the thin ice. It would be suicidal to expose it any further risk.

The need of the hour is that we should make a new beginning, educate our brothers and sisters in Kashmir about the true position in respect of their political, social and cultural freedoms and tell them that we as fellow country-men have already helped them to the tune of ₹ 95,000 crore from 1989-90 to 2009-10, and would continue to discharge our obligations in this respect in future also to make them a happy and prosperous community of the Union.

My Truth Speaks Again

Through the above analysis of the main events of the last one and a half years, my Kashmir truth has spoken once again. It has reinforced the validity of one of the key propositions formulated by me in this book; *viz.* the Indian decision makers in the arena of politics and the Indian opinion makers in the arena of media have, more often than not, played, *albeit* unwittingly, in the hands of forces inimical to Indian unity and well-being. The former is afflicted with the chronic malady of softness and the latter with the chronic weakness of appearing as liberal even if it involves blinking over stark facts and past experience. These deep-rooted infirmities could be cured only if national mindset undergoes a fundamental change and, as elaborated in the earlier chapters, healthy and constructive values are created to underpin the actions of the State and social groups.

---

*In this regard, attention of the reader is particularly drawn, apart from the three chapters on Roots (IV, V and VI), to sections/sub-sections, titled: *Short of Azadi: Maximum Autonomy; Hollowness of Approach; Nuts and Bolts of Working Relationship; Specious Arguments and An Healthy Feature of chapter XVIII;* and also section, titled: *Musharraf's Out of Box Suggestion* and its subsequent sub-sections and also to sections, titled: *Accession/Merger* and *Kashmir Identity–Real Threat* of chapter XXI. *Specious Arguments and An Healthy Feature of chapter XVIII;* and also section, titled: *Musharraf's Out of Box Suggestion* and its subsequent sub-sections and also to sections, titled: *Accession/Merger* and *Kashmir Identity–Real Threat* of chapter XXI.

CHAPTER XXIII

A Season for Inward and Outward Change: Undoing the Negative Politics of Article 370

Let us teach ourselves and others that Politics can be not only the art of the possible–especially if this means intrigues, 'deals and manoeuvring–but also the art of the impossible, namely, the art of improving ourselves.

*–Vaclav Havel**

On May 19, 2014, soon after the completion of the 16th Lok Sabha elections, I wrote to Prime Minister-designate, Narendra Modi: "From Your resounding victory of truly historic proportion, it seems to me that the much needed season for an inward and outward change could be approaching India, when confidence and commitment could claim a share with her prudence and when she could attain her highest wisdom by daring."

I do not know whether my expectations with regard to the 'much needed season' are overoptimistic, and whether they could be actualized in the near future or not. But I do know that unless such a season and accompanying inward and outward change come, India would not be able to rid herself of the deep-rooted maladies which she has contracted over the years. This is particularly true of the maladies

*An internationally reputed playwright, philosopher and propagator of humanitarian values, Vaclav Havel was first President of the Czech Republic. He was awarded Gandhi Peace Prize in 2003.

pertaining to the state of J&K. Here, from the very inception, the infections from multiple maladies have been reinforcing one another and adding to the weight of a hugely complex web of intractabilities.

At the time of release of the tenth (10th) edition of this book, a group-discussion was held at the India International Centre, where I made a short presentation, captioned: *Why Has My Frozen Turbulence in Kashmir Remained Frozen For So Long?* My proposition was that, over the last several years, India, in relation to its state of J&K, had acquired social, cultural and political ethos which were conducive to the growth of separatism, subversion and terrorism. Disruption and demagogy had penetrated deep into the texture of its democracy. And narrow ends of personal and political power had attained a total ascendancy. In this environment, I underscored, the chronic infections in the roots of the body-politic had remained, and erupted into high fever from time to time. Unless this environment undergoes an upward transformation and propels the ethos of the social and political leadership into a healthier orbit, there would be no basic improvement and the frozen turbulence would not blow away.

The outward facts of high fever, the internal and external forces providing frequent stimuli to the embedded infections, and the superficial treatment to which these high fevers and flared-up infections were subjected to in the past have all been brought out, in historical context, in the preceding chapters of the book; and need not be rearticulated here.

Article 370, too, has been discussed threadbare earlier. But with regard to it, new dimensions and new tone and tenor have emerged on the political firmament of the country, after the decisive victory of the Bharatiya Janata Party whose election manifesto had declared: "The Party reiterates its stand on Article 370, and will discuss this with all stake holders and remains committed to the abrogation of this article". In this context, the issue calls for examination from a somewhat different angle. Even otherwise, Article 370 has a chequered backdrop. It has moved from one complex stage to another, gathering layers within layers, and accommodating, *albeit* temporarily, different illusions amongst different actors on the stage. The prevailing position is hardly intelligible to the common man. He perceives it through his prism of social, political and religious biases which are further fed and strengthened, especially in the valley, by the power-hungry politicians, by way of emotional outbursts on selective ingredients in the Article. A recent example of this phenomenon is provided by the fulmination of Chief Minister Omar Abdullah: "Mark my words and save this tweet–long after Modi government is a distant memory, either J&K won't be part of India or Article 370 will still exist".

The threatening tone speaks for itself. Omar Abdullah could not have got away with it easily, had the public in general adequate information about the circumstances in which this Article was drafted and the manner in which it has travelled through the pages of history during the last several years. The whole issue needs to be put in perspective, from the very initial stage to date, and made clear to the common Kashmiri. Then alone, he would be able to assess for himself whether Article 370 has benefitted or harmed his interests, and to what extent he has been made a victim of a calculated campaign of disinformation launched by a caucus of political elite. Unfortunately, over the years, the issue has assumed such a complexity that it is extremely difficult for the common man to grasp it properly.

Perhaps, a simple question-answer form would be of great help in communicating the correct position to him. I would, therefore, raise relevant questions, in such a sequence that their answers would provide an all embracing picture which is also easily intelligible to the common man. After the 16th Lok Sabha elections, these questions have often been asked in public but in a rather diffused way and have seldom been answered effectively. I would deal with these questions, one by one.

Q: What led to the inclusion of Article 370 in the Indian Constitution, when most of the political leaders of the times viewed it unfavourably?

A: The inclusion of this Article was largely the result of Jawaharlal Nehru's misplaced trust in Sheikh Abdullah who, literally, had won his confidence by 'honest trifles' only to 'betray him in deepest consequences'. Quite a few perceptive observers of the times had noticed that Sheikh Abdullah was an overambitious leader, and also 'ambivalence incarnate'. Frank Moraes*, in his book, *Witness to an Era,* has given an interesting account of this:

Power had gone to Abdullah's head. Even when in Delhi in 1946 I had breakfast with him, he struck me as a highly egocentric individual,

**Frank Moraes: Witness To An Era* p.220. He was a celebrated journalist of his time, known for his perceptive and fearless observations.

personally very ambitious. Around 1951, I met him again in Bombay. Abdullah had been in power for three years, power had plainly infected his thinking and judgement, and I was surprised at the change in his political mood. He talked disdainfully of New Delhi.... As usual, however, he would not be drawn into any specific commitments. In the hindsight of after-events I have a feeling that even at that time his mind was moving towards independence for the Valley of Srinagar with himself as the Kashmiri equivalent of the Grand Mogul.

Unfortunately, Nehru had developed a one-eyed stance towards Abdullah. He refused to look at the warning signals, even when these were hoisted by eminent statesmen and political analysts.

Q: Does the issue boil down merely to misreading of Sheikh Abdullah's character by Nehru?

A: As I have described in detail in earlier chapters of this book, a number of mistakes were made in handling the Kashmir issue from the very beginning. But the most serious of all was the failure to judge the mind and motivation of Sheikh Mohammad Abdullah. For Abdullah, it was his ambition that got precedence over everything else. When it suited him, he kept proclaiming that accession of Kashmir to India was based on fundamental principles and was irrevocable. As soon as he saw another opening, he started sounding Anglo-US bloc for support to the idea of having an independent 'Sheikhdom'. As early as January 28, 1948, he discussed the subject with American officials. This is clear from the note of the same date sent by Warren Austin to the State Department after an interview with Sheikh Abdullah. The September 1950 report of Loy Henderson, the US Ambassador to India, also underlined: "In discussing future Kashmir, Abdullah was vigorous that it should be independent."

Q: Did it not amount to Sheikh's betrayal of Nehru's trust?

A: Certainly; it did. There is also a plethora of corroborative evidence. On May 3, 1953, Adlai Stevenson came to Srinagar and had a long meeting with Sheikh Abdullah. The New York Times, on July 5, published a map, hinting at independent status for the Valley. Clement Atlee also let it be known publicly: "Kashmir should neither belong to India nor Pakistan but should be independent." On July 10, speaking at Mujahid Manzil, Abdullah said: "A time will come, when I will bid goodbye to India."

All these events and pronouncements, taken together, should leave nobody in doubt that Sheikh Abdullah was scheming to become an independent ruler of Kashmir and the Anglo-US bloc was encouraging him.

Q: How did this scheme get thwarted?

A: Events took a fateful turn on June 23, 1953, when Shyama Prasad Mookerjee died as a detainee of the state government in the Srinagar Camp Jail at the relatively young age of 51. He had gone there to protest against a wholly unjust system under which even Indian citizens, including the President of India, could not enter, without a permit, the state of J&K. Mookerjee defied the system on May 11, 1953. Arrested, he remained in detention till his death, in circumstances that have, till date, left many valid questions unanswered.

Soon after Mookerjee's death, his mother, Jogmaya Devi, posed a poignant question to Prime Minister Nehru: "Had my son, a citizen of India, a member of the House of People, a leader of opposition, no fundamental right to enter Kashmir without any obstruction from any quarter?" This question alone raised the level of national consciousness so high that no government, howsoever stubborn, could afford to ignore the inconvenient reality about Sheikh Abdullah's attitude and outlook.

Mookerjee was the first to sense Abdullah's hidden ambition to bring about a 'virtual sheikhdom' of his own. In a letter written, about four months before his death, he told Abdullah in no uncertain words: "You are now developing a three-nation theory, the third being the 'Kashmir nation'. These are dangerous symptoms and not good for your state or the whole of India". On May 21, 1952, he also posed a pertinent question to Nehru in Parliament: "Are Kashmiris Indians first and Kashmiris next, or are they Kashmiris first and Indians next, or are they Kashmiris first, second and third and not Indian at all?" There was no reply. Mookerjee quipped: "Nehru claims to have discovered India. But he has yet to discover his mind."

Q: Was it not the expectation that Article 370 would provide only stop-gap arrangements?

A: When Sheikh Abdullah demanded a special status for the state of J&K, a number of senior Congress leaders and members of the

Constituent Assembly insisted that J&K should be treated as other princely states. To resolve the differences, Prime Minister Nehru asked Gopalaswamy Ayyangar to work out a compromise formula. Ayyangar suggested a draft that was later on included in the Constitution as Article 370. This draft, too, was strongly opposed, but Nehru was keen to have it adopted. Since he was going on tour abroad, he told Ayyangar to request Sardar Patel on his behalf, to use his influence to get the draft approved. To avoid embarrassment to Nehru, Patel obliged, though he was not personally convinced about the intrinsic soundness of Ayyangar's proposal. The tendency at that time was to gloss over the difficulties by way of interim measures, hoping that they would get sorted out at a later stage.

When V. Shankar, Secretary to Sardar Patel, expressed doubts about the wisdom of agreeing, *albeit* against his better judgement, to the draft of Ayyangar, Patel remarked; "After all, neither Sheikh Abdullah nor Gopalaswamy is permanent. The future would depend upon the strength and guts of the Indian government and if we cannot have confidence in our own strength we do not deserve to exist as a nation."

Nehru, too, considered Article 370 as an interim measure. Speaking in Parliament on 24 July 1952, he said: "We all wanted to leave it in a fluid condition because of the various factors and gradually develop the relation–legal and constitutional relations. As a result of this, a rather unusual provision was made in our Constitution. That provision is now Article 370, in Part XXI, Temporary and Transitional Provisions." On 7 August 1952, Nehru once again made it clear that Article 370 was not final, and it merely prescribed the manner in which additions could be made to the subjects.

Q: What did Nehru mean by saying that Article 370 merely prescribed the manner in which additions could be made to the subjects later?

A: The sum and substance of Article 370 is that, in addition to Defence, Foreign Affairs and Communication, the Union Parliament can make laws with regard to the items in the Union and Concurrent Lists, but only with the concurrence of the state government. And such laws can be extended to the state by an order of the President under this Article.

What laws and provisions of the constitution would be extended to the State of J&K was the subject matter of long discussions between the representatives of the Union and the State Government. By that time, as pointed out earlier, Sheikh Abdullah had, in connivance with Anglo-American bloc, started working for a plan to set up a 'Sheikhom' of his own. He raised several demands which were one-sided and disintegrative in impact. But Nehru was in no mood to assert, hoping that difficulties could be overcome later. A broad agreement, known as the Delhi Agreement of July 24, 1952, was arrived at.

Q: What were the provisions of the Delhi Agreement?

A: The provisions of the Delhi Agreement included abolition of the hereditary rulership; vesting of the residuary powers in the State; continuance of special citizenship rights for the 'State subjects'; flying of a separate flag for the state with the national flag also finding a distinct place; and, subject to certain restrictions and limitations, extension of provisions of the Indian constitution in respect of fundamental rights, emergency powers of the President and the jurisdiction of the Supreme Court.

Q: What reaction did these provisions evoke in the public?

A: There was a strong resentment in a large section of the people, especially the followers of Bharatiya Jan Sangh of which Shyama Prasad Mookerjee was the President. To him, grant of special status to J&K was an anathema. In Parliament, he vehemently criticized the Union Government for lack of clarity on the subject. On August 7, 1952, he posed a pertinent question to the Prime Minister: "Was Sheikh Abdullah not a party to the Constitution of India? Did he not accept this Constitution in relation to the rest of India, including about 562 Princely States? If it is good enough for all of them, why should it not be good enough for him in Kashmir?" Elaborating, he said: "Suppose some sort of fulfillment of the pledge that we are thinking of so literally in relation to Kashmir was demanded by other states, would we have agreed to give that? We would not have, because that would have destroyed India."

Mookerjee cautioned Parliament: "If you just want to play with the wind and say we are helpless and let Sheikh Abdullah do what he likes, then Kashmir will be lost. I say this with great deliberation that Kashmir will be lost." Parliament, unfortunately, did not rise to the occasion. It let the then Prime Minister do what clearly contained seeds for future troubles.

And these troubles came in abundance. Sorely disappointed, Mookerjee lent his powerful support to the Jammu-Praja-Parishad agitation and raised it to all-India level. The main plank of this agitation was that "in one country, two Constitutions; in one country, two Flags; in one country, two Prime Ministers;" would not be tolerated. About the flag, Mookerjee's lament was particularly sharp: "You cannot have a divided loyalty. It is not a question of 50-50. It is not a question of parity".

Q: What precisely led to Sheikh Abdullah's dismissal and detention?

A: While, on the one hand, Nehru suffered in public esteem, on account of criticism in Parliament and public agitations, on the other, he was deeply dismayed to find that he had been virtually 'foxed' by Abdullah who, after securing implementation of the Delhi Agreement clauses which suited him, referred the remaining clauses to the various sub-committees of the State Constituent Assembly. In his letters of 6 and 7 August, 1952 to Abdullah, he lamented that his position in Parliament would become untenable, if changes were made by the Kashmiri leaders in the Delhi Agreement. But Abdullah was unmoved. He was playing his own game. Again, on 23 June 1953, Nehru wrote to Abdullah: "To me it has been a major surprise that settlement arrived at between us should be by-passed or repudiated. That strikes at the root of all confidence. My honour is bound up with my word". But it made no impact on Abdullah who even avoided visiting Delhi for discussion, though he was invited by Nehru himself.

Nehru's appeasement of Sheikh Abdullah and the encouragement he had received from the Anglo-US bloc for the idea of independent Kashmir had made him still more ambitious and impatient. In the first week of August 1953, a speech written in Urdu by Sheikh Abdullah, and given for translation in English, came into the hands of intelligence authorities. In it, he described Kashmir's accession to India as 'conditional and temporary'. He referred to the roads and rivers that lead to Pakistan and raised the question of 'changing Kashmir's relationship with India in view of the international situation.'* This document served as the proverbial last straw that broke the camel's back. Nehru was left with no other option but to see Abdullah out of office by blinking over the means and methods which were used at the State Government level by the Sadar-i-Riyasat. Clearly, it was Sheikh Abdullah's ambition, ambivalence, fantasy of independence and disposition to abandon India and his friend Nehru that led to a rift in the State Cabinet and his eventual dismissal and detention in August 1953. In this regard, Josef Korbel's observations are pertinent: "The 'Lion of Kashmir', who thought as a socialist, acted as a dictator, manoeuvred as a petty Machiavellist, finally succumbed at the hands of his life-long associates by methods which he had often used himself."

After dismissal of Sheikh Abdullah on 9 August, 1953, Bakshi Ghulam Mohammad took over as Prime Minister. On assumption of office, in a radio broadcast, he explained why it had become necessary to take the extreme measure: "Betrayal of the country's interests was in the offing. An independent Kashmir, under the influence of an imperialist power, would be a grave threat to the freedom and independence of the Indian and Pakistani people. Another Korea may be staged here."

Q: Was any lesson learnt from Abdullah's politics of bluff and bluster that eventually led to the extreme step of his dismissal and detention, causing another set of complications?

A: Unfortunately, not. Nehru remained soft towards Sheikh Abdullah who had even become the patron of the Plebiscite Front which had been founded, in 1955, by his deputy, Mirza Afzal Beg, and had received clandestine help from across the border. The Kashmir Conspiracy Case, was also withdrawn, though the Magistrate had found sufficient evidence, during the commitment proceedings, to send the case for trial to the Sessions Court.

*S. Gopal, Nehru's official biographer: "After meeting the United States Ambassador in Srinagar in the spring of 1949, Sheikh Abdullah seems to have got the impression-as against what he had been told in New York in 1948- that the United Nations and Britain would favour an independent Kashmir and would provide it with international guarantees. Certainly from 1949 his mind worked clearly on these lines and in numerous speeches and statements he hinted at the advantages of such a development. He was even reported to have suggested this to Sir Owen Dixon in the summer of 1950 as one of the possible solutions of the Kashmir issue and to be contemplating bilateral negotiations with the leaders of 'Azad Kashmir'".

Abdullah was set free. But his disposition to keep his legs in more than one boat remained.

Duane R. Clarridge, in his book, *A Spy for All Seasons: My Life in The CIA,* has, recorded as follows:

> In 1964, Nehru released Sheikh Abdullah from prison. He immediately left for Paris. I flew to Paris to see him. He seemed a bit tentative, and nothing much came of the meeting, except for an agreement to meet again, this time in Jidda, Saudi Arabia, during the *Hajj*.
>
> Later, I flew to Jidda and contacted him. This time, Abdullah really did have something to say, and it was explosive. During his pilgrimage to Mecca, Saudi Arabia, for the *Hajj* and before my arrival in Jidda, Abdullah claimed he had been briefed on Pakistan's next moves on Kashmir, which would result in the first Indo-Pakistani War in the fall of 1965.
>
> The Lion of Kashmir basically gave me the whole plan of the Pakistanis for Kashmir. The Pakistanis were going to begin infiltrating small guerrilla units out of Azad Kashmir into Kashmir proper. Those units would then begin to stir things up. Once the insurrection got under way in Kashmir, regular Pakistani military forces would come to Kashmir's aid.

Around the same time, in February-March 1965, Sheikh Abdullah misused the opportunity, afforded by his *Hajj*-visit abroad, to indulge in anti-India propaganda. He also met Chou En-Lai on March 28, 1965, giving rise to apprehensions that the Pindi-Peking axis was in the offing, especially with regard to the Kashmir issue. His passport was cancelled. On return, he was arrested at the Delhi Airport in May 1965. Soon thereafter came the 1965 Indo-Pakistan War.

All these events, involving elements of distrust, disruptions and destabilization, could have been prevented had appropriate lessons been learnt from the happenings of 1950-1953, and steps taken to establish a cooperative, constructive and development-oriented relationship between the State of J&K and the Union.

Q: Were not some salutary measures in this direction taken after the State government came to be headed by Bakshi Ghulam Mohammad and, later on, by G.M. Sadiq and others?

A: Some measures were, indeed, taken. In any case, they were dictated by practical considerations and commitment of the State government under the Delhi Agreement. Apart from establishing financial links between the Union and the State, the jurisdiction of Comptroller and Auditor-General was extended in 1958. In 1960, the Supreme Court was given powers to entertain 'special leave to appeal' from the decisions of the J&K High Court. The supervisory role of the Election Commission of India was also allowed, though the elections continued to be held under the laws of the state. Articles 356 and 357 of the Indian Constitution were made applicable in 1965.

Q: What other changes needed to be made but were not made?

A: Though they brought some improvement upon the extremely limited relationship that obtained earlier, the changes did not touch the core issue: the infection in the roots, the separatist psyche that is embedded in Article 370. There is, moreover, a vast area that remains under the exclusive jurisdiction of the state government. This includes the Concurrent List and residuary powers. The citizens of India are not *ipso facto* the citizens of J&K. Even if they have been residing in the state for years, they cannot acquire right of settlement and hold property in the state. They have no right to vote in the election to the State Assembly or the local bodies or the Panchayats. What is worse, a woman citizen of J&K loses her property* and other rights if she marries a non-state subject.

Q: Some apologists for the grant of maximum autonomy to Kashmir often pose a question in the media: Why is an issue being made only of Article 370? What about Articles 371A, 371G and the like?

A: This is a misleading question, designed to plant doubts in the mind of the public by drawing a 'parallel' between the special provisions of Article 371A, 371G and the like on the one hand and the special provisions of Article 370 on the other. The 'parallel' is spurious and untenable. In states other than J&K, there is no separate constitution, no separate citizenship, no limited applicability of the fundamental rights guaranteed under the Indian Constitution, no exclusive vesting of residuary power, no separate commission for delimitations of constituencies, no

---

*Reasonable restrictions on the purchase of land by the outsiders can be imposed, as has been done by the state of Himachal Pradesh. Such restrictions are protected by the Indian Constitution.

appointment of Governor under the State Constitution and no fixation of his terms, salary and allowances, etc. under the said Constitution.

Q: Has not the relatively new political outfit, the People's Democratic Party, gone a step further by advocating 'self-governance'?

A: Apparently, the PDP is attempting to outcompete the National Conference by exploiting the constitutional illiteracy of the Kashmiri populace and by whipping up its anti-Union and pro-Pakistan biases, created over the years, by the National Conference for its own selfish and narrow ends of power.

No one is against the concept or principle of autonomy. But we must make a distinction between an autonomy that leads to efficiency in administration, speed in development and fuller realization of a creative potential of a community, and an autonomy that leads to separation, subversion and secession and provides a fillip to the forces of parochialism and chauvinism. Unfortunately, in the case of J&K State, the autonomy that has all along been asked for fall largely in the second category.

Q: Is it your proposition that negativity* is inbuilt in Article 370, and this negativity is vulnerable to exploitation by the state-level coteries of oligarchs who, in pursuance of their narrow ends of personal and political power, have severely undermined our national goal of establishing a development-oriented and poverty and illiteracy-free society?

A: Yes. But one needs to go still deeper into the fundamentals. Viewed dispassionately and in depth, Article 370 is virtually an item of disrespect to the Indian Constitution. Its initial insertion and subsequent retention assumes that our Constitution is not inclusive, liberal, humanistic and enlightened enough to safeguard the social, cultural, religious, linguistic and educational rights of the Kashmiri Muslims, and their identity and personality could be protected only by a separate Constitution framed behind the insulating wall of Article 370.

---

*The reader may have noted that some of the arguments pin-pointed here have already been brought out in detail in the earlier portion of the book, particularly in Chapter VI and Chapter XVIII. These are being repeated here, *albeit* briefly, to maintain the continuity of thought and cohesiveness of the narrative.

What, on the other hand, is the truth? What empirical evidence stares the objective observers in the face? And why are no satisfactory answers available to a number of pertinent questions, such as the following.

Has the distinct personality of various states of the Union, such as Bengal, Tamil Nadu and Kerala, not only remained intact but also advanced under the Indian Constitution? Why could not the same Constitution provide protection and progress to what is loosely called Kashmiriyat? What objections could be taken to the extension of the jurisdiction of Supreme Court or the Election Commission or the Comptroller and Auditor-General of India? Would not these extensions make available a stronger framework of delivery of justice, a better system of accounting and a more independent body for conducting elections? Why should there be a separate State Delimitation of Constituencies Commission for J&K? How would a common Kashmiri be benefitted by having a different nomenclature for the head of the State and the head of the government? What would happen if subjects of Defence, Foreign Affairs, and Communication alone are assigned to the Union Parliament/Government and the rest entrusted to the State Legislature/Government? How would J&K Government then meet its requirements of finances which at present are provided by the Union Government to the tune of 74 per cent, of its needs? Could the 'nuts and bolts' of security and governance structure be ignored in practice? Why do the persistent singers of Article-370 ode never sing a line about the huge financial assistance they get from the tax-collection of their fellow country-men from the rest of India? Is there not a purpose behind this silence? How many common Kashmiris know that they have been helped to the tune of ₹ 95,000 crore during the period 1989-90 to 2009-10, and the per capita central assistance that their state has got is many times more than the other states?

The plain truth is that a bogey, by way of Article 370, has been crafted by a handful of state-level coteries of ambitious oligarchs who have found it expedient to build their power base in the valley by whipping up religious biases and igniting parochial sentiments. At best, their politics is one of designed ambiguities; at worst, it is no different from that of an intimidating posture of a separatist.

Q. Is it correct to conclude that your intimate rub with various facets of life at the ground-level in Kashmir have convinced you that the current system is inherently disintegrative, unjust and generative of social and political tension?

A. Yes. It is regressive, and provides unending scope for exploitation. The extent to which narrow ends could be pursued under the current system and gross injustices perpetrated by the vested interests would strike any fair-minded individual like an arrow in his eyes when he views the provisions of Article 370 and Article 35-A of the Constitution of India in conjunction with the provisions of huge finances that are made available to the State for various development projects.

Take, for example, the miserable plight of a few thousand displaced persons and their families from West Pakistan, who settled in the State of J&K in 1947. They have been here for over seven decades. But these unfortunate persons, who were forced to migrate due to compulsions of circumstances beyond their control, have been denied elementary human rights. They, their children and grandchildren have no citizenship rights in J&K. They cannot participate in the elections to the State Assembly or municipality or panchayat. They cannot even secure loans from the State Government or its agencies. Young boys and girls cannot get admission to medical, engineering or agricultural colleges in State, even when these institutions are set up with financial assistance of the Union Government.

Is it not tragic that this is happening in a part of our country–a country that has been taking pride, in season and out of season, in its sense of social, economic and political justice, a country which of late has been scaling higher and higher peaks in the realm of constitutional liberalism, beginning from the concept of basic structure of the Constitution, as propounded in the Kesavananda Bharti case, to that of inalienability of privacy rights, and their core value, embedded in individual dignity, as laid down in the recent unanimous nine-judge Bench of the Supreme Court?

It should go without saying that a nation that tolerates such contradictions and turns such a timid face to the exploiters would find itself perpetually in a sea of trouble, and would be visited, from time to time, by waves of uncertainty and instability. The epicenter of these waves has been known for years. And its effective tackling can no longer be delayed.

Q: What could be done now? Have not some of the political commentators and jurists opined that legal and constitutional considerations rule out abrogation of Article 370?

A: Different views have been expressed by different commentators.* But the basic issue is not of technicality of law or its interpretation from a narrow or liberal perspective. It is really one of injustices, inequities, crudities and contradiction for the removal of which all modern laws and constitutions are framed or amended or subjected to dynamic and enlightened interpretation. If once the new ruling dispensation, which has won a decisive mandate, come to recognize the negativities of Article 370 and Article 35-A, it should have no hesitation in doing away with them, either by their abrogation, or by their effective dilution through extension of the provisions of the Indian Constitution, or by linking financial assistance for specific plan-projects with the acceptance of applicability of the Union laws to which the projects pertain.

But before taking any of the above measures, it must vigorously attend to the task of convincing the common man in Kashmir how artificial barriers have been created between the valley and the rest of India by a handful of coteries of oligarchs, at the state level, and how these coteries have managed to keep the common man in the dark about all that I have narrated and analysed above, and instead misled him by manufacturing a sense of victimhood. In other words, the chronic and deep rooted infections have first to be drained out from the body-politic. The 'inward changes' to rejuvenate the damaged soil and make it receptive to the healthy seeds offered by the new dispensation must precede the 'outward changes', that is, the changes in the laws and Constitution, relevant to Article 370.

From the above set of questions and answers, it should be clear that the negative politics of Article 370 should be done away with–the earlier the better. The 'changed season' provides us a rare opportunity

*My views would be found in the three chapters (IV-VI), titled Roots, especially chapter VI. They are reinforced by ground level examples, picked up from personal experience. The entire issue needs to be viewed holistically and interpreted on the principles of harmonious construction.

to prepare new soils and new seeds of commonalty and show to the common man in Kashmir and the rest of India that his true and lasting welfare lies in speedy development and not in the spurious stitch of Article 370, which has caused multiple infections and led to recurring maladies of dangerous proportion.

CHAPTER XXIV

Onward to a New Resolve

And do not think of the fruit of action.
Fare forward.

O voyagers, O seamen,
You who come to port, and you whose bodies
Will suffer the trial and judgment of the sea,
Or whatever event, this is your real destination.

–*T.S. Eliot**

New Helmsman

In the preceding chapter–numbered XXIII–I had, soon after Narendra Modi's government assumed office in May, 2014, reflected upon the expectations of a 'much needed season for inward and outward change'. In this chapter, I would examine in what direction have these expectations moved, and how have harsh and cruel realities on the ground been encountered during the eventful period of 33 months of the new regime, from May 26, 2014 to February 28, 2017.

In similar strain, I would cover, in the next chapter, events uptill January 2019; assessing, in the process, impact of several changes brought about by Narendra Modi regime during the aforesaid 33 months.

*T.S. Eliot: *Four Quartets, Dry Salvages.*

In my book, *Soul and Structure of Governance in India*, I had underscored:

> Notwithstanding the cultural renaissance witnessed in the late nineteenth century and the early twentieth century and the fervor generated by the movement for independence and injection of Gandhian ethics in the social and political environment, India, at the most crucial turning point in her history, failed to acquire great inspiration and produce a great helmsman who could create a consistent and coherent ideology for building a new India and constructing new institutions and reconstructing old ones on the motivation of that ideology.*

In this chapter, I would, in the background of India's 70 years of nightmarish Kashmir experience, assess whether the developments of the aforementioned period of 33 months hold out a promise of finding such a helmsman who could steer the 'boat' through stormy sea and turbulent winds and bring it safely to a calm and clean shore, from where a new journey, with a new mind and motivation, could begin. Before I do so, let me unfold the contours of these events and their inter-connections.

Nature's Revenge

When nature turns 'red in tooth and claw' and is preceded by man's cupidity and corruption and also by the rulers' ineptitude and lack of vision, a vast but wobbling stage is set up for a mind-boggling tragedy to be enacted. The tragic drama of this genre came to be played in full fury, with heavy fretting and fuming all around, during the last three months or so of the National Conference-Congress coalition government, headed by Omar Abdullah. These three months of Omar regime were particularly inglorious. They brought out in a telling manner the major flaws of its politics–its disposition to spend time and energy on contrived controversies, neglect solid administrative work and remain oblivious of nature's revenge against brutalization of its inviolabilities.

In August/September, 2014, the state witnessed the worst flood of the last 50 years. About 150 persons died. The economic losses to the state were staggering. Some estimates put the figure of loss as high as ₹ 1,00,000 crores. Undoubtedly, the disaster was caused by five days

*Jagmohan: *Soul and Structure of Governance in India.* (Second Edition. p. 101).

of continuous rains. But it was gravely compounded by the rampant corruption which had been manifesting itself, over the years, in the large scale illegal constructions and encroachment on public lands, including wetlands, embankments of lakes and river Jhelum and building of houses and hotels on the flood plains. The State Government had been turning a blind eye to all such reckless ventures. No law–civic, planning or environmental–was respected. The vested interests, including separatists and subversionists, derived huge financial benefits and used a portion of these to prop up insurgency in the valley.

In face of the heavy downpour, and sudden swelling in the level of water-bodies and blockages in the flow of natural drainage lanes, Omar Abdullah government found itself clueless. It was virtually paralyzed from top to bottom. Later on, Omar Abdullah himself admitted that his government went missing for a couple of days. At the peak of the floods (September 2 to 5, 2014), Prime Minister Narendra Modi had an aerial survey. He described the damage to life and property as a national calamity and announced a financial aid of ₹ 1,000 crores for relief and rehabilitation of the sufferers. Thousands of stranded families were rescued by the Indian Army, the Air Force and the Navy. About 30,000 troops were deployed in the state. By September 18, 2014, about 2,00,000 persons had been moved to safer places.

All this was a great humanitarian service, a historic feat, of which any country could be proud. Nevertheless, a number of pertinent questions continue to stare in the eyes of the experienced and thoughtful observers of the Kashmir scene. Would any lesson be learnt by the power-wielders of the state's political set up? Would ravaging of the wetlands and choking of the freeways of drainage be checked with a firm hand? And would new avenues be generated for the preservation of environmental assets? With all such questions remaining unattended, the state moved to the Assembly Elections.

State Assembly Elections

The development that followed the J&K State Assembly Elections* of December, 2014 once again showed the disparate range and dangerous depth of the multiple infections which had been bedeviling

*About 65 per cent of the voters cast their votes in this State Assembly Elections. The first phase of this five-phases elections commenced on November 25, 2014.

the body-politics of state for the last several years. The verdict of the electors was fractured. In a 87-member House, the Jammu-Kashmir People's Democratic Party secured 28 seats, the Bharatiya Janata Party 25, the Jammu-Kashmir National Conference 15, the Indian National Conference 12, the Jammu-Kashmir People's Conference 2, Independents 3 and others 2. The two main regions, Jammu and Kashmir Valley, threw up a fragmentation of another kind. The BJP, though it increased its percentage of total votes polled, drew a blank in the valley. But its predominance in the Jammu region was marked; its 25 candidates winning by huge margins, ranging from 10,000 to 45,000 votes.

PDP-BJP *Coalition Government*

With such a divisive spectrum emerging on the political horizon of the troubled state, managing the contradictions in the declarations made in the election manifestos of major political parties presented a formidable problem. It took two months of protracted negotiations between the two main parties, the People's Democratic Party and the Bharatiya Janata Party, to resolve this problem. Keeping in view the larger context of the practical options that could be exercised, these parties worked out a coalition arrangement on the basis of what was declared, on March 1, 2015, as Agenda of Alliance.

In the words of Mufti Mohammed Sayeed, who took over as Chief Minister, the two coalition partners, who were as distant in their basic ideologies, as 'north pole' and 'south pole', had joined hands to serve the common goals of the common man under a common minimum programme. It was, he underscored, the best way of converting a complex political challenge into an elevating opportunity, end regional strifes and conflicts and bring all round peace and prosperity to the State.

Agenda of Alliance

The basic principles and prominent features of the Agenda of Alliance could be summarised in the following propositions and pronouncements:

- The two partners recognize each other's concerns and admit their differences with regard to quite a few issues of fundamental importance. But they would keep aside these concerns and differences during the six-year period of the Coalition Government. In this period, all constitutional provisions pertaining to J&K, including its special status in the Constitution of India, would remain unaltered.

- While the final decision with regard to the continuance or withdrawal of Armed Forces (Special Powers) Act would rest with the Union Government, the State Government on its part, would examine the need for de-notifying 'disturbed areas'.
- Relief, rehabilitation and development schemes to provide succour to the flood affected families and areas would be speedily executed, and equitable and balanced benefits to all the regions ensured.
- Congenial and fear-free environment would be created and maintained to enable the Kashmiri Pandits to return to the Valley with dignity and confidence and lead a normal life.
- The pending issues concerning refugees from the Pakistan-occupied Kashmir, who moved to the State of J&K, during the 'wars' of 1947, 1965 and 1971, would be resolved under a 'one time settlement'.
- A beginning would be made in redressing the seven decades old grievances with regard to non-grant of State's citizens rights to thousands of the West Pakistan refugees and their families who fled to J&K consequent to 1947 partition riots. In the first phase of redressal, ration cards would be granted to them.
- A dynamic, honest and modern governance would be provided, not only to sweep away the fall-outs of the past incompetencies and indecisions but also to herald a new era of implementational will and vigour, ensuring, *inter-alia,* an effective pattern of decentralized administration at village Panchayat and city-Council levels.

Warding Off Unsavoury Legacies

From no angle, in theory, the above enunciations could be faulted. But the unsavory legacies of the earlier aberrations could not be warded off easily. Soon after taking oath as Chief Minister, on March 1, 2015, Mufti Mohammed Sayeed thanked 'pro-Pakistan Hurriyat and militants for allowing an atmosphere conducive to the holding of peaceful Assembly elections in the State'. Hardly had the misgivings caused by the aforesaid 'thanks' abated than another acute embarrassment was caused to the alliance partner, Bharatiya Janata

Party. Without taking into confidence any of his cabinet colleagues, orders were issued by the Chief Minister to release from detention Masarat Alam Bhat, head of the Muslim League, a constituent of hard-line Tehreek-Hurriyat of Syed Ali Shah Geelani. Masarat, as mentioned earlier in the book, was the principal instigator and organizer of the stone-throwing groups of youngsters who caused violent clashes in major towns of the valley, from June to October, 2010.

All this was seen as a subtle attempt by the Chief Minister to keep alive the forces of 'militancy and soft-separatism'. But the Bhartiya Janata Party leadership, both at the Centre and the State, lost no time in making it clear that issues of national security could not be trifled with and no further unilateral action by the People's Democratic Party in this area would be allowed to pass by. Being an experienced politician, Mufti Mohammad Sayeed, read the signal correctly. Without appearing to yield and adopting the strategy of allowing the controversy to lose its sting in a maze of clarifications and vague statements, he ensured that he and his party-functionaries were more circumspect in dealing with the issues which touched the raw nerves of their alliance partner.

On November 7, 2015, Prime Minister Narendra Modi visited Srinagar. At a public rally, he announced a package of ₹ 80,000/- crores for radically augmenting the social and economic infrastructure of the State. He underscored that the speedy development of the state would be the guiding star for his Government. When Mufti-Mohammad Sayeed, in his speech, said that he could offer a piece of advice to Prime Minister to act like an elder brother towards Pakistan, Narendra Modi's response was short and curt: "I do not need any one's advice in this regard." It was the first firm indication that the old game of the Kashmiri politicians of keeping one leg in India's boat and the other in Pakistan's would not work with the new government at the Centre.

There were quite a few bouts of consternations between the partners of the coalition government, such as the ones instanced above. But on the whole, the government worked on an even keel and performed well during the ten months period of Mufti Mohammad Sayeed's regime, from March 1, 2015 to January 7, 2016, when he passed away.

Interregnum: Between Mohammad Sayeed's Death and Assumption of Office by Mehbooba.

Mehbooba Mufti, President of the Peoples Democratic Party, was an obvious choice to succeed her father. But she procrastinated. It was first given out that she was in mourning. Thereafter, she publically expressed doubts whether she had the experience and practical wisdom to run the coalition government. This was, perhaps, Mehbooba's way of putting pressure on Peoples Democratic Party's alliance partner. Or was she apprehensive that her collaborators of the past would embarrass her with her own earlier eulogisation of 'our boys in the jungle' and labelling of the security force's action as state sponsored terrorism?

Be that as it may, after marking time for about three months, she met Prime Minister Narendra Modi in New Delhi. After the meeting, she declared she had been assured all help and cooperation of the Union Government. On return to Srinagar, she formally staked her claim, and was sworn in as Chief Minister of the Coalition Government on April 4, 2016.

In the interregnum, between January 7 and April 4, the State was placed under the Governor Rule. This period saw, apart from the sporadic events of subversion, a serious terror attack on February 22-24, 2016. A CRPF convoy was ambushed on Jammu-Srinagar National Highway, at Sempora, Pampore, near Entrepreneurship Development Institute. During the encounter that followed, the militants moved to the institute which had as many as five storeys and 60 rooms. They mixed with the students and other inmates who served as human shields, willingly or out of fear, and resorted to pro-militant and anti-India exhortations. Simultaneously, four mosques in the nearby localities played recorded encomium, praising the '*fidayeen*' and raising slogans: '*Jivey Jivey, Pakistan; Hum Kya Chahatya: Azadi*'. It took almost three days to clear the premises of the institute and eliminate the three terrorists. The Army lost three elite commandos and CRPF two members of its force. One civilian was also killed.

Another serious incident which happened at Handwara within a fortnight of Mehbooba's taking over charge as Chief-Minister of the State pertained to the mob-frenzy which had been aroused through an intentionally coined false story that a Rashtriya Rifles Jawan had raped a minor girl. Notwithstanding a clear denial by the girl on television of any such untoward incident, huge processions were organized, crowds incited and police and army units attacked. To control the wide-spread violence, firing had to be resorted to at some places. Five agitators lost their lives, inflaming the public passions further. An intensively surcharged atmosphere was created throughout the valley out of a 'rape incident' that never happened.

Pointers of Sempora/Pampore and Handwara

The above two events, one that occurred a few days before and the other a few days after assumption of office by Mehbooba, were pointers in themselves. The stance which the Peoples' Democratic Party had been pursuing for quite some times with regard to 'self-governance', 'soft-separatism', 'open borders', 'common currency', 'support for Hurriyat', 'laying out Rawalpindi road', etc. had resulted, at the ground level, in strengthening the fundamentalist and pro-Pakistan elements. May be, the stance was the outcome of its strategy to acquire an electoral edge over its rival party–National Conference–which, too, was following an anti-Union/separatist agenda in its own way. But, in the context of the goals set out by the Peoples' Democratic Party–Bharatiya Janata Party Coalition Government, this stance warranted a fundamental change. It was incumbent upon the Peoples' Democratic Party's leadership to fully recognize the damaging fall-outs of its past pursuits, reverse the trends and educate its cadres about the overwhelming need for taking a new initiative, beating back the negative forces and ensuring speedy development. But, unfortunately, no worthwhile step in this direction was forthcoming.

Intervening Development at Another Plane

Before the consequences of this omission are dealt with, it would be contextually relevant to indicate a few other intervening developments at another plane.

As promised to Mehbooba during her meeting with the Prime Minister at Delhi on the eve of her taking charge as Chief Minister at Srinagar, and also as an expression of his pragmatic approach, Narendra Modi visited the State soon after Mehbooba Mufti assumed office. The assurance for the speedy implementation of the development package of about ₹ 80,000 crore was reiterated, and the Government of J&K advised to gear up its administrative machinery for timely and effective utilization of funds. At the State level, Deputy Chief Minister Nirmal Singh, once again reminded the people: "Ours is neither a political alliance nor an ideological one; it is 'governance alliance'. The concentration is to be on development, employment and good administration."

The performance of the Mehbooba Mufti coalition regime, from April 4 to July 8, 2016, was, on the whole, encouraging. Tourists came in a large number. Business was on the upswing. The administration functioned fairly well. In the by-election from the seat which fell vacant, consequent to her father's death six months ago, Mehbooba Mufti registered an impressive victory on June 21, 2016, winning by a margin more than that of Mufti Sayeed in December 2014.

All this inspired hope and confidence. But those who looked at the seemingly happy position, with equanimity, had not taken into account the dark and destabilizing forces which had been injected, over the years, into the polity and mindscape of Jammu and Kashmir. The nature of these forces, the course they had taken in their tortuous journey of about 70 years, and overall destructive impact they had caused, have all been brought out in the earlier chapters* of the book, along with the tragic inability, in general, of the Indian public and politicians to learn from their past acts of omission and commission. These may not be recapitulated here.

Combined Impact of Lethal Forces: Setting up Stage for Burhan Wani

However, the two set of recent incidents, one relating to Sempora/Pampore and other to Handwara, which I have analyzed above, demand a brief recall. They had emitted warning signals which indicated, in no uncertain terms, the lethal impact of coordinated and cohesive convergence of pro-Pakistan, pro-separatists, pro-subversion and pro-Jihadist elements. But no lessons were picked up from these signals. The state of drift continued. Coupled with the reporting from disruptive and disinformation oriented section of the press and aroused by the motivational *Jihadi* literature of sacrifice and immortality, the circumstances were 'tailor made' for someone like Burhan Wani to appear at the centre of the stage and mesmerize the audience by his heightened sense of bravado and belief in his

*Chapters IV; V; VI, titled *Roots;* Chapter X, titled: *Nature and Pattern of Subversion and Terrorism.* Chapter XII, titled: *Whirlpool of Confusion and Contradictions;* and Chapter XV, titled: *A Deluge of Disinformation and Distortion;* are particularly relevant.

invincibility, and then end his 'short part' by getting himself, the 'stage' and a sizeable segment of his admirers burnt.

Burhan Wani, a school drop-out, was a handsome young man of Tral, in his early twenties, when he joined the ranks of militants in 2010. After three years, he was designated as Commander of Hizabul Mujahideen. He had acquired expertise in manipulating social media to propagate the ideology of his 'masters' and gain popularity amongst the youth.

On July 8, 2016, in a raid conducted by the security forces on a suspected terrorist hide out in South Kashmir, Burhan Wani, and two of his fellow militants, Sartaj Ahmed and Parvez, were killed in the encounter. A very large crowd joined Wani's funeral at Tral, and violence erupted in a number of towns and villages of the valley. The police stations, central forces out-posts, public buildings, and even army camps were attacked. In the very first phase of no holds barred disturbances, the buildings of about 50 police stations and local courts were burnt down.

The brazenness with which the crowds, mostly comprising youth of 15-20 years and backed by a few hard core, pro-Pakistani militants, caused acts of destruction could be seen from what happened at the police station of Damhal Hanjipora on July 9, 2016. Twenty policemen were held hostages for hours together, armoury was looted, and 40 automatic weapons were taken away or put to fire along with a sizeable part of the station. Even a bulldozer was brought to the site to raise the entire building to the ground.

Having remained unprepared, Mehbooba's regime found itself in a state of mental vacuum. Caught in the quagmire caused by the pronouncements of her pre-power days' past and her new power-days' obligations, she seemed to be struggling to acquire a touch of certainty. Initially, she contented herself by urging Pakistan to "change its policy of encouraging Kashmiri youth to resort to gun violence". Soon thereafter, however, she struck a different posture: "Had her government been aware that Burhan Wani would be killed, she would not have allowed the operation to take place." A week later, she took a still more discomforting turn: "These children who have gone, I promise you, I will not allow their sacrifice to go waste".

Clearly, this type of double speak was not the way of meeting a calculated onslaught of destabilizing forces both from within and outside the State. With violent disturbances showing no sign of abatement and with stark realities staring in the face of Chief Minister, practically every day, she started realising the strands of truth, do some plain speaking and put the blame where it belonged. She accused Pakistan of provoking "our children to pick up guns", and then tell them: "you will become our leader in case you get killed in an encounter"*. On another occasion, she underlined "It was important to differentiate between people (95 per cent) who want resolution of the problem through dialogue and people (5 per cent) who exploit small children, the children of the poor, to attack camps and take to streets with stones".** About the criticism with regard to excessive use of force, Mehbooba countered: "It is easy to say that the security forces could have exercised restraint, but when a mob attacks a police station with petrol bombs, stones and axes, it becomes difficult."***. She went on to assert: "The 2016 violence was a well-planned conspiracy hatched by vested interests to spread blood-shed in the State. Preparation for violence had been made well in advance. When issues like separate Kashmiri Pandit colony and Sainik colony did not work, they triggered the violence over the killing of Burhan Wani."****. Incensed by a pressman's sarcastic question, she minced no words in her reply. "Did the children go to the Army camp to buy toffees? Did the 15-year old boy in Dhamal Hanjipora go to fetch milk when he attacked the police station?"*****

Obviously, the conspiracy of disruptionist and destabilizing forces, which Mehbooba Mufti and her party had themselves fomented in the course of their search for state power had come to confront and virtually compel them to shed their double-speak and become more practical in facing the truth and fighting the destructive elements on the ground. The sagacity with which the Union government handled the crisis was also of great help to Mehbooba in locating the right path and sticking to it.

Union Government's Sagacious Handling

To acquire deeper insight into the ground level conditions and to assure the State Government of all help and cooperation, Home Minister Raj Nath Singh made three two-days visits to the State–first

*; **; ***; ****; *****The observations cited here are from Mehbooba Mufti's statement made in the State Assembly, on January 9, 2017, while replying to the adjournment motion tabled by the opposition. Earlier on August 25, 2016, reply on similar lines had been given by her to the questions asked at the press conference jointly addressed by Union Home Minister Raj Nath Singh and Mehbooba Mufti at Srinagar.

on July 23-24, 2016, the second on August 24-25 and the third as head of an all-Party delegation on September 4-5. Separately, on August 22, in an interaction with a deputation from Kashmir, led by former Chief Minister Omar Abdullah, Prime Minister Narendra Modi dwelt upon the need for all stake holders to join hands to work for bringing about complete normalcy. He underscored: "Those who have lost their lives during the recent disturbances are part of us, and it is a matter of distress whether lives lost are of our youth, security personnel or police". Later, on August 28, in a radio broadcast, and on September 2, in a television interview, he amplified the ideals of *ekkta* (unity) and *mamta* (compassion) and of *vikas* (development) and *vishwas* (trust) and alluded to their being virtual appendages to the ideals of *insaniyat, jamhooriyat, and kashmiriyat*. What was implied was that the framework of J&K solution could be created, within the Indian Union/ Constitution, on seven planks/principles: *insaniyat, jamhooriyat, kashmiriyat, ekkta, mamta, vikas and vishwas.* (Humanity; Democracy; Kashmiri culture; Unity; Compassion; Development and Trust)

In the meanwhile, with the commencement of the monsoon session of Parliament in August 2016, the prevailing conditions in Kashmir came up for discussion in the Rajya Sabha. Most of the speeches made by the participating Members were marked by generalities, and showed little depth in understanding either of the practicalities involved or of the sinister forces that had been pumping poison in Kashmir's political, social and cultural environment, both from inside and outside. In his reply to the debate, on August 12, Home Minister Raj Nath Singh, quoting facts and figures, put the records straight: "Despite the strategy framed by the so-called leaders, the manner in which the state Government is working under difficult circumstances in Kashmir must be appreciated'... The chief minister has taken full care of the conveniences of the people. There is sufficient stock of all types of commodities. More than 400 ambulances are working, despite 100 ambulances having been totally destroyed by stone-pelting... The security forces have been directed by the Government to maintain the maximum possible restraint in using pellet guns".

All-Party Parliamentary Delegation

Subsequently, at a meeting convened by Prime-Minister, it was decided that an all-Party Parliamentary delegation, headed by Raj Nath Singh, would visit the State on September 4-5, 2016. Before leaving New Delhi, the 26 member delegation had announced that they would meet whosoever wished to do so. Apart from it, Mehbooba Mufti, in her capacity as Chairperson of Peoples' Democratic Party, had invited the Hurriyat Leaders, for discussion with all-Party delegation. But the invitation was spurned.

At Srinagar, 30 groups, representing different shades of stakeholders, met the all-Party delegation and appraised the members of their point of view. A segment of the delegation– Yechury, Raja and Yadav–attempted, in their individual capacity, to meet the Hurriyat leaders. But at every place they were arrogantly turned away. Embarrassed by their own miscalculation, they could do hardly anything else than put up a brave face in public. But, inwardly, they must have come nearer to realization of truth about the obduracy of the forces that had, till then, resulted in 56 days of curfew-ridden unrest in the valley and 71 death of persons, mostly of youth in the age-group of 15-25 year, whose mind had been shackled for years together under an assiduously drawn programme of radicalization.

On return to Delhi, a follow-up meeting of the all-Party delegation was held under the Chairmanship of Raj Nath Singh. A simple statement was issued. Apart from reiterating that there could not be any compromise on the issue of national sovereignty and there was no place for violence in a civilized society, the statement appealed to all stake-holders to resort to only dialogue and discussion.

The calm, composed and confident way in which Home Minister Raj Nath Singh had handled a seemingly unmanageable situation during his three aforementioned visits to the State, and the manner in which he and Prime Minister had ensured that the Union government and the State government functioned on the same wave length, helped a great deal in overcoming a serious multi-rooted crisis.

INDIA-PAKISTAN RELATIONS

Attempted Detente

In the sphere of India-Pakistan relations, Prime-Minister Narendra Modi, from the beginning of his regime in May 2014, showed his keenness to take yet another initiative to build a shared vision of harmony and good will with Pakistan.

As indicated in sections titled: *'Killing a Routine'; 'Treacherous Drama'–Kargil war'; 'Peace Initiatives'; 'Attack on Parliament'* of

Chapter XIX; and section titled: *Oscillation of Chapter XX;* every attempt made by A.B. Vajpayee to assume 'the role of a bold and innovative designer for a future architecture of peace and prosperity', was followed by a virtual stab in the back of India. Experience of Dr. Manmohan Singh was no less frustrating. The assurance given to him by President Musharraf that 'he would not permit any territory under Pakistan's control to be used, to support terrorism in any manner', did not go beyond words. Similar was the fate of the agreement, jointly announced in September, 2006 by President Musharraf and Dr. Manmohan Singh, 'to set up an India-Pakistan anti-terrorism institutional mechanism to identify and implement counter-terrorism and initiatives and investigations'. Whatever little residue remained of all such announcements and assurances was blown out by the horrible Mumbai terror attack on November 26, 2008.

Despite a long history of 'disguised betrayals' by the wielders of power in Pakistan, Prime Minister Narendra Modi made an earnest effort towards dètente. Apart from inviting Pakistan Prime Minister Nawaz Sharif to his swearing-in-ceremony, he made an impromptu visit to Lahore on December 25, 2015– "a virtual dropping in, on his return journey from Kabul to New Delhi"–to wish Nawaz Sharif a happy birthday. But these gestures, though generative of outward goodwill and warmth, did not alter the crafty designs of the power caucus in Pakistan.

Attack on Pathankot Air-base

Within a week of bon-homie witnessed at Lahore, Pathankot air base was subjected to a serious terror attack on January 2, 2016, which had lasted for about 80 hours and caused death of 7 and injury to 37 Air-base's officials. The imprints of the Inter-Services Intelligence agency of Pakistan and its outfit, Jaish-e-Mohammad, were too glaring to be missed. A day later, the Indian Consulate at Mazar-i-Sharif, Afghanistan, was targeted. Also, immediately before Nawaz Sharif arrived at New Delhi to participate in the swearing-in-ceremony of Narendra Modi on May 26, 2014, the Indian Consulate at Herat had been attacked. What has all along been perplexing was that whenever any positive move was made by India to normalize relations with its neighbor, it was followed by a Pakistani sponsored incident which left a bitter trail in its wake and caused deep erosion of trust.

The Foreign Secretary level talks, the decision in respect of which was taken consequent to Narendra Modi-Nawaz Sharif friendly meeting on May 26, 2014, and the first phase of which was to be held on August 25, 2015, at New Delhi, were virtually scuttled by Pakistan High Commissioner Abdul Basit's insistence on fixing a meeting of the Kashmiri Hurriyat leaders with the head of the Pakistan delegation, Sartaj Aziz. The game of the Pakistani authorities was to present the Hurriyat as an umbrella organization which embodied the indigenous uprising of all Kashmiris against India. When Narendra Modi government refused to accept the contours of this game, Sartaj Aziz cancelled his visit to New Delhi. The ardour for building a new framework of conciliation stood diminished.

Another Attempt

After a couple of months, India made another earnest attempt to bring about a congenial environment. Her Foreign Minister, Sushma Swaraj, while participating in the Heart of Asia, Istanbul Process Ministerial Meeting on Afghanistan, at Islamabad, on December 9, 2015, said: "Let me take this opportunity to extend our hand to Pakistan as well. It is time we display the maturity and self-confidence to do business with each other and strengthen regional trade and cooperation. The entire world is rooting for a change. Let us not disappoint them". It was in continuation of this attempt of creating good will that Prime Minister Narendra Modi made the unscheduled visit, mentioned earlier, to Lahore on December 25, 2015.

These initiatives at the level of the Indian Foreign Minister and Prime Minister were taken, despite the occurrence of terrorism related events, such as the attacks on July 27, 2015, on a passenger bus as well as police station, Gurdaspur, in which seven persons were killed; and despite also the irritation caused to India by the 'hate speeches' made frequently by the likes of Masood Azhar and Hafiz Saeed. The extent, on the other hand, to which India could go to create an atmosphere of trust and cooperation, between the two countries, could be seen from the fact that, after the Pathankot attack, an investigation team from Pakistan, which included an officer of the Inter-Services Intelligence, was allowed to visit the site in March 2016. But, unfortunately, no reciprocal visit to the team from India was allowed by Pakistan, thereby obstructing the process of reaching the suspects/culprits of Jaish-e-Mohammad who had brazenly boasted of having successfully organized the attack.

Attack on Uri Brigade Headquarter

In fact, Pakistan had all along been deceitful. It never intended to be sincere in adhering to any joint-statement or declaration made by the two Heads of Governments. The latest to be trounced upon was the joint-statement, made at Ufa.* What to speak of cooperating with India to carry out joint investigation, Pakistan embarked upon another diabolical terror attack on the Indian soil by using the same terrorist outfit–Jaish-e-Mohammad–as was used by it in attacking Pathankot air-base. On September 18, 2016, the Army Brigade Headquarter, Uri, was targeted. 19 soldiers of the Indian Army were killed in what was reckoned as the most deadly and dastardly attack on the security forces.

The timing of the attack had its own pointer. With Chief Minister Mehbooba Mufti showing stronger disposition to be more candid in her criticism of the role of Pakistan in inciting the youth to resort to aggressive stone throwing, and with Home Minister Raj Nath Singh and Prime Minister Narendra Modi maintaining composure and firmness in facing all sorts of accusations of their denigrators, the propagators of the unrest found the morale of their followers sagging. By the middle of September, 2016, it had become clear that the violence-ridden agitation was petering out. It was to prop up this agitation that, apart from pursuing its long-term goal of bleeding India by 'thousand cuts', the Uri attack was planned and executed by Pakistan through its terror-outfits.

Momentarily, the attack on the Uri Brigade Headquarter produced a strong impact. But it soon became clear that the power-wielders in Pakistan had gravely miscalculated. They had taken it for granted that Narendra Modi's government was the chip of the same block of which earlier governments were made.

As brought out in this book, the first edition of which was published in 1990-91 and the 13th updated edition of which is now coming out, appeasement and wishful thinking have been the bane of the Indian government set-up. The successive governments, till the coming into being of Narendra Modi government, have remained, in one form or the other, prisoners of politics of superficiality and softness.

On the basis of my study of the prevailing political culture, and in the context of my close encounter in Jammu and Kashmir with the

*This joint statement was issued on July 10, 2015, at the Russian city, where the two Prime Ministers met on the sideline of another conference.

harsh ground level reality, I had been advocating, from the very beginning of my first tenure as Governor, that resolute practicality, accompanied by an attitude of fairness and firmness, was badly needed to drain out the accumulated infections in the system and transfuse fresh blood and elevated sense of values into it. But few lent any ear to this advocacy; those who listened did not have the steadiness and stamina to execute the task, or at least to propel the norms of polity and administration to a higher orbit. Consequently, the tyranny of shallowness, and poison sprouting out of the contaminated roots, continued to extract their heavy toll; from kidnapping of Rubaiya Sayeed, to the killing of Kashmiri Pandits, to broad day light shooting of four IAF Officers, to attack on Parliament, to carnage in Mumbai, to ambushing of CRPF convoys, to targeting of military installations, etc.

Pakistan's belief that the Narendra Modi Government would act in the same way as the previous governments, in general, had acted in the past was reinforced by it extending the hand of cooperation for joint investigation with regard to the Pathankot air base attack. It was here that the mind and motivation of Narendra Modi was misread. Undoubtedly, he was keen to establish harmonious relations with Pakistan and took several initiatives in this regard. But he could not be pushed beyond a point. Narendra Modi noted that in the Uri attack and in inflaming of the post-Burhan Wani violent agitation in the Kashmir Valley, Pakistan's perfidy had crossed all limits. For him, it turned out to be the proverbial last straw that made him to declare in anguish: enough is enough. Passivity or strategic restraint, whatever one may like to call it, had not yielded any result; it had only whetted the appetite of Pakistan and its terrorists' outfits.

Move Toward a New Resolve

Exasperated by Pakistan's repeated acts of trickery, Narendra Modi realized that it was time to hold the levers of history firmly in his hand and move them towards ushering in a new resolve. The planks of this resolve were to be fashioned out of the known doctrines of 'deterrences', of 'compellence', of 'activism', and of being 'offensive-defensive' in approach. Most important of all, the new resolve had to be put in practice diligently and with courage and consistency. So far, with the exception in the case of Kargil war, the 'mantra' of the Indian political decision makers had been the doctrine of 'strategic restraint'.

In most cases, it had been used to rationalize inaction or to cover innate timidity or to cater to the selfish dictates of internal vote-bank politics.

Now, a new beginning had to be made. Narendra Modi attended to this challenge immediately after the Uri tragedy. He assured the nation: "The perpetrators shall not go unpunished". Four days later, addressing BJP National Council at Kozhikode, Kerala, he repeated this assurance: "India would not forget the sacrifices of 19 soldiers killed in the Uri terrorist attack". From the same venue, he appealed to the people of Pakistan to free themselves from the vice-like grip of military rulers and their associates and enter into competition with India in a different kind of race–a race against poverty and unemployment. This was a double-edged move. One was to indicate that action would be taken against the killers, but at the time and place of India's choosing. The second was to remind the general public of Pakistan the strong vested interest of the Army in continuing with its policy of organizing terrorists' outfits and diverting limited financial resources from development to the destructive venture of spilling blood on the Indian soil.

NEW RESOLVE

Ingredients

What were to be the ingredients of the new resolve, and in what form and shape were they to be invoked? Clearly, by the very nature of challenges to be tackled, the new resolve had to be multi-directional, both in concept and ground-level application. Its fulcrum was to be offensive-defensive approach which would cover not only sphere of internal security but also the connected spheres of diplomacy and economic relations, etc. To cause wholesome impact, it was necessary to be pro-active in dealing with the corresponding issues that came up for consideration, in one form or the other, at the international, regional, multi-lateral and bilateral forums.

To facilitate easy understanding of the 'new resolve' and its core component of offensive-defensive approach, actions taken by Narendra Modi government in pursuance of this 'resolve', could be grouped into the following seven heads/sub-heads:

(I) To expose, thoroughly and persistently, at the United Nations General Assembly and other international fora, Pakistan as a state sponsor of terrorism and using it as an instrument of its policies.

(II) To declare the incompatibility of Pakistan's credentials to hold the 19th SAARC Summit scheduled for November 2016 at Islamabad on account of its unwillingness to curb terrorists' groups from attacking fellow members.

(III) To indicate firmly that hostility would be countered with hostility and comparatively liberal treatment that Pakistan is presently enjoying with regard to river-water distribution and trade-regimes could be withdrawn and the Indus Water Treaty and Most Favoured Nation Status revisited.

(IV) To demonstrate India's right to pre-empt terrorists from entering its territory by attacking their preparatory bases across the Line of Control/border.

(V) To continue earnest efforts to persuade the multi-lateral groups, such as BRICS, to denounce Pakistan as a malevolent force of terrorism which, apart from dehumanizing a large section of mankind, is undermining the basic objectives for the attainment of which such groups have been set up, namely, quick coordinated and cohesive development.

(VI) To show how Pakistan is providing sanctuaries of safe haven to a number of dangerous terror-organisations who are bleeding the Heart of Asian Region.

(VII) To take up vigorously the issues pertaining to the large scale violations of human rights by the Pakistan Army in Balochistan, Baltistan, Gilgit and Pakistan occupied Kashmir, and simultaneously counter Pakistan's diabolical disinformation campaign against India for 'committing atrocities and violations of human rights in Kashmir valley'.

In pursuance of the 'new resolve', action taken by the Narendra Modi's government with regard to items under each of the above heads/sub-heads is narrated and analyzed in paragraphs as set up hereinafter.

I. *Exposure of Pakistan at UN Assembly*

The session of the UN General Assembly was already on. Pakistan Prime Minister Nawaz Sharif was to address it on September 21, 2016. In his speech Nawaz Sharif talked of 'Indian atrocities' in Kashmir and claimed that Pakistan had repeatedly offered 'dialogue to address all outstanding issues', but India had put 'unacceptable pre-conditions'. He alleged: "A new generation of Kashmiris has risen spontaneously against India's illegal occupation. Burhan Wani, the young leader murdered by Indian forces, has emerged as the symbol of the latest Kashmiri Intifada".

Exercising India's 'right of reply',* her representative, Ms. Gambhir, exposed the crafty mind of Pakistan: "What we see today in Pakistan is a terrorist state, which channelizes billions of dollars, much of it diverted from international aid, to training, financing and supporting terrorist groups as militant proxies against it neighbours. Even today we have heard support by the Prime Minister of Pakistan for a self-acknowledged commander of a known terrorist organization, Hizbul Mujahideen".

India's Foreign Minister, Ms. Sushma Swaraj, in her speech* in the Assembly, five days later, (September 26) was even more forthright: "We must acknowledge that terrorism is undoubtedly the biggest violation of human rights. It targets the innocent and kills indiscriminately. Terrorism has gone way beyond affecting individuals or nations–it is a crime against humanity itself. But it is important to ask–who is behind this and who benefits from it? Terrorists do not own banks or weapons factories, so let us ask the real question: who finances these terrorists, who arms them and provides sanctuaries? We heard similar questions being asked by Afghanistan from this podium".

Leaving no one in doubt whom she was referring to, Ms. Sushma Swaraj underlined: "In our midst, there are nations that still speak the language of terrorism, that nurture it, peddle it, and export it. To shelter terrorists has become their calling card. We must identify these nations and hold them to account. These nations, in which UN designated terrorists roam freely, lead processions and deliver their poisonous sermons of hate with impunity, are as culpable as the very terrorists they harbour. Such countries should have no place in the comity of nations".

Replying to the insinuations about the 'pre-conditions' put by India for talks, Ms. Swaraj recounted the various initiatives taken, during the last two and a half years, by Prime Minister Narendra Modi's Government and asserted: "We have in fact attempted a paradigm of

*All statements/observations quoted here are from the Texts of the speeches made on September 21 and September 26 at the UN Assembly session.

friendship in the last two years which is without precedent. And what did we get in return? Pathankot, Bahadur Ali, and Uri. Bahadur Ali is a terrorist in our custody, whose confession is a living proof of Pakistan's complicity in cross-border terror".

Never before had such firm and confident assertions been made by India at the U.N. Forum. Never before a Pakistani spade had been called a spade so persuasively as at this juncture.

Pakistan Prime Minister Nawaz Sharif's speech, couched as it was with slant and slander, and his description of the local Commander of Hizab-ul-Mujahideen, a known terrorist organization, as a young Kashmiri freedom fighter, could hardly be distinguished from a self-incriminating statement of a guilty party. The special emissaries deputed to influential countries to canvas support for Pakistan's viewpoints could also not cut much ice anywhere. On the other hand, the U.S. State Department affirmed: "We have been very clear Pakistan must target all militant groups, including those that target Pakistan's neighbours and close all safe havens". U.S. National Security Adviser, Susan Rice, too, underscored: "Pakistan must take effective action to combat and delegitimize terrorists and terror groups". U.K., France, Germany and Russia deprecated, in their own way, terrorism oriented state policy of Pakistan.

II. *Boycott of 19th SAARC*

Simultaneous to the portrayal of Pakistan, at the UN, as an unabashed host to the Ivy League of terrorism, India announced its decision to boycott 19th Summit of SAARC scheduled for meeting at Islamabad in November, 2016. Sharing India's view, three other members–Afghanistan, Bangladesh and Bhutan–also pulled out of the Summit at about the same time. Sri Lanka, Maldives and Nepal soon followed suit. Clearly, a fundamental change in their attitude had occurred. Pakistan was left alone. Its isolation in the region was too stark to be glossed over. Summit-meeting was cancelled. It was a significant diplomatic triumph for India, a manifestation of its new-found assertion and confidence.

III. *(a) Revisiting Indus Water Treaty*

Signalling that efforts to promote good will would no longer be one sided, India declared that it would revisit the Indus Water Treaty

(1960). It could curtail the scale at which water is presently flowing into Pakistan. While remaining within the ambit of its international obligations, India could draw as much as 3.6 Million Acre Feet of additional water from the three western rivers*–Indus, Jhelum and Chenab.

India could take many other measures. It could straightway recommence Tulbul Navigation project which would be highly beneficial to the Indian State of J&K. This project provides for raising the level of water in river Jhelum/Wullar lake which would create round-the year facilities for navigation between Srinagar, Anantnag and Baramulla. The execution of the project was held over due to a few objections raised by Pakistan. But these objections have no validity in terms of Indus Water Treaty. The resumption of work on Tulbul project would not only put right kind of pressure on Pakistan but also expose its hypocrisy and show how it has been working against the true interests of the people of Kashmir.

India has a few other leverages in its hand. It could speed up the construction of three dams on river Chenab, namely, Pakul, Souvalkot and Bursan, and also take up extensive repair, of the headwork on the Indian side, which would prevent, due to leakages, flow of two million acre feet per annum to Pakistan from India's share.

On India's move to review the current position, Pakistan reacted with its usual bellicosity. "Revocation of Treaty could be an act of war". This threat was held out by Sartaj Aziz, foreign policy advisor to Pakistan Prime Minister. He failed to note, or omitted it by design, that India's action on new lines did not involve abrogation of Indus Water Treaty. It envisages changes only in the mechanism of implementation. Under the prevailing position, Pakistan is getting liberal treatment. Instead of expressing gratitude, it has been mounting terrorist attacks on the Indian soil through the so called non-state actors and their protégés. In this context, Prime-Minister Narendra Modi's declaration made on September 26, at the public forum at Kozhikode that "blood and water could not flow together" was unexceptionable. It fully captured the overall national mood of anger.

---

*According to Indus Water Treaty (1960), India has exclusive use of water of three eastern rivers–Sutlej, Beas and Ravi. It could also draw 3.6 million acre feet of water from three western rivers - Indus, Jhelum and Chenab which it is not drawing at present.

To hide its own grossly inefficient use* of water resources, Pakistan, especially its irresponsible and jingoist leadership, has been trying to mislead the people and accusing India of resorting to water terrorism. This leadership has not even bothered to go through the report of Pakistan's Senate Committee of July 9, 2015, in which it has been indicated that India is actually using less than its allocated share under Indus Water Treaty. The Chairman, Indus River System Authority clearly affirmed: "Reports in media about India getting more water is propaganda. India is using water only to produce electricity; the neighbours are getting less compared to their allocated share of water."

III. *(b) Reconsidering Most Favoured Nation Status*

In tune with the new hardline adopted towards Pakistan, it was publically declared that the Most Favoured Nation Status accorded to it from 2003-04, under International trade regime, would be reconsidered and the special concessions extended to it, one sided as they are at present, could be withdrawn.

Undoubtedly, India-Pakistan bilateral trade has gone up from $ 0.345 billion in 2003-04 to $ 2.6 billion in 2015-16, that is, about five times. But, seen in the context of overall volume of India's foreign trade, which stood at about $ 641 billion in 2015, this increase is insignificant and far below the potential.

What is worse, Pakistan is found to have been misusing the regime by importing impermissible items, such as California almonds, through three Trade Facilitation Centres of Salamabad, Uri and Chakkan-da-Bagh. Recent investigations carried out by the National Investigation Agency have shown that, under the cover of payments for these imports, substantial funds were made available to 'separatist and overground workers' to finance the violent agitation following the death of Hizbul Mujahideen Commander Burhan Wani on 8th July, 2016, in an encounter with the security forces. Obviously, if blood and

*Pakistan's productivity per unit of water is 0.13 kgm. It is one of the lowest in the world. It is one-third of India's and one sixth of China's. Indus Water Treaty (1960) is often cited as another example of India's negotiation and strategic naiveté. It virtually surrendered its full sovereign rights and agreed to assign about 80 per cent share of Indus-System waters to Pakistan. Now, it is legally extremely difficult for India to put "water pressure" upon Pakistan, even when the latter is pursuing the dangerous course of bleeding the former by way of thousand cuts.

water cannot flow together, how can a small trade benefit, under an assumed confidence building measure, be reconciled with the continued hostility of Pakistan, particularly when it is accompanied by the manipulation of the system to channel funds to the subversionists.

IV. *Surgical Strike: Pre-emptive Action*

After preparing the right kind of atmosphere at the international and regional forums and after indicating its intention to revisit Indus Water Treaty (1960) and Most Favoured Nation status for Pakistan, Narendra Modi government mustered political will to give a go-ahead signal to the Army to carry out 'surgical strike' on the Pakistan's side of Line of Control. On the night of 28th-29th September, 2016, the rubicon was crossed. In a multipronged action, using multiple special forces and backed by Commandos, seven terror launch pads, spread over 250 km length of 'Line of Control', were attacked and destroyed, inflicting a number of causalities on the terrorists and their associates.

Forthwith, a simple, yet telling, statement was issued by Lt. General Ranbir Singh, Director General Military Operations: "Based on receiving specific and credible inputs that some terrorist teams had positioned themselves at launch pads along the LoC to carry out infiltration and conduct terrorist strikes inside J&K and in various metros in other states, the Indian army conducted surgical strikes at several of these launch pads to pre-empt infiltration by terrorists. We do not have any plans for further continuation". The attacking troops returned safely to the Indian side of Line of Control.

It was a stunning operation, carried out with pinpoint precision and electrifying professional skill and coordination. The assumption of Pakistan that India would restrict itself to usual protests and warnings had been knocked out from its very bottom. Not only that, India's capability of acquiring accurate locational information and conducting 'retaliatory strikes' deep inside Pakistan had been effectively demonstrated. Clearly, from now onwards, it would be Pakistan and its proxies who would have to run for cover, in a state of uncertainty, from one point to another, not knowing where India's counter-strike would occur. All this, it is believed, would force Pakistan to abandon, after an initial face-saving spell* of retaliatory

*Pakistan has been virtually under a 'soft coup'. To ensure that the ascendency of Army in the politico military power-structure of Pakistan was maintained, the face-saving spells of

(Contd...)

action, its strategy of 'bleeding India by thousand cuts', a strategy that it has so far been pursuing with impunity but which could now become costly, both in terms of money and manpower. In relation to Pakistan, the surgical strike could be a moment of history for India–a turning point, from being bled and bullied to being confident and courageous. As rightly observed by Shiv Aroor and Rahul Singh, in their recent book, *India's Most Fearless*: "Not only had the surgical strikes of 28-29 September been the most audacious and dangerous peacetime attacks mounted by Indian forces, they had also been the cleanest. … A total of 38-40 terrorists and 2 Pakistan Army personnel were killed at the 4 targets. The 3 separate teams had simultaneously struck 4 launch pads across the LoC. Their entry into PoK had been coordinated and precisely timed".

The 29th September, 2016 surgical strike also showed the kind of extraordinary heroism and skill the Indian soldiers are capable of performing. As aptly underlined by General Bipin Rawat: "For all the decaying values we tend to be surrounded by, let nobody convince you that true heroes don't exist"*.

A section of the press and a group of opposition political parties attempted to belittle the significance of the 29th September surgical strikes, saying that such strikes had been conducted even earlier. This attempt was unfortunate. It was a product of entrenched biases and narrow politics. It virtually delivered a publicity coup to Pakistan. The stark truth is that, in terms of length, depth, impact and overall range of operation, the surgical strike was unprecedented. Marked by stealth, surprise, speed and sense of timing, it was a stupendous success not only militarily but also diplomatically. As a key element of 'new resolve', its successful culmination, announced by the Director-General of Military Operations with dignified restraint, served as a great morale booster to the nation. Years of diffidence had been shaken off with a determined mind.

(Contd...)

retaliatory actions were expected at least in the immediate future. And they did come about. Apart from quite a few heavy fire assaults, along the Line of Control, there was a serious terror attack across the international border on the Nagrotta Army Camp on November 29, 2016. In the Nagrotta attack seven defence personnel, including two officers, were killed.

*The observation, quoted here, has been made by General Bipin Rawat in the introduction to the book, *India's Most Fearless*.

The surgical strike also brought to surface Pakistan's increasing diplomatic isolation. The major members of the international community understood India's resort to pre-emptive action across the Line of Control. United States Ambassador to India, Richard Verma, in a press interview, said: "India took the action it thought was necessary to defend itself, which we understand". He further commented: "We have been quite tough on Pakistan... about the need.... to crack down on its safe havens, to crack down on the use of proxies to carry out terrorist attacks. We have to stand united and we stand in solidarity with India on that front". Russian Ambassador Alexander Kadakin, too, supported India's surgical strike of 29th September, 2016. No other country found fault with India's first ever counter-terror operation in the Pakistan-occupied Kashmir. Clearly, after a long time, a favourable wind had started blowing to move India's ship of destiny in the right direction.

V. *Baring the Ugly Face of Pakistani Bred Terrorism At Multilateral Forum of BRICS.**

After the adoption of the new resolve, Prime Minister Narendra Modi seized every opportunity that came in his way to draw attention of the members of regional and multi-lateral organizations to the plethora of evils embedded in Pakistan's use of terror as instrument of its policies. He did so with a sense of mission at the 8th BRICS SUMMIT, held at Goa, on October 15-16, 2016. In his address at the opening session, he described Pakistan as mother-ship of terrorism: "Terror modules around the world are linked to this mother-ship. This country shelters not just terrorists. It nurtures a mindset". On October 17, 2016, at the BRICS-BIMSTEC Outreach Summit, he reinforced his views by observing: "In South Asia and BIMSTEC,** all nations, barring one, are motivated to pursue a path of peace, development and economic prosperity for its people. Unfortunately, this country in India's neighbourhood embraces and radiates the darkness of terrorism. Terrorism has become its favourite child. And this child in turn has come to define the fundamental character and nature of its parents".

---

* BRICS constitutes a group of five important countries. They together cover a quarter of earth's land mass and 42 per cent of the global population. It produces 25 per cent of the world GDP, and represents about half of the global gold reserves and foreign exchange.

**The group of seven BIMSTEC countries comprises Bangladesh, India, Myanmar, Sri Lanka, Thailand, Bhutan and Nepal.

Though other members, notably China and Russia, did not go along with Narendra Modi in naming Pakistan or referring to terms, such as cross-border or state sponsored terrorism, the final declaration, named as Goa Declaration of October 16, 2016, contained a severe indictment of pursuit of terror as national strategy: "We strongly condemn the recent several attacks, against some BRICS countries, including that in India. .... We stress that there can be no justification whatsoever for any acts of terrorism, whether based upon ideological, religious, political, racial, ethnic or any other reasons. We call upon all nations to adopt a comprehensive approach in combating terrorism, which should include countering violent extremism, radicalization, movement of terrorists, blocking sources of financing and dismantling terrorist bases."

Though generally rated as a limited success from the point of view of India's campaign against Pakistan's propelled terrorism, there was something in between the lines of the Goa Declaration that could not be ignored. From the expression: 'recent attack, including that in India', one could understand who was attacked and by whom. There was also a reference to the terrorist organization named by the United Nations which include Jaish-e-Mohammad, a major outfit used against India by Pakistan. Even otherwise, India's advocacy for realization of the all round dangers posed to the regional and multilateral groups by Pakistan's pursuit of terror, including bedeviling of their development prospects, was getting registered.

China's extensive economic and military interests in Pakistan had made it to stand by its 'all weather friend'. Russia, too, had its own compulsions with regard to its involvement in Syria imbroglio. But this did not inhibit Narendra Modi in directing a beam of searchlight on the diseased spots of the Pakistani reared terrorism and the debilitating and dehumanizing impact it was having on the current civilization of the globe.

With an eye on Pakistan, whichever country Narendra Modi visited, in the post Uri attack period, be it Saudi Arabia or Qatar, he forcefully argued for de-legitimisation of terrorism and its supporters. The response from most members of the international community has been positive. Modi's mission is having its impact. Clearly, Pakistan is no longer in a position to pretend that the atmosphere of dislike against it is not getting thicker by the day and its standing in the comity of nation is not being rapidly undermined.

VI. *Deeper Exposure at HEART of Asia Conference.*

Prime Minister Narendra Modi's relentless efforts undertaken as items of his 'new resolve', to expose the terror-smeared practices that Pakistan has been following for several years, yielded all-round fruitful results at the Sixth Heart of Asia Conference–Istanbul Process, held at Amritsar on December 4, 2016. In the Amritsar Conference Declaration, not only the most deadly terrorist organizations, such as Jaish-e-Mohammad and Lashkar-e-Taiba, which are known for years to have been trained, equipped, financed and guided by the Inter-Services Intelligence of Pakistan, were specifically named, but also Pakistan's duplicitous behavior was openly sneered at.

When foreign policy Advisor to Pakistan's Prime Minister, Sartaj Aziz, offered $ 500 million as development assistance for reconstruction of Afghanistan, President Ashraf Ghani did not hide his pent up feelings over Pakistan's hypocrisy and double dealing. Turing down the offer with a touch of sarcasm, he said: "The money may be used for containing extremism, because without peace, no amount of assistance will help". He pointed out: "The period, between October 4 and November 20, saw a spike in Taliban offensives. This could not happen without terrorists receiving state-backed sanctuaries. Last year, too, Afghanistan suffered the highest number of causalities and civilian and military-related deaths in the world". In sharp contrast to Pakistan's deceitful behaviour, India's attitude of providing solid financial assistance*, followed by execution of solid projects on the ground, 'acting like a national partner',** was warmly applauded by the Afghan President.

On his part, Prime Minister Narendra Modi envisioned an 'Afghan-led, Afghan-owned and Afghan-controlled' process of developing Afghanistan as a vibrant hub of connectivity between South Asia and Central Asia. For actualizing such a vision and building a self-propelling engine of growth, he called for a 'resolute action not just against terrorists but those backing them'. He emphasized: "Silence and inaction against terrorism in Afghanistan and our region will only embolden terrorists and their masters".

Who have been the terrorists? And who have been their masters? Obviously, they are the politico-military rulers of Pakistan. With every

---

* Under the India-Afghanistan Economic Cooperation Programme, India *has already spent two billion dollars, and committed another one* billion dollar this year.

**This expression has often been used by the Afghan Ambassador to India, Shaida Abdali, to describe India's sincere efforts to help Afghanistan.

passing international and multi-lateral gathering, in the post- Uri attack period, the pretensions of these rulers have been falling by the wayside. Their credibility touched a new low at the Sixth Heart of Asia Conference, Amritsar.

VII. *Highlighting the Continued Violations of Human Rights in Balochistan and PoK, and Countering Pakistan's Diabolical Disinformation Campaign with Regard to Kashmir.*

In his address to the nation on August 15, 2016, Prime Minister Narendra Modi said: "Today, from the ramparts of Red Fort, I want to greet and express my thanks to some people. In the last few days, people of Balochistan, Gilgit and Pakistan-occupied Kashmir have thanked me and expressed gratitude and expressed good wishes for me. The people who are living far away, whom I have never seen, never met–such people have expressed appreciation for the Prime Minister of India".

Obviously, it was a subtle way of signalling a change in India's attitude towards what had been happening for long in the above mentioned areas as a result of an iniquitous and repressive regime imposed on the peoples by the Government of Pakistan. So far, India had shown only low-grade, intermittent, interest in the matter. Now, as an item of Prime Minister's 'new resolve', a wider, deeper and long-range strategy of dealing with the issues connected with Balochistan and areas under Pakistan-Occupied Kashmir is being evolved. Earlier, on August 13, 2016, at the all-Party meeting on Kashmir, Prime Minister had indicated his mind: "Time has come for Pakistan to answer the world on atrocities against the people in Balochistan and Pakistan-occupied Kashmir."

As a historical backdrop, it may be stated that the Khanate of Kalat, located on the north-western border of pre-partitioned India, had been for years together under the rule of the Khans, with strong tribal linkages. Before 1876, it was, for all intents and purpose, an independent entity. Before the second Anglo-Afghan war, the British-Indian Government sought a few facilities from the Khan, including a passage through the Bolan Pass and a garrison at Quetta. These facilities were agreed to. In 1876, a Treaty was signed between the two parties, namely the Khanate of Kalat and the British Indian Government. The latter used these facilities effectively to acquire an upper hand in its conflicts with Afghanistan.

With the Indian independence and carving out of a separate state of Pakistan in sight, the Treaty of 1876 was brought to a closure by the British Indian government on August 11, 1947, with the mutual agreement of both the parties. The status of un-encumbered independence, which the Khanate enjoyed before 1876, was thus restored.

The Khanate, it needs to be specially noted, was not a princely state within the British Empire. Nor was the Khan a member of the Chamber of Princes. It remained independent* from August 11, 1947 to March 11, 1948, when it was annexed by Pakistan through subterfuge and display of military might. The British connived at all this, as inclusion of Kalat in Pakistan suited their strategic interests. It could be of great help to them in checking the Russian expansionist designs in the Central Asia.

Annexation was bitterly resented by the tribal leaders and other Balochis, amongst whom were a few educated young men fired with the spirit of freedom. The nationalistic mood of the times found eloquent expression in the speech** delivered by Mir Ghaus Bux Bizenjo in the first Session of *dar-ul-awam* in mid-December, 1947: "We have a distinct civilisation. We have a separate culture like that of Iran and Afghanistan. We are Muslims but it is not necessary that by virtue of our being Muslims we should lose our freedom and merge with others... If Pakistan wants to treat us as a sovereign people we are

---

* The Khan of Kalat had engaged M.A. Jinnah as his lawyer who forcefully argued before the Cabinet Mission (1946) that the Khanate of Kalat must be treated as an independent State. Ironically, he, as a Governor General of Pakistan, was instrumental in denying that status to the Khanate.

** At the time of delivering the speech, Mir Ghaus Bux Bizenjo who had received his education in India at Aitchison College, was a young leader of about 30 years. Later on, he became famous as Baba-e Balochistan (Father of Balochistan). He refuted the two-nation theory. He consistently held the view: "At no time the Muslims were, are or would be a nation ever. Islam is a multi-national institution. It is not a national institution. An Indian Muslim is a Muslim. So is Afghan, Arab and Indonesian Muslim a Muslim. But they are not one nation. Islam is not a nation, it is an ummath (men of the same faith)." (Quoted from Martin Axmann's book on Back to the Future (Oxford p. 275). The quote from dar-ul-awam speech of Mir Ghaus Bux Bizenjo is also from the same book. (p. 230).

Mir Ghaus Bux Bizenjo also suffered imprisonment for years, including in the notorious Quli Camp in Quetta, where he was mercilessly tortured. One of the fellow prisoners recalled: "They kept Mir Ghaus Bux Bizenjo separate from us and tortured him so much that when he was brought back I didn't recognize him."

ready to extend the hand of friendship and co-operation. If Pakistan does not agree to do so, flying in the face of democratic principles, such an attitude will be totally unacceptable to us, and if we are forced to accept this fate then every Baloch son will sacrifice his life in defence of his national freedom".

The resentment of Balochis against annexation manifested itself in frequent spells of insurgencies–1948; 1958-59; 1962-63; and 1973-77. They were all suppressed ruthlessly by the Pakistani Army. In 1977, the former Chief Commissioner Province of Balochistan, the former Balochistan States' Union and the enclave of Gwadar, which was earlier purchased by Pakistan from Oman, were amalgamated to form a single unit–the Province of Balochistan as it stands at present.

Though the largest province–it covers about 43 per cent of Pakistan's total land area–Balochistan has relatively a small population of about 13 million. It is largely poverty-ridden. Households-wise, the incidence of 'poverty' and 'severe poverty' in Balochistan is 52 per cent and 35 per cent respectively. Since 1948, the area has seen little economic progress, though it is mineral rich and has huge deposits of coal, gold and copper. It could provide almost unlimited supply of natural gas. Much to the frustration of the indigenous people of Balochistan, its resources have largely been used for benefits of outsiders, especially the residents of Punjab. In terms of per capita GDP, the average annual rise has been 2.4 per cent in the case of Punjab and only 0.2 per cent in the case of Balochistan.

The frequent eruptions of insurgencies and seething anger of the people in general touched a boiling point after the commencement of the highly ambitious project of the China Pakistan Economic Corridor. It includes expansion and modernization of Gwadar sea port and building of 2400 km of rail and road infrastructure which would provide China access to all-weather deep water seaport* on the Arabian Sea. When, in 2001, President Pervez Musharraf announced the development of Gwadar port, and assigned the work to a Chinese

*Under an accord signed recently (May 16, 2016) between Iran, India and Afghanistan, Chabahar port in South-Eastern Iran is being developed. A number of urban centres of Afghanistan would get connected to this port through the Zeranj-Delaram road which India has built under an Afghan-assistance project. India, too, will get land access to Central Asia. Apart from serving a gateway to new markets, the modernized and technologically upgraded port of Chabahar could balance the strategic advantage which both Pakistan and China are seeking by establishing a military-naval base in Gwadar.

construction company, a wave of indignation swept across practically the whole of Balochistan.

It was the beginning of a new phase of insurgency–low intensity and lethal in impact and subversionist and separatist in outlook. Some Chinese engineers, doctors and construction workers were attacked and killed. Enraged, President Musharraf ordered a crackdown. Pakistan's Army and its sponsored terrorist outfits resorted to indiscriminate killing and violated human rights with impunity. Hundreds of Balochis, especially those who were suspected to have links with such groups as the Balochistan Liberation Army, the Baloch Liberation Front and the Baloch Republican Army, were arrested under draconian laws. Some of them fell victim to the infamous practice of 'kidnap, kill and dump'. Scores came to be included in the 'list of missing persons'. Even the Air Force was used. In an air and ground operation, in August 2006, the head of the most influential Bugti tribe, Nawab Akbar Khan Bugti, was killed, fuelling the turmoil manifold.

The rising tempo of the Balochi opposition notwithstanding, the Chinese Pakistan Economic Corridor was pushed ahead. In April 2015, President XI Jinping of China visited Islamabad and announced the upgraded project of One Belt One Road to Central Asia. The revised alignments of the road, rail and pipelines cover a large area of Gilgit, Baltistan and Pakistan-occupied Kashmir over which Pakistan has no legal right. The seeds of future troubles are thus being planted in diverse ways, and a new kind of Great Game could come to be staged in the Central and South Asia amongst China, Pakistan, Iran, Afghanistan and India.

As the massive project, which involves a Chinese assistance of about $ 46 billion, is acquiring larger dimensions, the opposition of the Balochis is becoming more bitter, and their apprehensions of being swamped by the Chinese and personnel from other provinces of Pakistan are growing. And so is their violence and militancy. The Pakistan Army and its sponsored terrorist outfits, brutal and vengeful as they are, fall upon, with beastly ferocity, on the Balochis–not only on suspected militants but also on their sympathisers.

Ahmed Rashid, a noted Pakistani author and journalist, has described the on-going turmoil in Balochistan as Pakistan's longest civil war. He has observed: "The Frontier Corps, the anti-Shia group Lashkar-e-Jhangvi and other groups are all enmeshed in a decade-long campaign of "pick up and dump" in which Baloch nationalists, militants or even innocent bystanders are picked up, disappeared, tortured, mutilated and then killed". The report of Brad Adam is no less revealing: "The surge in unlawful killings of suspected militants and opposition figures in Balochistan has taken the brutality in the province to an unprecedented level".* The Pakistan Human Rights Commission itself found that in the year 2012 alone, 57 persons went missing and are believed to have been bumped off.

Much has been made by Pakistan's propaganda machine about the 'human rights violations' in Kashmir. But little is said about the gross violations that have been perpetrated by Pakistan on the Balochis from the day–March 1948–when the Khanate of Kalat was annexed. Here, both in range and depth, the human rights have been trampled over in the worst way. And, as the data and documents cited above show, these violations have been committed not only in the form of physical torture but also in the form of depriving Balochis of fair share of their natural resources. They have remained shackled in severe poverty and abysmal illiteracy. And their capacities to improve their lot in future have been sapped from their roots. With the execution of CPEC projects gaining momentum, it is becoming increasingly clear that the Balochis are not likely to get 'anything more than the opportunities of fixing punctures on the Chinese trucks' engaged for construction works. The meager employment opportunities apart, the indigenous ethnic groups could soon find their majority being reduced to minority by influx of personnel from other provinces of Pakistan.

With regard to the allegations of large scale violations of human rights in Kashmir, the boot, for most part of it, would be found on the other leg. In the earlier chapters of this book, I have analysed a number of specific cases in which intentional falsification had been done to prop up the culture of radicalism, extremism and antagonism. They show how brutal concoctions, culled out of a brutalised mind, in an atmosphere brutalized by contrived feelings of victimhood are resorted to with impunity. While Pakistan and its valley-collaborators continue to spread their network of subversion and terrorism to serve their purpose of gobbling up Kashmir, it is the common folk who are put to all sorts of miseries.

Of late, the modus operandi that is being increasingly invoked is to weave a frame of mind around the youth in which he is driven to get

---

*Report of Brad Adam, Asia Director at Human Rights.

closer and closer to attack and injure the policemen and other security officials by way of a volley of stones, leaving little option to them but to rely upon punitive action, sometimes firing. In essence, a situation is induced, wherein human rights violations seemingly occur, providing additional quantity of lubricants to the propaganda machine to keep it running in the top gear.

Obviously, the planks of the tragedy are built elsewhere. And they would continue to be built and distributed all over in Kashmir till the crafty and cruel designs of Pakistan and its collaborators are laid bare in all their ramifications, especially the phenomenon of their 'double heartlessness'. One, they set the ball of terrorist act rolling, which in itself involves a savage violation of human rights of the innocent. Two, in their pursuit of gaining maximum publicity, they resort to psychological conditioning of the mind of immature youths, the overwhelming number of whom belong to the poor families, and goad them to expose themselves to risks of life in the name of militant Islam and Jihad.

It is, in fact, a cold blooded strategy of the leaders of the terrorists' groups. They ignite strands of militant Islam and inject a sense of bravado in the youths who are driven to believe that they are Davids who would bring down Goliaths. Not un-often, they, taking advantage of the concern of the security forces to avoid collateral damage, are able to cause gaps in the cordons of the security forces and facilitate escape of the besieged terrorists. When, however, some of the youths get hurt or killed, the tragedy is exploited to do extensive propaganda against 'the brute Indian security forces who are killing children.' That is why, over the years, increased efforts have been put in by the terrorists' leaders to ensure that the stone pelting is organised at or near every cordon-cum- encounter site. In the vicinity of such a site, all the mosques are promptly activated, and from these pre-recorded and synchronised exhortations are blared out, urging people to come out and attack the security forces by raining in stones on a large scale.

In essence, India is hit by a double whammy. It first suffers from a terror attack and then from the aftermath of induced violations and adverse publicity. The real source of all inhumanities is Pakistan's supermarket of terror commodities from which all sorts of evils are parcelled out. The devilish extent to which these evils are deployed should be clear from the blood-chilling manner in which, as detailed in earlier chapters, the human rights of practically the entire community of Kashmiri Pandits have been violated, and the most learned and advanced people made refugees in their own country.

Promise and Potential of New Helmsman

From the above analysis of events of the first 33 months of Narendra Modi regime, it could be asserted, with a fair degree of reasonableness, that India which, in relation to Kashmir issue, has been suffering, for years together, 'trials and judgments' of a turbulent sea, has, found a promising helmsman. He has shown the calibre to chart out a new sea-lane. He remains confident even when this lane is crossed by heavy winds and ominous clouds. The formulation and execution of seven items of new resolve have been the hallmarks of his dispensation. These also indicate a potential for undertaking constructive and elevating ventures in future.

APPENDIX

Appendix I

Sources of History of Kashmir

The main sources of Kashmir history are:

Group I: *Sanskrit Works*

(1) *Nilamata Purana,* (6th or 7th century A.D.); (2) *Kuttanimata Kavya,* said to have been written by Damodaragupta during the 8th century A.D.; (3) Ksemendra's *Samaya-matrka, Desopadesa-Narmamala* and *Desavataracarita;* (4) Kalhana's *Rajatarangini;* (5) Jonaraja's *Rajatarangini.*

Group II: *Kashmir Chronicles*

(1) *Tarikh-i-Kashmir* by Sayyid Ali; (2) *Baharistan-i-Shahi* by an unknown author; (3) *Tarikh-i-Kashmir* by Hasan B. Ali Kashmiri; (4) *Tarikh-i-Kashmir* by Haidar Malik Chadura; (5) *Tarikh-i-Kashmir* by Narayan Kaul Ajiz; (6) *Nawadir-ul-Akhbar* by Aba Rafi-ud-Din Ahmed; (7) *Waqiat-i-Kashmir* by Muhammad Azam; (8) *Tarikh-i-Hasan*by Pir Hasan Shah; (9) *Mukhtsar Tarikh-i-Kashmir* by Pt. Birbal Kachru.

Group III: *Delhi Sultanate Histories*

(1) *Tarikh-i-Mubarak Shahi* by Yahya, B. Ahmad B. Abdullah Sirhindi; (2) *Tarikh-i-Daudi;* and (3) *Tarikh-i-Khan-i-Jahani.*

Group IV: *Mughal Histories*

(1) *Ain-i-Akbari* by Abul Fazl; (2) *Akbar Nama,* also by Abul Fazl; (3) *Tuzuk-i-Jahangiri* by the emperor Jahangir; (4) *Maasirul Umara* by Shams-ud-Daula.

Group V: *General Histories*

(1) *Aabaqat-i-Akbari* by Nizam-ud-Din Ahmad; (2) *Tarikh-i-Firishta* by Muhammad Qasim Firishta; (3) *Muntakhab-ut-Tawarikh* by Abdul

Qadir Badauni; (4) *Haft Iqlim* by Amin Ahmad Razi; (5) *Majlis-ul-Muminin* by Qazi Nur Ullah Shustri.

Group VI: *Central Asian Histories*

(1) *Malfuzat-i-Timuri* by Timur; (2) *Zafar Nama* by Sharaf-ud-Din Ali Yazdi; (3) *Tarikh-i-Rashidi* by Mirza Haidar Dughlat.

Group VII: *Biographies of Sufis and Rishis*

(1) *Khulasatul Manaqib* by Nur-ud-Din Jafar Badakhshi; (2) *Tuhfatul Ahbab* by an unknown author; (3) *Hilyatul Arifin* by Khwaja Ishaq; (4) *Tazkira Mushaikh-i-Kashmir* by Baba Nasib; (5) *Nur Nama* by Baba Nasib-ud-Din Ghazi; (6) *Majmuadar Ansab, Mashaikh-i-Kashmir* and *Futuhat-i-Kubraviya* by Abdul Wahab.

Group VIII: *European Travellers*

Notes, letters and general accounts of (1) Father Jerome Xavier, (2) Benedict de Goes, (3) Francisco Pelsaert, (4) Bernier, (5) Father Desideri, and (6) Father Fryre.

Group IX: *Archaeological Excavations*

Kashmir is veritable treasure of archaeological remains. Apart from the pioneering work done by scholars and archaeologists like Sir Aurel Stein, General Cunningham and Major R.E. Cole, considerable headway has been made during the last 30 years or so, providing new insight into the ancient history and culture of the Valley. The excavations at Burzabom, district Srinagar; Gufkral, district Pulwama; Semthan, district Anantnag; and Harwan near Dachigam are particularly revealing.

Appendix II

Extracts from the Treaty of Lahore (March 9,1846) and Treaty of Amritsar (March 16, 1846)

A. *Treaty of Lahore* (March 9, 1846)

The British Government having demanded from the Lahore State, as indemnification for the expenses of the war, in addition to the cession of territory described in article 3, payment of one and a half crores of rupees; and the Lahore Government being unable to pay the whole of this sum at this time, or to give security satisfactory to the British Government for its eventual payment; the Maharaja cedes to the Honourable Company in perpetual sovereignty, as equivalent for one crore of rupees, all his forts, territories, rights and interests in the hill countries which are situated between the river Beas and Indus, including the provinces of Kashmir and Hazara.

B. *Treaty of Amritsar (*March 16, 1846)

The British Government transfers and makes over for ever in independent possession, to Maharaja Gulab Singh and heirs male of his body, all the hilly or mountainous country with its dependencies situated to the eastward of the river Indus and westward of the river Ravi, including Chamba and excluding Lahol, being part of the territories ceded to the British Government by the Lahore State according to provisions of Article IV of the Treaty of Lahore dated March 9, 1846 A.D.

Appendix III

Summary of the Programme of Naya Kashmir

The 'Naya Kashmir' plan envisaged a scheme of constitutional reforms for the State, a bill of rights and a frame of representative political institutions besides a national economic plan and a plan for cultural and educational development. The plan pledged to secure the people of the State, right to equality, right to self-determination, emancipation from oppression, poverty and ignorance and superstition and ensure them participation in the historic resurgence of the peoples of the East and the working masses of the world. The preamble of the plan read:

> We, the people of Jammu, Kashmir, Ladakh and the frontier regions, including Poonch and Chinani Ilaqas–commonly known as Jammu and Kashmir State–in order to perfect our Union in the fullest equality and self-determination, to raise ourselves and our children forever from the abyss of oppression and poverty, degradation and superstition from medieval darkness and ignorance, into the sunlit valleys of plenty ruled by freedom, science and honest toil, in worthy participation of the historic resurgence of the people of the East and the working masses of the world, and in determination to make this our country a dazzling gem upon the snowy bosom of Asia, do propose and propound the following Constitution of our State.

Appendix IV

Text of Sheikh Abdullah's letter of September 26, 1947

"May it please Your Highness,

It is after about one and half year's incarceration that–as long wished–I had an opportunity of having detailed talks with Thakur Nachint Chand Ji. What unfortunate things happened during this period in the State. I need not mention. But this is now realised by every well-wisher of the State that many of the regrettable happenings of the past have mainly been due to the misunderstandings which appear now to have deliberately been created by interested people in order to achieve their own ends. R.B. Ramchandra Kak, the ex-Prime Minister, through his mischievous methods and masterly manoeuvrings brought these misunderstandings to a climax and succeeded in his attempt, though temporarily, to a certain extent. He painted me and my organisation in the darkest colours and in everything that we did or attempted to do to bring Your Highness and your people closer, base and selfish motives were attributed to me. But God be thanked that all these enemies of Your Highness and the State stand exposed today.

In spite of what has happened in the past, I assure Your Highness that myself and my party have never harboured any sentiment of disloyalty towards Your Highness' person, throne or dynasty. The development of this beautiful country and the betterment of its people is our common aim and interest and I assure Your Highness the fullest and loyal support of myself and my organisation. Not only this, but I assure Your Highness that any party, within or without the State, which may attempt to create any impediments in our efforts to gain our goal, will be treated our enemy and will be treated as such.

In order to achieve the common aim set forth above, mutual trust and confidence must be tile mainstay. Without this it would not be possible to face successfully the great difficulties that beset our State on all sides at present.

Before I close this letter I beg to assure Your Highness once again of my steadfast loyalty and pray that God under Your Highness' aegis bring such an era of Peace, Prosperity and Good Government that it may be second to none and be an ideal for others to copy.

Your Highness' Most Obedient Subject
S.M. Abdullah"

Appendix V

The Resolution of the United Nations Security Council of August 13, 1948

Resolution of the Commission of August 13, 1948:

The United Nations Commission for India and Pakistan.

Having given careful consideration to the points of view expressed by the representatives of India and Pakistan regarding the situation in the State of Jammu and Kashmir; and

Being of the opinion that the prompt cessation of hostilities and the correction of conditions the continuance of which is likely to endanger international peace and security are essential to implementation of its endeavours to assist the Governments of India and Pakistan in effecting a final settlement of the situation;

Resolves to submit simultaneously to the Governments of India and Pakistan the following proposal:

Part I: *Cease-fire Order*

A. The Governments of India and Pakistan agree that their respective High Commands will issue separately and simultaneously a cease-fire order to apply to all forces under their control in the State of Jammu and Kashmir as of the earliest practicable date or dates to be mutually agreed upon within four days after these proposals have been accepted by both Governments.

B. The High Commands of the Indian and Pakistani forces agree to refrain from taking any measures that might augment the military potential of the forces under their control in the State of Jammu and Kashmir.

(For the purpose of these proposals forces under their control shall be considered to include all forces, organized and unorganized, fighting or participating in hostilities on their respective sides.)

C. The Commanders-in-Chief of the forces of India and Pakistan shall promptly confer regarding any necessary local changes in present dispositions which may facilitate the cease-fire.

D. In its discretion and as the Commission may find practicable, the Commission will appoint military observers who, under the authority of the Commission and with the co-operation of both Commands, will supervise the observance of the cease-fire order.

E. The Government of India and the Government of Pakistan agree to appeal to their respective peoples to assist in creating and maintaining an atmosphere favourable to the promotion of further negotiations.

Part II: *Truce Agreement*

Simultaneously with the acceptance of the proposal for the immediate cessation of hostilities as outlined in Part I, both Governments accept the following principles as a basis for the formulation of a truce agreement, the details of which shall be worked out in discussion between their representatives and the Commission.

A.

1. As the presence of troops of Pakistan in the territory of the State of Jammu and Kashmir constitutes a material change in the situation since it was represented by the Government of Pakistan before the Security Council, the Government of Pakistan agrees to withdraw its troops from that State.

2. The Government of Pakistan will use its best endeavour to secure the withdrawal from the State of Jammu and Kashmir of tribesmen and Pakistani nationals not normally resident therein who have entered the State for the purpose of fighting.

3. Pending a final solution, the territory evacuated by the Pakistani troops will be administered by the local authorities under the surveillance of the Commission.

B.

1. When the Commission shall have notified the Government of India that the tribesmen and Pakistani nationals referred to in Part II, A, 2 hereof have withdrawn, thereby terminating the situation which

was represented by the Government of India to the Security Council as having occasioned the presence of Indian forces in the State of Jammu and Kashmir, and further, that the Pakistani forces are being withdrawn from the State of Jammu and Kashmir, the Government of India agrees to begin to withdraw the bulk of its forces from that State in stages to be agreed upon with the Commission.

2. Pending the acceptance of the conditions for a final settlement of the situation in the State of Jammu and Kashmir, the Indian Government will maintain within the lines existing at the moment of the cease-fire the minimum strength of its forces which in agreement with the Commission are considered necessary to assist local authorities in the observance of law and order. The Commission will have observers stationed where it deems necessary.

3. The Government of India will undertake to ensure that the Government of the State of Jammu and Kashmir will take all measures within its power to make it publicly known that peace, law and order will be safeguarded and that all human and political rights will be guaranteed.

C.

1. Upon signature, the full text of the truce agreement or a communique containing the principles thereof as agreed upon between the two Governments and the Commission, will be made public.

Part III

The Government of India and the Government of Pakistan reaffirm their wish that the future status of the State of Jammu and Kashmir shall be determined in accordance with the will of the people and to that end, upon acceptance of the truce agreement, both Governments agree to enter into consultations with the Commission to determine fair and equitable conditions whereby such free expression will be assured.

Appendix VI

Summary of assurances given to India by United Nations Commission during the course of discussions and correspondence

(i) Responsibility for the security of the State of Jammu and Kashmir rests with the Government of India.

(ii) The sovereignty of Jammu and Kashmir Government over the entire territory of the State shall not be brought into question.

(iii) There shall be no recognition of the so-called Azad (Free) Kashmir Government.

(iv) The territory occupied by Pakistan shall not be consolidated to the disadvantage of the State of Jammu and Kashmir.

(v) The administration of the evacuated areas in the north shall revert to the Government of Jammu and Kashmir and its defence to the Government of India who will, if necessary, maintain garrisons for preventing the incursion of tribesmen, and for guarding the main trade routes.

(vi) Pakistan shall be excluded from all affairs of Jammu and Kashmir in particular in the plebiscite, if one should be held.

(vii) If a plebiscite is found to be impossible for technical or practical reasons, the Commission will consider other methods of determining fair and equitable conditions for ensuring a free expression of the people's will.

(viii) Plebiscite proposals shall not be binding upon India if Pakistan does not implement Parts I and II of the resolution of 13th August, 1948.

Appendix VII

Tashkent Declaration

Tashkent Declaration

The Prime Minister of India and the; President of Pakistan, having met at Tashkent and having discussed the existing relations between India and Pakistan hereby declare their firm resolve to restore normal and peaceful relations between their countries and to promote understanding and friendly relations between their peoples. They consider the attainment of these objectives of vital importance for the welfare of the 600 million people of India and Pakistan.

(i) The Prime Minister of India and the President of Pakistan agree that both sides will exert all efforts to create good neighbourly relations between India and Pakistan in accordance with the United Nations Charter. They reaffirm their obligation under the Charter not to have recourse to force and to settle their disputes through peaceful means. They considered that the interests of peace in their region and particularly in the Indo-Pakistan subcontinent and indeed, the interests of the peoples of India and Pakistan were not served by the continuance of tension between the two countries. It was against this background that Jammu & Kashmir was discussed, and each of the sides set forth its respective position.

(ii) The Prime Minister of India and the President of Pakistan have agreed that all armed personnel of the two countries shall be withdrawn not later than 25 February 1966 to the positions they held prior to 5 August 1965, and both sides shall observe the cease-fire terms on the cease-fire line.

(iii) The Prime Minister of India and the President of Pakistan have agreed that relations between India and Pakistan shall be based on the principle of non-interference in the internal affairs of each other.

(iv) Thc Prime Minister of India and the President of Pakistan have agreed that both sides will discourage any propaganda directed against the other country and will encourage propaganda which promotes the development of friendly relations between the two countries.

(v) The Prime Minister of India and the President of Pakistan have agreed that the High Commissioner of India to Pakistan and the High Commissioner of Pakistan to India will return to their posts and that the normal functioning of diplomatic missions of both countries will be restored. Both Governments shall observe the Vienna Convention of 1961 on Diplomatic Intercourse.

(vi) The Prime Minister of India and the President of Pakistan have agreed to consider measures towards the restoration of economic and trade relations, communications as well as cultural exchanges between India and Pakistan, and to take measures to implement the existing agreements between India and Pakistan.

(vii) The Prime Minister of India and the President of Pakistan have agreed that they will give instructions to their respective authorities to carry out the repatriation of the prisoners of war.

(viii) The Prime Minister of India and the President of Pakistan have agreed that the two sides will continue the discussions of questions relating to the problems of refugees and evictions/illegal immigrations. They also agreed that both sides will create conditions which will prevent the exodus of people. They further agree to discuss the return of the property and assets taken over by either side in connection with the conflict.

(ix) The Prime Minister of India and the President of Pakistan have agreed that the two sides will continue meetings both at highest and at other levels of matters of direct concern to both countries. Both sides have recognised the need to set up joint Indian-Pakistani bodies which will report to their Governments in order to decide what, further steps should be taken.

The Prime Minister of India and the President of Pakistan record their feelings, deep appreciation and gratitude to the leaders of the Soviet Union, the Soviet Government and personally to the Chairman of the Council of Ministers of the USSR for their constructive, friendly and noble part in bringing about the present meeting which has resulted in mutually satisfactory results. They also express to the Government and friendly people of Uzbekistan their sincere thankfulness for their overwhelming reception and generous hospitality.

They invite the Chairman of the Council of Ministers of the USSR to witness this declaration.

Prime Minister of India
Lal Bahadur Shastri
Tashkent, 10 January 1966

President of Pakistan
Mohammed Ayub Khan

Appendix VIII

Shimla Agreement

Shimla Agreement on Bilateral Relations between India and Pakistan signed by Prime Minister of India, Mrs. Indira Gandhi, and President of Pakistan, Mr. Z.A. Bhutto, in Shimla on July 3, 1972.

The Government of India and the Government of Pakistan are resolved that the two countries put an end to the conflict and confrontation that have hitherto marred their relations and work for the promotion of a friendly and harmonious relationship and the establishment of durable peace in the subcontinent, so that both countries may henceforth devote their resources and energies to the pressing task of advancing the welfare of their people.

In order to achieve this objective, the Government of India and the Government of Pakistan have agreed as follows:

(i) That the principles and purposes of the Charter of the United Nations shall govern the relations between the two countries.

(ii) That the two countries are resolved to settle their differences by peaceful means through bilateral negotiations or by any other peaceful means mutually agreed upon between them. Pending the final settlement of any of the problems between the two countries, neither side shall unilaterally alter the situation and both shall prevent the organisation, assistance or encouragement of any acts detrimental to the maintenance of peaceful and harmonious relations.

(iii) That the prerequisite for reconciliation, good neighbourliness and durable peace between them is a commitment by both the countries to peaceful co-existence, respect for each other's territorial integrity and sovereignty and non-interference in each other's internal affairs, on the basis of equality and mutual benefit.

(iv) That the basic issues and causes of conflict which have bedevilled the relations between the two countries for the last 25 years shall be resolved by peaceful means;

(v) That they shall always respect each other's national unity, territorial integrity, political independence and sovereign equality;

(vi) That in accordance with the Charter of the United Nations, they will refrain from the threat or use of force against the territorial integrity or political independence of each other.

Both Governments will take all steps within their power to prevent hostile propaganda directed against each other. Both countries will encourage the dissemination of such informations as would promote the development of friendly relations between them.

In order progressively to restore and normalise relations between the two countries step by step, it was agreed that:

(i) Steps shall be taken to resume communications, postal, telegraphic, sea, land including border, posts and air links including over-flights.

(ii) Appropriate steps shall be taken to promote travel facilities for the nationals of the other country.

(iii) Trade and cooperation in economic and other agreed fields will be resumed as far as possible.

(iv) Exchange in the fields of science and culture will be promoted.

In this connection delegations from the two countries will meet from time to time to work out the necessary details.

In order to initiate the process of the establishment of durable peace, both the Governments agree that:

(i) Indian and Pakistani forces shall be withdrawn to their side of the international border.

(ii) In Jammu and Kashmir, the line of control* resulting from the cease-fire of December 17, 1971, shall be respected by

*Neither the Karachi Agreement of 1949 nor the Shimla Agreement of 1972 refers to the Siachen Glacier, 74 km long, believed to be the world's largest in the non-polar regions, now turned into a battleground at altitudes from 15,000 and 20,000 feet since June 1984.

both sides without prejudice to the recognised position of either side. Neither side shall seek to alter it unilaterally, irrespective of mutual differences and legal interpretations. Both sides further undertake to refrain from the threat or the use of force in violation of this line.

(iii) The withdrawls shall commence upon entry into force of this agreement and shall be completed within a period of 30 days thereof.

This agreement will be subject to ratification by both countries in accordance with their respective constitutional procedures, and will come into force with effect from the date on which the instruments of ratification are exchanged.

Both Governments agree that their respective heads will meet again at a mutually convenient time in the future and that in the meanwhile the representatives of the two sides will meet to discuss further the modalities and arrangements for the establishment of durable peace and normalisation of relations, including the questions of repatriation of prisoners of war and civilian internees, a final settlement of Jammu and Kashmir and the resumption of diplomatic relations.

It remained undemarcated as no troops had ever been deployed there. Later Indian troops moved in when Pakistan was discovered encouraging foreign expeditions to go there. Pakistani contention is that the line of control resulting from the cease-fire of December 17, 1971, should go eastwards to meet the Karakoram Pass. India, on the other hand, maintains that Pakistan cannot have any right over undemarcated uninhabited area belonging to J&K State which is an Indian State. A succession of meetings at different levels during the past over three years to solve the dispute have proved futile with the result that confrontation for control of 4,000 sqkm of the inhospitable Siachen continues.

Appendix IX

Kashmir Accord (February 1975)

Agreed conclusions which led to Sheikh Mohammad Abdullah's accord with Mrs. Indira Gandhi, Prime Minister, and his subsequent assumption of office as Chief Minister in February 1975.

1. The State of Jammu and Kashmir which is a constituent unit of the Union of India, shall, in its relation with the Union, continue to be governed by Article 370 of the Constitution of India.

2. The residuary powers of legislation shall remain with the State; however, Parliament will continue to have power to make laws relating to the prevention of activities directed towards disclaiming, questioning or disrupting the sovereignty and territorial integrity of India or bringing about cession of apart of the territory of India or secession of a part of the territory of India from the Union or causing insult to the Indian National Flag, the Indian National Anthem and the Constitution.

3. Where any provision of the Constitution of India had been applied to the State of Jammu and Kashmir with adaptations and modifications, such adaptations and modifications can be altered or repealed by an order of the President under Article 370, each individual proposal in this behalf being considered on its merits; but provisions of the Constitution of India already applied to the State of Jammu and Kashmir without adaptation or modification are unalterable.

4. With a view to assuring freedom to the State of Jammu and Kashmir to have its own legislation on matters like welfare measures, cultural matters, social security, personal law and procedural laws, in a manner suited to the special conditions in the State, it is agreed that

the State Government can review the laws made by Parliament or extended to the State after 1953 on any matter relatable to the Concurrent List and may decide which of them, in its opinion, needs amendment or repeal. Thereafter, appropriate steps may be taken under Article 254 of the Constitution of India. The grant of President's assent to such legislation would be sympathetically considered. The same approach would be adopted in regard to laws to be made by Parliament in future under the Proviso to clause 2 of the Article. The State Government shall be consulted regarding the application of any such law to the State and the views of the State Government shall receive the fullest consideration.

5. As an arrangement reciprocal to what has been provided under Article 368, a suitable modification of that Article as applied to the State should be made by Presidential order to the effect that no law made by the Legislature of the State of Jammu and Kashmir, seeking to make any change in or in the effect of any provision of Constitution of the State of Jammu and Kashmir relating to any of the undermentioned matters, shall take effect unless the Bill, having been reserved for the consideration of the President, receives his assent; the matters are–

(a) the appointment, powers, functions, duties, privileges and immunities of the Governor, and

(b) the following matters relating to Elections namely, the superintendence, direction and control of Elections by the Election Commission of India, eligibility for inclusion in the electoral rolls without discrimination, adult suffrage and composition of the Legislative Council, being matters specified in sections 138, 139, 140 and 50 of the Constitution of the State of Jammu and Kashmir.

6. No agreement was possible on the question of nomenclature of the Governor and the Chief Minister and the matter is therefore remitted to the Principals.

Mirza Mohammad Afzal Beg G. Parthasarathi
New Delhi, November 13, 1974

Appendix X

Article 370 of the Constitution of India

Temporary Provisions with respect of the State of Jammu and Kashmir

(1) Notwithstanding anything in this Constitution:

(a) the provisions of Article 238 shall not apply in relation to the State of Jammu and Kashmir;

(b) the power of Parliament to make laws for the said State shall be limited to

(i) those matters in the Union List and the Concurrent List which in consultation with the Government of the State, are declared by the President to correspond to matters specified in the Instrument of Accession governing the accession of the State to the Dominion of India as the matters with respect to which the Dominion Legislature may make laws for that State; and

(ii) such other matters in the said Lists as, with the concurrence of the Government of the State, the President may by order specify.

1. *Explanation:* For the purposes of this Article, the Government of the State means the person for the time being recognised by the President as the Maharaja of Jammu and Kashmir acting on the advice of the Council of Ministers for the time being in office under the Maharaja's Proclamation dated the fifth day of March, 1948.

(c) the provisions of Article (1) and of this Article shall apply in relation to this State;

(d) Such of the other provisions of this Constitution shall apply in relation to that State subject to such exceptions and modifications as the President may by order specify:

Provided that no such order which related to the matters specified in the Instrument of Accession of the State referred to in paragraph (i) of sub-clause (b) shall be issued except in consultation with the Government of the State; Provided further that no such order which relates to matters other than those referred to in the last preceding proviso shall be issued except with the concurrence of the Government.

(2) If the concurrence of the Government of the State referred to in paragraph (ii) of sub-clause (b) of clause (1) or in the second proviso to sub-clause (d) of that clause be given, before the Constituent Assembly for the purpose of framing the Constitution of the State is convened, it shall be placed before such Assembly for such decision as it may take thereon.

(3) Notwithstanding anything in the foregoing provisions of the Article, the President may, by public notification, declare that this Article shall cease to be operative or shall be operative only with such exceptions and modifications and from such date as he may notify.

Provided that the recommendation of the Constituent Assembly of the State referred to in clause (2) shall be necessary before the President issues such a notification.*

---

*In exercise of the powers conferred by Article 370 the President, on the recommendation of the Constituent Assembly of the State of Jammu and Kashmir, declared that as from the 11th day of November, 1952, the said Art. 370 shall be operative with the modification that for the Explanation in cl. (1) thereof, the following explanation is substituted namely:

"Explanation–For the purpose of this article, the Government of the State means the person for the time being recognized by the President on the recommendation of the Legislative Assembly of the State as the *Sadar-i-Riyasat* of Jammu and Kashmir, acting on the advice of the Council of Ministers of the State for the time being in office."

Appendix XI

Particulars of the extensions of provisions of Indian Constitution to the State of Jammu and Kashmir

Sl. No	*Year*	*Particulars*
1.	1954	Financial integration effected through 1954 Presidential Order. The operations of Customs, Central Excise, Civil Aviation, Posts & Telegraph extended.
2.	1958	All-India Services–IAS and IPS–were introduced. Functions of Comptroller & Auditor General extended.
3.	1959	The legislative entry relating to census was applied as a result of which the census of 1961 could for the first time be conducted under the Central law.
4.	1960	The Supreme Court was given the powers to give special leave to appeal from the decisions of the High Court of Jammu and Kashmir. The elections to either House and the resolution of doubts and disputes relating to them were placed under the supervision of the Election Commission of India, although they continued to be conducted according to the laws of the State Legislature.
5.	1961	The Legislative entry relating to industries, the control of which by the Union is declared by law to be expedient in public interest was applied to the State and it enabled the extension of the Industries (Development and Regulation) Act, 1951, subsequently.

6.	1964	Articles 356 and 357 of the Constitution were applied to the State.
7.	1965	A number of legislative entries relating to the welfare of labour, trade unions, social security and social insurance, etc., were applied. As a result of this a number of Central labour laws were extended.
8.	1966	The provisions of the Constitution relating to the direct election of the representatives to Lok Sabha were applied.
9.	1968	Entry 72 of the Union List was applied in a modified form in relation to the appeals to the Supreme Court from the decisions of the State High Court in election petitions.
10.	1969	Article 248 and entry 97 of the Union List (relating to residuary powers of Legislature) of the Constitution were applied in a modified form and as a consequence, the Unlawful Activities (Prevention) Act, 1967, was extended subsequently.
11.	1971	Article 226 which relates to the powers of the High Courts to issue certain writs was made applicable.
12.	1972	Entry 60 of the Union List (relating to the sanctioning of cinematograph films) was applied on 24th February 1972.
13.	1986	Article 249 extended.

Appendix XII

Particulars of the Bomb Explosions in Kashmir Valley from August 15, 1983 to July 2, 1984

Date	*Place of occurrence*
15th August 1983	Srinagar Stadium
30th August 1983	India Coffee House
18th November 1983	Compound of Justice Anand's house
12th December 1983	Detection of a crude time bomb in Paladium Cinema
29th March 1984	Andernag Nagbal, Anantnag
11th April 1984	Administrative Block and Iqbal Library, Kashmir University
22nd April 1984	House of Shri Neelkanth Ganjoo, (Retd. Sessions Judge)
26th April 1984	Old RTC Bus Stand, Sopore

It was only after I started pursuing these cases at personal level that investigations were taken up in right earnest and the ring leader of the 'disruptionists', Shri Shabir Ahmed Shah, and 16 others were arrested, and the following arms, ammunition and explosives recovered:

(i)	.32 Revolvers	5
(ii)	.32 Cartridges	41
(iii)	.22 Pistol	1
(iv)	.22 Cartridges	5
(v)	Gelatine rods	322
(vi)	Detonators	5
(vii)	Hand Grenade with fuse	1

There were a number of other cases which indicated the increase in the activities of the anti-national elements. For instance, on 13th October, 1983, the one-day International Cricket Match was disturbed and an attempt was made to dig out tile pitch. Pakistani national flags were hoisted and the members of the Indian team harassed.

A large number of Curmat camps were also organised. There was reasonable ground to believe that, under the cover of religious preaching, training in the use of arms was given in these camps.

Again, after the execution of Maqbool Butt, a large number of highly objectionable anti-Indian posters appeared at various places. Practically, no action was taken against the offenders.

In regard to the conduct of June 1983 elections by Dr. Farooq Abdullah's Ministry, the Election Commission had, inter-alia, made the following observations:

The State Government authorities had assured the Union Home Secretary who had been sent as the Commission's observer, that it would implement his advice to use mixed police drawn from the Border Security Force, Central Reserve Police and its own forces both for patrolling and polling stations duty on the day of polling. However, except in isolated cases, the State Government did not utilise a mix of the Border Security Force and Central Reserve Police Force available with them either on joint patrolling or for duties at the polling booths on election day. The chart put up in the Police Control Room was impressive, but on the ground the Central Forces were kept immobilised or engaged on static or patrol duties only on the election day thus denying to the weaker sections a sense of security which had been assured to them by the Election Commission. It is this lack of security and protection to the electorate especially on the polling day, that enabled certain sections to commit election irregularities in some places.

Appendix XIII

An interview, published by the veteran journalist, Mulkh Raj Saraf, immediately after the end of the Governor/President Rule (November 1986). It is contemporaneous, and gives a brief idea of the work done.*

For the second time in the history of J&K the Governor's Rule was promulgated on March 7, 1986, under section 92 of the State Constitution. In the very scheme of a democratic polity, it could not be a permanent feature and it ended on November 7 the same year. Actually it was replaced by the Constitution on the recommendation of the Governor himself after a six-month tenure. Jagmohan during his brief tenure did a lot of good work which was hailed by the people at large. Jagmohan spoke to us as follows.

Q. 1 Could you, Mr. Governor, spell out what were the policy objectives which you intended to achieve during the Governor's Rule?

Ans. At the very commencement of the Governor's Rule (March 7, 1986) I had made it clear that my endeavour would be to provide even-handed justice to all; to reform, reorganise and humanise the Administration, and to make it an effective and dynamic instrument of service to the poor, the sick and the needy; to safeguard and improve the ecology and environment of the State; to introduce reforms in the field of

*reproduced from Saraf's *Year Book* (1987).

education, public health, and to radically upgrade the quality of life, both in the rural and urban areas; and to promote tourism which is the back-bone of the State's economy.

Q. 2 It what way have you reformed, reorganised and humanised the Administration?

Ans. First, All India Services, like Indian Administrative Service, Indian Police Service and Indian Forest Service, have been restructured, their cadres rationalised and their general morale given a boost.

Secondly, to make the process of recruitment fair and just an independent statutory Subordinate Service Selection Board has been established to select meritorious candidates for all categories of jobs which do not fall within the purview of the Public Service Commission.

Thirdly, for dealing with quasi-judicial matters, in which discretion is involved, independent Tribunals have been set up.

Fourthly, a vigorous drive against corruption has been launched and a lot of dead wood chopped off to infuse new life in the services. 22 senior officers have so far been compulsorily retired.

Fifthly, a system of public interviews has been introduced to enable even the poorest and the most resourceless to have direct access to the highest authority. This system not only helps in prompt disposal of public grievances but also acts as a "cat-scan" for the entire administrative machinery. It enables me to see clearly as to what is happening at different levels of the Administration. Under this system, I have so far met about 22,000 persons from different walks of life. This has made the entire machinery active, alert and responsive to the public needs and humanised it.

Q.3 What action have you taken on the Environmental front?

Ans. Top priority has been given to the cleaning of the Dal Lake. So far, 5500 metric tonnes of weed have been removed–3500 metric tonnes by indigenous doongas and 200 metric tonnes by using deweeding harvesters.

A massive dredger has also been fabricated, and this is dredging sill from the bed of the lake at the rate of about

20,000 cubic feet per day. This is equivalent to about 200 truck-loads of silt. So far, about 10 lakh cubic feet silt has been removed. In the current operation, 2 crore cubic feet of silt will be dredged, and this will clear depth of water upto 6 feet in areas where depth is only 6".

A special feature of this dredging is that the silt extracted from the bed is being used to reclaim the land lying between Shalimar Garden and the lake, and an extension of this garden will be developed on the reclaimed area. Thus, the Shalimar Garden will extend right upto the lake, thereby adding new lustre and charm to the entire environment around.

Another notable action taken on the environmental front is the establishment of the Srinagar City Forest which covers about 900 hectares of land including the slopes of Shankaracharya Hill, Zeathyar, Pari Mahal, Ziarat Syeed Mir Azam Saheb, etc. It will have four major zones–city forest zone; deer park zone; water fowl zone; and wilderness zone; including Conservation Training Centre for the children and students.

Three lakh trees are being planted this year, and under the overall scheme, 40 lakh trees will be planted. This will, besides providing a beautiful city forest, save the lake from the flow of nutrient and mud from the catchment area.

Likewise, in Jammu, a beautiful Tawi River Front is being developed and Mahamaya City Forest established.

To improve the overall environment, over five and a half crore trees are being planted in the State this year.

Q.4 What special work has been done in the field of Education?

Ans. I can most humbly claim that the State is currently witnessing something like an educational revolution. 1700 new school buildings, at the cost of about Rs. 15 crores, are fast coming up in the rural areas. 14 Model Schools, costing about Rs. 28 crores, are being established. Scores of existing schools have been upgraded, four new colleges and two Women Polytechnics set up.

Q.5 There has been some controversy in regard to your decision to ban private practice by the Government doctors. What have you to say about it?

Ans. Ban on private practice is another act of fundamental reform which will enable the poor, particularly those living in backward and far-flung areas, to secure really free medical service.

Let me make it clear that I am not against private practice. I am only against combination of public duty and private practice. This combination lends to various kinds of malpractices. It has, therefore, been abolished. Simultaneously, a number of incentives have been provided to the doctors, such as Non-practising Allowance 20% of pay, Special Incentive Allowance for the rural areas and increased stipend. Along with it, 15 Primary Health Centres, 152 Sub-Centres and 15 Evening Clinics have been set up.

A more significant step that has been taken in this regard is to substantially augment the supply of pure water, both in the urban and rural areas. In our State, most of the people suffer from water borne diseases. If supply of pure water is assured, sickness will be reduced and rush on hospitals and dispensaries will abate.

Q.6 What has been done to augment pure water supply?

Ans. This is another field in which new grounds have been broken and innovative techniques employed: Against about 40 villages, which were covered by rural water supply scheme during the last year, 170 villages have been provided with pure water supply during the first seven months of the current year. Special drilling machines have been installed to dig tube-wells and build under-ground water bank to supply potable water to the villages where none exists. In the urban areas, specially in the Srinagar city, this year, pure water supply has been considerably augmented by commissioning a number of new projects including Patshahi Bagh Water Treatment Plant, Ishber Tube-well, Nishat Water Treatment Plant and creating 6 lakh gallons per day capacity through underground water bank in Zainakote.

Q.7 It is sometimes said that not as much has been done in the rural areas as in the urban areas?

Ans. The truth is that much more is being done in the rural areas than in the urban areas. All the 1700 new school buildings, all the 14 Model Schools, all the 15 Primary Health Centres and 152 Sub-Centres are being put up in the rural areas. About 75% of the roads under improvement are in the rural areas. In the field of rural employment, it is unprecedented that even in a small State like ours, about 100 lakh man-days of employment are being created under National Rural Employment Programme and Rural Landless Employment Guarantee Programme. In regard to about 50% items pertaining to 20-Point Programme, which is basically a rural development and anti-poverty programme, our achievements have exceeded the targets, though only 7 months of the year have passed. By the year end we are confident of exceeding the targets in all the items of the 20-Point Programme. Prior to March 1986, the performance of the State Government in regard to the implementation of the 20-Point Programme has been one of the poorest in the country. In the background, the current achievement in the sphere of rural development must be reckoned as spectacular. We are also on the threshold of substantially extending the scope of the scheme for the welfare of the Scheduled Castes, Gujjars and Bakerwals and other weaker sections.

Q.8 What has been done to promote Tourism?

Ans. We are likely to have record number of tourists this season. Five and half lakhs of tourists have already visited the Valley. This is largely due to the vigorous steps taken to provide infrastructural facilities and to clean up the cities and tourist spots. A special drive has been launched to upgrade the civic life, construct roads through new technology and equip Municipal authorities with proper machines for removal of garbage, etc. A drive on the boulevard, along the Dal Lake or Maulana Azad Road is now a delight to experience. The tourist spots like Gulmarg, Pahalgam and Sonamarg have also been cleaned and improved. So are the places of cultural importance like Charisharief and Katra.

Q.9 Has anything been done in the field of social and cultural reforms?

Ans. I think, a lot has been done. For management of the Vaishno Devi Shrine, an entire area spreading from Katra to the

Bhavan, has been entrusted to an independent statutory Board, and radical improvements have been effected in the environment around in a short time. New roads and pony tracks have been laid and facilities for water, sewerage, electricity and other public conveniences, including medical treatment and resting places provided. The entire complex of the Shrine is being replanned and redeveloped.

An extremely significant project that is being undertaken is revival of Lalitaditya capital at Parihaspura. A large cultural complex, with due regard to its heritage, is planned to be established at the historical site. The Task Force comprising experts in different disciplines has been set up under my chairmanship to give a push to the project.

An artists village will be established at the aforesaid site or the site near Botanical Garden.

The Cultural Academy is also being reorganised. The Institute of Music and Fine Arts is being made apart of the Kashmir University and a new scheme to encourage and propagate different facets of Jammu, Kashmir and Ladakh culture is under consideration. An Open-Air Theatre is also proposed to be developed in Jammu.

Q.10 Lastly, what about the law and order problem?

Ans. The current atmosphere by and large is peaceful. The subversive elements stand isolated. Contrary to the impression created by propagandist and motivated stories, there are only 5 persons who have been detained under the Public Safety Act under the current drive against disruptionists. I have no doubt that overwhelming majority of the masses do not want that the unprecedented pace-of development generated in the recent times should be obstructed by a handful of trouble-makers. The various development programmes initiated are of special help to the poor, the sick and the needy and our endeavour would be to further extend these programmes so that the neglected sections of the society get their due share in the fruits of development.

Appendix XIV

Farooq Abdullah's written statement to the press (February 15, 1990)

J&K NATIONAL CONFERENCE

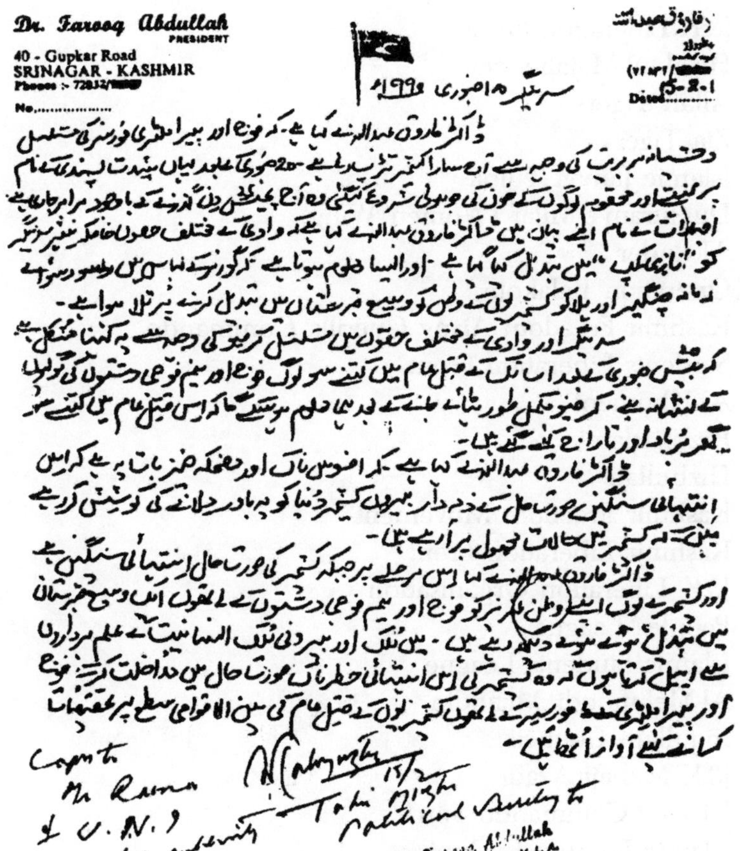

Dr. Farooq Abdullah
PRESIDENT

40 - Gupkar Road
SRINAGAR - KASHMIR
Phones :- 72832/

No.....................

Dated 15-2-1

سرینگر ۱۵ فروری ۱۹۹۰ء

ڈاکٹر فاروق عبداللہ نے کہا ہے کہ فوج اور نیم ملٹری فورسز کی مسلسل وحشیانہ بربریت کی وجہ سے آج سارا کشمیر تڑپ رہا ہے۔ ۲۰ جنوری کا [illegible] کے نام پر معصوم اور مظلوم لوگوں کے خون کی جو ہولی شروع کی گئی وہ آج پچیس دن گزرنے کے باوجود برابر جاری ہے۔ اخبارات کے نام اپنے بیان میں ڈاکٹر فاروق عبداللہ نے کہا ہے کہ وادی کے مختلف علاقوں خاص کر شہر سرینگر کو "نازی کیمپ" میں تبدیل کیا گیا ہے۔ اور ایسا معلوم ہوتا ہے کہ گورنر نے تاریخ کے رسوائے زمانہ چنگیز اور ہلاکو کی طرح لوگوں کے وطن کو وسیع قبرستان میں تبدیل کرنے پر تلا ہوا ہے۔

سرینگر اور وادی کے مختلف علاقوں میں مسلسل کرفیو کی وجہ سے یہ کہنا مشکل ہے کہ پچھلے جنوری کے بعد اب تک کے قتل عام میں کتنے سو لوگ فوج اور نیم فوجی دستوں کی گولیوں کے نشانہ بنے۔ کرفیو مکمل طور ہٹائے جانے کے بعد ہی معلوم ہو سکے گا کہ اس قتل عام میں کتنے سو گھر برباد اور تاراج کئے گئے ہیں۔

ڈاکٹر فاروق عبداللہ نے کہا ہے کہ افسوسناک اور مضحکہ خیز بات یہ ہے کہ اس انتہائی سنگین صورتحال کے ذمہ دار بیرون کشمیر دنیا کو یہ باور دلانے کی کوشش کر رہے ہیں کہ کشمیر میں حالات معمول پر آرہے ہیں۔

ڈاکٹر فاروق عبداللہ نے کہا اس مرحلے پر جبکہ کشمیر کی صورتحال انتہائی سنگین ہے اور کشمیر کے لوگ اپنے وطن عزیز کو فوج اور نیم فوجی دستوں کے بقول ایک وسیع قبرستان میں تبدیل ہوتے ہوئے دیکھ رہے ہیں۔ میں ملک اور بیرون ملک انسانیت کے علمبرداروں سے اپیل کرتا ہوں کہ وہ کشمیر کی اس انتہائی خطرناک صورتحال میں مداخلت کریں۔ فوج اور نیم ملٹری فورسز کے ہاتھوں کشمیری لوگوں کے قتل عام کی بین الاقوامی سطح پر تحقیقات کرانے کے لئے آواز اٹھائیں۔

Copy to
Mr Rama
& U.N.I
for authenticity

[signature] 15/2

Tahir [illegible]
Political Secretary to
Dr. Farooq Abdullah M.L.A.

Appendix XV

List of the Terrorist Organisations operating in the Kashmir Valley before my arrival on the scene (January 19,1990)

1. J&K Liberation Front
2. Hizab-ul-Majahedeen
3. Allah Tigers
4. Zia Tigers
5. Islamic Jamait Tulba
6. Dukhtram-e-Milat (Women Wing)
7. Al Bader
8. Operation Balakote
9. Kashmir Freedom Army Guerilla Commando
10. Students Liberation Front
11. Al-Khomeni
12. Hizbi Islami
13. Hizbullah
14. Kashmir Freedom Movement
15. Kashmir Liberation Front
16. J&K Liberation Organisation
17. Peoples League
18. Islamic Students League
19. Al-Mehmoodi Mijahdin
20. Inqullabi Council
21. J&K Mahaji Azadi
22. Victory Commando Force
23. Islamic Jamurie Kashmir

24. J&K Inquilabi Front
25. Kashmir Students Force
26. Peoples Liberation Organisation
27. Tehrike-Jahad
28. All J&K Soldiers Field Front
29. Hizab-Ullah-Islamic-Jammohuria J&K
30. Free Army
31. Ikhwan-ul-Musalmeen
32. Kashmir Liberation Tiger
33. Peoples Front
34. Hiz-ul-Zaheed .
35. National Muslim United Front
36. Al Hamzah
37. Ansor-ul-Islam
38. Muslim Student Front
39. Tehriqe Azadi
40. Jinnah Liberation Tiger
41. Kashmir Freedom KLF Wing
42. K.V.C.
43. T.F.
44. Al Qarblaie Group

Appendix XVI

Excerpts from My Interview with 'India Today'

"DISSOLVE THE ASSEMBLY"

JAGMOHAN has over the years developed the reputation of being a trouble-shooter. True to form, even at the very epicentre of the Jammu and Kashmir crisis, he remains composed and confident. Executive Editor INDERJIT BADHWAR *spoke to him in Srinagar. Excerpts:*

Q. *Farooq Abdullah is objecting to your appointment primarily on the ground thatyou had dismissed him on July 2, 1984.*

A. I am amazed at his stand. Farooq knows very well that, even on July 2, 1984, I had recommended the imposition of Governor's rule, and not the installation of the G.M. Shah ministry.

Q. What about the controversy over the search conducted in the early morning of January 20, 1990?

A. I was sworn in at Jammu in the evening of January 19, 1990, and the search took place in Srinagar in the early morning of January 20. Clearly, the decision was taken before I took over.

Q. *Do you think there was a conspiracy against you in regard to this search?*

A. It was a case of sheer political and administrative bungling and non-application of mind, so characteristic of the previous regime. I have already ordered an administrative inquiry into it.

Q. *Are searches and raids now being organised daily under your orders and personal supervision?*

A. I would do everything permitted by law to break the iron bars of the cage of terrorism.

Q. What about casualties?

A. Unfortunately, a section of the media, particularly the foreign media, has highly exaggerated the casualty figures. Actual casualties are less than 50. We propose to publish a list of casualties and then ask those who have given the exaggerated figures to supply full particulars. For me, whether A loses his life or B, it is the blood of all of us that spills. We must stop all this.

Q. Would you like to comment on the criticism about your appointment?

A. I have accepted the assignment solely with the motivation of lending a helping hand in overcoming a national crisis. I have exposed myself and my family to grave personal risk. I am not even drawing my pay. I have a broken and shattered administrative machinery at my disposal. If the commander is sniped at every day, the chances of success could well be imagined.

Q. *What is your basic approach to solving the crisis?*

A. The best way of solving the crisis is to assert the authority of the State and create an impression that, no matter what the cost, the subversionists and their collaborators will be firmly dealt with and eliminated. Also, it is important to adopt an absolutely just and fair approach to the people.

Q. *What about a political solution?*

A. First, we need a grace period to restore people's confidence by giving them an important freedom—freedom from corruption arid exploitation. I also recommend the State Assembly be dissolved and fresh elections be held after six months or so. By that time some of the subversive elements would be eliminated and some would prefer to give up the path of violence and participate in elections. A new leadership may emerge which would perceive the advantage of working within the Indian Constitution, the cornerstone of which is justice—political, social and economic.

Appendix XVII

Brief-particulars of cases registered on complaints and allegations during the period January 19 to May 26, 1990

Sl. No.	*Registration no. and Police Station*	*Nature of complaint/allegation*
1.	9/90 P.S. Ram Munshibagh	BSF personnel allegedly fired indiscriminately in Sonwar Bazar.
2.	23/90 P.S. Saddar	Indian Air Force personnel allegedly set a vehicle and a shop on fire.
3.	10/90 P.S. Maharaj Gunj	B Coy of 53 CRPF allegedly tresspassed into houses.
4.	10/90 P.S. Maharaj Gunj	CRPF personnel allegedly injured nimazees entering the shrine.
5.	12/90 P.S. Parimpora	One Army jawan allegedly beat the complainant Rashid Khan and snatched some cash.
6.	31/90 P.S. Saddar	BSF personnel allegedly beat some people.
7.	29/90 P.S. Maharaj Gunj	BSF 79 Bn. personnel allegedly opened fire indiscriminately.
8.	29/90 P.S. Shaheed Gunj	BSF personnel allegedly opened fire.
9.	67/90 P.S. Shergarhi	Army personnel allegedly fired upon civilian bus.
10.	34/90 P.S. Maharaj Gunj	CRPF 79 Bn. allegedly entered the shrine, injured the nimazees and caused damage to shrine.

11.	34/90 P.S. Maharaj Gunj	CRPF 67 Bn. personnel allegedly tress-passed into houses and caused injuries.
12.	45/90 P.S. Saddar	BSF personnel allegedly tresspassed into the house of Mohd. Farooq Rather.
13.	45/90 P.S. Saddar	CRPF personnel allegedly looted ornaments and cash and outraged.
14.	45/90 P.S. Maharaj Gunj	Case of cross-fire.
15.	24/90 P.S. Nowhatta	CRPF jawans allegedly entered the house of Mohd. Yunis and injured the inhabitants.
16.	34/90	CRPF personnel allegedly entered the house of Mohd. Unis Fazil forcibly.
17.	92/90 P.S. Saddar	Abdul Razak allegedly died during investigations by security forces.
18.	96/90 P.S. Shergarhi	Army personnel allegedly stole two golden rings and some cash from the house of Raja wife of Abdul Wahab during search operations.
19.	31/90 P.S. Karan Nagar	BSF personnel allegedly pelted stones at the house of Rtd. SI Jodh Singh resulting in damage to property.
20.	49/90 P.S. Maharaj Gunj	Alleged tresspass and molestation by security forces.
21.	49/90 P.S.	Army personnel allegedly stole Rs. 2000 from the house of Gh. Mohd. Sofi during search operation.
22.	68/90 P.S. Kulgam	Alleged death of a civilian in custody.
23.	51/90 P.S. Dooru	Alleged cross firing and rape.
24.	35/90 P.S. Nowhatta	CRPF personnel allegedly fired on a procession near Islamia College.

Appendix XVIII

Extracts from the Author's Suit

In the extracts, the plaintiff means the author, and defendant No. 1 refers to Inder Mohan. Annexure III means my book Island of Truth, *Annexure IV the* Sunday Magazine, *Annexure IV-A excerpts from my book and Annexure V-A means the impugned writing of Inder Mohan.*

The plaintiff give below fifteen (15) illustrations to demonstrate how grievously mental injury and pain has been caused to the plaintiff, and how the defendants, particularly defendant No. 1, have adopted a browbeating, bullying, arrogant, malevolent posture, and used highly derogatory and defamatory expressions, notwithstanding the fact that defendant No. 1 has made palpably false statement/assertions/reassertions.

(a) *Turkman Gate Incident*

In a write-up in *Seminar* (June 1977), Inder Mohan deliberately gave a false figure of 300 dead in Turkman Gate incident, that is, 50 times the actual number.

In the 'rejoinder' (Annexure V-A), Shri Inder Mohan, defendant No. 1, stated:

> All those concerned with such matters are convinced that the official figure of only six dead is a flagrant misrepresentation of facts. There is every reason for me to stick to the figures which have been quoted *on my behalf in a couple of publications.*

The defendant No. 1, thus, sticks to the figure of 300 dead as given by him in *Seminar*. The plaintiff submits that this assertion/reassertionis false. The falsehood of this assertion/reassertion would become self-evident if the defendant No. 1 is asked to submit his list of 300 dead persons, together with their names and addresses. The total number of slum houses cleared in the Turkman Gate area was about 120. The assertion/reassertion of the defendant No. 1 implies that two to three persons, on an average, died from each house. The plaintiff had given the names and addresses of the six persons (page 147 of the book–Annexure III) who lost their lives in the riots, and also indicated that, except for one person who came from the Turkman Gate area and where property was not affected by the clearance drive, all others were outsiders from Suinwala and Jama Masjid area, etc. (In this connection, the plaintiff would like to make it clear that he had nothing to do with firing, etc. That was the concern of the District Magistrate/Police, etc. The purpose of the plaintiff is to demonstrate the flasehood of the defendant No. 1's assertion/reassertion.)

(b) *Kalan Mahal*

In the book (Annexure III)/extract (Annexure IV-A), the plaintiff wrote:

> He (Shri Inder Mohan, defendant No. 1) also accused me falsely of demolishing Kalan Mahal supposedly a historic building where Shahjahan is rumoured to have stayed. The building was not a protected monument. It was in total ruin, and in occupation of squatters. It was acquired in 1965 by the Directorate of Education, Delhi Administration, for construction of two new school buildings at the site. The prejudice of Inder Mohan impelled him to accuse me even for the decision which the Delhi Administration took as far back as 1965.

In the 'rejoinder' (Annexure V-A), Shri Inder Mohan, defendant No. 1, stated:

> Jagmohan was not falsely accused of pulling down the invaluable portion of historic and ancient Kalan Mahal. Kalan Mahal should have been preserved and improved upon. In such matters a man has to have basic sensitivity and aesthetic interest. Jagmohan had neither.

The plaintiff submits that the defendant No. 1 again makes a false assertion/reassertion. This would be evident from the acquisition notification of the Delhi Administration and the award drawn by the Land Acquisition Collector (Award No. 1743, dated 24th October 1964. A sum of Rs. 2,34,382 was paid from the budgetory allocation of the Directorate of Education/PWD/Delhi Administration in July 1965). The defendant No. 1, in fact, adds insult to injury by casting false, malicious, unwarranted aspersions on the plaintiffs 'basic sensitivity' and 'aesthetic interest'.

(c) *'Painwala Estimate'*

In the book (Annexure III)/extracts (Annexure IV-A), the plaintiff wrote:

> Inder Mohan has tried to link me and Sanjay Gandhi to the Jama Masjid clearance plan by referring to the estimate of Rs. 1.80 crore for construction of a shopping complex in Painwala. The facts are that no project with any architectural and engineering drawing and other details had been formulated. The question of preparing any financial estimate, without any basic drawing and data, could never arise.

In the 'rejoinder' (Annexure V-A), Shri Inder Mohan, defendant No. 1, stated:

> Jagmohan knows that Painwala scheme had been finalised but given up because of strong opposition of shopkeepers.

The plaintiff submits that the falsehood of the defendant No. 1 would become self-evident if he is asked to produce or refer to the D.D.A.'s architectural and engineering drawing and other necessary details on which the financial estimate of Rs. 1.80 crore was made. The defendant No. 1 has coined the figure of Rs. 1.80 crore to lend credence to his false story of meeting the plaintiff and the plaintiff quoting the figure of Rs. 1.80 crore. In absence of any D.D.A.'s engineering/financial estimate, the question of the plaintiff giving the figure of Rs. 1.80 crore could not arise.

(d) *Vikas Minar Meeting*

In the book (Annexure III)/extracts (Annexure IV-A), the plaintiff wrote:

> The extent to which imaginary stories have been coined by Inder Mohan, and used by Uma Vasudeva, would be evident from her reference to Inder Mohan's meeting with me on September 19, 1975, in my 'spacious office'on the eighteenth floor of Vikas Minar.

She did not know that the D.D.A.'s office shifted to Vikas Minar in July 1976, that is, about nine months after Inder Mohan's alleged meeting with me. Even after shifting to Vikas Minar, my office was on the fifth floor. Inder Mohan obviously relied too much on his imagination.

In the 'rejoinder' (Annexure V-A), Shri Inder Mohan, defendant No. 1, stated:

> Jagmohan's jugglery regarding Vikas Minar and Vikas Bhavan cannot belie the fact that I had definitely met him on September 19, 1975 (at that time the office was a part of Vikas Bhavan).

The plaintiff submits that, according to the defendant No. 1's earlier version (given to Mrs. Uma Vasudeva), he met the plaintiff in the D.D.A.'s eighteen-floor building, Vikas Minar. In the second version quoted above, he changes the venue of the so-called 'meeting' to Vikas Bhavan and accuses the plaintiff of jugglery in regard to Vikas Bhavan and Vikas Minar. In this connection, the plaintiff submits that there could be no question of 'D.D.A.'s eighteen-floor building' with regard to Vikas Bhavan which had only five floors. The falsehood of the defendant No. 1's assertion/reassertion is self-evident. 'The plaintiff was 'Vice-Chairman' of Delhi Development Authority, and was not concerned with anybody's arrest or release, the matters in respect of which were the exclusive concern of the District Magistrate and Police authorities.

(e) *Short-term Assignment*

In the book (Annexure III)/extract (Annexure IV-A), the plaintiff wrote:

> "He, Inder Mohan, defendant No. 1, even persuaded me to give a short-term job in the D.D.A."

In the 'rejoinder' (Annexure V-A), Shri Inder Mohan, defendant No. 1, stated:

> "His (plaintiffs) assertion that I persuaded him to give me a short-term job is another blatant lie... I neither needed another job nor had any time for it."

The plaintiff submits that the falsehood of the defendant No. 1's assertion would be evident from the D.D.A.'s records in regard to payment received by the defendant No. 1.

The defendant No. 1 also imputed in Annexure V-A: "I soon discovered that Jagmohan had a communal mind and could undo any politician in double talk. I immediately withdrew myself." The falsehood and afterthought of this assertion is clear from the fact that the defendant had reviewed the plaintiff's book in the *I.I.C. Quarterly,* Volume No. 2, Number 2, of April 1975 (Annexure VI); in which he had commended the plaintiff's suggestions in regard to Rebuilding Shahjehanabad and removal of the social deprivation of the minority community. If defendant No. 1 had withdrawn from the plaintiff's thoughts and ideas in 1972, how could he commend his proposals in regard to the setting up of Second Shahjehanabad/Rebuilding Shahjehanabad in April, 1975? In fact, the plaintiff's book, *Rebuilding Shahjehanabad* (Annexure II) is nothing but an impassioned plea for the revival of healthy features of the old Mughal and Muslim culture.

(f) *Post of P.R.*O.

In the 'rejoinder' (Annexure V-A), Shri Inder Mohan, defendant No. 1, also asserted:

> I may mention in this context that as late as February 1975 when, according to Jagmohan, my bona fides were under doubt, he had offered me the post of a P.R.O. for D.D.A. I declined the offer.

The plaintiff submits that this is another imaginary, false, statement of the defendant No. 1. The D.D.A. had already a permanent and regular P.R.O., namely, Shri Tej B. Kumar (and still has the same officer). It is a matter of common knowledge that a public organisation like the D.D.A. cannot fill any post like that of P.R.O. without advertisement in the press or through a requisition on employment exchange. There was no financial sanction for the 'post' supposedly offered to the defendant No. 1. The Vice-Chairman was not competent to create such a 'post'. Nor could there be any question of recruiting a person of defendant No. l's age in Government or semi-Government organization.

(g) *Munirka Land etc.*

In the 'rejoinder' (Annexure V-A), Shri Inder Mohan, defendant No. 1, asserted:

> As regards the Munirka village land, the fact is D.D.A. made huge profits by acquiring it at throw-away prices and reselling it at a price which was more than one hundred times the original one. That is

> how posh colonies such as Vasant Vihar were set up. Anyone can get proof of this from the affected villagers who were duped, exploited and left high and dry.

This assertion is in relation to what the plaintiff had written in paras 10 and 11 of the extracts (Annexure IV-A). In this connection, the plaintiff submits that the actual facts are that undeveloped land as acquired by paying compensation determined by the courts, under the law of the land, on the basis of market' value prevailing at the time of notification, and two-bedroom flats, with separate living and dining room, kitchen, bath, lounge and verandah were allotted in the first phase to the individuals in the middle income group etc. at prices ranging from Rs. 40,000 to Rs. 45,000. This included the cost of development of land, provision of municipal services, and community facilities like parks and school sites, and construction of the flat itself. The disposal of flats was almost on no-profit no-loss basis. Moreover, the lands are acquired by the Delhi Administration for the planned development of Delhi, and thereafter placed at the disposal of the D.D.A. In computing the cost of its projects like the Munirka housing, the D.D.A. does not charge more than what it has to pay' to the Delhi Administration for the lands. In view of these facts, the question of 'D.D.A. making huge profits by acquiring the Munirka land at throw-away prices and re-selling it at price which was more than one hundred times the original one, and duping and exploiting the villagers', does not arise.

The assertion of the defendant No. 1: "that is how posh, colonies such as Vasant Vihar were set up", is also false. The correct position in this regard is that undeveloped lands were allotted to the house-building cooperative societies by the Delhi Administration in accordance with the decision of the Union Cabinet taken in early 1961. The orders of the Central Government in this respect are contained in the Home Ministry's letter No. 37/16/60-Delhi (i) dated May 2, 1961. The cooperative housing societies, like Government servants cooperative housing society (which developed Shanti Niketan and Vasant Vihar), were allotted land under the aforesaid order. Undeveloped lands were leased to the societies, for the purpose of development, after charging the cost of acquisition of land, as determined by the courts, plus a small additional charge prescribed under the aforesaid Government orders. The cost of development was to be met by the members of the housing societies directly.

In the context of these facts, the question of duping, exploiting and leaving anyone high and dry, and setting up posh colonies, could not arise.

(h) *Squatters' Death*

In the book (Annexure III)/extracts (Annexure IV-A) the plaintiff wrote:

> Nankekar also made some reckless statements. Without giving any details, he says, 'Hundreds of them (squatters) fell sick and died.' I can assert with confidence, and on the basis of records, that not a single person died due to shifting. From the comparison of the conditions prevailing in the pre-resettlement sites and the resettlement colonies, it would be clear even to the most prejudicial observer that the environments of the latter were far more conducive to healthy living than those of the former.

In the'rejoinder' (Annexure V-A), Shri Inder Mohan, defendant No. 1, stated:

> He (plaintiff) has the cheek to say that not a single person died due to shifting of 'squatters'. This is another of his fantastic lies."

The plaintiff submits that the falsehood of the defendant No. 1's assertion/reassertion would become self-evident if he is asked to furnish a list of persons, with addresses and other particulars, who died due to shifting of squatters.

(i) *'Wanton Destruction'*

In the 'rejoinder' (Annexure V-A), Shri Inder Mohan, defendant No. 1, stated/imputed:

> All the wanton destruction of human lives and properties that took place during those dark days as a consequence of bulldozing of property and forcible removal of people to far-away slums should weigh heavily on the conscience of Jagmohan–provided he has a conscience.

The correct position in this regard has been explained in the plaintiff's book (Annexure III), particularly in Chapters III, IV and V. Briefly, the position is:

i. It is incorrect to call the D.D.A.'s operations during the emergency as demolition operations;

ii. The programme was confined to removal of encroachments, illegal constructions and relocation of slums and squatters' settlements at the appropriate sites;
iii. The schemes of squatters' settlement and slum clearance were sanctioned much before the emergency and no fresh element, either by way of procedure or policy, was introduced during the emergency, except by way of liberalisation.
iv. The Union Cabinet, the Parliament and its Public Accounts Committee and Consultative Committee, the Planning Commission, and the Delhi Metropolitan Council–all approved and applauded the schemes, and the D.D.A. did nothing that was not in accordance with the approved policy and precedents.

As regards the plaintiff's motivation and connected issues, para 4 (p. 12), paras 1 and 2 (p. 13), para 4 (p. 14), para 1 (p. 15), paras 1 and 2 (p. 16), and para 3 (pp. 70-71) are relevant and need to be considered.

In view of these facts, the falsehood of the defendant No. 1's assertion in respect of "wanton destruction of human lives and properties etc." is quite clear.

(j) *'Mainstream' article*

In the book (Annexure III)/(Annexure IV-A) the plaintiff wrote:

> Taking advantage of the vitiated atmosphere and knowing full well that I had no access to the press to refute his false and frivolous allegations, Inder Mohan published a highly scurrilous article against me in *Mainstream.* The ostensible objective was to create prejudice against me in the minds of persons in authority,

In the 'rejoinder' (Annexure V), Shri Inder Mohan, defendant No. 1, asserted:

> I stand by, and own, every word of the article that had appeared in my name, under the caption: 'Jagmohan the Acrobat', in the issue of the *Mainstream* dated July 30, 1977. The article was written, with full sense of responsibility.

The aforesaid *Mainstream* article is added as Annexure VII. The following facts would show that this article (Annexure VII) is full of false statements, intentionally and knowingly made by defendant No. 1 to defame the plaintiff and cause *him acute mental pain and injury.*

(i) In the aforesaid *Mainstream* article (Annexure VII), the defendant No. 1 wrote:

> The father of the present Mayor is also reported to be throwing pressures in Jagmohan's favour. This is in return of a good turn done by Jagmohan some years ago. Hans Raj Gupta was given all the facilities by the D.D.A. to build a multi-storey commercial structure on a place of land near Basti Narnol, adjacent to Ajmeri Gate. This brought huge income to Gupta. The entire area was in fact earmarked for residential purposes under the Delhi Ajmeri Gate Scheme.

The plaintiff submits that this imputation is false. The area in question was covered by the Delhi Ajmeri Gate Slum Clearance Scheme. The Administration of the Slum Areas (Improvement and Clearance) Act, 1956, was, at the relevant time, the responsibility of the Delhi Municipal Corporation. In this connection, the plaintiff invites attention to the Lok Sabha Question No. 4606 answered by the Minister of Works and Housing, on April 22, 1974. A copy of the Question/Answer is added as Annexure VIII. It would be noticed that the D.D.A. or the plaintiff had nothing to do with the building plan or development of the land in question. The building plans for construction of the double-storeyed commercial building, known as "Raghushri Market" at Ajmeri Gate, were sanctioned by the Commissioner, Municipal Corporation of Delhi, on April 20 1971. And since the property was included in the slum area, the ad-hoc (Slum Clearance and Improvement) Committee of the M.C.D. permitted the owners of the property to re-develop it in accordance with the re-development scheme of the area. Under Section 53(1) of the Delhi Development Act, the provisions of the Act do not affect the operation of the Slum Areas (Improvement and Clearance) Act, 1956. Section 53(1) of D.D. Act, 1957, reads: "Nothing in this Act shall affect the operation of Slum Areas (Improvement and Clearance) Act, 1956."

(iii) In the aforesaid *Mainstream* article (Annexure VII), Shri Inder Mohan, defendant No. 1, wrote:

> So far Jagmohan never affixed his caste with his name. He is Malhotra; now it has come handy to him. One of his relatives, a political heavyweight in Delhi and of his own caste–Vijay Kumar Malhotra–is reported to be backing him.

The plaintiff submits that this assertion is absolutely false. The plaintiff is not in any way related to Shri Vijay Kumar Malhotra.

(iii) In the aforesaid *Mainstream* article (Annexure VII) Shri Inder Mohan, defendant No. 1, also wrote:

> He (Jagmohan) was favoured by the former Lt.-Governor of Delhi, the Late A.N. Jha, and was given the coveted post (of Vice-Chairman).

The plaintiff submits, that this is another false and mala fide statement. The actual position is that appointment to the post of Vice-Chairman is made by the Central Government, and this is done by the Appointment Committee of the Cabinet. Both the Secretary, Ministry of Works and Housing, and the Cabinet Secretary had recommended the plaintiff for appointment as Vice-Chairman, D.D.A. The Appointment Committee of the Cabinet, comprising Prime Minister, Home Minister and Works and Housing Minister, gave its approval. Therefore, the appointment of the plaintiff as Vice-Chairman, D.D.A. was notified by the Central Government, and he took charge of the post with effect from January 7, 1971. His appointment was continued from time to time by the Appointment Committee of the Cabinet, on the recommendations of the Cabinet Secretary. Prior to his appointment as Vice-Chairman (w.e.f. January 7, 1971), the plaintiff held a senior post of Commissioner (Implementation), Master Plan. Earlier, in the year 1964-65, the plaintiff was selected for advance training under the 'Reflective Training Programme for the Indian Administrators' organised by the Indian Institute of Public Administration/Ford Foundation. Under this programme, the plaintiff visited various countries, including U.K., U.S.A., Japan, Yugoslavia, etc. In the year 1965, the plaintiff was appointed as a special officer to reorganize the working of the D.D.A. On January 26, 1971, the plaintiff was awarded Padma Shri by the President of India of what his citation described as "Significant contribution in the formulation and implementation of Delhi Master Plan, for playing a pioneering role in planning and implementation of development projects, and for breaking new grounds in the matter of slum clearance."

The above facts show the extent to which defendant No. 1 has gone in defaming and maligning the plaintiff and causing him mental pain and injury. In his mala fide objective of defaming and degrading the plaintiff, the defendant No. 1 has not hesitated to cast aspersions on the Lt.-Governor, Late Dr. A.N. Jha, who died in January 1972.

(iv) In the aforesaid *Mainstream* article (Annexure VII) Shri Inder Mohan, defendant No. 1, wrote:

> What is Jagmohan's qualification to entitle him to function as a research scholar of such an institute? (the Institute of Urban Affairs).

This is another tendentious statement which reflects the mala fide intention of the defendant No. 1 to harm the plaintiff. In this connection, the plaintiff submits that the proposals to appoint the plaintiff as Research Fellow was considered by the Governing Council of the National Institute of Urban Affairs in its meeting held on June 12, 1977, and the minutes of the meeting contain, inter alia, the following:

> While the study/project should go as a document of the Institute and may require guidance of an expert group, a full-time senior researcher with necessary expertise and vision is required to take the responsibility for steering the project through. It was unanimously agreed that Shri Jagmohan has the required expertise to undertake the work... It was noted that the Ministry of Works and Housing were agreeable to the proposal, but since Shri Jagmohan is a permanent employee of the D.D.A., the President may write to the L.G. in this connection.

The said meeting of Governing Council was attended by Sarvshri Bhagwan Sahay, P.L. Verma, Gopalaswamy, N.K. Rewari, C.S. Chandershekhar, Syed S. Shafi and Prof. Dev Raj, and their decision was unanimous. In this connection, the plaintiff also submits that it was the Ministry of Works and Housing which decided in November 1975 to set up an autonomous body to be named as "National Institute of Urban Affairs". The plaintiff was merely a formal signatory to the formation of the Society under the Societies Registration Act. He never attended any meeting of tile Institute.

(v) In the aforesaid *Mainstream* article (Annexure VII), Shri Inder Mohan, defendant No. 1, stated:

> Jagmohan is undoubtedly an expert on demolitions, and in adding to the misery of one and half million slum dwellers of Delhi. His ruthlessness was at its peak during the emergency. In fact, he was a star performer, for which he should have been in prison by now, if the normal process of law was to take its toll for all his misdeeds."

The plaintiff submits that this is another derogatory, malicious and scurrilous statement. The correct position in regard to the so-called 'demolitions' has been indicated by the plaintiff in:

(i) above and the book (Annexure III).

(vi) In the aforesaid *Mainstream* article (Annexure VII), Shri Inder Mohan, defendant No. 1, stated:

> There is another 'distinction' that goes to Jagmohan's credit. All the resettlement colonies (a misnomer for them) which came into being fifteen years ago, or during emergency, first of all deprived hundreds and thousands of human beings of their livelihood. Secondly, they have been made to live in subhuman conditions as basic amenities have been denied. Colonies like Khichripur and Nandnagri are in low lying areas. Despite expert advice, Jagmohan insisted on pushing thousands of people there. They had to wade through knee-deep water during the rains of last year. When these colonies became scandalous, nearly fifty crores of rupees, if not more, were sunk to raise their level."

The plaintiff submits that this is yet another false and defamatory statement. In regard to the resettlement of the squatters, the plaintiff was one of the officers concerned with the Government programme and policy, which was in the overall interest of the squatters/slum dwellers and general public. The correct position in this respect has already been indicated above, and the details have been given in the book (Annexure III).

It is also false that, despite expert advice, the plaintiff insisted on pushing out thousands of people to Khichripur and Nandnagri, and when these colonies became scandalous, nearly fifty crores were sunk to raise their level. The correct position is that colonies of Khichripur and Nandnagri were planned and developed by senior technical experts of the D.D.A., viz. the Town Planners and Engineers who correspond to the Superintending Engineer and Chief Engineers of the C.P.W.D. These colonies were developed in the usual way, and the cost of levelling in Khichripur and Nandnagri was not even one-fiftieth of that has been alleged. During the rains of 1976-77, there has been no flooding of either Khichripur or Nandnagri.

Appendix XIX

Number and Nature of Crimes Committed

Number of people killed, yearwise:

Year	Number
1990	1,177
1991	1,393
1992	1,909
1993	2,560

In the year 1993 alone, 745 innocent persons were labelled as informers and killed, mostly after brutal torture.

A large number of persons were killed by resort to primitive savagery, such as hanging by trees, strapping bombs around the bodies of the victims and then exploding them.

Those who are resorting to terror are very well trained by the ISI. To see the extent to which the ISI could go, one should read the revelations of Brig. Yousaf in his book: *The Bear Trap.* Narrating ISI's activities in Afghanistan, he says: "During my four years, some 80,000 Mujahideen were trained; hundreds of tons of arms and ammunition were distributed, several billion dollars were spent on this immense logistic exercise and ISI teams regularly entered Afghanistan alongside the Mujahideen."

While talking of the human rights violations, one should not forget that the root cause of the problem is the large-scale violence of the militants to which the security forces have to react. Nor should different standards be applied for different countries. Why is there so little talk about what happened in Chile, Iraq, Vietnam, Haiti, etc. and what is happening in Somalia and former Yugoslavia and Kurdish area of Turkey?

Appendix XIX B

Particulars of a few Typical Cases of Ignorant and Superficial Reporting

G.S. Bhargava's write-up, *Sense and Nonsense,* published in the *Week* of October 24, 1993, betrayed his inexcusable ignorance about facts regarding migration of Kashmiri Pandits, Turkman Gate and removal of Dr. Farooq Abdullah. My rejoinder article, published in the issue of December 5, 1993, citing known documents, show the extent of careless and ignorant writing in a section ofthe Press.

The articles of Manishankar Aiyer on Kashmir, by and large, fall in the same category of ignorant and careless writing. As an example, his write-up in the *Sunday* (October 17-23, 1993) and my rejoinder, *Setting the Record Straight,* (November 7-13, 1993), may be seen.

See also

(a) Ms. Namita Bhandare's write-up on Governors in *Sunday* (December 5-11, 1993) and my rejoinder to it published in the issue of January 2-8, 1994.

(b) Amrik Singh's article *(Hindustan Times), "Kashmir–The Emotional Barrier"* (October 12, 1993) and my rejoinder, *"Then and Now"* (October 23, 1993).

Appendix XX

Accession

In his book, titled "Kashmir: A Disputed Legacy", Alastair Lamb attempts to formulate a proposition to the effect that the Indian forces landed at Srinagar airport before the Instrument of Accession was signed by the Maharaja.

Lamb's attempt is laboured, and based upon conjectures. It reflects pro-Pakistani bias in his thinking. For example, he refers to Mehar Chand Mahajan's book, "Looking Back", wherein the author, who was the Prime Minister of the State at that time, stated (p. 152):

> Around dinner time, the Prime Minister sent a message to me that with V.P. Menon, I should fly to Jammu to inform the Maharaja of this decision and also to get his signature on certain supplementary documents about the accession. I frankly informed him that I was not prepared to go to Jammu till I got news from my aerodrome officer at Srinagar that the Indian forces had landed there. Panditji did not insist and said, 'You can fly to Jammu next morning'.

From this statement mainly, Lamb infers that the Indian intervention took place before accession. Does this narration mean that V.P. Menon, too, did not go to the Maharaja earlier? What do words, "supplementary papers" denote? Do they not clearly mean that the main document had already been signed?

Lamb also omits to underscore what Mehar Chand Mahajan writes on page 151. He says:

> I was, however, adamant in my suhmission; the Prime Minister also was sticking to his own view, As a last resort Isaid, Give us the military force we need. Take the accession and give whatever power you desire to the popular party."

It is quite clear that Mehar Chand Mahajan, who had come to New Delhi with the full authority of the Maharaja, commits himself to accession.

Even if it be assumed, for the sake of argument, that the Instrument of Accession was formally signed afterwards, how does it invalidate the dispatch of Indian troops to the State? Could not a sovereign country extend help to a ruler who had asked for it? And could not an oral agreement be reduced to writing by the two parties and made applicable with effect from a particular date and time? What then, was the legal compulsion for 'manipulation of the document'?

Lamb has truly tried to make a mountain out of a mole-hill. What he has displayed is not scholarship but speculation.

Lamb also points to the presence of Patiala's troops in Jammu and Kashmir before October 27, 1947. This, too, is of little consequence. The Maharaja of Jammu and Kashmir was not precluded from obtaining troops from wherever he liked.

As regards Lamb's suggestion that there was some sort of 'conspiracy' between Nehru, Mountbatten and Radcliffe, the clinching evidence of the three chiefs and other facts, referred in the main Chapter, repel it. Lamb's capacity to stretch his imagination can be seen from the fact that the mere stay of Radcliffe at Viceregal lodge makes him think that Mountbatten had influenced the Chairman of the Boundary Commission in awarding three tehsils of Gurdaspur district to India.

If India had taken minor action in certain areas before October 27, 1947, how could it constitute conspiracy? After all, there was a possibility of J&K acceding to India which had never accepted the two nation theory. A few decisions to accommodate that possibility was nothing but natural.

Appendix XXI

Status of Different Areas

The Pakistan Occupied Kashmir could be divided into three broad units—(i) area which is administered by what is called 'Azad Kashmir' government; (ii) the northern territory of Gilgit and Baltistan which is directly administered by the central government; and (iii) the area which has been illegally occupied by China or illegally handed over by Pakistan to China.

"Azad Kashmir"

The first unit covers parts of the erstwhile districts of Muzaffarabad and Poonch. Its present population is about 20 lakh. Except for Muzaffarabad proper and plains of Mirpur, the soil is rugged, uneven and unproductive.

The government of 'Azad Kashmir' has really no legal status. Sometimes it is described as "local authority". It is argued that a sizeable number of Maharaja's subjects revolted and set up a government of 'Azad Kashmir'. Apart from the fact that this argument is based upon inaccurate facts, it does not provide Pakistan with any 'locus standi' to hold the area and establish a sort of State-Centre relationship between 'Azad Kashmir' government in Muzaffarabad and the Federal government in Islamabad. The entire affair is nothing but a constitutional mockery.

The so called "Azad Kashmir Republic" was set up under the 'presidency' of Sardar Ibrahim Khan, a local Muslim Conference leader. But the real powers were vested with the central ministry of 'Kashmir Affairs'. Its joint secretary was virtually the monarch of all that he surveyed—an executive, legislature and judiciary, all rolled in one.

In 1970, the Azad Kashmir Government Act was promulgated. Under it, a legislative assembly was created. In 1974, another Constitution came into being. It introduced a parliamentary system of government. The 'President of Azad Kashmir' was reduced to the position of a constitutional head, while the Prime Minister, who was made answerable to the legislative assembly, became the chief executive. Simultaneously, an 'Azad' Kashmir Council was set up in Islamabad. This Council has a jurisdiction over 52 items–"virtually everything of any importance." The Constitution of 1974 divided powers between the State government of Azad Kashmir in Muzaffarabad and 'Central Council of Azad Kashmir' in Islamabad.

Thus, for the first time, the Central government of Pakistan shared responsibility for the governance of 'Azad Kashmir'. These arrangements lend support to the view that at the time of Shimla Agreement (1972) there was a tacit understanding between the parties to partition the erstwhile State of Jammu and Kashmir along the line of actual control, and in pursuance thereof, Bhutto made 'Azad Kashmir' a constituent unit of federation.

The presence of local units of national political parties in Azad Kashmir is another feature that has tended to make it an adjunct of the central government. "Whatever happens in Pakistan also happens in 'Azad Kashmir'." Of late, however, there have been some muted voices of dissent, and leaders of 'Azad Kashmir' and central leaders have been singing slightly different tunes, particularly in regard to the status of northern territories and "struggle for self-determination". Accusations against Pakistan's Prime Minister of playing the 'Viceroy-like' role in regard to Azad Kashmir are also made occasionally.

Northern Territories

The 'northern territories' have been virtually annexed by Pakistan. Not even a fig leaf of separate entity has been provided to them. A number of leaders in Azad Kashmir have been protesting against this annexation/incorporation and claiming that northern territories are parts of 'Azad Kashmir'. Recently, the 'High Court' of Azad Kashmir has ruled that this claim is valid. The central government is unlikely to accept this verdict. Itmight file appeal in the Supreme Court of POK. The area of northern territories is about 60,000 square kilometres and its present population 900,000.

Chinese Occupation

China has occupied about 37,550 square miles of Jammu and Kashmir area illegally. In addition to this, Pakistan ceded, albeit illegally, 5,180 square miles of area from the northern territories. Thus, China has come to 'occupy' a total area of 42,730 square miles of the State of Jammu and Kashmir.

Void

India was a member of the United Nations prior to August 15, 1947. It was Pakistan who was admitted as a new member. The geographical area of the country which was admitted as a new member did not cover the Pakistan Occupied Kashmir. Therefore, the Pakistan's presence in and control over the aforesaid three units are ab initio void and violative of international law. Subsequent actions taken by the central government of Pakistan and the government of Azad Kashmir could not, and have not given, any legal or moral sanctity to it.

Area with India

While the entire erstwhile State of Jammu and Kashmir (2,22,236 sq. km) is a part of the Indian Union, as a consequence of irrevocable accession, the actual administration of the Union Government/State Government of J&K extend to the 'non-Pak' and 'non-Chinese occupied area.'

Appendix XXII

China's Stand

China's stand on Kashmir has been undergoing subtle shift from time to time, depending largely upon its foreign policy compulsions in Central Asia and South Asia.

During the early phase, 1950 to 1962, which was dominated by 'Panchsheel' and sentiments of 'Hindi-Chinibhai-bhai', China's stand was either neutral or a little favourable to India. It took special care not to offend India when it wanted to arrive at an understanding with Pakistan on border. In reply to India's protest note, China made it clear that "the negotiations did not involve the question of the ownership of Kashmir", and that "it has been the consistent position of the Chinese Government to be impartial and to wish that India and Pakistan should themselves reach a peaceful settlement".*

The position, however, underwent a change after India-China war (1962). In March 1963, China entered into an agreement with Pakistan without any reservation and secured possession of substantial part (5,180 sq. km) of the erstwhile State of Jammu and Kashmir, treating it as a settlement between the two countries. In February 1964, during his visit to Pakistan, Chou En-Lai supported Pakistan's stand and declared that "it would be of no avail to deny the existence of the dispute and adopt a big-nation chauvinistic attitude." During India-Pakistan war of September 1965, China tilted in favour of Pakistan. While it did not agree with President Ayub Khan's suggestion that it should occupy what now constitutes the State of Arunachal Pradesh, China issued an ultimatum on September 17, 1965 to India

*New China News Agency, June 4, 1962.

demanding that "aggressive military works on the Chinese side of China-Sikkim boundary" should be demolished within three days. This ultimatum contributed to the early cessation of hostilities and saving Pakistan from losing its face further.

At the time of Bangladesh war (1972), China repeated its' earlier performance of 1965. It denounced India but did nothing concrete to help Pakistan on ground.

By mid-seventies, China's support for Pakistan waned. New geo-political considerations made it adopt once again an even handed approach. In 1976, for instance, the Chinese foreign minister, in his speech to the United Nations General Assembly, did not include Kashmir in the list of the territories where self-determination had not been allowed. Presently, the general attitude of China is to keep, a studied distance from the Kashmir issue and make statements, whenever occasions so demanded, urging India and Pakistan to settle the matter peacefully and bilaterally.

Appendix XX III

Inter Services Intelligence

The Inter Services Intelligence of Pakistan has played a key role in weaving a web of subversion and terrorism in Kashmir. It has, over the years, turned out to be the most cool and calculating intelligence agency in the Third World. It has been singularly successful in exploiting American compulsions in Afghanistan and acquiring, in the process, enormous resources–financial, technical and military. In one year alone, 1987-88, it misappropriated 35 per cent of the American aid ($1.2 billion) meant for Afghan refugees.* According to another report, about 60 per cent of the sophisticated weapons, sent by the Americans for Afghan Mujahideens, were diverted by the ISI for its own use.

With regard to Kashmir, the ISI has been particularly innovative in evolving uncanny techniques of manipulating impressionable minds with modern gadgetry and using strands of militancy in Islam for creating an 'invisible army of Pakistan' for carrying out a war of attrition in the valley. In training and equipping this 'army', it has made extensive use of light but lethal weapons which it fell into its hands during the Afghan imbroglio.

The Inter-Services Intelligence was set up in 1948. Its primary task was to collect foreign intelligence. Under the military dictatorship of President Ayub Khan, it gained considerable ascendency, both in the internal and external fields. After the Bangladesh war, it was somewhat discredited. But under President Zia-ul-Haq, it became the most influential instrument of governance. Its present strength is about

*U.S. Congressional report.

25,000. It plays a crucial role in determining the power-structure of Pakistan.

India has been a special target of the ISI. The terrorist havoc caused by it in Punjab and Kashmir is too well-known to be dilated upon here. It has taken full advantage of India being a soft State.

The series of bomb blasts in Bombay on March 12, 1993, which killed about 300 persons appear to be the handiwork of this organisation. The subsequent recovery of huge quantities of explosives–2,380 kg. of RDX from Thane creek alone–lends support to this belief. If not checked by counter-measures, the ISI could seriously imperil India's security and stability.

Appendix XXIV

Fig 2: Press release of Hazbul Mujahideen faction of Kashmiri terrorists published in the morning edition of Urdu daily Aftab on 1/4/1990. Aftab is published from Srinagar. The headlines proclaimed: "The aim of present struggle is the supremacy of Islam in Kashmir, in all walks of life and nothing else. Anyone who puts any hurdle in our way will be annihilated."

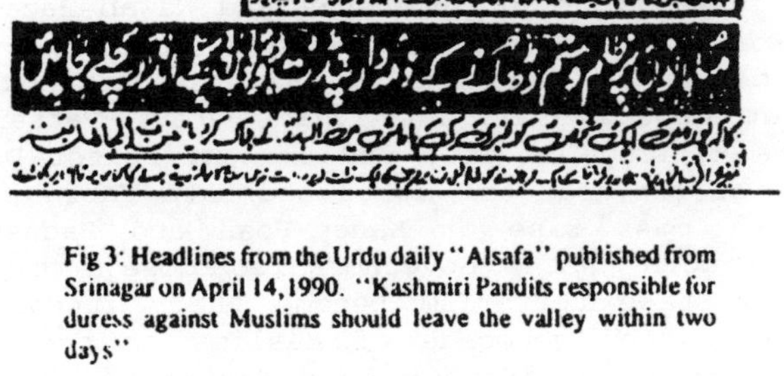

Fig 3: Headlines from the Urdu daily "Alsafa" published from Srinagar on April 14, 1990. "Kashmiri Pandits responsible for duress against Muslims should leave the valley within two days"

Appendix XXV

Memorandum[*]

TO EXCELLENCY THE GOVERNER J&K
GEN. KV KRISHNA RAO
JAMMU

We hope your Excellency may spare some time for going through the contents of the memorandum, wherein we sincerely and with clear mind mentioned some factors responsible for present grave of volcano situation in Jammu and Kashmir.

As it is known fact that since January 1990, Mr. Jagmohan was sent as Governor against the wishes of people and elected Government. A reign of terror started in Jammu and Kashmir. The sole aim of Mr. Jagmohan was to make genocide of Muslims on the directions of Hindu fundamentalist of India. For achieving the motive of the naked game of deaths and destruction started in Jammu and Kashmir in which thousands of innocents were also killed and locality after locality were razed into ground. Mr. Sexena successor of Mr. Jagmohan also follows footsteps of Jagmohan and incorporates his policy and planning in letter and spirit. Mr. Sexena was meeting Mr. Jagmohan whenever he visits Delhi and was getting directions from him for elimination of militancy at the cost of genocide the majority community and state terrorism.

Mr. Governor—The incidents of firing on Late Moulvi Mohd Farooq's funeral procession, senseless killings of innocents Matador Passengers at by-pass Srinagar and Fateh Kadal, criminal and barbaric killings of innocents and Nawab Bazarwhere those killed were sleeping in their homes, the naked death and destruction game in Handwara, Sopore and Batmaloc unwarranted killings at Chota Bazar, Khaniyar, Habak, Pattan Nishat,the unfortunate killings of able and eminent Doctor Dr. Ashie and permission of provacat and so called Ekta Yatra and shameless incidents of mass rape at Kanon-Posh and Badusgam are the sufficient proofs that Ex-Governors let loose a reign of terror, anarchy and State terrorism become their fundamental policy which aims planned genocide of Muslims on the direction of central Government, which in turn results

[*]Facsimile of opening paragraphs and the signatories (p. 762).

Farmer Ministers, members legeslative Assembly

Member legislative counsel and Member of Parliments.

1. Chaudhary Shabbir Ahmad Salaria Ex. M.P.

2. Ahmad Ali Mohammad Sagar Ex. Minister

3. Mr. Abdul Gani Vakil Ex. Minister

4. Ghulam Ahmad Shah Ex. MLA

5. Ch. B. A. NAZ - EX MLA
Mr. Bashir Ahmad NAZ - Ex MLA

6. Mr. Bali ... MLA

7. Mr. SADIQ ALI - MLC

8. Mr Chuni Lal Kotwal Ex MLC

9. Ahmad Ullah AZAD MLC LEH

10. Mr. Qamar Ali Akhoon Ex MLA Kargil

11. Ram Paul MLC
Mr. Ram Paul MLC

Farmer Ministers , members Legeslative Assembl ,

Member Legislative counsel and Member of Parliments.

11. Wali Mohd Itoo Ex-Speaker/Minister
M.L.C.

12.

13. Mr. Abdul Ahad Vakil (wani) Ex. MLA

14. ... MLC

15. Mr. Abdul Gani Mustafa ... Ex MLA

16. Pt. Gobind Ram Sharma (Ex MLA)
... MLC

17. Chodry ... Ramzan Ex - Minister

Appendix XXVI

Resolutions of the Kashmir Bar Association (September 28, 1993)

RESOLUTION NO. I

RESOLVED that Self-determination by the people, who are genuine permanent residents of the State of Jammu and Kashmir, is primarily the solution of Kashmir Problem.

RESOLUTION NO. II

RESOLVED that the State of Jammu and Kashmir be kept under the Trusteeship of United Nations for a period of five years, and as a consequence thereof, Governments of India and Pakistan, except Azad Kashmir be requested to withdraw their forces wherever they be, simultaneously from the State, and bring about re-unification of the State.

RESOLUTION NO. III

RESOLVED that during the 'period of five years, and after the withdrawal of last of the soldiers, appropriate interim arrangements be made by the U.N.O. to run the administration of the State.

RESOLUTION NO. IV

RESOLVED that till such time people of the State finally decided about the future of the State, provisional membership, be granted to the State in the United Nations.

RESOLUTION NO. V

RESOLVED that when the situation in the State is conducive, Referendum be held under the auspices of the U.N.O. on the question:

(a) Whether the people of the State want final disposition of the State in accordance with U.N. Resolutions dated August 13, 1948 and January 5th, 1949.
OR

(b) Should be given an option not to accede to either of two countries namely, India or Pakistan.

FURTHER RESOLVED that in the event of the majority of the people exercising their option in favour of clause (a) "Plebiscite" be held in the State in accordance with resolutions of the Security Council of the U.N.O.

Further resolved that in the event of Majority of the people opting for clause (b) the State of Jammu and Kashmir shall be an independent country and the Security Council of the U.N.O. shall be requested to modify its resolutions dated 13th of August, 1948 and 5th January 1949 accordingly.

RESOLUTION NO. VI

RESOLVED that with final determination, by direct majority Vote, the State's future disposition, be declared and U.N.O. be requested to extinguish its trusteeship over the State.

RESOLUTION NO. VII

RESOLVED that no other solution will be acceptable to the people of State, same and except above.

RESOLUTION NO. VIII

Further Resolved that pending peaceful settlement of Kashmir issue, 'occupational forces' be called upon to:

1. Stop catch and kill operations in the State;
2. Release all prisoners of conscience including Mr. Shabir Ahmad Shah and Mr. Mohammad Yaseen Malik and others.
3. Forbear and desist from the policy of repraisals and repression unleashed by them against the oppressed masses of Jammu and Kashmir.

Appendix XXVII

PART I

All India Kashmiri Pandit Conference
Central Office

Ganpatyar, Habbakadal Road, Srinagar, (Kmr.) (J&K State India) 190001

Corressponding Address: 218-M.L.A.'s Hostel, Jammu Tawi Phone: 47491

Camp Office:
N.D.M.C.
Community Centre
Lodhi Colony
Aligunj
New Delhi 110 003
October 13, 1993

To
The Editor-in-chief
"THE TRIBUNE"
Chandigarh

Sir,

The other day, I happened to see Kuldip Nayar's article in your esteemed daily of October 13, 1993, titled "Disinherited People". I am shocked at its deliberate distortion, falsehood and suppression of truth about the migration of my community from the Valley.

It is wholly incorrect that I and other Kashmir Pandits migrated from the Valley at the instance of Shri Jagmohan. The truth is exactly the opposite. Shri Jagmohan, in fact, did his level best to stop migration which had begun much earlier, when in broad day-light and on busy streets eminent and innocent leaders of Pandit's community were being brutally murdered and the Government of Dr. Farooq Abdullah was taking no action whatsoever or apprehending any culprit. Tikka Lal Taploo was shot dead on September 14, 1989, Judge N.K. Ganjoo on November 4 and journalist P.N. Bhatt on December 28, etc.

The terror-stricken Pandit community, in a memorandum dated January 16, 1990, to the then Governor, General (Retd.) K.V. Krishna Rao, pleaded:

> The ineffectiveness of the State Government has not been able to check loot, arson and killing of innocent people. Instead of the Government, it is the militants who are the de facto rulers in the Valley today. The ruling political forces are solely concerned with their own survival avoiding the wrath of the secessionists. Happenings in Anantnag, Sopore, Baramulla, Tral, Nurran, Pulwama, Ishber, Vicharnag, Shopian and other places in the Valley are indicative of the fundamentalists' designs regarding their planned targets of attack on the minorities. On 15th December 1989, in Shopian, men, children and old women of the minority community were mercilessly attacked and women-folk molested. The murder of Mahant Keshav Nath, Tikka Lal Taploo, N.K. Ganjoo, Prem Nath Bhat, Ajay Kapoor and others, was to create scare and awe among the minority community to force them to leave the Valley. The pace of exodus has further accelerated now.
>
> It is a sad commentary on the present administration that not even a single assailant of the minority leaders and others has either been identified or apprehended by the Police till now.

When Kashmiri Pandits were being regularly killed on the pretext that they were 'informers' and agents of the Central Government, I and some members of the All India Kashmiri Pandit Conference (A.I.K.P.C.) discussed the alarming situation. After discussion, I issued a press note on February 21, 1990 which was published in the newspapers on the following day. In this press note, I had appealed to the militants not to kill Kashmiri Pandits by labelling them as informers, and if they had suspicion on any Pandit, they should bring it to the notice of our organisation.

On February 28, my young and energetic secretary (Ashok Kazi, All India Kashmiri Pandit Conference) was done to death in most inhuman and savage manner. First he was shot in the knuckles. While he was bleeding profusely and crying 'end my agony by shooting me', the pitiless murderers enacted a sort of death-dance around him and hurled all types of abuses on Pandits. All this happened on a busy thoroughfare. But no one came to his rescue. It was only the distant siren of a police-van that made the killers to pump a number of bullets in Ashok Kazi's body and finish him and then disappear with easy pace.

On the same evening, I was violently abused on telephone in the most filthy and unprintable language. Referring to Ashok Kazi's torturous killing, the caller said: "Have you now got our reply to the press note? You, dog, will meet worse fate than Ashok Kazi." From that day onward, myself and the members of my community came to the conclusion that we were hoping against hope and must leave the Valley immediately to save our lives and the honour of our womenfolk. And the migration accelerated.

On the other hand, Governor Jagmohan tried very hard to persuade us not to leave. He fervently appealed to the Kashmiri Pandits, who had already migrated, to return to the Valley. He even offered to set up four temporary camps for them at Srinagar, Anantnag, Baramulla and Kupwara. This would be evident from his press note of March 7, 1990 which was widely published at that time. It is reproduced below:

> Jagmohan, Governor, J&K, has appealed to the members of Kashmiri Pandit community not to leave the Valley even temporarily. He said that law and order machinery was being rebuilt.
>
> With the appointment of Special Commisioners and Special DIGs for the newly created Divisions of Baramulla and Anantnag, the authority at the State was being re-established. The senior officers have been specifically charged with the duty of giving protection and safeguarding the minorities and restoring confidence amongst them.
>
> Jagmohan also appealed to the members of the community who have temporarily migrated to Jammu to return to the Valley. He offered to set up temporary camps at four places, namely, Srinagar, Anantnag, Baramulla and Kupwara for those who will return from Jammu. In these places Rest Houses or some other suitable buildings would be requisitioned.
>
> Jagmohan said that accommodation in these camps would be free and arrangements for food and other facilities would also be made. Necessary medical cover would also be provided in each camp. For going to their houses occasionally, a pool of vehicles will also be provided in each camp so that the members of the community could go to their houses with escort. For administering these camps and for attending to the problems of these camps, a separate Relief Commissioner would be appointed.
>
> Jagmohan requested the President and the Secretary of All India Kashmiri Pandit Association, who called on him today, to persuade those who have migrated to Jammu temporarily to return to the Valley.

A number of other energetic steps which have now become a part of history were taken by Shri Jagmohan to retrieve a hopeless situation. At great personal risk, he visited the police stations in thickly populated areas where the police machinery had totally broken down. To instil confidence in the highly demoralised Kashmir Pandit community, he even went to the house of young Satish Tikka in Habbakadal, a congested and highly terrorist-infested locality. He consoled the old parents of Satish who was brutally murdered after being called in the street by his 'erstwhile friends'. The Union Home Minister acknowledged all this when he said in the Parliament on April 25, 1990:

> Jagmohan had to function in a vacuum, in a situation where there was no respect for law or authority of the State government. He braved terrorists, instilled courage in government officials who had almost given up the situation as a lost case. It is very unfair for anyone to criticise Jagmohan for what he has done for the country.

When an all party Committee headed by Deputy Prime Minister Choudhry Devi Lal visited Srinagar, myself and Shri J.N. Sapru met him and the Union Law Minister Shri Dinesh Goswami, at the Centur Hotel, where the party was staying. We apprised them of our horrible plight—how we were living under continuous fear of death, how threats and hysterical slogans of Nizam-e-Mustafa, etc. were blared simultaneously from hundreds of loud-speakers installed on the mosques, how hit lists were being displayed on the notice boards and how our womenfolks were being dishonoured. We also met Shri Rajiv Gandhi and spoke to him on similar lines.

The waiters of the hotel, most of whom had turned collaborators of militants on account of internal subversion, were listening. The Director-General of Police and the Additional Director-General (CID) and the officials of the Intelligence Bureau came to know that the waiters had informed the militant leaders about what transpired at the aforesaid meetings. We were already on their 'hit list' and they decided to intensify their efforts to get us immediately, so that punishment for speaking about their atrocities was carried out speedily. The Director-General of Police and the Additional Director-General (CID) thought that there was no effective way of saving our lives except to shift us to Jammu till conditions improved for our safe return. I was moved out only on grounds of personal security, with a few clothes, and lodged in the MLA Hostel where a number of National Conference leaders had also taken refuge.

In the meanwhile, treacherous and brutal killings of innocent Kashmiri Pandits continued in the Valley. Those killed included prominent persons like Engineer B.K. Ganjoo, Poet Sarvanand Premi and his young son Virender Kaul, Prof. K.L. Ganjoo and his wife, Teacher C.L. Pandita. Press notices were prominently put out in widely-read dailies of Srinagar, namely, "Aftab" and "Alsafa", requiring Kashmiri Pandits to leave within 48 hours, failing which they would run the risk of being exterminated. Photo copies of these notices have been printed by Shri Jagmohan in his well-known book "MY FROZEN TURBULENCE IN KASHMIR".

On a number of occasions, we reiterated the true position. For instance, on February 8, 1991, addressing the All India Kashmiri Pandit Conference, I said that about 28,000 families of Pandits had moved out of the Valley during the Chief Ministership of Dr. Farooq Abdullah. The press report of February 9 stated, inter alia, as follows:

> He (H.N. Jattu) recalled that over 26,000 families of minority community had migrated here even when Dr. Farooq was Chief Minister of the State... Mr. Jattu alleged that Dr. Abdullah was the "chief architect" of the exodus of minority community from the Kashmir Valley.

Again, at the Delegate Session (February 15, 1991), General Secretary S.N. Sapru, in his working report (1989-90) said:

> "Before we do so the AIKPC would like to make it clear that AT NO STAGE, DID THE PARTY OR ITS LEADERSHIP MORE SO ITS PRESIDENT SHRI H.N.JATTU ADVISE ANYONE TO LEAVE THE VALLEY... Our present exodus is a movement of mourners where a brother has lost his sister; a family the only breadearner, old parents their only son and a child his parents. An exodus where blood of our youth was drained out of their bodies; where people were shot and strangulated. An exodus where our women were dishonoured."

The Resolution No.1 passed at the All India Kashmiri Pandit Conference opened with the following two sentences:

> The terrorist violence in Kashmir is sponsored by the fundamentalist organisation in Kashmir supported by Pakistan with the objective of cutting off Jammu and Kashmir from the rest of the country and annex it to Pakistan. The migration of Kashmiri Pandit was forced by the terrorist organisation on them, because they constituted the most stable support base of nationalism and secularism in the State.

And the Resolution No. 2 stated:

> The causes and the conditions which forced the migration of the Kashmiri Pandits in particular have been discussed in detail in this convention. To repeat the trauma of those days when the exodus from the land of our ancestors started does not need any repetition here. The truth of this un-precedented movement of a community at such a large scale under the threat of guns is a part of the history of mankind. A history which will remind the coming generations ofthe barbaric killings, hangings, strangulations, and torture to which their ancestors fell the victims. In which their mothers and sisters were dishonoured and desecrated.
>
> History will also record the lies and concoctions of some of the media-persons, and, a couple of self-styled Human Rights Activist who not only tried to paint us with a tarred brush but also projected their own country as the worst violators of human rights. We do not want to joint issue with these people here. But we put it on record for the entire world that the reports and the surveys of these "mediamen" and "human rights activists"

> will remain dark spots in the history of free press and free expression.

The Save Kashmir Pandit campaign Committee, the Kashmir Migrant Forum and General Appeal of Kashmiri Pandits to the people of India and hosts of interviews of the individuals published in "The Illustrated Weekly of India" contemporaneously—all vividly describe how an atmosphere of acute terror was created to drive out the Pandits from the Valley.

It is, indeed, inexcusable that Kuldip Nayyar and Balraj Puri and the like, despite the existence of documents and hard evidence, which are known to them, persist with their distortions.

In this connection, it is significant to note that at a public function held at Jammu early this year, which was attended by both Kuldip Nayyar and Balraj Puri, Dr. K.L. Chowdhry read a paper on "Press and the Present Crisis in Kashmir", in which the following observations, inter alia, appear;

> So far as the vigilance role is concerned, the press failed miserably. It was nowhere in evidence when 'maktabs' (schools for imparting religious teaching) were used for indoctrination of youth to carry on 'Jehad' (religious war) for the establishment of 'Nizame-Mustafa' (the Islamic governance in the State). It was nowhere in evidence when these motivated, indoctrinated youth were openly encouraged and prompted to board buses from Chattabal in Srinagar to Rawalpindi, when they started their journey with great fanfare receiving the blessings of their parents, friends and well wishers. And where was the press when the same boys returned after receiving arms training to the effusive, emotional and warm embraces of welcome by an admiring populace, with showering of petals, sweets, dates and coconuts as they alighted from the buses in jeans, jackets and jackboots with rifles hanging fearlessly from their shoulders. <u>There is no doubt that the police and vigilance agencies had failed or connived, the State and Central administration had abdicated. But what about the press?...</u>
>
> Some papers went ahead and published ultimatums by various organizations to the Kashmiri Pandits to quit the valley within 48 hours or face retribution and death. A community which had withstood the first shocking impact of the present crisis on the winter night of 19th January 1990, when thousands of mosques over the length and breadth of the valley switched on their loud speakers exhorting the Muslims to come out on the streets and declare the annexation of Kashmir to Pakistan without Kashmiri Pandits, but with their females, a community which had persevered with open threats in the form of

letters, telephone calls and hitlists pasted on their doors..."

In fact, the press remained silent about the murder and mayhem let loose on the Hindu community. On the contrary, it persisted with and perpetrated the disinformation that the Hindus were driven to exile not by the depreciations of the militants but by a pied piper named Jagmohan who wanted them out to safety of the exile so that he could bomb the valley. Isn't it the press which actually played the role of the pied piper by launching an offensive against the community and by delivering the threats of the militant organizations through their papers?

And yet, Kuldip Nayyar in his article indulges in patent falsehood about the cause of migration of Kashmiri Pandits. This shows his mala fides.

My entire community is very much pained and annoyed by intentional falsehood of Balraj Puri and Kuldip Nayyar. To assuage their hurt feelings, kindly publish the above facts in full, along with the documentary evidence cited, at the same prominent place at which you have published Kuldip Nayyar's article.

I am also sending copies of this letter to all leading national dailies. My Association (All India Kashmiri Pandit Conference) is also thinking of taking other forms of action.

Thanking you,

Yours faithfully,

(H.N. Jattu)

PART II

Apart from documents and contemporaneous records, cited in the above letter, there are many other pieces of concrete and unimpeachable evidence. The following may be particularly noted:

(i) Atmosphere of bloody terror built by such brutal and treacherous killings as that of Poet Sarvanand Kaul and his young son Virender (p. 451), Engineer B.K. Ganjoo (pages 448-449), Doordarshan Station Director Lassa Kaul (p. 491), Prof. K. Ganjoo (p. 450), etc. The tactics were clear: "Kill one and frighten one thousand; simultaneously, float calculated rumours, make reckless allegations and divide and demoralise the adversary".

(ii) Photo-copies of press notes given in Appendix XXIV vide which the Kashmiri Pandits were asked to leave within 48 hours.

(iii) The interviews of numerous persons contemporaneously recorded by the *Illustrated Weekly of India* (pages 452 to 454).

(iv) Resolutions/statements of various organisations/associations of Pandits other than All India Kashmiri Pandit Conference (p. 455 and 456); and also recent resolution of Panum Kashmir (no. PK/D/Pr/93/2022 dated November 4, 1993, which reads:

Panun Kashmir in its Executive Meeting viewed with deep anguish and concern motivated, false & mischievous articles of Sh. Kuldeep Nayyar & Sh. Balraj Puri published in 'THE TRIBUNE' & 'THE STATESMAN' of Oct. 13, 1993 & other dailies/magazines about the migration of KPs from the Valley and strongly condemned them.

These articles have acted as salt in our wounds which have been bleeding for the last four years. Apart from being false, such intentional distortions are unpatriotic & are bound to fan the forces of subversion and terrorism & serve as the instruments of the Pakistani propaganda Design.

The Executive Committee further resolved that the copy of the resolution be sent to all National Dailies.

Sd.
RAVI KAUL
PRESS Secretary

(v) Exposure of the network of lies, including one relating to migration of Pandits, built by the socalled human right bodies like "Committee on Initiative on Kashmir". (See for instance the statement of Chief Secretary R.K. Takkar (pp. 441-442).

(vi) The other pertinent questions which the propagators of the canard totally ignore are:

(a) Why are a number of leaders of the National Conference and the Congress staying, for most of the time, in Delhi and Jammu and why do they consider the Valley safe for the Pandits and not for themselves?

(b) If the Kashmiri Pandits had come away from the Valley at my instance, why did they not return after I demited office in mid-1990?

(c) What are the particulars of the trucks (registration number, etc.) which the Governor's Administration had hired?

(d) Which, and where, are the plots and houses which I had allotted, by way of inducements, to Kashmir Pandits?

(e) Why do the Kashmiri Pandits continue to live in miserable camps, under the scorching sun of Jammu and Delhi, if they do not apprehend kidnapping and killing in the Valley?

(f) When about sixteen families were induced to return to the Valley in June 1992, why were they threatened and made to flee for the second time by Hizbul Mujahideen and other militant groups within fifteen days?

Appendix XXVIII

The Delhi Declaration (World Kashmiri Pandits Conference)

The main demands included in The Delhi Declaration are:

I Creation of a separate homeland, in the north-east of river Jhelum, with the status of a Union Territory.

II Treating Pakistan as a terrorist State.

III Ensuring return of all Kashmiri Pandits.

IV Setting up of "Sharda Peeth", 'University in Exile', to preserve and promote Kashmiri art, architecture, literature, language, etc.

V Adoption of the Devanagiri script as an alternative script for the Kashmiri language.

VI Associating the Kashmiri Pandits with any talks that might be held about the future of Kashmir; and

VII Educating the world about the Human Rights violations of the Kashmiri Pandits and their 'ethnic cleansing' through terror and subversion.

Appendix XXIX

TOLL OF MILITANCY UPTO MAY 1996

	Progressive Total since 1989 to 1995	Jan.	Feb.	Mar.	Apr.	May	Total	Grand Total
1. Militants killed LAC	1405	21	3	5	6	14	49	1454
2. Elsewhere	5046	83	98	100	113	91	485	5531 6985
3. Civilians killed by Militants	4094	105	117	107	116	107	552	4646
4. Civilians killed in cross firing & maintenance of law and order	2240	3	10	5	11	7	36	2276
5. Security forces killed	1134	12	7	11	16	15	61	1195
6. Security personnel injured	4017	26	27	26	33	48	160	4177
7. No. of attacks on Security Forces	11557	106	236	131	137	165	775	12332
8. No. of crossfiring	8781	101	88	115	104	90	498	9279
9. Incidents of Militants firing	5919	137	237	133	-	-	507	6426
10. Explosions	6526	51	33	31	67	135	317	6843
11. Arsons	3885	47	44	57	46	63	257	4142
12. Rocket attacks	513	3	1	2	6	13	25	538
13. Abductions	2006	59	67	40	52	84	302	2308
14. Surrenders	1747	81	31	129	73	15	329	2076

DESTRUCTION BY MILITANCY IN 1996

	Progressive Total since 1989 to 1995	Jan.	Feb.	Mar.	Apr.	May	Total	Grand Total
1. Private houses gutted	6553	64	68	71	68	62	333	6886
2. Shops gutted	2030	12	13	-	-	-	25	2055
3. Bridges burnt	210	-	1	-	-	1	2	212
4. Schools burnt	529	3	3	12	11	18	47	576
5. Govt. bldgs. burnt	1588	6	1	9	12	7	35	1623
6. Hospital gutted	2	-	-	1	-	-	1	3
7. Mosque	2	-	-	-	-	-	-	2
8. Temples	31	-	-	-	-	-	-	31
9. Business Establishments	-	-	-	-	-	-	-	40

WEAPONS RECOVERED IN KASHMIR DURING 1996

	Progressive Total since 1989 to 1995	Jan.	Feb.	Mar.	Apr.	May	Total	Grand Total
AK Rifles	13294	216	159	299	237	143	1054	14348
UMGs/LMG/GPMG	627	11	7	7	12	7	44	671
R P Gs	415	5	-	4	-	4	13	428
Rev/Pistols	5216 +1 bag	117	72	109	116	79	493	5709 1 bag
Rocket launcher	328	-	-	4	6	1	11	339
Rockets	1531	10	2	23	33	68	136	1667
Magazines	33003	621	408	696	836	432	2993	35995
Ammunition	1819163 +686 boxes	26263	22172	28335	20233	18990	115993	1935156 686 boxes
Grenades	51680 +6 bags +57 sticks	289	244	476	387	281	1677	53357
Detonators	44459	436	277	447	278	1228	2666	47125
Wireless Sets	618	25	19	40	40	50	174	792
	(in Kgs.)							
Explosives	6439	302	72	168	542 800 G	205 800 G	7186 750 G	
RDX		5	5	-	45	55		
IED		25	6	18	98	147		
PKTS	1163	25	-	-	25			

Appendix XXX

As a part, of back channel diplomacy, a number of suggestions for the 'solution' of the Kashmir problem have been floated to ascertain the reactions of the peoples and the governments of India and Pakistan. In the main, these suggestions are:

(i) Formation of United States of Jammu and Kashmir.
(ii) Joint 'control' by both India and Pakistan.
(iii) Demilitarisation of 'Indian part' and 'Pakistan part' of the State and creation of soft-borders.
(iv) 'Self-Governance' for both the parts.
(v) Conversion of the present Line of Control into International border.
(vi) Modified version of (v) with borders adjusted along the flow of River Chenab.

All these suggestions are vague and unworkable. If, for example, self-governance means maximum autonomy, it already exists in the Indian part, as has been enunciated in chapter XVIII of this book.

None of these suggestions, moreover, takes into account the issue of financial viability. At present, the Indian part receives huge financial assistance in the shape of a special category state and in many other ways. The entire plan expenditure is met by the Central Government. The per capita financial assistance to the J&K citizen is about ten times more than the per capita assistance in other parts of the country. The Central Government is also directly financing a large number of development projects in the state. Its investment in on-going projects is about Rs. 250 billion.

To cap it all, no solution can be implemented on the ground, unless terrorism is first rooted out. If it remains even in a rudimentary form, forces of fundamentalism and fanaticism could raise their heads and subvert, from within, even the best of arrangements.

INDEX

G

JAMMU & KASHMIR
Area: 2,22,236 sq. km. out of which 78,114 sq. km. is under illegal occupation of Pakistan, 5,180 sq. km. illegally handed over by Pakistan to China, and 37,555 sq. km. is under illegal occupation of China.
TAJIKISTAN
AFGHANISTAN
CHINA
PAKISTAN
TIBET
JAMMU AND KASHMIR
KUNLUN MOUNTAINS
AGHIL MOUNTAINS
DEOSAI MOUNTAINS
GREAT HIMALAYA
LADAKH RANGE
ZASKAR MOUNTAINS
HINDURAJ
SRINAGAR
ISLAMABAD
LEH (LADAKH)
JAMMU
GILGIT
CHITRAL
KARGIL
SKARDU
BALTISTAN
AKSAI CHIN
SODA PLAINS
DEPSANG PLAINS
LINGZI TANG
CHANG CHENMO
Indus or Senge Khambab
Yarkand or Zarafshan